Jesus and Nicodemus

European University Studies

Europäische Hochschulschriften
Publications Universitaires Européennes

Series XXIII
Theology

Reihe XXIII Série XXIII
Theologie
Théologie

Vol./Bd. 711

PETER LANG

Frankfurt am Main · Berlin · Bern · Bruxelles · New York · Oxford · Wien

Paul Julian

Jesus and Nicodemus

A Literary and Narrative Exegesis of Jn. 2,23-3,36

PETER LANG
Europäischer Verlag der Wissenschaften

Die Deutsche Bibliothek - CIP-Einheitsaufnahme

Julian, Paul:

Jesus and Nicodemus : a literary and narrative exegesis of
Jn. 2,23-3,36 / Paul Julian. - Frankfurt am Main ; Berlin ; Bern ;
Bruxelles ; New York ; Oxford ; Wien : Lang, 2000
    (European university studies : 23, Theology ; Vol. 711)
    Zugl.: Würzburg, Univ., Diss., 2000
    ISBN 3-631-37224-8

D 20
ISSN 0721-3409
ISBN 3-631-37224-8
US-ISBN 0-8204-4836-2

© Peter Lang GmbH
Europäischer Verlag der Wissenschaften
Frankfurt am Main 2000
All rights reserved.

Printed in Germany 1 2 3 4 5   7

To my

Archdiocese of Chennai-Mylapore

and to my

Alma Mater, Sacred Heart Seminary, Chennai

Preface

Currently the fourth gospel attracts the attention of more scholars than any other book of the bible. Studying it with integrity and openness is indeed a spiritual adventure. This study was accepted as doctoral dissertation by the Catholic Theological Faculty of the Bavarian Julius-Maximilian University, Würzburg (Germany) in July 2000.

There are many people who have made this study possible. I am deeply grateful to my *Doktorvater*, Prof. Dr. Hans-Josef Klauck (Munich), who graciously encouraged me to pursue this research, for his attentive and wise guidance, prompt and painstaking corrections. I wish to thank in a special way Prof. Dr. Bernhard Heininger (Würzburg) for his critical evaluation of my dissertation and for preparing the *Zweitgutachten*.

Without the commission of my late Archbishop, Dr. Casimir Gnanadickam along with the staff of my *alma mater*, the loving encouragement of my Archbishop Dr. Arul Das James, and the initial grant of *Church in Need*, I would never have been able to begin this research. I must thank sincerely the diocese of Würzburg for welcoming me and allowing me to stay at Kloster Oberzell, Dr. Paul-Werner Scheele, Bishop of Würzburg, for his special grant to cover partially the publishing costs of this book, and Mrs. Gertrud Zahner, for her generous contribution and affectionate care during my visits to the University of Munich.

I would like to express my heartfelt gratitude to Sr. Reginarda Holzer, the Superior General of the congregation of the *Dienerinnen der Heiligen Kindheit Jesu*, for generously providing me with everything necessary to pursue my studies, besides the calm atmosphere and the warmth of care and concern of all the sisters, especially Sr. Veridiana, Sr. Basildis, Sr. Geralda, Sr. Luitgardis, Sr. Hildeberta, Sr. Peregrina and Sr. Leonis, at Kloster Oberzell.

The sharp and attentive eyes of Mrs. Hildegard Weigert spotted many an error in my draft manuscript. I am greatly indebted to her for her continuous encouragement and constant follow up of my work till the end. I should like to thank Mrs. Imelda Gersitz, who patiently read the early drafts of my work and her father, Mr. Alois Streitenberger, who, with meticulous care, made beautiful bound copies of the manuscript to be submitted to the faculty.

Finally, it is important that I thank the many friends who have helped me in the course of this research, especially Fr. Veit Dennert of Neunkirchen am Brand, who provided me with comfortable accommodation every year in the month of August, where I could continue my work undisturbed, and late Dr. Hubertus Wohl, Fr. Richard Körner, Fr. Bruno Zeißner, Prof. Dr. Stephan-Ernst Müller, Fr. Amalraj, Fr. Roy and Dr. Klaus Linsenmeyer for their loving company and friendship at Kloster Oberzell.

I hope you will find the book interesting and stimulating to interact with the depth and wealth of this gospel, and contributing a few fresh ingredients to stir up new insights in understanding it.

Würzburg, August 2000   Paul Julian

TABLE OF CONTENTS

PART I

LITERARY AND NARRATIVE EXEGESIS OF 2,23-3,36   25

Chapter 1

PERIMETERS OF 2,23-3,36   25

Chapter 2

SURVEY OF PAST RESEARCH   31

Chapter 3

LITERARY AND NARRATIVE ANALYSIS OF 2,23-3,36   47

Chapter 4

PLOT   227

Chapter 5

NARRATOR AND POINT OF VIEW   239

Chapter 6

NARRATIVE CHRISTOLOGY IN PARALLEL EPISODES   247

PART II

LITERARY DESIGN AND NETWORK OF 1,19-4,54   257

Chapter 1

DIVISION OF 1,19-4,54   259

Chapter 2

PERIMETERS OF UNITS AND SUB-UNITS 265

Chapter 3

LITERARY AND NARRATIVE CORRELATION BETWEEN THE UNITS

AND THE UNDERLYING NARRATIVE CHRISTOLOGY 275

Jn. 2,23-3,36

2,23a   Ὡς δὲ ἦν ἐν τοῖς Ἱεροσολύμοις ἐν τῷ πάσχα ἐν τῇ ε ορτῇ,
   b   πολλοὶ ἐπίστευσαν εἰς τὸ ὄνομα αὐτοῦ
   c   θεωροῦντες αὐτοῦ τὰ σημεῖα ἃ ἐποίει·
  24a   αὐτὸς δὲ Ἰησοῦς οὐκ ἐπίστευεν αὐτὸν αὐτοῖς
   b   διὰ τὸ αὐτὸν γινώσκειν πάντας
  25a   καὶ ὅτι οὐ χρείαν εἶχεν
   b   ἵνα τις μαρτυρήσῃ περὶ τοῦ ἀνθρώπου·
   c   αὐτὸς γὰρ ἐγίνωσκεν
   d   τί ἦν ἐν τῷ ἀνθρώπῳ.
3,1a   Ἦν δὲ ἄνθρωπος ἐκ τῶν Φαρισαίων,
   b   Νικόδημος ὄνομα αὐτῷ, ἄρχων τῶν Ἰουδαίων·
  2a   οὗτος ἦλθεν πρὸς αὐτὸν νυκτὸς
   b   καὶ εἶπεν αὐτῷ,
   c   Ῥαββί, οἴδαμεν
   d   ὅτι .... διδάσκαλος (ὅτι ἀπὸ θεοῦ ἐλήλυθας διδάσκαλος·)
   e   ἀπὸ θεοῦ ἐλήλυθας
   f   οὐδεὶς γὰρ δύναται ταῦτα τὰ σημεῖα ποιεῖν
   g   ἃ σὺ ποιεῖς,
   h   ἐὰν μὴ ᾖ ο θεὸς μετ' αὐτοῦ.
  3a   ἀπεκρίθη Ἰησοῦς καὶ εἶπεν αὐτῷ,
   b   Ἀμὴν ἀμὴν λέγω σοι,
   c   ἐὰν μή τις γεννηθῇ ἄνωθεν,
   d   οὐ δύναται ἰδεῖν τὴν βασιλείαν τοῦ θεοῦ.
  4a   λέγει πρὸς αὐτὸν [ο] Νικόδημος,
   b   Πῶς δύναται ἄνθρωπος γεννηθῆναι
   c   γέρων ὤν;
   d   μὴ δύναται εἰς τὴν κοιλίαν τῆς μητρὸς αὐτοῦ δεύτερον εἰσελθεῖν
   e   καὶ γεννηθῆναι;
  5a   ἀπεκρίθη Ἰησοῦς,
   b   Ἀμὴν ἀμὴν λέγω σοι,
   c   ἐὰν μή τις γεννηθῇ ἐξ ὕδατος καὶ πνεύματος,
   d   οὐ δύναται εἰσελθεῖν εἰς τὴν βασιλείαν τοῦ θεοῦ.
  6a   τὸ γεγεννημένον ἐκ τῆς σαρκὸς σάρξ ἐστιν,
   b   καὶ τὸ γεγεννημένον ἐκ τοῦ πνεύματος πνεῦμά ἐστιν.
  7a   μὴ θαυμάσῃς
   b   ὅτι εἶπόν σοι,
   c   Δεῖ υ μᾶς γεννηθῆναι ἄνωθεν.
  8a   τὸ πνεῦμα...πνεῖ (τὸ πνεῦμα ὅπου θέλει πνεῖ)
   b   ὅπου θέλει
   c   καὶ τὴν φωνὴν αὐτοῦ ἀκούεις,
   d   ἀλλ' οὐκ οἶδας
   e   πόθεν ἔρχεται
   f   καὶ ποῦ υ πάγει·
   g   οὕτως ἐστὶν πᾶς
   h   ο γεγεννημένος ἐκ τοῦ πνεύματος.

9a ἀπεκρίθη Νικόδημος καὶ εἶπεν αὐτῷ,
 b Πῶς δύναται ταῦτα γενέσθαι;
10a ἀπεκρίθη Ἰησοῦς καὶ εἶπεν αὐτῷ,
 b Σὺ εἶ ὁ διδάσκαλος τοῦ Ἰσραὴλ
 c καὶ ταῦτα οὐ γινώσκεις;
11a ἀμὴν ἀμὴν λέγω σοι
 b ὅτι ὃ οἴδαμεν
 c λαλοῦμεν
 d καὶ ὃ ἑωράκαμεν
 e μαρτυροῦμεν,
 f καὶ τὴν μαρτυρίαν ἡμῶν οὐ λαμβάνετε.
12a εἰ τὰ ἐπίγεια εἶπον ὑμῖν
 b καὶ οὐ πιστεύετε,
 c πῶς ... πιστεύσετε (πῶς ἐὰν εἴπω ὑμῖν τὰ ἐπουράνια πιστεύσετε;)
 d ἐὰν εἴπω ὑμῖν τὰ ἐπουράνια
13a καὶ οὐδεὶς ἀναβέβηκεν εἰς τὸν οὐρανὸν
 b εἰ μὴ ὁ ἐκ τοῦ οὐρανοῦ καταβάς, ὁ υἱ ὸς τοῦ ἀνθρώπου.
14a καὶ καθὼς Μωϋσῆς ὕψωσεν τὸν ὄφιν ἐν τῇ ἐρήμῳ,
 b οὕτως ὑ ψωθῆναι δεῖ τὸν υἱ ὸν τοῦ ἀνθρώπου,
15a ἵνα πᾶς ὁ πιστεύων ἐν αὐτῷ
 b ἔχῃ ζωὴν αἰώνιον.
16a Οὕτως γὰρ ἠγάπησεν ὁ θεὸς τὸν κόσμον,
 b ὥστε τὸν υἱ ὸν τὸν μονογενῆ ἔδωκεν,
 c ἵνα πᾶς ὁ πιστεύων εἰς αὐτὸν
 d μὴ ἀπόληται
 e ἀλλ’ ἔχῃ ζωὴν αἰώνιον.
17a οὐ γὰρ ἀπέστειλεν ὁ θεὸς τὸν υἱ ὸν εἰς τὸν κόσμον
 b ἵνα κρίνῃ τὸν κόσμον,
 c ἀλλ’ ἵνα σωθῇ ὁ κόσμος δι’ αὐτοῦ.
18a ὁ πιστεύων εἰς αὐτὸν
 b οὐ κρίνεται·
 c ὁ δὲ μὴ πιστεύων
 d ἤδη κέκριται,
 e ὅτι μὴ πεπίστευκεν εἰς τὸ ὄνομα τοῦ μονογενοῦς υἱ οῦ τοῦ θεοῦ.
19a αὕτη δέ ἐστιν ἡ κρίσις
 b ὅτι τὸ φῶς ἐλήλυθεν εἰς τὸν κόσμον
 c καὶ ἠγάπησαν οἱ ἄνθρωποι μᾶλλον τὸ σκότος ἢ τὸ φῶς·
 d ἦν γὰρ αὐτῶν πονηρὰ τὰ ἔργα.
20a πᾶς γὰρ ὁ φαῦλα πράσσων
 b μισεῖ τὸ φῶς
 c καὶ οὐκ ἔρχεται πρὸς τὸ φῶς,
 d ἵνα μὴ ἐλεγχθῇ τὰ ἔργα αὐτοῦ·
21a ὁ δὲ ποιῶν τὴν ἀλήθειαν
 b ἔρχεται πρὸς τὸ φῶς,
 c ἵνα φανερωθῇ αὐτοῦ
 d τὰ ἔργα ὅτι ἐν θεῷ ἐστιν εἰργασμένα.
22a Μετὰ ταῦτα ἦλθεν ὁ Ἰησοῦς καὶ οἱ μαθηταὶ αὐτοῦ εἰς τὴν Ἰουδαίαν γῆν
 b καὶ ἐκεῖ διέτριβεν μετ’ αὐτῶν
 c καὶ ἐβάπτιζεν.

23a ἦν δὲ καὶ ὁ Ἰωάννης βαπτίζων ἐν Αἰνὼν ἐγγὺς τοῦ Σαλείμ,
  b ὅτι ὕδατα πολλὰ ἦν ἐκεῖ,
  c καὶ παρεγίνοντο
  d καὶ ἐβαπτίζοντο·
24 οὔπω γὰρ ἦν βεβλημένος εἰς τὴν φυλακὴν ὁ Ἰωάννης.
25 Ἐγένετο οὖν ζήτησις ἐκ τῶν μαθητῶν Ἰωάννου μετὰ Ἰουδαίου περὶ καθαρισμοῦ.
26a καὶ ἦλθον πρὸς τὸν Ἰωάννην
  b καὶ εἶπαν αὐτῷ,
  c Ῥαββί,
  d ὃς ἦν μετὰ σοῦ πέραν τοῦ Ἰορδάνου,
  e ᾧ σὺ μεμαρτύρηκας,
  f ἴδε οὗτος βαπτίζει
  g καὶ πάντες ἔρχονται πρὸς αὐτόν.
27a ἀπεκρίθη Ἰωάννης καὶ εἶπεν,
  b Οὐ δύναται ἄνθρωπος λαμβάνειν οὐδὲν ἕν
  c ἐὰν μὴ ᾖ δεδομένον αὐτῷ ἐκ τοῦ οὐρανοῦ.
28a αὐτοὶ υμεῖς μοι μαρτυρεῖτε
  b ὅτι εἶπον
  c [ὅτι] Οὐκ εἰμὶ ἐγὼ ὁ Χριστός,
  d ἀλλ’ ὅτι Ἀπεσταλμένος εἰμὶ ἔμπροσθεν ἐκείνου.
29a ὁ ἔχων τὴν νύμφην
  b νυμφίος ἐστίν·
  c ὁ δὲ φίλος τοῦ νυμφίου
  d ὁ ἑστηκὼς
  e καὶ ἀκούων αὐτοῦ
  f χαρᾷ χαίρει διὰ τὴν φωνὴν τοῦ νυμφίου.
  g αὕτη οὖν ἡ χαρὰ ἡ ἐμὴ πεπλήρωται.
30a ἐκεῖνον δεῖ αὐξάνειν,
  b ἐμὲ δὲ ἐλαττοῦσθαι.
31a Ὁ ἄνωθεν ἐρχόμενος
  b ἐπάνω πάντων ἐστίν·
  c ὁ ὢν ἐκ τῆς γῆς
  d ἐκ τῆς γῆς ἐστιν
  e καὶ ἐκ τῆς γῆς λαλεῖ.
  f ὁ ἐκ τοῦ οὐρανοῦ ἐρχόμενος
  g [ἐπάνω πάντων ἐστίν·]
32a τοῦτο μαρτυρεῖ (ὃ ἑώρακεν καὶ ἤκουσεν τοῦτο μαρτυρεῖ,)
  b ὃ ἑώρακεν
  c καὶ ἤκουσεν
  d καὶ τὴν μαρτυρίαν αὐτοῦ οὐδεὶς λαμβάνει.
33a ὁ λαβὼν αὐτοῦ τὴν μαρτυρίαν
  b ἐσφράγισεν
  c ὅτι ὁ θεὸς ἀληθής ἐστιν.
34a ὃν γὰρ ἀπέστειλεν ὁ θεὸς
  b τὰ ρήματα τοῦ θεοῦ λαλεῖ,
  c οὐ γὰρ ἐκ μέτρου δίδωσιν τὸ πνεῦμα.
35a ὁ πατὴρ ἀγαπᾷ τὸν υἱόν
  b καὶ πάντα δέδωκεν ἐν τῇ χειρὶ αὐτοῦ.

36a ο πιστεύων εἰς τὸν υἱ ὸν
 b ἔχει ζωὴν αἰώνιον·
 c ο δὲ ἀπειθῶν τῷ υἱ ῷ
 d οὐκ ὄψεται ζωήν,
 e ἀλλ' η ὀργὴ τοῦ θεοῦ μένει ἐπ' αὐτόν.

Jn. 2,23-3,36 (NRSV)

2,23a When he was in Jerusalem during the Passover festival,
 b many believed in his name
 c because they saw the signs
 d that he was doing.
24a But Jesus on his part would not entrust himself to them,
 b because he knew all people
25a and needed no one
 b to testify about anyone;
 c for he himself knew
 d what was in everyone.
3,1a Now there was a Pharisee
 b named Nicodemus, a leader of the Jews.
 2a He came to Jesus by night
 b and said to him,
 c "Rabbi, we know
 d that you are a teacher
 e who has come from God;
 f for no one can do these signs
 g that you do
 h apart from the presence of God."
 3a Jesus answered him,
 b "Very truly, I tell you,
 c *no one can see the kingdom of God*[1]
 d *without being born from above.*"
 4a Nicodemus said to him,
 b "How can anyone be born
 c after having grown old?
 d Can one enter a second time into the mother's womb
 e and be born?"
 5a Jesus answered,
 b "Very truly, I tell you,
 c *no one can enter the kingdom of God*
 d *without being born of water and Spirit.*
 6a What is born of the flesh is flesh,
 b and what is born of the Spirit is spirit.
 7a Do not be astonished
 b that I said to you,
 c 'You must be born from above.'
 8a The wind blows
 b where it chooses,
 c and you hear the sound of it,

---

[1] The phrases in italics are not in the same order as they appear in the Greek text.

d   but you do not know
e   where it comes from
f   or where it goes.
g   So it is with everyone
h   who is born of the Spirit."
9a   Nicodemus said to him,
b   "How can these things be?"
10a   Jesus answered him,
b   "Are you a teacher of Israel,
c   and yet you do not understand these things?
11a   Very truly, I tell you,
b   *we speak of*
c   *what we know*
d   *and testify to*
e   *what we have seen;*
f   yet you do not receive our testimony.
12a   If I have told you about earthly things
b   and you do not believe,
c   how can you believe
d   if I tell you about heavenly things?
13a   No one has ascended into heaven
b   except the one who descended from heaven, the Son of Man.
14a   And just as Moses lifted up the serpent in the wilderness,
b   so must the Son of Man be lifted up,
15a   that whoever believes in him
b   may have eternal life."
16a   For God so loved the world
b   that he gave his only Son,
c   so that everyone who believes in him
d   may not perish
e   but may have eternal life.
17a   Indeed, God did not send the Son into the world
b   to condemn the world,
c   but in order that the world might be saved through him.
18a   Those who believe in him
b   are not condemned;
c   but those who do not believe
d   are condemned already,
e   because they have not believed in the name of the only Son of God.
19a   And this is the judgement,
b   that the light has come into the world,
c   and people loved darkness rather than light
d   because their deeds were evil.
20a   For all who do evil
b   hate the light
c   and do not come to the light,
d   so that their deeds may not be exposed.
21a   But those who do what is true
b   come to the light,
c   so that it may be clearly seen
d   that their deeds have been done in God.

22a   After this Jesus and his disciples went into the Judean countryside,
  b   and he spent some time there with them
  c   and baptised.
23a   John also was baptising at Aenon near Salim
  b   because water was abundant there;
  c   and people kept coming
  d   and were being baptised
24   John, of course, had not yet been thrown into prison.
25   Now a discussion about purification arose between John's disciples and a Jew.
26a   They came to John
  b   and said to him,
  c   "Rabbi,
  d   the one who was with you across the Jordan,
  e   to whom you testified,
  f   here he is baptising,
  g   and all are going to him."
27a   John answered,
  b   "No one can receive anything
  c   except what has been given from heaven.
28a   You yourselves are my witnesses
  b   that I said,
  c   'I am not the Messiah,
  d   but I have been sent ahead of him.'
29a   He who has the bride
  b   is the bridegroom.
  c   The friend of the bridegroom,
  d   who stands
  e   and hears him,
  f   rejoices greatly at the bridegroom's voice.
  g   For this reason my joy has been fulfilled.
30a   He must increase,
  b   but I must decrease."
31a   The one who comes from above
  b   is above all;
  c   the one who is of the earth
  d   belongs to the earth
  e   and speaks about earthly things.
  f   The one who comes from heaven
  g   is above all.
32a   He testifies
  b   to what he has seen
  c   and heard,
  d   yet no one accepts his testimony.
33a   Whoever has accepted his testimony
  b   has certified this,
  c   that God is true.
34a   He whom God has sent
  b   speaks the words of God,
  c   for he gives the Spirit without measure.
35a   The Father loves the Son
  b   and has placed all things in his hands.

36a   Whoever believes in the Son
  b   has eternal life;
  c   whoever disobeys the Son
  d   will not see life,
  e   but must endure God's wrath.

1

INTRODUCTION

In his magnificent study of the fourth Gospel, Raymond E. Brown describes it as the "pearl of great price among the New Testament writings."[1] It is a NT writing that continues to command wide interest. The waves of scholarship on the fourth Gospel persist in their relentless assault on the 'enigma'[2] of this Gospel. It is certainly one of the most beloved and belaboured, revered and explored, of all NT documents, and yet there are dimensions and depths in this valuable work that still have not been sufficiently explored.

A. Ever Increasing Studies on the Fourth Gospel

Many scholars have written extensively on "this perennially fascinating Gospel."[3] The flood of monographs and articles offers new and enlightening views of this Gospel. A quick glance at the number of commentaries and works of study that have appeared under interesting titles vouch for it.[4] It has been named a Gospel of Belief,[5] Gospel of Glory,[6] Gospel of Signs,[7] Gospel of Truth,[8] Gospel of Wisdom,[9] Definitive Gospel,[10] Martyr's Gospel,[11] Maverick Gospel,[12] Missionary Gospel,[13] Post-Modern Gospel,[14] Prophetic

---

[1] R. E. Brown, *The Gospel according to St. John* (AncB 29) (New York 1966) I, 18. Regarding footnotes, at the first occurrence the author's name will appear with the initials of his/her first name(s) with full title etc. as given above. From the second instance onwards only the surname and the corresponding page(s) will be given. If there is more than one author under the same surname the initials will also be repeated all through. If the same author has more than one book and/or article quoted in this dissertation, then a key word or phrase of the respective title, too, will be given.

[2] G. R. Beasley-Murray, *John* (WBC 36) (Waco 1987) xxxii; and cf. R. Eisler, *The Enigma of the Fourth Gospel* (London 1938).

[3] J. Ashton, *Studying John. Approaches to the Fourth Gospel* (Oxford 1994) 1.

[4] E.g. G. van Belle (*Johannine Bibliography 1966-1985: A Cumulative Bibliography on the Fourth Gospel* [BEThL 82] [Leuven 1988]) lists 6300 publications for the period of 20 years covered in his bibliography.

[5] M. C. Tenney, *John: The Gospel of Belief. An Analytic Study of the Text* (Grand Rapids 1988); see also F.-J. Moloney, *Belief in the Word. Reading the Fourth Gospel: John 1-4* (Minneapolis 1993).

[6] R. E. Brown (*op. cit.*, 2 Vols. [AncB 29/29a] [New York 1966/70]) and F.-J. Moloney (*The Gospel of John* [SPS 4] [Collegeville 1998]) treat the fourth Gospel dividing it into two sections, namely 'Book of Signs' and 'Book of Glory' which is widely accepted by many scholars. M. Gourgues (*Pour que vous croyiez. Pistes d'exploration de l'évangile de Jean* [Paris 1982]) names the 'Book of Glory' as the 'Book of the Hour.'

[7] Cf. R. T. Fortna, *The Gospel of Signs. A Reconstruction of the Narrative Source Underlying the Fourth Gospel* (MSSNTS 11) (Cambridge 1970). As signs are not restricted to 1,19-12,50, from a broader perspective, such a view, according to me, is not incorrect. 20,30-31 makes it clear that from the evangelist's perspective the whole Gospel is a book of signs. In fact, I would say that the account of the passion and resurrection of Jesus is to be viewed as the ultimate sign of the 'lifting up' of the Son of Man and, hence, one could call it also a 'Gospel of Signs.'

[8] Cf. J. Kreyenbühl, *Das Evangelium der Wahrheit* (Berlin 1900); see also I. de la Potterie, *La vérité dans S. Jean*, 2 Vols. (AnBib 73/74) (Rome 1977).

[9] B. Witherington, III, *John's Wisdom. A Commentary on the Fourth Gospel* (Westminster 1995).

[10] Tenney, 35.

[11] P. S. Minear, *John, the Martyr's Gospel* (New York 1984).

[12] R. Kysar, *John. The Maverick Gospel* (Louisville, Westminster 1993).

[13] See W. Oehler, *Das Johannesevangelium. Eine Missionsschrift für die Welt* (Gütersloh 1936); and his *Zum Missionscharakter des Johannesevangeliums* (Gütersloh 1941).

[14] P. Counet and J. E. Chatelion, *John, a Post-Modern Gospel: Introduction to Deconstructive Exegesis Applied to the Fourth Gospel* (Leiden 2000).

Gospel,[15] Selective Gospel,[16] Spiritual Gospel,[17] Universal Gospel,[18] an Apologetic Gospel,[19] Attested Gospel,[20] Effective Gospel,[21] Evangelistic Gospel,[22] Interpretative Gospel;[23] and the list could be lengthened further.

A kaleidoscope makes various forms emerge as one turns it, yet remains the same kaleidoscope. The same could be said of the fourth Gospel; it is often sufficient to tilt the angle of approach to discover a new vision of things, yet it is always one and the same Gospel. Various commentators and research scholars, in kaleidoscopic fashion, view the Gospel from different angles. Some see in this Gospel a narrative that reflects the situation of the Church at the time in which it was written. Others see in it a narrative that reflects the life and beliefs of a special segment of the Church that they call the *Johannine Community*. They observe in this Gospel the result of a long line of historical development; and these commentators try to trace the major ideas of the Gospel back to historical sources.[24] Pastors, on the other hand, may look to the Gospel for its ethical and pastoral teachings. The fourth Gospel proves to be "a treasure-house of psychological and spiritual insight."[25]

J. Ashton, at the beginning of his book *Understanding the Fourth Gospel*, thanking his teacher X. Léon-Dufour, says that he owes him the "dawning realisation" of the fact that "there is more in the Gospel of John than meets the eye."[26] Studying a pericope or a theme of the fourth Gospel and attempting to say something new is certainly not an easy task, as it has aroused a special attraction among scholars since a number of decades. The

---

[15] A. T. Hanson, *The Prophetic Gospel. A Study of John and the Old Testament* (Edinburgh 1991).

[16] Tenney, 34.

[17] This designation of the fourth Gospel goes back to Clement of Alexandria, according to Eusebius, *Hist. Eccl.* 6.14.7 = *Sources chrétiennes* 41 (Paris 1957) 107. M. F. Wiles, *The Spiritual Gospel. The Interpretation of the Fourth Gospel in the Early Church* (Cambridge 1960); and H. van den Bussche, *Jean. Commentaire de l'Évangile Spirituel* (Bruges 1967); see also G. Zevini, *Commentaire spirituel de l'Évangile de Jean* (Montréal, Paris 1995); and X. Léon-Dufour, *Lecture de l'Évangile selon Jean* (PD) (Paris 1988) I, 12-15.

[18] Cf. Kysar, *Maverick Gospel*, 128-35.

[19] Tenney, 35.

[20] *Ibid.*, 34.

[21] *Ibid.*, 36.

[22] D. A. Carson, *The Gospel according to John* (Grand Rapids, Leicester 1991) 8.

[23] Tenney, 35. The fourth Gospel interprets the life of Jesus in terms of the Messiah predicted in the OT and awaited by the Jewish nation.

[24] Cf. J. D. Kaestli, J.-M. Poffet and J. Zumstein (eds.), *La communauté johannique et son histoire. La trajectoire de l'évangile de Jean aux deux premiers siècles* (MB) (Geneva 1990); P.-Y. Ruff, "La communauté johannique et son histoire," *RTP* 123 (1991) 79-92; R. A. Culpepper, *The Johannine School. An Evaluation of the Johannine School Hypothesis Based on an Investigation of the Nature of Ancient Schools* (SBL.DS 26) (Missoula 1975); and G. L. Renner, *The Life-World of the Johannine Community: An Investigation of the Social Dynamics which Resulted in the Composition of the Fourth Gospel* (Boston 1982). See also J. L. Martyn, "Glimpses into the History of the Johannine Community. From its Origin through the Period of its Life in which the Fourth Gospel was Composed," in: M. de Jonge (ed.), *L'Évangile de Jean. Sources, rédaction, théologie* (BEThL 44) (Leuven 1977) 149-75. There are a lot more studies done on the Johannine Community.

[25] J. A. Sanford, *Mystical Christianity. A Psychological Commentary on the Gospel of John* (New York 1993) 1.

[26] J. Ashton, *Understanding the Fourth Gospel* (Oxford 1993) ix.

amount of published work on it is proliferating every day and the subject is vast. "No other book of the New Testament has attracted so much attention from commentators."[27]

B. Christology – the Dominating Theme

H. Weder asserts that "Christology is the central and decisive process of reflection within the *corpus Iohanneum*. It is the central theme of hermeneutical reflection in these writings."[28] The question relating especially to the Christology of the fourth Gospel has been the most dominating and fascinating theme of many of the recent works.[29] R. Schnackenburg rightly observes that "one of the most mature fruits of reflection on Jesus Christ in early Christianity is Johannine Christology. There is no end to works that deal with it."[30] The titles and terms applied to Jesus in the fourth Gospel again and again encapsulate the early Christian understanding of the role and status of Jesus. While none of them on its own sums up the full revelation of God contained in Jesus, each of them contributes distinctively and complementarily to the multi-faceted picture of Jesus portrayed by the fourth evangelist.

---

[27] Moloney, *John*, xi.

[28] H. Weder, "Deus Incarnatus: On the Hermeneutics of Christology in the Johannine Writings," in: R. A. Culpepper and C. C. Black (eds.), *Exploring the Gospel of John. In Honour of D. Moody Smith* (Louisville, Westminster 1996) 327.

[29] For a survey of recent research see M. J. J. Menken, "The Christology of the Fourth Gospel: A Survey of Recent Research," in: M. C. de Boer (ed.), *From Jesus to John. Essays on Jesus and New Testament Christology. FS M. de Jonge* (JSNT.S 84) (Sheffield 1993) 292-320; see also M. Hengel, *Studies in Christology* (Edinburgh 1998).

[30] R. Schnackenburg, *Jesus in the Gospels. A Biblical Christology* (Louisville 1995) 219. Even for the last 25 years it is almost impossible to give an exhaustive list of authors. See especially van Belle, *Johannine Bibliography*. All the same, I shall list a few that have attracted my attention: J. Rinke, *Kerygma und Autopsie. Der Christologische Disput als Spiegel johanneischer Gemeindegeschichte* (HBS 12) (Freiburg 1996); P. N. Anderson, *The Christology of the Fourth Gospel. Its Unity and Disunity in the Light of John 6* (WUNT 78) (Tübingen 1996); W. Loader, *The Christology of the Fourth Gospel* (BET 23) (Frankfurt ²1992); J. H. Neyrey, *An Ideology of Revolt. John's Christology in Social-Science Perspective* (Philadelphia 1988); U. Schnelle, *Antidoketische Christologie im Johannesevangelium. Eine Untersuchung zur Stellung des vierten Evangeliums in der johanneischen Schule* (FRLANT 144) (Göttingen 1987); J.-A. Bühner, *Der Gesandte und sein Weg im 4. Evangelium. Die kultur- und religionsgeschichtlichen Grundlagen der johanneischen Sendungschristologie so wie ihre traditionsgeschichtliche Entwicklung* (WUNT II/2) (Tübingen 1977); J. Becker, "Ich bin die Auferstehung und das Leben. Eine Skizze der johanneischen Christologie," *ThZ* 39 (1983) 136-51; R. Baum-Bodenbender, *Hoheit in Niedrigkeit. Johanneische Christologie im Prozeß Jesu vor Pilatus (Joh 18,28-19,16a)* (FzB 49) (Würzburg 1984); M.-É. Boismard, *Moïse ou Jésus. Essai de christologie johannique* (BEThL 84) (Leuven 1988); M. de Jonge, *Jesus. Stranger from Heaven and Son of God. Jesus Christ and the Christians in Johannine Perspective* (SBibSt) (Missoula 1977); G. Mlakuzhyil, *The Christocentric Literary Structure of the Fourth Gospel* (AnBib 117) (Rome 1987); F.-J. Moloney, *The Johannine Son of Man* (BSRel 14) (Rome ²1978); U. B. Müller, *Die Geschichte der Christologie in der johanneischen Gemeinde* (SBS 77) (Stuttgart 1975); T. E. Pollard, *Johannine Christology and the Early Church* (MSSNTS 13) (Cambridge 1970); W. Thüsing, *Die Erhöhung und Verherrlichung Jesu im Johannesevangelium* (NTA 21) (Münster ³1979); R. Kysar, *The Fourth Evangelist and His Gospel* (Minneapolis 1975) esp. 178-206; J. P. Miranda, *Die Sendung Jesu im Vierten Evangelium. Der Vater, der mich gesandt hat. Religions- und theologiegeschichtliche Untersuchungen zu den johannneischen Sendungsformeln* (SBS 87) (Stuttgart 1977); de la Potterie, *La vérité*, I, 117-278; M. L. Appold, *The Oneness Motif in the Fourth Gospel* (WUNT II/1) (Tübingen 1976); M. Theobald, *Die Fleischwerdung des Logos* (NTANF 20) (Münster 1988); K.-J. Kuschel, *Geboren vor aller Zeit? Der Streit um Christi Ursprung* (München 1990); and K. Scholtissek, "Mystagogische Christologie im Johannes-evangelium? Eine Spurensuche," *GuL* 68 (1995) 412-26.

4

It is generally acknowledged that the most characteristic elements of the Christology of the fourth Gospel are bound up with the concept of the Son of God; and a striking feature of the presentation of the Son in the fourth Gospel is its close liaison with the Son of Man.[31] According to W. R. G. Loader, Christology lies at the heart of the theology of the fourth Gospel. He tries to identify the basic structure of the Christology underlying the various motives and themes of the Gospel. He uses the results of his analysis to re-examine Christological issues and their significance for a better understanding of the Gospel.[32] P. Létourneau in his doctoral dissertation on the conversation of Jesus with Nicodemus and the second witness of the Baptist, making use of the tool of 'structural analysis' above all, has done an excellent study in analysing the pattern of Christology underlying Jn. 3 in particular, and the fourth Gospel in general. He shows how the Christology of the fourth Gospel is developed around the two fundamental themes of looking at Jesus as *the Son of Man come down from heaven* and of affirming that he is *the Son of God sent by the Father*. This pattern of a double-Christology in the fourth Gospel furnishes the framework for understanding most of the Christological terms, statements and schemes of this Gospel, and helps to appreciate the originality of the fourth evangelist's presentation of the death of Jesus better.[33] P. Anderson, in his recent book on the Christology of the fourth Gospel, exposes that Jesus is presented as both human and divine causing tension and provoking debate. He explores in his work the origins and character of the unity and disunity of the Christology of this Gospel, especially from the point of view of Jn. 6.[34]

The fourth evangelist himself, in his conclusion, states explicitly the purpose of his Gospel as Christocentric:[35] "Now Jesus did many other signs in the presence of his disciples which are not written in this book. But these are written so that you may come to believe that Jesus is the Messiah, the Son of God, and that through believing you may have life in his name" (20,30-31). The aim of my dissertation is to plunge deeper into the unit chosen for my study (2,23-3,36), explore and unearth, investigate and appreciate further the inexhaustible riches of the Christology buried here, and especially in the narrative sequence and network of the first section of this Gospel (1,19-4,54), as key to understanding a passage often lies outside it.

C. Choice of the Unit of my Study

According to O. Hofius, the conversation of Jesus with Nicodemus belongs not only to the theologically important, but also to the exegetically controversial pericopes of the fourth

---

[31] Cf. Beasley-Murray, *John*, lxxxii.

[32] Loader, *Christology*. The book is rich on the various elements of the Christology of the fourth Gospel and devotes a large section to the compilation of different points of view on the subject. See also his article: "The Central structure of the Johannine Christology," *NTS* 30 (1984) 188-216.

[33] P. Létourneau, *Jésus fils de l'homme et fils de Dieu* (RNS 27) (Montréal, Paris 1992). For a critical appreciation of this book see M. Gourgues, "Notes critiques: Sur la structure et la christologie de Jean 3. Approche et apport d'un ouvrage récent," *ScEs* 46 (1994) 221-27.

[34] Cf. Anderson.

[35] See the recent work of G. A. F. Knight, *Christ the Centre* (Grand Rapids 1999); and Mlakuzhyil.

Gospel.[36] Because of the numerous themes dealt with in Jn. 3, J. Becker considers it as containing the first exposition of the central themes of the theology of the fourth Gospel.[37] F. Porsch finds in it a magnificent and concentrated summary of the Christian faith. He would even call it a catechism of faith in the form of a dialogue.[38] For K.-M. Bull Jn. 3 is the key text of the fourth Gospel containing in a few verses the basic statements of Johannine theology.[39] E. Ruckstuhl and P. Dschulnigg, too, find Jn. 3 to be typically Johannine in character comparing it with the whole Gospel.[40] Among the many pericopes in the fourth Gospel having a Christological argumentation, such as 2,23-3,36; 5,19-30; 6,22-59; 8,21-30 and 17, the first and, perhaps, the most attractive, according to me, is the encounter of Nicodemus (2,23-3,21) and the second witness of John the Baptist (3,22-36). I am sure Jn. 3 contains a synthesis of the fourth evangelist's Christology and soteriology and, therefore, could serve as a key to understanding the overall Christological scheme of the Gospel. These are some of the main reasons for the choice of this unit for my study.

D. Methodology

The choice of a method of appropriate analysis constitutes an essential factor for the advancement of research. The fourth Gospel is a multi-story phenomenon calling for a multi-disciplinary methodology. A current methodology that attracts me is the one used by M. W. G. Stibbe in his doctoral dissertation published in 1992 entitled *John as Storyteller* and in his commentary on the fourth Gospel.[41] Rejecting '*a-historical*' literary criticism he develops a multi-faceted criticism that integrates 'diachronic' and 'synchronic' methods of biblical criticism. It is a comprehensive exegetical approach treating the fourth Gospel from a literary, as well as an historico-theological perspective, calling it 'narrative criticism'– a *text, context and pre-text*[42] method. He likes to name it an "intergrated"[43]

---

[36] Cf. O. Hofius, "Das Wunder der Wiedergeburt. Jesu Gespräch mit Nicodemus. Jn. 3,1-21," in: O. Hofius and H.-C. Kammler (eds.), *Johannesstudien: Untersuchungen zur Theologie des vierten Evangeliums* (WUNT 88) (Tübingen 1996) 33.

[37] J. Becker, *Das Evangelium nach Johannes. Kapitel 1-10* (Gütersloh, Würzburg ³1991) 153; see also D. J. Hawkin, *The Johannine World: Reflections on the Theology of the Fourth Gospel and Contemporary Society* (Albany 1996).

[38] F. Porsch, *Johannesevangelium* (SKK.NT 4) (Stuttgart 1988) 39.

[39] K.-M. Bull, *Gemeinde zwischen Integration und Abgrenzung. Ein Beitrag zur Frage nach dem Ort der johanneischen Gemeinde(n) in der Geschichte des Urchristentums* (BET 24) (Bern, Frankfurt, New York, Paris 1992) 67.

[40] E. Ruckstuhl and P. Dschulnigg, *Stilkritik und Verfasserfrage im Johannesevangelium. Die johanneischen Sprachmerkmale auf dem Hintergrund des Neuen Testaments und des zeitgenössischen hellenistischen Schrifttums* (NTOA 17) (Fribourg, Göttingen 1991) 216-41.

[41] M. W. G. Stibbe, *John as Storyteller. Narrative Criticism and the Fourth Gospel* (MSSNTS 73) (Cambridge 1992); and his *John* (RNBC) (Sheffield 1993). In fact, many of the modern commentaries follow this method of narrative criticism; see also Moloney, *John*, 13-20; his *Belief in the Word*, 1-7; *Signs and Shadows. Reading John 5-12* (Minneapolis 1996); *Glory not Dishonor. Reading John 13-20 (21)* (Minneapolis 1998); Léon-Dufour, *Lecture*, I, 21-26; and G. L. Borchert, *John 1-11* (NAC 25A) (Louisville 1996) 50-59.

[42] Stibbe, *Storyteller*, 1. Moloney (*John*, 13-14 and 18-20) speaks of 'world behind the text, world in the text and world in front of the text.' For a recent study on a multi-faceted perspective see A. J. Köstenberger, *Encountering John: The Gospel in Historical, Literary, and Theological Perspective* (EBS) (Grand Rapids 1999).

[43] Stibbe, *op. cit.*, 1-2. He integrates literary and theological questions in chapter I, structuralism and historical criticism in chapter II, and literary and sociological areas of enquiry in chapter III. I would like to

approach. His method seems promising and his exegesis is often provocative. I believe, there could be no more apt description of the story of the fourth evangelist than narrative Christology. In fact, the aim expressed by the author in Jn. 20,31 using terms of narrative categories can be paraphrased as follows: every detail of this narrative has been selected and expressed in such a way that you might accept its fundamental Christological belief, that Jesus is the Christ.

The years 1920-1960 were marked by the historical-critical method whose specific object was the history of the formation of the text and dissection of the text into minimal units (diachronics) based on their function to the different literary strata they belong to. The new tendencies of research of the fourth Gospel, in the past couple of decades, have revolutionised its exegesis. The hermeneutics of today give primacy to the final text as one has it and take for granted that there is a general uniformity of style throughout the Gospel – that it is a unitary composition and contains all the elements necessary for its interpretation. Given this tradition, and given also the preferred starting point of modern literary and narrative criticism, it seems best to me to start with the supposition that the text is a unity.[44] In the last few decades there has been a shift of emphasis in exegesis. In the following pages let me, briefly, survey the various exegetical methods (old and new) and seek to justify my methodology.

1. Shift of Emphasis in Exegesis

a. Theological Approach

For many centuries the emphasis in the interpretation of the fourth Gospel was on its *theological meaning*.[45] Though there was considerable diversity, particularly between the literal and symbolic interpretations, there was, however, certain unanimity on basic presuppositions. It was taken for granted that the text was an inspired unity,[46] and that, when properly interpreted, it provided reliable insights into the ultimate meaning of life. The task of the scholar was to elaborate that insight.

b. Historical-Critical Method

During the nineteenth and twentieth-centuries the process of theological exposition of the fourth Gospel was developed and enriched, particularly in the commentaries of B. Westcott, E. C. Hoskyns, R. Butmann, R. E. Brown and R. Schnackenburg; but very often the dominating interest of these years was in *history*. Historical questions were put on a pedestal and asked often not 'what does it mean?' but 'did it happen?' The result was a fundamental change of focus – shift of attention from the text to its background, to the reconstruction of events and of earlier texts. The entire process of interpretation became so dominated by the single question of history that the acceptable interpretative procedure

---

call it 'modern literary and narrative criticism'; see also I. J. du Plessis, "Integrating Historical and Literary Study: Luke a Case Study," Paper read at 1995 SNTS meeting.

[44] See also J. W. Voelz, *What Does This mean? Principles of Biblical Interpretation in the Post-Modern World* (Saint Louis ²1997).

[45] See esp. C. R. Seitz and K. Greene-McCreight (eds.), *Theological Exegesis: Essays in Honour of Brevard S. Childs* (Grand Rapids 1999).

[46] See esp. S. M. Schneiders, *The Revelatory Text: Interpreting the New Testament as Sacred Scripture* (Collegeville 2000).

came to be known as the *historical-critical method*[47] or, quite simply, the *historical method*.

The historical method's quest for history has met with mixed success.[48] It had achieved a major break through, in establishing with considerable certainty, that both Matthew and Luke depended on Mark. But in the twentieth-century, as it moved even further and writers composed unified texts and entered into the worlds of *form criticism* (based on the concept of *oral tradition*), the *history of religions approach* (looking at the influence of first-century philosophical and religious movements on the fourth evangelist), *source criticism* (attempting to uncover the original sources used in the composition of the Gospel) and *redaction criticism* (working tentatively toward a reconstruction of the Johannine Community from evidence within the Gospel and the Johannine Epistles), historical criticism became vague in its central concepts – *oral tradition* and *redaction*. There has been no clear agreement on how oral transmission actually works;[49] nor is there a clear understanding of the role of editors.[50] The result has been a proliferation of complex and unverifiable 're-constructions' of how the various texts originated and developed.[51] Since the emphasis on history tended to lead people away from the final text and back into a world of 're-constructions,' which at times seemed fragile and hollow, some scholars began to protest against the dominance of the historical method.[52] As Culpepper rightly asserts "the future of the Gospel in the life of the Church will depend on the Church's ability to relate both story and history to truth in such a way that neither has an exclusive claim to truth and one is not incompatible with the other."[53] In an argument of great urgency, N. Fyre rightly appeals to biblical scholars to "relax from their obsession with the Bible's historicity"[54] and to give other hypotheses a chance.

---

[47] See esp. J. G. Prior, *The Historical Critical Method in Catholic Exegesis* (Rome 1999).

[48] I think F. W. Dobbs-Allsopp ("Rethinking Historical Criticism," *BibInt* 7 [1999] 271) is over-optimistic when he says that "historical criticism remains alive and well, and its theoretical base is healthy and vigorous today as ever before and, perhaps, more so." See also J. B. Rogers and D. K. McKim, *The Authority and Interpretation of the Bible: An Historical Approach* (Eugene 1999).

[49] See W. Kelber, *The Oral and Written Gospel. The Hermeneutics of Speaking and Writing in the Synoptic Tradition, Mark, Paul and Q* (Philadelphia 1983) 1-14.

[50] See esp. J. A. Miles, "Radical Editing... and... Willed Confusion," in: B. Halpern and J. D. Levenson (eds.), *Traditions in Transformation* (Winona Lake 1981) 9-31.

[51] See e.g. T. R. Hatina, "Intertextuality and Historical Criticism in New Testament Studies: Is There a Relationship?," *BibInt* 7 (1999) 28-43; A. Dauer, "Schichten im Johannesevangelium als Anzeichen von Entwicklungen in der (den) johanneischen Gemeinde(n) nach G. Richter. Darstellung und Kritik," in: A. E. Hierold, V. Eid, I. Escribano-Alberca, O. Fuchs and N. Glatzel (eds.), *Die Kraft der Hoffnung. Gemeinde und Evangelium. FS J. Schneider* (Bamberg 1986) 62-83; A. J. Mattill, "Johannine Communities Behind the Fourth Gospel: Georg Richter's Analysis," *TS* 38 (1977) 294-315; M. Schmidl, *Jesus und Nikodemus: Gespräch zur johanneischen Christologie* (BU 28) (Regensburg 1998); and C. Dekker, "Grundschrift und Redaktion im Johannesevangelium," *NTS* 13 (1966) 66-80.

[52] Cf. W. Wink, *The Bible in Human Transformation. Toward a New Paradigm for Biblical Study* (Philadelphia 1973) 1; see also R. E. C. Johnston, *From an Author-Oriented to a Text-Oriented Hermeneutic: Implications of Paul Ricoeur's Hermeneutical Theory for the Interpretation of the New Testament* (Leuven 1977) 1-23.

[53] R. A. Culpepper, *Anatomy of the Fourth Gospel. A Study in Literary Design* (Philadelphia 1983) 236.

[54] See N. Fyre, *The Great Code. The Bible and Literature* (London, New York 1981) 40-42. Shortly after R. Kysar brought out his *John's Story of Jesus* (Philadelphia 1984). Then came J. L. Staley's *The Print's First Kiss: A Rhetorical Investigation of the Implied Reader in the Fourth Gospel* (SBL.DS 82) (Atlanta 1988).

c. Sociological Approach

Just when the historical method seemed destined to take a more modest role, in the mid-1970s, the *sociological* approach found vigorous life within a vast new undertaking. This is a method which has had considerable influence on the studies of the fourth Gospel. The essence of sociology is that it examines not just one aspect of society but the amalgamation of all the aspects. History by comparison has been narrow – a report on, say, politics and religion – and, as such, it has, sometimes, been seen as a sub-discipline of sociology. History, for instance, may say that people were poor, but sociology goes further; it asks why; it seeks to trace all the underlying factors and the complex connections between those factors. Sociological method helps to analyse the social history of early Christianity and renders a valuable service to understand and interpret the text.[55] This approach enables the reader to interpret the Gospel in a way that would be fair to its original author and audience, because the distance between to-day's reader and the bible is as much social as it is temporal and conceptual.[56] Such a social distance includes radical difference in social structures, social roles, values and general cultural features.

d. Canonical Criticism

Given the ability of historical criticism and of social analysis to lose sight both of theology and of the text, advocates of *canonical criticism* protested. Their basic point was simple and central: whatever the merits of history and sociology, the essential meaning of scripture is to be sought in the theological message which is contained in its final canonical form.[57]

e. Literary Criticism

The essence of this method is to look not at the background of the text (its author and origins), but at the text itself, the finished work – its integrity and structure, its interrelation of form and content. Texts are to be regarded not as windows, as ways of looking at something beyond and at distant events, but as mirrors and surfaces which contain coherent

---

[55] See M. Hasitschka, "Sozialgeschichtliche Anmerkungen zum Johannesevangelium," *PzB* 1 (1992) 59-67. See also D. G. Horrell (ed.), *Social-Scientific Approaches to New Testament Interpretation* (Edinburgh 1999); and J. D. Kingsbury (ed.), *Gospel Interpretation: Narrative-Critical and Social-Scientific Approaches* (Minneapolis 1999). For reviews and assessments, see esp. D. J. Harrington, "Sociological Concepts and the Early Church: A Decade of Research," *TS* 41 (1980) 181-90; C. Osiek, "The New Handmaid. The Bible and the Social Sciences," *TS* 50 (1989) 260-78; see also H. C. Kee, *Knowing the Truth. A Sociological Approach to New Testament Interpretation* (Minneapolis 1989) 32-64; B. Holmberg, *Sociology and the New Testament. An Appraisal* (Philadelphia 1990); and P. F. Craffert, "Relationships between Social-Scientific, Literary, and Rhetorical Interpretation of Texts," *BTB* 26 (1996) 45-53.

[56] Cf. B. J. Malina and R. L. Rohrbaugh, *Social-Science Commentary on the Gospel of John* (Minneapolis 1998) 1-2. One has to keep in mind that the meaning communicated by means of written or spoken language derive ultimately from a social system. See J. H. Elliot, *What is Social-Scientific Criticism?* (GBSNT) (Minneapolis 1993).

[57] See esp. B. S. Childs, *The New Testament as Canon* (Philadelphia 1985); and J. Sanders, *Canon and Community. Guides to Biblical Scholarship* (Philadelphia 1984); for a critique, see R. E. Brown, "Hermeneutics," *NJBC*, 71; cf. also D. M. Smith, "John, the Synoptics, and the Canonical Approach to Exegesis," in: G. F. Hawthorne (ed.), *Tradition and Interpretation in the New Testament. Essays in Honour of Earl Ellis for his 60th Birthday* (Tübingen 1987) 166-80; and his, "Prolegomena to a Canonical Reading of the Fourth Gospel," in: F. F. Segovia (ed.), *'What is John?' Readers and Readings of the Fourth Gospel* (Atlanta 1996) 169-82.

worlds of meaning.[58] The impetus for this shift, from the author's world to the finished text, has come also from other literary circles, particularly from the French method of *'explication de textes'* and the Russian formalists.[59] *Structural criticism* (can be considered a part of literary criticism) has had the effect of strengthening the shift from a concentration on the author to an insistence on the finished text.[60] The impact of modern literary criticism on Gospel studies first began to emerge clearly about 1974. It was also the year of the launching of the experimental journal *Semeia*. The entire story of literary criticism's impact on the interpretation of the Gospels has since been chronicled in detail in S. D. Moore.[61] Since 1974, both in *Semeia* and in other publications, a growing number of scholars have examined biblical texts, not by regarding them as edited collections of fragments or by focusing on their origins, but by taking seriously the unity of the finished text.

All these skills have been used in biblical interpretation. However, all these methods include some degree of incompleteness. Every approach, according to me, has tendencies toward certain excesses. The theological emphasis, presupposing that its method was correct and comprehensive, had sometimes tended toward arbitrary symbolism, the historical – sometimes tending to regard all that preceded as pre-critical – toward disproportionately long footnotes; the literary, on the other hand, tended toward a complex terminology appearing, at times, to be autocratic.[62] The danger is acute of losing the biblical text in a mountain of endless historical and philological notes. However limited one or another method may be, the fact is that, ultimately, each represents a skill which is not only valid but valuable.[63] Any thorough study of the bible or a biblical passage, I feel, should use all the necessary skills and tools at its disposal, and do so in an appropriate way.

2. Short Description of 'Modern Literary Criticism'

In assessing the relationship between the Gospel's literary and theological aspects, though the theological is the most essential and first in ultimate value, it is not methodologically. The literary is what demands one's initial attention.[64] Paradoxical as it may sound, the

---

[58] Cf. W. Weren, *Windows on Jesus. Methods in Gospel Exegesis* (Philadelphia 1999). However, the text is, paradoxically, both mirror and window.

[59] Cf. A. Jefferson, "Russian Formalism," in: A. Jefferson and D. Robey (eds.), *Modern Literary Theory. A Comparative Introduction* (Totowa 1982) 16-37. It has been further underlined by P. Ricoeur, *Interpretation Theory: Discourse and Surplus of Meaning* (Fort Worth 1976); see also R. E. C. Johnston, and P. Henry, *New Directions in New Testament Study* (Philadelphia 1979) 59-69; and R. Wellek and A. Warren, *Theory of Literature* (London, New York ³1977) 139-40.

[60] Cf. J. D. Culler, *Structuralist Poetics: Structuralism, Linguistics and the Study of Literature* (Ithaca 1975).

[61] S. D. Moore, *Literary Criticism and the Gospels. The Theoretical Challenge* (London, New Haven 1989).

[62] Cf. J. Becker, "Das Johannesevangelium im Streit der Methoden (1980-1984)," *ThR* 51 (1986) 7.

[63] Cf. M. Sternberg, *The Poetics of Biblical Narrative. Ideological Literature and the Drama of Reading* (Bloomington 1985) 17.

[64] There is now a greater interest among scholars to approach each single document, however limited and flawed it might be, as a work of art; see D. A. Templeton, *The New Testament as True Fiction: Literature, Literary Criticism, Aesthetics* (Sheffield 1999). E. V. McKnight and E. S. Malbon (eds.), *The New Literary Criticism and the New Testament* (Minneapolis 1994). Culpepper's *Anatomy* is considered as one of the pioneering works in this direction. I prefer to call it 'Modern Literary Criticism' to distinguish it from the ancient, to avoid confusion, and to show that it is an integrated or a comprehensive method of including the

historical method, as commonly practised, is not the surest way of making progress in historical research. These methodologies were not concerned with the aesthetic qualities of the final form of the text as it is. Hence, it is becoming more and more clear that literary appreciation – ancient and modern – is crucial to understanding the very nature of the NT documents, including their value as history. Any investigative method which does not adequately consider such basic data does not do justice to the cause of historical research. The literary approach, therefore, will dominate my method of research. In its broadest sense, literary criticism encompasses all questions which arise pertaining to the text itself, including its authorship, historical setting, various aspects of the language and content of the text. Historically, literary criticism in traditional biblical studies has had a rather narrow focus referring, primarily, to source or documentary analysis.

In general literary studies, literary criticism denotes a broad range of topics:[65] the compositional structure and character of a text, techniques of style, the employment of images and symbols by an author, aesthetic and dramatic effects in a work,[66] and so on. All these factors are involved in reading and understanding biblical texts. The bible is more than literature, but it is certainly literature.

The field of 'modern literary criticism' has three major methodological segments: 1) Structuralism which involves an analysis of the implied structures – such as deep structures at the root of human realities – inherent in a story; 2) rhetorical criticism, which involves the canons of rhetoric or the effectiveness of communication – the study of which goes back to Aristotle and Quintillian; 3) narrative criticism[67] whose focus is on the story, the formal content element involving the dimensions of characterisation, plot, setting and point of view.

a. Structural Criticism[68]

In a play it is helpful, at first, to know the very simple fact that it consists of many acts and scenes. But in the case of the fourth Gospel the basic divisions are not indicated;[69] therefore, before launching into theological exposition, it is, first, necessary to attend to the literary task of trying to discern how the Gospel is organised or structured. The structure of a book is like the anatomy of a body; it gives a foundational sense of the work's

---

structural, rhetorical and narrative analysis in the exegesis of a biblical text; see J. Zumstein, "Analyse narrative, critique rhétorique et exégèse johannique," in: P. Bühler and J.-F. Habermacher (eds.), *La narration. Quand le récit devient communication* (LiTh 12) (Geneva 1998) 37-56; and Carson (*Gospel*, 35) calls it "new criticism."

[65] See the work of N. Fyre, *Anatomy of Criticism* (Princeton 1971).

[66] Cf. N. M. Flanagan, "The Gospel of John as Drama," *BiTod* 19 (1981) 264-70; see also C. Rau, *Struktur und Rhythmus im Johannesevangelium* (SzR) (Stuttgart 1972); and D. W. Wead, *Literary Devices in John's Gospel* (ThDiss 4) (Basel 1970).

[67] According to S. D. Moore (*Literary Criticism*, 176-77) narrative analysis may well be the most successful aspect of literary analysis in dealing with the Gospels.

[68] One does still not have a complete, definitive and comprehensive exposition of this method. Here are some that are useful: J. Calloud, "Toward a Structural Analysis of the Gospel of Mark," *Semeia* 16 (1980) 133-65; D. Via, *Kerygma and Comedy in the New Testament. A Structuralist Approach to Hermeneutic* (Philadelphia 1975); A. Vanhoye, "Les indices de la structure littéraire de l'Épître aux Hébreux," in: *Studia Evangelica II* (TU 87) (Berlin 1964); M. Girard, *Les Psaumes. Analyse structurelle et interprétation, Tome 1, 1-50* (Montréal, Paris 1984) 11-51; and R. Meynet, *L'analyse rhétorique: une nouvelle méthode pour comprendre la Bible. Textes fondateurs et Exposé systématique* (Paris 1989) 23-74.

[69] The divisions into chapters and sub-divisions into verses were done in the sixteenth-century.

organisation and contents. Hence, the most basic literary feature which my study seeks to discern is the text's structure – the structure (design or plan) of the Gospel as a whole and the structure of its various parts and sections.

i. Emphases of Structural Criticism

First of all, according to structural analysis, a text is to be considered *ahistorical* or, perhaps, more accurately *atemporal.* A text is to be read without reference to the element of time unless it is a particular concern of the text. One should assume nothing more than that it exists. In this sense the text read is timeless. It exists in his own right, and is to be interpreted on its own terms. Only the *final form* of the text is of consideration. It is accepted as a finished piece awaiting interpretation. There is no interest to inquire into its pre-history, or distinguish between earlier and later forms of the text, or identify parts of the text that might be later interpolations – the work of later redactors or editors. Though a structural critic recognises that a text may exist in different versions, this is inconsequential. Obviously structuralists assume that a text was written by someone, at some time, in some place and setting. But these facts are of no concern in structural criticism. They are bracketed out. Whatever meaning is being conveyed through the text is not being conveyed from an author through the text, but from the text itself.

Hence, structural criticism has preference for *synchronic* over *diachronic* analysis. Literally, these two frequently used terms mean 'with' or 'at the same time' and 'through time' respectively. Diachronic analysis presupposes that one can conceive of a text as having existed and developed 'through time.' It implies a linear model of investigation, one that allows to chart development and progress along a time line. Synchronic analysis, by contrast, is *atemporal* or *ahistorical,* and considers a literary work to possess its own meaning.[70] Synchronic method is preferred, because the work of an exegete is not reduced to establishing the original text – which, however, is also important – but what is more essential is its message.

Secondly, structural analysis of biblical texts recognises that a text, passage or pericope generally forms part of a larger whole – document, book, section or unit – of which it is a segment.[71] Being a component in a larger whole, the part both contributes to the meaning of the whole, and derives meaning from the sense of the whole. A text, however, usually has a number of literary contexts. There is, of course, the immediate context of the passage, or its location between what precedes and what follows. The passage and its immediate context may be components within a larger unit or section. This explains the necessity and importance of my treatment in Part II.

Thirdly, structural criticism is based on a view that tries to understand all forms of human experience and behaviour as concrete manifestations of certain ordering principles, or structures that are considered universals.

Therefore, the structural critic operates, first, with an expanded understanding of the concept *language.* Rather than seeing language as communication through words,

---

[70] However, I would consider that these two methods are complementary. It would be an error to consider them mutually exclusive; cf. Léon-Dufour, *Lecture,* I, 21-22.

[71] As some words appear often, to void confusion, to ensure clarity and to be precise, I shall use the following words in this descending order of hierarchy: document, book, part, section, sub-section, block, unit, sub-unit, pericope/episode, segment, verse, phrase, and term.

structuralists understand it as a set of ordered symbols, verbal or non-verbal, through which meaning is conveyed.

Then, not only is language understood in a very broad sense, but also the language of any given text is seen to contain *varying levels of meanings.* Accordingly, this method of criticism distinguishes between 'surface structures' and 'deep structures' in the reading of a text. *Surface structures* refer to those contours of a text which one can visibly trace, such as the outline of an argument, or the flow of a story. Beneath the surface structures, a text reflects *deep structures* of conviction. They are understood as being encoded so that the exegete must understand that the language of a text is functioning as a code. A text should be read and analysed in order not to determine the referent in any given case, but the deep structures from which it ultimately stems and to which it indicates. Deep structures are those underlying, ordering principles and features that come to concrete expression in the text, but are not actually stated in the text. For example, I may use good principles of grammar as I speak without being conscious of the rules of syntax in arranging my words. And yet the underlying principles of grammar and syntax that govern what I say can be deduced from my actual use of language.

Further, one of the important principles of structural criticism that is used to interpret all empirical forms of social behaviour and their deep structure is the *principle of binary opposition.* In analysing texts using this method one works with categories of opposites. Certain pairs of opposites (dualism) are considered fundamental to all human experience, and may be at work in producing a given text. This would include such binary oppositions as light/darkness, truth/error, life/death, salvation/condemnation, good/evil, divine/human, above/below, heaven/earth, etc.

ii. Structural Patterns

The fourth evangelist has employed a number of structural patterns based on the principles of repetition and balance. The following five patterns are found in the fourth Gospel:

α. Parallelism

Parallelism is the fundamental principle of OT poetry. The fourth evangelist employs parallelism frequently in the dialogues and discourses of Jesus. One can identify four different variations of them: a) *Antithetic Parallelism* – where the second line or verse is contrasted, or balanced with the first. b) *Staircase Parallelism* – where one line takes up the last principal word of the preceding line,[72] or where the successive lines are connected by hook-words to form a sort of steps of a staircase.[73] It is rather frequent in the fourth Gospel. c) *Synonymous Parallelism* – where there is a repetition of words or ideas, in a single verse or neighbouring verses, in different synonymous words.[74] d) *Synthetic Parallelism* – where "the sense flows on from one line to another."[75]

---

[72] R. E. Brown, *Gospel*, I, cxxxii.

[73] Mlakuzhyil, 124-25.

[74] R. E. Brown, *op. cit.*; cf. Mlakuzhyil, 122-23; and also A.-J. Festugière, *Observations stylistiques sur l'évangile de S. Jean* (EeC 84) (Paris 1974) 48-63.

[75] R. E. Brown, *op. cit.*; see also Mlakuzhyil, 124.

β. Chiasmus

The most unfamiliar, yet an important aspect of the structure of the fourth Gospel is its intricate use of the device known as chiasmus or chiastic structure. It was widely used in antiquity in the bible and in the non-biblical literature.[76] It is, basically, an inverted parallelism, or a passage in which the second part is inverted and balanced against the first.[77] A simple example would be: "The Sabbath is made for man, not man for the Sabbath" (Mk. 2,27). A chiasm is a portion of the text in which the words are arranged to form two inverted parallel panels (e.g. a b//b^1 a^1; a b c//c^1 b^1 a^1; etc.). The fourth Gospel contains a number of chiastic constructions in single sentences (e.g. in 3,31b; 3,32d-33a and 18,36bc), pericopes (e.g. 5,19-30) and whole sections (Jn. 2-4; 5-10; 13-17 and 18-20),[78] though, I would say, chiasmus is often in the eye of the beholder rather than in the text itself.

γ. Concentric Structure

Many authors include the 'concentric structure' in chiasmus.[79] But they have two different structural patterns. The concentric structure, though somewhat similar to the chiastic, has a central element around which other elements are arranged in a parallel manner (e.g. a *b* a^1; a b *c* b^{1}a^1; etc.). This type of structures are quite common in the fourth Gospel. The purpose is to draw attention in a passage to the centre as the focal point of the surrounding verses. I shall deal with some such patterns in my forthcoming chapters.

δ. Ring Composition (Inclusion)

This refers to the practice of restating or paraphrasing the opening and leading idea or phrase at the conclusion in order to re-emphasise the point being made, or the position being advocated. The fourth Gospel often mentions a detail, or makes an allusion at the end of a passage to recall something mentioned at the beginning of the passage, so knitting the unit together.[80]

ε. Spiral Structure

Some scholars of the fourth Gospel hold the view that the development of thought in the fourth Gospel is not linear but spiral. Kysar, for example, finds that the thought of the fourth evangelist seems to move in circles or spirals, doubling back upon itself.[81] De La Potterie compares this pattern of composition to a spiral staircase. The one who climbs it

---

[76] Cf. J. W. Welch (ed.), *Chiasmus in Antiquity. Structures, Analyses, Exegesis* (Hildesheim 1981).

[77] Cf. M. Dahood, "Chiasmus," *IDB. Supplementary Volume*, 145.

[78] For more examples see Mlakuzhyil, 125-29. See also X. Léon-Dufour, "Trois chiasmes johanniques," *NTS* (1960/61) 249-55.

[79] Stibbe, *Storyteller*, 20.

[80] E.g. the references to the two Cana miracles (2,11 and 4,46.54); the references to the Transjordan (1,28 and 10,40); and the two implied references to the Passover lamb (1,29 and 19,36). See B. M. Newman, Jr., "Some Observations Regarding the Argument, Structure and Literary Characteristics of the Gospel of John," *BiTr* 26 (1975) 234-39.

[81] Kysar, *Fourth Evangelist*, 176.

besides going round and round also climbs higher and higher.[82] One can even compare it to an advancing wave in the sea.

Besides these, there are several literary criteria which help one to understand the fourth Gospel better from its structural point of view: introductions, conclusions, inclusions, characteristic vocabulary, geographical and chronological indications, liturgical feasts, transitions, bridge passages, hook-words, techniques of repetition, change of literary genres (narrative, dialogue, discourse), etc. I do not intend to treat each of them in detail with examples here. As and when I make use of them in the following chapters, I shall provide the necessary explanations, too, with corroborating examples. All these factors help in a special way in the determination of the perimeters of a pericope or a section.

I am convinced that a thorough study of literary structure provides new insights into the Christology of the Gospel. Of course, one must have recourse to multiple types of indices with a view to discerning and establishing the structure. However, the study of the literary structure[83] should not be understood as a master key to open all the doors, and resolve all the exegetical problems.

b. Rhetorical Criticism[84]

Rhetorical criticism is closely related to literary criticism. Rhetoric was not some specialised interest, limited to one department of Greco-Roman schooling or politics. It pervaded the entire process of educated expression, and was intimately linked with writing. Promoted by both the Greeks and the Romans, rhetoric "encapsulated the most ancient, central, and pervasive tradition of verbalisation and of thought known to mankind at least in the West."[85] What is now becoming more and more clear is that the NT has considerable affinity with ancient rhetoric and, thus, with ancient Greco-Roman literature.[86] For a long time such a link had not been suspected, or at least not emphasised. The basic idea of the connection between the NT and rhetoric, in my opinion, makes sense. If the NT has influenced literature and may, profitably, be regarded as literature, then it must have been formed in connection with some kind of literary context; and the pervasive literary context of the first-century was that of rhetoric.[87]

---

[82] I. de la Potterie, "L'evangelo di san Giovanni," in: G. Rinaldi and P. Benedetti (eds.), *Introduzione al Nuovo Testamento* (Brescia 1971) 894. For an example of spiral structure in Jn. 1-18, see S. A. Panimolle, *Il Dono della Legge e la Grazia della Verità. Gv. 1,17* (Rome 1973) 96; see also Mlakuzhyil, 131-34.

[83] Cf. F. Kemper, "Zur literarischen Gestalt des Johannesevangeliums," *ThZ* 43 (1987) 247-64.

[84] M. Davies, *Rhetoric and Reference in the Fourth Gospel* (JSNT.S 69) (Sheffield 1992); and G. A. Kennedy, *New Testament Interpretation Through Rhetorical Criticism* (Chapel Hill, London 1984) are valuable books on this subject. See also D. L. Stamps, "Rhetorical Criticism and the Rhetoric of New Testament Criticism," *JLT* 6 (1992) 268-79; B. L. Mack, *Rhetoric and the New Testament* (GBSNT) (Minneapolis 1990); and W. Wuellner, "Where is Rhetorical Criticism Taking Us?," *CBQ* 49 (1987) 448-63.

[85] Cf. W. J. Ong, *Rhetoric, Romance and Technology* (Ithaca, London 1971) 214.

[86] See e.g. H.-J. Klauck, *Die antike Briefliteratur und das Neue Testament* (UTB 2022) (München, Paderborn, Wien, Zürich 1998).

[87] A. N. Wilder (*Early Christian Rhetoric. The Language of the Gospel* [Cambridge 1971]) was the pioneer in identifying to students of the NT the language of the Gospel as early Christian rhetoric. In relation to the fourth Gospel see J. Beutler, "Johannesevangelium und Rhetorikkritik. Zu einem neueren Buch," in: his *Studien zu den johanneischen Schriften* (SBAB 25) (Stuttgart 1998) 233-46.

Most of the biblical literature seeks to persuade the reader about certain truths, positions and courses of action and is, thus, subject to rhetorical analysis.[88] It was produced for very particular rhetorical situations. A rhetorical situation involves an audience, a speaker or writer, a topic or issue of mutual concern and an occasion for communication. The speaker or writer seeks to convince the audience to accept a particular interpretation or course of action.

Ancient authors employed often devices and techniques of rhetoric within the text itself to assist in the comprehension of the message of a text, and to persuade the hearer or reader of the truth presented there. As the biblical documents were written, originally, to be read aloud, this rhetorical dimension was an important ingredient in their composition. The authors were aware of the difficulty hearers and readers had in following an extended argument or narrative. They, therefore, supplied periodic summaries throughout the narrative to facilitate the reader in following the argument or story.

Ancient rhetoric paid attention to speaker, audience and discourse called *ethos, pathos* and *logos*. Ethos denoted the character – the speaker's credibility and trustworthiness. Pathos referred to the feelings and reactions of the audience. Much of the imagery used in the bible tries to appeal to the audience's emotions and feelings and, thus, gain a response. Logos dealt with logical developments within the discourse.[89] In the exegesis of a biblical text, alertness to the literary and rhetorical dimensions of a text is necessary. Emphasis on compositional techniques and rhetorical features help in understanding the development of the writing, the way structure and style contribute to its presentation, and the objectives the writer may have had in mind.

c. Narrative Criticism[90]

Contemporary Gospel studies are showing an increasing interest in narrative criticism. It is interesting, indeed, to observe that a good number of the recent commentaries on the fourth Gospel have preferred the use of narrative methodology. For example, Carson in the introduction to his commentary says: "The analysis that follows attempts to weigh the development of the Gospel *as a narrative* against the more formal considerations of structure."[91] Moloney, too, in his recent commentary clearly expresses his method: "The following commentary works from the conviction that it is possible to identify a strong narrative unity across the Fourth Gospel."[92] Borchert in his recent commentary on the fourth Gospel praises narrative criticism, quoting S. Moore, who maintains that narrative analysis may well be "the most successful"[93] aspect of literary analysis in dealing with the Gospels.

---

[88] See J. L. Staley, *Reading with a Passion. Rhetoric, Autobiography, and the American West in the Gospel of John* (New York 1995).

[89] See J. H. Hays and C. R. Holladay, *Biblical Exegesis. A Beginner's Handbook* (Atlanta 1987) 73-83.

[90] Cf. M. A. Powell, *What is Narrative Criticism. A New Approach to the Bible* (London 1993); and M. C. de Boer, "Narrative Criticism, Historical Criticism, and the Gospel of John," in: J. Ashton (ed.), *The Interpretation of John* (Edinburgh ²1997) 301-14.

[91] Carson, *Gospel*, 104; my italics.

[92] Moloney, *John*, 13.

[93] Borchert, 51. Cf. S. D. Moore, *Literary Criticism,* 176-77.

Narrative criticism is distinguished from earlier methods by a consistent vision of the Gospels as stories, and the desire to reach a better understanding of how these stories are told. It is a method of interpreting biblical narratives with the help of modern and ancient literary theory. It approaches the biblical narrative not as an historical source for something that lies behind the text, but as a literary text that may be analysed in literary terms (characterisation, plot, point of view in narration, etc.) like other works of literature. Narrative criticism tends to view the narrative as an interactive whole, with harmonies and tensions which develop in the course of narration. It is usually concerned with the possible effects of the literary techniques on the reader or hearer. Narrative criticism is, sometimes, subsumed under the broader label 'literary criticism.'[94]

i. Authors and Readers

S. Chatman proposes that in approaching a narrative, one needs to understand that on the author's side are the *real author*, the *implied author* and the *narrator*. On the reader's side are the *real reader*, the *implied reader* and the *narratee*.[95]

The *real author* refers to the person(s) who actually wrote the Gospel, and who may not be the first line of concern for understanding it. More important is the *implied author* – the person who seems to emerge in the story as the one who directs the reader's thinking. He is an ideal or literary figure created by the real author. He is always distinct from the real author, and is evoked by a narrative. The fourth Gospel, therefore, has an implied author simply by virtue of its being a narrative. He chooses, consciously or unconsciously what is to be read. From the narrative the reader infers him as an ideal, literary, created version of the real man. The whole of the fourth Gospel conveys to the reader an impression of the implied author, not the real flesh and blood author, but the literary artist or creative intellect at work in the narrative. He never speaks in the story, and never communicates directly with the reader.

This role is reserved for the *narrator* who will, periodically, provide information to the reader so that he/she can sense the story. The *narrator* is a rhetorical device[96] (the voice of the implied author) that actually tells the story, addresses the reader, and resorts to explanatory asides. Since the narrator shares the author's point of view, the two are not usually distinguished. The narrator introduces dialogues, provides explanations, translates terms, introduces characters, tells the reader what the characters knew or did not know, guides him/her through the narrative, and provides the proper perspective from which the action is to be viewed. As the narrator makes comments to the reader – which interrupt the flow of the narrative – he is intrusive. The reader has a clear sense of his presence, and relates to him as a person. Moreover, the narrator is self-conscious in the sense that he is aware of speaking to a reader or audience.[97] As it is the narrator who tells the story, and because of the way he tells it, the reader accepts him as a reliable guide to understand the Christological argumentation of the narrative.

---

[94] For a critical view of this method, see Ashton, *Studying John*, 141-65.

[95] See S. Chatman, *Story and Discourse. Narrative Structure in Fiction and Film* (Ithaca 1978); and Culpepper, *Anatomy*, 205-27.

[96] Culpepper, *op. cit.*, 18.

[97] Cf. A. Reinhartz, "Great Expectations. A Reader-Oriented Approach to Johannine Christology and Eschatology," *LT* 3 (1989) 61-76.

Now, the text is the means by which communication takes place between the *real author* and the *real reader*.[98] But the *real author* does not know who the *real reader* will be. Instead, the *real author* has in mind some person(s) who is envisaged to be the potential reader(s), and that potential reader is the *implied* or *imagined reader* with whom the *real author* has been attempting to communicate.[99] The *narratee* in literary studies is a little more vague, and difficult to perceive, but he/she may be thought of as the one in a story who receives narrative insights, and comments on behalf of the implied reader.[100]

ii. Internal Context and Question of Truth

The next step is to understand the literary or internal context of the story. Each story should be understood primarily from within the context of the text's construction and order.[101] Indeed, it is a crucial factor for understanding the fourth Gospel; it is a matter that has led many to misunderstand it. In reading the fourth Gospel many have imported into it the order of events from the Synoptics or *vice versa*, and have not allowed it to be what it is. The fourth Gospel has its own internal logic. At this point, however, it is crucial to add a note about historical matters. While the fourth evangelist assumes the factual reality of his statements, his concern is to deal with the acceptance or rejection of Jesus as the turning point of history (the focus of Jn. 1,1-18).[102] Therefore, the main task of an exegete should be to explore and try to understand the truth the evangelist seeks to communicate. When one takes this approach, he/she does not stand above the text either as being for or against it. Instead, he/she accepts its truth, and tries to understand how and why it is seeking to communicate truth in the way it does.[103] Taking this approach does not mean, for example, the historical and sociological studies are *passé*. On the contrary, one brings to bear on the story everything one can learn about it so that one might more effectively enter its context along with the ancient implied reader.

iii. Characterisation

From the action narrated the fourth evangelist makes emerge of it the complete characterisation. Characters are not just introduced or developed in his Gospel for their own sake. They serve as yardstick in understanding his Christology.[104] There is an inseparable link between his characterisation and Christology. All through his Gospel the characters are portrayed through their speech and behaviour in such a manner as to increase the reader's understanding of who Jesus really is. The *reader* may also be led to

---

[98] See esp. W. Vorster, "The Reader in the Text: Narrative Material," *Semeia* 48 (1989) 21-39.

[99] According to Staley (*Print's First Kiss*, 25-26) the real author does not know for certain how the real reader will respond; hence, an implied reader is envisioned to present the story.

[100] For further understanding of these literary figures see also Moloney (*John*, 14-16) who explains with a simple example from life.

[101] Cf. E. Malbon, "Texts and Contexts. Interpreting the Disciples in Mark," *Semeia* 62 (1993) 82-84.

[102] Even the fine commentaries by R. E. Brown and Schnackenburg seem to be driven repeatedly to defend the historical legitimacy of the fourth evangelist. R. A. Culpepper ("Story and History in the Gospels," *RExp* 81 [1984] 467-78) pleads to direct the study of the Gospels away from searching for facts but to a hermeneutic that treats the Gospels as narrative or story.

[103] See D. Marguerat, "Raconter Dieu. L'évangile comme narration historique," in: Bühler and Habermacher, *La narration*, 104-5.

[104] R. Alter, *The Art of Biblical Narrative* (New York 1981) 116.; see also Culpepper, *Anatomy*, 101-48.

react to each of the characters in a particular way, and to identify with facets of their characterisation. Much of the power of the fourth Gospel comes from its vivid characterisation and its effects upon the reader.

iv. Plot and Structure

A plot is created when the author structures the episodes coherently to make of it a narrative whole with a beginning, a middle and an end.[105] Defining plot, H. White observes that the plot with its ending gives the events "the order or the ideal."[106] As actions occurring after the beginning are the result or the natural consequence of what preceded, plot, inevitably, is connected with time and causality. For Stibbe plot is the organising principle providing order and meaning to separate events, and "structure is the architectural end-product of this arrangement of parts into a whole."[107] There are two aspects of this plot because there are two aspects of the person of Jesus – the human and the divine. Plot is, therefore, used by the fourth evangelist Christologically. While plot is the organising principle which gives order and meaning to separate events, structure is the architectural end-product of this arrangement of parts into a whole; and the evangelist uses it to suit his Christological scheme.

v. Narrative Techniques

I shall, in the following pages, try to give a brief explanation of the narrative techniques employed in the fourth Gospel in order to facilitate a better understanding of the methods used in this study, and to give a chance to refer back for clarifications as and when needed. The most important among them are:

α. Irony

Irony is a literary device employed often in the fourth Gospel. Characters are frequently presented as saying and/or doing something which they do not fully grasp, but the reader understands. The essential idea of irony lies in the fact that words convey a sense that is more or other than their literal meaning.[108] Irony ties in with the device of dualism. It is a "two-story phenomenon."[109] There is the lower level of appearance or apparent meaning, and there is a higher perspective, or belief that is contradictory or incompatible with the lower. Through irony the reader is invited by the author to leap to a higher level.[110]

---

[105] Cf. F. J. Matera, "The Plot of Matthew's Gospel," *CBQ* 49 (1987) 235. See also P. Ricoeur, *Time and Narrative* (Chicago 1984) ix.

[106] H. White, "The Value of Narrativity in the Representation of Reality," *CI* 7 (1980) 24.

[107] Stibbe, *Storyteller*, 26. Cf. Culpepper, *Anatomy*, 79-98.

[108] Cf. R. A. Culpepper, "Reading Johannine Irony," in: Culpepper and Black, *Exploring the Gospel of John*, 194-207. Much has been written on this subject in the recent past; see for example: P. D. Duke, *Irony in the Fourth Gospel* (Atlanta 1985). For the shape and function of this literary device see G. W. MacRae, "Theology and Irony in the Fourth Gospel," in: M. W. G. Stibbe (ed.), *The Gospel of John as Literature. An Anthology of Twentieth-Century Perspectives* (Köln, Leiden, New York 1993) 103-13. See also Culpepper, *Anatomy*, 165-80; and H. Clavier, "L'ironie dans le quatrième évangile," in: K. Aland (ed.), *Studia Evangelica I* (TU 73) (Berlin 1959) 261-76.

[109] D. C. Muecke, *The Compass of Irony* (London 1969) 19; and his *Irony* (The Critical Idiom 13) (London 1970). See also W. C. Booth, *A Rhetoric of Irony* (Chicago 1974) 36-39.

[110] Cf. D. W. Wead, "Johannine Irony as a Key to the Author-Audience Relationship in John's Gospel," in: F. O. Francis (ed.), *AAR Biblical Literature, 1974* (Missoula 1974) 33-50.

19

β. Double Meaning

One of the unique literary devices used by the fourth evangelist is double meaning.[111] He uses two meanings of a word, both of which are distinct enough that they could not convey one aspect of thought. He, probably, did not intend to present an 'either-or' situation wherein a reader must make a choice of meaning. More likely he was following a pattern of usage found in the OT wherein two meanings were intended to be conveyed through one expression.[112] He employs numerous ambiguous expressions or terms of double meaning. I shall explore in Part I the expressions of double meaning found in 2,23-3,36.

γ. Misunderstanding

Misunderstanding also is closely linked to irony. It appears that almost everyone in the fourth Gospel misunderstands Jesus. The purpose is to challenge the mind, to suggest that something is wrong or being missed or misunderstood, and to bring the reader to life. Because the characters in the story of the fourth Gospel repeatedly misunderstand who Jesus is, the reader is, by the very process of misunderstanding, encouraged to understand more fully the message being presented through the Gospel story. Brodie calls it an "anti-superficiality technique."[113]

δ. Dualism

The *Westminster Dictionary of Theological Terms* defines dualism as "any view that is constituted by two basic or fundamental principles such as spirit and matter or good and evil."[114] And *The New International Dictionary of New Testament Theology* formulates its definition as "any doctrine which asserts that there are two ultimate powers or principles."[115] The whole system of religious thought presented in the fourth Gospel hangs within a dualistic framework that contains two anchoring points between which the evangelist has woven the thought of his Gospel.[116] The fourth evangelist's view of

---

[111] F. Manns ("Les mots à double entente. Antécédents et fonction herméneutique d'un procédé johannique," *SBFLA* 38 [1988] 39) calls this device of double meaning *"la technique johannique."* See also D. W. Wead, "The Johannine Double Meaning," *RestQ* 13 (1970) 106-20.

[112] Cf. S. Cohen, "The Political Background of the Words of Amos," *HUCA* 36 (1965) 153-60.

[113] T. L. Brodie, *The Gospel according to John. A Literary and Theological Commentary* (New York, Oxford 1993) 17.

[114] D. K. McKim (ed.), *Westminster Dictionary of Theological Terms* (Westminster 1996) 83.

[115] C. Brown, "Glossary – Dualism," *NIDNT*, I, 55.

[116] The understanding of Johannine dualism is at present extremely diverse among the scholars of the fourth Gospel. H. Conzelmann (*Grundriß der Theologie des Neuen* Testaments [UTB 1446] [Tübingen ⁶1997] 355) states that in spite of the antithetical terminology in the fourth Gospel, only carefully should one speak of Johannine dualism. He, therefore, treats this theme briefly and only at the periphery of his work. On the contrary, L. Schottroff (*Der Glaubende und die feindliche Welt. Beobachtungen zum gnostischen Dualismus* [WMANT 37] [Neukirchen-Vluyn 1970]) considers dualism to be the basis of Johannine theology. Though there have been various short studies on dualism in general and in the fourth Gospel, most of them have treated some selected dualistic symbols occurring in the fourth Gospel. E.g. O. Schwankl (*Licht und Finsternis. Ein metaphorisches Paradigma in den johanneischen Schriften* [HBS 5] [Barcelona, Basel, Freiburg, New York, Rome, Wien, 1995]) treats elaborately the dualistic symbols of *light and darkness*; and H. Merklein ("Gott und Welt. Eine exemplarische Interpretation von Joh 2,23-3,21; 12,20-36 zur theologischen Bestimmung des johanneischen Dualismus," in: T. Söding [ed.], *Der lebendige Gott. Studien zur Theologie des Neuen Testaments. FS für W. Thüsing zum 75. Geburtstag* [NTA 31] [Münster 1996] 287-305) deals with the dualistic symbol *'world.'* There has been no monograph treating comprehensively the phenomenon of dualism in the fourth Gospel. However, see J. Becker, "Beobachtungen zum Dualismus im

salvation is both vertical and horizontal. The vertical dimension pertains to his dualism (heavenly/earthly, above/below, descent/ascent, spirit/flesh, truth/falsehood, life/death, salvation/condemnation, light/darkness, etc.) whereas the horizontal dimension pertains to the incarnation of the Word in human flesh and in salvation history. Dualistic pairs of images denote same realities, offer the same ethical choice, and point to Jesus as the centre, the personal centre of the fourth evangelist's ethic.[117]

ε. Symbolism

Symbolism is a more positive technique by which various ordinary elements and events are used to indicate the presence of greater realities, many of them unseen. For example, light, water, bread and wind are among the most common and day-to-day elements of life, but through them the Gospel opens up a new realm. The evangelist uses an earthly symbol as a vehicle to direct the mind of the reader to a divine reality. For example, the event at Cana is referred to as a sign (2,11), and the cleansing of the Temple appears to be a symbolic action (2,13-22). Symbols act as connecting links between two levels of meaning in a story. Throughout his Gospel the evangelist connects images with abstract meanings.[118] The fundamental structure of the symbolism of the fourth Gospel is twofold. The primary level of meaning concerns Jesus; the secondary level concern discipleship. The movement from Christology to discipleship is apparent in symbolic images and actions throughout the Gospel.[119] Symbolic meanings in the fourth Gospel, at their heart, according to me, should be focused on Jesus, who in turn symbolically represents God.

ζ. Number Patterns

The fourth evangelist uses this as a narrative strategy.[120] One finds in his Gospel a special narrative strategy preferring to structure the material into units of seven and/or three. For examples of seven: the seven discourses (3,16-2; 4,5-27; 5,19-47; 6,27-58; 7-8; 10,1ff. and 14-17), the seven signs/miracles in Jn. 1-12 (2,1-11; 4,46-54; 5,1-15; 6,1-15; 6,16-21; 9,1-7 and 11,1-44), and the seven Ἐγώ εἰμι sayings (6,35; 8,12; 10,7; 10,11; 11,25; 14,6 and 15,1). For examples of threes: the three passovers (2,13; 6,4 and 13,1), Pilate's threefold

---

Johannesevangelium," *ZNW* 65 (1974) 71-87; and his *Johannes*, 174-79; the latter is restricted to the Nicodemus pericope 2,23-3,21. Ashton (*Understanding*, 205-37) studies briefly six Johannine dualistic symbols. J. H. Charlesworth ("A Critical Comparison of the Dualism in 1 QS 3:13-14:26 and the 'Dualism' Contained in the Gospel of John," in: his *John and Qumran* [London 1972] 76-106) has done an elaborate comparative study of dualism in 1 QS 3,13-4,26 and the fourth Gospel which is praiseworthy; I shall refer to it and others in the following pages. O. Böcher (*Der johanneische Dualismus im Zusammenhang des nachbiblischen Judentums* [Gütersloh 1965]) studies Johannine dualism from the angle of the late-biblical Jewish tradition, while R. Bergmeier (*Glaube als Gabe nach Johannes. Religions- und theologiegeschichtliche Studien zum prädestinatianischen Dualismus im vierten Evangelium* [BWANT 112] [Stuttgart 1980]) treats the predestination dualism of the fourth Gospel. T. Onuki (*Gemeinde und Welt im Johannesevangelium: Ein Beitrag zur Frage nach der theologischen und pragmatischen Funktion des johanneischen 'Dualismus'* [WMANT 56] [Neukirchen-Vluyn 1984]) treats Johannine dualism from the theological and pragmatic perspectives.

[117] Cf. G. Stemberger, *La symbolique du bien et du mal selon saint Jean* (Paris 1980) 21.

[118] See esp. the study of R. Kieffer, *Le monde symbolique de saint Jean* (LeDiv 137) (Paris 1989).

[119] Cf. C. R. Koester, *Symbolism in the Fourth Gospel. Meaning, Mystery, Community* (Minneapolis 1995) 2-4 and 13.

[120] Cf. M. J. J. Menken, *Numerical Literary Techniques in John. The Fourth Evangelist's Use of Numbers of Words and Syllables* (Leiden 1985).

protestation of Jesus' innocence (18,38; 19,4 and 19,6), and the three equal sections of the passion narrative (18,1-27; 18,28-19,16a and 19,16b-42), etc.

η. Narration and Dialogue

Relationship between narration and dialogue is a special feature of the fourth Gospel as a whole. This narrative technique of the fourth evangelist deepens the reader's interpretation of details in the narrative sequences. For example, the lengthy discourse on the Bread of Life in 6,27-58 follows almost immediately after the multiplication of the loaves in 6,1-15. In the two episodes of 2,23-3,36, as I shall demonstrate in detail in Part I, the narrator's report and dialogue are immediately followed by the discourses of Jesus and John the Baptist respectively.

θ. Narrator's Asides

The explanatory asides, found often in this Gospel, explain names (1,38.42) and symbols (2,21; 12,33 and 18,9), correct possible misunderstandings (4,2 and 6,6), remind the reader of related events (3,24 and 11,2), and re-identify the characters of the story (7,50 and 21,20). There are about sixty of these asides, and they are a further evidence of the evangelist's uniform literary style.

ι. Style

A number of narrative strategies are used consistently, throughout the fourth Gospel, for the same purpose of Christological persuasion. This is an argument that suggests an overall unity in the fourth evangelist's narrative. Basing on thirty-three stylistic features characteristic of the fourth evangelist's narrative, but uncommon in the rest of the NT, E. Schweizer concludes that there is a uniformity of style throughout the fourth Gospel.[121] There is a long list of several such narrative techniques employed in the fourth Gospel. I do not attempt to treat each one of them here. They will be dealt with in the forthcoming chapters as and when necessary. I shall just enumerate a few of them here: narrative summaries, the trial motif, narrator and point of view, reader and point of view, narrative echo effects, change of scenes, technique of alternating scenes, technique of double-stage action, introduction of *dramatis personae*, change of *dramatis personae*, the law of stage duality, technique of vanishing characters, technique of diptych scenes, sequence of action–dialogue–discourse, etc.

κ. Themes

Selected and repeated themes such as remaining, knowing, believing, following, signs and works, glory, hour, life, love, truth, commands, etc. are often used by the fourth evangelist to knit together the different episodes and parts of his narrative.

Conclusion

The detection of all these structural patterns, literary criteria and narrative techniques opens the way for a better theological understanding of the story of Jesus as portrayed by

---

[121] Cf. E. Schweizer, *Ego eimi. Die religionsgeschichtliche Herkunft und Bedeutung der johanneischen Bildreden, zugleich ein Beitrag zur Quellenfrage des vierten Evangeliums* (FRLANT 38) (Göttingen 1939) 180.

the fourth evangelist. However, they should be used with discretion and discipline, because it is possible that the biblical writers had certain notions of unity rather different from my own. Ultimately the Gospel's techniques defy complete analysis and classification. Language, after all, is an art, not an exact science, and so it is inevitable that some of the openness of art be found in the Gospel.

My proposed literary and narrative exegesis of 2,23-3,36 as explained above, focuses on the text, its composition, structure, style and mood. This method involves taking the text seriously as a literary unit. My aim is to contribute to the understanding of the fourth Gospel as a narrative text – what it is and how it works. The emphasis will be upon analysis and interpretation, and the focus on reading the text from within.

The problem is not just that the text is difficult and the secondary literature vast, but that there is an aspect of the fourth Gospel which almost lies beyond literary and theological commentary. In spite of the refinement of different exegetical methods, interpretation of a biblical passage is subjective given the difficulty of the nature of the text itself, which can only be imperfectly translated as one cannot enter into the mind of the author to understand what he actually meant. Further, the cultural distance prejudices a clear perception. That is, the specificity of the literary techniques in the Jewish and Greco-Roman cultures in the Old and NT times, the plurality of authors, the religious character of writings, forms and contents pose enormous amount of problems to an exegete. Therefore, nothing is more crucial than reading a text thoroughly, closely, sympathetically and with both an eye and an ear to the internal dimensions of the text which may serve as most useful clues to understanding it.

I shall, therefore, give much attention to the literary shape of each pericope surrounding the unit 2,23-3,36, and demonstrate the way each episode flows logically from what went before, and leads directly into what follows. Besides, in order to show the consistency of the underlying point of view of the fourth evangelist who has shaped and told a story of the life of Jesus in a new way, I shall analyse the roles of various characters in the story, the passing of time, and the unresolved puzzles that emerge forcing one to look farther into the narrative to tie these puzzles together.

My study shall, therefore, consist of two parts. The most important stage of my research would consist in analysing the internal structure of 2,23-3,36, and subjecting it to a thorough exegesis using, principally, the tools of literary and narrative analyses. I shall undertake this in Part I in chapters 3, 4 and 5, and expose its narrative and parallel Christological scheme in chapter 6. These are preceded by two chapters. Chapter 1 justifies the delimitation of the unit chosen for my study and chapter 2 summarises, briefly, the results of the research done in the past; its only purpose is to orient my study better.

However, it is a known fact that the unity of Jn. 3 is strongly doubted. In order to prove the presence of a coherent Christology in such a debated pericope, one has, above all, the task of establishing its literary unity and integrity. I shall take up this exploration in chapter 3 of Part II, and demonstrate it convincingly by situating 2,23-3,36 in the narrative and structural context of its section (1,19-4,54). I shall do so, first by demarcating the perimeters of the units and sub-units of 1,19-4,54, and then by analysing the literary and narrative correlations among them. This will help to detect the place and orientation of 2,23-3,36 in its context as well as to determine its Christological scheme against the background of its network, since Christology functions as the primary unifying thread in the fourth Gospel. That Jesus is the centre of everything in the fourth Gospel is an obvious truism that is clear from simply looking at the number of times Ἰησοῦς occurs in the fourth Gospel.[122] The fourth evangelist rarely says at once all that he has to say on a particular theme, but proceeds often over successive waves, each of them adding some new elements to the elaboration of the precedent waves.[123]

As the same two episodes – 2,23-3,21 and 3,22-36 – will be analysed repeatedly from various literary and narrative aspects, a certain amount of overlapping or repetition may be inevitable, if the exegesis has to be comprehensive from all perspectives. However, I have tried my best to reduce such repetitions to the minimum while trying to be faithful, and do maximum justice to the methodology chosen.

---

[122] The name *Jesus* appears in the NT a total of 919 times, only in 6 references to persons other than Jesus of Nazareth. It occurs 244 times in the Gospel of John. See G. Schneider, "Ἰησοῦς," *EDNT*, II, 180-84.

[123] E.g. in 1,5; 3,14-15; 6,62; 8,28; 12,31-34 and 19,17-37 the fourth evangelist uses the narrative technique of 'frequence.' Like a ladder having rungs to climb up, the fourth Gospel amplifies the themes progressively. Thus, J. Zumstein ("L'Évangile johannique: une stratégie du croire," *RSR* 77 [1989] 225-27) speaks of a hermeneutic of several levels ("herméneutic étagée").

PART I

LITERARY AND NARRATIVE EXEGESIS OF 2,23-3,36

In this Part, I shall analyse the inner literary and narrative structure of 2,23-3,36 by establishing its inner structural demarcations or perimeters that facilitate such a study, and then expose and appreciate its literary and narrative organisation. Besides treating the large cluster of Johannine themes enriching the Nicodemus pericope, and the episode of the second testimony of John the Baptist, the literary and narrative devices like characterisation, double meaning, misunderstanding, irony, symbolism, dualism, reader and point of view, plot, and narrator and point of view – employed by the fourth evangelist to drive his point home – will be studied in detail. Let me, first of all, justify the perimeters of the unit chosen for my exegesis.

Chapter 1

PERIMETERS OF 2,23-3,36

A. 2,23-3,21

In many ways, the account of the purification of the Temple (2,12-22) is rounded off by a return to the themes raised in 2,13 – the presence of Jesus in Jerusalem for the Passover feast (2,23a). The reader then learns of the movement of many people toward Jesus in an action of *belief* because they saw the signs he did. Strangely, no signs have been reported and the initial reaction of 'the Jews' (2,20) would seem to discourage such a mass movement of believers toward Jesus. However, the reader must accept the word of the narrator.[1] A major new section begins with Jesus' refusal at the Passover to entrust himself to people (2,23-25).[2] At first sight this may seem unlikely. The story appears to move smoothly from the cleansing of the Temple (2,12-22) to the subsequent verses concerning Jesus' hesitancy; there is no change of time or place (one is still in Jerusalem during the Passover festival – 2,23). However, the essential content of 2,23-25 indicates an important turning point. From the appearance of the first disciples in Jn. 1,35 till the reference to the post-resurrectional faith in 2,22, the evangelist has described a drama of progressive believing (ἐπίστευσαν – 2,22). But in the aftermath of the cleansing of the Temple, just when Jesus' signs start generating an enthusiasm for belief in him, there is a new dynamic: "Ἰησοῦς οὐκ ἐπίστευεν..." (2,24); note the use of the same verb for 'believing.' The text signifies the entry of doubt. At one level, of course, the incident seems almost insignificant, an obscure reference to a moment of hesitation; and the subsequent comment that Jesus "knew what was in everyone" (2,25) seems even more brief and cryptic. But

---

[1] This is a Johannine version of what G. Genette (*Narrative Discourse: An Essay in Method* [Ithaca 1980] 35-47) calls 'anachrony.' The story has not reported the 'signs' in Jerusalem, and these 'signs' upset the numbering of a first and a second miracle at Cana (see 2,11 and 4,54); but the ongoing narrative takes it for granted that they happened. The reader can only accept this uncomfortable information. See also the apt remarks of R. Schnackenburg, *The Gospel according to St. John* (London 1980) I, 342.

[2] Cf. R. Bultmann (*The Gospel of John. A Commentary* [Philadelphia 1971] 111 and 130) observes that the major section – which concludes in Jn. 6 – begins in 2,23-25; see also L. J. Topel, "A Note on the Methodology of Structural Analysis in Jn. 2:23-3:21," *CBQ* 33 (1971) 216-17.

πιστεύω is the *heartbeat* of the fourth Gospel (cf. 20,30-31), and the negation of it, for the first time in the Gospel, and that also on the lips of Jesus, means that in some sense the heart has missed its beat.

In the encounter with Nicodemus which occupies the first half of Jn. 3, one notices a *threefold pattern* of question and reply.[3] The author reveals a predilection for *tripartite structures*. Moreover, 3,1-21 is enclosed by the antithetic limits found in 3,2 and 3,21 – 'coming by night' and 'coming to light' respectively. This *inclusion* is all the more evident as Jesus himself is considered to be the true light (cf. 1,7-9; 8,12). On the one hand, Nicodemus comes to Jesus by night (3,2a), and on the other, 'those who do what is true come to the light' (3,21ab). This inclusion can, perhaps, be completed by the connection between the performance of *signs* proving *the presence of God* in Jesus (3,2) and '*deeds done in God*' (3,21d) leading to the *light*. The entire pericope seems to place Nicodemus in contrast with Jesus. Besides, in the arrangement of 3,1-21 several examples of inclusion are evident:[4]

v.1	ἄνθρωπος	//	ἄνθρωποι	v.19
v.2	ἦλθεν πρὸς αὐτὸν (Jesus)	//	ἔρχεται πρὸς τὸ φῶς	v.21
v.2.	νυκτὸς	//	σκότος	v.19
v.2.	ποιεῖν ἃ σὺ ποιεῖς	//	πράσσων	v.20
v.2	ᾖ ὁ θεὸς μετ' αὐτοῦ.	//	ἐν θεῷ.....εἰργασμένα	v.21

There are, however, other clues indicating that the pericope 3,1-21 is not a complete unit and demanding the consideration of 2,23-25 as belonging to it to form a unity. Because of the way the chapters have been divided, there is a tendency, especially in some translations (e.g. JB, NAB), to regard the brief account of Jesus' ministry in Jerusalem (2,23-25) as a conclusion or sequel to the cleansing of the Temple. No doubt, 2,23-25 is a demonstration of the ability of the fourth evangelist to use a passage both as conclusion and introduction.[5] Yet on close examination it is clear that these verses are not so much a conclusion to Jn. 2, but an introduction to the Nicodemus episode in Jn. 3.[6] Several words used in 2,23-25 offer an interpretative background for the dialogue to follow between Jesus and Nicodemus. In other words, the narrator's reference to Jesus' knowledge of what is in a person (ἄνθρωπος – 2,25) prepares the way for the next statement: "There was an "ἄνθρωπος named Nicodemus" (3,1).

---

[3] Even though Nicodemus' questions, especially when taken with their introductions, become shorter (cf. 3,1-2; 3,4 and 3,9) the replies of Jesus become longer (cf. 3,3; 3,5-8 and 3,10-21); see R. E. Brown, *Gospel*, I, 136; W. Rebell, *Gemeinde als Gegenwelt. Zur soziologischen und didaktischen Funktion des Johannes-evangeliums* (BET 20) (Bern, Frankfurt, New York 1987) 146ff.; and Schmidl, 83.

[4] Cf. R. E. Brown, *op. cit.*, 136-37.

[5] The significance of this literary device should not be underestimated. The evangelist often uses passages as both conclusion and introduction. Stories in the fourth Gospel are often open ended. A. Vanhoye praises the work of Mlakuzhyil saying that his discovery of 'bridge-passages' is interesting and convincing, and permits one to resolve many problems of composition which otherwise would remain inextricable; see Mlakuzhyil, xviii.

[6] Cf. E. C. Hoskyns, *The Fourth Gospel* (London ²1947) 201; Bultmann, *op. cit.*, 130; C. H. Dodd, *Historical Tradition in the Fourth Gospel* (Cambridge 1963) 235; Schnackenburg, *op. cit.*, 358; R. E. Brown, *op. cit.*, 126; E. Haenchen, *John* (Hermeneia) (Philadelphia 1984) I, 192; and Beasley-Murray, *John*, 43 and 47.

B. 3,22-36

In themselves 3,22-30 do not pose much difficulty. After the encounter with Nicodemus the narrator provides a brief itinerary fragment (3,22). It suits perfectly well as the beginning of a scene. The initial "Μετὰ ταῦτα" serves frequently to introduce a new section in the fourth Gospel as pointed out already.[7] One can also observe that these verses (3,22-30) serve as a bridge in switching over from discourse style to a narrative one. The scene has a change of place and action: Jesus goes from Jerusalem to the Judean countryside and starts baptising. However, the problem lies in fixing the end of the unit. There are three possibilities. One can conclude it with the words of the Baptist in 3,30 or 3,36 or with the transitional note in 4,1-3 on the baptismal activity of Jesus and on his departure for Galilee. The last possibility (4,1-3) is practically not found among scholars.[8] It is preferred rather as an introduction to the following section (4,4-42) as it begins with a temporal phrase "Ὡς οὖν ἔγνω" (4,1) and a change of place (4,3).

Moreover, the two sub-units (3,1-21 and 3,22-36) are parallel to each other in structure and Christological exposition. Besides, the observation of a diptych of parallel and complementary scenes in 2,23-3,21 and 3,22-36, each having a similar tripartite structure seems to defend the unity of Jn. 3:[9]

In Jerusalem (2,23-3,21):
2,23-3,1	- a report, serving as an introduction to the Nicodemus episode
3,2-10	- a dialogue between Jesus and Nicodemus
3,11-21	- a monologue (discourse)

In Judea (3,22-36):
3,22-25	- report, serving as an introduction to the second testimony of the Baptist
3,26-30	- a dialogue between the Baptist and his disciples
3,31-36	- a monologue (discourse)

C. Debate

The logical sequence of Jn. 3 and the question at what point the dialogue of Jesus with Nicodemus and that of the Baptist with his disciples pass into the reflections of the fourth evangelist, have always troubled scholars. The debate concerning the composition and literary unity of 2,23-3,36 continues. Much has been written to transpose the entire pericope or parts of it using theories of dislocation which are abundant. Almost all the commentaries on the fourth Gospel deal with this problem. I shall treat only very summarily the discussions concerning these theories of dislocation and transposition as bypassing it may not give a comprehensive outlook to my treatment of 2,23-3,36.

---

[7] Cf. 5,1; 6,1; 7,1; and 19,28.38.

[8] Exception: W. Howard-Brook, *Becoming Children of God. John's Gospel and Radical Discipleship* (New York 1994) 94-99. P. F. Ellis (*The Genius of John. A Compositional-Critical Commentary on the Fourth Gospel* [Collegeville 1984] 29 and 60-61) notices a chiastic structure in 1,19-4,3 and 3,23-4,3; see also Schmidl.

[9] See H. Thyen, "Aus der Literatur zum Johannesevangelium," *ThR* 44 (1979) 112; Y. Ibuki, "Καὶ τὴν φωνὴν αὐτοῦ ἀκούεις - Gedankenaufbau und Hintergrund des 3. Kapitels des Johannesevangeliums," *BSU* 14 (1978) 9-33; Léon-Dufour, *Lecture*, I, 282-84; and Beasley-Murray, *op. cit.*, 47. However, I have a slightly different division of these verses (2,23-3,2; 3,3-10; 3,11-21 and 3,22-26; 3,27-30; 3,31-36); for details see my chapter 3.

1. Dislocations and Transpositions

For some scholars of the fourth Gospel, 3,31-36 do not seem to be in continuity with the preceding second testimony of the Baptist because of their Christological themes. Hence, it is important to determine whether the testimony of the Baptist concludes in 3,30 or in 3,36. Many scholars consider that the verses 31-36 belong to the pericope 3,11-21 and therefore, transpose them either after 3,12 or 3,13 or 3,21.[10] In the following paragraphs, I shall examine briefly some such proposals without going into details of their arguments:

One of the pioneers of such proposals is Gourbillon[11] who favours the following sequence: 3,1-13.31-36.22-30. He recognises an important separation between 3,13 and 3,14 based on the chronological aspect and change of theme. He finds the theme of the elevation of the Son of Man at this place to be superfluous and so attaches it to 12,31. Thus, the gap created by such a transposition is filled in by placing 3,31-36 before 3,22-30. Such a shift of 3,14-21 to Jn. 12 remains an isolated hypothesis without support among other scholars.

Mendner, on the other hand, considers that the dialogue with Nicodemus was originally placed after the narrative in 7,51.[12] Bligh is of the opinion that the discourse to Nicodemus was originally written to stand after the cure of the man born blind.[13] Without removing 3,14-21, Bernard and Bultmann are satisfied to transpose 3,22-30 to the end of the chapter creating a large unit with the two discourses of Jesus (and/or commentaries of the evangelist), viz., 3,11-21 and 31-36. This transposition, I find, while resolving one problem creates another. In fact, trying to eliminate the abrupt interruption of the discourse of Jesus by the testimony of the Baptist in 3,22, an important thematic rupture is created between 3,21 and 3,31.

Schnackenburg maintains that the original order of this section was 3,1-12.31-36. 13-21. That is to say, Jesus' dialogue with Nicodemus comprises only 3,1-12. Then the evangelist attached the kerygmatic discourse (3,31-36 and 13-21). He argues that the disciples of the evangelist divided the kerygmatic discourse into two parts and attached 3,13-21 to 3,12 because these two passages echo the common theme of the 'ἐπουράνια.'[14]

---

[10] Cf. Schnackenburg, *op. cit.*, 380-81; M.-J. Lagrange, *Évangile selon saint Jean* (EtB) (Paris 1964) 96; See also J. H. Bernard, *A Critical and Exegetical Commentary on the Gospel according to St. John*, Vol. 1 (ICC) (Edinburgh ⁶1962); Bultmann, *op. cit.*; and J. Blank, *Das Evangelium nach Johannes* (GSL.NT 4/1a) (Düsseldorf 1981) *ad loc.* For a summary treatment see Létourneau, *Jésus*, 53-54; and Schmidl, 399-404.

[11] J.-G. Gourbillon, "La parabole du Serpent d'airain et la 'lacune' du ch. III de l'Évangile selon S. Jean," *VivPen* 2 (1942) 213-26.

[12] S. Mendner, "Nicodemus," *JBL* 77 (1958) 293-323. Schnackenburg (*op. cit.*, 360-63) and R. E. Brown (*op. cit.*, 135) rightly reject Mendner's argument.

[13] J. Bligh, "Four Studies in St. John, II: Nicodemus," *HeyJ* 8 (1967) 40.

[14] Cf. R. Schnackenburg, "Die 'situationsgelösten' Redestücke in Joh 3," *ZNW* 49 (1958) 88-99; and his *Gospel*, I, 47; 55; 360-63 and 380-81. Contrary to his view, G. Richter (*Studien zum Johannesevangelium*, J. Heinz [ed.] [BU 13] [Regensburg 1977] 337) maintains that 3,31-36 are surely not *situationsgelöste Rede*. He contends that they neither belong to the Nicodemus episode nor to another place in the Gospel. They are, on the contrary, "*sehr situationsbezogen.*" They have been intentionally placed by the evangelist to correct the immediately preceding second testimony of the Baptist on Jesus (3,25-30); see also U. Wilckens, "Rezension Richter, Georg: Studien zum Johannesevangelium," *ThLZ* 106 (1981) 815-17. I would say that the evangelist here makes the Baptist testify to the heavenly origin and the divine Sonship of Jesus; I shall demonstrate it in detail in chapter 3. Schnackenburg and others, I believe, fail to sense the force of the summation of the fourth evangelist in 3,31-36.

Schnackenburg's argument contains some persuasive suggestions, but, as a whole, it is unconvincing and does not satisfactorily explain the rupture between 3,36 and 3,13.

Rejecting the argument of Dodd[15] that the editor wanted to use 3,31-36 to recapitulate the whole of 3,1-30 and to summarise both the Nicodemus and the Baptist scenes, Brown sounds sceptical about all these transposition theories and believes that "what was once an isolated discourse of Jesus ... has been attached to the scenes of chap. iii as an interpretation of those scenes."[16] I do not go into further minute details as to who proposes which transposition; such details do not bring any advantage to the literary and narrative methodology chosen by me. Moreover, such displacements are not universally accepted and many modern exegetes are of the opinion that one should treat the text as it is. Besides, the new arrangements are always hypothetical and are often insufficient. The different hypotheses of the literary critic lead to an earlier stage of the text anterior to the final (transmitted in the manuscripts) and there is no verification of this fact.

2. Speaker of 3,31-36

There has been considerable discussion over the speaker of these words. Some suggest that the Baptist is still speaking,[17] while others claim that Jesus has entered the scene.[18] Considering the nature of the terms used a few scholars argue that the narrator addresses the reader.[19] Placed at the end of Jn. 3, they form a kind of summary of the principal themes treated already. Though the abrupt shift from narrative to discourse style lacking a redactional link betrays an interruption in the structure between the verses 30 and 31, I see in it the intention of the evangelist to bring the Baptist into the scene a second time to testify to the revelation of Jesus; because, according to the Jewish Law, only a testimony with two witnesses is valid and binding.[20] Moreover, in the absence of the mention of a change of speaker in 3,31, it is only logical that the same interlocutor (the Baptist) continues, just as in the case of 3,13-21, where these words are intended by the evangelist that the reader hears them from the mouth of Jesus and, hence, mentions no change of speaker.

---

[15] Cf. C. H. Dodd, *The Interpretation of the Fourth Gospel* (Cambridge 1963) 308-11.

[16] R. E. Brown, *op. cit.*, 160.

[17] Cf. W. Bauer, *Das Johannesevangelium erklärt* (HNT 6) (Tübingen ³1933) 63-65; C. K. Barrett, *The Gospel according to St. John* (London ²1978) 224; J. Wilson, "The Integrity of John 3:22-26," *JSNT* 10 (1981) 36-38; D. K. Rensberger (*Johannine Faith and Liberating Community* [Philadelphia 1988] 58 and 63) considers it as a continuation of the Baptist's speech challenging his disciples to accept Jesus as the Son of God. See also Létourneau, *Jésus*, 54; J. Schneider, *Das Evangelium nach Johannes. Aus dem Nachlaß herausgegeben unter Leitung von Erich Fascher* (ThHK Sonderband) (Berlin 1976) 105; Ibuki, "Καὶ τὴν," 26; Richter, *Studien*, 337; and M. Stowasser, *Johannes der Täufer im Vierten Evangelium. Eine Untersuchung zu seiner Bedeutung für die johanneische Gemeinde* (ÖBS 12) (Klosterneuburg 1992) 176.

[18] Cf. Schnackenburg, *Gospel*, 380-81; and his, "Die 'situationsgelösten' Redestücke," 88-99.

[19] See e.g. Lagrange, 96; B. F. Westcott, *The Gospel according to Saint John: The Greek Text with Introduction and Notes* (London ²1908) I, 60; and R. E. Brown, *op. cit.*, 159-60. See also the commentary of van den Bussche, L. Morris (*The Gospel according to John* [rev. ed.] [NIC] [Grand Rapids 1995]). Whether the speaker is the Baptist, Jesus, or the narrator, finally what is being expressed here is the point of view of the evangelist. He can, to some extent, choose his disguises, but never choose to disappear; see W. C. Booth, *The Rhetoric of Fiction* (Chicago 1983) 20. For the centrality of the narrator in the Gospels, see S. D. Moore, *Literary Criticism*, 25-40.

[20] I shall come back to this point later.

Conclusion

The task of an exegete is to get into the mind of the evangelist and try to discern his purpose in composing the text as it is now found rather than trying to read one's own modern mind into a text of the past. He/she must always bear in mind that what he/she thinks as an appropriate sequence need not necessarily be the one the evangelist would have adopted. I am convinced that the present sequence is justifiable as it reflects the evangelist's *Sitz im Leben*.[21] I shall demonstrate, in Part II, that the sequence of Jn. 3 fits into the narrative sequence of its section.

---

[21] Cf. K. Tsuchido, "The Composition of the Nicodemus-Episode, John ii 23 – iii 21," *AJBI* 1 (1975) 91-103; see also Thyen, "Aus der Literatur," 112.

Chapter 2

SURVEY OF PAST RESEARCH

As Ashton rightly contends "the sequence of thought in Jn. 3 is notoriously hard to follow."[1] Many scholars have proposed various ways of 're-arranging' this chapter. Any understanding of the text, no doubt, must depend on how one envisages its structure. Basing on formal criteria some have proposed literary structures, while others, using thematic criteria, have proposed various divisions of Jn. 3. I shall throw a quick glance at some of the important observations of the research in the recent past in order to orient my study. I do not, however, intend to dwell long on this survey, nor do I attempt here a comprehensive and exhaustive study of the past research. As the focus of my study is limited to the literary and narrative aspects, I shall stick on only to these. In order to evaluate meaningfully the structural patterns proposed in the past, it is, however, inevitable to quote the proposed structures, as briefly as possible. Hence, it will inevitably occupy a few pages.

A. Thematic Divisions

Jn. 3 contains the first of the extended theological discourses of Jesus – one of the hallmarks of the fourth Gospel. Each of the discourses contains an event, an encounter, questions or a dialogue around which the discourse is focussed. Each discourse contains one or more key statements by Jesus which summarise some aspects of the Christian faith. Many of these key statements are so well conceived that they are easily remembered like frequently quoted maxims. Such is the case in statements such as: "You must be born again" (3,7), "God so loved the world..." (3,16), and "He must increase, but I must decrease" (3,30).

Most scholars divide 2,23-3,36 into two scenes: the encounter with Nicodemus (3,1-21) and the second testimony of the Baptist (3,22-36).[2] According to some scholars, 2,23-25 operates as a bridge passage between Jn. 2 and Jn. 3, serving as an introduction to the narrative.[3] Some make a division between 3,15 and 3,16.[4] Scholars like Morris, Braun and Westcott argue that the two scenes mentioned above conclude with a commentary of the evangelist, namely 3,16-21 and 3,31-36 because of the evangelist's retrospective view

---

[1] Ashton, *Understanding*, 374.

[2] See R. E. Brown (*Gospel*), Morris (*Gospel*), A. Schlatter (*Der Evangelist Johannes, wie er spricht, denkt und glaubt. Ein Kommentar zum vierten Evangelium* [Stuttgart ³1960]), S. Schulz (*Das Evangelium nach Johannes* [NTD 4] [Göttingen ¹⁵1983]), J. Gnilka (*Johannesevangelium* [NEB] [Würzburg 1989]), Moloney, Malina and Rohrbaugh, Carson (*Gospel*), Beasley-Murray (*John*), Borchert, U. Wilckens (*Das Evangelium nach Johannes* [NTD 4] [Göttingen ¹⁷1998]), H. Ridderbos (*The Gospel of John: A Theological Commentary* [Grand Rapids 1997]), L. Schenke (*Johanneskommentar* [Düsseldorf 1998]), C. L'Èplattenier (*L'Évangile de Jean* [BPP] [Geneva 1993]), Léon-Dufour (*Lecture*), Mlakuzhyil, Létourneau (*Jésus*), and many others.

[3] On this, see I. de la Potterie, "'Naître de l'eau et naître de l'Esprit.' Le texte baptismal de Jean 3,5," *ScEc* 14 (1962) 417-43 ; Léon-Dufour, *op. cit.*, 280-82; M. de Jonge, "Nicodemus and Jesus: Some Observations on Misunderstanding and Understanding in the Fourth Gospel," *BJRL* 53 (1971) 340-41; G. C. Nicholson, *Death as Departure. The Johannine Descent-Ascent Schema* (SBL.DS 63) (Chico 1983) 65. Most scholars mentioned in the preceding footnote, too, share this view.

[4] Morris, Ridderbos, Carson, Stibbe, Schenke, L'Éplattanier, Ruckstuhl, Moloney, Lagrange, Braun, Westcott and van den Bussche; see their commentaries or studies *ad loc.*

in the use of past tense of the verbs 'δίδωμι, ἀποστέλλω, ἔρχομαι' in these two segments, and because of the presence of phrases which are typical of the fourth evangelist.

These two arguments for the designation of the above two segments as the evangelist's commentaries, I believe, are not convincing and acceptable because, first of all, the evangelist is bound to speak in the past tense while referring to the moment of Jesus' coming or his being sent – Jesus is on earth already when the event is described; secondly, the hand of the evangelist is omnipresent in the dialogues, in the discourses of Jesus as well as in the narratives and summaries. Besides, the characteristic elements of the fourth evangelist are scattered all over Jn. 3.

There are others who subdivide the two scenes of Jn. 3 into smaller segments or divide the two pericopes differently. A glance at the table of contents of the various commentaries proves that there is no unanimity among scholars with regard to the division or structure of the Jn. 3 as well as its contents. Schmidl in his recent monograph on 2,23-4,3 provides in three pages such a bird's eye view of the divisions of this unit by 14 scholars as found in the table of contents of their commentaries or studies.[5] Létourneau evaluates the thematic divisions of de la Potterie, Vouga, Leidig and Michel.[6] He stresses the Christological aspect of the episodes while Blank notices a basic catechism there.[7] I shall, therefore, not to make this part unnecessarily long, avoid an evaluation of those mentioned above and take up only a short evaluation of the studies of A. Gabriel, L. Walter and E. Ruckstuhl.

Gabriel contends that faith leading to life – the central theme and purpose of the fourth Gospel (20,31) – is also the focus of the scene of Nicodemus and, thus, finds the following thematic pattern in this episode:

---

[5] See Schmidl, 9-11. He does not evaluate the various divisions found in the commentaries. It is only helpful to have a quick glance of how differently Jn. 3 is being viewed by various scholars. As I have warned already in the exposition of my methodology, a slight tilt of angle can bring completely different results, which only proves how rich and profound the fourth Gospel is, and how difficult it is to bring it under one single pattern to explore and understand its meaning in its depth.

[6] See Létourneau, *Jésus*, 103-8. See also the series of articles of I. de la Potterie, "Structura primae partis Evangelii Johannis," *VD* 47 (1969) 130-40; his, "Ad dialogum Jesu cum Nicodemo (2,23-3,21). Analysis litteraria," *VD* 47 (1969) 141-50; and his, "Jesus et Niocodemus: de revelatione Jesu et vera fide in eum (Jo 3,11-21)," *VD* 47 (1969) 257-83; he establishes an antithetic correspondence between the introduction 2,23-3,2 and the third revelation of Jesus (3,11-21): the theme of the imperfect faith of the Jews is put in contrast with the perfect faith of the Christians – faith accompanied by fruits of salvation. He notices also a strong parallelism between 3,11-21 and 3,31-36. See also F. Vouga, *Le cadre historique et l'intention théologique de Jean* (BeRe) (Paris 1977) 15-36; he views the text from the angle of the literary device 'misunderstanding and irony' and considers the interventions of Jesus introduced by the double-*amen* formula – which, on two occasions, replies to the explicit questions of Nicodemus – as the criterion for the structure. E. Leidig (*Jesu Gespräch mit der Samaritanerin und weitere Gespräche im Johannesevangelium* [ThDiss 15] [Basel 1979] 162-65 and 186-87) believes to have recognised in the fourth Gospel a new literary genre which she calls "*Glaubensgespräche*". This study, however, lacks a formal literary stress and takes into account neither the dialogue nor the discourse character of 3,11-21. M. Michel ("Nicodème ou le non-lieu de la vérité," *RevSR* 55 [1981] 227-36) takes up and polishes the principles found in the proposals of Brown, Vouga and Leidig having recourse to the narrative structure: *report, dialogue and discourse* favouring the division of the text into 3,1-2; 3,3-10 and 3,11-21. She favours a further tripartite division of 3,11-21 which seems sensible; see esp. 230-231.

[7] Blank, *Johannes*, 222.

2:23-25	-	Presentation of the theme: the question of the correct type of faith.
3:1-2	-	Nicodemus, a perfect representative of the traditional Jewish faith meets Jesus. He speaks of the *signs* done in Jerusalem.
3:3-10	-	Nicodemus is confronted with deeper questions related to faith: 'rebirth' or 'birth from above.'
3:11-15	-	Jesus as the true revealer (and the greatest of his *signs*: vv.14-15).
3:16-21	-	Belief – eternal life; unbelief – condemnation.[8]

No doubt, the Nicodemus episode deals with the question of true faith rendering eternal life. This article, short and limited in its scope, does not elaborate the Christological aspect but concentrates only on faith leading to baptism and rebirth. The role of Christ is reduced to that of a revealer alone; faith in him gives eternal life. This thematic plan is rather sketchy and, therefore, does not bring out the full substance of the pericope strongly.

Walter presents a different and more detailed thematic plan of 3,1-21. His plan (see below) revolves around the central theme of faith. He divides the pericope into three parts (3,1-8; 9-18;19-21) and exposes the unity of its doctrine:

I.   "Being born from above:"
   a) Main affirmation: Jn 3,3.5
   b) Flesh and Spirit: Jn 3,6-8
   c) Jn 3,1-8 according to faith:
      1. *Word and Spirit*
      2. *Faith and Baptism*

II. "Not to judge, but to save:" (Jn 3,9-18)
   a) Heavenly things
   b) Son of Man
      1. *Just as Moses lifted up the serpent in the wilderness,*
      2. *so must the Son of Man be lifted up, that whoever believes in him may have eternal life.*
      3. *Cross and faith*
   c) The alternative: Life or Judgement
      1. God so loved the world that He gave his only Son,
      2. so that everyone who believes in him may not perish but may have eternal life.

III. Doing what is true: (Jn 3,19-21)
   a) Light and Judgement
      1. The time of light
      2. Refusal to believe
   b) Light and Truth
      1. Doing what is true
      2. Coming to light[9]

---

[8] A. Gabriel, "Faith and Rebirth in the Fourth Gospel," *BiBh* 16 (1990) 210; see also 205-15. The thematic plan of de la Potterie has some similarities with this as both seem to revolve around the axes of faith and revelation.

[9] L. Walter, "Lecture d'Évangile. Jean III,1-21: selon la foi et l'incrédulité," *EeV* 87 (1977) 369-78 and 385-90. This is a part of his dissertation entitled *Foi et incrédulité selon saint Jean* and defended at l'Institut Catholique de Paris in May 1975.

In the first part, the main theme of being begotten from above, born of water and Spirit or to be baptised in water and Spirit in order to have eternal life and the correlation between faith and baptism, are clear; but one does not find any reference to word in the pericope. His explanation is very vague and not well founded. The second sub-unit (3,9-18) treating the Christology, soteriology and eschatology is well exposed. Though Walter recognises 3,11-21 as a discourse, he believes that 3,19-21 has to be treated specially.[10] It is, however, surprising that he does not give any reason for such a division and separate treatment. His plan rightly observes the dualism between flesh and Spirit but does not mention the dualism between heavenly and earthly things, above and below, light and darkness, life and judgement or salvation and condemnation; hence, it is incomplete. His concluding observation, however, that Christology is at the centre of the doctrine of the pericope is to be acknowledged.[11]

Ruckstuhl, on the other hand, proposes a thematic plan to the whole of Jn. 3. He, too, observes parallels between the two episodes in Jn. 3:

3,1-21	**3,22-36**
3,3-10: Rebirth from above through baptism.	3,22-25: Jesus and John the Baptist baptise.
3,11-13: The eye-witness of the heavenly world demands true belief.	3,27-30: The Baptist testifies in favour of Jesus
3,14-15: True belief is possible through the lifting up of the Son of Man on the cross.	3,31-36: Jesus is the only witness of the heavenly world. One must believe in him.
3,16-21: Where there is belief, there is life and salvation; where unbelief, there is judgement and rejection.	3,31-36: The incomparable superiority of Jesus. Where there is belief, there is salvation; where unbelief, there is wrath.[12]

He considers *signs-faith and true faith, rebirth from above (baptism) and testimony from above* as leitmotiv of the whole chapter, and 2,23-25 as an introduction. The observation of all the parallel themes such as belief, rebirth (baptism?) testimony, Christology, soteriology and eschatology, in both the episodes, is praiseworthy. But his exposition of parallels between the two episodes is insufficient, unfounded and not fully compatible.

B. Structural Patterns

1. Parallel Structures

Malina and Rohrbaugh observe a parallel structure between 3,1-21 and 3,22-36 largely focused on the themes appearing in the two scenes (see below):

1. Born ἄνωθεν (from above) (3,3.7)	1. One coming ἄνωθεν is above all (3,31)
2. Jesus: the one who came down from sky (3,13)	2. Jesus who comes down from sky (3,31b)

---

[10] *Ibid.*, 374.

[11] *Ibid.*, 389-90.

[12] E. Ruckstuhl, "Abstieg und Erhöhung des johanneischen Menschensohns," in: R. Pesch and R. Schnackenburg (eds.), *Jesus und der Menschensohn. FS Anton Vögtle* (Basel, Freiburg, Wien 1975) 314-15.

3. Opposing types of people – flesh and spirit (3,6); earthly and celestial (3,12)	3. Opposing types of people – earthly and celestial (3,31)
4. "We speak of what we know and testify to what we have seen, yet you do not accept our testimony" (3,11)	4. "He testifies to what he has seen and heard, yet no one accepts his testimony" (3,32)
5. God sent the Son (3,17)	5. the one whom God has sent (3,34)
6. "that whoever believes in the Son may have eternal life" (3,15.16)	6. "Whoever believes in the Son has eternal life" (3,36)
7. Judgement (3,19-21)	7. Judgement (3,36)[13]

Even a quick glance at this structure betrays that 3,1-2.4-5.8-10.14.18.22-30. 33 are completely ignored and their position in the proposed thematic parallel structure is not exposed. Verses from the Nicodemus episode are picked up out of the narrative sequence of the evangelist (see the column on the left) to match with the same themes 're-treated' in 3,31-36. This parallelism is, often, restricted to certain terms and phrases repeated in both episodes. Very little has been attempted at the explanation of the proposed structure.

Stibbe, on the other hand, observes that just as 3,1-15 is followed by the narrator's commentary, so also 3,22-30 is followed by a summary. According to him, in 3,31-36, the narrator recalls some of the earlier themes of 3,1-15. Stibbe acknowledges the evangelist's artful compilation of his material:

Subject	**3,1-15**	**3,31-36**
From above	ἄνωθεν (3.3.7)	ἄνωθεν (3,31)
Heavenly origins	ἐκ τοῦ οὐρανοῦ (3,13)	ἐκ τοῦ οὐρανοῦ (3,31)
Earth/heaven	ἐπίγεια/ἐπουράνια (3,12)	ἐκ τῆς γῆς/ἐκ τοῦ οὐρανοῦ (3,31)
Witnessing to what has been	ὃ ἑωράκαμεν μαρτυροῦμεν (3,11)	ὃ ἑώρακεν.... μαρτυρεῖ (3,32)
Failure to receive the testimony	τὴν μαρτυρίαν ἡμῶν οὐ λαμβάνετε (3,11)	τὴν μαρτυρίαν αὐτοῦ οὐδεὶς λαμβάνει (3,32)
The Spirit	πνεῦμα (3,8)	πνεῦμα (3,34)
Faith and Life	πιστεύων/ζωὴν (3,15.16)	πιστεύων/ζωὴν (3,36)[14]

I find this structure of Stibbe, too, to be evidently incomplete as it picks up some verses of 3,1-15 in an order different from that of the evangelist to suit his discovery of parallel themes. Just as in the structure of Malina and Rohrbaugh the verses 1-2.4-6.9-10. 14.18-21 and 33 are conveniently forgotten. Moreover, both the structures are, in some parallels, just reduced to the recurrence of a word or phrase. One cannot, therefore, accept the above two proposals as complete literary structures.

R. Beauvery[15] finds a unique structure in 3,1-21. I shall call it a tripartite structure (3,1-8; 9-15; and 16-21) each element of the triptych having a double phase – i) attitude of man (vv.1-2; 9-11 and 16-17) and ii) revelation of Jesus (vv.3-8; 12-15 and 18-21). The criterion he uses to analyse these verses is exclusively thematic. He also observes here a Trinitarian thematic structure – 3,1-8: new birth as work of the *Spirit*; 9-15: testimony and

---

[13] Malina and Rohrbaugh, 93.

[14] M. W. G. Stibbe, *John* (RNBC) (Sheffield 1993) 61.

[15] R. Beauvery, "Jean 3,14-21. Accueillir le dessein d'amour de Dieu révélé en Jésus," *EeV* 8 (1970) 114 - 15.

elevation of the *Son* of Man; and 16-21: plan of salvation of the *Father*. But Beauvery, in this structural exposition, does not convincingly prove any formal link established between the elements in the tripartite division. His study does not help as a basis for a correct literary structure of the episode.

The most comprehensive study so far in the structural analysis of 2,23-3,36 has been done by Létourneau. He presents the following interesting parallel structure:[16]

A	2,23-3,2	A[1]	3,22-26
B	3,3-10	B[1]	3,27-30
C	3,11-21	C[1]	3,31-36

Between A and A[1] he observes formal links in the parallel expressions that Nicodemus "came to Jesus...and said to him: 'Rabbi'" (3,2), and the disciples of the Baptist "came to John and said to him: 'Rabbi'"(3,26). He finds also a correspondence between "οὗτος ἦλθεν πρὸς αὐτὸν" (3,2) and "πάντες ἔρχονται πρὸς αὐτόν" (3,26) as Nicodemus seems to be one of the 'many' who "believed in his (Jesus') name because they saw the signs that he was doing" (2,23). Thus, he argues for a formal link between the "many (who) believed in his name" (2,23) and the "all (who) are going to him" (3,26). Besides, he observes a number of verbal correspondences between A and A[1] as shown in the structural studies of other scholars above.[17] Between B and B[1] he notices a syntactic structure in 3,3.5 and 3,27. In 3,3 and 3,5 one finds the structure 'ἐὰν μή τις + subjunctive, οὐ δύναται + infinitive.' The same structure is found inverted in 3,27: 'Οὐ δύναται + infinitive, + subjunctive.' Of course, he observes many other verbal parallels between B and B[1].[18] Finally, between C and C[1], like most of the scholars, Létourneau, too, acknowledges the maximum number of correlations.[19]

Now, to comment on the proposal of Létourneau, it is to be appreciated that he is the first one who finds such a large number of structural parallels between the two episodes of Jn. 3 taking into consideration both episodes completely together with the transitional passage (2,23-25). His structural analysis, in many aspects, is precise and profound. But I wonder if such a parallel correspondence, based solely on the material identity of terms without taking their theological significance into consideration, is perfectly valid? Very often he falls back on the literary device of inclusion for support of parallelism. Such a study, leaning exclusively on the pure formal elements and identical terms and expressions, runs the risk of deviating from the theological significance of the pericope.[20] One has to acknowledge, however, that the study of Létourneau has opened new avenues for further research, which I intend to take up in my next chapter.

---

[16] Létourneau, *Jésus*, 119-28.

[17] Cf. *Ibid.*, 120-21.

[18] Cf. *Ibid.*, 122-23.

[19] *Ibid.*, 125-28.

[20] For a detailed critique of his study see Gourgues, "Notes critiques."

2. Chiastic, Concentric and Spiral Structures[21]

At this juncture it is fitting to quote Howard-Brook who has written a commentary on the fourth Gospel based on chiastic and concentric structures: "The process of looking for parallels is an effective reading strategy for inculcating skills of close and disciplined reading."[22] I shall evaluate here only the studies of J. Bligh, M. Vellanicakal and G. Gaeta. Bligh,[23] divides the encounter with Nicodemus into three separate concentric structures. According to him, the first presents the scene (2,23-3,2):

A 23 When he was in Jerusalem (at the Passover) at the feast, many believed in his name,
　　　　seeing the *signs* that he was doing.
B 　　　24 Jesus, however, did not entrust himself to them,
C 　　　　because he *knew* all men,
D 　　　　　25 and had no need that anyone should bear witness to him concerning man,
C[1] 　　　　for he *knew* what was in man.
B[1] 　　　3:1 There was a man of the Pharisees, Nicodemus by name, a ruler of the Jews.
　　　　　2 He came to him by night and said to him:
A[1] 'Rabbi, we know that you have come from God as a teacher, for no one could do
　　　　these *signs* that you are doing, if God were not with him.'

One can easily notice that Bligh is employing thematic and formal criteria simultaneously. The correspondence between A-A[1] and C-C[1] are based on the verbal recurrences. The link between B and B[1] is not clear at all. Moreover, 2,25 as the centre and focus of the structure is doubtful. In his second concentric structure, Bligh contends, Jesus speaks about baptism (3,2-11):

A 2 '*Rabbi*, we know that you have come from God as a teacher,
B 　　　for no one could do *these signs* that you are doing, if God were not with him.'
C 　　　　3 Jesus replied and said to him: 'I tell you truly, unless a man is *born anôthen*,
　　　　　　he cannot see the kingdom of God.'
D 　　　　　4 Nicodemus said to him: 'How can a man be *born* again when he is old?
E 　　　　　　Can one enter into his mother's womb and be *born* a second time?'
F 　　　　　　　**5 Jesus replied: 'I tell you truly, unless a man is *born* of water and**
　　　　　　　　Spirit, he cannot enter the kingdom of God.
E[1] 　　　　　6 What is born of the flesh is flesh; what is *born* of the Spirit is spirit.
D[1] 　　　　　7 You should not be amazed because I said to you: You must be *born*
　　　　　　anôthen.
C[1] 　　　　8 The Spirit like the wind blows where it wills; you hear its voice, but you do not
　　　　　　know where it is coming from or where it is going. So it is with everyone who
　　　　　　is *born* of the Spirit.'
B[1] 　　　9 Nicodemus replied and said to him: 'How can *these things* happen?'
A[1] 10 Jesus replied and said to him: "You are a *master* in Israel and yet ignorant of that?
　　　　11 I tell you truly, we speak of what we know and we bear witness to what we have
　　　　seen; but you do not accept our witness.

---

[21] However, one has to remember the scholarly objection to chiasm that it often seems to be in the eye of the interpreter rather than in the text. See Stibbe, *John*, 20. Howard-Brook (39), too, does not hide the fact that "chiasm is a somewhat controversial aspect of Johannine literary design."

[22] Howard-Brook, 40.

[23] Bligh, "Four Studies," 40-51.

The correspondence between A and A[1] is centred on the recurrence of the term 'Rabbi'; however, the inclusion of 3,11 in the dyad, caused, perhaps, by the word οἴδαμεν, unnecessarily breaks the connection of 3,10-11 with 3,12-13 because the οἴδαμεν of 3,2 has been replied already by the οὐ γινώσκεις addressed to Nicodemus in 3,10. The parallel between B and B[1] seems to rest solely on the repetition of the words δύναται ταῦτα which are but secondary. Though the question of Nicodemus implies the signs performed by Jesus, and the reply of Jesus was on birth from above, such a link between B and B[1] based on δύναται ταῦτα is acceptable only if the same is stressed in the rest of the parallels. In fact, the link between C-C[1], D-D[1] and E-E[1] is based on the recurrence of the verb γεννάω which appears in each of the verses of 3,3-8. In such a case anyone of these verses can be put in parallel relation with any other verse containing the term γεννάω. The structure presented by Bligh seems to ignore the stronger parallels between 3,5 and 3,7; 3,6 and 3,8; and between 3,4 and 3,9.

In his third concentric structure (see below) Bligh argues that Jesus here speaks of his incarnation and of its purpose and effects (3,11f-21):

A 11f But you do not accept our witness. 12 If I have told you earthly things and you do not believe them, how will you believe if I tell you heavenly things?

B 13 No one has been up to heaven except him who came down from heaven, the Son of Man.

C 14 And as Moses raised up the serpent in the desert, so must the Son of Man be raised up,

D 15 in order that everyone who believes in him may have eternal life."

E **16 For God so loved the world that he gave his only Son,**

D[1] in order that everyone who believes in him may not perish but have eternal life.

C[1] 17 For God sent his Son into the world, not to condemn the world, but that the world might be saved by him.

B[1] 18 He who believes in him escapes condemnation; he who does not believe is condemned already, because he has not believed in the name of the only Son of God.

A[1] 19 This is the judgement: the Light has come into the world, and men have loved darkness rather than light, because their works were evil. 20 Whoever does evil hates the light and does not come to the light, in order that his works may not be shown up; 21 but the man who does the truth comes to the light, in order that it may be seen that his works have been done in God.

The dyads A-A[1] and D-D[1] seem to be based on sound literary links. But I find no parallel correspondence between B (the descent of the Son of Man) and B[1] (faith and condemnation). In the same way the relation between *the elevation of the Son of Man* (C) and *God sending his Son into world* is not evident (C[1]). Hence, the concentric structures of Bligh are incomplete as not all the correspondences are related as presented in his diagram. It is, therefore, weak and partly unacceptable.

M. Vellanickal finds an interesting circular or spiral structure in 3,2-10 and a concentric structure in 3,11-21:

3,2 A			Nicodemus said ...WE KNOW ...YOU ARE A TEACHER come ...
B			No one CAN do THESE signs ... unless ...
3,3	C		Jesus said ... UNLESS ONE IS BEGOTTEN FROM ABOVE
		D	HE CANNOT (οὐ) SEE (ἰδεῖν) THE KINGDOM OF GOD
3,4 B^1			Nicodemus said ... HOW CAN
	C^1		A MAN BE BEGOTTEN when he is old
		D^1	CAN HE ENTER (εἰσελθεῖν) INTO the womb ...
3,5	C^2		Jesus ... I say ... UNLESS ONE IS BEGOTTEN FROM WATER AND SPIRIT
		D^2	HE CANNOT ENTER (εἰσελθεῖν) INTO THE KINGDOM OF GOD
3,6		E	That which is BORN OF the flesh IS flesh
			That which is BORN OF THE SPIRIT IS SPIRIT
3,7	C^3		Do not ... I said ... YOU must BE BEGOTTEN FROM ABOVE
3,8		D^3	The Wind (Spirit) blows ... You do not know (οὐκ οἶδας) whence it comes (ἔρχεται) ...
		E^1	So is everyone who IS BORN OF THE SPIRIT
3,9 B^2			Nicodemus replied ... HOW CAN THESE THINGS BE
3,10 A^1			Jesus replied ..YOUR ARE A TEACHER .YOU DO NOT KNOW[24]

This structure, as I see, is rather complex. I observe the repetitive and progressive presentation of the same elements BCD//B^{1}C^{1}D^1, C^{2}D^{2}E//C^{3}D^{3}E^1, with the inclusion AB//B^{2}A^1 which serves as a delimitation marking off the segment (3,2-10) from what follows. Moreover, the verbal parallels (given in capital letters) are clearly noticeable between A-A^1, B^1-B^2, C-C^3, C^1-C^2, D-D^3, D^1-D^2 and E-E^1. Vellanickal sees the main theme of this passage as 'rebirth' marked by the verb 'γεννάω' which appears in all the central verses of 3,3-8; and the different elements occurring in this passage revolve around this verb and go to specify it. In my observation, this structure is dependent mostly on the recurrence of a simple word or particle and so does not convincingly expose the structural network of the passage.

The concentric structure of the segment 3,11-21, on the other hand, seems to contain a lot of parallel elements based not only on formal verbal links but also supported by the themes of those parallels simultaneously. I shall compare this with the following chiastic structure proposed by G. Gaeta and evaluate at the end of the two presentations.

3,11 A	Amen ... WE SPEAK ... BEAR WITNESS ... YOU DO NOT RECEIVE ...
3,12 B	If ... you DO NOT BELIEVE, how YOU BELIEVE ...
3,13 C	No one has ... he who descended from heaven SON of Man
3,14 D	And ... Moses ... so must the SON of Man be lifted up
3,15 E	That WHOEVER BELIEVES MAY HAVE ETERNAL LIFE IN HIM
3,16 D^1	For God ... gave his only SON that ... may have ... life
3,17 C^1	For God sent the SON into ... world ... might ... him
3,18 B^1	He who BELIEVES is not ... he who DOES NOT BELIEVE ...
3,19-21 A^1	This ... the Light has come ... men ... does not come to ... Light ...[25]

---

[24] M. Vellanickal, *The Divine Sonship of Christians in the Johannine Writings* (AnBib 72) (Rome 1977) 165-66. About a repetitive spiralling manner of arranging the Nicodemus episode see also Kysar, *John's Story*, 27-28.

[25] Vellanickal, 208.

Gaeta presents a concentric structure of 3,11-21 based on the themes the evangelist treats in those verses:[26]

A - 3,11 - opposition to the testimony
   B - 3,12 - lack of faith in the word   action of the Son
      C - 3,13 - descent of the Son of Man
         D - 3,14 - elevation of the Son of Man
            E - 3,15 - salvation
         D^1 - 3,16 - gift of the Son
      C^1- 3,17 - sending of the Son   action of the Father
   B^1 - 3,18 - lack of faith in the Son
A^1- 3,19ff. - opposition to the light

To the credit of these structures one can mention that they have more valid correlations than those of the preceding ones. B and B^1 are linked by the verb 'πιστεύω' which occurs twice in B and thrice in B^1. In the same way there is a parallel between the descent of the Son of Man (C) and the sending of the Son (C^1), and the elevation of the Son of Man (D) corresponds to the gift of the Son (D^1) because there is an allusion to death in the gift of the Son. One of the positive aspects of these two structures is that it rightly sees at its centre the important theme of 'ζωὴ αἰώνιος' (the soteriological aspect).

Roustang,[27] for example, proposes a tripartite structural arrangement of 3,1-21. 3,1-2, according to him, serves as a brief introduction and forms an inclusion with the conclusion (3,19-21).[28] The scene is introduced by a word of Jesus (3,3) which provokes Nicodemus to raise two questions (3,4). Jesus replies the two questions but in the inverse order: the distinction between the two types of birth (3,5-8) and the how of the birth from above (3,9-15). Each of the interventions of Jesus is introduced by a solemn double-*amen* formula. This proposal of Roustang follows simultaneously a thematic plan in its structure. I have remarked already that the three interventions of Jesus introduced by the double-*amen* formula, as well as the questions of Nicodemus must certainly have a rhetoric function in the text. I am disappointed to notice that Roustang takes a bad orientation in mixing, from the beginning, the literary and the thematic criteria. He makes a profound distinction between the questions in 3,4bc and 3,4de and considers synonymously those of 4bc and 9b. This basis, thematically founded, appears to be insufficient to introduce the idea of inversion between the questions of Nicodemus and the replies of Jesus. The questions raised in 3,4 seem to belong together as they manifest the surprise and incomprehension of Nicodemus confronted with the possibility of an old man to be

---

[26] G. Gaeta, *Il dialogo con Nicodemo. Per l'interpretatione del capitolo terzo dell'evangelo di Giovanni* (SB 26) (Brescia 1974) 100. See also H. Maneschg, *Die Erzählung von der ehernen Schlange (Num 21, 4-9) in der Auslegung der früheren jüdischen Literatur. Eine traditionsgeschichtliche Studie* (EHS.T 157) (Bern, Frankfurt 1981) 385-96.

[27] See F. Roustang, "L'entretien avec Nicodème," *NRTh* 78 (1956) 337-58.

[28] The inclusive relation between 3,1-2 and 3,19-21 is based on three elements: first, 'Nicodemus came to Jesus by night' (3,2) corresponds to the expression 'coming/not coming to light' of 3,20 and 3,21; second, the designation of Jesus as 'teacher come from God' (3,2) is to be noted in the affirmation of the coming of the light into the world (3,19); third, there is a parallel relation between 'signs done with the presence of God' (3,2) and 'deeds done in God' (3,21).

physically reborn. I have no intention of making an exhaustive survey of all the structural studies of the past.[29]

C. Narrative Patterns

By far one of the pioneering and influential studies in the narrative world of the fourth Gospel has been Culpepper's *Anatomy of the Fourth Gospel*. "The experience of reading the text," according to him, "is more important than understanding the process of its composition."[30] It is precisely through narrative elements, he contends, that the fourth Gospel communicates its confessed aim of moving the reader to new insights and to faith in Jesus as the Son of God (Jn. 20,31).

He analyses at length the development of the plot of the fourth Gospel chapter by chapter. Jn. 1,19-2,11 is regarded as "a dramatic introduction to Jesus and his work."[31] Jesus' cleansing of the Temple in Jerusalem and the discussion provoked by the Jews on the issue of the destruction and rebuilding of the *Temple*, which is an allusion to Jesus' death and resurrection, move the plot forward (2,13-22). The problem posed by Jesus' reluctance to trust those who believed in his name (2,23-25) complicates the plot somewhat and sounds a less optimistic tone.[32] The dialogues and discourses in Jn. 3 disclose further dimensions of Jesus' identity, mission and significance, and the causes and consequences of belief and unbelief. After establishing the existence of a plot, Culpepper describes its development around the central figure, Jesus Christ, the divine Logos who became a human being to reveal the Father and who was rejected by the Jews and welcomed in faith by a few. The progressive but episodic character of the development of plot is underlined. He argues that "each episode has essentially the same plot as the story as whole... The story is repeated over and over."[33]

His careful analysis of the dramatic-episodic plot is enlightening. But one of the weaknesses of his analysis is that it is mostly done chapter by chapter, as though the author of the fourth Gospel had divided it into 21 chapters.[34] He does not sufficiently stress the principal stages of the development of plot, though some of them are hinted at. Moreover, Semitic literary devices such as 'inclusion,' or 'chiasm' for the division of a narrative are hardly ever mentioned by Culpepper. Since the primary purpose of Culpepper in his book is not to establish the literary structure of the Gospel, I point out this observation not as a defect but as a limitation that has to be complemented.[35]

---

[29] For further structural studies on 3,1-10; 3,1-21 and 3,22-4,3 see Howard-Brook, 86-99; on 2,23-3,21 see G. Korting, *Die esoterische Struktur des Johannesevangeliums* (BU 25) (Regensburg 1994) I, 156-80.

[30] Culpepper, *Anatomy*, 5.

[31] *Ibid.*, 89.

[32] *Ibid.*, 90.

[33] *Ibid.*, 89; see also his "The Plot of John's Story of Jesus," *Interp.* 49 (1995) 347-58.

[34] Cf. *Ibid.*, 89-94. Only a few chapters are grouped together (1,19-2,11; 9-10; 13-17 and 18,28-19,42).

[35] There have been moves toward such a contribution such as Ellis's *The Genius of John* which broke some new ground and R. Kysar's very short and popular book *John's Story of Jesus* which paved the way toward a predominantly text-immanent commentary. See also L. Schenke, *Das Johannesevangelium. Einführung – Text – dramatische Gestalt* (UB 446) (Stuttgart 1992).

♦ Narrative-Parallel Patterns

Having surveyed some of the structural patterns let me explore some narrative patterns which could throw some more light on the literary structure of the unit of my study. Not many have studied in the past 2,23-3,36 from a narrative structural perspective. However, I turn to some of the studies that seem to be closer to or containing narrative elements in their patterns. Interestingly all of them see a parallel relation between the two episodes: 3,1-21 and 3,22-36. The first narrative pattern taken up for my study is that of Malina and Rohrbaugh:[36]

3,1-21	//	**3,22-36**
1. Occasion		1. Occasion
a) a Pharisee		a) A Judean
b) born of water/spirit		b) over purification
c) with Jesus		c) with John's disciples
2. Address: "Rabbi..."		2. Address: "Rabbi..."
3. Christology: "A teacher from God"		3. Christology: "He who was with you... to whom you bore testimony, here he is baptising, and all are going to him."
4. Reply of Jesus		4. Reply of John the Baptist
a) unless you are born ἄνωθεν (from above/again)		a) unless it is given him from the sky
b) metaphor of wind (spirit) (v.8)		b) metaphor of bridegroom (v.29)
5. Nicodemus and his eminence: "You a teacher of Israel do not know this?" (v.10)		5. John the Baptist and Jesus' eminence: "He must increase and I must decrease" (v.30)

Malina and Rohrbaugh, here, seem to aim at showing that the parallel scenes develop rather identically. The observation of the setting, the characters involved, the beginning of the conversation, the themes of the dialogue in question and answer form in both episodes are worth noting. Unfortunately, the authors do not provide any further explanation to this structure in their commentary. First of all, it clearly appears to be a very incomplete pattern as it does not take into consideration all the parallels in the narrative of the diptych 3,1-21 and 3,22-36, nor do they give the verse references to the parallels all through. The observation of the narrative structure in the elements, such as the occasion leading to the narrative or dialogue (cf. 1 in the diagram above), and the mode of addressing (cf. 2 in the diagram above) and the reply (cf. 4 in the diagram above) are well noticed, though in a very inadequate manner. The dialogue pattern is not clearly exposed. What is presented as Christology in both the parallels is disappointing. The soteriological aspect is passed under silence. As a narrative pattern, I believe, this exposition is rather superficial and incomplete.

Let me now turn to a study made by J. Wilson which is also closer to a narrative pattern:[37]

---

[36] Malina and Rohrbaugh, 93.

[37] Wilson, 34-41, esp. 37.

Discourse of Jesus	//	**Discourse of the Baptist**

1. Approach to Jesus vss. 1-2
   a. question
   b. title of ʿΡαββι
2. Reply of Jesus vs. 3
   a. γεννηθῇ ἄνωθεν
3. Further Replies vss. 5-8, 11-12
4. Change of Tone vss. 13-21 (first to third person)
   a. ἐκ τοῦ οὐρανου
   b. vss. 16-18: ζωὴν αἰώνιον/κρίνεται
5. The Spirit vss. 6 and 8
   ὁ γεγεννημένος ἐκ τοῦ πνεύματος

1. Approach to Baptist vss. 25-27
   a. question
   b. title of ʿΡαββι
2. Reply of Baptist vs. 27
   a. δεδομένον … ἐκ τοῦ οὐρανοῦ
3. Further Replies vss. 29-31
4. Change of Tone vss. 31-36 (first to third person)
   a. ὁ ἄνωθεν ἐρχόμενος
   b. vss. 35-36: ζωὴν αἰώνιον/ὀργὴ
5. The Spirit vs. 34
   δίδωσιν τὸ πνεῦμα

Like the previous one this is also a parallel narrative structure. It is praiseworthy that Wilson exposes a parallelism in the narrative structure not only between 3,11-21 and 31-36 but between the whole of 3,1-21 and 25-36. 3,22-24, absent in the column on the right, according to him, serves as a bridge between the two parallel sub-units as Jesus and the Baptist are presented as engaged in baptising. The correlation between 3,1-2 and 3,25-26 as noticed by Wilson is literally founded and is, therefore, something to be appreciated. The elements of movement, addressing and questioning in 1, and the observation of replies in 2 and 3, change from first to the third person in 4 are also noteworthy elements contributing toward establishing the narrative structure of the sub-units. However, in 3, in both episodes (3,5-8; 11-12 and 29-31) the correlation is not sufficiently demonstrated; moreover, one can also observe strong parallels between 3,11-12 and 3,31-34 which Wilson seems to ignore.

Following the pattern suggested by Ibuki and Thyen,[38] Mlakuzhyil in his monograph, *Christocentric Structure of the Fourth Gospel*, presents the parallel elements in the narrative structure of 2,23-3,21 and 3,22-36:[39] I shall present his narrative structure in the form of a diagram as given below:

2,23-3,21	//	**3,22-36**

2,23-3,1: short narrative
3,2-10: dialogue on birth from above
(here he presents each of the verbal
3,11-21: discourse on eternal life

3,22-25: short narrative
3,26-30: dialogue on the groom from above
parallels between the two episodes)
3,31-36: discourse on life

The parallels in the *short narrative* in both the episodes (2,23-3,1 and 3,22-25), and in the two dialogues (3,2-10 and 3,26-30) are evident; there is also agreement among many

---

[38] Cf. Ibuki, "Καὶ τὴν," 9-33; and Thyen, "Aus der Literatur," 112.

[39] Cf. Mlakuzhyil, 198-99. I do not quote all the verbal parallels observed by him. He does not, however, comment or explain further his presentation, as he believes that "the parallels between the two passages are so numerous and so striking that it is unnecessary to comment on them." I shall take up the detailed exegesis in my next chapter dealing with narrative and structural analysis.

modern scholars about the same.[40] But his reduction of the central theme of the monologue or discourse in 3,11-21 and 3,31-36 to eternal life – soteriological aspect – alone is insufficient.

Moloney presents a little more detailed narrative pattern under the same basic tripartite division and elements:[41] I present it in the form of a diagram as given below:

3,1-21   //   3,22-36

3,1-21	**3,22-36**
I. 3,1-2a: Introductory passage (setting: time and characterisation)	I. 3,22-24: Introductory passage (setting: time, location and activity of the main characters)

II. 3,2b-11/12: Dialogue between Jesus and Nicodemus:
  a. 3,2b: Opening statement of Nicodemus (his understanding of Jesus' person and role)
  b. 3,3-8: Response of Jesus– teaching on rebirth in the spirit
  c. 3,9-10: Nicodemus' final intervention and Jesus' response.
  d. 3,11-12: Bridge verses
	II. 3,25-30: Discussion between the Baptist and his disciples
	  a. 3,25-26: Opening statement- question about the relationship between Jesus and the Baptist.
	  b. 3,27-30: Response of the Baptist– the bridegroom

III. 3, 13-21: Discourse of Jesus
  a. 3,13-15: Theme 1: revelation of the heavenly in the Son of Man
  b. 3,16-21: Theme 2: salvation or condemnation
	III. 3,31-36: Commentary of the narrator
	  a. 3,31-35: Theme 1: revelation of the heavenly in the Son
	  b. 3,36: Theme 2: salvation or condemnation

I find that the narrative shape of 3,1-21 is repeated in 3,22-26. Both have an introduction to a dialogue that leads to a discourse. One observes a thematic and literary unity in these two episodes; both episodes deal with the response of the Jews (Nicodemus and the Baptist) to Jesus. But Moloney surprisingly leaves out the important prelude (2,23-25) in his introduction leading to the Nicodemus episode; 2,23-25 presents precious information about the character of Nicodemus, the themes of signs and faith and, thus, provides the immediate setting for the following episode. Moreover, his classification of 3,11-12 as bridge verses is groundless and therefore not convincing.

Stibbe, on the other hand, presents a slightly different structure: dialogue (3,1-15//3,23-30); narrator's commentary (3,16-21//3,31-36); itinerary fragment (3,22//4,1-3).[42] He straight away starts with the aspect of dialogue and fails to notice the location and occasion (2,23), and the background (2,24-25) leading to the Nicodemus episode; he also ignores the aspect of introduction of the character of Nicodemus (3,1) and the setting of time (3,2a) leading to the encounter and dialogue. Though one could certainly observe a parallel between the itinerary fragments 3,22 and 4,1-3, 3,22 along with 3,23-24, just like 2,23-25, suits better as an introduction (of characters, occasion, place, etc.) to the

---

[40] Cf. e.g. Léon-Dufour, *op. cit.*, 282-84; Beasley-Murray, *op. cit.*, 46. See also W. Klaiber, "Der irdische und der himmlische Zeuge: Eine Auslegung von Joh 3.22-36," *NTS* 36 (1990) 211-13 who divides as: *Bericht – Gespräch – Die Stimme Christi.*

[41] Moloney, *Belief in the Word*, 106-7 and 122-23. See also his *John*, 90 and 104.

[42] Stibbe, *John*, 59.

forthcoming episode (3,26-36). No doubt, the itinerary fragment 4,1-3 forms an *inclusio* with 3,22-23 repeating the baptismal activity of Jesus and his disciples, besides giving the itinerary details. Hence, the two narrative patterns of Moloney and Stibbe – in spite of the fact they contain the basic narrative shape of the two episodes – need to be improved.

Conclusion

Like many other facets of the fourth Gospel, its basic structure seems fairly simple until one starts to explore it. This complexity hidden in simplicity is the reason why scores of studies on the structure of the fourth Gospel have been published in the last three decades. One of the reasons why critics find so many mutually exclusive structures is the evangelist's repeated handling of only a few themes. At the end of this survey, I feel, one point emerges clearly: the great disparity of results. Whether thematic, symbolic, structural or narrative, none of the proposed patterns seem to be vital with evidence. They either ignore one or the other theme, or fail to observe one or the other literary aspect. However, the profound richness of 2,23-3,36 comes to the fore in all these studies. I should conclude that there is unanimity among scholars about the presence of parallel elements between the Nicodemus and the Baptist episodes, though all of them – except Létourneau and Moloney – include only parts of Jn. 3 in their observations. However, most scholars seem to accept the parallel narrative structural pattern of *introduction – dialogue – monologue/discourse/ commentary* as the basic design of 2,23-3,36, though they differ in the sub-division of the verses.

Chapter 3

LITERARY AND NARRATIVE ANALYSIS OF 2,23-3,36

A text, once conceived and formulated, acquires a life of its own, and can become an object of investigation in its own right. The fourth evangelist has arranged each narrative and discourse with meticulous artistry and noticeable literary design. The literary and narrative exegesis should lead to a sort of open heart surgery of the text in order to lay bare these aspects and help understand the rhythm of its heart-beat. I shall explore 2,23-3,36 from its intra-structural and narrative points of view, first, by subjecting the chosen text to a thorough and systematic analysis of the two episodes (2,23-3,21 and 3,22-36) separately, and then, by observing the parallel structure between them in view of extracting the underlying Christological argumentation and the soteriology flowing from the text.

A. Literary and Narrative Analysis of 2,23-3,21

The study of the fourth Gospel as a narrative demands that one attends to its structure in order to articulate its plot-line. The author of the fourth Gospel is "a literary architect of rare excellence."[1] Let me begin the analysis of the episode dealing with the encounter of Nicodemus with Jesus under three subdivisions: (A) 2,23-3,2; (B) 3,3-10; and (C) 3,11-21.[2] From the narrative perspective it begins with an *introduction*, followed by a *dialogue* that leads to a *discourse (monologue)*. One can also observe here a concentric structure in which the first (A) and the third (C) sub-units are linked to each other. First of all, I shall try to explore and expose the transition of the narrative from (A) to (C) through (B).

As the thematic coherence of the episode is not evident, my aim is to establish it through structural and narrative analysis. All the attempts to understand the pericope must be done keeping in mind the rapport between the dialogue on rebirth (3,3-10) and the coupling of the introduction (2,23-3,2) with the Christological discourse (3,11-21). In other words, the link between the statements of Jesus in 3,3.5-8 and the words of Nicodemus in 3,2 must be established first; and then the link between Jesus' dialogue with Nicodemus and the discourse of Jesus must be explored. Let me draw the attention to the tripartite structure of the text in order to observe the verbal recurrences and demonstrate the formal link among them:

A (2,23-3,2)

^{2,23} Ὡς δὲ ἦν ἐν τοῖς Ἱεροσολύμοις ἐν τῷ πάσχα ἐν τῇ ἑορτῇ, <u>πολλοὶ ἐπίστευσαν</u> <u>εἰς τὸ ὄνομα</u> αὐτοῦ <u>θεωροῦντες</u> αὐτοῦ *τὰ σημεῖα ἃ ἐποίει·* ^{24} αὐτὸς δὲ Ἰησοῦς <u>οὐκ ἐπίστευεν</u> αὐτὸν αὐτοῖς διὰ τὸ αὐτὸν <u>γινώσκειν</u> πάντας ^{25} καὶ ὅτι οὐ χρείαν εἶχεν ἵνα τις μαρτυρήσῃ περὶ τοῦ <u>ἀνθρώπου·</u> αὐτὸς γὰρ <u>ἐγίνωσκεν</u> τί ἦν ἐν τῷ <u>ἀνθρώπῳ.</u> $^{3:1}$ Ἦν δὲ <u>ἄνθρωπος</u> ἐκ τῶν Φαρισαίων, Νικόδημος ὄνομα αὐτῷ,

---

[1] G. Østenstad, "The Structure of the Fourth Gospel: Can it be Defined Objectively?," *StTh* 45 (1991) 33.

[2] Scholars like R. E. Brown, Mlakuzhyil and Léon-Dufour contend that the dialogue of Nicodemus begins already with 3,2, while others like de la Potterie, Vouga and Leidig see Jesus taking the initiative in the dialogue (3,3). The separation between dialogue and discourse, too, creates problems. My literary and narrative analysis in this chapter will demonstrate well that the *introduction* ends at 3,2, the *dialogue* begins at 3,3 and the *discourse* at 3,11. However, there is ambiguity between 3,9 and 3,10. Though they formally belong to the dialogue (3,3-10), they seem to serve also as an introduction to the Christological discourse that follows and so act as 'bridge-verses.'

ἄρχων τῶν Ἰουδαίων· ² οὗτος ἦλθεν πρὸς αὐτὸν νυκτὸς καὶ εἶπεν αὐτῷ, Ῥαββί, <u>οἴδαμεν</u> ὅτι ἀπὸ θεοῦ ἐλήλυθας <u>διδάσκαλος</u>· *οὐδεὶς* γὰρ δύναται *ταῦτα τὰ σημεῖα ποιεῖν ἃ σὺ ποιεῖς,* ἐὰν μὴ ᾖ ὁ θεὸς μετ' αὐτοῦ.

B (3,3-10)

³,³ ἀπεκρίθη Ἰησοῦς καὶ εἶπεν αὐτῷ, <u>Ἀμὴν ἀμὴν λέγω σοι,</u> ἐὰν μή τις γεννηθῇ ἄνωθεν, οὐ δύναται <u>ἰδεῖν</u> τὴν βασιλείαν τοῦ θεοῦ. ⁴ λέγει πρὸς αὐτὸν [ὁ] Νικόδημος, <u>Πῶς</u> δύναται <u>ἄνθρωπος</u> γεννηθῆναι γέρων ὤν; μὴ δύναται εἰς τὴν κοιλίαν τῆς μητρὸς αὐτοῦ δεύτερον εἰσελθεῖν καὶ γεννηθῆναι; ⁵ ἀπεκρίθη Ἰησοῦς, <u>Ἀμὴν ἀμὴν λέγω σοι,</u> ἐὰν μή τις γεννηθῇ ἐξ ὕδατος καὶ πνεύματος, οὐ δύναται εἰσελθεῖν εἰς τὴν βασιλείαν τοῦ θεοῦ. ⁶ τὸ γεγεννημένον ἐκ τῆς σαρκὸς σάρξ ἐστιν, καὶ τὸ γεγεννημένον ἐκ τοῦ πνεύματος πνεῦμά ἐστιν. ⁷ μὴ θαυμάσῃς ὅτι εἶπόν σοι, <u>Δεῖ</u> ὑμᾶς γεννηθῆναι ἄνωθεν. ⁸ τὸ πνεῦμα ὅπου θέλει πνεῖ καὶ τὴν φωνὴν αὐτοῦ ἀκούεις, ἀλλ' οὐκ οἶδας πόθεν ἔρχεται καὶ ποῦ ὑπάγει· οὕτως ἐστὶν πᾶς ὁ γεγεννημένος ἐκ τοῦ πνεύματος. ⁹ ἀπεκρίθη Νικόδημος καὶ εἶπεν αὐτῷ, <u>Πῶς</u> δύναται ταῦτα γενέσθαι; ¹⁰ ἀπεκρίθη Ἰησοῦς καὶ εἶπεν αὐτῷ, Σὺ εἶ ὁ <u>διδάσκαλος</u> τοῦ Ἰσραὴλ καὶ ταῦτα οὐ <u>γινώσκεις;</u>

C (3,11-21)

³,¹¹ <u>ἀμὴν ἀμὴν λέγω σοι</u> ὅτι ὃ <u>οἴδαμεν λαλοῦμεν</u> καὶ ὃ <u>ἑωράκαμεν μαρτυροῦμεν,</u> καὶ τὴν <u>μαρτυρίαν</u> ἡμῶν οὐ <u>λαμβάνετε.</u> ¹² εἰ τὰ ἐπίγεια εἶπον ὑμῖν καὶ <u>οὐ πιστεύετε,</u> πῶς ἐὰν εἴπω ὑμῖν τὰ ἐπουράνια <u>πιστεύσετε;</u> ¹³ καὶ *οὐδεὶς* ἀναβέβηκεν εἰς τὸν οὐρανὸν εἰ <u>μὴ</u> ὁ ἐκ τοῦ οὐρανοῦ καταβάς, ὁ υἱὸς τοῦ ἀνθρώπου. ¹⁴ καὶ καθὼς Μωϋσῆς ὕψωσεν τὸν ὄφιν ἐν τῇ ἐρήμῳ, οὕτως ὑψωθῆναι <u>δεῖ</u> τὸν υἱὸν τοῦ ἀνθρώπου, ¹⁵ ἵνα πᾶς ὁ <u>πιστεύων</u> ἐν αὐτῷ ἔχῃ ζωὴν αἰώνιον. ¹⁶ Οὕτως γὰρ ἠγάπησεν ὁ θεὸς τὸν κόσμον, ὥστε τὸν υἱὸν τὸν μονογενῆ ἔδωκεν, ἵνα πᾶς ὁ <u>πιστεύων εἰς αὐτὸν</u> μὴ ἀπόληται ἀλλ' ἔχῃ ζωὴν αἰώνιον. ¹⁷ οὐ γὰρ <u>ἀπέστειλεν ὁ θεὸς τὸν υἱὸν</u> εἰς τὸν κόσμον ἵνα κρίνῃ τὸν κόσμον, ἀλλ' ἵνα σωθῇ ὁ κόσμος δι' αὐτοῦ. ¹⁸ ὁ <u>πιστεύων εἰς αὐτὸν</u> οὐ κρίνεται· ὁ δὲ <u>μὴ πιστεύων</u> ἤδη κέκριται, ὅτι <u>μὴ πεπίστευκεν εἰς τὸ ὄνομα τοῦ μονογενοῦς υἱοῦ τοῦ θεοῦ.</u> ¹⁹ αὕτη δέ ἐστιν ἡ κρίσις ὅτι τὸ φῶς <u>ἐλήλυθεν</u> εἰς τὸν κόσμον καὶ ἠγάπησαν <u>οἱ ἄνθρωποι</u> μᾶλλον τὸ σκότος ἢ τὸ φῶς· ἦν γὰρ αὐτῶν πονηρὰ τὰ ἔργα. ²⁰ πᾶς γὰρ ὁ φαῦλα *πράσσων* μισεῖ τὸ φῶς καὶ <u>οὐκ ἔρχεται πρὸς τὸ φῶς,</u> ἵνα μὴ ἐλεγχθῇ τὰ ἔργα αὐτοῦ· ²¹ ὁ δὲ ποιῶν τὴν ἀλήθειαν <u>ἔρχεται πρὸς τὸ φῶς,</u> ἵνα φανερωθῇ αὐτοῦ τὰ ἔργα ὅτι ἐν θεῷ ἐστιν εἰργασμένα.

The central sub-unit (B) is linked to the first (A) in the formal recurrence of the terms θεωροῦντες/ἰδεῖν, ἄνθρωπος, διδάσκαλος, γινώσκεις common to both sub-units; and to the third (C) in the recurrence of the terms: ἀμὴν ἀμὴν λέγω σοι, πῶς, δεῖ, and οἴδαμεν. Furthermore, there are a number of elements common to the sub-units A and C: first of all, there is the repeated occurrence of the verb πιστεύω which is completely absent in B. It is also to be observed that there is a formal link between the phrases: "ἐπίστευσαν εἰς τὸ ὄνομα αὐτοῦ" (2,23b) and "πεπίστευκεν εἰς τὸ ὄνομα τοῦ μονογενοῦς υἱοῦ τοῦ θεοῦ" (3,18e). There is also a rapport between the signs done by Jesus, because God is with him (cf. 3,2 and 2,23) and the 'deeds done in God' (3,21; cf. 3,19-20).[3] In the wake of this tie between 3,2 and 3,21, the use of the verb ποιέω (2,23c; 3,2f and 3,21a) and the occurrence of its synonym πράσσω (3,20a) are to be noted.

---

[3] Although signs are specific to Jesus, they make part of his deeds (cf. 5,16-17.36; 6,30 and 7,21-23). He tells his disciples that those who believe in him will also do the same deeds and even greater (cf. 14,12).

In the exposition of the inclusion which holds the unit (2,23-3,21) together, I have pointed out already (cf. chapter 1), the formal link between 3,2 and 3,20-21 in the expressions 'came to Jesus by night' and 'do not come to the light...come to the light' respectively. In approaching Jesus, Nicodemus comes toward the light; however, he has some reservations, because he comes by night. In fact, it is evident that the οἴδαμεν expressed by Jesus in 3,11b resumes explicitly the οἴδαμεν of Nicodemus in 3,2c. The knowledge of Nicodemus in confessing Jesus merely as 'a teacher come from God' is restricted. On the contrary, the οἴδαμεν that is spoken of in 3,11b has reference to the identity of Jesus as the 'Son of Man come down from heaven' (cf. 3,13-14) and 'Son sent by the Father' (cf. 3,16-17). Jesus is not just a teacher but the 'Son of Man' and the 'only Son of God.' To leave the night (darkness) and reach fully the light, Nicodemus must make a bold step forward that would lead him from the conception of the Pharisees to the true confession of faith. The ruler of the Jews rightly acknowledges that 'God is with Jesus;' but God is not present as He was present to the great personages of Israel in its tradition. The presence of God in Jesus is unique – perfect union between the sending Father and His only Son-sent (cf. 3,16-17).

Finally, in the same line of correlation, one must go a step ahead in comparing the seeing (θεωρέω) of signs (2,23c) and the seeing (ὁράω) of the real mystery of the person of Jesus who is the object of testimony (3,11d). Note also the formal recurrence of the verb 'μαρτυρέω' (2,25a and 3,11e) and the substantives 'μαρτυρία' (3,11f) and 'ἄνθρωπος' (2,25a. d; 3,1a and 3,19c), and the syntactic structure 'οὐδεὶς ... ἐὰν/εἰ μή' (3,2 and 3,13).

1. 2,23-3,2: Scene Setting (Introduction/Report)

There is no unanimity among scholars for such a grouping of verses. Many of them, in fact, begin the episode with the appearance of Nicodemus, the dialogue partner of Jesus, in the scene. Though there appears to be a break with 2,25 at 3,1, that does not, in my opinion, necessarily imply a change of literary unit. On the contrary, formal literary indications compel to consider 2,23-3,2 as a literary unit. This is supported, first of all, by an *inclusion* between 2,23 and 3,2 which is sufficient to establish the literary unity of this sub-unit (see the diagram on the next page):

a. Chiastic Structure

There is a correspondence between A and A[1] which is evident in the recurrence of the terms 'his name' in 2,23b (ὄνομα αὐτοῦ) and 3,1b (ὄνομα αὐτῷ), and the expressions 'signs that he was doing' (τὰ σημεῖα ἃ ἐποίει – 2,23c) and 'these signs that you do' (ταῦτα τὰ σημεῖα ποιεῖν ἃ σὺ ποιεῖς – 3,2fg). Thus, the whole sub-unit has an inclusive structure. Nicodemus appears as one of the 'many who believed in his name' (2,23b). Consequently, there is a probable relation between the general flocking of the πολλοί toward Jesus 'believing in his name' and the acknowledgement by Nicodemus that Jesus is a 'teacher[4] come from God' (3,2de). In fact, the faith evoked solely by seeing signs[5] is not profound as it restricts their consideration of Jesus only as a prophet or as a master enjoying divine

---

[4] H.-J. Klauck ("Gemeinde ohne Amt? Erfahrungen mit der Kirche in den johanneischen Schriften," *BZ* 29 [1985] 205) is of the opinion that the style of speech here seems to reflect that of the Johannine School.

[5] See M.-É. Boismard, "Rapports entre foi et miracles dans l'évangile de Jean," *EThL* 58 (1982) 357-64.

assistance – as Nicodemus does (3,2). Just as Jesus does not entrust himself to the faith of the πολλοί, 'because he knew (γινώσκω) all people' (2,24b; cf. 2,25cd), he does not seem to be taken up by the faith of Nicodemus acknowledging him merely as a 'Rabbi' and 'teacher who has come from God' and in whom there is the presence of God (3,2). This is evident also in the later ironic rebuke of Jesus: "Are you a teacher of Israel, and yet you do not understand (γινώσκω) these things?" (3,10bc).

A 2,23: Ὡς δὲ ἦν ἐν τοῖς Ἰεροσολύμοις ἐν τῷ πάσχα ἐν τῇ ἑορτῇ, πολλοὶ ἐπίστευσαν εἰς τὸ ὄνομα αὐτοῦ θεωροῦντες αὐτοῦ τὰ σημεῖα ἃ ἐποίει·

    B 2,24-25ab: αὐτὸς δὲ Ἰησοῦς οὐκ ἐπίστευεν αὐτὸν αὐτοῖς διὰ τὸ αὐτὸν γινώσκειν πάντας καὶ ὅτι οὐ χρείαν εἶχεν ἵνα τις μαρτυρήσῃ περὶ τοῦ ἀνθρώπου·

    B¹ 2,25cd: αὐτὸς γὰρ ἐγίνωσκεν τί ἦν ἐν τῷ ἀνθρώπῳ.

A¹ 3,1-2: Ἦν δὲ ἄνθρωπος ἐκ τῶν Φαρισαίων, Νικόδημος ὄνομα αὐτῷ, ἄρχων τῶν Ἰουδαίων· ² οὗτος ἦλθεν πρὸς αὐτὸν νυκτὸς καὶ εἶπεν αὐτῷ, Ῥαββί, οἴδαμεν ὅτι ἀπὸ θεοῦ ἐλήλυθας διδάσκαλος· οὐδεὶς γὰρ δύναται ταῦτα τὰ σημεῖα ποιεῖν ἃ σὺ ποιεῖς, ἐὰν μὴ ᾖ ὁ θεὸς μετ' αὐτοῦ.[6]

In B and B¹ there is a synonymy between the affirmation that Jesus 'knew all people' (γινώσκειν πάντας – 2,24b) – those who saw Jesus' signs – and the statement that he 'knew what was in everyone' (ἐγίνωσκεν τί ἦν ἐν τῷ ἀνθρώπῳ – 2,25cd). Jesus is the subject of the verb γινώσκω here. He does not entrust himself to the πολλοί in Jerusalem who believed in his name, because he *knew* their hearts and was aware of their type of faith and perceived how far it could lead to. Finally, just as the elements A and B are linked through the verb πιστεύω (2,23 and 24), the elements B¹ and A¹ are hooked through the word ἄνθρωπος (2,25 and 3,1).[7]

However, the above mentioned chiastic structure and the observation of an inclusion are not the only criteria to prove the literary unity of 2,23-3,2. One can easily observe that Jesus does not intervene until 3,3, which implies that the expression 'πρὸς αὐτὸν'[8] of 3,2a must be linked to its referent in the context, *viz.*, 'αὐτὸς δὲ Ἰησοῦς' (2,24a). Furthermore, one can fall back on the literary genre – *introduction* – in 2,25-3,2 (see the narrative structure below). Finally, the conjunction δέ in 3,1-2 places 2,23-25 in contrast: 'In Jerusalem, at the Passover, many believed in his name...*But*[9] there was a *man* among the Pharisees... who came to him.' These different indications show that between 2,25 and 3,2 there is no change of scene, but rather an implicit plan. This is demonstrated further in the explanation of the narrative structure below.

---

[6] See also Létourneau, *Jésus*, 52. The words underlined and in bold face are the hook-words.

[7] This link in words and expressions are obscured in the English translation. Hence, I prefer to quote the Greek text in the chiastic structure.

[8] In the NRSV it is translated as: "he came to Jesus," though the word *Jesus* does not appear as yet there, but only implied. See Létourneau, *op. cit.*, 116; and Schmidl, 85.

b. Argumentative Narrative Structure

2,23a	Outline of the occasion (specification of place and time)
b	Establishing the fact: ἐπίστευσαν
cd	Reasoning: seeing the σημεῖα
24a	Restriction (specification): δὲ ... οὐκ
b	Reasoning 1: διὰ
25	Reasoning 2: καὶ ὅτι οὐ ... γὰρ
3,1-2a	Introduction/*description of the person* and *details of time* (comp. 2,13.23a; 4,45; 6,4; 11,55; 12,1 and 13,1)
2b	Speech opening: εἶπεν
2c-h	First intervention of Nicodemus (a brief *description of his faith/stand in relation to the signs performed by Jesus*; cf. 2,23cd)
2c	Addressing: Ῥαββι
2cde	Affirmation: οἴδαμεν ὅτι
2fgh	Reasoning of the argumentation: γὰρ; ἐάν μὴ; σημεῖα

c. Thematic Argumentation

Having established the formal and narrative structures of the text, I must now explore the thematic argumentation supported by these structures. The main contribution of any structure should be to indicate the thematic orientation of the text. Such a separation of the two aspects is justified, because the determination of a structure using formal criteria could, at times, eclipse or ignore the themes contained in the text. Once the perimeters of a text are established, an exegete must search to place its thematic argumentation on a solid basis. A structure that does not expose the thematic argumentation of a text is a doubtful one.

The determination of the perimeters of the first sub-unit (2,23-3,2) reveals that the first words of Nicodemus do not form part of the *dialogue* but belong to the introductory exposition. This can explain, at least partially, the thematic separation[10] between the affirmation of Nicodemus in 3,2 and the first words of Jesus in 3,3.[11] Though Nicodemus

---

[9] Cf. *The Darby Bible* (1884/1890).

[10] F. P. Cotterell ("The Nicodemus Conversation: A Fresh Appraisal," *ET* 96 [1984/85] 239) observes that Nicodemus here offers Jesus four topics for consideration: 1) The concept of Rabbi; 2) The implication of Jesus being recognised as a teacher; 3) The significance of the qualifying 'ἀπὸ θεοῦ;' 4) The significance and provenance of the 'σημεῖα.'

[11] The expression 'ἀπεκρίθη' on the lips of Jesus in 3,3a gives the impression that a question has preceded it. But 3,2, in my opinion, has a character of confession and does not contain an explicit question. Against see A. Wikenhauser (*Das Evangelium nach Johannes* [ReNT 4] [Regensburg ²1957]120) and W. C. Grese ("'Unless One is Born Again:' The Use of a Heavenly Journey in John 3," *JBL* 107 [1988] 690f), who are of the opinion that Nicodemus implicitly poses the question of salvation. B. Lindars (*The Gospel of John* [NCB] [Grand Rapids ²1981] 150) and J. Painter ("Quest and Rejection Stories in John," *JSNT* 36 [1989] 25) think that it can be the intention of the evangelist that Jesus knows the question before it is asked, because of his special insight (cf. 2,24b.25cd). Nicodemus approaches Jesus attracted by the signs Jesus performs and with a positive confession. There is no controversy or debate on a particular miracle performed on a Sabbath as in 9,14. Some exegetes see that a break between 3,2 and 3,3 is intended by the evangelist to criticise radically Nicodemus and his confession; see G. R. Beasley-Murray, *Baptism in the New Testament* (Grand Rapids 1981) 226; and W. Lütgehetmann, *Die Hochzeit von Kana (Joh 2,1-11). Zu Ursprung und Deutung einer Wundererzählung im Rahmen johanneischer Redaktionsgeschichte* (BU 20) (Regensburg 1990) 195. Some consider this apparent break as an expression of the fourth evangelist's dualism. Jesus transposes the question to a higher level; the questioner is raised from the level of the sensible to the spiritual plane, on which alone can there be true knowledge of the Messiah; see R. E. Brown, *Gospel*, I, 138; and S. Agrelo, "A Propositio de Jn 3,1-3," *Anton.* 60 (1985) 233. On the contrary, Vellanickal (206) exposes a chiastic structure in 3,2-3

intervenes first, it is Jesus who actually opens the real dialogue.[12] It is he who decides on the theme; he is the revealer.[13]

Now, the inclusive character of the dyad A-A[1] and the explanatory function of the dyad B-B[1] (διά, καὶ ὅτι, γάρ), apparently, make *faith based on seeing signs* the main theme of the sub-unit. Between the elements A and A[1], one notices that A[1] deals with a specification or particularisation of the general statement made in A: from the πολλοὶ in 2,23 one moves on to an ἄνθρωπος – a Pharisee named Nicodemus, a leader of the Jews in 3,1. In the same way, the statement 'believed in his name' (2,23b) is made precise by the reasoning behind such a belief, namely *because* he is 'a teacher come from God' (3,2de). Such a movement – from general to particular and indeterminate to specific – is not clear without the inclusion of 3,2 into the thematic of this sub-unit which introduces the episode.

If such is the case, the affirmation of Nicodemus must be made the object of a special attention. It is made up of two parts: a confession about Jesus introduced by a 'we know' (3,2c) of an almost official character,[14] and a justification, linked to that confession through an explanatory 'γάρ' (3,2f). The syntactic construction of Nicodemus' confession insists on the terms 'ἀπὸ θεοῦ ἐλήλυθας;' in fact, it is the *divine origin of Jesus* which forms the main object of his confession. But the term 'διδάσκαλος' (3,2d), which is added at the end of the phrase,[15] spells out the reasoning of Nicodemus: he interprets the divine mission of Jesus as that of a 'διδάσκαλος.'[16] The reasoning is further clarified by the

---

showing the continuity and not a break. Leidig (185) speaks of a '*Schocktherapie*' for Niocdemus; see also Rebell, 139f. Létourneau (*op. cit.*, 352), on the other hand, sees that there is perfect logic in the movement from the signs (3,2b) to the perfect sign (3,14-15) through the intervention of the access to salvation (3,3). In my argument 3,2 does not belong to the dialogue but to the narrative part as my analysis demonstrates.

[12] Dodd (*Historical Tradition*, 317) observes that, contrary to the dialogues in the Synoptics, it is Jesus who normally opens the dialogues in the fourth Gospel. This is an added reason to argue that the actual dialogue begins with the intervention of Jesus in 3,3; and 3,2 still belongs to the exposition of the situation and introduction of the dialogue partners; see also M. Morgen, *Afin que le monde soit sauvé. Jésus révèle sa mission de salut dans l'évangile de Jean* (LeDiv 154) (Paris 1993) 45; and her, "Le Fils de l'homme élevé en vue de la vie eternelle (Jn 3,14-15 éclairé par diverses traditions juives)," *RevSR* 68 (1994) 5-17.

[13] Cf. J. Heer, "Johanneische Botschaft (VI). Der Offenbarer und Nikodemus (Jo 3,1-12)," *SuS* 32 (1967) 439.

[14] Such a use of plural on the lips of an individual is in agreement with the rabbinic usage "in which the form of speech is determined by the individual's consciousness of belonging to a community" (Bultmann, *Gospel*, 134, n. 3). But in the immediate context it is only probable that he is representing the 'πολλοὶ' who have come to believe in Jesus after seeing his signs (2,23) and to which Nicodemus refers to (3,2); see Barrett, 171. Such a view seems to be all the more reasonable as Nicodemus represents, in the next two appearances (7,47-52 and 19,38-39), those who have begun to believe in Jesus, but were afraid of open confession for fear of being expelled from the synagogue.

[15] As is evident from the second person singular form of the verb 'ἐλήλυθας,' the term 'διδάσκαλος' is not the grammatical subject of the sentence but a pronoun of the second person singular. Moreover, the stress of the sentence is on the coming of Jesus 'ἀπὸ θεοῦ.' In the context, the meaning of the sentence could, probably, be as follows: 'we know that you have come from God as teacher.'

[16] In the Jewish tradition 'διδάσκαλος' is one who reveals the will of God from the Law and the prophets (cf. K. H. Rengstorf, "διδάσκαλος," *TDNT*, II, 151-53). Such a designation must be set in relation with the circle of the Scribes and the Doctors of the Law who replaced the prophets in the Jewish tradition after the return from exile. Hence, it was in the study of the Torah and not in the inspired words of the prophets that God's will had to be sought; see J. Giblet, "Prophétisme et attente d'un Messie Prophète dans l'ancien Judaïsme," in: L. Cerfaux (ed.), *L'attente du Messie* (RechBib 1) (Bruges 1954) 98. According to Deut. 34,10, "Never has there arisen a prophet in Israel like Moses." In this line of thought, the confession of Nicodemus, a Pharisee, cannot refer to a prophetic mission of Jesus; (against this view see M.-É. Boismard and A. Lamouille, *L'Évangile de Jean* [*Synopse des quatres évangiles en français*] [Paris 1977] III, 118). But the phrase 'come from God' (3,2) (cf. Ex. 3,10; 1 Sam. 15,1 and 16,1; 2 Chr. 24,19; Jer. 1,7 and 25,15;

syntactic construction 'no one can do.... *apart from* (ἐάν μή).'[17] The main proposition that 'Jesus does signs which no one else can do' is explained with the condition that 'God is with him.'[18] In this logic, the sign really fulfils its function of being an indicator: the signifier (the signs performed by Jesus) reveals the signified (the presence of God). The position of Nicodemus rests, therefore, entirely on the presence of God with Jesus. From this presence he deduces the sending of Jesus by God, which is interpreted in terms of the function of a διδάσκαλος.[19] In other words, the confession of Nicodemus in Jesus as an authorised teacher or one sent by God is based on his traditional belief that Jesus' performance of signs prove a special presence of God with him; this is too vague and says very little about his true origin, identity and mission.

Passing on to the central part of the chiasm (B-B[1]), 2,24 is linked to 2,23 with the adversative conjunction δέ, which marks a contrast in the general order. The whole of 'αὐτὸς δὲ Ἰησοῦς' with the use of an emphatic personal pronoun and 'δέ' beside the name 'Ἰησοῦς,' attracts one's attention to the reaction of Jesus who is confronted with the faith mentioned in 2,23: "Many believed in his name..., *but* Jesus on his part would not entrust himself to them"[20] (2,23-24). The first motive for the distrust of Jesus is supplied in 2,24b introduced by a causal 'διὰ:' he would not entrust himself to them, "*because* he knew all

---

and Ezek. 2,4) as well as the performance of signs refer to the sending of a prophet. Hence, it is possible to understand the word διδάσκαλος in terms of a prophet. According to W. J. Bittner (*Jesu Zeichen im Johannesevangelium: Die Messiaserkenntnis im Johannesevangelium vor ihrem jüdischen Hintergrund* [WUNT II/26] [Tübingen 1987] 103-8), Judaism attributed to the awaited Messiah a '*Lehrfunktion*.' On this point see also R. Riesner, *Jesus als Lehrer. Eine Untersuchung zum Ursprung der Evangelienüberlieferung* (WUNT II/7) (Tübingen ³1988) 304-30; and O. Betz, *Jesus. Der Messias Israels* (WUNT 42) (Tübingen 1987) 413. Hence, in the Nicodemus' confession of Jesus as διδάσκαλος in 3,2 Jesus could be recognised as the awaited Messiah; see W. A. Meeks, *The Prophet-King. Moses Traditions and Johannine Christology* (NT.S 14) (Leiden 1967); and W. Nicol, *The Semeia in the Fourth Gospel. Tradition and Redaction* (NT.S 32) (Leiden 1971) 83-90. What is exactly meant by the term in 3,2 is difficult to determine. But what is clear is that, in the opinion of the evangelist – for whom Jesus is the Son of Man and the Son sent by the Father, such a confession of Nicodemus is insufficient.

[17] The use of an explanatory 'γάρ' by Nicodemus illustrates the depth of his confession. The reasoning of Nicodemus is stressed and intensified with a double negation. Such is the case with sentences dealing with wisdom-teaching and norms. For an analysis of sentences with the structure 'ἐὰν μή... οὐ μή' see Bittner, *op. cit.*, 132.

[18] The presence of God is a sign of dignity of the personages in Israel: God is with Isaac (Gen. 26,24), Jacob (Gen. 28,15 and 31,3), Joshua (Deut. 31,23), and the Judges (e.g. Gideon: Judg. 6,12.16). This presence of God is characteristic of the prophets (cf. Is. 41,10; and Jer. 1,18), and is, in a special way, applicable to Moses (Ex. 3,12). The prophet-motif is further stressed by the signs which are directly connected with the authentication of the sending of the prophets (cf. Ex. 3,12 and 4,1-9.30-31; 1 Kings 18,36-39; and Is. 7,14). See also H. Riedl, *Zeichen und Herrlichkeit. Die christologische Relevanz der Semeiaquelle in den Kanawundern Joh 2,1-11 und Joh 4,46-54* (RSTh 51) (Frankfurt 1997) 208-10; and D. Burkett, *The Son of the Man in the Gospel of John* (JSNT.S 56) (Sheffield 1991) 88.

[19] Schmidl (113) feels that Nicodemus' acknowledgement of Jesus (having a Jewish background) as 'Ραββί' shows the awaiting of a Prophet-Messiah of the end times. This, in my opinion, is unacceptable, because Deut. 13,1-6 stipulates that a sign is not a criterion of decisive discernment; above all, the word of a prophet must conform to the Law of the Lord. One finds the same argument in Jn. 9,16 where there is a division among the Pharisees; some of them accept the divine mission of Jesus based on his signs, and others consider him a sinner as he does not respect the Sabbath.

[20] The 'πιστεύω τινί τι' construction signifies normally 'entrusting something to another' (cf. LSJ, 1408). The BBE translates 2,24 as "Jesus did not have faith in them..." which is milder than "he did not believe them." As it is often found in the NT, the simple personal pronoun replaces the reflexive pronoun; thus, one can have αὐτὸν for ἑαυτόν. The meaning is changed to 'trust' someone. Hence, most of the translations adopt "he did not entrust himself to them."

people." This motive is continued in 2,25ab, which begins with 'καὶ ὅτι:'[21] 'and (he) needed no one to testify about anyone.' This statement does not add any new motive; it is rather a continuation and a consequence of the first motive; that is, because Jesus 'knew all people' (2,24b), 'he needed no one to testify about anyone' (2,25ab). In fact, 2,25ab only stress the unique, personal and extraordinary aspect of the knowledge of Jesus about all people. He possesses this knowledge; it does not come to him from the testimony of others.

Finally, it is the use of the conjunction 'γὰρ' in 2,25c, which connects what precedes, and justifies the distrust of Jesus: "*because* he himself knew what was in everyone" (2,15cd).[22] The syntactic construction of the two verses (2,24 and 2,25) expresses the distrust of Jesus. Both verses begin with phrases having the emphatic pronoun αὐτὸς[23] at the beginning: *αὐτὸς δέ ... διὰ ... καὶ ὅτι ... αὐτὸς γάρ...* After the statement in 2,24a, the causal chain leads progressively to the emphatic phrase 'αὐτὸς γάρ.' Thus, from the formal and narrative structure, one is able to demonstrate the thematic argumentation of this sub-unit.

Let me now reconsider some of the significant elements. First of all, one notices that the entire sub-unit of *introduction/report* is composed of three main statements, each of which is immediately followed by a reasoning or justification. The statement in 2,23b (A) expresses the coming to faith of the πολλοὶ in the name of Jesus, the reason being the witness of signs performed by Jesus (2,23cd). The statement in 2,24a (B) mentions the distrust of Jesus in such a faith, the reason being the personal knowledge of Jesus about people in general[24] (2,24b-25ab); this knowledge is further specified (in B¹) as a knowledge about the heart of a person (2,25cd).[25] Finally, A¹ exposes implicitly the deeper reasons for the hesitation of Jesus, *viz.*, the affirmation of Nicodemus about the origin (ἀπὸ θεοῦ ἐλήλυθας), identity ('Ραββί) and mission of Jesus (διδάσκαλος) (cf. 3,2) which fall short of his true origin, identity and mission.

Moreover, just as there is a semantic transition from the πολλοὶ to 'an ἄνθρωπος named Nicodemus,' there is another more important movement from 'believing' to 'knowing.'[26] In the case of the πολλοὶ, their faith (ἐπίστευσαν)[27] in the name of Jesus is the

---

[21] The explanation of Barrett (168) seems to be acceptable on this issue: "καὶ ὅτι with a finite verb continues διά and the articular infinitive. It is an unusual but readily understood construction *ad sensum*, and there is no need for conjecture (e.g. καθότι for καὶ ὅτι)."

[22] The judgement of Jesus is right, because he is the one whom 'God has sent,' who 'speaks the words of God,' and posseses the 'Spirit without measure' (cf. 3,34). One may also observe here an allusion to Is. 11,2-3 where it is said that the Spirit of Yahweh (Spirit of wisdom and understanding, the Spirit of counsel and might, the Spirit of knowledge and the fear of the Lord) will rest on the shoot from the stump of Jesse.

[23] In the first case , the pronoun functions as an adjective and qualifies the grammatical subject (Jesus). In the second instance, the pronoun stresses the subject contained in the verb.

[24] W. Klaiber ("Der irdische und der himmlische Zeuge. Eine Auslegung von Joh 3,22-36," *NTS* 36 [1990] 212) sees the reason for the distrust of Jesus in the fact that for Jesus a faith aroused by seeing the signs performed by him is not sufficient to recognise who he is and to understand what God does through him.

[25] The extraordinary knowledge of Jesus in 2,24-25 can, perhaps, explain the answer of Jesus in 3,3 to an unexpressed question of Nicodemus. Jesus could, through his extraordinary knowledge, read what was in the mind of Nicodemus. See Schmidl, 86; J. Painter, "Quest Stories in John 1-4," *JSNT* 41 (1991) 57; and his, "Quest and Rejection Stories," 25; see also P. Rolland, "Jésus connaissait leurs pensées," *EThL* 62 (1986) 118-21.

[26] J. Gaffney, "Believing and Knowing in the Fourth Gospel," *TS* 26 (1965) 215-41.

direct and immediate outcome of seeing (θεωροῦντες) the signs performed by Jesus. It is a sort of instinctive faith generated by signs. Mere seeing of signs does not lead automatically to faith. In the case of Nicodemus, a Pharisee and ruler of the Jews – hence a knowledgeable man – asserts (οἴδαμεν) his knowledge about the identity of Jesus. He interprets the signs performed by Jesus theologically as manifestations of the presence of God with him, and this presence of God, in turn, is further explained as an authentication of the divine *origin* of Jesus' mission as διδάσκαλος. It is the insertion of this theological reasoning which explains the movement from the level of ἐπίστευσαν to the level of assurance of the οἴδαμεν.

What remains is to clarify what the 'name'[28] means; that is the real *identity* of Jesus as the Son of Man and the Son sent by the Father, in order that this faith could progress and lead to eternal life.[29] Thus, the central theme of the sub-unit is, in the heart of it, a Christological one.

d. Characterisation

Having detected from the structural and narrative argumentation that the theme of the sub-unit is, at the heart of it, Christological, let me turn to the narrative aspect of characterisation which strengthens my contention. One of the most interesting elements of any story is the cast of characters which populate it. Characters are defined and shaped for the reader by what they say, as well as what is said about them by the narrator or by other characters. F. Kermode is right in his observation that narratives generate characters, and the characters generate new narratives.[30] Culpepper affirms that characters give the narrative richness and power; they make the plot of the story alive.[31]

In the fourth Gospel diverse types of characters are introduced and made to interact with Jesus in order to draw out the manifold aspects of Jesus' true identity successively.

---

[27] 'Πιστεύειν εἰς' is an expression that has not been found in secular Greek or even in the Septuagint. Within the NT itself, by far the largest number of instances of 'πιστεύειν εἰς' are Johannine, and 'πιστεύειν εἰς τὸ ὄνομα' is entirely Johannine and in every instance refers to faith in Jesus; see Z. C. Hodges, "Problem Passages in the Gospel of John. Part 2: Untrustworthy Believers – John 2:23-25," *BS* 135 (1978) 140. According to him, the use of 'πιστεύειν εἰς' is a favourite expression in the fourth Gospel for regenerating faith (e.g. 1,12; 3,16.18.36; 4,39; 6,29.35.40, 7,38.39; etc.). For the fourth evangelist the contrast is between belief and unbelief, not between full belief and something less than that. Hence, the new believers in 2,23 are to be categorised as those who are not ready for fuller disclosures from Jesus whom they had just trusted. Looking with supernatural discernment into their hearts, Jesus did not regard them as truly prepared.

[28] There is no agreement among scholars about the meaning of the expression 'ἐπίστευσαν εἰς τὸ ὄνομα αὐτοῦ.' In the Semitic understanding, the term 'name' stands for the identity of a person. Name functions as a symbol of one's personality (cf. Dodd, *Interpretation*, 184). As the name (Jesus) in 2,23 is not specified, it represents an imperfect faith which does not confess the true identity of Jesus. On the contrary, the word 'name' in 3,18e deals with true faith as it is specified further as representing 'the only Son of God;' see Schnackenburg, *Gospel*, I, 357-58; and de la Potterie, "Naître de l'eau." Cf. esp. the detailed study of F. G. Untergaßmair (*Im Namen Jesu: Der Namensbegriff im Johannesevangelium. Eine exegetisch-religionsge-schichtliche Studie zu den johanneischen Namensaussagen* [FzB 13] [Stuttgart 1973] 174 and 364) on this subject.

[29] This procedure is followed in the healing of the blind man in Jn. 9: starting from an immediate but insufficient acceptance of Jesus after the sign performed by Jesus, he learns a little later about the identity of Jesus as the Son of Man and believes (cf. 9,35-38); see the detailed treatment of M. Rein, *Die Heilung des Blindgeborenen (Joh 9). Tradition und Redaktion* (WUNT II/73) (Tübingen 1995); and J. Resseguie, "John 9: A Literary-Critical Analysis," in: Stibbe, *Gospel of John as Literature*, 115-22.

[30] F. Kermode, *The Genesis of Secrecy: On the Interpretation of Narrative* (Cambridge 1979) 98-99.

[31] Culpepper, *Anatomy*, 148.

Since Jesus is the centre of all exchanges, the minor characters are rarely seen interacting with each other.[32]

In this sub-unit one meets two characters, *viz.*, the πολλοί and Nicodemus. As Nicodemus appears further in the pericope I shall analyse his character portrayal at the end of the dialogue. However, he is introduced as a Pharisee[33] and as a leader of the Jews (οἱ Ἰουδαῖοι). Besides, in 3,25 there is a dispute between a Jew(s) and the Baptist's disciples. Let me, therefore, take up the πολλοί and οἱ Ἰουδαῖοι for my analysis at this juncture.

i. Πολλοί

According to J. Jeremias, in many NT instances, πολλοί is used to describe the circle of people to whom the saving work of Jesus applies.[34] The fourth evangelist observes often that many (πολλοί) or multitudes (ὄχλος πολύς) believed in Jesus or followed him, because they saw the signs he performed (2,23; cf. 6,2; 7,31;10,42;11,45 and 12,11). The first such πολλοί that Jesus encountered was in Jerusalem at the Passover feast, where the reaction of Jesus was that he 'would *not entrust himself*[35] (2,24) to them, since they believed in him only because they saw the *signs* he performed (2,23-25).

This is preceded by a conflict between Jesus and the Jews[36] regarding his action at the Temple and their demand for a *sign* from Jesus (cf. 2,18-20). The disciples did not understand the meaning of Jesus' sign or words at that time, but after his resurrection (cf. 2,22). Thus, a reference to the death and resurrection of Jesus is present (cf. 3,13-16). The narrator's comment reads that Jesus 'himself knew what was in everyone' (cf. 2,22-25) of the πολλοί – a reference to the supernatural knowledge of Jesus.[37]

Each of these elements – the setting of a feast, enthusiasm of the πολλοί for signs, Jesus' negative reaction to their acclaim – help the reader discern the typical character of this group.[38] Added to these, one finds that such instances are accompanied by the following narrative elements: conflict with the Jews, a hint at Jesus' death/glorification,

---

[32] Even in the few exceptions (e.g. John the Baptist and his disciples interact in 3,25-26) the purpose is to show that Jesus is greater than the Baptist. The Pharisees and the blind are made to interact in 9,15ff.; the response of the blind man's parents serve as a contrast for their son's response to the Jews, which is, at the same time, a response to Jesus. Peter's exchange with the servant girl in 18,17 is a foil for Jesus' response to the chief priest. See J. A. du Rand, "The Characterisation of Jesus as Depicted in the Narrative of the Fourth Gospel," *Neotest.* 19 (1985) 18-36.

[33] The term 'Pharisees' in the fourth Gospel is virtually a synonym for 'Jews.' K. Wengst (*Bedrängte Gemeinde und verherrlichter Christus: Der historische Ort des Johannesevangeliums als Schlüssel zu seiner Interpretation* [BThSt 5] [Neukirchen-Vluyn 1981] 42), in this careful and thorough discussion, rightly observes that the two concepts appear together and are mutually explanatory. According to him, an inspection of all the relevant texts shows that Judaism emerges as a one-dimensional phenomenon – Pharisaic in kind.

[34] J. Jeremias, "πολλοί," *TDNT*, VI, 536.

[35] Hodges, "Untrustworthy Believers," 148. There is, in the fourth Gospel, a dynamic of hide-and-seek going on all the time. People seek Jesus, but often he hides from them; see M. W. G. Stibbe, "The Elusive Christ: A New Reading of the Fourth Gospel," *JSNT* 44 (1991) 232.

[36] Cf. M. de Jonge, "The Conflict between Jesus and the Jews, and the Radical Christology of the Fourth Gospel," *PRSt* 20 (1993) 341-55.

[37] For a detailed treatment see Rolland, 118-21.

[38] On the function of the chorus as an actor, see P. W. Harsh, *A Handbook of Classical Drama* (Palo Alto 1944) 20-22.

disciples who do not understand Jesus at the instance but later, and Jesus' supernatural knowledge and elusiveness.

The repetition of the same pattern in 5,1-6,14; 7,1-51 and 12,1-36[39] makes me conclude that the typical character of the πολλοί, as portrayed in 2,23, enhances the reader's understanding of the implied author's plot in evoking the πολλοί's amazement for Jesus and drawing their attention to the central figure of his story – Jesus. Every instance of the astonishment of the πολλοί on seeing the sign(s) of Jesus is carefully and skilfully structured and exploited by the implied author to drive home his Christology – an ascent and descent Christology, depicting the death of Jesus as glorification of the Son of Man.[40]

ii. Οἱ Ἰουδαῖοι

The common Synoptic distinction into Scribes, Pharisees, and Sadducees are found less frequently in the fourth Gospel.[41] Moreover, one of the strange facts about the fourth Gospel is that, while the Synoptics each refer to 'the Jews' five or six times, the fourth evangelist has over seventy such occurrences. Only ten of them occur in Jn. 1-4. I do not intend to make a comprehensive study of the characterisation of 'the Jews' in the entire Gospel. I restrict my analysis to those aspects that concern the themes of 2,23-3,36 and in brief reference to the first section of the Gospel (1,19-4,54) in which the unit of my study is inserted.

'The Jews' in the fourth Gospel are, first of all, representatives. The designation has no reference to any ethnic distinction. Thus, it is possible to read into 'the Jews' – the enquiry commission from Jerusalem[42] (cf. 1,19ff.) – a sense of religious hostility.[43] Besides, such opposition of 'the Jews' arises from their essential Jewishness,[44] for example, from their attachment to the Temple (cf. 2,18.20).

'The Jews' are *stylised types* of those who reject Jesus. Through them the fourth evangelist explores the heart and soul of unbelief. As representatives of unbelief, their

---

[39] I do not go into details of demonstrating the pattern in all these three other instances not to make the dissertation long.

[40] On this subject see K. P. M. Kuzenzama, "La conception johannique de la 'montée-descente' du Fils de l'Homme. Étude sémantique," *RAT* 1 (1977) 207-18; and M. C. de Boer, *Johannine Perspectives on the Death of Jesus* (Pharos 1996).

[41] See T. M. Dowell, "Jews and Christians in Conflict: Why the Fourth Gospel Changed the Synoptic Tradition," *LouvSt* 15 (1990) 19-37; and J. D. G. Dunn (ed.), *Jews and Christians. The Parting of the Ways A. D. 70 to 135* (WUNT 66) (Tübingen ²1999).

[42] See U. C. von Wahlde, "The Gospel of John and the Presentation of Jews and Judaism," in: D. P. Efroymson, E. J. Fisher and L. Klenicki (eds.), *Within Context. Essays on Jews and Judaism in the New Testament* (Collegeville 1993) 67-84; and his, "The Johannine 'Jews': A Critical Survey," *NTS* 28 (1982) 33-60.

[43] W. Pratscher, "Die Juden im Johannesevangelium," *BiLi* 59 (1986) 178; see also J. C. O'Neill, "The Jews in the Fourth Gospel," *IBSt* 18 (1996) 58-74; K. Scholtissek, "Antijudaismus im Johannesevangelium? Ein Gesprächsbeitrag," in: R. Kampling (ed.), *"Nun steht aber diese Sache im Evangelium..." Zur Frage nach den Anfängen des christlichen Antijudaismus* (Paderborn 1999) 151-81; F. Vouga, "Antijudaismus und Johannesevangelium?" *ThGl* 83 (1993) 81-89; M. Brumlik, "Johannes: Das judenfeindliche Evangelium," *Kul* 4 (1989) 102-13; and W. R. Farmer (ed.), *Anti-Judaism and the Gospels* (Minneapolis 1999).

[44] For a detailed discussion see Ashton, *Studying John*, 36-70; and his, "The Identity and Function of the ΙΟΥΔΑΙΟΙ in the Fourth Gospel," *NT* 27 (1985) 40-75; see also E. Gräßer, "Die antijüdische Polemik im Johannesevangelium," *NTS* 11 (1964/65) 74-90; and D. M. Smith, "Judaism and the Gospel of John," in: J. H. Charlesworth (ed.), *Jews and Christians. Exploring the Past, Present, and Future* (New York 1990) 76-99.

misunderstanding touches all the vital issues. For example, Jesus' origin and identity and mission are the central issues to the evangelist. 'The Jews' misunderstand them (cf. Jesus' origin and identity revealed in Jn. 3 in the ascent and descent motifs, and in the Son of Man and Son of God titles).[45] The pathos of their unbelief is that they are the religious people,[46] some even the religious authorities like Nicodemus, who have had all the advantages of the heritage of Israel, but misunderstand Moses and the prophets. They legalistically maintain their observance of ritual purification (cf. 3,25) and festivals.

Moreover, 'the Jews' are portrayed as standing on the negative pole of the *dualistic scheme* as examples of unbelief. It may be that the positive pole of the dualistic pair in this case is 'Israel.' The Baptist declares the purpose of his coming was to reveal the Messiah to *Israel* (1,31); Jesus calls Nathanael a true *Israelite* "in whom there is no deceit" (1,47); and Nathanael acknowledges Jesus as 'the King of *Israel*' (1,49). Further, Jesus is said to have been greeted as 'King of *Israel*' upon entering Jerusalem.[47] Note that Nicodemus is introduced as ἐκ τῶν Φαρισαίων, and as ἄρχων τῶν Ἰουδαίων[48] by the narrator in 3,1; but in 3,10 the surprising rebuke, expressed in the words of Jesus, seems to imply that Nicodemus does not deserve the positive title ὁ διδάσκαλος τοῦ Ἰσραὴλ, because his religious understanding was that of a Φαρισαῖος and of the Ἰουδαῖοι. The evangelist is, thus, introducing Nicodemus more as a 'Jew' than as a guileless 'Israelite,' at least, at his first appearance in the Gospel, because a teacher of Israel is not in need of exegetical explanations, but of a new birth.

It is also interesting to observe that οἱ Ἰουδαῖοι is selected along with κόσμος to serve as the central *symbol of negativity*.[49] Although there is, in the fourth Gospel, no formal identification of οἱ Ἰουδαῖοι and κόσμος,[50] in both cases the reader is invited by the context to make the identification for himself. In the context of the Nicodemus episode, too, it can be seen readily that the point of the story is the inability of the people of this world,[51] pre-eminently 'the Jews,' to understand and accept Jesus.[52]

It was the pressure of the concrete *historical situation*[53] that caused the selection of the expression 'the Jews' as a *type of unbelief.* One may even assume that the author of the

---

[45] Cf. J. W. Pryor, "The Johannine Son of Man and the Descent-Ascent Motif," *JETS* 34 (1991) 341-51.

[46] See e.g. G. Caron, "Exploring a Religious Dimension: The Johannine Jews," *SR* 24 (1995) 159-71.

[47] Cf. M. Lowe, "Who were the Ἰουδαῖοι?," *NT* 18 (1976) 118-19.

[48] See U. C. von Wahlde, "The Terms for Religious Authorities in the Fourth Gospel: A Key to Literary Strata?," *JBL* 98 (1979) 234.

[49] See W. Trilling, "Gegner Jesu – Widersacher der Gemeinde – Repräsentanten der 'Welt'. Das Johannesevangelium und die Juden," in: H. Goldstein (ed.), *Gottesverächter und Menschenfeinde? Juden zwischen Jesus und frühchristlicher Kirche* (PPB) (Düsseldorf 1979) 190-210.

[50] See N. H. Cassem, "A Grammatical and Contextual Inventory of the Use of κόσμος in the Johannine Corpus with Some Implications for a Johannine Cosmic Theology," *NTS* 19 (1972) 81-91.

[51] I shall treat this in detail under dualism.

[52] See W. A. Meeks, "The Man from Heaven in Johannine Sectarianism," in: Ashton, *Interpretation*, 181; see also L. Schenke, "Der 'Dialog Jesu mit den Juden' im Johannesevangelium. Ein Rekonstruktionsversuch," *NTS* 34 (1988) 573-603.

[53] See J. Maier, *Jüdische Auseinandersetzung mit dem Christentum in der Antike* (EdF 177) (Darmstadt 1982) 4; 137 and 141; S. J. Joubert, "A Bone of Contention in Recent Scholarship: The 'birkat ha-mimim' and the Separation of Church and Synagogue in the First-Century A. D.," *Neotest.* 27 (1993) 351-63; S. T. Katz, "Issues in the Separation of Judaism and Christianity after 70 C.E.: A Reconsideration," *JBL* 103 (1984) 43-76; and H. C. Kee and L. H. Cohic (eds.), *Evolution of the Synagogue: Problems and Progress* (Minneapolis 1999).

fourth Gospel is of Jewish ancestry, or at least that a large number of those in the local Christian community were Jewish. Hence, the Gospel is not issuing a judgement on the Jewish people as an ethnic group.[54] It implies, however, that the Jewish opponents of the Church at that time and place were *typical of the human failure* to accept Jesus. The Gospel represents that kind of rejection with the symbol of 'the Jews,' casting them as the *symbol of unbelief.*[55] The symbol is a part of the broader Johannine dualism. Those who fail to see that in Jesus there is a fulfilment of the heritage of the OT, cling to their pride in themselves and cannot accept the self-understanding presented in the revelation of God in Jesus – they are the persons represented in the symbol 'the Jews.' In short, I would say that characterisation serves as yardstick in understanding the evangelist's Christology, the central theme of the sub-unit.

e. Reader and Point of View

In my introductory chapter I have remarked that a text should be studied also as a *mirror* and not only as a *window* to the past.[56] Instead of being author-centred as so much of earlier literary and biblical criticism had been – instead of answering questions such as what is the historical and biographical context that best explains what an author is trying to do? – reader-response criticism claims to be reader-oriented.[57] It is interested in the effect of a narrative on the reader. It is keenly interested in describing and analysing the persuasive side of literature.[58] This new approach, in my opinion, could bridge the growing gap between the academician studying the text as artifact and the layperson reading it as article of faith.[59]

The reader feels that the prologue is still ringing in his/her ears. He/she has heard the testimony of the Baptist, watched Jesus call his first disciples, and made note of the demand of Jesus for greater faith as a necessary condition for the promise of seeing 'greater things' (1,50-51), and was astonished at the miracle of Cana where Jesus transformed water into wine. Except for a hint at the rejection of the hero of the story (1,10-11) and even a mention of his death (2,22), everything has worked toward encouraging a simple optimism and excitement in the reader. This excitement is enhanced as the reader next learns of the movement of *many* people toward Jesus in an action of

---

[54] Cf. P. J. Hartin, "A Community in Crisis. The Christology of the Johannine Community as the Point at Issue," *Neotest.* 19 (1985) 37-49.

[55] T. L. Brodie, *The Quest for the Origin of John's Gospel. A Source-Oriented Approach* (New York, Oxford 1993) 151.

[56] On this subject see S. R. Moore, "'Mirror, Mirror...:' Lacanian Reflections on Malbon's Mark," *Semeia* 62 (1993) 165-71.

[57] S. Mailloux (*Rhetorical Power* [Ithaca 1989] 19-36) is especially helpful at situating this historical shift within the context of institutional rhetoric. See also S. R. Suleiman and I. Crosman (eds.), *The Reader in the Text: Essays on Audience and Interpretation* (Princeton 1980) 3-4.

[58] See R. M. Fowler, *Let the Reade Understand: Reader-Response Criticism and the Gospel of Mark* (Minneapolis 1991) 9-12; Powell, *What Is Narrative Criticism?*, 6-21; R. Detweiler and V. K. Robbins, "From New Criticism to Post-structuralism: Twentieth-Century Hermeneutics," in: S. Prickett (ed.), *Reading the Text: Biblical Criticism and Literary Theory* (Cambridge 1991) 248-52; and H. Boers, "Narrative Criticism, Historical Criticism, and the Gospel of John," *JSNT* 47 (1992) 37-38 and 43-44.

[59] See B. F. Meyer, "The Challenges of Text and Reader to the Historical-Critical Method," in: W. Beuken, S. Freyne and A. Weiler (eds.), *The Bible and its Readers* (Philadelphia 1991) 3-12; and W. Wuellner, "Is There an Encoded Reader Fallacy?," *Semeia* 48 (1989) 41.

60

belief[60] (2,23). But warned by Jesus' reaction to Nathanael's initial faith (cf. 1,49-51), the reader is now vigilant of a quality of faith based on seeing *signs*. The reader has learned this already from the Jews' request for a *sign*, and their inability to accept the *sign* they were offered (cf. 2,18-20). He/she is aware that Jesus asks more from those who would be his followers.[61] He/she is now on the way to understanding the relational quality of true faith. However, the narrator's aside that "Jesus on his part would not entrust himself to them" (2,24) begins to temper the reader's enthusiasm.[62] The reader is, thus, warned not to show a hasty sympathy for the πολλοί.

The initiative of Nicodemus to come to Jesus and acknowledge that Jesus must be "a teacher who has come from God" (3,2) because of the quality of his wondrous works attracts the reader immediately, because he/she shares his view of Jesus. This rekindles the reader's optimism.[63] Nevertheless, the reader senses in Nicodemus' addressing of Jesus in 3,2 a repetition of sentiments found in the expressions of insufficient faith based on signs (cf. 2,23-25). The reader is able to look further back to recall the limited response of the first disciples in 1,35-51. These two passages, however, provide the reader with the means to understand the limitations of Nicodemus' confession. Nicodemus is a new character for the reader. However, the reader is encouraged to see that a prominent 'Pharisee' and 'a leader of the Jews' (3,1) will come to understand Jesus and believe in him, and the story will continue to unfold the pattern of Jesus' glorious success; because the reader is aware that there has been a progression from the open hostility shown toward Jesus by 'the Jews' who arrogantly rejected his word (2,18-20). Though, the reader's sympathy for Nicodemus is reinforced, he/she is warned not to see a complete confession of faith in the statement of Nicodemus.

Thus, the narrative is carefully structured to hold up to the readers' investigation two models of response to Jesus in order to warn them of Jesus' reluctance to such an inadequate recognition of his origin, identity and mission. The purpose of the evangelist is to attract the attention of the reader to respond to Jesus as Christology is the central concern of his story.

2. 3,3-10: Dialogue

a. Argumentative Narrative Structure

3,3ab	Speech opening and change of speaker
3cde	*Jesus' first intervention*

---

60 See Y. Ibuki, "Viele glaubten an ihn – Auseinandersetzung mit dem Glauben im Johannesevangelium," *AJBI* 9 (1983) esp. 132-33 and 138-39.

61 I think, the use of the verb 'πιστεύω' twice by the narrator to report Jesus' response to a faith based on signs, indicates to the reader the dynamic quality of true faith. The second use of 'πιστεύω' in 2,24 is a reflexive use of the verb found only here in the NT. See Barrett, 202; and Schnackenburg, *Gospel*, I, 359. Westcott (I, 45), however, points out the nuance that "there is at the same time a contrast of tenses. The first verb marks a definite, completed act; the second a habitual course of action."

62 In 2,23-25 the narrator draws back from narrative to speak directly to the reader in a commentary on the quality of a faith based on seeing the miracles of Jesus. See G. Genette, *Nouveau discours de récit* (Paris 1983) 22-25. However, this commentary of the narrator enables the author to lead the reader into the next example of faith among the Jews: Nicodemus.

63 Moloney (*Belief in the Word*, 108) suggests that the implied reader (on the basis of 1,5) recognises Nicodemus' coming out of the darkness into the light. Hence, the reader is even more optimistic about this meeting of the two figures.

	3c	Double-amen formula (of authority)
	3de	Conditional sentence (ἐὰν μή); dialogue theme
		Determination of purpose/goal (ἰδεῖν)
4a		Speech opening and change of speaker
4b-e		*Nicodemus' second intervention*
	4bc	Question one (Πῶς δύναται;)
	4de	Question two (μὴ δύναται;)
5a		Speech opening and change of speaker
5b-8		*Jesus' second intervention*
	5b	Double-amen formula (of authority)
	5cd	Conditional sentence (ἐὰν μή); dialogue theme variation
		Determination of purpose (εἰσελθεῖν)
6-8		*Commentary on 5cd*
	6	Antithetical parallelism
	7a	Order of prohibition
	7b	Introduction to a quotation
	7c	Quotation; dialogue theme (cf. 3,3e.5d)
	8	*Word of wisdom* (theme: πνεῦμα)
	8a-f	Pictorial or figurative part
	8gh	Subject matter (οὕτως)
9ab		Speech opening and change of speaker
9c		*Nicodemus' third intervention*
		Question (Πῶς δύναται; cf. 4b)
10ab		Speech opening and change of speaker
10cd		*Jesus' third intervention*
	10c	Subordination (σὺ εἶ)
	10d	Ironic question of retort

Even a quick glance reveals the global scheme of the dialogue: a word of Jesus makes Nicodemus to raise a question betraying his surprise and misunderstanding. Jesus resumes his word and clarifies his thought, which provokes Nicodemus to raise another question. This necessitates the final words of Jesus which clarify the theme. Narratively, this argumentative scheme emerges from the words of Jesus solemnly introduced by the formula "Ἀμὴν ἀμὴν λέγω σοι"[64] (3,3.5.11), the questions raised by Nicodemus beginning with the interrogatory phrase 'πῶς δύναται' (3,4.9), and the concluding words of Jesus to Nicodemus.

---

[64] According to K. Berger (*Die Amen Worte Jesu. Eine Untersuchung zum Problem der Legitimation in apokalyptischer Rede* [BZNW 39] [Berlin 1970] 19 and 28), this formula comes from the Hellenistic-Jewish Christian milieu. It exposes the revelatory character of the words introduced. In the fourth Gospel, the words introduced by this formula designate Jesus as the founder of the tradition and the Johannine Community as the second transmitter. Moreover, this formula gives to the words the certitude of testimony. The massive presence of the *amen*-words in the fourth Gospel is due to their close connection to the *Sendungschristologie* of the fourth evangelist (cf. *ibid.* 116); Jesus, as the one sent by the Father, speaks only what he has heard from his Father (the same is true of the disciples, sent by Jesus). As far as 2,23-3,36 is concerned, I may, briefly, say that the formula plays an important role in the argumentative development of the text; it introduces the interventions of Jesus which explain and clarify further what preceded and adds a new development at every stage. Thus, 3,3 is linked to 3,2; 3,5-8 to 3,4; and 3,11-12 to 3,9-10. On this subject see

b. Parallel Structure

No literary study of 3,3-10 can ignore the strong formal and thematic correlation between 3,3 and 3,5-8. Besides, there is also a close rapport to be observed between the questions of Nicodemus in 3,4 and 3,9. The thematic correspondence in the narrative structure of this sub-unit (3, 3-10) becomes evident in the parallel structure between the two interventions each of Jesus and Nicodemus as one can observe in the diagram below:

<table>
<tr><td align="center">A</td><td align="center">//</td><td align="center">B</td></tr>
</table>

A	B
³,³ ἀπεκρίθη Ἰησοῦς καὶ εἶπεν αὐτῷ, Ἀμὴν ἀμὴν λέγω σοι, ἐὰν μή τις γεννηθῇ *ἄνωθεν*, οὐ δύναται <u>ἰδεῖν τὴν βασιλείαν τοῦ θεοῦ</u>.	³,⁵ ἀπεκρίθη Ἰησοῦς, Ἀμὴν ἀμὴν λέγω σοι, ἐὰν μή τις γεννηθῇ ἐξ ὕδατος καὶ πνεύματος, οὐ δύναται <u>εἰσελθεῖν εἰς τὴν βασιλείαν τοῦ θεοῦ</u>.
	⁶ τὸ γεγεννημένον ἐκ τῆς σαρκὸς σάρξ ἐστιν, καὶ τὸ *γεγεννημένον ἐκ τοῦ πνεύματος* πνεῦμά ἐστιν. ⁷ μὴ θαυμάσῃς ὅτι εἶπόν σοι, Δεῖ ὑμᾶς γεννηθῆναι ἄνωθεν. ⁸ τὸ πνεῦμα ὅπου θέλει πνεῖ καὶ τὴν φωνὴν αὐτοῦ ἀκούεις, ἀλλ' οὐκ οἶδας πόθεν ἔρχεται καὶ ποῦ ὑπάγει· οὕτως ἐστὶν πᾶς ὁ *γεγεννημένος ἐκ τοῦ πνεύματος.*
³,⁴ λέγει πρὸς αὐτὸν [ὁ] Νικόδημος, <u>Πῶς δύναται ἄνθρωπος γεννηθῆναι</u> γέρων ὤν; μὴ δύναται εἰς τὴν κοιλίαν τῆς μητρὸς αὐτοῦ δεύτερον εἰσελθεῖν καὶ γεννηθῆναι;	³,⁹ ἀπεκρίθη Νικόδημος καὶ εἶπεν αὐτῷ, <u>Πῶς δύναται ταῦτα γενέσθαι</u>;

Moreover, 3,3 and 3,4 are encompassed by an inclusion. There is a synonymous correspondence between 'γεννηθῇ ἄνωθεν' (3,3) and 'δεύτερον εἰσελθεῖν καὶ γεννηθῆναι' (3,4). As I shall examine in the following pages, the words of Nicodemus reflect a mere physical or earthly interpretation of the statement of Jesus. Similarly 3,5-8 are also encompassed by an inclusion. There is a dependent relation between 'γεννηθῇ ἐξ.......... πνεύματος' (3,5) and 'γεγεννημένος ἐκ τοῦ πνεύματος' (3,8).

In fact, 3,3 and 3,5 are identical except for a replacement or re-interpretation of the term 'ἄνωθεν' (3,3) using the expression 'ἐξ ὕδατος καὶ πνεύματος' (3,5), as well as a re-interpretation of the verb 'ἰδεῖν' (3,3) using 'εἰσελθεῖν' (3,5). Moreover, the expression 'γεννηθῇ ἄνωθεν' (3,3) is repeated in 3,7 with an additional emphasis of 'Δεῖ...γεννηθῆναι ἄνωθεν.'

Furthermore, 3,4 and 3,9 are linked by the questions raised by Nicodemus: πῶς δύναται ..? Both questions have the same syntactic structure: auxiliary, subject and infinitive. Considering the vocabulary used, I notice the recurrence of the expression 'Πῶς δύναται' and the synonymous phrases 'ἄνθρωπος γεννηθῆναι' and 'ταῦτα γενέσθαι.' While the verb 'γενέσθαι' is related to the order of things (ταῦτα), the verb 'γεννηθῆναι' is related to the order of beings (ἄνθρωπος).

---

also Bernard, I, 66-67; V. Hasler, *Amen: Redaktionsgeschichtliche Untersuchung zur Einführungsformel der Herrenworte "Wahrlich, ich sage euch"* (Stuttgart, Zürich 1969); and Moloney, *Son of Man*, 48.

I notice also that 3,5-8, which is more elaborate and developed than its parallel 3,3, has an interior structure of its own (3,5//3,7; and 3,6//3,8). While 3,5 and 3,7 contain the synonymous expressions 'γεννηθῇ ἐξ ὕδατος καὶ πνεύματος' and 'γεννηθῆναι ἄνωθεν,' the expression 'γεγεννημένος ἐκ τοῦ πνεύματος' recurs in 3,6 and 3,8.

c. Thematic Argumentation of 3,3-8

In 3,3 Jesus affirms: "ἐὰν μή τις γεννηθῇ ἄνωθεν, οὐ δύναται ἰδεῖν τὴν βασιλείαν τοῦ θεοῦ." This assertion of Jesus can be interpreted differently depending on the different possible combinations between the two meanings of the verb γεννάω (born/begotten) and the double meaning of the adverb ἄνωθεν (again/above).[65] As the continued discussion between Jesus and Nicodemus shows, the four theoretical possibilities finally boil down to two real interpretations – either 'born again' (interpretation of Nicodemus), and 'begotten from above' (meaning intended by Jesus). As the structure of the phrase indicates (ἐὰν μή), this 'γεννηθῇ ἄνωθεν' is proposed as a necessary condition to see (ἰδεῖν) the kingdom of God, that is, participation in salvation. There is no temporal distinction between the present and the final (the already and the not yet): as soon as the condition is fulfilled, the present is realised; in other words, as soon as someone is begotten from above, he/she has the capacity to *see* the kingdom of God (cf. 3,18.36).

Jesus' statement provokes the double question of Nicodemus which exposes his misunderstanding and surprise simultaneously: "How can anyone be born after having grown old? Can one enter a second time into the mother's womb and be born?" (3,4). One observes easily that 3,4bc apply the condition of 3,3 (γεννηθῇ ἄνωθεν) to the concrete case of an old man (ἄνθρωπος...γέρων ὤν). The argumentative interest of this first question of Nicodemus is that it manifests his misunderstanding: the Pharisee interprets the verb γεννάω wrongly as 'born' instead of 'begotten.' In this sense, one may notice that Nicodemus ignores the adverb ἄνωθεν used by Jesus; out of the affirmation of Jesus he takes up exclusively the verb γεννηθῆναι on which alone his question seems to rest. In fact, Nicodemus should have asked: 'Πῶς δύναται ἄνθρωπος γεννηθῆναι ἄνωθεν γέρων ὤν;' Based on a false interpretation of the statement of Jesus, Nicodemus formulates an objection, like a teacher in a rabbinic discussion, a provoking exaggeration forcing Jesus to take a stand.[66] I would like to paraphrase his argumentation thus: 'your statement has no meaning; how can a man be born when he is already old?'

However, it is only the second part of 3,4 which makes one perceive clearly the interpretation made by Nicodemus of the verb γεννάω to mean exclusively 'born.' In fact, one cannot give to this verb the significance of 'being begotten' when it is used to refer to the act of being brought out of the mother's womb, as it is the case in 3,4d. Once the meaning 'born' is attributed to the verb 'γεννηθῇ' in 3,3, the adverb 'ἄνωθεν' logically means 'again.' Nicodemus substitutes the expression 'kingdom of God' with 'mother's womb.' Hence, to apply it to the action described by 'γεννηθῇ ἄνωθεν,' one must undergo a 'δεύτερον εἰσελθεῖν.' This substitution illustrates well the position of Nicodemus which belongs to the level of the material, physical or earthly understanding.

---

[65] See my elaborate treatment under double meaning and misunderstanding.

[66] G. Maier, *Johannesevangelium* (EdC.B 6) (Neuhausen, Stuttgart 1984) I, 113.

d. Inverted Parallel Structure

I observe also a double and inverted parallel structure (see the diagram below) in Jesus' response to the double question of Nicodemus (3,4de//3,5-6 ; and 3,4abc//3,7-8). The first part of the reply of Jesus (3,5-6) answers to the second absurd objection of Nicodemus: "Can one enter a second time into the mother's womb and be born?" (3,4de), while the second part of the reply of Jesus (3,7-8) answers to the surprise and misunderstanding of Nicodemus manifested in his first question (3,4bc):

^{3,4de} μὴ δύναται εἰς τὴν κοιλίαν τῆς μητρὸς αὐτοῦ *δεύτερον* <u>εἰσελθεῖν</u> καὶ *γεννηθῆναι;*	^{3,5-6} ἀπεκρίθη Ἰησοῦς, Ἀμὴν ἀμὴν λέγω σοι, ἐὰν μή τις *γεννηθῇ* ἐξ ὕδατος καὶ πνεύματος, οὐ δύναται <u>εἰσελθεῖν</u> εἰς τὴν βασιλείαν τοῦ θεοῦ. ⁶ *τὸ γεγεννημένον ἐκ τῆς σαρκὸς σάρξ ἐστιν,* καὶ τὸ ἐγεννημένον ἐκ τοῦ πνεύματος πνεῦμά ἐστιν.
^{3,4abc} λέγει πρὸς αὐτὸν [ὁ] Νικόδημος, Πῶς δύναται ἄνθρωπος γεννηθῆναι γέρων ὤν;	^{3,7-8} μὴ θαυμάσῃς ὅτι εἶπόν σοι, Δεῖ ὑμᾶς <u>γεννηθῆναι ἄνωθεν.</u> ⁸ τὸ πνεῦμα ὅπου θέλει πνεῖ καὶ τὴν φωνὴν αὐτοῦ ἀκούεις, ἀλλ' οὐκ οἶδας πόθεν ἔρχεται καὶ ποῦ ὑπάγει· οὕτως ἐστὶν πᾶς ὁ γεγεννημένος ἐκ τοῦ πνεύματος.

The first part (3,5-6) tries to clarify that the statement of 3,3 is about spiritual begetting and not a simple physical rebirth.[67] Wikenhauser rightly comments that the man who wants to be saved must become another and new man. As he is, he cannot enter the kingdom of God.[68] Haenchen goes another step forward to clarify the same and says that a man must become a new being with a new existence and receive a new eye that can see the handwork of God.[69] The relation of 3,5-6 to 3,4de is to be noticed in the repetition of the same categories: the recurrence of verb εἰσελθεῖν; and the birth in flesh is taken up again in 3,6. Nicodemus tries to find the meaning of Jesus' words in his own tradition, and as a realist, tries to understand it only rationally and logically.[70] In 3,5-6 Jesus shows Nicodemus that he must not interpret the statement in 3,3 in an exclusively temporal and material or physical (fleshy) way.[71] The adverb ἄνωθεν does not mean only 'again;' that is why it must be replaced by the terms 'ἐξ ὕδατος καὶ πνεύματος,' which designate the divine principle operating in the action defined by the verb γεννηθῆναι. Moreover, if γεννηθῆναι refers to a spiritual principle (3,5) of heavenly origin (3,3), the verb must be rightly interpreted to mean 'being begotten.'[72] Vellanickal observes that the aorist form

---

[67] I prefer to use the term 'begetting' – which reflects more of a spiritual sense – instead of 'born' – which gives rise to a more physical understanding.

[68] Wikenhauser, 86.

[69] Haenchen, I, 200.

[70] Tsuchido, 99; see also Rebell, 140; H. J. Holtzmann, *Evangelium des Johannes* (HC 4.1) (Tübingen ³1908) 83; and K. Wengst, "Nikodemus. Bemerkungen zu Joh 3,1-5," *NStim* 31 (1978) 39.

[71] A. Stimpfle, *Blinde sehen. Die Eschatologie im traditionsgeschichtlichen Prozeß des Johannesevangeliums* (BZNW 57) (Berlin, New York 1990) 46. See also J. A. Trumbover, *Born from Above. The Anthropology of the Gospel of John* (HuTh 29) (Tübingen 1992).

[72] Haenchen, I, 200.

γεννηθῇ in 3,3 and 3,5 indicates a definite point of beginning.[73] He adds that the fourth evangelist actually speaks of the divine begetting in the aorist only in Jn. 3. On all the other occasions he makes use of the perfect tense γεγέννηται or γεγεννημένος. It shows that, unlike a human parent, God does not impart His life to the begotten only once and for ever. He continues to strengthen it habitually by His divine influence.

Moreover, 3,6 makes it more precise saying that there are two levels of reality, and Nicodemus must not limit himself to the first to interpret Jesus' words. Material (fleshly) begetting produces a being in flesh, that is, leads to birth in flesh. On the contrary, spiritual begetting produces a spiritual being, making possible an entrance into the kingdom of God. This distinction of two levels of reality explains the correction made by Jesus in 3,5 in answering to the question of Nicodemus. Moreover, one must *not* '*enter*.....and be born' – level of flesh, but 'be begotten...to *enter*' – spiritual level. The place to enter is not the mother's womb but the kingdom of God. These two statements belong to two different levels of reality (earthly and heavenly respectively),[74] which are clearly distinguished in 3,6. Only a spiritual begetting, which does not belong to this world, allows entrance into the kingdom of God.

Having corrected and clarified the interpretation of Nicodemus expressed in 3,4de, Jesus answers to the question raised in 3,4bc. His answer (3,7-8) is introduced by a repetition of the earlier expression in 3,3 (γεννηθῆναι ἄνωθεν), as well as an allusion to the reaction of Nicodemus. "μὴ θαυμάσῃς ὅτι εἶπόν σοι, Δεῖ ὑμᾶς γεννηθῆναι ἄνωθεν" (3,7). In relation to the statement of Jesus in 3,3 an evident transformation has been made in 3,7. The second clause of 3,3cd speaking about seeing the kingdom of God, introduced by a conditional conjunction 'ἐὰν μή,' is replaced in 3,7 by an auxiliary verb 'δεῖ.' The meaning, however, is not affected by this change in grammar, but only underlines the necessity of being begotten from above in the divine salvific plan; the entrance into the kingdom of God is to be understood as a reference to salvation. One may observe that the author could have completed 3,7c introduced by δεῖ, by repeating the theme of entrance into the kingdom with a conjunction ἵνα, to render the statement as follows: 'You must be begotten from above, in order to enter into the kingdom of God.' In my opinion, the absence of 3,3d regarding the kingdom of God in 3,7 shows that 3,7 – in its expression γεννηθῆναι ἄνωθεν – answers to the question raised in 3,4bc. In fact, this first question of Nicodemus is not concerned with the salvific aspect as in the statement of Jesus in 3,3d. Structurally, the theme of astonishment (μὴ θαυμάσῃς) in 3,7a reminds one of 3,4bc, where Nicodemus was surprised (πῶς δύναται); and the expression "ὅτι εἶπόν σοι, Δεῖ ὑμᾶς γεννηθῆναι ἄνωθεν" (3,7bc) reminds one of 3,3 which was misunderstood by Nicodemus. A new reduction of the expression to a material sense is impossible, because 3,7 is structurally put in parallel with 3,5 which affirms clearly that it is a birth from water[75] and Spirit.

---

[73] Vellanickal, 170 and 194.

[74] The two levels of reality are not opposed to each other but complementary. In fact, one must, first of all, be begotten and born in this world before being begotten from above which leads to the begetting into the kingdom of God. Jesus, thus, tries to lead Nicodemus from the initial material level to attain the final spiritual level.

[75] About the meaning of water see my elaborate treatment under symbolism.

In 3,8 Jesus will, therefore, reply to the objection raised by Nicodemus in 3,4bc taking into account the correction made already in 3,5-6. It is now the turn of Jesus to expose the meaninglessness of the objection of Nicodemus. One need not be surprised regarding the necessity of a new begetting from above in order to enter into the kingdom of God, even in the case of an old man, because "the wind/Spirit blows where it chooses....so it is with everyone who is born of the Spirit." This comparison, which superimposes the reality of the wind on that of the Spirit,[76] serves to demonstrate that the begetting by the Spirit, in spite of its mysterious character, does not make it a lesser reality. The proof of it is that, even if one is not able to discern the mysterious reality of the wind,[77] one cannot doubt its presence, because one feels its effects. It is the same with the begetting by the Spirit.[78] Nicodemus, therefore, must not be astonished.[79]

Although this demonstration of the reality of spiritual begetting is an important function of 3,8, I feel that the argumentative content of this verse leads further on. In the literary structure of 3,3-8, I notice that 3,6 and 3,8 have some parallels; the purpose of this parallelism intended by the author is not to be reduced to the aesthetic realm alone. It has also an argumentative function. In 3,6 Jesus distinguishes two levels of interpretation of the begetting which is necessary to see the kingdom of God (cf. 3,3): there is the material (physical) level which leads to interpreting it as a new physical birth; and there is the spiritual level, according to which it is a new begetting from above (from water and Spirit). Moreover, behind these two levels two distinct conceptions of access to salvation are hidden. In the Jewish tradition, of which Nicodemus is the mouth piece, it is Abraham and his descendants who could receive the blessing of the promised land. The inheritors of the promise are, therefore, those who belong by physical birth to the descendants of

---

[76] See M. Görg, "Vom Wehen des Pneuma," *BN* 66 (1993) 5-9. F.-M. Braun (*Le mystère de Jésus-Christ* [Paris 1966] III:1, 88) affirms that, in the biblical tradition, wind served as a profound analogy in relation to the Spirit of Yahweh, and between the two terms, the breath of Yahweh served as the middle one. The breath of Yahweh is, first of all, the life-giving principle that God gives to man according to his choice; cf. Gen. 2,7 and Job 34,14. But it is also the wind whose howling one hears whose violence overwhelms nature; cf. Ex. 15,8; Ps. 18,14; and Is. 40,7).

[77] The mysterious aspect of the wind is expressed by its mysterious origin and destination. That is why Haenchen (I, 201) contends that the comparison is inappropriate. According to him, in the case of the wind, one can feel whence it comes and whither it goes. Against such an affirmation, I make two observations: first of all, the evangelist does not stress here on the meteorological knowledge, but on the tradition of the OT which used the mystery of the wind to symbolise the impenetrability of the ways of God (cf. Eccles. 11,5; Prov. 30,4; and Sir. 16,21). Secondly, by connecting the begetting by the Spirit to the mystery of the origin and destination of the wind, the evangelist tries to allude, in anticipation, to the Christological basis of salvation. In fact, all along the fourth Gospel, the mystery of the person of Jesus is expressed in terms of his origin and destination (descent and ascent): to believe in Jesus is to recognise that he has come from the Father/heaven and must return to him. Those who do not believe do not know where he comes from (cf. 9,29) and do not understand his departure (cf. 8,22). In the same way, to understand the regenerative action of the Spirit and the salvation which flows from it, one must answer to the question 'where it come from and where it goes to,' applying it first to Jesus and then to the Spirit. See also C. H. Smith, "Οὕτως ἐστὶν πᾶς ὁ γεγεννημένος ἐκ τοῦ πνεύματος (Jn 3,8)," *ET* 81 (1969/70) 181.

[78] 1 Jn. 3,9-10 enumerates the perceivable effects of the action of the Spirit: sinlessness, holiness and fraternal love.

[79] Nicodemus, being a learned Pharisee who is well versed in the Scriptures, must have, at least, interpreted the affirmation of Jesus in connection with the announcement of the eschatological renewal operated by the Spirit in the intimacy of one's heart (Is. 59,21; Ezek. 36,24-27; Joel 3,1; and Ps. 51,12f.) – renewal conceived as a new creation (cf. H. L. Strack and P. Billerbeck, *Kommentar zum Neuen Testament aus Talmud und Midrasch. Band 2: Das Evangelium nach Markus, Lukas und Johannes und die Apostelgeschichte erläutert aus Talmud und Midrasch* [München ⁸1983] 421-23).

67

Abraham.[80] On the contrary, according to the statement of Jesus in 3,3, clarified in 3,5-6, the entrance into the kingdom does not depend on a physical birth enabling one to belong to the descendants of Abraham, but rather on a begetting from above and on a spiritual level.[81] One must be begotten from above, from God (3,3; cf. 1,13) and become a child of God (1,12).[82] In this perspective, one understands better the message of 3,8. In the physical order (3,6a; cf. 3,4), the access to salvation is not a mystery; it is easy to notice the physical belonging to the descendants of Abraham. Moreover, circumcision has been given as a visible sign of covenant between God and the descendants of Abraham (cf. Gen. 17,9-14). But in the order of the Spirit, in which one must be begotten to have access to salvation, it is not so. "The wind/Spirit blows where it chooses.... you do not know where it comes from[83] or where it goes" (3,8). The Spirit cannot be understood in human or physical categories. Nicodemus must renounce his earthly assurances and accept the proper process of the spiritual order. This leads me to the final question of Nicodemus (3,9) and the reaction of Jesus (3,10).

---

[80] One can understand better the astonishment and ironic answer of Nicodemus who interprets the expression 'γεννηθῆναι ἄνωθεν' against this background. However, even from the Jewish-tradition point of view it must have been possible to understand the allusion to a new generation. In fact, the rabbinical tradition knows the idea of new generation of man, of his transformation into a new creature (cf. καινὴ κτίσις: Gal. 6,15; and 2 Cor. 5,17) if God heals him of his infirmities, if He saves him from his misery, or if He forgives his sins (cf. Strack-Billerbeck, II, 421-22).

[81] 3,11-21 will clarify that it is through faith that a man accedes to this begetting from above. In this sense, the thematic of 3,3ff. is surprisingly similar to that of Rom. 4 and Gal. 3,6-29, where Paul, without denying the principle of belonging to the descendants of Abraham in order to inherit the promise, explains through a type of rabbinical exegesis, that it is the faith and not the birth which introduces one into the descendants of Abraham. A similar argument is used in 8,31-47. Being the son of someone is not just belonging to his descendants; it is also doing his works. Moreover, if salvation belongs to those who have Abraham as father, and through him God, only those who do the works of their father will be saved, that is the works of Abraham and of God. But the Jews do neither the works of God nor of Abraham (8,39-40.42). They have the devil as father (8,44) and do his works (8,41); see E. Gräßer, "Die Juden als Teufelssöhne in Johannes 8,37-47," in: W. Eckert (ed.), Antijudaismus im Neuen Testament? Exegetische und systematische Beiträge (ACJD 2) (München 1967) 157-70; and S. Motyer, Your Father the Devil? A New Approach to John and the Jews (Exeter 1997).

[82] See D. Patte, "Jesus' Pronouncement about Entering the Kingdom like a Child: A Structural Exegesis," Semeia 29 (1983) 3-42.

[83] In the fourth Gospel, the adverb 'πόθεν' is often employed to expose the ignorance of the people on the realities of salvation. Thus, Nathanael does not know *from where* Jesus knows him (1,48); the master of the banquet does not know *from where* the good wine (2,9) comes; Nicodemus does not know *from where* the wind/Spirit comes (3,7); the Samaritan woman does not know *from where* Jesus draws the living water (4,11); the disciples do not know *from where* the bread comes (6,5). From Jn. 7 onwards, the adverb expresses the ignorance of the people or of the Jews about the person of Jesus: either they think that they know (7,27) or they do not know (7,28 and 9,29-30) *where* Jesus is *from*. In such an ambiguity, only Pilate will directly ask Jesus: "*Where* do you come *from*?" (19,9). The formula 'που + verb go/leave' is frequently used to indicate the wrong interpretation of the departure of Jesus (cf. 7,35; 8,14; 13,36; 14,5 and 16,5). The double expression 'πόθεν ...and που' reveals the real mystery of the person of Jesus. Understanding his person is to know *where* he comes *from* (from the Father) and *where* he goes *to* (to the Father). Believing in Jesus, the Son sent by God, is to accept this origin and destination. In revealing the words of the Father to the world, Jesus gives to the humans the possibility to accept and to know truly 'that he has come from the Father,' and to 'believe that God has sent him' (cf. 17,8.25).

e. Transition from Dialogue to Discourse

In the dialogues of the fourth Gospel, it is customary that the last intervention of Jesus is developed into a Christological discourse[84] (3,11-21; cf. Jn. 5; 6; 8; etc.). Though 3,10 may seem not to fit well into the formal structure of 3,3-9, its function lies in bridging the dialogue (3,3-9) with the discourse that follows (3,11-21). That is why it is linked to 3,9 in the recurrence of the term 'ταῦτα'and the repetition of the formula "ἀπεκρίθη ... καὶ εἶπεν αὐτῷ," and to 3,11 in the transition form 'οὐ γινώσκεις' (3,10c) to 'οἴδαμεν' (3,11c). As 3,10 contains the last response of Jesus addressed to Nicodemus as an individual, formally it belongs to the dialogue. From 3,11 onwards, Nicodemus appears no more in the scene as Jesus shifts to the plural form (οἴδαμεν and λαμβάνετε) as is seen below:

3,9 *ἀπεκρίθη* Νικόδημος *καὶ εἶπεν αὐτῷ,* Πῶς δύναται *ταῦτα* γενέσθαι;

10 *ἀπεκρίθη* Ἰησοῦς *καὶ εἶπεν αὐτῷ,* Σὺ εἶ ὁ διδάσκαλος τοῦ Ἰσραὴλ καὶ *ταῦτα οὐ γινώσκεις;*

11 ἀμὴν ἀμὴν λέγω σοι ὅτι ὃ *οἴδαμεν* λαλοῦμεν καὶ ὃ ἑωράκαμεν μαρτυροῦμεν, καὶ τὴν μαρτυρίαν ἡμῶν οὐ *λαμβάνετε.*

Moreover, 3,10 serves as an immediate preparation for the discourse of Jesus to follow in 3,11-21. This discourse is narratively commanded by the demand made in 3,9. One can, therefore, think that Jesus is going to explain the foundation of salvation, that is, how it is possible to receive the Spirit who begets from above and enables the attainment of the kingdom of God. In this sense, 3,9 constitutes an announcement of the subject that is to follow. On the one hand, 3,10 makes an immediate preparation for 3,11 thanks to the opposition between the 'you do not know' that is addressed to Nicodemus (3,10) and the 'we know' of Jesus (3,11). On the other hand, the pronoun 'ταῦτα' in 3,9 refers to the preceding discussion. One understands, thus, the real function of the sub-unit 3,9-10 is a preparation for the forthcoming Christological discourse while remaining simultaneously a part of the dialogue on begetting from above for salvation.

f. Argumentation of 3,9-10

Now, if the purpose of the question in 3,9 is to introduce the discourse beginning in 3,11, it must announce the subject; that is, it must lead to specifying the theme of the discourse. To interpret the orientation of 3,9 rightly, one must, above all, specify the referent of the pronoun 'ταῦτα' (3,9c). One can either suppose that the pronoun refers to what precedes it – that is to the content of 3,5-8 – or to what Jesus has just explained in 3,8 regarding the necessity of accepting the mysterious aspect of the reality of a spiritual begetting. The question "how can these things be?" has a rhetoric function at this juncture of the dialogue. The question in 3,9 does not fulfil its structural function of making the discussion progress, if it were a mere repetition of the question raised in 3,4 and dealt with the interpretation of the expression 'γεννηθῇ ἄνωθεν.' In such a case it would only demonstrate the obstinacy of Nicodemus and make the whole discussion futile.

---

[84] Cf. U. Schoenborn, "'Im Wechsel der Worte das Wort'. Oder: Dialog und Offenbarung in Johannes 3," in: S. M. Pfürtner and U. Schoenborn (eds.), *Der bezwingende Vorsprung des Guten. Exegetische und theologische Werkstattberichte, FS Wolfgang Harnisch* (Hamburg, Münster 1994) 108-25.

In my opinion, there seems to be only one referent to the pronoun ταῦτα in 3,9. It hints at the theme of being begotten ἄνωθεν by the Spirit. Through the question, 'how these things can happen?' Nicodemus asks Jesus: 'how can one receive the Spirit who begets from above and be saved?' Thus, the question leads to the theme of salvation.

The use of the interrogative adverb 'πῶς,' in my opinion, stresses the reference to salvation in the question of Nicodemus. In fact, in the fourth Gospel, the use of this adverb on the lips of someone other than Jesus expresses, almost always, the complete ignorance or the total incomprehension of the identity of Jesus or his saving mission.[85] In 3,9 the use of the adverb 'πῶς,' therefore, serves to underline the fact that Nicodemus, a master of Israel, does not know how it is possible to obtain the Spirit and salvation definitively.[86] Contrary to the scribe in Mk. 12,28-34 who inquires about the greatest commandment (Mk. 12,28), but shows that he knew the response (Mk. 32-33), Nicodemus seems to be completely ignorant.

g. Culpable Ignorance of Nicodemus – Ironic Retort of Jesus

The ignorance of Nicodemus betrayed by his question in 3,9 provokes immediately the ironic reply of Jesus: "Σὺ εἶ ὁ διδάσκαλος τοῦ Ἰσραὴλ καὶ ταῦτα οὐ γινώσκεις" (3,10). One can notice easily the strong relation between this verse and 3,2 pronounced by Nicodemus. Such a correspondence between 3,2 and 3,10 constitutes an inclusion of the whole dialogue between Jesus and Nicodemus underlining the 'knowing' and yet 'not understanding' of Nicodemus. To Nicodemus who claimed to know (οἴδαμεν) that Jesus was a teacher (διδάσκαλος), Jesus retorts that even Nicodemus, a known teacher of Israel (ὁ διδάσκαλος τοῦ Ἰσραὴλ), however, does not even know what concerns salvation (ταῦτα οὐ γινώσκεις). Moreover, it is the quality of a teacher to know and to teach what he knows. The ignorance of Nicodemus is a culpable one. The irony is much more evident in the fact that it is a shameful crime to be ignorant about salvation, as it belongs to the primary domain of the knowledge of a teacher of Israel. He is supposed to be a specialist of the Law whose observance leads to salvation. He must have, at least, asked Jesus about the relation of his teaching to that Law; but his question "how can these things be?" only betrays his *ignorance*.

Going a little deeper, one could even think that Nicodemus, as a qualified teacher, should not be ignorant of spiritual regeneration. Already in the OT, the prophets had announced the new covenant in terms of regeneration or of new creation of the people of Israel, and this has, often, been attributed to the Spirit of Yahweh (cf. Jer. 31,31-34; and Ezek. 11,19-20 and 36,24-27). Is. 66,7-14 describes even the coming of New Israel in using the metaphor of a mother giving birth. In the same line, a midrashic interpretation of the Canticle of Canticles 8,2 says: "Why does he call Sinai 'house of my mother?' Because, it is there that the Israelites became new born children."[87] Nicodemus, therefore,

---

[85] E.g. the adverb shows complete ignorance concerning his descent from heaven (6,42), the gift of his flesh to eat (6,52), Jesus' knowledge of the Scriptures (7,15), liberation by truth (8,33), the recovering of sight (9,21; cf. 9,10.15.19.26), the operation of signs (9,16), the elevation of the Son of Man (12,34), and the vision of the Father (14,5.9).

[86] In 3,4 the second part of the question shows clearly a lack of understanding on the part of Nicodemus with regard to a statement of Jesus. In 3,9 it is rather a lack of knowledge of the teacher.

[87] Cf. Vellanickal, 24, n. 57.

has no reason to be surprised of a 'begetting from above' to attain salvation. He must not be surprised anymore of a 'water and Spirit begetting,' because the prophets had spoken of a superabundant pouring of the Spirit of God as a characteristic of the Messianic times (cf. Is. 4,4; 32,15 and 59,21; Zach. 12,10 and 13,1; and Joel 3,1), which will have the effect of a true interior transformation (cf. Ezek. 11,19-20 and 36,24-27) – qualified by the Rabbis as a new creation and a new birth.[88] In some texts like Is. 44,3; Jer. 31,33; and Ezek. 36,25-27 and 47,1-2, the symbolism of water is even directly associated with the Spirit.

h. Characterisation of Nicodemus

As Jesus' dialogue with Nicodemus apparently ends in 3,10, I shall analyse the character portrayal of Nicodemus at this juncture which might throw more light to understand the meaning of this sub-unit. H. James asks, "What is character but the determination of incident? What is incident but the illustration of character?"[89] Plot and character blend almost inseparably in the fourth Gospel. Plot and character are relevant for interpreting the life of an historical personage.

There is no unanimity among scholars as to how much of the fourth Gospel is *history* and how much *fiction*. Though one can bring in the argument that there are various concepts of characterisation, the question persists: how can one apply the concept of *characterisation* to the description of persons in an historical and biographical narrative like the Gospels? On the other hand, one can also understand characterisation as a literary art and technique through which a writer shapes the portrayal of a person convincingly.[90] What remains important for us, however, is the *how* of the portrayal[91] rather than whether the portrayed person is historical or fictitious. I am concerned about the understanding of the author in the choice of persons and their role in a sequence of events, and how he communicates to the reader convincingly through such a portrayal. What is significant is the relationships between author and text, and text and reader rather than the historical origin of the characters. As Abrams rightly states, characters are shaped by what the narrator describes about them as he introduces them, what the characters themselves say or do, and how the other characters interact with them.[92]

The implied author introduces craftily into the narrative the person of Nicodemus as a representative of the official Judaism and of partial faith in Jesus on the basis of signs.[93] Such an illustration seems to be logical after examples of more satisfactory faith (the disciples at Cana – cf. 2,11) and of complete lack of faith ('the Jews' at the Temple – cf.

---

[88] Cf. Léon-Dufour, *Lecture*, I, 292; Schnackenburg, *Gospel*, I, 370; R. E. Brown, *Gospel*, I, 140; U. Horst, "Heilsverlangen und Wiedergeburt. Zu Joh 3:1-12," *AnzKG* 88 (1979) 408; and H. A. Hoyt, "The Explanation of the New Birth," *GrJ* 8 (1967) 14-21; see also E. Sjöberg, "Wiedergeburt und Neuschöpfung im palästinischen Judentum," *StTh* 4 (1951) 83.

[89] H. James, "The Art of Fiction," in: L. Edel (ed.), *Henry James: Selected Fiction* (New York 1953) 597.

[90] See L. Cantwell, "The Quest for the Historical Nicodemus," *RelSt* 16 (1980) 482.

[91] For example, the principles or norms used to select such persons, the devices used to bring them into the narrative, and make them part of a uninterrupted and continuous story are important. See G. R. O'Day, "Narrative Mode and Theological Claim: A Study in the Fourth Gospel," *JBL* 105 (1986) 661-62.

[92] Cf. M. H. Abrams, *A Glossary of Literary Terms* (New York [4]1981) 21; see also D. Rhoads, "Narrative Criticism and the Gospel of Mark," *JAAR* 50 (1982) 417; and Alter, 116-17.

[93] See P. Mourlon-Beernaert, "Nicodème et les croyants. Trois méthodes de lecture (Jn 3)," *Tel* 42 (1985) 11-20; and L. Walter, "Lecture d'Évangile. Jean III,1-21: selon la foi et l'incrédulité," *EeV* 87 (1977) 369-78 and 385-90.

2,18-20). The presence of Jesus in Jerusalem[94] for the Passover feast (2,23) and the Jewish context is strongly maintained. As with 2,1-12 and 2,23-25, there is an insistence on the Jewishness of the character who meets Jesus. Thus, the context of Nicodemus' visit, his background and social status, the time of his approach, his way of addressing, his lack of understanding – all play a role in understanding his character, and through this characterisation the implied author's narrative Christology is exposed.

Nicodemus is unknown to the Synoptic tradition, but he might well have been known among the *Rabbis* with whom the fourth Gospel seems to be in constant dialogue. The Babylonian Talmud cites a man named Naqai among a group of five disciples of Jesus. Naqai is a shortened form of the Hebrew name, Naqdimon, which would be the equivalent of the Greek name which is transliterated as Nicodemus. He has sometimes been identified with Naqdimon ben Gurion,[95] a wealthy citizen of Jerusalem who supplied water to pilgrims at the principal feasts, and who is known to have lived at the time of the destruction of Jerusalem (70 AD).[96] Jn. 3,4 gives me a hint that Nicodemus, perhaps, was an old man when he encountered Jesus; but the arguments for this identification are quite inconclusive.[97]

Whatever his identification may be in extra-biblical literature, what is sure for me is his name, his belonging to the party of the Pharisees,[98] his position in society (ἄρχων τῶν Ἰουδαίων – 3,1), and his qualification (ὁ διδάσκαλος τοῦ Ἰσραὴλ – 3,10). The fourth evangelist does not give the age or physical characteristics of any character. He provides the reader with the barest minimum information of their past.[99] Though they are individualised by their position in society and by their interaction with Jesus, the implied author is, however, very cautious about individualising him so much as to have a 'personality.' This gives the impression that he may easily become a type or representative figure.[100] Nevertheless, his position in the society and his interactions with Jesus are realistic. The implied author portrays him in such a manner that the reader may accept him, more important, accept his characterisation of Jesus.

There are two theories among scholars about Nicodemus: first, that he was a sincere inquirer; second, that he came as a representative of the Pharisaic class, of which he was a

---

[94] The setting of 3,1-21, although not explicitly given, must be taken as Jerusalem, as there has been no indication of movement away from the city since Jesus' arrival there (cf. 2,13.23).

[95] Cf. R. Bauckham, "Nicodemus and the Gurion Family," *JThS* 47 (1996) 1-37.

[96] That would make Naqdimon a very young man forty years earlier, during the ministry of Jesus, probably too young to have been a member of the Sanhedrin and a teacher of Israel unless he was exceptionally talented and popular. Cf. Carson, *Gospel*, 186.

[97] E. Reinmuth, "Nikodemus," *ZdZ* 39 (1985) 53.

[98] See J. S. King, "Nicodemus and the Pharisees," *ET* 98 (1986/87) 45.

[99] For example, the lame man had been afflicted for thirty-eight years (5,5), and the blind man had been blind from birth (9,1).

[100] Notwithstanding the careful presentation of Nicodemus and the attestation of Nicodemus in the rabbinical tradition, in my opinion, there can be little doubt that the implied author is more interested in the role of Nicodemus as a representative figure than seeing in him an historical person who belonged to Jesus' entourage. See R. F. Collins, "The Representative Figures of the Fourth Gospel," *DR* 94 (1976) 36-37; his, "Jesus' Conversation with Nicodemus," *BiTod* 93 (1977) 1409-19; and D. M. Stanley, "Israel's Wisdom Meets the Wisdom of God," *Worship* 32 (1958) 281-82. Against this view, K. Hanhart ("The Structure of John I 35 - IV 54," in: *Studies in John. Presented to J. N. Sevenster on the Occasion of his Seventieth Birthday* [NT.S 24] [Leiden 1970] 35) and M. D. Goulder ("Nicodemus," *SJTh* 44 [1991] 156) consider Nicodemus as a well known historical person.

member, either trying to find a way to come to terms with Jesus or a way to disparage what he stood for.[101] If the former is the case, I have to assume that Nicodemus was a man looking for a deeper truth but was limited by his literalism and concretistic way of thinking. If the latter is the case, I have to assume that his questions to Jesus and behaviour toward him were diplomatic and not sincere.[102]

The case for the second point of view is strengthened by the narrator's omniscient view of Jesus' internal attitudes toward the people around him in Jerusalem at the Passover (cf. 2,23-25). He does not trust them, does not need their testimony, and knows them only too well.[103] Out of this distrusting atmosphere steps out one of them to speak with Jesus privately. The juxtaposition of τῷ ἀνθρώπῳ in 2,25 and ἄνθρωπος in 3,1 identifies Nicodemus precisely as one of those Jesus knows and does not need testimony from. Upon this negative narrative signal is added the identification of Jesus' visitor as a Pharisee, one of the party who asked the Baptist hard questions in the wilderness (cf. 1,19-25). Is Nicodemus coming to Jesus on a similar mission to investigate an unknown and untrained teacher, having seen the equally illegal acts performed at the Temple (2,14-16)? Nicodemus is identified not only as a Pharisee but also as ἄρχων τῶν Ἰουδαίων (3,1), that is a member of the Sanhedrin, the highest Jewish court permitted by the Romans and radiated legal authority from Jerusalem throughout Palestine. How fitting that the fourth Gospel's Jesus addresses his own reference to 'the kingdom of God' (3,3.5) to a 'ruler of the Jews' (3,1)!

Moreover, the narrator tells the reader that Nicodemus came 'at night,' the time of darkness. This does not promise to be a joyous encounter. With this dark introduction, Nicodemus opens the conversation in 3,2 by addressing Jesus as *Rabbi*, just as Jesus' first disciples did (cf. 1,38.49). Could Nicodemus be coming as a prospective disciple? He continues by speaking in the plural as he gives Jesus precisely the testimony that Jesus does not need: "we[104] know that you are a teacher who has come from God; for no one can do these signs that you do apart from the presence of God" (3,2). Added to that, Nicodemus' attraction for Jesus is based on signs, precisely what Jesus does not trust (cf. 2,24-25). It is now clear that Nicodemus is one and apparently represents others of those described in 2,23 who believed in Jesus, because they saw the signs he performed in Jerusalem.

Furthermore, Jesus' replies to his questions sound curt and Nicodemus' responses appear to be argumentative and even ridicule what Jesus is saying. Thus, when Nicodemus

---

[101] The very scantiness of information concerning Nicodemus might tempt one to supply unknown facts from fancy and to give a picture of a secret disciple – sympathetic but weak or (alternatively) tenacious and cunning – or of a sympathising outsider who did not, after all, acquire the true faith and contented himself with paying the last honour to a man whom he revered and whom he considered to have been condemned to death unjustly.

[102] See also Goulder, 156.

[103] A. Pangritz ("Der 'maskierte Christus.' Nicodemismus und Antinikodemismus in der italienischen Reformation," *EvTh* 54 [1994] 9) even speaks of a certain *Nikodemismus*.

[104] Gaeta (45) claims that the expression indicates not a personal opinion but a doctrinal declaration. As is often pointed out, the plural is used to indicate Nicodemus' representative status. See also A. von Harnack, "Das 'Wir' in den Johanneischen Schriften," in: his *Kleine Schriften zur alten Kirche. Berliner Akademie-schriften 1908-1930* (Opuscula IX/2) (Leipzig 1980) 626-43. I notice in this affirmation a note of self-confidence based on the traditions and culture of Israel.

says, "How can anyone be born after having grown old? Can one enter a second time into the mother's womb and be born?" (3,4) – this can be interpreted as sarcasm. Similarly, Jesus' final statement to Nicodemus in 3,10, "Are you a teacher of Israel, and yet you do not understand these things?" – can be thought of as a blunt dismissal of a man whom Jesus perceived to be incompetent or insincere.[105] His silent disappearance[106] from the scene seems to support it further. If this is the case, in my opinion, it is a study in the futility of a spiritually minded person trying to carry on a discussion about spiritual matters with someone whose underlying motive is to refute and ridicule spiritual beliefs. People who find themselves in such a situation would do well to follow Jesus' example and cut the conversation short.

However, there are also good arguments for the other point of view that Nicodemus was sincere. He seems to be underestimated by modern commentators.[107] His role is important: he is the instigator of Jesus' first discourse in the fourth Gospel.[108] He may be regarded by the evangelist as one of the many of 2,23. It is probable, however, that the Greek conjunction δέ[109] (3,1) with which this narrative is connected with the preceding chapter has adversative force: '*but* there was one of the Pharisees....' It is not that Nicodemus is guilty of a false faith, but a miracle-based faith is inadequate. Such a faith, in my opinion, is only the first step toward Jesus: it has not yet seen him in his true significance, and it is, therefore, not yet fully established. The chief cause of the inadequacy is that one cannot understand or confess who Jesus truly is, unless one really understands whence comes and whither he goes. Nicodemus, like the others, had been impressed by the signs whose deeper significance he did not realise, *but* there was in him a sincere willingness to learn more, to which Jesus responded by 'entrusting himself' to him more than he did to many others. Jesus, with his unerring intuition into human character, perceived at once the earnestness of Nicodemus.

Then there is the little detail that he came 'by night.'[110] It is reasonable to suppose that he came by night to avoid being seen, but if he was sent by the Pharisees he would not have cared if he was seen or not. The night visit to Jesus suggests a man who is nervously inquiring about something that he senses might have some truth to it, but does not want to

---

[105] See E. F. F. Bishop, "'The Authorised Teacher of the Israel of God.' John 3:10," *BiTr* 7 (1956) 83.

[106] For a detailed study see F. Eckert, *Das Schweigen des Nikodemus. 19 Wortmeldungen eines Grenzgängers* (Basel, Freiburg, Wien 1990).

[107] See e.g. the short treatment of M. Davies, 336-37; and Culpepper, *Anatomy*, 134-36.

[108] Cf. M. de Jonge, "Nicodemus and Jesus: Some Observations on Misunderstanding and Understanding in the Fourth Gospel," *BJRL* 53 (1971) 337-59.

[109] Besides *but*, δέ could mean: *to the contrary, rather, and, now.* RSV, NRS, NASB, NAS, NIV, BBE and some other English translations render it as 'now' which is an idiomatic adaptation. The Darby Bible (1884/1890) renders it rightly as 'but.' See also Carson, *op. cit.*, 185-86; and F. F. Bruce, *The Gospel of John. Introduction, Exposition and Notes* (Grand Rapids 1994) 81.

[110] Even at this early stage of the narrative the reader is able to look back to the conflict between the φῶς and σκοτία of 1,5. The evangelist recalls this detail in 19,39 because of its symbolic import. The best clue lies in the fourth evangelist's use of 'night' elsewhere: in each instance (3,2; 9,4; 11,10 and 13,30) the word is either used metaphorically for moral and spiritual darkness. Darkness and night symbolise the realm of evil, untruth, and ignorance. In 13,30 Judas leaves the light to go out of the darkness into the night of Satan; Nicodemus, on the other hand, comes out of the darkness into the light (3,19-21). On a purely natural level, the night-time visit may have been a stealthy expedient for fear of the Jews; or it may reflect the rabbinic custom of staying up at night to study the Law. See R. E. Brown, *op. cit.*, 130; Carson, *op. cit.*, 186; and K. Stasiak, "The Man Who Came by Night," *BiTod* 20 (1982) 84-89.

risk offending or angering his fellow Pharisees who see Jesus as an enemy (cf. 2,18ff.), and so goes to some length to keep his visit secret. The Pharisee may have chosen this time in order to be sure of an uninterrupted,[111] leisurely, tranquil, and profound interview. During the day Jesus would be busy and there would be crowds of common people around him. At any rate the visit of Nicodemus to Jesus is "a brave act in itself."[112]

Many motives have been ascribed to him, of one kind or another,[113] but I am inclined to believe, from the turn of the conversation, that Nicodemus was not moved by a purely intellectual curiosity. He does not begin his conversation with a question but with a statement of admiration for Jesus. His words of greeting express his high esteem for Jesus: "*Rabbi*, we know that you are a *teacher* who has *come from God*; for no one can do these signs that you do apart from the *presence of God*" (3,2).[114] Nicodemus seems to claim he can *see* something of who Jesus is in the miracles. He, like other Jews, wants to set up criteria by which one can assess who Jesus is. But Jesus seems to reject the priority of Nicodemus, and radically question his qualifications for sorting out 'heavenly things' (3,11). At one level Nicodemus' assessment of Jesus must be judged disappointing. He does not suggest Jesus is a prophet, still less *the* prophet or the Messiah,[115] but simply a teacher endowed with God's power. He is openly curious about Jesus, but still falls a long way short of confession that he is uniquely the promised Messiah. He comes to Jesus prepared to accept him as part of his own world. Jesus insists none can *see* the saving reign of God at all, including through the display of miraculous signs, unless begotten ἄνωθεν. Jesus himself reaches beyond the signs and speaks of (seeing/entering) the kingdom of God. He, thereby, places his public conduct in a context in which God is with him in another, superior, and more decisive way than Nicodemus and the ἄνθρωποι in Jerusalem are, apparently, aware of.

It is of importance for the understanding of this story that one keeps in mind, throughout, the position of Nicodemus and the high esteem in which he must have been held by his fellow-countrymen. He was not only a man of education and blameless character (cf. 7,50-51), but also of such marked ability that he had been chosen a member of the *Sanhedrin*, the highest civil and ecclesiastical court of the land. Nicodemus wants to maintain this position of honour and influence. His visit manifests that he must have taken part in Jesus' work and teaching which was causing great discussions everywhere. At any rate he confesses that he knew what they were, and had formed his own conclusions about

---

[111] Beasley-Murray, *John*, 47.

[112] A. Watson, *Jesus and the Jews. The Pharisaic Tradition in John* (Athens, London 1995) 40.

[113] For Barrett (202) "Nicodemus appears before Jesus but never even states the purpose of his coming."

[114] This recognition of Jesus as a teacher come from God is certainly not a confession of Jesus' pre-existence. Though the qualifications Nicodemus uses of Jesus ('come from God,' and 'God is with him' – 3,2) appear to be similar to what Jesus says of himself (e.g. 8,29 and 16,32), what Nicodemus means in 3,2 is that God is peculiarly with Jesus, very much as he was with Moses or Jeremiah (cf. Ex. 3,12; and Jer. 1,8). Prophets in the OT were considered to be coming from God; their mission received authority and authenticity in their being sent by God. The acknowledgement of Nicodemus here is to be understood against this background. See Bernard, I, 101; and Barrett, 205. See also G. Reim, *Studien zum alttestamentlichen Hintergrund des Johannesevangeliums* (MSSNTS 22) (Cambridge 1974) 199-200.

[115] See M. de Jonge, "Jewish Expectations about the 'Messiah' according to the Fourth Gospel," *NTS* 19 (1972) 248; see also M. Hengel, "Jesus als messianischer Lehrer der Weisheit und die Anfänge der Christologie," in: *Sagesse et Religion. Colloque de Strasbourg, Octobre 1976* (Paris 1979) 148-88.

them. The implied author, thus, seems to demonstrate that there were exceptions among the hostile Jews who were attracted by Jesus' teaching.

Another important clue to understand the character of Nicodemus is the fact that the narrator brings him twice more into the story. In Jn. 7,50-51 he sympathises with Jesus when he advocates a fair hearing for Jesus according to the Jewish Law.[116] Only a little need be said here about the background to this second intervention. The Pharisees and chief priests send officers to arrest Jesus, perhaps, for blasphemy (cf. 7,32). The officers fail because, they say, "Never has anyone spoken like this" (7,46). The Pharisees ask if the officers were also deceived and, further, if any of the rulers or Pharisees believed in Jesus (7,47f.). The people who do not know the Law[117] are cursed, say the Pharisees (7,49). Nicodemus intervenes: "Our Law does not judge people without first giving them a hearing to find out what they are doing" (7,51). The Pharisees respond angrily in terms of their well known antagonism.

Nicodemus is presented here, too, not as an individual person, but as belonging to a larger group – as *one* of the many. He belongs to the Pharisees, and as such he pleads Jesus' cause with his colleagues.[118] Though Nicodemus advocates precision in legal procedure in dealing with Jesus, the implied author is clearly portraying Nicodemus, here too, as the one exception among the rulers and the Pharisees who shows extreme generosity of spirit toward Jesus.[119] Nicodemus' intervention is deeply moving. He, a Pharisee, is distancing himself in a pointed way from those who want Jesus' death. My contention that the Greek conjunction δέ of 3,1 – translated as *but* – is presenting Nicodemus as an exception among those to whom Jesus did not entrust himself in 2,23-25, seems to corroborate the presentation of Nicodemus as an exception among the many in 7,48-51.[120] One can also suspect that Nicodemus, while he was open to a discussion with Jesus, was, like other Pharisees, wholly satisfied that the Law was the only divine means of salvation. The implied author, perhaps, wants to disclose to the reader how fatal it could be to be satisfied with one's religious attainments, social position, learnedness and riches. The

---

[116] Cf. F. Wessel, "'Der Mensch' in der Verteidigungsrede des Nikodemus Joh 7,51 und das 'Ecce Homo'," *SNTU* 17 (1992) 199-200.

[117] See S. Pancaro, *The Law in the Fourth Gospel: The Torah and the Gospel, Moses and Jesus, Judaism and Christianity according to John* (NT.S 42) (Leiden 1975) 138-40.

[118] Mendner (294-323) suggests that the authentic setting for the Nicodemus-story is in 7,51. He supposes that only after Nicodemus had spoken on Jesus' behalf, he went to investigate him. Hence, the visit of Nicodemus to Jesus must follow 7,50-51. I would say that it was his first encounter with Jesus that made him come out of the darkness, to a certain extent, about the identity of Jesus. His encounter with Jesus enabled him later in 7,51 to intervene in favour of Jesus. However, the analysis of Jn. 7 is directly relevant to the question concerning the attitude of the implied author toward Nicodemus.

[119] Though Nicodemus' remark does not deal with Jesus' teaching and acts as such and only emphasises the legal requirement that the accused should be granted a proper hearing (cf. Deut. 1,16; 13,14; 17,4 and 19,18), he unmasks the hypocrisy of his fellow Pharisees who scoff at "this crowd, which does not know the Law" (7,49) and evidently have no regard for the Law themselves if that is more convenient to them.

[120] Note also that in 7,48 and 12,42 the 'οἱ ἄρχοντες' are distinguished from the Pharisees, that in 12,42 secret believers are reported to have been among them, who feared the Pharisees, and that in 7,26 the crowd supposes that 'οἱ ἄρχοντες' have recognised that Jesus is the Messiah. However, J. L. Martyn's (*History and Theology in the Fourth Gospel* [Nashville ²1979] 74-76) hypothesis that 'οἱ ἄρχοντες' is used in the fourth Gospel always for those members of the Sanhedrin who believed secretly cannot be substantiated. But it is clear that Jesus' preaching has caused a split among the Jewish leaders, just as it had caused a 'σχίσμα' among the ordinary people a little earlier (7,43). A schism among the Jews is also mentioned in 9,16 and 10,19.

conversation with Jesus ends leaving the bewildered ruler in the dark. Nicodemus' silent disappearance from the scene betrays his indecisiveness.[121] A comparison of the indecisiveness and the silent and sad departure of the rich young man of the Synoptics, who kept the Law perfectly but could not decide to commit himself to Jesus (cf. Mt. 19,21; Mk. 10,22; and Lk. 18,23), with that of Nicodemus might throw some light to understand the character of Nicodemus better.

In my opinion, only when one considers all the three appearances of Nicodemus together one understands the narrator's portrayal of the character of Nicodemus correctly. The implied author undoubtedly wants his readers to connect all three mentions of Nicodemus, since he calls his reader's attention to the initial conversation between Jesus and Nicodemus when he introduces the latter at 7,50 and 19,39.[122] At his last appearance in 19,39, where he joins Joseph of Arimathea in burying Jesus, he brings a large quantity of myrrh and aloes to give an honourable burial to Jesus.[123] The second and the third appearances of Nicodemus are connected with the first one by means of redactional remarks in 7,50, "who had gone to Jesus before," and in19,39, "who had at first come to Jesus by night."[124] This shows that the implied author wants to indicate a connection between these three interventions of Nicodemus.[125] Moreover, it is evident that in the second and third interventions Nicodemus appears to be distanced from his colleagues. In 19,39 Nicodemus' social rank and religious affiliation are not mentioned, but it may not be farfetched to suppose that the implied author wants the reader to deduce that he was, by then, a μαθητὴς τοῦ Ἰησοῦ κεκρυμμένος δὲ διὰ τὸν φόβον τῶν Ἰουδαίων like Joseph of Arimathea whose companion he had become.[126]

---

[121] R. Schnackenburg's ("Die Messiasfrage im Johannesevangelium," in: *Neutestamentliche Aufsätze. FS J. Schmid* [Regensburg 1963] 240-64) view, I think, is borne out by my analysis of the Nicodemus passages. The sympathetic, even believing Jews like Nicodemus are on their way to Jesus. But they should know, and Christians who speak with them should know, that a far more incisive decision will have to be made before they really understand who Jesus is and what salvation he brings. Conversion from Judaism to Christianity (as the fourth Gospel understands it) requires a complete rethinking, a rebirth which is a begetting ἄνωθεν. And the Church which is confronted with Judaism should not only realise that Jewish expectations have been fulfilled in Jesus, but also emphasise that these have to be re-interpreted fundamentally, because the new revelation is radically different from the old. Therefore, the central question here, in my opinion, is Christological.

[122] J.-M. Auwers, "La nuit de Nicodème (Jean 3,2; 19,39) ou l'ombre du langage," *RB* 97 (1990) 500-3.

[123] See D. D. Sylva, "Nicodemus and his Spices (John 19.39)," *NTS* 34 (1988) 148-51.

[124] There are many textual variants at this point. There is no need to suppose that א*, which omits this phrase altogether, represents the original text; in 19,39 all manuscripts have a similar cross-reference (with some variation). Auwers (*op. cit.*) considers the night visit of Nicodemus to Jesus at Jerusalem to be the night of the Passover. See also M. Meinertz, "Die 'Nacht' im Johannesevangelium," *ThQ* 133 (1953) 400-7.

[125] P. Dschulnigg, "Nikodemus im Johannesevangelium," *SNTU* 24 (1999) 103-18

[126] B. Hemelsoet ("L'Ensevelissement selon Saint Jean," in: *Studies in John*, 47-65) argues convincingly that Joseph and Nicodemus who 'ἔλαβον οὖν τὸ σῶμα τοῦ Ἰησοῦ' are regarded as true believers. They have accepted the Word (see the ἔλαβον αὐτόν in 1,12) while accepting the body of Jesus as that of the new paschal lamb. He sets great store by the fact that λαμβάνειν (with the meanings of 'take' and 'accept') is used only in connection with Joseph and Nicodemus, not with the Jews and the soldiers. J. N. Suggit ("Nicodemus – the True Jew," *Neotest.* 14 [1981] 102-4) also makes much of the use of 'ἔλαβον' in 19,40. He claims that it indicates Nicodemus' total acceptance of Jesus which, I contend, is farfetched. The opinion of de Jonge ("Nicodemus and Jesus," 343) – that in the fourth Gospel Joseph and Nicodemus are pictured as having come to a dead end, regard the burial of Jesus as definitive, and have not been able to look further than the tomb in the garden near the place where Jesus was crucified – is, I contend, not acceptable for such a presentation does not serve the goal of the implied author (20,30-31).

Even if it is possible that Nicodemus was a hostile inquirer[127] in the story the fourth evangelist narrates in Jn. 3, I have reasons to assume that Nicodemus went through a radical change of heart later on. The first curious element in the third intervention is the absence of the disciples, Mary the mother of Jesus, and Mary Magdalene. Properly, they should be responsible for the anointing and burial of the body of Jesus, not the hitherto unknown Joseph of Arimathea and the rebuffed Nicodemus. The implied author here, probably, is making a point about Nicodemus' behaviour in contrast to that of the disciples.

A second curious omission is that there is no mention that, by touching the corpse, Nicodemus has made himself ritually unclean for seven days, an important consequence for a Pharisee and member of the Sanhedrin. This ritual uncleanness must be stressed. Num. 19,11 lays down: "Those who touch the dead body of any human being shall be unclean seven days."[128] Purification rites were required on the third day and seventh day (Num. 19,12), but the person who touched the corpse was unclean for the whole seven days. Nothing he did could shorten that period of time; and an unclean person could not celebrate Passover, and for Nicodemus Passover would fall within that period (cf. 19,14.31). It was on that account that the Jews would not enter the Roman praetorium when Jesus was taken there: "They themselves did not enter the headquarters, so as to avoid ritual defilement and to be able to eat the Passover"(18,28).[129] Nicodemus could eat the Passover a month later (cf. Num. 9,6ff.), but that is not the same thing at all. Nicodemus has cut himself off from his fellow Pharisees and members of the Sanhedrin for the greatest celebration of the Jewish year, and that to respect the body of Jesus, who apparently slighted him in life and is now defeated in death.

In view of these two more appearances, it is more reasonable to believe that Nicodemus is an extremely good and kind man who is very respectful of Jesus and extraordinarily generous toward him. However, in his first intervention he appears as an awkward, but sincere and somewhat nervous inquirer. His statements to Jesus do not reflect hostility but show the difficulty his literal and legal mind has in understanding what Jesus is saying; and Jesus is not rebuffing him but going to some lengths to try to enlighten him. For my purpose, I am going to assume that this is the way it really was. Taking all the three appearances of Nicodemus in the Gospel story together, I can notice a sort of gradualness or progression in the portrayal of the character of Nicodemus as a secret believer. Selected as an exception from among the sceptical believers[130] on seeing the signs of Jesus (cf. 2,23-25), he is gradually shown to have found sympathy for the person of Jesus (7,50-51), but lacked courage to openly confess his faith, and had finally became a secret disciple at the last stage.

The conversation of Nicodemus with Jesus seems to reveal also a sense of hunger for spiritual truths when he acknowledges Jesus as a teacher come from God. Nicodemus

---

[127] J. M. Bassler ("Mixed Signals: Nicodemus in the Fourth Gospel," *JBL* 108 [1989] 636-37) claims that already at the beginning of the narrative (3,1) the term 'Jew(s)' has acquired the connotation of non-receptivity and even hostility toward Jesus. In my opinion, she seems to overstate her case.

[128] See also Num. 19,16 and 31,19.

[129] The reason for defilement for entering the praetorium is the subject of much debate: see e.g. R. E. Brown, *op. cit.*, II, 846.

[130] Cf. P. Mourlon-Beernaert, "Nicodème et les croyants. Trois méthodes de lecture (Jn 3)," *Tel* 42 (1985) 11-20.

wished to understand what this new movement meant, wished to get to the heart of it, to study it and to study it at the source. Moreover, he knew that a private conversation was the best method of attaining his object. Sensing it, Jesus says to him: "Very truly, I tell you, no one can see the kingdom of God without being born from above" (3,3). In his question, Nicodemus is presented, apparently, as one who is not capable of opening himself to the mystery of the words of Jesus, but as belonging purely to temporal dimensions by using the word δεύτερον (3,4).[131] Nicodemus replies to Jesus' words about being begotten again with a question: "How can these things be?" (3,9). Jesus replies with a question of his own: "Are you a teacher of Israel, and yet you do not understand[132] these things?" (3,10). The verb used is γινώσκειν; it implies a knowledge that comes through experience. The implied author is trying to portray that Jesus and Nicodemus speak on entirely different wavelengths, if not about completely different subjects. He is coming with a prejudiced mind which prevents intimate knowledge of Jesus. His position of honour in society and his sense that he was stooping from it were against his getting at any real comprehension of Jesus. Very few men of education and refinement can lightly put aside what it has cost them a whole lifetime to build up, so as to listen with an open mind to what a young working man from a country village has got to say about the very subject which they have studied most deeply. In addition to that, the very religion of the Pharisee would make it difficult for him to listen with appreciation to the new teaching. He had been trained from his earliest days in the Law, to believe that men were saved by strict obedience to commandments, through reverence for the traditions of the elders, and through shaping one's whole conduct by a complicated system of rules. He, therefore, had an idea of God which closed his mind against the free spirit of Jesus. Nicodemus' approach is well-intentioned but theologically inadequate.

In the narrative, Nicodemus is also characterised symbolically as one living in a conflict between the light he perceives and the darkness he seems to prefer. Through the dark streets of Jerusalem Nicodemus steals along until he reached the house where Jesus lodged. He enters and is in the presence of the Son of God. The antithetic inclusion of night (darkness) (3,2) and light (3,21), in my opinion, portrays indirectly that Nicodemus, who is living in darkness comes toward light as he comes to Jesus.[133] His encounter with Jesus seems to have made an impact on him in favour of Jesus.

Finally, the entire dialogue is best seen in terms of the narrative time of the Johannine Community rather than the story time of Jesus. All the statements are made in terms of Nicodemus as a representative character. The Johannine Jesus challenges this ἄρχων τῶν Ἰουδαίων and those he represents to give up their status, their worldly glory, and join the Johannine Community. Nicodemus should be seen as a type of the

---

[131] See J. Bishop, "Encounters in the New Testament," in: G. Louis and R. R. Kenneth (eds.), *Literary Interpretations of Biblical Narratives* (Nashville 1982) II, 293.

[132] Misunderstanding is not a matter of understanding incompletely or inaccurately; it reveals a fundamental lack of understanding.

[133] Moloney (*Belief in the Word*, 108) feels that as the narrative unfolds, the implied reader will associate Nicodemus with a movement from darkness to light. Against this view see Rensberger, 37-41 and 54-59; and de Jonge, "Nicodemus and Jesus," 341-46. For an over-optimistic understanding of the character of Nicodemus, see Suggit, "Nicodemus," 90-110; see also J. Sahi, "Nicodemus Comes to Christ by Night," in: C. Duraisingh and C. Hargreaves (eds.), *India's Search for Reality and the Relevance of the Gospel of John. Papers from a Conference held in Pune in February 1974* (Delhi 1975) 78-79.

sympathetic Jewish seeker, yet one who is still in the dark and remains in the synagogue.[134] Nicodemus is the first full-fledged example in the fourth Gospel of the types of seekers and people in need Jesus meets, and his story is meant to be seen as an example of one who is on a pilgrimage toward a full and proper faith in Jesus but has not yet arrived, as the misunderstanding shows.

To conclude, the episode of Nicodemus in not only the story of a leading figure from Judaism who can only come to partial faith because of his inability to forsake his own criteria. It is, above all, a dense instruction for the reader on the uniqueness of the revelation that Jesus brings and the consequences of accepting or rejecting such revelation as is clear from the discourse that follows (cf. 3,11-21) and the second testimony of the Baptist (cf. 3,27-36).

i. Reader and Point of View

In the narrative of the fourth Gospel the individuality of minor characters like Nicodemus is determined by their encounter with or relation to Jesus. He is portrayed in such a way that he reflects the misunderstanding or the response the reader may share with regard to the person of Jesus and to guide the reader to examine the alternatives. The shape of the narrative and the voice of the narrator lead the reader to identify or interact variously with the character portrayed.[135]

In this sub-unit (3,3-10) the reader is shocked by the solemn and stern statement of Jesus (3,3) which seems to block the chance of winning over an influential leader of the Jews. The reader is utterly puzzled by the necessity of being begotten ἄνωθεν in order to see the βασιλεία τοῦ θεοῦ. The juxtaposition of γεννηθῇ and ἄνωθεν, creates misunderstanding. The reader is perplexed by the ambiguity[136] of the term ἄνωθεν and is forced to consider how one might be begotten either *from above* or *once again*, and feels distanced from Jesus as he/she cannot understand Jesus' words and feels threatened by the sense of confusion. There is the fear that the reader feels alienated from Jesus with whose cause he/she has become identified so far.

Moreover, Jesus redefines the issue of the conversation about entering the βασιλεία τοῦ θεοῦ. The reader hears that such an entrance depends on an ἄνωθεν birth. But the βασιλεία τοῦ θεοῦ itself has its own ambiguities.[137] It evokes a whole series of references

---

[134] The fourth Gospel presupposes the existence of Christian and Jewish communities side by side, definitely different, often not on speaking but on debating terms; cf. G. Reim, "Zur Lokalisierung der johanneischen Gemeinde," *BZ* 32 (1988) 79-80. The fourth evangelist never allows the identification of Jesus as Mosaic Prophet-Messiah to occupy centre stage without causing it shortly thereafter to be replaced by the motif of the Son of Man. See also Martyn, *History and Theology*, 338-51.

[135] See M. W. Newheart, "Toward a Pyscho-literary Reading of the Fourth Gospel," in: Segovia, *What is John?*, 43-58.

[136] By ambiguity I mean the verbal nuance which gives room for alternative reactions to the same piece of language. See W. Empson, *Seven Types of Ambiguity* (New York 1966) 1. See also my treatment under double meaning and misunderstanding.

[137] Moloney (*op. cit.*, 110) feels that to the reader, however familiar he/she may be with the Jewish notion of God as King, something different is being introduced by these words of Jesus to Nicodemus. For a provocative discussion on the metaphorical character of 'βασιλεία τοῦ θεοῦ' see N. Perrin, *Jesus and the Language of the Kingdom* (Philadelphia 1976) 29-32. For Patte (41), the realm of the kingdom of God is nothing else than the Johannine Community of faith. Onuki (*Gemeinde und Welt*, 63-64) argues for 3,5 as a reference to the ritual of baptism through which a person crossed a social barrier upon entering into the Johannine Community. Regarding the *kingdom of God* in the fourth Gospel referring to eternal life, see my

such as God's power, the ideal human society, a political transformation. The reader is now faced with one vague image (being begotten ἄνωθεν) used along with another (βασιλεία τοῦ θεοῦ); one puzzle refers the reader to another. He/she is forced to ask how being begotten ἄνωθεν could empower one to experience the βασιλεία τοῦ θεοῦ.

Now the question of Nicodemus triggers several different responses in the reader and puts him/her somewhat at ease, as Nicodemus, too, is puzzled by Jesus' ambiguous words. Like Nicodemus, the reader wonders how it is possible, feels drawn to him, identifies himself/herself with the role of Nicodemus in his confusion, becomes a coinquirer, and even hopes that with his help the obscurity of the saying will be clarified. Thanks to Nicodemus' question the reader feels clarified that the literal meaning is to be eliminated and that being begotten ἄνωθεν cannot refer to a second physical birth.[138] For a short time the reader even feels superior to Nicodemus. Nicodemus has come to Jesus prepared to accept him as part of his own world. On the basis of the narrative to this point the implied reader knows that such an understanding about Jesus falls short of the idea.

The intent of Jesus' words in the following verses (3,5-8) at first seems to confirm the reader's renewed sense of companionship with Jesus. That new affirmation is, however, shortlived. Once again the reader hears a solemn statement of Jesus and prepares himself/herself for difficulty. Being begotten ἄνωθεν is further compared to a begetting 'ἐξ ὕδατος καὶ πνεύματος.' The puzzle is now enriched, but the reader is confused and again pushed away from Jesus. Little more achieved than to replace the puzzle of ἄνωθεν with that of ἐξ ὕδατος καὶ πνεύματος. But the reader has learned already of a close association between water and the Holy Spirit from the reliable witness of the Baptist. The reader could recall the Baptist's distinction between his baptism with water and Jesus' baptism with the Holy Spirit (1,33).[139] As Nicodemus is being challenged to make that journey, the reader is being asked to recognise the transcendent nature of the events leading to true faith in Jesus. The reader must make a decision; he/she has sufficient information and experience already to be aware that the right decision is to commit oneself to the word of Jesus. The reader finds further light shed on Jesus' use of the expression βασιλεία τοῦ θεοῦ.

3,6 narrows down the possible reference to the mysterious begetting ἄνωθεν. Confirming Nicodemus' false impression that the birth is physical, Jesus distinguishes

---

treatment on dualism. See also the essays in H. B. Huffmon, F. A. Spina and A. R. W. Green (eds.), *The Quest for the Kingdom of God: Studies in Honour of George E. Mendenhall* (Winona Lake 1983); and J. Weiss, *Jesus' Proclamation of the Kingdom of God* (Ames 1999).

[138] According to Moloney (*op. cit.*), the implied reader, at home in Koine Greek, knows the double meaning of ἄνωθεν. Unless both words are given the translation loses this.

[139] The second day of 1,29-34 was marked by the absence of a specified audience. This indicates that the narrator was speaking, through the words of the Baptist, to the reader. F.-J. Moloney ("When is John talking about Sacraments?," *ABR* 30 [1982] 10-33), however, thinks that there is considerable diachronic debate over 3,5. The rest of 3,5-8 concentrates on *Spirit*; and *water* does not appear again. He argues that historically it was added to the text at some stage of the journey of the Johannine Community. The earliest form of this text spoke only of a rebirth in the Spirit as necessary for entry into the community. But the community's break with the synagogue and its growing awareness of its uniqueness led to the introduction of an explicit reference to the ritual of water baptism, a public sign that *externally* marked their *internal* experience and commitment to the beliefs of the Johannine Community. This must have occasioned both the temporal and the spiritual meaning of ἄνωθεν. See also de la Potterie, "Naître de l'eau." For a good presentation of the intersecting vertical and horizontal perspective involved here, see J. Calloud and F. Genuyt, *L'Evangile de Jean (I): Lecture sémiotique des chapitres 1 à 6* (Lyon 1989) 61-62.

between being begotten of the flesh and begotten of the Spirit.[140] The reader is encouraged to read on for the light of clarification. But the word σάρξ clouds the light and introduces yet another of the accumulating ambiguous terms for the reader. He/she has heard already in the prologue the distinction between born of God and born of the flesh (cf. 1,12-13). Nicodemus has not been informed of this begetting ἄνωθεν for those who believe in Jesus, nor did he hear the Baptist's testimony about baptism with water and Jesus' baptism with the Holy Spirit; but the reader is equipped with such knowledge. However, the questions – what more precisely a spiritual or divine begetting is and how such a begetting is possible – compel the reader in his/her pursuit of reading.

The reader has by now managed to squeeze some satisfaction out of Nicodemus' question and Jesus' distinction between spiritual and physical birth. But Jesus' words in 3,7 seem to mock both Nicodemus and the reader in their lack of understanding. How can they not be astonished? Now the reader senses that he/she once again stands with Nicodemus in his/her struggle to understand. The reader's alienation from Jesus is re-established.

Yet Jesus goes on now, seeming to promise clarification. His words concerning the πνεῦμα in 3,8 encourage the reader to expect an elucidation of entering βασιλεία τοῦ θεοῦ through an ἄνωθεν birth by the Spirit. Spirit is the key to lay bare the meaning hidden in Jesus' image. But the brief parabolic saying in 3,8 stretches the mind of the reader between πνεῦμα as spirit and wind. Jesus speaks of the freedom of the πνεῦμα, the perception of the sound of the wind, but the mystery[141] of its origin and destination. An implicit comparison of wind and spirit is supposed to illumine the begetting ἄνωθεν by water and the Spirit. But precisely the 'how' of it still evades the reader.

The reader feels that Nicodemus is inside his/her mind and speaks for him/her. His/her identification with Nicodemus in his puzzlement and their mutual alienation from Jesus is complete. The reader, too, is forced to repeat Nicodemus' question, "How can these things be?" (3,9) – these things referring to the entire discussion so far. Consequently, Jesus' stern reprimand of Nicodemus is intended by the narrator to be the reprimand of the reader as well: 'Are you a teacher of Israel (or have you read thus far), and yet you do not understand these things?' (3,10).

The reader is gradually lead through the reading, made to identify himself with the Nicodemus in his struggles, success and failures to understand Jesus. Through ups and downs his search for a clearer understanding of Jesus and his revelation makes progress. He/she has read the earlier part of the Gospel and so is better equipped in his journey of recognising the true identity of Jesus. The character portrayal of Nicodemus expresses much about the Johannine Community's simultaneous heartfelt desire to bring the religious leaders into commitment to Jesus and their doubt, based on hard experience, that this was

---

[140] F. Manns, "Nicodème ou la nécessité de renaître de l'Esprit," *TS(F)* 3 (1990) 107-10.

[141] The wind (πνεῦμα) is a mystery: one can experience it; it is a part of life, but one can never pin down its origins or its end (cf. Eccles. 11,5; and Sir. 16,21). Some commentators claim that 3,8abc have a double meaning, wind and Spirit, particularly on the basis of the use of the word 'φωνή;' some others consider 3,8abc referring to the natural wind, and only 3,8d as an application to the Spirit. See my treatment under double meaning.

likely to happen.[142] For the readers, it provides an archetypal encounter challenging a person – powerful in the eyes of the world – to convert and become powerful in the eyes of God.

It is also important to note that at no stage of the narrative does Nicodemus take the word of Jesus and reject it. The ongoing reading experience of the reader will eventually reveal that Nicodemus will make his own journey into faith. The figure of Nicodemus is used by the storyteller of the fourth Gospel as an example of partial faith for the implied reader. At this stage of the narrative, Nicodemus must be seen as not rejecting Jesus but still falling short of belief in Jesus' word. What is striking about the characterisation of Nicodemus is that – though he actually appears in only seventeen verses in this Gospel, and he speaks only sixty three words – I feel one knows him rather well, and apparently the audience is meant to develop a certain sense of kinship or identity with him.

j. Implicit Commentary

The fourth evangelist achieves his most subtle effects through his implicit commentary, that is, the devices and passages in which he communicates with the reader by implication and indirection. Here the text says more than it ever makes explicit. Stibbe rightly remarks that one cannot speak of plot and structure of a narrative without speaking of its implicit commentary.[143] The impact of the fourth Gospel's characterisation is only one aspect of the silent communication between author and reader. The fourth evangelist exhibits the art of saying something without really saying it. He says a great deal without actually saying it. In a dialogue such communication proceeds through the meaningful pause, the knowing glance, the frown, the nod, the wink, and gestures as well as through the implications of a carefully chosen word or a surprising turn of phrase. What seems clear and simple on the surface is never so simple for the perceptive reader because of the obscure and complex nature of the fourth Gospel. Various textual features such as double meaning, misunderstanding, irony, dualism, and symbolism serve the implied author as more than stage props for his story to lead the reader to a different point of view. These sub-surface signals allow the Gospel to be read again and again with profit and pleasure. I shall explore in the forthcoming pages the use of these above mentioned narrative devices in 3,3-10 to understand their meaning further.

i. Double Meaning

α. Double Meaning on the Basis of the Greek Alone

The alternative meanings of ἄνωθεν are very clear and very much debated.[144] One group of scholars claims that the word can only mean 'again' or 'anew.' These commentators[145]

---

[142] J. Nissen, "Rebirth and Community. A Spiritual and Social Reading of John 3,1-21," in: P. Bilde, H. K. Nielsen and J. P. Sorensen (eds.), *Apocryphon Severini. FS Sören Giversen* (Aarhus 1993) 121-39.

[143] Stibbe, *Storyteller*, 27.

[144] B. Lindars ("John and the Synoptic Gospels: A Test Case," *GrJ* 27 [1980/81] 291) observes that, in the NT, ἄνωθεν has the following meanings: 'from the top' (Mt. 27,51; Mk. 15,38; and Jn. 19,23); 'from above' (Jn. 3,31 and 19,11; and Jas. 1,17 and 3,15.17); 'from the first' (Lk. 1,3 and Acts 26,5); and 'again' (Gal. 4,9).

[145] T. Zahn, *Das Evangelium des Johannes* (KNT 4) (Leipzig ⁶1921) 183f.; and R. Bultmann, *Das Evangelium des Johannes* (KEK 2) (Göttingen ²¹1986) 95, n. 2.

83

follow the early Syriac (Peshito), Memphitic, Ethiopic, and the Latin versions including the Vulgate, which translates ἄνωθεν with *denuo*, and words corresponding to it.[146] Luther uses the translation '*von neuem*' also following this trend. These commentators may point to Gal. 4,9, where ἄνωθεν is used by Paul to mean 'again.' They may also point to Justin,[147] who gives one of the earliest patristic citations of this verse, substituting ἀναγεννασθαι for the more ambiguous term chosen by the fourth evangelist.

The other group of scholars claims that the word can mean only 'from above.' These scholars[148] point to the Hebrew word מִלְמָעְלָה (Josh. 3,13.16) meaning 'from above' which, probably, lied behind ἄνωθεν. מִלְמָעְלָה is not capable of meaning other than 'from above.' Such an argument always seems tenuous, because it involves the postulation of a term as antecedent. The evangelist emphasises that the birth mentioned is a spiritual begetting of divine origin. The Greek writers from Origen on generally use this translation. In addition, there are the translations of the Harclean Syriac, Armenian, and the Gothic versions, not to mention the Züricher Bibel which uses '*von oben herab*.' The context of the fourth Gospel provides other uses of the word ἄνωθεν, all of which are translated as 'from above.' In 3,31 and 19,11 the reference is to divine origin. In 19,23 the reference is to the continuous weave in Jesus' robe 'from the top' throughout.

The third group of scholars follow the course suggested by Bauer in his lexicon: "3. *wiederum, von neuem, ... Absichtl. doppelsinnig* ἀνὰ γεννηθῆναι '*von oben her*' *gezeugt und so wiederum geboren werden, 3:3,7.*"[149]

In my opinion, ἄνωθεν is capable of two meanings and here, it has both. It may mean 'from above' and 'anew, afresh, again.' The begetting required is certainly a second birth, but it is not a mere repetition of a person's second birth, but a begetting from God, from above. The adverb ἄνωθεν connected with the verb γεννηθῆναι has a chronological or temporal (again) and a local or spatial (from above) meaning. What is meant is not a choice between the two. The misunderstanding of Nicodemus, as if it is dealing with a birth ἐκ τῆς κοιλίας τῆς μητρὸς (3,4), is concerned only with the verb γεννηθῆναι, and not the interpretation of ἄνωθεν in the sense of δεύτερον. According to the opinion of the evangelist, it is the mind of Jesus that the verse here deals with a real rebirth (cf. 3,7). There is no doubt that here, as in 3,31 and 19,11, ἄνωθεν means also 'from above,' and Nicodemus has not understood it.

---

[146] Cf. Westcott, I, 63.

[147] Justin the Martyr, *Apology*, I, 61.

[148] Most exegetes understand the term in 3,3.7 has having the meaning 'from above/from God.' See Strack-Billerbeck, II, 421; Richter, *Studien*, 338; Schnackenburg, *Gospel*, I , 366-68; D. Mollat, *L'Évangile selon Saint Jean* (BiJer) (Paris ³1973); and F. Büchsel, *Das Evangelium nach Johannes* (NTD 4) (Göttingen ⁵1949), *ad loc*. Lindars (*Gospel*, 150-51) rigorously defends the meaning 'from above' as the only sense intended. However, I must point out that Lindars is not fully correct when he says: "The misunderstanding does not depend on the two possible meanings of ἄνωθεν, but on a literal, as opposed to a metaphorical idea of birth."

[149] W. Bauer, *Griechisch-Deutsches Wörterbuch zu den Schriften des Neuen Testaments* (Berlin, New York ⁵1971) *ad loc*. In this latter group, I find Barrett, O. Cullmann ("Der johanneische Gebrauch doppeldeutiger Ausdrücke als Schlüssel zum Verständnis des vierten Evangeliums," in: his *Vorträge und Aufsätze* 1925-1962 [Zürich 1966] 176-86), A. M. Hunter (*The Gospel according to John* [CNEB] [Cambridge 1965]), R. Tasker, *The Gospel according to St. John. An Introduction and Commentary* [TNTC] [London 1960]); and Blank (*Johannes*, 227).

With this reference to the local or spatial meaning ('from above') the following verses (12ff.) show the Christological foundation of rebirth: "No one has ascended into heaven except the one who descended from heaven, the Son of Man" (3,13). The interconnectedness of these two meanings is, thus, clear: in order to be born *again*, the Son of Man who has come down (whose coming according to 7,39 and 16,7 contains also his exaltation) from heaven must re-ascend into heaven, so that the begetting by the Spirit *from above* is possible (3,5).[150] The adverb ἄνωθεν comes to emphasise not only what may be visibly happening, a begetting out of water, but also what happens unseen – a begetting from above through the Holy Spirit. Nowhere does the evangelist choose between the two meanings. By means of this literary device the fourth evangelist is able to synthesise two fundamental truths of the Christian experience: the believer must be begotten again/anew from above.

β. Double Meaning in a Parabolic Saying

The fourth evangelist has developed the use of a short parabolic saying which involves a double meaning.[151] This use relies on a primary meaning to the word for the literal part of the saying. The application or figurative element comes from the secondary meaning of the word. Both aspects of the parabolic saying are bound up with the actual meanings of the same words. A good illustration of this is found in the short parabolic saying contained in 3,8: "The wind blows where it chooses, and you hear the sound of it, but you do not know where it comes from or where it goes. So it is with everyone who is born of the Spirit." This saying has a direct parallel in Eccles. 11,5: "Just as you do not know how the breath (πνεῦμα) comes to the bones in the mother's womb, so you do not know the work of God, who makes everything." Here I find the same ambiguity. J. H. Bernard shows the possibility of translating the noun πνεῦμα as *wind* or *spirit* and the verb πνέω either as the action of the wind or of the spirit.[152] I find here a word picture and its meaning is so closely united that the two meanings cannot be separated. The unknown action of the wind expresses the unknowable actions of the Spirit. The parabolic saying in 3,8 speaks of the atmospheric element (wind) to explain the mystery of the divine life engendered in a person through the power of the Spirit. The mystery of the wind is not to be compared to the action of the Spirit in the world but to the behaviour of the person begotten by the Spirit.[153] However, the double meaning cannot apply to those γεγεννημένος ἐκ τοῦ πνεύματος.

The meaning here is not, 'as the wind blows so the spirit works.' The relationship between wind and spirit in the fourth Gospel is not that of the one between picture and reality, but more real and concrete and it is proved also by 20,22, where the resurrected

---

[150] Cf. Grese, 677-93.

[151] See E. Richard, "Expressions of Double Meaning and their Function in the Gospel of John," *NTS* 31 (1985) 103.

[152] See Bernard, I, 264. The use of 'πνεῦμα' is readily understood in view of the imagery of the passage; however, the occurrence of 'πνέω' in this context must be viewed as intentional ambiguity since the fourth evangelist could have employed 'ἐμφυσάω' (breathe upon), as he does in 20,22: "He breathed on them and said to them, 'Receive the Holy Spirit.'" See also Cullmann, "Johanneische Gebrauch," 364; Richard, *op. cit.*, 102; and J. D. Thomas, "A Translation Problem – John 3:8," *RestQ* 24 (1981) 219-24.

[153] B. Buetubela, "Jn 3,8: L'esprit saint ou le vent naturel?," *RAT* 4 (1980) 63.

Lord *breaths* (ἐνεφύσησεν) to impart the Holy Spirit to his disciples. Acts 2,2 also stands as a proof that the Holy Spirit is not only comparable to the wind, but just like wind. As water and Spirit (ἐξ ὕδατος καὶ πνεύματος – 3,5) are related, and in the fourth Gospel, 'water' is explicitly a symbol of the 'Spirit' (cf. 7,38-39), the word πνεῦμα has both meanings 'wind' and 'Spirit.' Hence, here Jesus speaks of a 'begetting by the Spirit' as well as a 'begetting out of water and the wind.'[154]

This close union of terminology brings the dilemma of the translator once more clearly into view. This situation presents no problem in the Hebrew (רוּחַ), Aramaic (רוּחָא), Syriac, or Greek where the words for wind and spirit are the same.[155] But when one comes to the Latin, one is beyond the languages where the terminology permits the double meaning. Thus, the Latin translators have been forced to make a choice.[156] The Vulgate uses *"spiritus ubi vult spirat,"* but immediately the double meaning is lost. The English bible translators have been forced to make a choice, which they have usually done with 'the wind blows where it wills.' They also have lost the force of the double meaning. One of the deficiencies of translation comes when one attempts to bring out the full meaning of terminology into another language that does not carry exactly the meanings of the original. The double meaning is a refinement of the technique the fourth evangelist uses to develop the historical interpretative elements of his theology. It shows the words of the text are carefully, not carelessly, chosen and bring new depth of meaning to the text.

ii. Misunderstanding

Misunderstanding is a literary device used by the composer of the fourth Gospel to assist the presentation of his story. First a statement is made, then it is given a preliminary examination by being misunderstood, and then it is restated in a more emphatic and effective form. It may even be argued that misunderstanding is a necessary feature of the composer's theological intention. Through form-critical analysis Leroy defines 'misunderstanding' in the fourth Gospel as *concealed riddles*[157] which, according to me, is too rigid a definition. That misunderstanding arises out of an expression having a double meaning and the interlocutor choosing the one not meant by Jesus is, in my opinion, incorrect. If one examines closely he/she will find that the misunderstanding of the interlocutor arises very rarely from a word having double meaning.[158] Generally it is the whole statement of Jesus that is misinterpreted; Jesus speaks of spiritual realities and the interlocutor understands them on the material plane. In general one observes the following

---

[154] Cullmann, *op. cit.*

[155] See G. Schwarz, "'Der Wind weht, wo er will'?," *BN* 63 (1992) 48, see also M. Görg, "Vom Wehen des Pneuma," *BN* 66 (1993) 5-9.

[156] See J. Doignon, "L'esprit souffle où il veut (Jn III,8) dans la plus ancienne tradition patristique latine," *RSPhTh* 62 (1978) 345-59.

[157] H. Leroy, "Das johanneische Mißverständnis als literarische Form," *BiLe* 9 (1968) 196-207. According to him, all the misunderstandings arise from a concept with a twofold meaning (*einem doppeldeutigen Begriff*) which usually belongs to the peculiar vocabulary (*Sondersprache*) of the Johannine Community; see also his *Rätsel und Mißverständnis. Ein Beitrag zur Formgeschichte des Johannesevangeliums* (BBB 30) (Bonn 1968) 46 and 157-60. For a criticism of Leroy see D. A. Carson, "Understanding Misunderstandings in the Fourth Gospel," *TynB* 33 (1982) 72-78.

[158] The only two actual cases of the sort are the expression 'γεννηθῆναι ἄνωθεν' in 3,3 and the verb 'ὑψόω' in 3,14; 8,28 and 12,32.34.

characteristic elements in this literary device called 'misunderstanding:' 1) Jesus makes a statement which is ambiguous, metaphorical, or contains a double meaning in his conversations; 2) his dialogue partner responds either in terms of the literal meaning of Jesus' statement or by a question, scoff, challenge or request which shows that he/she has not grasped the intended deeper meaning of Jesus' words; 3) at times Jesus explains, in other instances the narrator comments or the conversation moves on with the implicit assumption that the reader can resolve the misunderstanding. Misunderstandings, therefore, provide an opportunity to explain the meaning of Jesus' words and develop significant themes further.

Moreover, the effect on the reader is greater than if the meaning had, merely, been stated plainly from the beginning. The reader who resolves the Gospel's misunderstandings, finds himself or herself drawn again toward a fuller comprehension of the narrator's theological point of view. The fourth evangelist develops and integrates misunderstanding into his Gospel artistically. Besides, misunderstanding arises from his concept of revelation; inevitably those who did not accept Jesus misunderstand him.[159] One of the distinctive features of the fourth Gospel is the frequency with which its secondary characters misunderstand Jesus. Note that Nicodemus sees in Jesus a 'Rabbi' or 'a man come from God,' (3,2). If he had penetrated beneath the surface he would have seen its truth. He is not prepared to dare; he is submerged in his traditions; the fear of danger to his position and the consequences of losing his social standing block his sight from seeing the truth. In short I can say that the misunderstanding motif is historically based, dramatically developed and has a pedagogical purpose ('pädagogisches Mittel'[160]) in the structure of the fourth Gospel. What is important is not whether misunderstanding is described as a 'motif,' 'technique,' or 'device' but the recognition of its frequency, variability and effects. Hence, my concern is to explore the function of misunderstanding and its effect upon the reader in this sub-unit.

α. Γεννηθῇ ἄνωθεν

Mendner thinks that the Pharisee seems to be primitive and does not have the minimum idea of logic.[161] Jesus tells Nicodemus 'unless one is begotten ἄνωθεν he cannot see the kingdom of God' (3,3). It is considered the *locus classicus* of the use of misunderstanding in the fourth Gospel. Which is the meaning intended here – one or the other, or even both? Jesus' speech is apparently plain and open, but his words are a trap for those not intended to understand? Stibbe calls Nicodemus "the embodiment of misunderstanding."[162] He takes

---

[159] Cf. Vouga, *Le cadre historique*, 32-33 and 36. Becker (*Johannes*, I, 135-36) contends that misunderstanding (*Mißverständnis*) is characteristic of unbelieving Jews, and is to be sharply distinguished from the non-understanding (*Unverständnis*) of the disciples, who do not misunderstand by adopting an earthly meaning, but simply lack instruction – a lack Jesus promptly makes up.

[160] Cf. F. Moser, "Mißverständnis und Ironie in der johanneischen Argumentation und ihr Gebrauch in der heutigen pfarramtlichen Praxis," in: M. Rose (ed.), *Johannesstudien. Interdisziplinäre Zugänge zum Johannesevangelium. Freundesgabe der Theologischen Fakultät der Universität Neuchâtel für Jean Zumstein* (Zürich 1991) 53.

[161] Mendner, 298.

[162] Stibbe, *John*, 54. Against this view R. H. Strachan (*The Fourth Gospel. Its Significance and Environment* [London ³1960] 133) contends that Nicodemus, probably, understood only too well both the spiritual and moral demand made on him; he must have understood that to be born when he is old means a

the wrong meaning of the term 'again' and understands birth in a literal, physical or earthly sense.[163] But the misunderstanding of Nicodemus does not arise only from a temporal understanding of the adverb ἄνωθεν instead of giving to it also a spatial sense. The real misunderstanding of Nicodemus consists in the fact that he falsely understands the preceding word, the verb γεννάω, which could mean to 'be born' or 'begotten.' He interprets the verb as a *birth* from a mother's womb. It is precisely this choice of Nicodemus which makes him to interpret the adverb ἄνωθεν with a temporal meaning (again). In fact, it is easy to imagine a new birth, but not a begetting from above.

There is no protective intervention by the narrator as in the case of the previous misunderstanding in 2,21. Instead, Jesus moves on to restate the matter in other terms: "unless one is born of water and the Spirit" (3,5).[164] In 3,5-6 Jesus corrects this misinterpretation of the verb γεννάω. It is not a new birth in flesh which would necessitate an entrance into the mother's womb to be born a second time; it is rather an entrance (being begotten) into the kingdom of God, which necessitates a begetting out of water and the Spirit (3,5), a new begetting from above. The double meaning (temporal and spatial) of the adverb ἄνωθεν must be maintained but only one meaning of the *verb* must be retained. I would like to paraphrase the statement of Jesus with the help of the following comparison: 'just as a birth in flesh is necessary to enter into this world, a spiritual begetting (from above, out of water and the Spirit) is necessary to enter (be begotten) into the kingdom of God.' To pass from this world to the kingdom of God, a new begetting, not as in the case of the first birth, but one from above is necessary. In choosing exclusively the meaning 'to be born' for the verb γεννάω, Nicodemus had no other choice but to consider the adverb ἄνωθεν as involving a second birth (born again).

Jesus rectifies the misinterpretation of Nicodemus further: "Do not be astonished that I said to you: Δεῖ ὑμᾶς γεννηθῆναι ἄνωθεν" (3,7). The actual answer of Jesus is to be found in 3,8: though the spiritual begetting is a mystery it is not far away; it is like the wind whose sound one hears (indication of reality) but one does not know whence it comes or whither it goes (mysterious nature).[165] Nicodemus must be, therefore, not surprised; the Spirit can beget a man again from above even if he is old. The character of misunderstanding as a misinterpretation of a 'heavenly' metaphor[166] with an 'earthly' meaning is implied by a still later response of Jesus: "If I have told you about *earthly* things and you do not believe, how can you believe if I tell you about *heavenly* things?" (3,12).

β. Effects of Misunderstanding on the Reader

The most significant function of misunderstanding is to teach readers how to read the Gospel and to enforce a marked distinction between those who understand the elusive implication of Jesus' revelatory discourses and those who have rejected Jesus. His purpose

---

revolutionary change of a man's personal relationship to God and toward his fellows. But the majority of exegetes see a misunderstanding here on the part of Nicodemus.

[163] Cf. V. Hasler, "Glauben und Erkennen im Johannesevangelium. Strukturale und hermeneutische Überlegungen," *EvTh* 50 (1990) 285.

[164] RSV translation.

[165] Cf. the elaborate study of M. A. Chevallier, *Souffle de Dieu. Le Saint-Esprit dans le Nouveau Testament* (PoTh 54) (Paris 1990).

[166] Cf. J. G. van der Watt, "The Dynamics of Metaphor," *SNTU* 23 (1998) 43-44.

in writing, as he has always said, was to foster belief "that Jesus is the Messiah, the Son of God" (20,31).[167] Since the Jews represent complete lack of understanding of Jesus from the point of view of the fourth evangelist, it is not surprising that they are the victims of misunderstanding. Jesus, the heavenly revealer, is totally incomprehensible to those whose understanding is bound to the earth. In this respect, Nicodemus is the paradigm of the Jews' inability to grasp the meaning of Jesus' metaphorical discourse.[168] The character of Nicodemus, in my opinion, is not arbitrarily chosen; the misunderstanding sharpens his characterisation and enhances the representative value of his character. Besides, the device of misunderstanding serves partly to show the progress from darkness to light, and partly to warn and to persuade the reader that plain statements conceal complex realities. [169]

A further effect of the misunderstandings is to remove the doubt or misperception about key points in the Christology and soteriology of the fourth Gospel. Nicodemus and other *dramatis personae* do not offer a model of how one is to understand. They serve rather as representatives of the consequences of failure to do so. Jesus' responses to them guide the reader around some of the Gospel's characteristic metaphors. Misunderstanding is related to the use of irony in the Gospel.

iii. Irony

The fourth evangelist has been characterised repeatedly as a master of irony.[170] The silent communication between narrator and reader assumes its most fascinating form in the ironies of his Gospel. One of the most comprehensive treatments of irony in the fourth Gospel is the dissertation by P. D. Duke.[171] The principal obstacle in the way of a simple definition of irony is the fact that it is not a simple phenomenon. Jesus' exhortation, "do not judge by appearances, but judge with right judgement" (7,24) could be considered a sort of definition of irony. In irony though, on the surface level, something appears to be true, in reality its opposite is true. It is a matter of perception and it must, to become manifest, be seen by an observer or it does not exist. The foundational irony of the fourth

---

[167] See E. Tobler, *Vom Mißverstehen zum Glauben. Ein theologisch-literarischer Versuch zum vierten Evangelium und zu Zeugnissen seiner Wirkung* (EHS.T 395) (Bern, Frankfurt, New York, Paris 1990).

[168] Cf. R. Kysar, "The Making of Metaphor: Another Reading of John 3.1-15," in: Segovia, *What is John?*, 21-41.

[169] K. Grayston, "Who Misunderstands the Johannine Misunderstandings?," *ScrB* 20 (1989) 14.

[170] W. A. Meeks ("The Divine Agent and His Counterfeit in Philo and the Fourth Gospel," in: E. S. Fiorenza [ed.], *Aspects of Religious Propaganda in Judaism and Early Christianity* [Notre Dame 1976] 59) refers to him as "that unknown master of irony and drama."

[171] Duke (*Irony*) shows how irony is used repeatedly in the fourth Gospel to lead the reader into that dimension of truth about Jesus which most of the characters within the narrative world seem to miss. Among the recent articles on the treatment of irony in the fourth Gospel the following four studies are interesting: S. D. Moore, "Rifts in (a reading of) the Fourth Gospel, or: Does Johannine irony still collapse in a reading that draws attention to itself?," *Neotest.* 23 (1989) 5-17; it is a critique of Johannine irony. He contends that there is no homogeneity in Johannine irony. G. Johnston, "*Ecce Homo!* Irony in the Christology of the Fourth Evangelist," in: L. D. Hurst and N. T. Wright (eds.), *The Glory of Christ in the New Testament. Studies in Christology* (Oxford 1987) 125-50; it is not a comprehensive study of irony but restricted to Christological questions. J. E. Botha, "The Case of Johannine Irony Reopened I: The Problematic Current Situation," *Neotest.* 25 (1991) 209-20; it is a call to reconsider Johannine irony. He criticises the treatments of Duke and Culpepper on irony in their respective works. See also K. Scholtissek, "Ironie und Rollenwechsel im Johannesevangelium," *ZNW* 89 (1998) 235-55.

Gospel is that the Jews rejected the Messiah they eagerly expected: "He came to his own home, and his own people received him not" (1,11).

α. Participants of Irony

Irony usually has three participants: the ironist, the victim, and the reader.[172] Through the use of this device the implied author (ironist) seems to smile, wink, and raise his eye-brows as the story progresses. He guides the implied reader into responding with understanding and faith where certainly the Jews misunderstand and disbelieve.

The Jews, especially their teachers like Nicodemus, Pharisees, and priests are the most frequent victims of irony. They should have recognised the Messiah; hence, there is wilfulness in their blindness: they 'love darkness rather than light,' 'their deeds are evil' (3,19), "they loved human glory more than the glory that comes from God" (12,43; cf. 5,44) and, in fact, they see but reject what they see (9,39-41). The greater the victim's blindness the more striking the irony.

Never is the reader the victim of irony in the fourth Gospel. As he/she shares more and more common ground with the implied author, he/she simultaneously feels the duality of his position as observer over against the victimised characters.[173] He/she is able to see the Jews' blindness and Jesus' glory through the eyes of the evangelist. The reader – who sees and hears – understands that the narrator conveys more than he says and that characters like Nicodemus do not understand what is happening or what they are saying. The shock of incongruity which the reader often observes in irony creates a detachment between the reader and the values and appearances of the unbelieving world. Irony is calculated, therefore, primarily to include readers among the circle of believers. It is not designed to extract the truth, but to expose it and to include the observer in the circle of those who have recognised it. In short, irony for the fourth evangelist consists in the fact that the reader can see that Jesus should be the true teacher and the expected Messiah; hence, Christological in purpose.

β. Instances of Irony in 3,1-10

The fourth Gospel's pervasive use of dramatic irony, in which the contrast between appearances and reality is underscored, is to be found in the ignorant speeches of the characters like Nicodemus. For such an irony to be fully effective, the reader need to know at the outset how the play would end.[174] Hence, MacRae is right in his observation that the heart of the fourth evangelist's theology is itself the irony of the Logos becoming flesh.[175] The revelation of Jesus' *identity* at the outset (prologue) provides, therefore, a firm footing for the reader's reconstruction of hidden meanings suppressed behind the backs or over the heads of the characters (e.g. the heavenly origin of Jesus [cf. 3,13.31], his identity [cf. 3,2], and his mission through death and glorification [cf. 3,16-17]). Although it lies at the core of most of the ironic passages in the fourth Gospel, the *identity* of Jesus (Son of Man and

---

[172] Culpepper, *Anatomy*, 177.

[173] Cf. Muecke, *Compass of Irony*, 218.

[174] Koester, *Symbolism*, 36.

[175] MacRae, 94.

Son of God) and the various ways it is manifested and announced are frequently the specific object of irony.

The basic feature of every irony is a "contrast between a reality and an appearance."[176] Nicodemus, for example, appears to *know* who Jesus is and calls him 'a teacher come from God' (3,2), but Nicodemus' subsequent comments reveal that he really does *not know* what he is talking about (3,10). Irony warns that appearances are deceiving and that truth often runs the contrary to ordinary perceptions.

The mention of the categorical οἴδαμεν ('we know') of Nicodemus (3,2) constitutes a case of irony. Many indications justify this affirmation. First of all, the reasoning of Jesus in 3,10 places the stress on the 'not-knowing' of Nicodemus. Secondly, I have explained already that the reasoning of Nicodemus contains an apparent and unacceptable theological error in the eyes of his colleagues among Pharisees and Scribes: the signs do not indicate necessarily the presence of God (cf. 9,16.24.29). Finally, one can easily note that, on the lips of the Jews, the verb οἴδαμεν is, almost always, used ironically (cf. 6,42: "*We know* his father and mother;" 7,27: "*We know* where he comes from;" 9,24: "*We know* that this man is a sinner;" 9,29: "*We know* that God spoke to Moses, *we do not know* where he is from"). From all these examples, it is evident that the οἴδαμεν of Nicodemus in 3,2 is pregnant with irony. It is the mode of the evangelist to attract the attention of the reader to the insufficient character of his Christological confession.

Ironic development of various aspects of the theme of Jesus being rejected by his own (cf. 1,11) permeates the narrative. The Jews should recognise Jesus, because Moses and the prophets bore witness to him (1,45). The responsibility and culpability of the leaders of the Jews is repeatedly driven home with sharp thrusts from irony. Nicodemus, a *teacher of Israel*, cannot understand even earthly things (3,10.12). How can he, then, understand the final meeting place of heaven and earth (cf. 1,51 and 3,13-14) – Jesus who is God and man, and the expected Messiah?

γ. **Purpose of Irony**

The evangelist's use of irony is to make the relationship between reader and narrator attractive.[177] Through his irony, the evangelist lifts the reader to the point of view of the narrator so that the reader knows what others in the story have not yet discovered and can feel the humour and bite of meanings they miss. Irony creates an intimate relationship among those who are committed to faith in Jesus. In the hands of the fourth evangelist irony is, therefore, not a *sword*, but used more like a *net* in which readers are caught and drawn toward the goal of his Gospel (20,31). Finally, I must say that irony is so crucial to the message of the fourth evangelist that unable to grasp it is unable to grasp his Gospel.

iv. **Symbolism**

No understanding of the fourth Gospel is possible without an appreciation of the part played by symbolism as the whole of the fourth Gospel, narrative and discourse, is bound together by an intricate network of symbolism. Misunderstanding is a dramatic portrayal of

---

[176] Muecke, *Irony*, 30.

[177] Culpepper (*op. cit.*, 180) says that irony "sweetens and spices the fellowship between reader and narrator."

the plight of those whose understanding is limited to the earthly. The ironies of the story more subtly invite the reader to share the implied author's higher vantage point. Symbolism, on the other hand, opens even richer and more stimulating views into the order and mystery of the world above. Culpepper sees in them "the ladder on which readers, like the angels of Jacob's dream, may ascend and descend while moving to and from the heaven opened by the story"[178] (cf. 1,51). Symbols, like the images, metaphors, motifs, and themes to which they are related, often carry the principal burden of the narrative and provide implicit commentary and directional signals for the reader. Unlike a sign, a symbol is not arbitrary but bears some inherent analogical relationship to that which it symbolises. The reader understands that the symbol means or expresses something more or something else than its plain or superficial meaning.

Besides separating personal from impersonal symbols, W. Hinderer observes two categories of impersonal symbols: core symbols and peripheral symbols.[179] The core symbols are those whose centrality is demonstrated by their higher frequency of recurrence and their appearance in more important contexts. Three such core symbols of the fourth Gospel are light, water, and bread. Each of these points to Jesus' revelatory role and carries a heavy thematic load. To these are related several co-ordinate symbols, metaphors, and concepts in different passages: darkness, flesh, life, wine, etc. Subordinate symbols can also be gathered around each. For example, among the subordinate symbols for light are lamps, fires, torches, lanterns, day (and night), morning, and seeing. They are drawn from everyday life, but derive their significance from the rich associations they have acquired in the OT and apocalyptic literature.

J. Painter observes that the symbols of the fourth Gospel are drawn from those applied to the Law by Judaism and are *re-interpreted Christologically*. They are "focal points of the conflict"[180] with Judaism and "vehicles of revelation."[181] Symbols point to Jesus, who is himself a symbolic revelation of God.[182] For example, recognising Jesus as the Son of God is a symbolic operation which, by means of faith, connects the past and present, Jesus and the Son of God.

Among the symbols that are present in 2,23-3,36 *water* and *light* are the core symbols. In this section, I shall study the symbolism of water alone in a rather detailed manner as there is a lot of controversy about the interpretation of this verse (3,5) among scholars, and treat the rest of the symbols (world, light, truth, life, etc.) under dualistic symbols.

♦ **Symbolism of Water**

The symbol of water appears surprisingly frequently and with the most varied associations of any of the fourth evangelist's symbols. It is a dominant motif and an expanding core

---

[178] Culpepper, *op. cit.*, 181.

[179] W. Hinderer, "Theory, Conception, and Interpretation of the Symbol," in: J. Strelka (ed.), *Perspectives in Literary Symbolism* (YBCC 1) (University Park 1968) 108.

[180] J. Painter, *John: Witness and Theologian* (London ²1979) 20-21; 48 and 139.

[181] J. Painter, "Johannine Symbols: A Case Study in Epistemology," *JTSA* 27 (1979) 32.

[182] Cf. X. Léon-Dufour, "Toward a Symbolic Reading of the Fourth Gospel," *NTS* 27 (1980/81) 442.

symbol in the fourth Gospel.[183] There are conversations about water, water jars, rivers, wells, springs, the sea, pools, basins, thirst, and drink in the fourth Gospel. Context and discourse provide clues to the symbolic value of water in the various passages.[184]

The symbol of water binds the first four chapters of the fourth Gospel. Early in the Gospel, water is associated with baptism and *cleansing*. Water is mentioned in relation to the baptism administered by the Baptist and the Holy Spirit in 1,26.31.33 and in connection with Jewish *purification* rites in 2,6. Water as a means of washing or external cleansing points to the inner cleansing which occurs when one accepts the Baptist's testimony. But it is given temporary or secondary status by the promise of cleansing by the Spirit (cf. 1,33).

Symbolism in 2,23-3,36 is *developed gradually*. One notices how the narrator initially makes the suggestive observation that Nicodemus comes to Jesus 'by night' (3,2) but does not disclose the significance of the darkness until later (cf. 3,19-21). Similarly, water is mentioned only briefly at the beginning of the chapter in connection with new birth (3,5),[185] but its import is made clearer in the subsequent discussion on baptism (3,22-26). The theme of water developed in Jn. 1-2 reaches a confluence in Jn. 3. The two sub-themes flow together in Jn. 3, when a dispute over purification breaks out between the disciples of the Baptist and a Jew(s). As the debate subsides, the significance of water becomes clearer through a connection with the baptism administered by Jesus and his disciples (3,22 and 4,2). Jesus tells Nicodemus, "Very truly, I tell you, no one can enter the kingdom of God without being *born of water and Spirit*" (3,5). There is difference of opinion as to what 'γεννηθῇ ἐξ ὕδατος καὶ πνεύματος' means. Interpretations may be grouped according to the following six categories: ritualistic, symbolic, physiological, dualistic, cosmological and figurative.

α. Ritualistic Views of Water

The sudden reference to water in the dialogue between Jesus and Nicodemus appears to be peculiar, but the wider literary context shows that water connotes *ritual washing*. Ritualistic views of water fall into either of the two levels of interpretation: (a) those which assume a basic contrast between water and spirit, water relating to an aspect of Jewish ceremonial legalism and spirit referring to Christian baptism: and (b) water and spirit seen as a double reference to Christian baptism.[186]

---

[183] Cf. T. Söding, "Wiedergeburt aus Wasser und Geist. Anmerkungen zur Symbolsprache des Johannes-evangeliums am Beispiel des Nikodemusgesprächs (Joh 3,1-21)," in: K. Kertelge (ed.), *Metaphorik und Mythos im Neuen Testament* (QD 126) (Basel, Freiburg, Wien 1990) 168-219.

[184] See the recent work of L. P. Jones (*The Symbol of Water in the Gospel of John* [JSNT.S 145] [Sheffield 1997]) on this subject.

[185] For a summary discussion on the relationship between water and Spirit in 3,5, see G. M. Burge, *The Anointed Community: The Holy Spirit in the Johannine Tradition* (Grand Rapids 1987) 161-65.

[186] For a discussion see P. J. Bayens, *'Begotten of Water and Spirit' (John 3:5): Baptism in the Johannine Tradition* (DissA Marquette) (Milwaukee 1993).

a) Jewish Ritualism

i) Anti-Essene Polemic

The phrase "γεννηθῇ ἐξ ὕδατος καὶ πνεύματος" (3,5) is seen by Mowry as an explanatory note of cultic character, introduced by the fourth evangelist to teach the Essenes that they must move beyond the legalism of their ceremonial washings (ὕδωρ) and enter the realm of new birth (ὕδωρ and πνεῦμα) through Christian baptism.[187] However, although the importance of purification at Qumran may be related to the fourth evangelist's emphasis on water, the internal evidence offered for such anti-Essene polemic is not conclusive. Besides, Nicodemus being clearly stated as a Pharisee would be does not support the view that the fourth evangelist's main purpose was to refute Essenism.

ii) Jewish Religion

This is a favourite interpretation of D. W. B. Robinson, who bases his view on the theological coherence of Jn. 1-4.[188] According to him, γεννηθῇ ἐξ ὕδατος, characterises the entire system of Jewish ceremonial practice while πνεῦμα represents the transforming work of God through the Spirit. Couched in a parable, Jesus is teaching that Judaism is without life but for the work of the Spirit as depicted in Ezek. 37,8-10.

Endorsement for this view is found in Jn. 1 where the Baptist, as the last representative of the old religion with his 'water' baptism, is set in contrast with the coming work of the Spirit (1,26. 31. 33).[189] In Jn. 2,6 water stands for the purificatory observances of the Jews; in Jn. 3 born of the flesh is contrasted with born of the spirit; and in Jn. 4 worship centred around the patriarchal well of Jacob is contrasted with worship in spirit and truth (4,23-24).

Though this seems to be an attractive solution to the strange phrase, it is not tenable for the following seven reasons: i) It breaks the parallelism of 3,3.5.6b and 7. ii) The single preposition ἐκ and the conjunction καὶ form a conceptual unity, not two contrasting entities (γεννηθῇ ἐξ ὕδατος καὶ πνεύματος). iii) Water and spirit are not contrasted, as in 1,26.31.33, but co-ordinated (καὶ). iv) It would be plausible only if Nicodemus had made some reference to Jewish ritualism in 3,4. v) It agrees neither with the notion γεννηθῇ of the σάρξ (3,4) nor with γεννηθῇ of the πνεῦμα. vi) The comparison in Jn. 4 is between two types of living water (4,10) – physical and spiritual – and not between water and spirit. vii) Γεννηθῇ ἐξ ὕδατος to be understood as being 'born under the law' has no contemporary supportive evidence.

iii) Baptism of John the Baptist

Some other advocate the view that 'γεννηθῇ ἐξ ὕδατος καὶ πνεύματος' refers explicitly to the rite of water baptism administered by the Baptist. Westcott contends that it can scarcely be questioned that as Nicodemus heard these words, *water* carried with it a reference to the

---

[187] Cf. L. Mowry, "The Dead Sea Scrolls and the Background for the Gospel of John," *BA* 17 (1954) 92.

[188] D. W. B. Robinson, "Born of Water and Spirit: Does John 3:5 Refer to Baptism," *RTR* 25 (1966) 20.

[189] Of the twenty-one instances of the term 'ὕδωρ' in the Gospel, the first three occur, not surprisingly in Jn. 1 in connection with the baptising activity of John the Baptist. In all three instances, the word occurs in the same prepositional phrase 'ἐν ὕδατι.' Furthermore this phrase is used in connection with the action done by, not to, John the Baptist. He baptises and he does so with water; see M. C. de Boer, "Jesus the Baptiser: 1 John 5:5-8 and the Gospel of John," *JBL* 107 (1988) 94.

baptism of the Baptist which was a divinely appointed rite (1,33).[190] As a Jew, this would have been the only baptism with which Nicodemus would have been familiar. Moreover, it would be relevant since Nicodemus would have rejected this rite being himself a Pharisee. As a leader of the Jews (cf. 3,1) in Jerusalem, he belongs to the group that sent an enquiry commission to question the Baptist about his identity and baptismal practices (1,19.24). His baptism was also producing at that time such a sensation in Palestine that the mere mention of *water* would, certainly, have immediately turned Nicodemus' thoughts to that baptism.

Although contextual support is found in the conjunction of water and Spirit baptism in 1,26.31.33 and in the references to the baptism of the Baptist in 3,23, in my opinion, Nicodemus' response is unintelligible. If Jesus were insisting on the need for Nicodemus to accept the Messianic forerunner's baptism, as a Pharisee he would have rejected a call to repentance (cf. Lk. 7,29-30) – a message common to all the OT prophets. The promise of the outpouring of the Spirit must have been familiar to Nicodemus. Nicodemus' response is not a refusal manifesting an attitude of disobedience but one of misunderstanding (3,4), astonishment (3,7) and incomprehension (3,9-10.12).

One wonders why Jesus uses the obscure ἐξ ὕδατος καὶ πνεύματος, instead of the familiar terminology of 'baptism with water' (1,26.31.33), if he was referring to the baptism of the Baptist. The solution has to be sought in the fact that the baptism of the Baptist is refered to in Jn. 1 and 3 mainly to to show its relative unimportance (1,23.26; cf. 3,30). Moreover, baptism does not fit into the overall theme of spiritual begetting in Jn. 3, for it can hardly be classified as a spiritual source (ἐκ) that can effect an ἄνωθεν begetting.

b) Christian Ritualism

i) Jesus' Baptism

One could also see in water a reference to Jesus' baptism (as a fore-runner and model for Christian baptism) drawing inspiration from the placing together of water and Spirit at the descent of the dove (1,32-34). Though seems agreeable, however, for the Synoptic Gospels which record Jesus' baptism in detail, this view, in my opinion, remains unaccepable for the fourth Gospel which does not describe the event itself, but only its theological import (cf. 1,29-34).

ii) Christian Baptism[191]

The dominant view among exegetes seems to be that water in 3,5 cannot but mean the water of Christian baptism.[192] To quote Dodd: "The instructed Christian reader would imme-

---

[190] Cf. Westcott, I, 108; on the baptism of John the Baptist, see also F. L. Godet, *Commentary on the Gospel of John* (Grand Rapids 1969) I, 379.

[191] Baptism with water was widely practised by early Christians. It is reflected in the letters of Paul, the risen Christ's commission to baptise when making disciples of all nations (Mt. 28,19), the missionary activity of the disciples described in Acts and other sources. The Spirit was regularly associated with baptism, but the mode of connection varied. In some cases people were touched by the Spirit before being baptised (Acts 10,44-48); in other cases the Spirit came through the laying on of hands after baptism (Acts 19,5-6); and in still others the Spirit was said to work in and through baptism (1 Cor. 12,12-13).

[192] J. D. G. Dunn (*Baptism in the Holy Spirit. A Re-examination of the New Testament Teaching on the Gift of the Spirit in relation to Pentacostalism Today* [London 1970]), Beasley-Murray (*Baptism in the New*

diately recognise a reference to baptism as the sacrament through which the Spirit is given to believers and by which they were initiated into that new age of life described as the kingdom of God, historically embodied in the Church."[193]

In spite of the fact that many authors incline to believe that in water there is a hint at Christian baptism, there is difference of opinion concerning the relationship between water and spirit as well as water's exact symbolic significance. For example, Hammer understands Christian baptism as an inseparable union of nature (ὕδωρ) and grace (πνεῦμα) similar to the incarnation. Baptism with water points to the affirmation of creation and human life; baptism with the 'Spirit' to the power of God and that is at work in His creation to bring cleansing and new life.[194] B. A. Mastin and J. N. Sanders understand 3,5 to be the fourth evangelist's own comment on Jesus' words, identifying baptism as the occasion of new birth conveying the gift of the Spirit.[195]

Now the question is whether there is in 'γεννηθῇ ἐξ ὕδατος καὶ πνεύματος' a reference to the Christian sacraments either primarily or secondarily. Based primarily on the sacramental references made elsewhere in the Gospel some respond affirmatively. They are of the opinion that the evangelist has had a lot to say about the Baptist already, especially that the Baptist was sent to baptise with 'water' (1,26.31.33). 1,33 constitutes the relationship between water and spirit. The significance of water is made clearer in the second and parallel scene that explicitly mentions baptism (3,22-30).[196] The episode refers to disputes[197] involving the three different persons or groups that have been prominent in the first three chapters: 1) Jesus and his disciples are baptising in Judea (3,22); a later comment explains that only the disciples performed baptism (4,2),[198] but the text clearly associates the practice of baptism using water with Jesus and his followers.[199] 2) The

---

Testament), Zahn, Bauer, Barrett, Bernard, P. L. Hammer ("Baptism with Water and the Spirit," *ThLS* 8 [1965] 35-43), Dodd, Tasker and Lindars favour this interpretation.

[193] Dodd, *Interpretation*, 309.

[194] Hammer, 38-42. Without a reference to the Spirit the baptismal doctrine of the fourth evangelist is not intelligible; see also I. de la Potterie, "Jesus et Nicodemus: de necessitate generationis ex Spiritu (Jo 3,1-10)," *VD* 47 (1969) 193-214.

[195] B. A. Mastin and J. N. Sanders, *A Commentary on the Gospel according to St. John* (BNTC) (London 1968) 124. For a survey of positions relating water and Spirit, see Vellanickal, 181-86; and Burge, 165-69; see also F. M. Braun, "Le don de Dieu et l'initiation chrétienne (Jn. 2-4)," *NRTh* 86 (1964) 1025-48.

[196] H. Zimmermann ("Die christliche Taufe nach Joh 3. Ein Beitrag zur Logoschristologie des vierten Evangeliums," *Cath[M]* 30 [1976] 84ff.) is convinced that Christian baptism is the central theme of the dialogue with Nicodemus (3,1-12) and of the last witness of the Baptist (3,22-30).

[197] The disputes in this episode show how difficult it is to distinguish the ritual washings used by the Jews, by the disciples of the Baptist, and by the followers of Jesus. The differences are not readily apparent at the level of practice and can be understood only in terms of the contrast between the heavenly and the earthly. The passage places the Baptist's disciples and their Jewish interlocutor in the same category. Despite their disagreements, both seem to approach questions of purification on the same earthly plane. Like other Jews, the followers of the Baptist belong to the earth and speak from an earthly perspective, and both groups resent the popularity of the baptism administered by Jesus and his disciples (3,26 and 4,1-3). Jesus, however, has come from above, and people receive his baptism because it has been granted from heaven (3,27.31). What makes Jesus unique is not the rite that he and his followers perform but his own divine origin – a truth that can be grasped only by faith in the testimony borne to Jesus (3,33).

[198] M. Cambe, "Jésus baptise et cesse de baptiser en Judée (Jean 3/22-4/3)," *ETR* 53 (1978) 98-102; see also G. Gander, "Jean III,22 à IV,3 parle-t-il d'un baptême administré par Jésus?," *RTP* 36 (1948) 133-37.

[199] 3,22.26 and 4,1-2 seem to contradict what is reported in 1,33, where it is also said that Jesus was a baptiser but in a way different from John the Baptist. Whereas the latter baptised with water, Jesus baptised 'with (ἐν) the Holy Spirit.' It may be noted, first of all, that this distinction between the baptism of the Baptist

Baptist is baptising at a place called Aenon near Salim, where there is much water (3,23). Many people come to him for baptism, and some of his disciples are with him. 3) There is a brief but significant mention of a Jew(s) who is engaged in a controversy with the disciples of the Baptist over issues of purification done with water (3,25; cf. 2,6). Jesus' own baptismal ministry is said to have exceeded that of the Baptist (cf. 3,26.30). It is also claimed that references to the Eucharist in Jn. 6 support seeing the sacraments elsewhere in the fourth Gospel.[200]

It must be clearly seen, however, that those who opt for ὕδωρ as Christian baptism are viewing the text as a didactic creation on the part of the evangelist to communicate spiritual truth to the Church at large about the value and necessity of baptism.[201] The teaching of Jesus then becomes irrelevant to Nicodemus and his contemporaries. Moreover, I think the identification of water and baptism might well be classed as a common exegetical *faux pas* as it reflects neither a careful consideration of the evangelist's thought nor the contextual considerations. There is nothing in the immediate context to warrant such an interpretation of ὕδωρ: 1) It is little short ridiculous to imagine Jesus reprimanding Nicodemus in 3,10 for his failure to understand the necessity of a rite yet to be instituted. 2) Reference to baptism as an essential condition for entering the kingdom of God makes incomprehensible the dropping of ὕδωρ on repetition of his statement in 3,6. In fact, ὕδωρ is neither mentioned nor expanded in the verses that follow (but cf. πνεῦμα).[202] 3) A reference to baptism would introduce an incongruity into the flow of a text which is

---

and that of Jesus is paralleled in the Synoptic Gospels (the very same terminology being employed) and is thus, probably, traditional (Mk. 1,7-8; Mt. 3,11; Lk. 3,16; and Acts 1,5 and 11,16). Second, the point of this distinction may, simply, be that whereas John the Baptist's baptismal activity did not involve the instrumentality of the Spirit (cf. Acts 19,3-6), the baptising action of Jesus did; see de Boer, "Jesus the Baptiser," 95.

[200] Cf. M. Gourgues, "Section christologique et section eucharistique en Jean VI: une proposition," *RB* 88 (1981) 515-31; and C. H. Cosgrove, "The Place where Jesus is: Allusions to Baptism and the Eucharist in the Fourth Gospel," *NTS* 35 (1989) 522-39.

[201] Wellhausen, Bultmann and E. Lohse ["Wort und Sakrament im Johannesevangelium," *NTS* 7 (1960/61) 116-25] consider 'ὕδατος καὶ' as a later ecclesiastical interpolation after the final redaction of the Gospel. Braun, Leon-Dufour, Feuillet, Van den Bussche, Mollat, Bernard and Vellanickal think that these words go back to the evangelist himself, though not to Jesus in his conversation with Nicodemus.

[202] In his initial encounter, Jesus gives washing with water a place in the process of new birth, closely connecting it with the work of the Spirit (cf. 3,5); but the emphasis falls on the Spirit (cf. 3,8) rather than on water. Jesus' preceding remark to Nicodemus states that one must be begotten ἄνωθεν but mentions nothing about water (3,3). His subsequent comments sharply distinguish between birth from the flesh and birth from the Spirit and repeatedly stress the need to be begotten ἄνωθεν and of the Spirit, but he does not mention water again (3,6-8). See D. Ewert, "Born of the Spirit. John 3,1:-8," in: G. R. Brunk (ed.), *Encounter with the Holy Spirit* (Scottdale 1972) 16-25. All critics agree in their consideration that Nicodemus could have had no idea of such a baptism. And so, they come to the conclusion that the mention of water is an addition to the text which originally would have spoken only of rebirth through the Spirit. It is all the more so because water is no longer mentioned in the following part of the dialogue. Therefore, according to de la Potterie ("Naître de l'eau," 424-25), the text should be read with two redactional steps in mind: the rebirth through the Spirit and then the rebirth through baptism and the Spirit. He urges that in the earliest Johannine catechism there was question only of regeneration by the Spirit, and that could reflect what Jesus actually said; but, in the light of the instruction of the Risen Lord and the Christian practice of baptism, the evangelist added ὕδατος καὶ, by way of commentary, to indicate to the reader how new life of the Spirit is gained. However widespread this interpretation may be, in my opinion, it cannot claim to be anything more than a hypothesis without critical basis. The excision of the words 'ὕδατος καὶ' would not be supported by textual criticism. Moreover, I think that a sound literary criticism in no way forces that excision upon us. The present text could have been written by the evangelist both in a sacramental perspective and in a non-sacramental one. See also Léon-Dufour, "Toward a Symbolic Reading," 449-50.

concerned not with submission to an external rite but with the realities of γένεσις, πνεῦμα, σάρξ and the nature of βασιλείαν τοῦ θεοῦ. 4) It does not form a ready parallel with γεννηθῇ ἄνωθεν (3,3) nor with γεγεννημένον ἐκ τοῦ πνεύματος (3,6). 5) One also wonders what 'baptism' and the analogy of 'how the wind blows' (3,8) have in common.[203]

Further, if the evangelist did mean ὕδωρ to be an indirect reference to Christian baptism, it is indeed incredible that he elsewhere neglected the opportunity to say this directly.[204] As regards the conjunction of water and Spirit in 1,26.31.33, it should be noted that they are contrasted in 1,33 while co-ordinated (καί) in 3,5. Additionally, if baptism and the gift of the Spirit are so essentially bound to one another, as supporters of this position claim, it is indeed remarkable that one finds no mention of baptism in Jn. 14-16 nor in 20,22 where the Spirit is given independently of water baptism.[205] Nor do the themes of repentance and forgiveness, associated with water baptism in the Synoptic Gospels, occur.[206] Given, moreover, the fourth evangelist's strong emphasis on faith[207] as the basis of salvation (e.g. 20,30-31), it would be inexplicable why in 3,5 he would suddenly appear to confine salvation to an outward sign.

β. Symbolic Usage of Water

a) Water as Torah

Some scholars see in water a symbol for the Torah. It is claimed that water is interpreted symbolically most often of the Torah in rabbinic literature. The NT also speaks of "birth through the word" (Jas. 1,18; and 1 Pet. 1,23-25) and "washing through water and the word" (Eph. 5,26). It must, however, be pointed out that while ὕδωρ ζῶν is found in rabbinic literature as a symbol for the Torah,[208] ὕδωρ *per se* is not the symbol used often of the Torah. בְּאֵר (well) and not ὕδωρ is the symbol most often used of the Torah: "But when Isaac's servants dug in the valley and found there a well of spring water" (Gen. 26,19) refers to the third book of the Torah, Leviticus, because this book is full of great *traditions*.[209] If water and the Torah are related, it is to compare the Torah with the life-sustaining and purifying capabilities of water: "Just as water is life to the world so the words of the Torah are life to the world.... Just as water brings out the unclean out of his impurity so the words of the Torah bring man from the evil way to the good way..."[210] 'Birth out of water,' however, is a concept that is foreign to rabbinic literature, making improbable, therefore, the association in 3,5 of water and the Torah. Moreover, given also

---

[203] Cf. G. Richter ("Zum sogenannten Tauftext Joh 3,5," *MThZ* 26 [1975] 101; 110 and 123) calls it "ein Irrtum" to say that 3,5 speaks of Christian baptism.

[204] Cf. Z. C. Hodges, "Problem Passages in the Gospel of John. Part 3: Water and Spirit - John 3,5," *BS* 135 (1978) 209.

[205] Dunn, *Baptism in the Holy Spirit*, 195.

[206] Cf. J. W. Pryor, "John 3.3,5. A Study in the Relation of John's Gospel to the Synoptic Tradition," *JSNT* 41 (1991) 71-95.

[207] Jn. 2,23-3,2 speaks of the imperfect faith of the Jews; 3,11-21 speaks of the authentic faith of the believers. Cf. Vellanickal, 164.

[208] Cf. L. Belleville, "'Born of Water and Spirit:' John 3:5," *TrinJ* 1 (1980) 130.

[209] *Ibid.*

[210] *Ibid.*

that Jesus refers to the life-giving properties of τὰ ῥήματα αὐτοῦ (his words) in 6,63, it would be inexplicable why ὕδωρ and not ῥῆμα would find its way into the text of 3,5.[211]

b) Water as Renunciation of the 'Old Man'

'Γεννηθῇ ἐξ ὕδατος καὶ πνεύματος' has been taken by some to symbolise a two-stage process of regeneration – ὕδωρ standing for the renunciation of the *old man* and πνεῦμα for the *new life* (Rom. 6,1-7).[212] This interpretation, however, presupposes in ὕδωρ καὶ πνεῦμα a primary reference to Christian baptism and early Christian symbolism that attended the act of immersion, which, in my opinion, is foreign to the imagery, text, and theology of the fourth Gospel.

γ. Physiological Views

a) Embryonic Fluid

The physiological interpretation argues that 'entering a second time into the mother's womb' (3,4), 'γεννηθῇ ἐξ ὕδατος' (3,5), and 'γεννηθῇ ἐκ τῆς σαρκὸς' (3,6) are parallel statements. It is claimed that 'γεννηθῇ ἐξ ὕδατος' is a suitable and appropriate description of physical birth, since human birth is preceded by the rupturing of the bag of fluid surrounding the baby in the womb of the mother. Hence, every birth is a birth ἐξ ὕδατος. Water referring to the embryonic fluid can be closely linked to (born from above) γεννηθῇ ἄνωθεν in 3,3 and to Nicodemus' reference to the mother's womb in 3,4. It also expands the content of ἄνωθεν while clarifying simultaneously Nicodemus' question regarding a second birth, as no other interpretation of water can can.[213] It is also argued that water as referring to birth maintains the structural balance between 3,5 and 3,6, σάρξ referring back to ὕδωρ and τὸ πνεῦμα to πνεῦμα. It also accounts for the dropping of ὕδωρ in 3,6-8 if subsumed under γεννηθῇ ἐκ τῆς σαρκὸς. While it is not true to say that no one can enter the kingdom without baptism, it is true to say that no one can enter without being born twice.[214]

There are several obstacles to this interpretation. We do not find any parallels either in ancient or in contemporary writings to support that 'water-birth' corresponds to 'physical birth'. Moreover, if Jesus wanted to speak of physical birth, it is reasonable to assume that he would have used either 'γεγεννημένος ἐκ τῆς σαρκὸς' (3,6) or 'γεννηθῇ ἐξ αἱμάτων' ('born of blood' – 1,13). Besides, this interpretation contradicts the syntax of 'ἐξ ὕδατος καὶ πνεύματος' as a conceptual unity and disrupts the parallelism in 3,3.5.6b.7.[215]

---

[211] Cf. Hodges, "Water and Spirit," 214.

[212] See L. Goppelt, "Taufe und neues Leben nach Joh 3 und Röm 6," *SOrth* 4 (1970) 51-53; and 5 (1970) 36-41; and M. Mees, "Das 3. Kapitel des Johannesevangeliums in frühchristlicher Sicht," *Laur.* 27 (1986) 121-37.

[213] R. M. Fowler ("Born of Water and Spirit [John 3:5]," *ET* 82 [1970/71] 82) says that there is nothing in the context to connect it with baptism but much to connect it with two births – a physical and a spiritual birth. See also D. G. Spriggs, "The Meaning of 'Water' in John 3:5," *ET* 85 (1974) 149-50.

[214] It is also claimed that if 'ἐξ ὕδατος' refers to physical birth, 1 Jn. 5,6-8 is also illumined. Seeing 'water' exclusively in reference to the baptism of Jesus is criticised by Thüsing, 165-74; see also H.-J. Klauck, *Der erste Johannesbrief* (EKK XXIII/1) (Neukirchen-Vluyn, Zürich 1991) 293-94.

[215] Nor is 1 Jn. 5,6 a supportive parallel. While the ascensive sense of καὶ is spelled out in 1 Jn. 5,7, there is no such clarification following Jn. 3,5. Instead, I find σάρξ and πνεῦμα (3,6) to be antithetical rather than ascensive.

Furthermore, the inclusion of physical birth as a condition for entrance into the kingdom would appear to contradict other statements of the evangelist, notably 1,13 where 'to become children of God' is not the result of any process comparable with that of physical birth, and 6,63 where it is stated that the "flesh is useless; only the Spirit gives life."

b) Male Semen

This reading of γεννηθῇ ἐξ ὕδατος is based on the rabbinic use of טיפה (a drop) for the male semen: "Knowest whence those camest? From a fetid drop (טיפה). What smell of a woman born is this and what taste of a white drop (טיפה) that ascends to the high heavens?" (3 Enoch 6,2).[216] As the readers of the fourth Gospel would not have been aware of such rabbinic nuances, Spriggs rightly questions if such an interpretation of water in terms of the semen.[217]

δ. Dualistic Views

The contrast between 'τὰ ἄνω' (things above) or 'τὰ ἐπουράνια' (heavenly things), and 'τὰ κάτω' (things below) or 'τὰ ἐπίγεια' (earthly things) (cf. 3,12.31) is crucial to understand the fourth evangelist's thought. This leads to interpreting 'γεννηθῇ ἐξ ὕδατος καὶ πνεύματος' / 'γεννηθῇ ἄνωθεν ' as reflective of such a spatial dualism. Vellanickal speaks of a temporal and sptial dualism.[218]

Belleville views water and spirit as representative of liquid and pure elements in opposition to the earthly and gross nature of man. According to him 3,5 teaches that one must leave behind the heavy and weighty mass of flesh and become like water and wind so as to move upwards.[219]

In rabbinic and Jewish mystical literature 'טיפה' (drop) and 'water,' 'rain' and 'dew' are used literally of the male procreative 'σπέρμα' (seed)[220] and symbolically to indicate the spiritual or divine begetting from the world 'ἄνω.' In this context H. Odeberg views 3,5 with a strong emphasis on the contrast between the two worlds of πνεῦμα and σάρξ, similar to the one between τὰ ἐπουράνια/τὰ ἐπίγεια, ἄνω/κάτω and οὐρανός/κόσμος. He contrasts γεννηθῇ ἐξ ὕδατος καὶ πνεύματος (the divine begetting) with Nicodemus' reference to the physical/earthly birth in 3,4 (i.e. the earthly or sarcical seed). Odeberg is convinced that a similar idea is in the mind of the fourth evangelist as, according to him, there is 1) the σάρξ/πνεῦμα contrast throughout the dialogue, 2) the use made of the idea of spiritual seed in 1 Jn. 3,9 (cf. 1 Pet. 1,23), and 3) the thought of life-giving water in 4,10.14 and 7,38-39.[221] But Odeberg's citations of rabbinic and Jewish mystical sources, however, are not persuasive as none of the sources he quotes are used in conjunction with the concept of regeneration. Also, the connection drawn between ὕδωρ and σπέρμα appears stretched.

---

[216] Cf. Barrett, 209.

[217] Spriggs, 150.

[218] Vellanickal, 166.

[219] E.g. Belleville, 132.

[220] Water is that which, in the spiritual process of birth, corresponds to the semen in the sarcical process. Cf. H. Odeberg, *The Fourth Gospel. Interpreted in its Relation to Contemporaneous Religious Currents in Palestine and the Hellenistic-Oriental World* (Amsterdam 1968) 50. See also Morris, *Gospel*, 192. For him γεννηθῇ ἐξ ὕδατος καὶ πνεύματος is a hendiadys for spiritual or heavenly σπέρμα (in contrast with physical semen or σάρξ).

[221] Cf. Gen. 1,2; Acts of Thomas 52; cf. also Strachan, 134.

Although the sources cited associate ὕδωρ with the generation of life, the further association that Odeberg draws between ὕδωρ and spiritual semen is his own and not that of his sources.[222]

ε. Cosmological

Jesus, no doubt, must be using water and spirit to call forth OT imagery which must have been familiar to Nicodemus, a teacher of Israel and a learned Pharisee (3,1.10). Based on this assumption Hodges prefers to understand water and spirit in their natural meanings of 'water' and 'wind' respectively,[223] a double metaphor alluding to and subsumed under the work of τὸ πνεῦμα explicitly mentioned in 3,6 and 3,8. 3,8 evidently demonstrays that πνεῦμα can be rendered as both 'wind' and 'Spirit,' in the frequent association of water and wind as elements in the physical world, and in the vital and vivifying use of water and wind in the OT as divine figures and instruments.[224] The main difficulty with this interpretation is its consistency. Hodges must translate πνεῦμα in 3,5 and 3,6 in the same fashion. In scuh a case the translation thus rendered sounds absurd in the context: 'very truly, I tell you, no one can enter the kingdom of God without being born of water and *wind*. What is born of the flesh is flesh, and what is born of the *wind* (spirit) is *wind*.'

ζ. Figurative Applications

Some exegets in the line of Origen, consider γεννηθῇ ἐξ ὕδατος καὶ πνεύματος as referring to the purifying work of God's Spirit. Exegetically, καὶ is understood as either epexegetic ('water, namely the Spirit') or co-ordinate ('water as the Spirit's instrument of purification and renewal').[225] The affinity of 'water' with 'Spirit' in the OT as symbols of cleansing and renewal is recurrent.[226] There is also a specail accent laid in Judaism on the Spirit and his eschatological function concerning an inner change of heart. Apocryphal and rabbinic writings demonstrate that the concepts of purification and creation by God's Spirit were active in Jesus' time.[227] This interpretation also explains the dropping of 'water' in 3,6-8, and couches for the flow of the text and argument. It is also harmonious with the internal symbolism of the Gospel which uses water to illustrate the operation of the Spirit, yet without any direct connection with literal baptism (e.g. water and Spirit are associated in 7,37-39). Westcott, however, contends that καὶ in the fourth Gospel can only be co-ordinating and not epexegetic, thereby denying any position that treats water as merely

---

[222] Moreover, the contrast of ὕδωρ, πνεῦμα, τὰ ἐπουράνια, and τὰ ἄνω with σπέρμα, σάρξ, τὰ ἐπίγεια, and τὰ κάτω, respectively, is neither textually nor theologically demonstrable. Τὰ ἐπίγεια (3,12) refers to the whole of the preceding verses (3,2-11) and includes, therefore, ὕδατος καὶ πνεύματος. Σάρξ and πνεῦμα are spatially dualistic in the Gospel but rather qualitatively antithetical.[222] The contrast between τὰ ἄνω and τὰ κάτω is based on the view that ἄνωθεν (3,3) means 'from above;' and this cannot be sustained given 3,4. See also my discussion on double meaning and misunderstanding. This interpretation, in my opinion, assumes far too much of the reader as well as of Nicodemus, namely, the association of ὕδωρ with σπέρμα, an implied σπέρμα in 3,6.

[223] Hodges, "Water and Spirit," 206-20.

[224] Cf. the promise of the future pouring out of God's Spirit on the dry ground of man's soul (Is. 44,3ff.) and the breathing of God's Spirit on the slain (Ezek. 37,9).

[225] For epexegetical or explicative καὶ, see *BAGD*, 393.

[226] Cf. G. E. Ladd, *A Theology of the New Testament* (Grand Rapids 1974) 284.

[227] Job 1,16.23 and 5,12; Pss. Sol. 18,16; Enoch 92,3-4 and 10,16; and 1QS 3,21and 10,10-11.

figurative and descriptive.[228] But it is to be objected, on either reading of καί, that 'water' interpreted as inanimate in contrast to an animate 'Spirit' disturbs the syntax of the pericope.

η. A Fresh Investigation

a) Style and Syntax

Water and spirit in 3,5 are governed by a single preposition (ἐκ) and connected by the conjunction καί indicating that the phrase is to be viewed as a conceptual unity, *viz.*, 'water-spirit.'[229] One is dealing, therefore, with a water-spirit source as the origin of man's second γένεσις. Both nouns 'water' and 'spirit' describe rather than specify or identify, emphasising the nature or quality of the second γένεσις.[230] Jn. 3,5; 3,6b and 3,7 are parallel statements – a typical characteristic of the fourth Gospel.[231] The parallelism between γεννηθῇ ἐξ ὕδατος καὶ πνεύματος (3,5c) and τὸ γεγεννημένον ἐκ τοῦ πνεύματος (3,6b), indicates that conceptually water and spirit are so closely interconnected that Jesus can subsume both under the auspices of the singular spirit in 3,6b.

b) Milieu

i) Teacher of Israel

It is as ὁ διδάσκαλος τοῦ Ἰσραὴλ (teacher of Israel) that Nicodemus is expected to know ταῦτα (these things – 3,10) of which Jesus has been speaking, which means that a knowledge of the OT is presupposed for a right comprehension of this water-spirit γένεσις in 3,5. The OT, therefore, can be regarded as the primary domain of investigation for inquiring into the conceptual milieu of the phrase γεννηθῇ ἐξ ὕδατος καὶ πνεύματος and thereby search, explicate and account for the exact meaning of 3,5.[232]

ii) Kingdom of God

A scrutiny of the passages containing the term 'water' in the fourth Gospel – placed on the lips of Jesus – betrays that all have in common a double link among ὕδωρ, πνεῦμα, and γένεσις or ζωή. Unique to 3,5 is the fact that ὕδωρ, πνεῦμα, and γένεσις are further linked with and qualify the expression 'kingdom of God'[233] (3,3.5). The result of the new begetting is described by the evangelist as 'seeing' and 'entering' the kingdom of God. The concept of a 'kingdom of God' was evidently known to Nicodemus. That is why he does

---

[228] Westcott, I, 108.

[229] See M. J. Harris, "Prepositions and Theology in the Greek New Testament," *NIDNT*, III, 1178.

[230] The focus would, therefore, not be on the person of the πνεῦμα, but on his nature and activity. Cf. 6,63 and 4,23-24. Nor does the article with πνεῦμα in 3,6 warrant explaining away the anarthrous πνεῦμα on the basis of Johannine stylistic variation. As M. Zerwick (*Biblical Greek Illustrated by Examples* [Rome 1963] 47) points out, the neuter τὸ of 3,6 is used of persons where the emphasis is on quality of function. Further, the neuter gender lays down an absolute and universal principle based on the distinct separateness of the natural and supernatural orders.

[231] The fourth evangelist characteristically introduces slight variations when similar statements or themes of spiritual import are repeated. Cf. L. Morris, *Studies in the Fourth Gospel* (Grand Rapids 1969) 313.

[232] Cf. the detailed study of C. Westermann, *The Gospel of John in the Light of the Old Testament* (Peabody 1997).

[233] The Synoptics employ the form 'kingdom of heaven.'

not ask Jesus, '*What* do you mean by the kingdom of God?' His response is, rather, "*How* can these things be?" (3,9).

In the Judaism of Jesus' days there were two concepts of the kingdom that were current: the present reign of God and the future eschatological coming of the kingdom of God.[234] However, although the notion of the 'kingdom of God' occurs in the OT, the expression itself does not occur. When a *kingdom* is ascribed to Yahweh it is the abstract sense of reign or rule. Only derivatively does it mean the rule of God over His people. This rule, to a pious Jew, is especially accomplished in the Law. To take up the 'yoke of the kingdom of heaven' means to pledge obedience to Law. In the prophets, there begins to emerge alongside the concept of a present rule of God the concept of a kingdom that is *yet to come*. The belief arises that in the last days the Messiah will restore the splendour of the Davidic kingdom and will subject to himself all nations. The expectation of the coming kingdom of God becomes synonymous with Messianic nationalism.[235]

The phrase οὐ δύναται εἰσελθεῖν (ἰδεῖν – 3,3) εἰς τὴν βασιλείαν τοῦ θεοῦ of 3,5d fits neither of these popular and prevailing concepts of the kingdom.[236] This difference hints at a redefining of the 'kingdom of God' by Jesus along characteristic lines, which the preceding examination of the syntax and style has shown. This redefining involves three essential realities that were unknown to the prevailing views of the kingdom. First, the condition for participation in the kingdom requires a begetting ἄνωθεν. Second, the nature of this kingdom is spiritual and not physical (3,6). The 'flesh' of human existence is discontinuous with and antithetical to participation.[237] Third, the nature of God's kingdom is not merely one of rule but of sphere: 'entrance' into it is required for participation.[238] Nicodemus is excluded from this kingdom at present. As a Rabbi and Pharisee and by virtue of his obedience to the Law, Nicodemus must have considered himself already as participating in God's kingdom.

iii) Begotten of Water and Spirit

α) Milieu

The phrase 'γεννηθῇ ἐξ ὕδατος καὶ πνεύματος' (begotten of water and Spirit) has no precedence in the bible. Spiritual begetting of man with God as Father is a phenomenon that is unique to the NT. Neither γεννηθῇ ἐκ πνεύματος nor γεννηθῇ ἐκ τοῦ θεοῦ is found in the OT. Birth in the OT is either physical and national or by election. Israel being named as God's first born (cf. Ex. 4,22; Deut. 32,6; and Hos. 11,1), it is a sonship based on covenant choice, not due to divine procreation. Begetting by God occurs only with regard

---

[234] See C. C. Caragounis, "The Kingdom of God in John and the Synoptics: Realized or Potential Eschatology?," in: A. Denaux (ed.), *John and the Synoptics* (BEThL 101) (Leuven 1992) 473-80.

[235] E.g. Mic. 4,7-8; Ps. 102,19 and 144,11.13. Cf. Wis. 6,4 and 10,10; and Dan. 3,54 and 4,3. See B. Klappert, "βασιλεία," *NIDNT*, II, 377.

[236] On this subject see R. J. White, *The Kingdom of God in the Fourth Gospel* (Louisville 1982).

[237] It is similar to Paul's "flesh and blood cannot inherit the kingdom of God" (1 Cor. 15,50). It is significant that elsewhere in the fourth Gospel, where Jesus is approached on the basis of 'signs' (comparable to 2,23-3,2), these 'signs' are linked with the kingdom of God and the prevailing popular beliefs regarding a Messianic kingship; cf. Jn. 6,14-15.

[238] Cf. Patte, 3-42; M. Pamment, "John 3:5: 'Unless One is Born of Water and the Spirit, He Cannot Enter the Kingdom of God'," *NT* 25 (1983) 189-90; and G. R. Beasley-Murray, "John 3,3.5: Baptism, Spirit and the Kingdom," *ET* 97 (1985/86) 167-70.

to Messianic expectation (e.g. Ps. 2) but even this is on the basis of election.[239] Although the phrase γεννηθῇ ἐκ πνεύματος is not found in the OT, the wider concept of ζωή, especially the infusion of spiritual life (πνεῦμα) is basic to the prophetic promises and foundational to Jewish intertestamental eschatological expectation.[240]

We may even say that Jesus is drawing his usage of γεννάω partially from the everyday experience of childbearing. This would harmonise with Jesus' practice of drawing examples from day-to-day life for his teaching as he does elsewhere in the NT.[241] It would also be compatible with his use in 3,8 of an analogy drawn from nature itself (i.e. "The wind blows where it chooses, and you hear the sound of it, but you do not know where it comes from or where it goes"). In this case 'γεννηθῇ ἄνωθεν' (3,3) will refer to the necessity for man to undergo a spiritual begetting as against a material one.

β) Fourth Evangelist's Application

Although the concept of divine begetting is rare in the OT, it is frequent in the Johannine literature. The evangelist's familiar expression regarding the believer's relationship to God is that he 'γεγέννηται ἐκ τοῦ θεοῦ' (is born of God – 1,13). To be 'born of God' in 1,13 is antithetical to being born of the σάρξ. It means receiving the very nature of God, for being born of God results in the doing of righteousness (1 Jn. 2,29), in not sinning (1 Jn. 3,7-10), in love (1 Jn. 4,7), and in overcoming the world (1 Jn. 5,4). 'Γεννηθῇ ἐξ ὕδατος καὶ πνεύματος,' if equal to 'γεγέννηται ἐκ τοῦ θεοῦ,' involves the imparting of God's nature and a work of regeneration in man. This would *a priori* rule out any ritualistic understanding of 3,5 (e.g. baptism) as well as any physiological interpretation of water. Neither can effect spiritual begetting or regeneration.

iv) Spirit

The word 'spirit' is repeated five times in 3,3-12. This betrays a pneumatological emphasis of these verses. Let us examine the OT and rabbinic milieu that could throw some light on Jewish expectation regarding the 'spirit' which Nicodemus could have had in mind to understand Jesus' pneumatological statements.

α) OT Milieu

The OT presents πνεῦμα consistently as the principle of life. The Spirit of Yahweh, compared often to the wind, as the source of life was a very ancient concept in Israel. Just as God gave physical life to man, when He breathed into him the breath (πνεῦμα) of life (Gen. 2,7 and 6,3; and Job 34,14), so also God will at some future point breathe spiritual

---

[239] See R. E. Brown, *Gospel*, I, 139. According to A. Ringwald ("γεννάω," *NIDNT*, I, 177), the absence of this verb in contexts regarding the father-son relationship or with God as the Father of Israel is indicative of the OT's attempt to dissociate itself from the procreation myths of Israel's surrounding Canaanite culture.

[240] The concept of rebirth is not found either in the Qumran Scrolls or in the Damascus Document. Only in the post-exilic period does one find pious individuals designated as "sons of God" (e.g. Wis. 2,13.16.18 and 5,5; Pss. Sol. 17,30; and Sir. 4,10 and 23,1.4). The term γεννηθῇ ἐκ τοῦ θεοῦ, however, is not found. See R. E. Brown, *op. cit.*; see also the recent study of J. Baumgarten, E. G. Chazon and A. Pinnick (eds.), *The Damascus Document: A Centennial of Discovery. Proceedings of the third International Symposium of the Orion Centre for the Study of the Dead Sea Scrolls and Associated Literature, 4-8 February, 1998* (Leiden 1999).

[241] E.g. Mt. 13 and Lk. 18.

life into His people and put His πνεῦμα within them "that they might live" (cf. Ezek. 37,1-4). The association of 'birth' and 'life' with the πνεῦμα is something that is well-known to the OT.[242]

The OT also eagerly awaits a new dispensation of the πνεῦμα marked by: 1) an outpouring of the Spirit on all mankind (Joel 2,28) resulting in divine blessing, peace, and righteousness (Ezek. 36,25-26 and 39,29; Is. 32,15-20 and 44,3), and 2) an indwelling of the Spirit which insures cleansing from idolatry, obedience to God's commandments, and participation in the 'people of God' (Ezek. 36,26-27 and 11,19-20). Such an outpouring of the Spirit of God was pivotal to Jewish eschatological hope and indicated the arrival of Messianic times. Any allusion to the Spirit by Jesus would have hinted at the advent of this Messianic era.

Moreover, for israel, the Spirit of Yahweh is parallel to the word of Yahweh; both accomplish the same in a similar way (cf. Is. 11,4 and 34,16; Ps. 147,18). In Ps. 33,6 רוּחַ and דָּבָר are parallels and are expressed in equivalent terms. Nicodemus must have been at home with the understanding of the Spirit as working through the Word of God.

β) Rabbinic Milieu

In leter Judaism, too, the role of the Spirit in prifying and renewing the life of individuals through the truth and the law of God was current.[243] The notion of birth through the Teacher (i.e. through the Word) and through the Spirit (power) of God is also found in later Judaism.[244] These concepts too must have been familiar to Nicodemus. But in none of these texts does one find a mention of a begetting of an *individual* through the Spirit, but a always a *community* which makes the misunderstanding of Nicodemus clear. It is perhaps the newness of Jesus' teachaing.[245]

One notices in rabbinic literature a link between the Spirit and a life which is obedient to God: "He who undertakes a command in faith is worthy that the Holy Spirit rest on him."[246] "He who studies with the intention of doing it deserves the gift of the Holy Spirit."[247] The sequence here is significant. The Spirit is viewed as the proper reward for a righteous life. However, in 3,5 one finds just the reverse. The Spirit is viewed not as a reward but as a necessary condition for participation in God's kingdom. Nor is the work of the Spirit a mere matter of purification from sin and idolatry. The operation of the Spirit in man demands nothing less than a second begetting – a begetting that has the nature of spirit. One of the reasons for such a nature of spirit is that the backbone of worship under the new covenant is spirit and truth (cf. 4,23), in conformity with the nature of God as Spirit (4,24). The believer participates in God's nature, because he is begotten of the Spirit (3,36).

---

[242] Cf. R. E. Brown, *op. cit.*, 140; and E. Kamlah, "πνεῦμα," *NIDNT*, III, 692.

[243] Cf. I QS 3,4-9; 4,20f.; 7,29-31; 9,30-36 and 11,10-12; Jub. 1,23-25.

[244] Cf. I QH 3,1-18.

[245] Cf. Vellanickal, 175.

[246] E. Sjöberg, "רוח in Palestine Judaism," *TDNT*, VI, 383.

[247] *Ibid.*

v) Water

In the OT the theme of renewal and the theme of catharsis are predominantly and inseparably linked to the concept of water.

α) Renewal

Water in the Near East was scarce and, hence, was a precious element. Being a vital necessity for life, it is not surprising that the OT uses water as a symbol of God's operation in arousing people to life.[248] It is often regarded as an instrument of renewal and blessing. Joel (2,28-29) refers to the assurance that God will *pour* out his Spirit on all flesh in the last days. Prophet Isaiah (32,15; 44,3-4) speaks of a time when the Spirit will be *poured* on the people from on high.

β) Catharsis

The idea of purification by water is something central to the OT theology.. The prophets preached an eschatological sprinkling with clean water that would cleanse both land and people of an idolatrous spirit. The symbolic expression 'to sprinkle with clean water' is borrowed from from the levitical purification rites.[249] The prophetic spiritualisation of OT legal and ritual cleansing is mirrored in the Judaism of the intertestamental period, too: "I will create in them a holy Spirit and I will cleanse them...I will be their father and they shall be my children" (Jub. 1,23-25). In Philo and Josephus, purification with water became a symbol for the purification of soul and conscience.[250] The Pharisees developed the OT stipulations of Lev. 11-15 into a complicated system of ritual purification.[251] The Covenanters, too, looked forward to the day when God would "purify in His truth all the works of man, rooting out iniquity and purifying man's flesh of all impurity by a holy Spirit."[252] Against this background I am inclined to believe that the mention of water in 3,5 recalls God's saving activities of cleansing and renewal, which is an eschatological motif conspicuous both in the OT and the environment of Jesus' time.

γ) Faith

The meaning of begetting through water and the Spirit should, moreover, be understood in terms of faith. In 1 Jn. 3,9 the 'divine begetting' is attributed to the 'seed of God remaining in us,' which is to be understood as the 'Word of God' received and accepted in faith under the influence of the Spirit. In the primitive Christian tradition we find two series of texts, one pointing to the Word of God as the principle of this begetting (cf. 1 pet. 1,22-23 and 3,23; James 1,17-18), and the other to the Spirit as the source of this begetting (cf.

---

[248] E.g. Is. 55,1-3; Jer. 2,13 and 17,13; Zech. 14,8; Ezek. 47,9; Is. 32,15-17 and 44,3-5; Joel 2,28; and Job 1,33.

[249] O. Böcher, " Ὕδωρ," *NIDNT*, III, 989; and his, "Wasser und Geist," in: O. Böcher and K. Haacker (eds.), *Verborum Veritas. FS Gustav Stählin zum 70. Geburtstag* (Wuppertal 1970) 197-209. Cleansing from defilement involved sprinkling with water prepared with the ashes of a red heifer. See Num. 19,17-19. Cf. Ps. 51,9.

[250] *Ibid.*

[251] See Strack-Billerbeck, I, 695-702 for discussion and references; see also A. Opeke, "λούω," *TDNT*, IV, 301; and R. Meyer, "καθαρός," *TDNT*, III, 418-20.

[252] 1QS 4,21-24. Cf. also 1QS 3,6-8; 11,10-14; 7,6; 9,32; 12,12; 16,12 and 17,20 regarding Qumran purification rites which were an outward sign of inward cleansing and renewal.

Rom. 8,15-16; Gal. 4,6 and Tit. 3,5). One should, in fact consider them as complementary and not as exclusive. It is through the Word of God that the Spirit works in us, and it is the Spirit, who begets faith in the word of God and gives dynamism to it. Being begotten ἄνωθεν means, therefore, coming to faith in Jesus, who came down from above. Faith is new birth, because through it people enter into relationship with God that issues in eternal life.[253] The visible anchor point for faith is the cross (3,14-16).[254] Those who believe discern in Jesus' crucifixion the perfect and supreme expression of God's love for the world. They also come to know that Jesus resumed his heavenly glory through his physical elevation on a cross.[255] Those who do not believe cannot recognise the transcendent reality that Jesus conveys through his earthly speech (cf. 3,12). Their understanding is restricted by what is below, and they face the prospect of perishing under divine condemnation (3,18).

The second episode (3,22-36) says that the willingness to come to Jesus for baptism shows that God is at work already; they come because it has been granted 'from heaven' (3,26-27; cf. 6,44.65). Here, baptism does not initiate God's activity but is the fruit of His activity; it is the consequence of a faith engendered through testimony borne to Jesus (cf. 3,28-29.32.34). It is the material sign of the Spirit's work.

δ) **Baptism and Discipleship**

Another important point to be noted is that the fourth evangelist maintains important connections and makes critical distinctions between water and Spirit and between baptism and discipleship. After joining water and Spirit in the process of new birth, the text immediately stresses the Spirit's freedom to 'blow where it chooses;' the Spirit's activity is connected with baptism but cannot be confined to baptism (3,5-8).[256] The narrative context of the second episode indicates that Jesus and his disciples practised baptism with water, while recognising that there were forms of cleansing that do not convey the Spirit. The emphasis of 'water and Spirit' in 3,5 could also be seen as: not that baptism is necessary[257] but that any baptism which does not involve cleansing by the Spirit is defective.[258] Similarly, baptism is associated but not equated with discipleship. The text says that 'Jesus is *making* and baptising' disciples (4,1). This means that a disciple of Jesus will be baptised, but not that the reverse was true; one cannot assume that everyone who came for baptism automatically became a true disciple. The next verse adds that 'Jesus himself did not baptise, but his disciples did' (4,2). This qualification maintains the vital tension between baptism and discipleship. Jesus' followers may have performed baptism (4,2), but

---

[253] See Gabriel, 205-15. As the structure of Jn. 3 betrays the evangelist is stressing here the fundamental condition of passing from the imperfect faith of the Jews (2,23-3,2) to the authentic fatih 83,11-21).

[254] For B. Bonvin ("Nicodème ou l'invitation à renaître. Jn 3.1-21," *NV* 64 [1989] 70) faith is a "decision in front of the elevated Jesus."

[255] See Koester, *Symbolism*, 209-14.

[256] See C. D. Osburn, "Some Exegetical Observations on John 3:5-8," *RestQ* 31 (1989) 129-38.

[257] B. Witherington III ("The Waters of Birth: John 3.5 and 1 John 5,6-8," *NTS* 35 [1989] 155) is demonstrating a plausible non-sacramental reference for the word 'water' that makes sense of both passages.

[258] Cf. Culpepper, *Anatomy*, 193.

Jesus alone could make disciples (4,1); the two actions were not identified.[259] Water in this episode helps to integrate the Gospel's first three chapters while introducing the fourth.

To summarise the above discussion, Jn. 3,5 both sums up and goes beyond the OT concepts of kingdom, begetting, spirit and water. Whereas the OT speaks of cleansing and renewal through the outpouring and indwelling of God's Spirit, Jesus speaks of an entirely new beginning (γεννηθῇ ἄνωθεν – 3,3), a second begetting whose nature is ὕδωρ καὶ πνεῦμα as opposed to σάρξ (3,5-6). It is reasonable to assume that in water there is a reference to the eschatological cleansing (as envisioned by the prophets – Ezek. 36,26-27) accomplished through God's Spirit (3,6) – the spiritual counterpart to the Levitical rites of purification. In πνεῦμα one does not have a reference to the Holy Spirit as such, but a reference to the imparting of God's nature as πνεῦμα (cf. 4,24). It is the twofold work of the Spirit (3,6) to purify and impart this nature to man. Only τὸ γεγεννημένον ἐκ τοῦ πνεύματος as πνεῦμα (3,6) can 'see' and 'enter' the kingdom of God (3,3.5), for the kingdom of God is spiritual in nature just as God Himself is Spirit (cf. 4,23-24). This implies for Nicodemus a fundamental adaptation of Jewish kingdom concepts, for the *kingdom* of Jn. 3,3-5 implies not only reign but also spiritual realm. The basis for these changes is given in 3,12-21 in response to Nicodemus' "Πῶς δύναται ταῦτα γενέσθαι;," as the saving work of the Son of God.

Conclusion

Through symbolism the author tells the reader that things are more than they seem to be. Everything is considered 'from above.' He invites the reader to focus the portrait of Jesus, understand the non-answers he gives to his dialogue partners, and grasp the revelation embodied in Jesus. The metaphors and symbols are misunderstood by Nicodemus, creating a setting for irony and underlining the importance of perceiving the symbolic meaning of Jesus, his words, and his works. This interweaving of themes through misunderstanding, irony, and symbolism, is the imprint of the evangelist's insight and skill. They also point to the central conflict in the Gospel – the conflict between that which is 'from above' and that which is 'from below.' Primarily the conflict is between Jesus, who is 'from above,' and those who cannot and will not recognise his identity. Understanding of the symbols is, therefore, an index to the position and movement of the characters. The symbols are one of the primary means by which the fourth evangelist presents and interprets Jesus to the reader.

3. 3,11-21: Discourse

The third authoritative double-*amen* statement of this chapter (3,3.5.11; cf. 1,51) introduces the first of the extended didactic sections related to Jesus in the fourth Gospel. The overall motif of this section deals with the purpose of Jesus' coming and with the importance of receiving or believing in him. As I have mentioned already in chapter 1, some scholars contest the literary unity of these verses and have proposed rearrangement

---

[259] See the perceptive treatment by T. Okure, *The Johannine Approach to Mission: A Contextual Study of John 4,1-42* (WUNT 31) (Tübingen 1988) 81-83; and A. J. Köstenberger, *The Missions of Jesus and the Disciples according to the Fourth Gospel: With Implications for the Fourth Gospel's Purpose and the Mission of the Contemporary Church* (Grand Rapids 1998).

108

of the chapter to the aid of 3,31-36, and many others have suggested transpositions. I shall, through my method of narrative and structural analysis, expose and demonstrate that 3,11-21 is well organised and forms a literary unit well structured in a chiastic form AB//B¹A¹. I shall first observe, briefly, the general structure of this sub-unit (3,11-21) and then go into details of smaller segmental structures within this sub-unit and analyse them from the narrative and structural perspectives.

The outer elements A-A¹ of the chiastic structure rest on a number of synonymous correlations. The first of these correlations links 3,11f-12 with 3,19c-21 (see below).

A (3,11-13)
¹¹ ἀμὴν ἀμὴν λέγω σοι ὅτι ὃ οἴδαμεν λαλοῦμεν καὶ ὃ ἑωράκαμεν μαρτυροῦμεν, καὶ _τὴν μαρτυρίαν ἡμῶν οὐ λαμβάνετε._ ¹² εἰ τὰ ἐπίγεια εἶπον ὑμῖν καὶ _οὐ πιστεύετε,_ πῶς ἐὰν εἴπω ὑμῖν τὰ ἐπουράνια πιστεύσετε; ¹³ καὶ οὐδεὶς ἀναβέβηκεν εἰς τὸν οὐρανὸν εἰ μὴ ὁ ἐκ τοῦ οὐρανοῦ καταβάς, ὁ υἱὸς τοῦ ἀνθρώπου.

> B (3,14-15)
> ¹⁴ καὶ καθὼς Μωϋσῆς ὕψωσεν τὸν ὄφιν ἐν τῇ ἐρήμῳ, οὕτως ὑψωθῆναι δεῖ τὸν υἱὸν τοῦ ἀνθρώπου, ¹⁵ ἵνα _πᾶς ὁ πιστεύων ἐν αὐτῷ ἔχῃ ζωὴν αἰώνιον._

> B¹ (3,16-18)
> ¹⁶ Οὕτως γὰρ ἠγάπησεν ὁ θεὸς τὸν κόσμον, ὥστε τὸν υἱὸν τὸν μονογενῆ ἔδωκεν, ἵνα _πᾶς ὁ πιστεύων εἰς αὐτὸν μὴ ἀπόληται ἀλλ' ἔχῃ ζωὴν αἰώνιον._ ¹⁷ _οὐ_ γὰρ ἀπέστειλεν ὁ θεὸς τὸν υἱὸν εἰς τὸν κόσμον ἵνα _κρίνῃ_ τὸν κόσμον, ἀλλ' ἵνα _σωθῇ_ ὁ κόσμος δι' αὐτοῦ. ¹⁸ ὁ πιστεύων εἰς αὐτὸν _οὐ κρίνεται·_ ὁ δὲ μὴ πιστεύων ἤδη κέκριται, ὅτι μὴ πεπίστευκεν εἰς τὸ ὄνομα τοῦ μονογενοῦς υἱοῦ τοῦ θεοῦ.

A¹ (3,19-21)
¹⁹ αὕτη δέ ἐστιν ἡ κρίσις ὅτι _τὸ φῶς ἐλήλυθεν εἰς τὸν κόσμον_ καὶ _ἠγάπησαν_ οἱ ἄνθρωποι μᾶλλον _τὸ σκότος ἢ τὸ φῶς·_ ἦν γὰρ αὐτῶν πονηρὰ τὰ ἔργα. ²⁰ πᾶς γὰρ ὁ φαῦλα πράσσων _μισεῖ τὸ φῶς_ καὶ _οὐκ ἔρχεται πρὸς τὸ φῶς,_ ἵνα μὴ ἐλεγχθῇ τὰ ἔργα αὐτοῦ· ²¹ ὁ δὲ ποιῶν τὴν ἀλήθειαν _ἔρχεται πρὸς τὸ φῶς,_ ἵνα φανερωθῇ αὐτοῦ τὰ ἔργα ὅτι ἐν θεῷ ἐστιν εἰργασμένα.

As is evident in these verses, 'not receiving the testimony' (3,11f) and 'not believing the earthly things...and the heavenly things' (3,12) are in parallel correlation with 'loving darkness more than the light' (3,19c) (see the diagram below). Because light is a metaphor signifying the revelation brought by Jesus, preferring darkness to light is an indication of refusal of that revelation, that is, not receiving the testimony borne regarding earthly and heavenly things. I can, evidently, add to this the 'hating of light and not coming to the light' of 3,20bc, as well as its antithesis 'coming to light' of 3,21b. One who refuses the testimony and loves darkness 'hates the light and does not come to the light.' Note also that the noun 'light' plays the role of inclusion in 3,19-21.

¹¹f-12 yet you *do not receive* our testimony. ¹² If I have told you about earthly things and you *do not believe*, how can you believe if I tell you about heavenly things?

¹⁹c-21 and people *loved darkness* rather than **light** because their deeds were evil. ²⁰ For all who do evil *hate the* **light** and do _not come to the **light**,_ so that their deeds may not be exposed. ²¹ But those who do what is true _come to the **light**,_ so that it may be clearly seen that their deeds have been done in God.

The second parallel correspondence revolves around the *coming of Jesus into the world:*

[13] No one has ascended into heaven except the one who *descended from heaven, the Son of Man.*

[19ab] And this is the judgement, that *the light has come into the world;*

A synonymy is to be observed in the 'descent of the Son of Man' and in the 'coming of the light into the world' (cf. 1,9). In both cases, it is the unique event of the entrance of Jesus into the world that is referred to. Now, the inner elements B-B[1] of the chiastic structure demonstrate, in two different Christological statements, the soteriological aspect of this revelatory coming of the light into the world. This structure revolves around the theme of belief and salvation:

[14-15] And just as Moses lifted up the serpent in the wilderness, so must the **Son of Man** be lifted up, [15] that *whoever **believes** in him may have eternal life.*

[16-18] For God so loved the world that he gave his **only Son**, so that *everyone who **believes** in him* <u>may not perish</u> but *may have eternal life.* [17] Indeed, God did <u>not</u> send the **Son** into the world <u>to condemn</u> the world, but in order that *the world might be saved through him.* [18] Those who **believe** in him <u>are not condemned</u>; but those who do ***not believe*** are condemned already, because they have ***not believed*** in the name of the **only Son of God.**

The positive expression "whoever believes in him *may have eternal life*" (3,15) recurs first *per nagationem* and then positively stressed in 3,16: "that everyone who believes in him *may not perish* but may *have* eternal life." 3,16 expresses, therefore, the consequences both of believing and not believing. The same echoes (positively) in the expression "in order that the world might be *saved* through him" (3,17) as well as (negatively) in "those who believe in him are *not condemned*" (3,18). If the 'lifting up of the Son of Man from the world' (3,15), 'the gift of the only Son of God' (3,16), and the 'sending of the Son into the world' (3,17) – all three have the same goal of salvation – then, all three acts are closely related to each other despite their belonging to different semantic and Christological categories.[260] I shall demonstrate that all the three events have a common denominator, namely the crucifixion of Jesus. Finally, it is to be noticed that 3,16-18 are enclosed by the recurrence of the title 'only (begotten) Son (of God)' and the verb 'believe.'

Before analysing in detail the thematic argumentation of this section, let me just mention that the regrouping of the units are based on two different Christological perspectives. The elements A and B are held together by the figure of the Son of Man (3,13 and 14). It is not just the recurrence of the title 'Son of Man' but also the vertical manner in which it is inserted into the structure demonstrates this unity. In 3,13 it is the question of the descent (from heaven) of the Son of Man and 3,14 speaks of his being lifted up (on to the cross and into heaven). The same perspective of a dualistic verticality (heaven-earth) is

---

[260] See F. Mußner, "Die 'semantische Achse' des Johannesevangeliums. Ein Versuch," in: H. Franke-mölle and K. Kertelge (eds.), *Vom Urchristentum zu Jesus, FS J. Gnilka* (Basel, Freiburg, Wien 1989) 246-55.

found in the antithesis between 'earthly and heavenly things' (3,12).[261] In the elements A[1] and B[1] (3,16-21), an horizontal structure substitutes the vertical. It is no more a question of the descent from heaven, but a coming into the world (cf. 3,19).[262] Accordingly, there is change in the titles attributed to Jesus: from the 'Son of Man' one moves to the 'Son (of God)' and the symbol of 'light.'[263]

Having observed the general structure of the entire sub-unit (3,11-21) briefly, let me now take up each of the elements of the above chiastic structure and explore their progressive thematic argumentation from the narrative and structural perspectives.

a. 3,11-13:

i. Argumentative Narrative structure

11a	Formula of authority (ἀμὴν ἀμὴν λέγω σοι)
11b-d	Affirmation (οἴδαμεν – synonymous parallelism)[264]
11f	Contrasting word of result (καὶ... οὐ)
12	Question of argument (εἰ ... καὶ οὐ ... πῶς ἐὰν – antithetical parallelism)[265]
13	Shift of argumentation (antithetical parallelism)[266]
13a	Negative statement (καὶ οὐδεὶς)
13b	Affirmative presentation (εἰ μὴ)

Besides, 3,11-13 are also structured chiastically as shown below:

a   [11a-e] Very truly, I tell you, we speak of what we know and testify to what we have seen;

    b   [11f] yet you do not receive our testimony.

    b[1] [12] If I have told you about earthly things and you do not believe, how can you believe if I tell you about heavenly things?

a[1]   [13] No one has ascended into heaven except the one who descended from heaven, the Son of Man.

The dyad a-a[1] rests on an essentially thematic relation which can be described as: testimony and its authority. In fact, in 3,11a-e Jesus and the Baptist (perhaps also the disciples) are shown as the only witnesses and revealers of the heavenly things. 3,13 gives

---

[261] Note also this verticality in the previous sub-unit in the physical/spiritual begetting ἄνωθεν (3,3-8). On a formal level 3,13 is linked to 3,11-12 through the strong connection between ἐπουράνια - οὐρανὸν/οὐρανοῦ (3,12 and 13), and to 3,14 through the recurrence of the title 'Son of Man.' However, the theme of 3,13 is closer to that of 3,11-12 than to that of 3,14-15. The Son of Man, as the only one having had an heavenly sojourn, is the qualified and unique witness of the heavenly things.

[262] See Bühner, 199.

[263] The designation of Jesus as 'light' (titular use, comp. 3,19 with 8,12) is related rather to the title 'Son' than to the title 'Son of Man.' In the prologue, the titles 'Logos' and 'light' are closely related (cf. 1,5.9; comp. 6-7 and 14-15). Moreover, in 1,14-18, the incarnated Logos itself is identified as Jesus Christ, as he is the only begotten Son of God, a qualification which is attributed only to the Son in the Gospel (cf. 3,16.18), but never to the Son of Man. This identification of the Logos (and, therefore, of the light) with the only Son of God is corroborated by Boismard and Lamouille, 72; Schnackenburg, *Gospel*, I, 279-80; and Barrett, 141.

[264] One's speech corresponds to what one knows and his/her testimony corresponds to what he/she has seen. Speech and testimony are synonymous just as knowledge and sight are synonymous.

[265] Just as believing and not believing are in contrast to each other, earthly and heavenly things are dualistic opposites of each other.

[266] The antithesis is to be noticed in the opposite movements of *ascending* and *descending* as well as in the opposite directions expressed by the prepositions 'into' (εἰς) and 'from' (ἐκ).

a reason (authority) for this affirmation: no one has ascended into heaven to be able to know and reveal the heavenly things; Jesus knows and can reveal them, because he is the Son of Man descended from heaven. The central elements (B-B¹), on the other hand, mention the refusal of this revelation by Nicodemus and the Jews whom he represents. There is a formal synonymous correspondence between 'not *receiving* our testimony' (3,11f) and the scepticism expressed in "*how can* you *believe*...the heavenly things?" (3,12c). One can equally see a synonymous correspondence between the expressions '*not receiving* the testimony of what we have seen' (of the *heavenly things* – 3,12d)[267] and '*not* (even) *believing* the *earthly things*' (3,12a). Besides, there is a dualistic correspondence of two extreme or opposed realities of a series (*viz.*, earthly and heavenly things). While admitting that the testimony of Jesus in 3,11 refers to the heavenly things, believing neither the affirmations on the earthly things nor the testimony on the heavenly things (3,12) is the rejection of *all* that Jesus reveals and manifests, both earthly and heavenly.

As I have indicated already, the whole discourse is introduced by the solemn formula "ἀμὴν ἀμὴν λέγω σοι" (3,11a). The triple mention of this formula in the text (3,3.5.11) has the same function of introducing a new phase of encounter in relation to what preceded. Such a link with what preceded is, however, established by the theme of knowledge. In fact, the proposition "we speak of what *we know*" in 3,11bc entertains an antithetical rapport with 3,10: "Are you a teacher of Israel, and yet *you do not understand* these things?" Contrary to the teacher of Israel who *does not understand* 'these things,' Jesus *knows* and reveals them.

ii. The Plural Form

The literary and grammatical structures of 3,10-11 imply more antithesis than the one between the above mentioned 'not knowing of Nicodemus' and the 'knowledge' of Jesus. In order to understand the semantic contribution of the text, one must explain the plural form used by Jesus and clarify the content as well as the relation between the expressions 'what *we* know' (ὃ οἴδαμεν) and 'what *we* have seen' (ὃ ἑωράκαμεν).[268]

There have been many attempts to explain the use of the plural here. There are divergent interpretations. Some, like H. Hegermann contend that the evangelist, here, is slipping into a dialogue between the Church ('we' – *pluralis ecclesiasticus*) and the Synagogue ('you' – pl.).[269] Though R. E. Brown and Ridderbos are of the opinion that some of the fourth evangelist's thoughts are addressed apologetically to the Synagogue, reject this view, because the evangelist returns to the singular 'I' in 3,12, even though he keeps the 'you' plural. They contend that if the Church is speaking, it cannot be only for

---

[267] A comparison of 3,11c: "...and *testify* to what we have *seen*" with 3,31-32: "The one who comes from *heaven* is above all. He *testifies* to what he has *seen* and *heard*, yet no one accepts his testimony;" 3,34: "He whom God has sent *speaks* the words of God," and 6,46: "The one who is from God, he has *seen* the Father," makes it clear that the reference here is to the heavenly things.

[268] Comp. 3,11 with 3,32: "He *testifies* to what he has *seen and heard*, yet *no one accepts his testimony*" which repeats in singular virtually 3,11. Rinke (*Kerygma und Autopsie*, 50-59) calls Jn. 3,11 as a "crux exegetica."

[269] H. Hegermann ("Er kam in sein Eigentum. Zur Bedeutung des Erdenwirkens Jesu im vierten Evangelium," in: E. Lohse, B. Schaller and C. Burchard [eds.], *Der Ruf Jesu und die Antwort der Gemeinde. Exegetische Untersuchungen. FS Joachim Jeremias zum 70. Geburtstag* [Göttingen 1970] 120); see also Dodd, *Historical Tradition*, 328; and Léon-Dufour, *Lecture*, I, 296.

one verse.[270] However, in my opinion, it is true that the fourth Gospel theologically can be read at *two levels*: the level of human reality and the level of a deeper spiritual reality. The issue of the plurals here brings up another question for the interpreter: can the reader of the Gospel also recognise the presence of a discussion at *two levels* historically? Those two intermingled contexts are the context at the time of Jesus and the context after his resurrection when the evangelist was writing.[271] If the reader is able to recognise this pattern, then the Gospel can become an exceedingly vital testimony and a model of how stories of Jesus can be applied to Church situations. The basic problem with such an approach, however, is not the Gospel itself but the way in which some scholars seek to deal with the Gospel. They try to divide the Gospel into those verses that go back to Jesus from those that go back to the early Church. From my perspective, that type of study is an unproductive quest for the historical Jesus. The fourth Gospel is a magnificent testimony that affirms both its testimonial nature and the fact that it is deeply rooted in history (21,24). Such a testimonial work allows, I believe, no such separation between history and theology as though one could strip off the layers of the testimony and get back to some isolated core of history. Trying to strip of layers from the Gospel is like peeling an onion that really has no core.

Schnackenburg rejects also the opinion that the evangelist uses a *pluralis majestatis* here to mark Jesus' consciousness of his high dignity, because, when the fourth Gospel' Jesus gives utterance to his full dignity, he uses ἐγώ; and the only comparable text in the Gospel (9,4) is inapposite, because, there, Jesus is addressing the intimate circle of his disciples.[272] Some others argue that Jesus, here, identifies himself with the prophets.[273] This view, in my opinion, is weak as one has to consider "what we have seen" in 3,11 as referring to visions, which certainly do not fit Jesus. Most standard commentaries discuss the various opinions. Hence, I do not want to enumerate all those opinions and refute each one of them with counter arguments. I shall, however, defend my view in the following pages.[274]

Now, from the orientation furnished by the structural organisation of the text, I shall analyse also in detail the content of these verses. The first part of the synonymous parallelism (3,11b-e) is composed of two assertions placed parallel to each other and linked by the conjunction καὶ: ὃ οἴδαμεν λαλοῦμεν καὶ ὃ ἑωράκαμεν μαρτυροῦμεν. The first assertion is about the declaration 'what we know.'

---

[270] Cf. R. E. Brown, *op. cit.*, 132; and Ridderbos, 133.

[271] See the study of G. Sellin, "'Die Auferstehung ist schon geschehen'. Zur Spiritualisierung apokalyptischer Terminologie im Neuen Testament," *NT* 25 (1983) 220-37.

[272] Cf. Schnackenburg, *Gospel*, I, 376.

[273] For a discussion on various opinions, see the commentaries of Bauer, Strachan, Barrett, Wikenhauser, Schnackenburg, Bernard and A. Loisy, *Le quatrième Évangile. Les Épîtres dites de Jean* (Paris 1921).

[274] For a bird's eye view of the various opinions and their supporters see the chart of Schmidl (217, n. 743). Létourneau (*Jésus*, 158-59, n. 109) regroups all the opinions into three important ones: 1) Echo of the plural in 3,2 for contrasting the knowledge of Jesus and Nicodemus; 2) Jesus and his disciples as the most natural; 3) *Pluralis ecclesiasticus*. Though he favours the second one, he argues that all the three opinions complement each other.

α. Οἴδαμεν

The clue to a right interpretation of this verse is to be found, first of all, in the structure of the text itself. On the one hand, the form 'ὃ οἴδαμεν' used by Jesus in 3,11, structurally takes one to its verbal form 'οἴδαμεν' used by Nicodemus in 3,2. In my opinion, there is logic in observing in 3,11 an ironic echo of the οἴδαμεν of 3,2 as already been pointed out earlier. Just as in 3,10 Jesus picks up the theme of 'teacher' from Nicodemus' words in 3,2, so also in 3,11 Jesus picks up the οἴδαμεν from 3,2 and turns it against Nicodemus. R. E. Brown contends that the οἴδαμεν is a "parody of Nicodemus' hint of arrogance."[275] I shall come to a plausible solution to the plural form at the end of the discussion on this verse in the following pages.

In my opinion, a mere ironic repetition of the οἴδαμεν in 3,2 and 3,11 cannot indicate the contrast between Nicodemus and Jesus. It is rather the *knowledge* itself of the two dialogue partners which is placed in opposition. Though there seems to be a confrontation between Jesus and Nicodemus, the emphasis is no longer (negatively) on the inadequacy of Nicodemus' knowledge but (positively) to another knowledge on the basis of which Jesus speaks (3,11). Nicodemus is the representative of the knowledge of his group; he comes to Jesus and makes his knowledge – that he shares with those whom he represents – known to Jesus. Like those mentioned in 2,23, he has seen the signs performed by Jesus. Being a Pharisee and a ruler of the Jews, he knows that the signs confirm normally the presence of God and that they attest the divine mission and sending by God. His knowledge, though inadequate, concerns the person and the mission of Jesus.[276] The repetition of the οἴδαμεν in 3,11 is not, therefore, purely formal and empty of meaning, but indicates a Christological revelation of the discourse introduced here.

Moreover, the ὃ οἴδαμεν in 3,11 stands in antithesis to the affirmation οὐ γινώσκεις 3,10.[277] To the unmasked and exposed οὐ γινώσκεις of Nicodemus, the ὃ οἴδαμεν of Jesus in 3,11 is placed in opposition.[278] But in order that the opposition may be significant in its argumentation, the object of οὐ γινώσκεις and ὃ οἴδαμεν must be the same. This leads to the assumption that there must be a thematic continuity in the narration of the dialogue – between 'these things' (ταῦτα) in 3,9-10 and 'what we know' (ὃ οἴδαμεν) in 3,11. Moreover, the question of Nicodemus in 3,9 must be understood as dealing with the process of salvation as such. Following the explanation of Jesus on the spiritual nature of

---

[275] R. E. Brown, *op. cit.*, 132. See also Carson, *Gospel*, 199; and Léon-Dufour, *op. cit.*

[276] Nicodemus has found Jesus' teaching hard to understand (cf. 3,10), but Jesus turns that incredulity into a fundamentally Christological question. Nicodemus had approached Jesus with a certain amount of respect (3,2), but he had not even begun to appreciate the real identiy of Jesus. In fact, the failure of Nicodemus and his group was not a failure of intellect but a failure to believe the testimony of the Baptist (cf. 1,19-27 and 3,23-25) and that of Jesus (3,11). The Jews at large did not receive the testimony. The present tense "you do not receive our testimony" (3,11f) must be given its full force. This was no occasional thing, but the regular habit. The failure to believe was more reprehensible than the lack of knowledge or the failure to understand, since it betrayed a fundamentally inadequate appreciation of the identity of Jesus.

[277] For a discussion on these two terms see I. de la Potterie, "οἶδα et γινώσκω. Les deux modes de la connaissance dans le quatrième évangile," *Bib.* 40 (1959) 709-25. See also J. H. Neyrey, "John III – A Debate over Johannine Epistemology and Christology," *NT* 23 (1981) 118-22.

[278] Létourneau (*op. cit.* 160, n. 112) argues that the position of 'ὃ οἴδαμεν' at the beginning of the phrase (3,11b) before the verb is an emphasis. The more the 'οὐ γινώσκεις' of Nicodemus is exposed by the irony in 3,10 the more the 'ὃ οἴδαμεν' of Jesus is brought emphatically to the forefront.

the necessity of begetting ἄνωθεν to enter into the kingdom of God, Nicodemus finally asks how one could enter into the kingdom of God; that is, how could one receive the Spirit which begets ἄνωθεν? (cf. 3,9). The *knowledge* in 3,11 which is the object of revelation must, therefore, be concerning this question of salvation. These results, thus, lead me to the first deduction that 3,11 reveals the person and the mission of Jesus (link with 3,2) as well as the process of attaining salvation (link with 3,9-10).

β. Λαλοῦμεν

The verb λαλέω, in the fourth Gospel, stands for revelation.[279] This is all the more so when the verb is applied to Jesus in the singular (cf. 8,38). It is, however, legitimate to ask if the *plural form* includes in some way the disciples of Jesus.[280] One may suspect that such, apparently, may be the case in 3,11. In fact, in 15,15 Jesus tells his disciples: "I have called you friends, because I have made known to you everything that I have heard from my Father." Provided with this knowledge, the disciples can be associated with the revelatory mission of Jesus. After the departure of Jesus, they would continue this mission with the assistance of the Paraclete, the Spirit of truth (cf. 14,25-26). However, there remains a difference between Jesus and his disciples; Jesus is the initiator of revelation; the disciples are associated with him as the first recipients of that revelation.

γ. Ἑωράκαμεν

The use of the present tense of the verb 'ἑωράκαμεν' must also be interpreted in this sense. Apart from 3,11, the perfect of the verb 'ἑώρακεν' has Jesus as subject thrice (3,32; 6,46; 8,38; and implicitly 1,18). On two occasions 'what he has seen' is not determined but implies Jesus' situation when he was with his Father or in heaven (8,38; cf. 3,31-32); in the other cases, 'what Jesus has seen' is his Father himself (1,18 and 6,46). Other uses of the verb in the perfect tense serve either to deny the vision of the Father by anyone other than the Son (1,18; 5,37 and 6,46), or positively, to express the 'seeing' which is fixed on the person of Jesus during his presence on earth (6,36; 9,37; 14,7.9; 19,35 and 20,18.25.29). In some of these cases, one may be led to think that the verb expresses the perception of faith, because the 'seeing' can lead to the Father who dwells in Jesus (14,7.9).[281] However, it is always the historical person of Jesus who is the immediate object of 'seeing.'

---

[279] Cf. de la Potterie, "de revelatione," 259. See also R. E. Brown, *op. cit.*; and J. Beutler, *Martyria. Traditionsgeschichtliche Untersuchungen zum Zeugnisthema bei Johannes* (FTS 10) (Frankfurt 1972) 311. This verb, in the fourth Gospel, refers often to the teaching of Jesus, who has been appointed the only revealer of the Father, and who "speaks the words of God" (3,34); he declares to the world what he has heard from his Father (8,26); his Father has instructed him (8,28); has seen in his Father's presence (8,38) what He has commanded him (12,49); what he says is the truth that he has heard from his Father (8,40). Moreover, he speaks just as the Father has told him (12,50); he does not speak on his own, but the Father who dwells in him does his works (14,10). Even after his return to his Father, he will continue to speak (17,13), plainly (16,25.29), through the Paraclete – the Spirit of truth (16,13).

[280] Ridderbos (134), along with Westcott and Barrett defends this opinion substantially. Létourneau (*op. cit.*, 161), too, favours this interpretation. See also Morris, *Gospel*, 196. Schnackenburg (*Gospel*, I, 376), though seems to accept this as a plausible solution, observes, all the same, that such a view does not account for the fact that Jesus is the unique revealer (cf. 3,32) and the disciples are not to be considered revealers in the same sense as Jesus. See also Boismard and Lamouille, 122.

[281] C. Traets (*Voir Jésus et le Père en lui selon l'Évangile de saint Jean* [AnGr 159] [Rome 1967] 50-52) argues that each verb can express in its own way the depth of the visual perception leading to a vision of

Under these circumstances, it may imply that, if the disciples are associated with Jesus in the plural form in 3,11, the content of their testimony concerns their experience of the person of Jesus during his earthly ministry. Though their *seeing* could have, through faith, recognised the true mystery of the person of Jesus, it is to the eye-witness account of his earthly life that they are called to testify (cf. 15,27). This thematic takes me back to 1,14 which expresses, in other words, that the 'seeing' of the believer is directed to the Word made flesh, discerning in it the glory of the only Son of God. One could equally invoke the text of 19,35 which concludes the story of the crucifixion. Once again, the seeing is directed to the concrete event of the life of Jesus and leads to the perception of faith. That is what is the object of testimony[282] here (cf. 1 Jn. 1,1-3).

δ. Μαρτυροῦμεν

Now, I must ask if the second part "ὃ ἑωράκαμεν μαρτυροῦμεν" (3,11de) allows the same association of the disciples with Jesus. Here, the text speaks of the *testimony*[283] to what has been *seen*. In the fourth Gospel, the verb 'μαρτυρέω' is used in different ways. When it is Jesus himself who testifies, the object of his testimony is often his own person (8,12-14) or a truth belonging to the order of salvation inaccessible to human beings (cf. 3,32 and 18,37). The authority of his testimony is, first of all, based on the fact that 'he *knows* where he comes from and where he goes' (cf. 8,14); secondly, it is based on his heavenly *origin* (cf. 3,31-32). In this perspective, it will be difficult to include the disciples as the subject of the testimony in the same level as that of Jesus. Moreover, 3,13 forbids one from such an understanding as '*no one* has ascended into heaven *except* ...., the Son of Man.'

But the verb 'μαρτυρέω' is also used to refer to the testimony of others on Jesus. The verb is, thus, applied to God (5,32.37 and 8,18), the Paraclete – the Spirit of truth (15,26), the Baptist (1,7.8.15.32.34; 3,26 and 5,33), the Samaritan woman (4,39), the works (5,36 and 10,25), the Scriptures (5,39), and the disciples (15,27 and 19,35). In this category, the application of the verb to the Baptist, the Samaritan woman and the disciples is particularly significant for my purpose in the network of the first section of the Gospel, which I shall treat in Part II in detail. The testimony of these three witnesses is essentially based on the experience of an event in the ministry of Jesus: the Baptist *testifies*, because he has *seen* the Spirit descending and remaining on Jesus (1,32-34); that of the Samaritan woman is based on the fact that Jesus *told* her "all that she had done" (4,39); in the same way the disciples can testify, because Jesus has *promised* them of a sight of "greater things" (1,51); he revealed his glory to them and they believed in him (2,11), and "they have been with Jesus from the beginning" (15,27), that is, they have been eye-witnesses of his ministry (cf. 19,35).

All these seem to imply that the disciples can be associated with Jesus in "ὃ ἑωράκαμεν μαρτυροῦμεν" in 3,11 only with difficulty. When Jesus testifies to what he has seen and heard, it is to his seeing the Father and to his knowledge about the heavenly

---

faith. Hence, one must, according to him, pay attention to the context and tense in which the verb is employed.

[282] It is to be remembered that the testimony of the members of the Johannine Community was essentially based on the earthly sojourn of the Word made flesh.

[283] For a discussion on testimony here, see A. A. Trites, *The New Testament Concept of Witness* (MSSNTS 31) (Cambridge 1977) 95-97. See also Klaiber, 205-33.

things; he is the only one who could testify to it, because he has come down from heaven.[284] When the disciples are called to testify, they announce only what they have seen of the incarnated Word on earth. But one must not forget that, in a certain limited way, it is this vision of the Word incarnate who gives them access to the world above.[285] However, for the following reasons, I find it more reasonable to see the plural referring to Jesus and the Baptist:

1) In the narrative context of the story, it makes more sense that Jesus has the Baptist in mind in the "we know" and "we testify" in 3,11 rather than his disciples. At this early part of the story, the disciples are still in the beginning stage of following him and have not yet been sufficiently initiated to know and to testify to the person of Jesus. Though, they are with Jesus in Jerusalem (2,12), have seen the miracle at Cana (2,2.11) and have even been promised sight of greater things (1,51), nowhere else in the first three chapters are they presented as testifying to Jesus. Only in Jn. 4 they are sent out by Jesus in Samaria (to buy food) which could have a faint reference to the beginning stage of their being sent out to bear witness to Jesus.

2) In the context of the dialogue with Nicodemus, it is logical that Jesus refers to the testimony of the Baptist, as Nicodemus (a Jerusalem based Pharisee and ruler of the Jews) belongs to the Jewish enquiry commission from Jerusalem sent to investigate the activity of the Baptist (1,19; cf. 3,1). The disciples are not known to Nicodemus.

3) Nicodemus and his colleagues apparently did not accept the testimony of the Baptist (cf. 1,19-25) and this is echoed in the 'non acceptance of *our testimony*' (3,11f).

4) Besides this narrative context, the formal verbal evidence also supports my view: ὃ οἴδαμεν (3,11b) of Jesus echoes the Baptist's κἀγὼ οὐκ ᾔδειν αὐτόν (1,31.33); καὶ ὃ ἑωράκαμεν (3,11d) of Jesus echoes the Baptist's κἀγὼ ἑώρακα (1,34); and μαρτυροῦμεν (3,11e) of Jesus again echoes the Baptist's καὶ μεμαρτύρηκα (1,34). Added to this, I must also refer to the following parallels: ὃ οἴδαμεν (3,11b) of Jesus is parallel to στηκεν ὃν ὑμεῖς οὐκ οἴδατε (1,26) of the Baptist to the enquiry commission from Jerusalem, and the similar οὐ γινώσκεις (3,10) of Jesus to Nicodemus, who represented the Jerusalem authorities.

Let me also go back to the prologue where Jn. 3 has parallels in a special way (comp. e.g.: the symbol of light in 1,4.5.7-9 with 3,19-21):

1,5b καὶ ἡ σκοτία αὐτὸ <u>οὐ</u> κατέλαβεν // 3,11f καὶ <u>*τὴν μαρτυρίαν*</u> ἡμῶν <u>οὐ</u> λαμβάνετε.

1,7a οὗτος ἦλθεν εἰς *μαρτυρίαν*

1,7b is almost identical with 1,8b: ἵνα μαρτυρήσῃ περὶ τοῦ φωτός

1,11b καὶ οἱ ἴδιοι αὐτὸν <u>οὐ</u> παρέλαβον.

---

[284] A. Denaux, "The Q-Logion Mt 11,27/Lk 10,22 and the Gospel of John," in: his *John and the Synoptics*, 194.

[285] In 14,6 Jesus reveals that he is the way, the truth and the life, and no one can go to the Father except through him. Immediately after, that is, 14,7 shows that this way to the Father is not to be found in an eschatological future far away, but is open already: from now on the disciples know the Father and see Him. To Philip who does not understand and asks Jesus to show him the Father, Jesus replies: "Have I been with you all this time, Philip, and you still do not know me? Whoever has *seen* me has *seen* the Father" (14,9). During the time spent with Jesus, the disciples had access to know and

Let me now consider the object of this *sight*. Besides the formal parallelism, the content of the parallels also supports the comparison. The testimony of the Baptist was not a random testimony to something, nor to a vision (1,32: τεθέαμαι τὸ πνεῦμα καταβαῖνον), but a testimony to which God Himself had given proof (1,33: Ἐφ' ὃν ἂν ἴδῃς τὸ πνεῦμα καταβαῖνον). Moreover, it is accompanied by God's word (1,33: ἐκεῖνός μοι εἶπεν).

Now, what all these have to do with 3,11? From his 'not knowing' (1,31.33: οὐκ ᾔδειν) the Baptist has received a sight (1,32: τεθέαμαι), so that he could later testify to it: κἀγὼ ἑώρακα, καὶ μεμαρτύρηκα (1,34). In the perfect form the past is assumed into the present; and the knowledge of the Baptist, hence also his testimony, are reliable as they result from a *sight* he had. The object of the sight in 3,11 must also be related, though not be identified with, to the immediately preceding 'being begotten ἄνωθεν by the Spirit' (3,3-8).

However, in my formal and narrative structure I have included 3,11 to the discourse part of the Nicodemus episode, which goes beyond the first part on begetting ἄνωθεν. Where does it go beyond? Recalling the testimony of the Baptist, he saw Jesus as one on whom the Spirit descended. The theme of begetting ἄνωθεν by the Spirit leads to the mediator of this begetting, Jesus himself in 3,11. The object of the sight in 1,29-34 is the same as that of 3,11, *viz.*, Jesus in his relation with the Father, in his Spirit-being as God's only Son (cf. 3,34: "He gives the Spirit without measure;" and 3,35: "The Father loves the Son and has placed all things in his hands").

5) Finally, another important support strengthens my argument: The evangelist brings the Baptist into the scene once again immediately after this episode and makes him testify to Jesus a second time to authenticate the authority of Jesus beyond doubt. See the parallels between 3,11-13 and 3,31-36, and the recurrence of the terms, witnesses, testify and testimony in 3,26.28.32.33; of the terms hear, speak, and see in 3,32.34; and of above/below, heaven/earth, and heavenly things/earthly things in 3,31.

Concluding this first part, I must say that the plural form of 3,11 is not just a literary artifice devoid of meaning, serving to balance structurally the words of Jesus, and of Nicodemus and his group in 3,2. I must also admit that the evangelist, here, is making use of the occasion to make Jesus prove the authority of the testimony of the Baptist. Although Jesus is the unique revealer, the special vision of the Baptist had equipped him with first hand information and knowledge about heavenly things; he must, therefore, be also associated with him as an authorised agent of testimony.

If one accepts the interpretation of 3,11, according to which the Baptist is included with Jesus in the plural form, one must also admit that the content of the testimony is the same for both subjects; in other words, the expressions 'what *we* know' and 'what *we* have seen' must have a unique referent in the case of Jesus and the Baptist. The testimony, therefore, can only be about the heavenly things, which is also confirmed by the rest of the structure as I shall show in the following pages. For the moment, it is sufficient to accept that the Baptist is associated with Jesus as witness of heavenly things in the plural form.

iii. Logic of 3,12

However, the testimony about what has been *known* and *seen* is *not received* (3,11f). 3,12 leads me to the reasoning behind the testimony being rejected:

"**If** *I*[286] have told you about earthly things and *you* (pl.) do not believe
how can you believe **if** *I* tell *you* (pl.) about heavenly things?"

3,12 uses an argument *a minori ad maius*. The argumentation of this verse rests on
the attachment of the two conditional propositions (if), of which the first becomes the
premise of the second. In the first case, one has a factual or real situation in the past tense
(εἰ + aorist indicative). The fact that the statement refers to a past action implies its
completion and even verification. It refers to what has actually happened. Therefore, it can
serve as the valuable basis for the conditional proposition in the second part of the verse,
which speaks of a future event (ἐὰν + subjunctive). It does not contain any implication
about the fulfilment of the condition. The reasoning is the following: when Jesus spoke of
the (simple) 'earthly things,' they did not believe; it will not, therefore, be surprising if
they will not believe if he speaks of the heavenly things.

In spite of the simple construction, the verse carries an ambiguity of interpretation
which needs to be clarified.[287] The first way to understand 3,12 can be illustrated by the
following rendering: 'when I spoke to you about the earthly things (which are simpler to
understand) you did not believe, how will you be able to, then, believe if I speak to you
about heavenly things (which are far more difficult to understand)?' In such an
interpretation, the verse paves the way for Jesus to announce the heavenly things, which he
is about to reveal, though his listeners like Nicodemus will not believe.

Now, inserted into the narrative sequence of the story, this statement of Jesus
implies forcefully that Jesus has not yet spoken of the heavenly things. All that he has said
so far is about the earthly things; and the experience of refusal to believe them serves as
sufficient proof to expect the same result of unbelief when the heavenly things will be
revealed. The narrative chain of 3,11-12 forces me to take into consideration the testimony
made in 3,11 to what has been *known* and *seen*. Moreover, the study I made above on the
fourth evangelist's use of the verbs λαλέω, ὁράω and μαρτυρέω as applied to Jesus, helps
me to deduce that they qualify the content of the testimony as referring to 'earthly things.'

There is, however, another way of interpreting 3,12, which consists in
understanding it as a principle of the general order, serving exclusively to explain the
statement 3,11. In this perspective, the principal function of 3,12 is not to initiate the future
announcement about the heavenly things in the following verses. As I have remarked
before, the announcement of the revelation has been made already in 3,11, which – in
serving as an answer to the question raised by Nicodemus in 3,9 about the attainment of
salvation – opened the Christological discourse of Jesus: "We speak of what we know and
testify to what we have seen" (3,11b-e). Already at the beginning of his discourse, Jesus
makes it clear to his dialogue partner the profound character of his revelation presented as
a testimony about the heavenly things; and he does not mince words in reproaching
Nicodemus and his colleagues for not accepting his testimony (3,10c.11f.). Thus, 3,12
comes to clarify this affirmation: 'it is not surprising that you did not receive our

---

[286] This shift again to the singular has evoked little interest among the scholars in their works. The
attention of the exegetes is concentrated on the 'earthly' and 'heavenly things' as well as on the disbelief.
However, for a discussion on the change in number see Rebell, 169; and Schmidl, 228.

[287] See C. Saayman, "The Textual Strategy in John 3:12-14: Preliminary Observations," *Neotest.* 29
(1995) 27-48.

testimony, because you did not believe even the earthly things that I spoke to you; how will you, then, believe if I speak to you about heavenly things?' The evidence of refusal to believe the testimony borne to things known and seen (3,11b-e) and the earthly things told (12a) serves as the argumentative basis for the reproach on the assumed refusal to believe the heavenly things. On the one hand, the first proposition (3,12ab) about unbelief in the earthly things is the basis for the logical consequence expressed in the second proposition (3,12cd). On the other hand, the whole of 3,12 serves to justify the statement made in 3,11f; it might, then, mean that the testimony (to "what we have seen") in 3,11de must correspond to the heavenly things of 3,12cd. Thus, there is a narrative flow and logical sequence between 3,11 and 3,12.

◆ Earthly and Heavenly Things

Now, what remains to be clarified is: what are these earthly and heavenly things?[288] If the argumentation of 3,11-12 rests on the refusal to believe the earthly things told already, and 3,11 has initiated already the discourse on the revelation of the heavenly things, what could be the narrative content of the earthly things that Jesus refers to.[289] The only possibility that remains is to search the narrative referent to the 'earthly things' in the subject of the preceding dialogue between Jesus and Nicodemus on begetting ἄνωθεν.[290] This is the opinion of a vast majority of exegetes.[291] Some reject this interpretation as begetting out

---

[288] The distinction between earthly and heavenly things is often used in wisdom and apocalyptic traditions as a kind of technique to avoid or to reproach in addressing a student who desires to know things that lie beyond his capacity, or a man who wants to reach heaven by penetrating the heavenly secrets. (cf. Wis. 9,16-17 and 4 Esdr. 4,10-12, and Sanhedrin 39a). For a further discussion on this see Schnackenburg, *Gospel*, I, 377-78; he reminds that there are in the NT degrees in the knowledge of salvation as suggested in 1 Cor. 3,1-3 and Heb. 6,1. On 4 Esdr. 4,10-12, see J. H. Charlesworth (ed.), *The Old Testament Pseudepigrapha* (Garden City 1983) I, 530. For more remote parallels cf. 3 Enoch 10,4-5 and 11,2-3 (see Charlesworth, *op. cit.*, 264). See also E. Schweizer, *Erniedrigung und Erhöhung bei Jesus und seinen Nachfolgern* (AThANT 28) (Zürich ²1962) 179-80. The distinction Jesus makes between the earthly and heavenly things must be seen not only as an argument to reproach Nicodemus for his unbelief but also as an attraction for Nicodemus and his colleagues to encourage a probe into higher realities. For the evangelist, it is a technique of leading the reader to further revelation on the identity of Jesus.

[289] The contrast between the 'earthly things' and the 'heavenly things' is not easy to determine; see R. E. Brown, *op. cit.*, 132. He also observes a spatial dualism here. However, he differentiates it from the flesh/ Spirit dualism since 'earthly' does not have any derogatory meaning. Some take the 'earthly things' to refer to physical elements such as wind and natural birth, while 'heavenly things' refer to the lofty subject like begetting ἄνωθεν But no one disbelieves in 'earthly things' such as wind and physical birth. A subtler variation of the same interpretation takes 'earthly things' to refer to birth and the blowing of the wind, but takes the clause 'and you do not believe' (3,12a) to mean 'you do not trust and recognise God in these events, nor see how they point parabolically to begetting ἄνωθεν.' Even such an interpretation, in my opinion, is unacceptable, for natural birth and the blowing of the wind do not function in the narrative as objects of faith by which one gains spiritual insight, but illustrations or analogies of spiritual realities. Besides, there are all sorts of wild speculations as to the explanation of the 'earthly' and 'heavenly things;' e.g. Thüsing (225ff.) argues strongly that the 'earthly things' cover Jesus' whole ministry on earth; the 'heavenly things' do not refer to the content of 3,13-15 but to the post-ascensional words of Jesus spoken through the Paraclete. Such a view has little support in the text. For a critique of this view cf. Létourneau, *op. cit.*, 166, n. 124. For a brief summary of the opinions of various scholars see Schmidl, 229-35.

[290] Calling it as the "simplest explanation," R. E. Brown (*op. cit.*) asserts that what Jesus has said already comes under 'earthly,' and what he is going to say falls under 'heavenly.'

[291] To mention a few, see J. Blank, *Krisis. Untersuchungen zur johanneischen Christologie und Eschatologie* (Freiburg 1964) 62-63; Barrett, 212; Schnackenburg, *op. cit.*, 377; Bauer, *Johannesevangelium*, 55; Becker, *Johannes*, I, 139; Bernard, I, 110; Bultmann, *Gospel*, 149; Hoskyns, 205; Morris, *Gospel*, 196-97; Ridderbos, 134; and Gaeta, 77.

'of water and the Spirit' is 'begetting ἄνωθεν, and it can scarcely be considered an 'earthly thing.' But it is 'earthly' in that it takes place here on earth when people are begotten. R. E. Brown rightly adds that the contrast here is "between two types of divine action, one more heavenly and mysterious than the other."[292] Schnackenburg, too, observes here "not a matter of contrast but of degree."[293] However, in my opinion, the general explanation of the terms 'earthly' and 'heavenly' is to be sought in the fourth evangelist's way of looking at things vertically and dualistically.

More important, Jesus' teaching on begetting ἄνωθεν is about the elementary point of entry into the kingdom of God. In this context, Carson argues that the 'heavenly things' refer to the "splendours of the kingdom."[294] The 'earthly things' apparently are the matters that have been discussed in the preceding dialogue and not believed by Nicodemus. The dialogue was taking place on earth and concerned a process with effects discernible on earth. To be sure, the subject matter had, then naturally, to deal with begetting ἄνωθεν, but in a perspective that was restricted to humanity and the earth, and things that one would assume a teacher in Israel could understand and believe.[295] In fact, the 'earthly things' are realities of the terrestrial domain linked with salvation and are accessible already according to the revelation made in the OT; and Nicodemus as a teacher of Israel should know them. But the revelation remains incomplete as long as it is not fulfilled in Jesus. As I have observed earlier, the regeneration in the Spirit on the day of Yahweh has been announced by the prophets. Having first reminded Nicodemus of that teaching (which could be called earthly things), Jesus continues to expose that such a regeneration is possible only through the elevation of the Son of Man (3,13-15) and through faith in the Son of God (3,16-18). These are the 'heavenly things' concerning the fulfilment of salvation in the person of the Son of Man and Son of God. It is a mystery inaccessible until now;[296] and only Jesus can reveal it as he has come down from heaven (3,13).

Nevertheless, the question of the *how* of the earthly things cannot be resolved without faith and insight into the heavenly things of which Jesus is about to speak. For in the light of the heavenly things it will become clear that being begotten ἄνωθεν out of 'water and Spirit,' is not a miracle from above but something that occurs through faith in him who came from above or, as 3,13 has it, 'descended from heaven.'

iv. Authority of Jesus' Testimony (3,13)

This first part of Jesus' discourse (3,11-13) concludes with a proof of Jesus' unique authority to speak of heavenly things (3,13). Echoing 'the heavenly things' in 3,12, it mentions 'heaven' twice, both times in connection with (the ascent and descent of) the Son of Man. Moreover, connected to the preceding verse by καί, 3,13 provides the explanation for the fact that Jesus is able to speak authoritatively of 'heavenly things.' Jesus has affirmed that he is the revealer of the heavenly things, and regrets that his testimony is not

---

[292] R. E. Brown, *op. cit.*

[293] Schnackenburg, *op. cit.*, 378.

[294] Carson, *Gospel*, 199.

[295] Cf. Léon-Dufour, *Lecture*, I, 298-99; and J. T. Forestell, *The Word of the Cross. Salvation as Revelation in the Fourth Gospel* (AnBib 57) (Rome 1974) 42-43.

[296] On the mystical aspect of the fourth Gospel see J. Kanagaraj, *'Mysticism' in the Gospel of John: An Inquiry into its Background* (JSNT.S 158) (Sheffield 1998).

received. It is not surprising that his listeners do not even accept his words about the earthly things which are accessible already; how will they believe in his words about the heavenly things? However, they must believe, because he is the only *authentic witness* who could speak about them *authoritatively*, because no one has ever ascended into heaven (cf. Prov. 30,4). But Jesus has come down from there. The fourth evangelist insists, throughout his Gospel, on Jesus' heavenly origin.[297] This is one way in which he brings out his point that Jesus is the Messiah. Here, his heavenly origin marks Jesus off from the rest of humanity.[298] People are, as Paul puts it, "from the earth, of dust" (1 Cor. 15,47); they cannot raise themselves to heaven.[299] But Jesus is from heaven, and he has brought heavenly realities to the earth (cf. 1,51). To understand about heavenly realities, therefore, the God-given means is through 'no one *but* the one' (εἰ μὴ ὁ) who has descended from heaven. This argument is strongly reflected in 3,13:

<blockquote>
"No one has ascended into heaven

except the one who descended from heaven, the Son of Man."
</blockquote>

The same is made all the more evident in the chiastic structure of this verse:

No one	A	οὐδεὶς
has ascended	B	ἀναβέβηκεν
into heaven	C	εἰς τὸν οὐρανὸν
but[300] he who	D	εἰ μὴ ὁ

---

[297] Cf. R. E. Brown, *op. cit.*, 133; see also O. Michel, "Der aufsteigende und der herabsteigende Gesandte," in: W. C. Weinrich (ed.), *The New Testament Age. Essays in Honor of Bo Reicke* (Macon 1984) II, 335-61.

[298] R. Bultmann (*Theology of the New Testament* [London 1955] II, 37; see also Vol. 1, 166ff.) explains this passage in terms of the Gnostic myth of the descent of the Redeemer. He cites no evidence, and takes the truth of his assumption for granted. But, I feel that strong objection can be raised against it. There is no real evidence that the Gnostic myth existed at the time the fourth Gospel was written. The only first-century literature to which Bultmann appeals is the NT itself. See C. Scholten, "Probleme der Gnosisforschung: alte Fragen – neue Zugänge," *IkaZ* 26 (1997) 481-501; E. Yamauchi, "Gnosticism and Early Christianity," in: W. E. Helleman (ed.), *Hellenisation Revisited. Shaping a Christian Response within Graeco-Roman World* (London 1994) 29-61; C. H. Talbert, "The Myth of a Descending-Ascending Redeemer in Mediterranean Antiquity," *NTS* 22 (1976) 418-40; R. G. Hamerton-Kelly, *Pre-existence, Wisdom and the Son of Man* (MSSNTS 21) (Cambridge 1973) 225-38; and M. E. Willett, *Wisdom Christology in the Fourth Gospel* (San Francisco 1992). The text here is rooted in an affirmation that the heavenly realities (3,12) are being opened to humanity because the divine Son of Man descended (καταβάς) into history. The aorist tense is intended to enumerate an event in history quite unlike any concept of the Son of Man in Enoch 68,2-6 or Dan. 7,14. The descent here obviously picks up the theme of a pre-existent Son of Man in those earlier Jewish texts, but the descent and ascent of the Son of Man in the fourth Gospel is clearly unlike anything in Jewish or Hellenistic literature. See P. Borgen, "Some Exegetical Traditions as Background for Son of Man Sayings in John's Gospel (Jn. 3:13-14 and context)," in: de Jonge, *L'Évangile de Jean*, 243-58; E. M. Sidebottom, "The Ascent and Descent of the Son of Man in the Gospel of John," *AThR* 39 (1957) 115-22; and S. S. Smalley, "The Johannine Son of Man Sayings," *NTS* 15 (1968/69) 291-94. This descent of Jesus, the Son of Man, made him actually become human (σάρξ – cf. 1,14) – an idea totally rejected by the later Gnostics and, although hinted at in texts like Is. 53, actually missed by Jewish interpreters. Indeed, it was hardly understood by Jesus' own disciples – until after the resurrection.

[299] It was part of the sin of the "son of Dawn" that he said in his heart, "I will ascend to heaven" (Is. 14,12-13). But he could not do it. It remained a boast and an ambition. However, since in the context there is the thought of begetting ἄνωθεν, and since there are references to seeing and entering the kingdom of God, one should, probably, understand the verse also to mean that ascent into heaven is, in fact, possible. But this can be done only by the new begetting ἄνωθεν which the Son of Man in some sense effects. It is not a human possibility. Thus, a further argument for the narrative flow and sequence with 3,3-10 is established.

[300] Cf. RSV translation. The NRSV translation has 'except' (giving the false interpretation of an 'exception').

from heaven	C¹	ἐκ τοῦ οὐρανοῦ
descended	B¹	(ὁ) καταβάς
the Son of Man	A¹	ὁ υἱὸς τοῦ ἀνθρώπου[301]

α. Εἰ μή

a) Translation

Εἰ μή is often misunderstood, primarily because it can be translated more than one way. Εἰ μή, often translated as 'except,'[302] can introduce an exception to the general idea that has been introduced, without providing an exception to what is explicitly stated in the immediately preceding clause. English usage in such cases often demands 'but,'[303] 'but rather,' or 'but only.'

b) Other Occurrences of εἰ μή in the NT

Comparing with "but nothing unclean will enter it, nor anyone who practices abomination or falsehood, *but* (εἰ μή) only those who are written in the Lamb's book of life" (Rev. 21,27), clearly those written in the Lamb's book of life are not thought to be impure, shameful or deceitful; the translation would be highly misleading in this context if εἰ μή were rendered by 'except' (cf. 6,22.46; 14,6; 17,12 and 19,15; Mt. 12,4; Lk. 4,27; and Gal. 1,19).[304] In all these cases the one in the εἰ μή clause proves to be the only one that does the action described in the first clause. In the example from Rev. 21,27, only those whose names are written in the book of life actually enter the holy city. Applying this to Jn. 3,13, it might be taken to mean that the one who has ascended is the one who has descended. But the flow of the argument and the peculiar perfect ἀναβέβηκεν (has ascended) conspire to focus the 'exception' rather differently. Jesus can speak of heavenly things (3,12), and (καί) no one (else) has ascended into heaven and remained there (so as to be able to speak authoritatively about heavenly things) *but only* the one who has come down from heaven (is equipped to do so).[305] Jesus insists that no one has ascended into heaven in such a way as to return to talk about heavenly things. He can speak of heavenly things, not because he ascended to heaven from a home on earth and then descended again to tell others of his

---

[301] For the chiastic structure see Bligh, "Four Studies," 48. In a few Greek manuscripts, the Latin and some Syriac versions (Aᶜ K Δ Θ Π fᶦ·¹³ itᵉ syrᶜ syrˢ and some others) the phrase 'ὁ ὤν ἐν τῷ οὐρανῷ' (who is in heaven) is found. According to R. E. Brown (*op. cit.*), the textual evidence is not strong, but the phrase is so difficult that it may well have been omitted in the majority of manuscripts (P⁶⁶·⁷⁵ ℵ B L Wˢᵘᵖᵖ and many others) to avoid difficulty. The choice is difficult as the better traditions favour an omission. Those who favour the additional phrase argue that it complements the perfect ἀναβέβηκεν and refers to the ascension of Jesus, 'who is (now) in heaven' (cf. Bultmann, *Gospel*, 151). The addition is better explained if one understands 3,13 not as an affirmation of the ascent of the Son of Man, but rather as a statement on his descent from heaven; to indicate that the Son of Man finally re-ascended into heaven, one could have added these controversial phrase. Lagrange, Boismard, and Wikenhauser are also among those who accept the additional phrase. Schnackenburg (*Gospel*, I, 394) considers the original phrase as an unnecessary later addition, though well supported in the textual tradition. For this study I adopt the Alexandrian tradition, which omits this phrase, as the original. For a further and detailed discussion on this subject see also D. A. Black, "The Text of John 3:13," *GTJ* 6 (1985) 49-66. For a list of those who accept the phrase or reject it, see Létourneau, *op. cit.*, 166, n. 125.

[302] Cf. DBY, NRSV and YLT translations.

[303] Cf. ASV, BBE, KJV, NASB, NAS, NKJV, RSV, RWB and WEB translations.

[304] This is only a sample list of a few similar occurrences.

[305] Cf. J. Coppens, "Le Fils de l'homme dan l'évangile johannique," *EThL* 52 (1976) 47; Moloney, *Son of Man*, 53-59; Carson, *op. cit.*, 200; Lagrange, 110-11; and Westcott, I, 53.

experiences, but because heaven was his home in the first place, and, therefore, he has in himself the fullness of heavenly knowledge. He is the one who came from heaven; he is the revelatory Son of Man.

β. 'Αναβέβηκεν

One may see a difficulty caused by the perfect form of the verb ἀναβέβηκεν[306] on the lips of Jesus, which gives the impression that the ascent in question has been accomplished already. How can he say, still being on earth, that no one *has* ascended into heaven (and continue to be there) *except* the Son of Man? Hence, the reference to the descent from heaven, which preceded the ascent, is noteworthy.[307] Many explanations have been given to account for the difficulty.

a) Anachronism?

Supposing that the verb refers to the historical ascension of Jesus, one defended it as a probable reflection of the primitive community, placed anachronically[308] on the lips of Jesus, and made of his ascension a past event but still efficacious. Carson doubts if the evangelist would create so clumsy an anachronism when he is frequently so careful to distinguish between events *during* Jesus' ministry and understanding that took place only after the resurrection/exaltation.[309] I think, even in the immediate context (3,14), the evangelist goes on to treat the resurrection of Jesus as *future* to the stance at which he has placed Jesus. Moreover, this appeal to anachronism does not explain why the evangelist has so tightly tied this verse to the preceding one. The major difficulty arises from the fact that it is not explained why the redactor did not harmonise 3,13 and 3,14 with the same chronology. In the actual text the ascension of Jesus seems to be juxtaposed as a past event (3,13) with the elevation on the cross as a future event (3,14).

To remedy this chronological tension between 3,13 and 3,14, some scholars have preferred to exclude an explicit reference to the future ascension of Jesus.[310] For example, Boismard has proposed to give to the perfect ἀναβέβηκεν the meaning of a present. Only the Son of Man, who has descended from heaven to communicate the wisdom and the

---

[306] Ridderbos (134) finds 3,13 to be pivotal text for the entire context and says that it is very hard to exegete. The perfect ἀναβέβηκεν is unexpected. Morris (*Gospel*, 197) thinks that the meaning is: "No man has gained the heights of heaven." There is the thought of continuing possession. R. E. Brown (*op. cit.*, 132), too, observes in the fourth evangelist's references to Jesus a strange timelessness or indifference to normal time sequence which must be reckoned with. But the primary reference of the words may well be spiritual rather than physical as Godet speaks of Jesus' entering into communion with God, whereby he possesses an intuitive knowledge of divine things, in order to reveal them to others. Only to him heaven has opened. These interpretations, in my opinion, are not incorrect, but fall short, however, of a satisfactory explication of the ἀναβέβηκεν.

[307] Grese (687) finds here the rejection of the idea of a heavenly journey found in a number of documents in antiquity. In my opinion, 3,13 reserves the claim to a heavenly knowledge exclusively for Jesus.

[308] For proponents, see Bauer, *Johannesevangelium*, 56; R. E. Brown, *op. cit.*, 145; Barrett, 177; Bultmann, *op. cit.*, 149-51; Loisy, 165; van den Bussche, 168-69; Wikenhauser, 73; O. Cullmann, *The Christology of the New Testament* (London ²1963) 185; esp. Nicholson, 91-98; and P. Borgen, *Logos Was the True Light and Other Essays on the Gospel of John* (Trondheim 1983) 133-48.

[309] Carson, *op. cit.*

[310] Tsuchido (92-93) tries to arrive at a solution by distinguishing the time of Jesus from the time of the evangelist. But such an interpretation does not reduce the problem of the literary order, *viz.*, perfect ἀναβέβηκεν.

Word, can at any moment reascend, precisely because he descended from there.[311] This position has an advantage of eliminating the anachronism of Jesus having ascended into heaven already, and maintaining simultaneously the reference to the future ascension of Jesus: that is, Jesus' reascension is not yet an accomplished fact. However, new difficulties emerge. First of all, if such an interpretation is accepted, the accent of the verse is placed more on the *ascent*; but the context (cf. 3,11) demands rather the need of a *descent*; in fact, it is not his capacity to ascend into heaven that gives the testimony of Jesus an authority, but the fact that he has descended from heaven. Moreover, it is difficult to attribute to the perfect of the verb ἀναβέβηκεν the meaning of a continuous present. That is, 3,13 effectively makes allusion to an ascent into heaven, seen under a continuous aspect, but realised already at the present moment.

b) Pre-existence of Jesus?

Another solution consists in understanding the perfect ἀναβέβηκεν as a reference, not to the ascension of Jesus after his elevation on the cross, but to another ascension referring to the pre-existence of Jesus,[312] preceding his missionary descent and the later return to the same state. This is primarily the position of P. Borgen[313] who contends, basing on the argument of a grammatical comparison with 6,46 and 17,12, that the verb ἀναβέβηκεν of the principal clause must normally be understood in co-ordination with the subordinate clause of exception. He, thus, proposes the following meaning as a possible solution:

No one has ascended into heaven
except the one who descended from heaven, the Son of Man
(who has ascended into heaven).

There is evidence of popular stories in the Judaism of Jesus' days about great personages of Israel like Moses, Elijah or Isaiah who had ascended into heaven and received special insight into God's ways and plans.[314] It is, therefore, possible that the evangelist wanted to refute such a popular conception and insist that neither Moses, nor Elijah, nor anyone else has ascended into heaven, in such a way as to return and talk about heavenly things, *except* the one who has descended, the Son of Man. If so, I cannot, resolve the difficulty of the perfect ἀναβέβηκεν, having recourse to the argument of the pre-existence of Jesus. Such a use here will remain an isolated case and that also in an indirect way. Moreover, when the fourth evangelist wants to speak of the authority of Jesus' mission coming from his pre-existence, he uses the scheme of *sending the Son* (cf. 3,17).

c) Plausible Interpretation

Moloney has an interesting solution. In his opinion the use of εἰ μή is a substitute for ἀλλά, which gives to the phrase a semantic structure of the type, 'not... but.' Εἰ μή is not a restriction of the content of the preceding clause. Rather, there is a continuation in the development of the idea, through the introduction of a new element in contrast to what

---

[311] Boismard and Lamouille, 122-23; Wikenhauser (124) also tries to explain by giving the meaning of a present to the perfect ἀναβέβηκεν; see also C. Williams, *He Came Down from Heaven* (Grand Rapids 1984).

[312] Cf. Kuschel.

[313] See Borgen, "Jewish Exegetical Traditions," 243-58; see also Hamerton-Kelly, 230-31.

[314] Cf. Meeks, *Prophet-King*, 110-11 and 192-95 and 235-36; and K. Haacker, *Die Stiftung des Heils. Untersuchungen zur Struktur der johanneischen Theologie* (AzTh 47) (Stuttgart 1972) 111.

went before.[315] In this perspective, 3,13 means: 'No one has ascended into heaven, *but* someone has descended from there, the Son of Man.' Nicholson rejects this view on two grounds. First, there is the use of two different verbs in the main (ἀναβέβηκεν) and subordinate (καταβάς) clauses. In the fourth Gospel, in fact, phrases of this type have always the form 'οὐδεὶς + verb ... εἰ μὴ + verb....'[316] Second, the interpretation of Moloney demands a consideration of the nominal participial clause 'ὁ ἐκ τοῦ οὐρανοῦ καταβάς' as a true verbal clause, as if the verb 'καταβάς' were in the indicative.[317]

E. Ruckstuhl's reconstruction of 3,13 falling back on the context in 3,12, in my opinion, helps to explicate considerably this grammatical problem:

No one has ascended into heaven,

(and has seen heavenly things there – cf. 3,12d),

only the Son of Man who descended from heaven

(has seen them).

He assumes that the first clause in 3,13 refers not to the Son of Man but to 'οὐδεὶς' whoever that may be.[318] Such a conception of the verse has the advantage of taking into account most of the remarks formulated above. There is no temporal distortion in the story, as it is no more the question of the ascension of Jesus but his descent from heaven that is stressed. Only in 3,14 the necessity of his future elevation will be affirmed. This interpretation renders justice also to the value of the perfect. Referring to an action accomplished in the past, the statement affirms that there has never been an ascent of anyone into heaven. The durative aspect of the perfect stresses that this ascent implies a long sojourn to get to know of the heavenly mysteries.[319]

In this perspective, one can understand better the unity of 3,11-13. Structurally, I have observed that 3,11a-e and 13 are parallel.[320] This argumentation is supported by the syntactic structure of 3,11a-e. The emphatic position of the syntagms 'ὃ οἴδαμεν' and 'ὃ ἑωράκαμεν' imply already, in some way, the authority of the testimony. We can paraphrase the statement in the following way: 'it is what we know that we say and it is what we have seen that we testify to.' The accent is on the truthfulness and reliability of the testimony.[321] Moreover, what gives authority to the testimony is the knowledge of the eye-witness. For this the witness must demonstrate his competence. This is the major difficulty regarding the heavenly things. That is why 3,13 is essential to the argumentation hooked with 3,11a-

---

[315] See Moloney, *Son of Man*, 55-56.

[316] Nicholson, 94. On the contrary, Lagrange (80), is of the opinion that it is possible that εἰ μη imposes a restriction in 3,13 which does not agree with what precedes. The logic behind the syntactic construction οὐδεὶς ... εἰ μὴ implies that the subordinate clause affirms that which is denied in the principal clause. He cites Jn. 3,27; Mt. 12,4; Lk. 4,27; and esp. Rev. 21,27.

[317] Nicholson, *op. cit.*

[318] See Ruckstuhl, "Abstieg," 325; see also 314-41. Though the sentence construction is somewhat clumsy, it resolves to a great extent the problem of the perfect ἀναβέβηκεν.

[319] In the same way the prolonged stay of Moses on Mount Sinai was thought of as necessary for God to communicate the prescription of the Law (cf. Ex. 32,1 and 34,28).

[320] Schnackenburg (*Gospel*, I, 377) and Gaeta (76) consider the καὶ that introduces 3,13 as having an adversative meaning ('but'). This verse, therefore, must be interpreted in relation to 3,11-12: "You do not receive our testimony" (3,11f)....; yet (you must accept because) "no one has ascended into heaven..." (3,13).

[321] See the detailed work of W. Grundmann, *Der Zeuge der Wahrheit. Grundzüge der Christologie des Johannesevangeliums* (Berlin 1985) on this subject.

e. The ultimate basis for a testimony to heavenly things can only be a direct access to the world above, either through intrusion of one into heaven or by descent to earth of a heavenly being. Moreover, 3,13a excludes all the eventuality of the former possibility: 'no one has ever ascended into heaven (to get to know the heavenly things).' On the contrary there is one from heaven who has come down, the Son of Man (3,13b). He is the competent witness, because he could confirm the mysteries from above.

Consequently, if neither Moses, nor any of the prophets, nor anyone else has ascended into heaven in order to re-descend with revelation, all the other testimonies except that of the Son of Man become secondary and cannot hold weight in the balance. The argumentation of narrative and structural analysis of 3,11-13 can be summarised in a synthesised form in the following chiasm:

A   3,11a-e   Authority of the testimony (knowing-seeing)
   B 3,11f Refusal of the testimony
   B¹ 3,12 Justification (disbelief in earthly things leads to disbelief in the heavenly)
A¹   3,13   Authority of testimony (heavenly origin of the revealer)

v. Implicit Commentary – Irony

The debate between Jesus and his opponents often returns to the theme of his *origin*. Jesus' heavenly *origin* (cf. 3,13.31) is so important to the theological point of view of the evangelist that it is underscored by irony as well as misunderstanding. One of the author's favourite devices is to allow Jesus' opponents to speak the truth unawares. But the irony is not a simple one; it has a deeper level. Whether Jesus is from Galilee (cf. 1,46 and 7,52) or Bethlehem (cf. 7,41-43) is a trivial matter in comparison with the questions whether he is ἐκ τῶν ἄνω or ἐκ τῶν κάτω (8,23),[322] whether he is or not from God (ἀπὸ θεοῦ – 3,2). This is Jesus' real origin (cf. 1,1-2), but ironically Nicodemus and the Jews do not see it. They neither understand his teaching nor that he is the Son of God.

Irony in the fourth Gospel depends on the reader being able to maintain a hierarchical separation of the two levels: heavenly/earthly, spiritual/material, figural/literal, etc. The one that discloses the irony of the fourth evangelist is the result of an oscillatory pull and tug in his Gospel between a descending and ascending, vertical and horizontal Christology. There are earthly matters (τὰ ἐπίγεια) and heavenly matters (τὰ ἐπουράνια – 3,12). Jesus is from above (ἄνω – 3,31); his opponents are from below (κάτω – 8,23) or from the earth (ἐκ τῆς γῆς – 3,31). The higher plane is associated with truth and the lower with falsehood, deception, and error (cf. 3,20-21). Nicodemus, a foil for Jesus' revelation[323] of what is from above, is naively or blindly unaware of the higher plane.

vi. Reader and Point of View

In this segment (3,11-13) the distance between Jesus and the reader increases. It begins again with the signal that what follows is important and demanding: "Ἀμὴν ἀμὴν λέγω

---

[322] See the remarks of J. Schneider, "(βαίνω), ἀναβαίνω, καταβαίνω, μεταναβαίνω," *TDNT*, I, 518-23.

[323] Cf. R. F. Collins, *These Things Have Been Written. Studies on the Fourth Gospel* (LThPM 2) (Grand Rapids, Louvain 1990) 66.

σοι." The first person plural[324] of 3,11 is not troublesome for the reader as he/she acknowledges the plurality of the speakers/witnesses thus far in the narrative (Jesus and the Baptist). However, beginning with this verse, the reader experiences the dialogue opening into a community. Jesus speaks, but now from within a group that has *seen*, *heard* and *bears witness* to its experience.[325]

The chasm becomes wider. The reader wonders what these *earthly things* are, and what the *heavenly things* might be? The reader's mind is driven back to the flesh-Spirit distinction.[326] Added to the dilemma loaded on the reader already, by the discussion thus far, comes another distinction: *ascending and descending*;[327] and with the distinction a title, Son of Man. For the reader it is a restatement, in terms of the Son of Man, of what was said of the Son in 1,18: "No one has ever seen God. It is God the only Son, who is close to the Father's heart, who has made him known." Here, the reader recalls also Jesus' promise to Nathanael: "You will see heaven opened and the angels of God *ascending and descending* upon the Son of Man" (1,51). But now it is the Son of Man who *descends and ascends*. The connection between the two, plus the encouragement of the prologue to the narrative, nurtures the reader's identification of Jesus with the Son of Man. The descent, the reader understands of course, speaks in a veiled way of the Logos' becoming flesh. The reader is, however, forced to ask himself: 'What might be the ascent? And what has all of these to do with begetting ἄνωθεν?'

The story of Nicodemus provides a profound combination of theology and history. It calls on the reader to think theologically about the meaning of the coming of Jesus and to reflect on the implications of that coming. It reminds him/her that Jesus conversed in terms of 'earthly' realities, because earth was the place where he came to minister. Created, earthly people were the objects of his conversation. But if earthly people like Nicodemus (and by implication the readers of the Gospel) have difficulty in understanding spiritual truth in human terms (τὰ ἐπίγεια – about which Jesus was speaking), what would happen to human receptive capacities if Jesus were to have started talking about 'the heavenly things' (τὰ ἐπουράνια)? Human beings think in human and space-time bound terms, but God and heaven do not fit their terminology. To think like Jesus the reader needs a transformation which can begin on earth by being begotten ἄνωθεν (3,3).

---

[324] Moloney (*Belief in the Word*, 115) is of the opinion that Jesus here speaks to both Nicodemus and the reader. According to Patte (41 and 18-19), "the readers are invited to become the addressees of the discourse and to be become listeners."

[325] This discourse provides the reader with a synthesis of the Gospel message on Jesus as the unique revealer of the 'heavenly things' (3,11-15) and the subsequent salvation or condemnation which flows from an acceptance or refusal of this revelation.

[326] For a Jewish reader the idea of life in 'the Spirit' which transcends all that the human spirit can control or understand is not new. It was a part of his religious tradition (cf. Ex. 15,8; Is. 40,7; 44,3 and 59,21; Ezek. 11,19-20 and 36,26-27; Joel 28,29; Job 34,14; Pss. 18,15 and 51,10; Wis. 9,16-18; and 1 QS 3,13-4,26). See R. E. Brown, *op. cit.*, 139-41.

[327] Jesus affirms the uniqueness of his revelatory role in terms of the Son of Man (3,13). In strong contradiction (οὐδείς) to any suggestion that the great revealers of Israel had been to heaven to learn the secrets they eventually revealed, Jesus affirms that *only* the Son of Man has come down from heaven. He alone is able to reveal the things he has seen (cf. 3,11-12). Cf. Boismard, *Moïse ou Jésus*, 78-79.

b. 3,14-18

The connections between 3,14 and the preceding verses are two: first, Jesus moves from an explanation of being begotten ἄνωθεν in terms of 'water' and 'Spirit' to a narrative passage. Second, the deepest point of connection between the bronze serpent and Jesus is the act of being *lifted up*: if in 3,13 the Son of Man is the revealer and the one who descended from heaven, here it transpires, that it is precisely in the matrix of suffering and exaltation, that God most clearly reveals Himself in the person of His Son. In the fourth Gospel these themes – divine revelation, obedient suffering of the Son, and his exaltation – constantly revolve around the title 'Son of Man.' From 3,14 onwards Jesus speaks more specifically about heavenly things regarding the question of Nicodemus on the attainment of salvation (cf. 3,9). Having analysed, in the preceding pages, the distinction on the narrative content between the earthly and heavenly things, I shall now specify the Christological component of the discussion on being begotten ἄνωθεν.

i. Thematic Argumentative Structure

Here, I notice the following thematic and argumentative structure with the Christological events at its centre, soteriology as its intertwined purpose,[328] and belief in Jesus as the *sine qua non* condition:

Christological Event	Soteriological Purpose	Condition
3,14-15: *Elevation* of the Son of Man	Salvation	Belief
3,16: God's love in the *gift* of his Son	Salvation	Belief
3,17-18: God *sending* his Son	Salvation	Belief[329]

We can observe here in a nutshell a hint at the entire Christology (his pre-existent origin, incarnation, crucifixion and glorification) which is intrinsically bound up with its soteriological mission and the response of faith expected of the readers to attain this salvation.[330]

ii. Bipartite Parallel Structure

While exploring the global literary structure of the sub-unit (3,11-21), I have established already that the mini-segment 3,14-18 constitutes a bipartite sub-structure placing the segments 3,14-15 and 3,16-18 parallel to each other (see the diagram on the next page):

Let me inspect the fundamental bipartite construction of this unit from the point of view of theme and structural homogeneity between 3,14-15 and 3,16-18. In the first segment (3,14-15), the discussion is on the *elevation* of the *Son of Man* and the *soteriology* that flows from it through *belief* in him. It represents the ascending Christology. The second segment (3,16-18) speaks of the *gift/sending* of the *only Son of God* – event whose *soteriological* purpose   through *belief* in him is repeatedly insisted upon. It represents the

---

[328] See the detailed work of R. R. Moore, *Soteriology and Structure. A Study of the Relation Between the Soteriology and Present Literary Structure of the Fourth Gospel* (Altanta 1982).

[329] Notice here an example of emphasis by repetition; the verb 'believe' is mentioned three times in 3,18 and is, thus, shown to be important.

[330] M. Rodriguez Ruiz, *Der Missionsgedanke des Johannesevangeliums. Ein Beitrag zur johanneischen Soteriologie und Ekklesiologie* (FzB 55) (Würzburg 1987).

descending Christology, as God *sending* His Son into the world (3,17a) hints at his incarnation. Moreover, the second segment (3,16-18) is also marked by an *inclusion* in the repetition of the title 'only Son of God' at the beginning and at the end (cf. 3,16b and 3,18e), besides the whole sub-unit (3,14-18) being enclosed by the two titles 'Son of Man' (3,14) and 'Son of God' (3,18), which represent the ascending and descending movements respectively.

^{3,14} And just as Moses *lifted up* the serpent in the wilderness, so must the **Son of Man** be *lifted up*, ¹⁵ that (ἵνα) whoever <u>believes</u> in him **may have eternal life.**	^{3,16ab} For God so loved the world that he *gave* his *only Son,* ^{17a} Indeed, God *sent* the Son into the world... ^{16cde} so that (ἵνα) everyone who <u>believes</u> in him **may not perish** but **may have eternal life.** ^{17bc} ... **not to condemn** the world, but in order that (ἵνα) the world **might be saved** through him. ¹⁸ Those who <u>believe</u> in him are **not condemned**; but those who do <u>not believe</u> are **condemned** already, because they have <u>not believed</u> in the name of the *only* **Son of God.**

Moreover, the *elevation* of the Son of Man – presented in the form of a typology of the bronze serpent of the OT – is related to the *giving and sending* of the only Son of God in 3,16 and 3,17 respectively. The saving death of Jesus on the cross – which is simultaneously his glorification – signifies the loving *gift* of God sent to humanity. The only *purpose* of this supreme act of love of God is the *salvation* of humanity. But *belief* in the Son as the *conditio sine qua non* for such a salvation is clearly and repeatedly mentioned all along in both segments. However, the *soteriological* aspect is emphasised more in the second segment (3,16-18) by repeating it both positively (may have eternal life/to save) and *per negationem* (may not perish/not to condemn). The fourth evangelist sets perishing (death) and life starkly over against each other. He knows no other final state.

iii. Synonymous Compound Parallel Structure

We notice also a synonymous parallelism of the structural formula – ab//a¹ b¹//a²b² as the diagram below shows (see the diagram on the next page):

The elements a, a¹ and a² state the fundamental salvific event in the two different Christological fields. In a, it is the lifting of the Son of Man (upward movement), and in a¹ and a², it is the gift/sending of the only Son by God (downward movement). The elements b, b¹ and b² indicate the soteriological goal of the two movements of the vertical Christological events described in a, a¹ and a². While a, a¹ and a² describe the *initiative of God* carried out in and through His only Son, b, b¹ and b² with the conjunction of finality (ἵνα)[331] – placed at the beginning of the phrases, as well as the verb πιστεύω – posed as the only condition, demand the *response of humanity* to attain salvation. I also notice that this insistence on the

---

[331] Cf. H. Riesenfeld, "Zu den johanneischen ἵνα-Sätzen," *StTh* 19 (1965) 213-20.

soteriological aspect gradually increases in the length of the phrases from b to b¹ and from b¹ to b².

<table>
<tr><td>

(a) [14] And just as Moses lifted up the serpent in the wilderness, so must the Son of Man be *lifted up*,
    (b) [15] that (ἵνα) whoever believes in him may *have eternal life*.

</td><td>

(a) Christology (↑)

(b) Soteriology (→)

</td></tr>
<tr><td>

(a¹) [16] For God so loved the world that he *gave*[332] his only Son,
    (b¹) so that (ἵνα) everyone who believes in him may *not perish* but may *have eternal life*.

</td><td>

(a¹) Christology (↓↑)
(b¹) Soteriology (→)

</td></tr>
<tr><td>

(a²) [17a] Indeed, God did not *send*[333] the Son into the world
    (b²) [17bc] (ἵνα) to condemn the world, but in order that (ἵνα) the world might be *saved* through him.[18] Those who believe in him are *not condemned*; but those who who do not believe are condemned already, because they have not believed in the name of the only Son of God.

</td><td>

(a²) Christology (↓)
(b²) Soteriology (→)[334]

</td></tr>
</table>

iv. Argumentative Narrative Structure

3,14   A comparison (καθώς[335] - οὕτως) – synonymous parallelism
      14a   An historical reference (Μωϋσῆς ὕψωσεν τὸν ὄφιν ἐν τῇ ἐρήμῳ)
      14b   Conclusion with a "must" (δεῖ)[336]
3,15   15a   Note of interpretation (ἵνα); outline of relation
      15b   Objective (ἐν αὐτῷ)
3,16   16ab   Stress on God's action (Οὕτως ..., ὥστε)
      16a   Reasoning (γάρ); God's positive action (ἠγάπησεν)
      16b   God's positive action (ἔδωκεν)
      16c   Note of interpretation (ἵνα); positive action (πιστεύων); objective (εἰς αὐτόν)
      16d   Result affirmed *per negationem* (μὴ ἀπόληται)

---

[332] God *giving* his only begotten Son to the world refers to his incarnation as well as to God's giving him on the cross and glorifying him for the salvation of mankind. In this giving, both the descending and ascending aspects of Christology are implicit.

[333] The purpose of the mission of Jesus on earth expressed in such terms as 'have eternal life,' 'not perish,' 'saved,' and 'not condemned' refers to his saving work on earth which is intrinsically connected with as well as achieved in and through his descending and ascending.

[334] As hinted at already in the introduction of my study, one has here, a clear exposition of a U-shaped (↓→↑) Johannine Christology.

[335] The fourth evangelist uses καθώς 31 times compared to 3 times in Matthew, 8 times in Mark, and 17 times in Luke. Clearly the fourth evangelist is fond of making comparisons.

[336] Δεῖ is a strong expression. The stress in the text falls on the fact that Jesus was operating according to a divine imperative. There is no other way than that of the lifting up of the Son of Man (cf. 12,34). He was under necessity to be crucified (cf. Mk. 8,31; and ἔδει in Lk. 24,26). So also in 3,7, there is no other way than that of being begotten ἄνωθεν. The fourth evangelist uses it again of the necessity of the resurrection (20,9), of the things Jesus did in the execution of his ministry (4,4; 9,4 and 10,16), and of the eclipse of the Baptist before Jesus (3,30). The term is also used of worship (4,20.24). See W. Grundmann, "δεῖ," *TDNT*, II, 24; and E. Fascher, "Theologische Beobachtungen zu δεῖ," in: *Neutestamentliche Studien für R. Bultmann* (BZNW 21) (Berlin 1957) 228-54. See also Schnackenburg, *Gospel*, I, 395.

	16e	and contrasted (ἀλλά) positively (ἔχῃ ζωὴν αἰώνιον)
3,17	17a	Reasoning (γάρ); God's positive action *per negationem* (οὐ...ἀπέστειλεν);
	17b	Negative purpose affirmed in the positive (κρίνῃ)
	17c	Contrast (ἀλλά); note of interpretation (ἵνα); positive purpose (σωθῇ); objective (δι' αὐτοῦ)
3,18	18a	Positive action (πιστεύων); objective (εἰς αὐτόν)
	18b	Result affirmed *per negationem* (οὐ κρίνεται)
	18c	Contrast (δέ); negative action (μὴ πιστεύων)
	18d	Result affirmed positively (κέκριται)
	18e	Reasoning (ὅτι...); objective (εἰς τὸ ὄνομα)

v. Typology of the Bronze Serpent

The first element of the parallelism contains a typology[337] based on the story of the lifting up of the bronze serpent by Moses in Num. 21,4-9.

καὶ καθὼς Μωϋσῆς ὕψωσεν   τὸν ὄφιν ἐν τῇ ἐρήμῳ,

οὕτως   ὑψωθῆναι δεῖ τὸν υἱὸν τοῦ ἀνθρώπου,

Most commentators generally agree in saying that the *tertium comparationis* is in the lifting up (ὑψόω) itself.[338] The fourth evangelist makes use of an image – that of the lifting up of the bronze serpent, which had a healing effect, to show that another lifting up – that of the Son of Man, has also a saving effect (3,15). But there are fundamental differences between the two with regard to the effects and the way they are produced: in the case of the serpent, the result was a healing from a mortal bite (physical healing), whereas, in the case of the Son of Man, the effect is eternal life (more than a mere physical healing); the physical healing in the OT was effected by Yahweh and not by the serpent on the pole, whereas, in the NT it is the one on the pole of the cross (ἐν αὐτῷ – 3,15) who brings about salvation.[339]

α. Ἐν αὐτῷ

Here, I would like to draw attention to the phrase ἐν αὐτῷ which puts Jesus in quite a different category from the bronze serpent. Every reader of the OT knew that eventually the bronze serpent had to be destroyed by King Hezekiah, before too many people treated it as if it had some inherent magical power (cf. 2 Kings 18,4). What spared the Israelites from the mortal threat of the desert snakes was God's power and grace; the sign was the bronze serpent. But I must say more than that about Jesus. The Father has granted the Son to have life in himself (cf. 5,26); he himself is the resurrection and the life (11,25), and

---

[337] Nicholson (99) argues that the formula 'καθὼς ... οὕτως' need not necessarily imply a typology. Such a use of typology is also found in Lk. 11,30 and 17,26. Other uses in the NT (e.g. Jn. 12,50; 14,31 and 15,4; 2 Cor. 1,5; 8,6 and 10,7; Col. 3,13; 1 Thess. 2,4; Heb. 5,3; and 1 Jn. 2,6) deal with a more general comparison. However, in my opinion, 3,14 contains all the elements of a typology: a concrete event in the OT is used as a type for an event in the NT that is connected with the person of Christ (anti-type) who realises perfectly and definitively what was anticipated in the OT.

[338] See e.g. Barrett, 214; Meeks, *Prophet-King*, 292; Odeberg, 100-11; Schnackenburg, *op. cit.*, 395-96; Ridderbos, 136-37; Borchert, 182; and Léon-Dufour, *Lecture*, I, 302.

[339] For a detailed discussion see J. Frey, "'Wie Mose die Schlange in der Wüste erhöht hat...' Zur frühchristlichen Deutung der 'ehernen Schlange' und ihrer christologischen Rezeption in Johannes 3,14f.," in: M. Hengel and H. Lohr (eds.), *Schriftauslegung im antiken Judentum und im Urchristentum* (WUNT 73) (Tübingen 1994) 153-205; and R. R. Marrs, "John 3,14-15. The Raised Serpent in the Wilderness: The Johannine Use of an Old Testament Account," in: J. E. Priest (ed.), *Johannine Studies. FS F. Pack* (Malibu 1989) 132-47.

those who believe have life *in him*. Here, then, is the frankest answer to Nicodemus' question, "how can these things be?" (3,9): the kingdom of God is seen or entered into, being begotten ἄνωθεν is experienced, and eternal life begins, through the saving cross-work of Christ, received by *faith in him*. Hence, though there are close similarities, the comparison is not identical in all respects. Majority of the commentators recognise that the phrase 'ἐν αὐτῷ'[340] must not be attached to 'πιστεύων,' but rather to 'ἔχη.'[341] They are of the opinion that the position of ἐν αὐτω *after* the verb is to lay the accent on the mediatory function of the lifted-up Son of Man in giving eternal life.[342] In fact, the fourth evangelist employs the verb πιστεύω, almost always, with εἰς (cf. 1,12; 2,11.23; 3,16.18.36; 4,39; 6,29; etc.) or still in the absolute form, without object (cf. 1,7.50; 3,12.18b; 4,41.42.53; 5,44; 6,36.47.64; etc.). On the contrary, the expression 'ἔχειν ἐν' appears often in the Johannine writings (cf. 14,30; 16,33 and 20,31; and 1 Jn. 4,16). It is, therefore, in my opinion, in and through Jesus – the Son of Man lifted up – the believer obtains eternal life.

β. Σημεῖον

Besides, the fourth evangelist, here, exploits an element contained already in the OT story. In fact, the Greek version of Num. 21,8 reads thus: "ποίησον σεαυτῷ ὄφιν καὶ *θὲς αὐτὸν ἐπὶ σημείου* καὶ ἔσται... πᾶς ὁ δεδηγμένος ἰδὼν αὐτὸν ζήσεται." The pole on which the serpent is lifted up is designated as 'σημεῖον.' It is, therefore, looking at the *sign* – which is lifted up – that the Israelites were saved. On the other hand, the evangelist is not alone or the only one, to have made maximum profit of such an understanding of the text. In Wis. 16,5-7 one finds the earliest commentary on this bronze serpent passage:

> [16,5] For when the terrible rage of wild animals came upon your people and they were being destroyed by the bites of writhing *serpents*, your wrath did not continue to the end; [6] they were troubled for a little while as a warning, and received a *symbol* of deliverance to remind them of your *law*'s command. [7] For the one who turned toward it was saved, not by the thing that was beheld, but by you, the Saviour of all.

As the text indicates clearly, the bronze serpent lifted up on the 'sign,' was given to the Israelites as a *symbol* of deliverance and to remind them of God's command in the Law. Maneschg concludes that, for the author of Wisdom, the serpent is only an external sign through which God brought about the act of salvation.[343] Turning toward the serpent signified a true conversion (cf. ἐπιστραφεὶς – Wis. 16,7) to the will of God. It is, therefore, not the serpent which brought salvation (οὐ διὰ τὸ θεωρούμενον) but God Himself, the

---

[340] Many manuscripts read ἐν αὐτῷ. Others (e.g. P[66]) have ἐπ' αὐτῷ; still others read εἰς αὐτόν. This last reading looks like assimilation of 3,16. Ἐν αὐτῷ appears to be the most original (e.g. P[75]; Vaticanus); see R. E. Brown, *op. cit.*, 133. Some interpreters take it with ἔχη, and as qualifying the ζωή αἰώνιος (cf. also ASV, NAS, NASB, BBE translations), partly on account of the distinction from εἰς αὐτόν for belief in him (cf. 3,16); see e.g. Carson, *Gospel*, 202. In my opinion, the emphasis still, probably, lies on the object of faith and in this connection there need not be a pronounced difference between ἐν and εἰς in the context here.

[341] Some manuscripts have imported μὴ ἀπόληται ἀλλ' from 3,16 and have placed it between ἐν αὐτῷ and ἔχη in 3,15. Thus, some English translations (KJV, NKJV, WEB, RWB, DBY, YLT) include this additional phrase in 3,15.

[342] Cf. Bultmann, *Gospel*, 152; Barrett, 179; R. E. Brown, *op. cit.*; Schnackenburg, *op. cit.*, 397; and Nicholson, 103. Against, see Bernard, I, 116, who prefers 'εἰς αὐτόν' as object of the verb 'πιστεύω.'

[343] Maneschg, 122 and 127.

only saviour (ἀλλὰ διὰ σὲ τὸν πάντων σωτῆρα).[344] As one can notice, the re-interpretation of the fourth evangelist lies in the same line, but goes beyond. In the fourth Gospel, the sign is 're-interpreted' Christologically: the lifting up is not only a sign of salvation given by God, but a sign which also manifests plainly Jesus as the saviour. The elevation of the Son of Man on the cross is the *sign* of his elevation into heaven from where he operates this salvation; it is through the Son of Man ascended into heaven that the believer obtains eternal life.

γ. 'Seeing' and 'Believing'

This salvific value attached to the lifting up of the Son of Man flows equally from the typological comparison with the lifting up of the bronze serpent in the OT. In fact, the fourth evangelist 're-interprets' Num. 21,8: "πᾶς ὁ δεδηγμένος ἰδὼν αὐτὸν ζήσεται," and Num. 21,9: "καὶ ἐπέβλεψεν ἐπὶ τὸν ὄφιν τὸν χαλκοῦν καὶ ἔζη." In the episode of the desert, it was the question of *seeing* the serpent lifted up in order to save one's *physical life*. In the story of the fourth evangelist, it is not enough to see but must *believe* (more than mere seeing),[345] (cf. also 2,23-25). The argumentation is that, if the simple looking at the lifted up Son of Man is not sufficient, and must go beyond it through a sight of faith, the salvific reality must also, therefore, go beyond the physical appearance. What is visible is the lifting up of the Son of Man on the cross; what must be perceived through faith is his lifting up into heaven. It is faith in the power of him who is powerless in the flesh and in the eyes of the flesh. One could, thus, say that the physical lifting up of the Son of Man is the visible *sign* of his being lifted up into heaven. But to be able to *see* and to *believe* in the heaven-descended and cross-exalted Son of Man – one needs a different set of eyes, and for that one must be begotten ἄνωθεν.

δ. Ὑψόω – Double Meaning and Misunderstanding

In 3,14 I find the first usage of ὑψόω.[346] One cannot deny that the verb 'ὑψόω' reminds specifically of the event of crucifixion – involving the pole (the common denominator between the two events) of the cross – without which the typological comparison with the lifting up of the serpent will have no similarity. The word ὑψόω appears five times in the fourth Gospel (3,14 [twice]; 8,28 and 12,32.34) in three passages, each time with connotations which lead to the double meaning of the literal exaltation on the cross and the

---

[344] Many Rabbinical texts interpret that the look of the Israelites at the bronze serpent lifted up on the pole was a form of turning their hearts to God. See R. Le Déaut (ed.), *Targum du pentateuque III Nombres* (SC 261) (Paris 1979); and G. Reim "Targum und Johannesevangelium," *BZ* 27 (1983) 1-13.

[345] T. F. Glasson (*Moses in the Fourth Gospel* [SBT 40] [London 1963] 34-35) points out that the idea of *seeing* is central in Num. 21. Though it is not mentioned explicitly here, it is implied; all the more so since the idea of *seeing* is so pronounced in the fourth Gospel.

[346] Ὑψόω is used fifteen times in the NT outside the fourth Gospel. In each case it has the meaning of exaltation. On the human level it refers to the exaltation of a person or a town either in his or its own time or in the time to come (Mt. 11,23 and 23,32; Lk. 1,52; 10,15; 14,11 and 18,14; 2 Cor. 11,7; James 4,10; and 1 Pet. 5,6). In Acts 2,33 and 5,31 u'yo,w refers to the exaltation of Christ to the right hand of God after his ascension. ʽUyo,omai is used for the changing of Jesus' sphere of being in the same way as ἀναβαίνω (3,13 and 6,62), πορεύομαι (7,35) and ὑπάγω (7,33 and 8,14.21f.). The term ὑψόω is always used in relation to the Son of Man, suggesting his heavenly character (glorification); see H. Hollis, "The Root of the Johannine Pun – Ὑ Ψ Ω Θ Η Ν Α Ι," *NTS* 36 (1989) 475-78.

metaphorical exaltation into heaven.[347] As the typological comparison rests, basically, on the lifting up, one must further specify to what exactly this lifting up of the Son of Man in the fourth Gospel is similar.

The task of establishing the meaning of ὑψόω involves a long discussion. Many scholars have supposed the existence of a double meaning of it: a literal meaning indicating the crucifixion and a metaphorical meaning signifying the exaltation. I can summarise the results under five types of interpretation about the use of ὑψόω in the fourth Gospel:[348]

i.   ὑψόω = σταυρόω, meaning 'to crucify.' The verb refers uniquely to Jesus' crucifixion.[349]
ii.   ὑψόω = σταυρόω + something more. The verb refers particularly to Jesus' crucifixion, but leaves room for an aspect of exaltation.[350]
iii.   ὑψόω means Jesus' crucifixion as such, as the first act of ascension/exaltation.[351]
iv.   ὑψόω refers primarily to exaltation into heaven. The verb implies, however, that this exaltation is realised through an elevation onto the cross.[352]
v.   ὑψόω never refers to Jesus' crucifixion.[353]

Now, the question is to know if the verb ὑψόω refers to Jesus' crucifixion, to his exaltation, or to a superimposition of the two concepts which could, however, prefer one to the other. The comparison in 3,14 is between the lifting up of the serpent in the desert (Num. 21,8ff.) and the lifting of the Son of Man. In fact, if the 'lifting up' itself is the *tertium comparationis* in the two events,[354] it is to be noted that the verb 'ὑψόω' appears neither in the MT (שׂים), nor in the LXX (τίθημι). If the fourth evangelist wanted to refer only to the lifting up onto the cross or the crucifixion of Jesus, he could have just used the verb τίθημι of LXX or used the verb σταυρόω (cf. Mt. 26,2; Lk. 24,7; and Jn. 19,6.10.15-20). The deliberate choice of 'ὑψόω' here implies the intention of the evangelist to mean more than the lifting up onto the cross.

Nicholson is right in his affirmation that the verb ὑψόω must be interpreted in relation to the characteristic 'descent-ascent' (of the Son of Man) scheme of the fourth Gospel.[355] Hence, the lifting up of the Son of Man must correspond to his ascent into heaven. There are many indications that support this point of view. Acts 2,33 and 5,31[356]

---

[347] Cf. G. Bertram, "ὕψος," *TDNT*, VIII, 610.

[348] See Nicholson, 21-22; and Létourneau, *op. cit.*, 388-93.

[349] Cf. Bernard, I, 113; 303 and 442.

[350] Cf. Moloney, *Son of Man*, 60-64; Morris, *Gospel*, 199-200; Ruckstuhl, "Abstieg" 332-33; and Thüsing, 3-12.

[351] See Barrett, 213-14; Blank, *Krisis*, 81-85; R. E. Brown, *op. cit.*, 145-46; 350-51; Forestell, *Word of the Cross*, 61-65; Lindars, *Gospel*, 157; Schnackenburg, *op. cit.*, 394-96; and J. Schneider, 98.

[352] See Dodd, *Interpretation*, 247; 306; 376 and 379; Bultmann, *Gospel*, 152; and T. Müller, *Das Heilsgeschehen im Johannesevangelium. Eine exegetische Studie, zugleich der Versuch einer Antwort an Rudolf Bultmann* (Frankfurt, Zürich 1958) 50.

[353] See Odeberg, 99 and 111.

[354] See Barrett, 214; and Schnackenburg, *op. cit.*, 396.

[355] Nicholson, 21-75., esp. 75.

[356] Acts 2,33-36 is interesting for my proposal as it uses the verb ὑψόω (v. 33) and σταυρόω (v. 36) at the same time, as well as the expression ἀνέβη εἰς τοὺς οὐρανούς (v. 34). This text plays on the contrast between two opposed actions, the crucifixion by the Jews and exaltation by God. "This Jesus whom you crucified" (v. 36) is put in opposition to the one who is "exalted at the right hand of God" (v. 33) and whom

use ὑψόω to refer to Jesus' ascension. I observe in 3,13 that the Son of Man has descended from heaven. Besides, in 6,62, Jesus announces the ascent of the Son of Man to the place where he was before, which can only refer to heaven, his place of origin. Moreover, as there is no independent report of the ascension of Jesus in the fourth Gospel[357] (cf. Acts 1,2.9.11.22 on Jesus' ascension), it seems that the event announced in 6,62 coincides with the lifting of the Son of Man in 3,14; 8,28 and 12,32.34.

The use of the verb ὑψόω along with the words 'from the earth' (ἐκ τῆς γῆς) in 12,32 is another indication in favour of this interpretation. In fact, the expression ἐκ τῆς γῆς in the fourth Gospel expresses the world below as opposed to the world above. The key statement of this distinction is found in 3,31: "The one who comes from above is above all; the one who is of the earth (ἐκ τῆς γῆς) belongs to the earth (ἐκ τῆς γῆς) and speaks about earthly things (ἐκ τῆς γῆς)." The same distinction is made in 8,23 using other words: "You are from below, I am from above; you are of this world, I am not of this world." Thus, it is evident that the lifting up ἐκ τῆς γῆς is not a simple elevation from the ground but a lifting up from this world to a world above.[358]

It seems, therefore, clear that the lifting up of the Son of Man refers to the ascent into heaven, his place of origin. In this sense, the fourth evangelist uses the term of Luke in Acts who makes use of the verb 'lift up' to speak of Jesus' ascension. For Luke, too, sees Jesus' ascension under the aspect of exaltation/glorification: having been lifted up to heaven, Jesus is enthroned at the right hand of God (cf. Ps. 110,1; and Acts 2,34-35), who "has made him both Lord and Messiah" (Acts 2,36; cf. Phil. 2,9), and "exalted him at his right hand as Leader and Saviour" (Acts 5,31). In fact, Jn. 12,31-34 demonstrates that the same association is made in the fourth Gospel. The lifting up/elevation of the Son of Man into heaven corresponds to his glorification.[359] He can draw all men to him.[360] The elevation is, therefore, an enthronement of the Son of Man, the beginning of his rule on the believers (drawn to him). In other words, the elevation is the hour of glorification of the Son of Man (12,23).

But the fourth evangelist does not use the verb 'lift up' in an entirely similar fashion as Luke does it. The narrator's aside in 12,33 gives an explanation of the verb 'lift up' used in 12,32: "He said this to indicate the kind of death he was to die." With this remark the narrator attracts the attention of the reader to the fact that the lifting up/elevation does not indicate only the ascent into heaven of the Son of Man; the moment of his death, his elevation on the cross is contained in it.[361]

"God has made both Lord and Messiah" (v. 36). It is also to be noted that in Acts 1,9 Jesus' ascension is expressed by the verb ἐπαίρω, which is a synonym for ὑψόω.

[357] See W. J. P. Boyd, "Ascension according to John," *TLon* 70 (1967) 207-11; and M. McNamara, "The Ascension and Exaltation of Christ in the Fourth Gospel," *Scrip.* 19 (1967) 65-73.

[358] See Thüsing, 24.

[359] Cf. P. Létourneau, "La gloire de Jésus: Gloire et glorification dans le IV. Évangile," *LTP* 51 (1995) 551-72; and W. Grossouw, "La glorification du Christ dans le quatrième évangile," in: *L'évangile de Jean. Études et problèmes* (Paris 1958) 131-45.

[360] See R. Beauvery, "Jésus élevé attire tous les hommes à lui (Jean 12,20-33)," *EeV* 80 (1970) 117-19.

[361] Some scholars contend that in 12,33 the verb ὑψόω is used primarily to refer to Jesus' crucifixion/ elevation on the cross (cf. Moloney, *Son of Man*, 229; Ruckstuhl, "Abstieg," 332; and S. Schulz *Untersuchungen zur Menschensohnchristologie im Johannesevangelium. Zugleich ein Beitrag zur Methodengeschichte der Auslegung des 4. Evangeliums* [Göttingen 1957] 108). This is not acceptable as

Such a double significance of the moment of lifting up is also supported by the occurrence of the verb ὑψόω in 8,28: "When you have lifted up the Son of Man..." On the one hand, the active form of the verb – which attributes the act of lifting up of the Son of Man to the Jews – can only refer to the physical elevation, that is, lifting Jesus onto the pole of the cross. But, on the other hand, the elevation is given as an answer to the question of the Jews regarding the identity of Jesus: "Who are you?" (8,25a); therefore, the lifting up must be seen as the moment of revelation of the identity of Jesus as the one sent by the Father ("....then you will realise that I am he" – 8,28). Such a revelation supposes the return of the Son of Man into heaven – to the sender. In fact, a mere lifting up of the Son of Man onto the cross does not reveal as such the identity of Jesus as the one sent by God. It is the exaltation of the crucified into heaven that reveals his true identity:[362] the cross is, thus, the return of the *one sent* to his Father; it is the place of total union of the Son with his Father.

With these results let me now move on to examine, from close quarters, the text 12,32-34 – the only case where the use of the verb ὑψόω results in a misunderstanding on the part of the Jews, the dialogue partners of Jesus. Jesus claims that if he is 'lifted up' he will draw all men to himself (12,32). The question of the Jews in 12,34 shows that they misunderstand this lifting up of Jesus as referring exclusively to his death: if the Son of Man is lifted up (i.e., *dies*), he cannot be the Messiah who remains for ever[363] (i.e., does not die; cf. Ps. 88,4.36 and 110,4). Even the dominion of Son of Man in Dan. 7,13-14 "is an everlasting dominion that shall not pass away, and his kingship is one that shall never be destroyed." In this case, what type of Son of Man is he? The error of the Jews lies in not recognising the true meaning of the lifting of the Son of Man. They do not understand that the death of Jesus is what precisely makes him rule for ever.

This has been explained in 12,23-26 which are parallel to 12,31-36. The elevation of the Son of Man is the hour of his glorification (12,23). But this glorification is achieved through the visible act of his death. The grain of wheat must fall to the ground and die in order to bear fruit (12,34). This image is then applied to Jesus and those who want to follow him: "Those who love their life lose it, and those who hate their life in this world will keep it for eternal life" (12,25). Giving up one's life on earth leads him to eternal life. In the same way, the death of the Son of Man makes him live for ever; his elevation onto the cross is his elevation into heaven, where he will rule for ever (12,31-32).[364]

In order that the true meaning of Jesus' claim in 12,32 may not escape the comprehension of the crowd, the narrator is brought in to explain to the crowd that Jesus is indicating the manner of his death (12,33); because a major concern of the fourth

---

12,33 does not make a distinction between elevation and crucifixion. Nicholson (137) rightly notes that such a distinction will make the expression 'ποίῳ θανάτῳ' insignificant. These words indicate that the choice is not between exaltation and crucifixion, but between different types of death: the elevation into heaven coincides with the death of Jesus – a death by elevation (on the cross).

[362] J. Riedl, "Wenn ihr den Menschensohn erhöht habt, werdet ihr erkennen (Joh 8,28)," in: Pesch and Schnackenburg, *Jesus und der Menschensohn*, 355-70.

[363] Cf. G. Caron, "The Lifting Up of the Human One and the Johannine Jews," *EeT(O)* 26 (1995) 327ff.

[364] See the explanation of A. Charbonneau, "Jésus en croix (Jn 19,16b-42); Jésus élévé (3,14ff.; 8,28f.; 12,31ff.)," *ScEs* 45 (1993) 5-23 and 161-80. See also M. Morgen, "Le Fils de l'homme élevé en vue de la vie éternelle (Jn 3,14-15 éclairé par diverses traditions juives)," *RevSR* 68 (1994) 5-17.

evangelist is to interpret Jesus' death as a triumph rather than a humiliation.[365] Surprisingly the crowd responds: "We have heard from the Law that the Messiah remains for ever. How can you say that the Son of Man must be lifted up? Who is this Son of Man?"(12,34). The introduction of the title 'Son of Man' here is unexpected. The last occurrence of the term was in Jesus' answer to Philip in 12,23, but it is used in both of the earlier references to Jesus being lifted up: "...so must the Son of Man be lifted up,..."(3,14), and "When you have lifted up the Son of Man..." (8,28). The conversation with the crowd, therefore, assumes information given already to the reader who should recall these earlier sayings. The crowd was not present when Jesus spoke to Nicodemus (3,14) or in 8,28. The crowd does not, apparently, understand that this exaltation will coincide with Jesus' death on the cross, and it is precisely this point that the implied author is intent on conveying to the reader. Correlation of the themes of the misunderstandings with the study of the narrator's point of view reveals that the themes selected for emphasis or explication by this form of discourse generally arise from the narrator's ideological and temporal point of view. The theme that appears most frequently in the misunderstandings is Jesus' death, resurrection and glorification.[366] The meaning of this event lies at the heart of the narrator's ideological point of view[367] and his interpretation of it reflects his position.

What is to be remembered from this example of misunderstanding is that the right understanding of the statement of Jesus in 3,14 is not choosing one meaning and excluding the other. The key to the interpretation lies in the superimposition of one meaning on the other: lifting up of the Son of Man does not mean either his crucifixion, or his ascension but his elevation into heaven through the medium of his elevation onto the cross.[368] The fourth evangelist's originality lies precisely in the fact that the ascension/glorification of Jesus is traced back to the moment of his being lifted up onto the cross.[369] The reason, obviously, is that Jesus' suffering and death were the way in which he would return to God and be glorified by Him, and the way he would grant eternal life to those who believe in him (cf. 3,15). For the fourth evangelist, the Pauline 'scandal' of the cross is not overcome only by the subsequent resurrection, but by the majesty and saving power of the cross itself. This last point again, in my opinion, ties in clearly with Num. 21: just as gazing at the serpent was the God-given means of life, a sign both of God's will to save and of his power over death, so also Jesus, as the Son of Man, in his suffering and death on the cross, embodies God's will to save and his power over death.

---

[365] Cf. the detailed work of M. C. de Boer, *Johannine Perspectives on the Death of Jesus* (Pharos 1996).

[366] Eight times: 2,19-21; 6,51-53; 7,31-36; 8,21-22; 12,32-34; 13,36-38; 14,4-6 and 16,16-19.

[367] Most of the other misunderstandings develop another of the Gospel's primary concerns; that is, the identity and nature of the children of God: their birth (3,3-5), their bread (6,32-35.51-53; cf. 4,31-34) and water (4,10-15), their freedom (8,31-35), their passage through death (8,51-53; 11,11-15 and 11,23-25), their vision of the Father (14,7-9), and Jesus' continuing presence with them (16,16-19; cf. 12,32-34 and 14,4-6).

[368] The theological connection between resurrection and exaltation is not infrequent in the NT: e.g. Rom. 8,34; Eph. 1,20 and 2,6; Col. 3,1 and 1 Pet. 1,21. The fourth evangelist goes farther, and theologically ties together the crucifixion, resurrection and ascension. For the fourth evangelist, the lifting up of the Son of Man on the cross is not what is fundamental, but his ascension into heaven, from where he descended. Only then is Jesus' mission completed.

[369] Schnackenburg (*Gospel*, I, 396) rightly contends that the evangelist here is taking "a most important step in Christology."

But the problem is still not solved, because the debate in determining which of these two meanings is the first in the intention of the fourth evangelist continues. In my opinion, this remains a false problematic. There could be no less futile controversy than the dispute whether, in these passages (3,14; 8,28 and 12,32), it is the crucifixion or the exaltation that is meant first. I contend that, for the fourth evangelist, the cross of shame is the throne of glory. The suffering and struggle of Jesus are only alternative names for his glory. In fact, glory hurts. It is when it hurts and is accepted that it becomes glory. Moreover, one need not search resolutely a distinction between a first and a second meaning of the verbal root. This must remain semantically open to two possibilities, without one or the other being preferred as the first. If the fourth evangelist wanted to insist on the crucifixion, he could have used σταυρόω or still τίθημι. For the exaltation into heaven, he could have used the verb ἀναβαίνω, or still one of the two verbs which Luke makes use of in the passive, viz., ἀναλαμβάνω (Acts 1,2.11.22) or ἐπαίρω (Acts 1,9). The choice of the verb ὑψόω demonstrates that the fourth evangelist did not want to distinguish the two meanings, and consequently, the two events. For him the death and glorification are simultaneous. The 'hour' fixed by the Father for his death (cf. 7,30 and 8,20), on which his gaze is fixed (cf. 12,23; 13,1 and 17,1), is – in contrast to the Synoptics (cf. Mk. 14,41 and Lk. 22,53) – only superficially the hour of darkness (cf. 13,30) and of disturbance (cf. 12,27). In reality it is the hour of his passing from this world to the Father (13,1) and the hour of his glorification (12,23 and 17,1). Many scholars have observed that 3,14 is related to the passion predictions in the Synoptics (cf. Mk. 8,31; 9,31; 10,33-34 and parallels).[370] What is significant of the fourth evangelist is the transformation he makes of the event of crucifixion. For him the glorious ascent of the Son of Man into heaven, made possible through the cross, is what is necessary for salvation. There is only one lifting up of Jesus in the fourth Gospel, and that is his ascension into heaven. However, the evangelist wants to make the reader understand that this ascension is effected through the concrete medium of the cross. This is suggested, not only through the semantic import of the verb, but also through the context which places in parallel the lifting up of the Son of Man and of the bronze serpent on the pole.[371]

Nicodemus, of course, could not have been expected to grasp both these connections at that time. But the first one should have been clear. He was being challenged to turn to Jesus in order to be begotten ἄνωθεν in much the same way as the ancient Israelites were commanded to turn to the bronze serpent for new life. Only when Nicodemus saw Jesus on the cross or, perhaps, only in his later reflection on the cross, the words of Jesus must have become clearer to him.[372]

---

[370] See e.g. B. Lindars, *Jesus Son of Man. A Fresh Examination of the Son of Man Sayings in the Gospels in the Light of Recent Research* (Grand Rapids 1984) 145-47; see also M. Morgen, "Jean 3 et les évangiles synoptiques," in: Denaux, *John and the Synoptics*, 514-22.

[371] See J. D. M. Derrett, "The Bronze Serpent," *EstB* 49 (1991) 311-29; R. J. Burns, "Jesus and the Bronze Serpent," *BiTod* 28 (1990) 84-89; and A. Greiner, "Le serpent d'Airain et le Crucifié. Quelques réflexions relatives à deux textes bibliques conjoints," *PosLuth* 34 (1986) 22-27; see also Maneschg, 425; M. Mees, "Erhöhung und Verherrlichung Jesu im Johannesevangelium nach dem Zeugnis neutestamentlicher Papyri," *BZ* 18 (1974) 35; and V. Mannucci, "Amour de Dieu et foi de l'homme (Jn 3,14-21)," *ASeign* 17 1970) 44.

[372] Cf. The Characterisation of Nicodemus.

ε. The Purpose of Ὑψόω

An important aspect to be treated concerns the liaison between 3,14 and 3,15. The argumentation proceeds from the grammatical construction 'δεῖ... ἵνα...' The lifting of the Son of Man into heaven through the event of his crucifixion/exaltation is a *necessity* for *eternal life* offered to humanity. 3,15 reads as follows: "ἵνα πᾶς ὁ πιστεύων ἐν αὐτῷ ἔχῃ ζωὴν αἰώνιον." The expression 'eternal life' here makes its first appearance in the fourth Gospel. It is not an endless duration of being in time, but being of which time is not a measure. It is always, in this Gospel, the life of the believer. Neither the Father nor the Son is said to have it. The Father 'has life in Himself' and he has granted this also to the Son (5,26). The Son is 'the life' (11,25 and 14,6). But 'eternal life' is reserved for the gift of life bestowed on believers. It originates in a divine action, the action wherein one is begotten. It is the gift of God and not a human achievement. This will be dealt with further in detail under dualism.

ζ. Irony

Everyone familiar with the fourth Gospel will be struck by the correspondence between the components of irony and the ways it is employed by the fourth evangelist. The contrast between levels of meaning is sharpest in the Gospel's pervasive use of irony. A vital tension exists between the aspects of the Gospel that stress the *contrast* between levels of meaning and those that disclose the *connections* between the levels of meaning. A verb like 'lift up' (ὑψόω – 3,14; 8,28 and 12,33-34) emphasises the *connection*, rather than the *contrast*, between the physical and the divine levels of meaning. As I have elaborated already in the treatment under double meaning, the term ὑψόω can mean either to elevate something in a physical sense or to exalt someone in honour and glory. In one sense Jesus' comment anticipates that he would be 'lifted up' physically onto the cross to die. Yet in the context of my unit of study as well as in the other two instances, the evangelist prepares the reader to see that the 'lifting up' is not only Jesus' elevation on the cross but also his exaltation in glory. The cross was both the culmination of Jesus' work on earth and the inauguration of his return to glory in heaven.

. A more specific, yet even more fundamental, example of irony occurs in the fourth Gospel's transformation of the triple prediction of the passion into the threefold allusion to the 'lifting up' of the Son of Man (3,14-15; 8,28 and 12,32-34). Here, there is a consummate irony in choosing the image of the bronze serpent on a pole (Num. 21,8-9) to suggest the mystery of the cross. The incongruity of the serpent, instrument of death (in the OT context), as source of life, parallels the incongruity of the scandalous death of Jesus on a cross as source of eternal life. But again, the irony reveals a deeper perception of reality that is contrary to the appearance, for the fourth evangelist accepts the fundamental Christian belief in both the incarnation and the reality of the passion. That Jesus' glorification should begin with his death on the cross (elevation) is an incongruity which one would not expect the fourth evangelist to let pass unnoticed. The descent and ascent motifs (cf. 3,12-14) are comprehensible to the reader as he/she knows the end of the story. Life triumphs through death – glorification through crucifixion; that is both the fundamental irony of the fourth evangelist's faith and the foundational irony of

Christianity. The evangelist's interpretation of the death of Jesus as exaltation and return to the Father – the 'lifting up of the Son' – is his unique and crowning irony.

vi. Argumentation of 3,16-18

After the statement on the necessity of the lifting up of the Son of Man to obtain eternal life (3,14-15), the *Christological* discourse is pursued at a new level in 3,16-18. For the first time in the chapter, one meets the title 'Son (only begotten) of God,' as well as the terms 'world,' 'condemn,' 'give,' and 'send.' It is equally a question of the active role of God, not mentioned since 3,2 ("No one can do these signs that you do apart from the presence of God"). I have exposed already the compound parallelism (ab//a^{1}b^1//a^{2}b^2) which binds 3,14-18. The πᾶς of 3,15 explains the πᾶς and κόσμος of 3,16. This establishes the continuity of 3,15 with 3,16ff.

When turning to 3,16-18, which contains what, probably, is the best known verse in the New Testament (3,16),[373] the reader finds one of the primary theological summaries concerning salvation in the NT.[374] 3,16 reduces everything to its deepest underlying cause and to its ultimate simplicity. What Moses did at God's instruction in the wilderness, *viz.*, lift up the serpent, was great and marvellous. But nowhere else does one see more clearly the difference between what God gave through Moses, and the grace and truth that came through Jesus Christ (cf. 1,17 and 6,32). Yet, one must take great care not to lose the marvellous balance in this wonderful summary. Interpreters, I feel, should deal with a minimum of these three verses, *viz.*, 3,16-18. I am treating them together, because it takes at least that many verses here to obtain the correct meaning. 3,16 serves as a *statement of fact involving the agency*[375] – the Son – God used to bring salvation to the world. The key to salvation is faith in the only Son of God; there is, therefore, no *soteriology* without *Christology* in the plan of God.[376] The text, however, does not specify or explain in what way the gift of the Son brings about salvation. Although salvation is rooted in the love of God for the world in its totality, it is accessible only to the believers (πᾶς ὁ πιστεύων εἰς αὐτόν). In an implicit way, one can suppose already that one who refuses to believe is destined to perish and not obtain eternal life. This principle is then explained in 3,17-18, which indicates the connection of these verses through the conjunction 'γάρ' at the beginning of 3,17. In fact, one could consider 3,17-18 as a paraphrasing of 3,16.

On the one hand, 3,17 explains God's intention and clearly identifies *God's purpose* in sending the Son. It also reaffirms the universal dimension of the salvific love of

---

[373] Bruce (89) comments: "If there is one sentence more than another which sums up the message of the fourth Gospel, it is this." See also J. Sudbrack, "Denn Gott hat die Welt so sehr geliebt, daß er seinen einzigen Sohn dahingab (Joh 3,16)," *GuL* 53 (1980) 382-86.

[374] See J. Beutler, "So sehr hat Gott die Welt geliebt (Joh 3,16). Zum Heilsuniversalismus im Johannesevangelium," *GuL* 66 (1993) 418-28; and H. Ritt, "'So sehr hat Gott die Welt geliebt...' (Joh 3,16). Gotteserfahrung bei Johannes," in: *'Ich will euer Gott werden.' Beispiele biblischen Redens von Gott* (SBS 100) (Stuttgart 1981) 207-26.

[375] For a detailed discussion on agency see P. Borgen, "God's Agent in the Fourth Gospel," in: J. Neussner (ed.), *Religions in Antiquity. Essays in Memory of E. R. Goodenough* (SHR 14) (Leiden 1968) 243-58; and A. E. Harvey, "Christ as Agent," in: Hurst and Wright, *Glory of Christ*, 239-50.

[376] Cf. G. A. Turner, "Soteriology in the Gospel of John," *JETS* 14 (1976) 271-77.

God.[377] In 3,16 there was a *reduction* of the perspective between the love of God for the world and the effective gift of eternal life *only* to the believers. 3,17 restores the *universal* perspective ("in order that the *world* might be saved through him") of salvation. Such an argumentative orientation of 3,17 is also supported by the syntactic structure ("οὐ γὰρ...ἵνα ..ἀλλ᾽ ἵνα...") which places the whole stress on the last clause: ἀλλ᾽ ἵνα σωθῇ ὁ κόσμος δι᾽ αὐτοῦ. The object of the love of God in giving His only Son is those to whom He sends His Son; his mission is their salvation. There is, therefore, no distinction between those whom God loves and those whom He wants to save. The salvific will of God is universal.

On the other hand, 3,17 reformulates the statement of 3,16cde on the salvific goal of the gift of the Son. In fact, the statements "ἵνα ... μὴ ἀπόληται ἀλλ᾽ ἔχῃ ζωὴν αἰώνιον" (3,16cde) and "οὐ ... ἵνα κρίνῃ .... ἀλλ᾽ ... σωθῇ[378] ..." (3,17) are obviously synonyms. In the fourth Gospel 'perish' and 'have eternal life' are in opposition.[379]

God's Son is sent into the world not to judge it but to save it. 'Κρίνειν' and 'σῴζειν'[380] seem to be directly opposed to each other; one must, thus, give to the verb κρίνειν the meaning of condemning.[381] Under this aspect of condemnation, judgement is often opposed to eternal life in the fourth Gospel,[382] in the sense that in 3,18, the expression 'not condemned' can be applied to the believer as a substitute for 'having eternal life.' 3,17 is a repetition of 3,16 with substitution of terms. The goal of the substitution of terms is, simply, to specify certain implicit elements of 3,16: the gift of the Son (3,16) is characterised as sending (3,17) into the world; the mission of the Son has an universal scope (3,17), because it finds its basis in the love of God for the world (3,16). Because of such a foundation, this mission cannot have for goal the condemnation of the world but only its salvation; the obtaining of eternal life is, in fact, the concrete and the

---

[377] See the elaborate treatment of A. Feuillet, *Le mystère de l'amour divin dans la théologie johannique* (Paris 1972); and F. F. Segovia, *Love Relationships in the Johannine Tradition. Agape/Agapan in I John and the Fourth Gospel* (SBL.DS 58) (Chico 1982) on this subject. See also R. Schnackenburg, "Die Agape Gottes nach Johannes," in: T. Franke (ed.), *Creatio ex amore: Beiträge zu einer Theologie der Liebe. FS Alexandre Ganoczy zum 60. Geburtstag* (Würzburg 1988) 36-47; and W. E. Hull, *Love in Four Dimensions: John 3:16. Divine Love in Human Life* (Nashville 1982).

[378] Except for the occurrences in 11,12 and 12,27, which do not refer to eternal salvation as such, all other occurrences of the verb 'σῴζω' are found in the immediate context of a reference to eternal life; comp. 5,34 with 5,39-40; 10,9 with 10,10; and 12,47 with 12,50.

[379] Cf. 6,27.39-40; 10,10.28 and 12,25.

[380] The verb 'σῴζειν' (save) is used only six times (3,17; 5,34, 10,9; 11,12 and 12,27.47) in the fourth Gospel, and 'σωτήρ' (4,42) and 'σωτηρία' (4,22) each once. The meaning of 'save' undoubtedly carries the idea of deliverance or coming to wholeness as in the OT (see G. Fohrer, "σῴζω and σωτηρία in the Old Testament," *TDNT*, VII, 970-80). The more usual expression in the fourth Gospel involves 'eternal life' or 'life.' For further treatment see under dualism.

[381] Cf. R. E. Brown, *op. cit.*, 134; and Barrett, 181. Blank (*Krisis*, 42) observes that the theme of judgement (κρίσις, κρίμα, κρίνω) carries a double significance in the fourth Gospel, one of judgement (*Gericht*) in the sense of the eschatological judgement, and the other of decision (*Entscheidung*). There is always an idea of separation.

[382] The most evident parallel is found in 12,47-48: "I do not judge anyone who hears my words and does not keep them, for I came not to judge the world, but to save the world. The one who rejects me and does not receive my word has a judge; on the last day the word that I have spoken will serve as judge." Rejecting the words of Jesus is to be condemned by the same word, because it is the Father's commandment, which is eternal life, that Jesus speaks (12,49-50). Rejecting this word is rejecting life. "Whoever keeps my word will never see death" (8,51). In the same way in 5,24: "Anyone who hears my word and believes him who sent me has eternal life, and does not come under judgement, but has passed from death to life." There is, therefore, only one alternative: having eternal life or being condemned.

only goal of the divine and universal salvific will of God. Hence, if all are not saved, the responsibility does not lie on God.

Only one aspect of 3,16 has not been developed in 3,17, *viz.*, 'πᾶς ὁ πιστεύων' and its negative and implicit counterpart. The explanation why a part of the world is condemned is fulfilled in 3,18, immediately after the affirmation of the universal scope of the salvific mission of the Son in 3,17. This reality, which has been implicitly affirmed in 3,16 by the movement from 'τὸν κόσμον' to 'πᾶς ὁ πιστεύων,' is repeated and developed in 3,18:

3,16	ἠγάπησεν ὁ θεὸς τὸν κόσμον	- πᾶς ὁ πιστεύων
3,17-18	ἵνα σωθῇ ὁ κόσμος δι᾽ αὐτου	- ὁ πιστεύων ... ὁ δὲ μὴ πιστεύων

After having reaffirmed God's universal salvific will, the evangelist turns (in 3,18) again to the effective impact of the mission of the Son on the addressees. But this time, the whole κόσμος is included in the perspective; he divides humanity into two camps: those who will be saved (ὁ πιστεύων) and those who will not be saved (ὁ δὲ μὴ πιστεύων). The latter is only implicit in 3,16. In 3,18 the reason for their exclusion from salvation is explicitly stated: "because they have not believed in the name of the only Son of God."[383] God offers salvation to the whole of humanity in sending His Son into the world; the world, however, remains free to accept or reject this salvation, and this freedom is exercised in the choice between believing and not believing.

But the scope of 3,18 does not stop here. Not only the verb 'condemn' is resumed from 3,17 to express the double result – positive and negative – of the mission of the Son, but its actualisation in the present. Those who believe in him are not condemned; but those who do not believe are condemned *already*. Though the Son has not come to condemn but to save the world, his presence brings inevitably a judgement, a separation between those who are saved and those who are condemned. In this sense, Jesus could say that he came to this world for a judgement (cf. 9,39), without, however, contradicting the affirmation of 3,17. In the fourth Gospel, salvation and condemnation are, therefore, present realities, related to the encounter with the Son-sent. The moment an individual takes the decision to look at the Son, his destiny is eternally fixed; the final judgement, that is, the eschatological separation between the saved and the condemned, those who have believed and those who have refused to believe, is realised already.[384]

---

[383] The verb 'believe' (πεπίστευκεν) in the perfect form here indicates an obstinate refusal to believe: the one who refuses to believe, and persists in his unbelief, is judged already. Moreover, the object of the verb is no more 'him' (the Son) but 'the name of the only Son of God.' In the Semitic world the name is a symbol of personality (cf. Dodd, *Interpretation*, 184; Bultmann, *Gospel*, 59, n. 2; and Schnackenburg, *Gospel*, I, 357-58). 'Believing in the name of the only Son of God' means recognising in Jesus, the Son (of God) sent by the Father for the salvation of the world.

[384] Cf. J. S. Henning, "Realized Eschatology: A study of John's Gospel and Gestalt Therapy," *BiTod* 68 (1973) 1332-34. Some passages of the fourth Gospel seem to be marked by the presence of a futuristic traditional eschatology, which is transparent in the statements on the final judgement or resurrection on the last day (cf. e.g. 5,28-29; 6,39-40.44.54 and 12,48). Some scholars tried to solve the contradiction by attributing the realised eschatology to the evangelist and the futuristic eschatology to a later ecclesiastical redactor (cf. O. Cullmann, *Heil als Geschichte* [Tübingen 1965] 245ff.; esp. G. Richter, "Präsentische und futurische Eschatologie im vierten Evangelium," in: P. Fiedler and D. Zeller [eds.], *Gegenwart und Kommen des Reiches. Schülergabe A. Vögtle zum 65. Geburtstag* [SBB] [Stuttgart 1975] 117-52). A less hypothetical solution is proposed by R. E. Brown and Schnackenburg among others. They propose a conception of the evangelist which announces the presence of an eschatological salvation but awaiting its future

3,18 provides, thus, a pointed 'reality-statement' concerning the present nature of judgement, a reality no reader should fail to understand. Only when the three verses are allowed to hang together does the reader begin to grasp the full meaning of the coming of Jesus and the fourth evangelist's message of salvation expounded here.

α. Measure of God's Love

All the emphasis in 3,16 seems to lie on the 'οὕτως' ('so,' 'in this manner,' 'in this measure'). This word refers back to the 'how' of the lifting up of the Son of Man, but it also directs the reader's attention to the measure of God's love underlying that lifting up. In reality, all the terminology is attuned to God's love. The syntactic framework of the argument in 3,16 is supported by the connection of the terms 'Οὕτως... ὥστε... ἵνα...' The love of God for the world is the reason for the *gift* of His only begotten Son, whose goal is salvation. In fact, "God so *loved* the *world...*" (3,16) is derived directly from "so that *everyone* who believes in him may have eternal life" (3,15). The exposition of the love continues the exposition of the gift of the bronze serpent, for it was *given* through *love*, as a medicine.

The fourth Gospel does not offer the world a superficial idea of the love of God in salvation. The Greek construction puts some emphasis on the actuality of the gift: it is not 'God loved *enough* to give,' but 'God loved *so that* He gave.' The Greek construction Οὕτως + ὥστε[385] + indicative (ἔδωκεν) instead of the infinitive (ὥστε + δοῦναι), which might have been expected, emphasises the intensity of that love. The verbs 'loved'[386] and 'gave' here express the genuine self-giving nature of God in having 'sent' His 'only Son'[387] on an unrepeatable mission into the world (cf. 1,14.18). It is God who takes the

---

accomplishment. See also Okure, 168. In my opinion, in the fourth Gospel, there is a realised eschatology, but it has a present (life begun already by faith in Jesus and the gift of the Spirit) and a future perspective (the hour of definitive victory by Jesus' elevation); see also F. Hahn, "Das Glaubensverständnis im Johannesevangelium," in: E. Gräßer and O. Merk (eds.), *Glaube und Eschatologie. FS Werner Georg Kümmel zum 80. Geburtstag* (Tübingen 1985) 61; and S. Pancaro, "A Statistical Approach to the Concept of Time and Eschatology in the Fourth Gospel," *Bib.* 50 (1969) 511-24. For a recent study see J. Frey, *Die johanneische Eschatologie. Band II: Das johanneische Zeitverständnis* (WUNT 110) (Tübingen 1998).

[385] See R. H. Gundry and R. W. Howell, "The Sense Syntax of John 3:14-17 with Special Reference to the Use of οὕτως ...... ὥστε in John 3:16," *NT* 41 (1999) 25-25 and 38-39. This is the fourth evangelist's only use of ὥστε, so that one has no means of knowing how often he would have used one construction in preference to the other. But 'ὥστε' is found in the NT 84 times, only 21 times with the indicative, 15 of which are in Paul. The fourth evangelist's use, I find, is rather unusual and in all probability emphatic.

[386] This is the fourth evangelist's first use of 'ἀγαπάω,' a verb he will employ 36 times, more than twice the number in any other book of the NT except 1 John (which has it 31 times; next is Luke with 13 times). He also uses 'φιλέω' more than anyone else, though the figures are smaller (John 13 times, then Matthew 5 times; the NT total is 25 times). It is interesting that the fourth evangelist uses both verbs more than twice as often as anyone else. Clearly 'love' matters a good deal to the fourth evangelist (though I should accept that Paul's total use of love-words is higher). For a detailed discussion see L. Morris, "Love in the Fourth Gospel," in: J. I. Cook (ed.), *Saved by Hope. Richard C. Oudersluys FS* (Grand Rapids 1978) 27-43; and his *Testaments of Love* (Grand Rapids 1981); see also M. Lattke, *Einheit im Wort. Die spezifische Bedeutung von 'ἀγάπη,' 'ἀγαπᾶν' und 'φιλεῖν' im Johannesevangelium* (StANT 41) (München 1975) 64.

[387] LXX translates the Hebrew יחיד in two ways: 1) by the adjective 'well-beloved' (ἀγαπητός - cf. Gen. 22,2. 12; Jer. 6,26; Amos 8,10 and Zech. 12,10); and 2) by the adjective 'only' (μονογενής – cf. Jud. 11,34; Ps. 22,21and 35,17). Qualifying a 'son' with יחיד can, therefore, mean both 'only' and 'well-beloved;' cf. Bernard, I, 23-24. For a detailed discussion see G. Pendrick, "ΜΟΝΟΓΕΝΗΣ," *NTS* 41 (1995) 587-600; R. Roberts, "The Rendering 'Only Begotten' in John 3:16," *RestQ* 16 (1973) 2-22; and J. V. Dahms, "The Johannine Use of Monogenes Reconsidered," *NTS* 29 (1983) 222-32.

initiative and makes the *all-embracing* sacrifice for the *world*. It is distinctly Christian idea that God's love is wide enough to embrace *all people*. His love is not confined to any national group or spiritual elite. It is a love that proceeds from the fact that He is love (cf. 1 Jn. 4,8.16). It is His nature to love. The fourth evangelist does not make further analysis of why God loves this way. The text's exclusive concern is the *fact* and the *magnitude* of God's love.[388] No sacrifice was too great to bring its unmeasured intensity home to humanity. The best that God had to give, He gave – His only begotten Son, His well-beloved. The pathos of the words 'His only Son' should remind the reader of the pathos in the story of Abraham when he was told by God to take his son, his 'only son Isaac,' and sacrifice him at Moriah (Gen. 22,2).[389]

3,15 reads, "that whoever believes in him (the Son)...." The starting point of faith does not lie in the fact that the world returned to God in the ascent of the Son of Man, but in the fact that, in the incarnated man Jesus, God put the world on the track of true humanity ('not perish,' but 'have eternal life'). God, in His eternal love, returned to the world as to His own, loved it in the surrender of His only begotten Son (cf. 3,35), and loved His Son, because he gave his own life (cf. 10,15) in a love that persisted to the end (cf. 13,1ff.). Note that the cross is not said to show the love of the Son (as in Gal. 2,20) but that of the Father. The atonement[390] proceeds from the loving heart of God.

β. ' Ἔδωκεν' **and** ''Απέστειλεν'

One question, however, which comes to the fore here is that of the relation between the verbs 'give' (16b) and 'send' (17a). Because 3,16 is sandwiched between 3,14-15 and 3,17, the fact that God gave His only Son is tied both to the Son's incarnation (3,17) and to his death[391] and glorification (3,14-15). Another passage where the Hebrew background of a double meaning word can be observed is 3,16. The meaning of ἔδωκεν here is questionable. Does it refer to the incarnation in the sense of ἀποστέλλω or does it refer to Calvary in the sense of παραδίδωμι? 3,17 (God sending His Son into the world – cf. 1 Jn. 4,9)[392] emphasises the first and 3,14-15, where the Son of Man is lifted up, points up the second (cf. Rom. 8,32).[393] The key to this is found in the OT use of נתן (to give) in Is. 53,12: "giving up to death because he poured out himself to death." In this passage

---

[388] As J. Marsh (*The Gospel of John* [PGC] [Baltimore 1978] 183) puts it, "the magnitude of the love is matched by the magnitude of the gift...God loved all there was, and gave all he had." See also K. Scholtissek, "Ein Vater, der Mit-Liebende sucht. Beobachtungen zum johanneischen Gottesbild," *Beiträge zu Pastoral, Katechese & Theologie* 11 (1999) 25-31.

[389] The comparison with the sacrifice of Isaac is to be seen in the fact that in both cases it is a father who gives his son up to death and that death has a positive effect on nation/humanity (cf. Gen. 22,18 and Sir. 44,21). See F.-M. Braun, "Le sacrifice d'Isaac dans le quatrième évangile d'après le Targum," *NRTh* 4 (1979) 483-97; Barrett, 180; Bernard, I, 118; R. E. Brown, *op. cit.*, 147; and Wikenhauser, 126.

[390] See M. Turner, "Atonement and the Death of Jesus in John. Some Questions to Bultmann and Forestell," *EvQ* 62 (1990) 99-122; see also the recent study of C. J. den Heyer, *Jesus and the Doctrine of the Atonement: Biblical Notes on a Controversial Topic* (Minneapolis 1998).

[391] On the theology of cross and incarnation see H. Kohler, *Kreuz und Menschwerdung im Johannesevangelium. Ein exegetisch-hermeneutischer Versuch zur johanneischen Kreuzestheologie* (AThANT 72) (Zürich 1987).

[392] See Klauck, *Der erste Johannesbrief*, 250.

[393] Cullmann, "Johanneische Gebrauch," 366; and Schnackenburg, *Gospel*, I, 399.

παρεδόθη (LXX) is a translation of the Hebrew נָשָׂא meaning to lift up, to bear or to carry, etc.

In typical fashion of the fourth Gospel 'gave' is used in two senses. God gave the Son by sending him into the world, but God also gave His Son on the cross. I may say that the Son is God's gift to the world, and moreover, he is *the* gift. However, do the two verbs refer to the same event? Some scholars suggest that the verb 'give' (δίδωμι) must, probably, be interpreted to mean 'give up' or 'surrender' (παραδίδωμι – cf. Rom. 4,25 and 8,32; Gal. 2,20; and Mk. 9,31), namely death on the cross: God literally gives up His Son to death on the cross.[394] In this perspective, this verse could refer to the expiatory sufferings of the Servant of Yahweh (cf. παρέδωκεν in Is. 53,6.12) or still to the sacrifice of Isaac. But this interpretation of the verb δίδωμι poses some hurdles. It is difficult to explain why the fourth evangelist here has not directly used the verb παραδίδωμι[395] to explain the death of Jesus on the cross.

In my opinion, the parallelism between 3,16ab and 17a directs me to another synonymous interpretation of the two verbs. 'Send'[396] is used also in other places in this Gospel. It is only here that the sending is described as a 'giving.' Moreover, in the place of the Son of Man (3,13) one now reads 'the Son,' because of the motif of surrender: 'the Son' implies a (pre-existent) personal relationship, while 'the Son of Man' implies a salvation-historical function.[397] In the perspective of the sending Christology,[398] it is the

---

[394] Cf. B. H. Grigsby, "The Cross as an Expiatory Sacrifice in the Fourth Gospel," *JSNT* 15 (1982) 51-80.

[395] The fourth evangelist uses this verb often to qualify the betrayal of Judas or the act of Jews delivering Jesus to Pilate (cf. 6,64.71; 12,4; 13,2.11.21; 18,2.5.30.35.35 and 19,11). Only once does the verb explicitly refer to the crucifixion: "τότε οὖν παρέδωκεν αὐτὸν αὐτοῖς ἵνα σταυρωθῇ" (19,16). See also B. H. Grigsby, "The Cross as an Expiatory Sacrifice in the Fourth Gospel," *JSNT* 15 (1982) 51-80.

[396] Westcott (*ad loc.*) distinguishes ἀποστέλλω from πέμπω in that it conveys the accessory notions of a special commission, and so far a delegated authority in the person sent. The simple verb marks πέμπω nothing more than the immediate relation of the sender to the sent. K. H. Rengstorf ("ἀποστέλλω [πέμπω]," *TDNT*, I, 398ff.) makes a similar distinction. E. A. Abbott (*Johannine Vocabulary* [London 1905] 1723) reverses the distinction saying that ἀποστέλλω means 'sending away into the world at large,' but πέμπω indicates 'sending on a special errand.' More recently C. Mercer ("'Αποστέλλειν and Πέμπειν in John,"*NTS* 36 [1990] 619-24) has argued that the distinction of Westcott and Rengstorf is correct, but he does not notice that variation in expression without significant difference in meaning is a characteristic of Johannine style. In my opinion, it may be doubted whether a sharp distinction between the two words is legitimate. The fourth evangelist uses ἀποστέλλω in the aorist and perfect indicative active and the perfect participle passive, whereas he uses πέμπω in the present, the future, and the aorist active participle. The difference is not one of meaning but of the evangelist's consistent choice of certain parts only of each of these verbs. That there is no difference of meaning is also to be noticed in the way the verbs are used. Both are used of purely human sending (ἀποστέλλω in 1,24 and πέμπω in 1,22), of the sending of the Baptist (ἀποστέλλω 1,6 and πέμπω 1,33), and of Jesus' sending of the disciples (ἀποστέλλω 17,18 and πέμπω 13,20). In both, the primacy is for the Father's sending of the Son (ἀποστέλλω 17 times out of 28 occurrences, and πέμπω 24 times out of 32). The verbs occur together in 7,28-29 and 20,21; and both roots in 13,16. No real difference of meaning is apparent. Both words occur in the fourth Gospel more often than in any other NT writing: ἀποστέλλω 28 times as against 22 times in Matthew, 20 times in Mark, and 25 times in Luke; πέμπω 32 times as against 4 times in Matthew, once in Mark, and 10 times in Luke. These statistics show that the thought of mission is important to the fourth evangelist.

[397] Cf. Ridderbos, 138; Schnackenburg, *op. cit.*; R. E. Brown, *op. cit.*, 134; Bultmann, *Gospel*, 153, n. 3; and Wikenhauser, 126.

[398] Cf. Miranda, 31.

whole mission of the Son that is important for salvation,[399] including, of course, the final act which concludes the mission. But the crucial moment remains the sending, the moment where the one sent receives his mandate that empowers him with all the necessary authority to accomplish his mission.

In the first part of the parallelism, the evangelist presents the fundamental event of salvation in the Christological perspective of the Son of Man (= lifted up on the cross/into heaven – 3,14-15). But in the interior of the Christological scheme of the Son-sent, it is the sending as such which is the most significant moment and which serves as the basis for the rest of the mission. One cannot, therefore, simply identify 'δίδωμι' (3,16) with 'ὑψόω' (3,14). If one has to distinguish a particular event which will explain the aorist form of the verb 'give' (ἔδωκεν), it cannot just be the sending of the Son on a mission as the parallel verb 'send' in 3,17 suggests it. There is difference of opinion among scholars regarding this sending. W. Kramer affirms that the evangelist here makes use of the traditional double-formula of faith (*Glaubensformeln*) of the early Christians, *viz.*, the formula of gift (*Dahingabeformel*) and the formula of sending (*Sendungsformel*).[400] In my opinion, this view is not acceptable as he simply 're-interprets' the gift of the Son in 3,16 with the traditional formula of sending in 3,17. E. Schweizer, on the other hand, observes rightly that in Paul and John this formula of sending supposes a pre-existence Christology (a sending from heaven), which has its roots in the Judeo-Hellenistic thought on Wisdom in the OT (e.g. Wis. 9,9-11.13-18).[401] In this context, the title 'Son of God' is to be distinguished from its use in the Davidic-Messiah tradition (cf. Ps. 2,7).[402] J. Blank finds a prophetic tradition in the sending of the Son. He observes an analogy between the tragic destiny of the prophets and Jesus.[403] According to him, the motif of sending is not mythical but *heilsgeschichtlich-prophetisch*.[404] In connection with his prophetic mission, the title 'Son'[405] is linked to the office of a messenger. Jesus is the last messenger of God, the eschatological prophet.[406]

---

[399] Cf. H. Weder, "L'asymétrie du salut. Réflexions sur Jean 3,14-21 dans le cadre de la théologie johannique," in: J. Zumstein, J.-D. Kaestli and J.-M. Poffet (eds.), *La Communauté Johannique et son histoire. La trajectoire de l'évangile de Jean aux deux premiers siècles* (Geneva 1990) 167.

[400] See W. Kramer, *Christos Kyrios Gottessohn. Untersuchungen zu Gebrauch und Bedeutung der christologischen Bezeichnungen bei Paulus und den vorpaulinischen Gemeinden* (AThANT 44) (Zürich 1963) 108-20.

[401] Cf. M. Morgen, "Les traditions sapientielles à l'arrière-plan de Jn 3," in: J. Trublet (ed.), *La Sagesse biblique de l'Ancien au Nouveau Testament* (LeDiv 160) (Paris 1995) 385-412.

[402] See E. Schweizer, "Zum religionsgeschichtlichen Hintergrund der 'Sendungsformel' Gal 4,4f. Röm 8,3f. Joh 3,16f. I Joh 4,9," *ZNW* 57 (1966) 208.

[403] See also K. Berger, *Die Auferstehung des Propheten und die Erhöhung des Menschensohnes. Traditionsgeschichtliche Untersuchungen zur Deutung des Geschickes Jesu in frühchristlichen Texten* (StUNT 13) (Göttingen 1976).

[404] J. Blank, "Die Sendung des Sohnes. Zur christologischen Bedeutung des Gleichnisses von den bösen Winzern Mk 12,1-12," in: J. Gnilka (ed.), *Neues Testament und Kirche* (Freiburg 1974) 17.

[405] *Ibid.*, 33-35. On the meaning of this title see also K. Berger, "Zum traditionsgeschichtlichen Hintergrund christologischer Hoheitstitel," *NTS* 17 (1971) 413-25.

[406] Cf. J. Coppens, "Le prophète eschatologique. L'annonce de sa venue. Les relecture," *EThL* 49 (1973) 5-35.

From the point of view of the history of traditions, I feel, it is probable that the formula of sending, as used by Paul and John,[407] betray a combination of the wisdom (cf. Schweizer) and the prophetic (cf. Blank) traditions. Jesus, the one sent by the Father, is not only the eschatological prophet, but also the pre-existent Son of God.[408] The fourth evangelist could have used the verb *give*, simply, to stress the root cause (depth) of 'sending' on a mission lying in the divine love for the world (3,16a). Thus, in my opinion, the notion of 'giving' and 'sending' characterises not just the crucifixion and exaltation, but also the entire salvific mission of Jesus. In other words, for the fourth evangelist's Christology is inseparably bound up with soteriology.

vii. Dualistic Symbols

One need not have to read far into the fourth Gospel before he is struck with the evangelist's use of dualistic symbols. The prologue presents a dualism of light and darkness: 'the light shines in the darkness, and the darkness did not overcome it' (1,5; cf. 3,19-21). Of course, such pairs of opposites are not unusual in the NT or in the Hebrew Bible. What is unusual in the fourth Gospel is their prominence. It would appear that the whole system of religious thought, presented in the fourth Gospel, hangs within a dualistic framework that contains two anchoring points between which the evangelist has woven the thought of his Gospel. The discourse of Jesus (3,11-21) is rich in dualistic symbols.

α. Κόσμος

a) Context

The easiest point of entry into the subject of dualism is a concept peculiar to the fourth Gospel – that of the word κόσμος.[409] This is not a simple concept, because the fourth Gospel's use of the term is not consistent.[410] One must watch the *context* in which this word is used, for it can have a variety of meanings. There are two quite distinct oppositions implied by the term κόσμος, and although these may coincide, they also differ significantly. Sometimes ὁ κόσμος appears to mean earth as opposed to heaven, *down below* as opposed to *up above*[411] (cf. 'earthly things' and 'heavenly things' – 3,12). Often it is used to distinguish the heavenly *origin* of Jesus as opposed to the earthly: the Son of Man has

---

[407] The difference between the Pauline and the Johannine use of the formula of sending lies in the fact that John develops more the juridical aspect of the notion of sending; see Bühner, 172, n. 51; and M. Waldstein, "Die Sendung Jesu und der Jünger im Johannesevangelium," *IKaZ* 19 (1990) 203-21.

[408] Cf. R. H. Fuller, "New Testament Roots to the Theotokos," *MarSt* 29 (1978) 46-64.

[409] In the Johannine literature the word κόσμος appears 105 times, 78 times in the fourth Gospel, 24 times in the three Johannine epistles, and 3 times in Revelation. The frequency of use, therefore, is two and a half times that of the entire remainder of the NT taken together. The word appears in the fourth Gospel almost six times more frequently than it does in the Synoptics. Useful summaries of how the term is used can be found in the work of R. E. Brown, *op. cit.*, 508-10; and F.-M. Braun, "Le péché du monde selon saint Jean," *RThom* 65 (1965) 181-201; the latter provides, perhaps, the most comprehensive effort to catalogue the various ways in which 'κόσμος' is used in the fourth Gospel. For a grammatical analysis of the appearance of the term 'κόσμος' see also Cassem, 81-91.

[410] In eleven texts the 'κόσμος' is connected with the polar concept of love-hatred. Five among them where the κόσμος hates the disciples (15,18.19 x 2; 17,14 and 1 Jn. 3,13) and one where it cannot (7,7), two where God loves either it (3,16) or those in it (13,1), one where it loves only its own (15,19), and two in which the disciples are exhorted not to love it (1 Jn. 2,15 x twice). This again clearly establishes the ambivalence with which the concept 'κόσμος' is used in Johannine theology.

[411] See J. A. Loewen, "The 'World' in John's Gospel Through West African Eyes," *BiTr* 34 (1983) 409.

'descended (on earth) *from heaven*' (3,13), and "the one who is of *the earth* belongs to the earth...The one who comes *from heaven* is above all" (3,31).[412]

b) Vertical Opposition

This meaning, which implies what one may call a *vertical opposition*, is also present in the numerous allusions to Jesus' entry into the world: 'God sent His Son *into the world*' (from his heavenly domain) – 3,17; 'the light has come *into the world*' (from his heavenly domain – 3,19); he does not come into the world like the rest of mankind, he is *sent* (3,17); he arrives *from another place*.[413] But it is to be stressed that the world he enters is the world of mankind.[414] The immediate source of this vertical opposition is the relative location of heaven and earth, respectively above and below, something one is in danger of forgetting, because it is always, simply, assumed.

I have yet to wrestle with the fully dualistic uses of the term. In 8,23 and 13,1 this world is set over against another realm. In both cases the point is that Jesus' home is not this world but another. "You are of this world, I am not of this world" (8,23; cf. 3,31). "Jesus knew that his hour had come to depart from this world and go to another" (13,1). Here the world is a sphere of being distinct from the sphere of the divine, and it would seem that this distinction is synonymous with several others in the fourth Gospel: for instance, earth and heaven, below and above. Jesus' home is in that other place, and he comes into the worldly sphere only temporarily. He has brought heavenly things to the world (3,12). His Father has sent him into the world (3,17). He ascends back from here to where he was (3,13-14). The distinction is between the world as the human-natural region over against the uncreated, divine realm. The first is dependent needing to be saved (cf. 3,17) while the second is his proper dwelling place where he belongs to.

This use of the world as a sphere distinct from the heavenly realm along with the use of other polarities like above and below, or heaven and earth suggests an important point. It would seem that the fourth evangelist embraced a cosmic dualism of two worlds. Nowhere else is the cosmic dualism so evident as in the fourth Gospel.[415]

c) Horizontal Opposition

Contrasted with this there is a *horizontal opposition*, which is played out on earth. This is genuinely dualistic, but this dualism is moral or ethical, not cosmological or metaphysical, what Bultmann calls it a 'dualism of decision' (*Entscheidungsdualismus*).[416] The prologue

---

[412] Thus, Jesus can say of his disciples that "they do not belong to the world, just as I do not belong to the world" (17,16) and inform Pilate that his kingdom is 'not of this world' (18,36). In these two instances the ἐκ of 'ἐκ τοῦ κόσμου' indicates the nature of what Jesus confronts.

[413] J. A. T. Robinson (*The Priority of John* [London 1985] 370) affirms that the expression "'to come into the world' is the equivalent of being 'born' or 'born into the world' (16,21) which is applied to Jesus (where?) and to any woman's child." This, I feel, is surely either obtuse or perverse.

[414] Only in two instances (17,5.24) does 'κόσμος' bear the meaning 'cosmos.'

[415] Much of the NT literature implies a kind of three-story universe: God and the angels in the highest level, Satan and the demons in the lowest, with human beings and nature stuck between the two. See Y. Ibuki, "Über den johanneischen Kosmosbegriff," *BSU* 18 (1981) 27-55.

[416] Bultmann, *Theology*, II, 21. Schottroff (231, n. 3), who otherwise offers an uncompromisingly Gnostic interpretation of the fourth Gospel, endorses Bultmann's view here. Many scholars rightly emphasise the incompatibility of Judaism with true Gnosticism: "We have always to keep in mind that Gnosticism was a religious phenomenon diametrically opposed to everything Jewish: in fact, the God of the Jews was

appears to identify the world with darkness (1,5.10). The same is reflected in 3,19 where the world (mankind or 'people) loved darkness rather than light.' And those who did receive the Logos (1,12) may be conceived as not belonging to the world. Later, in the farewell discourse, the unreceptivity of the world toward the Spirit of truth (14,17) follows and matches its response to the Logos (1,10). However, the fourth evangelist does not have a gloomy view of the physical world itself. When he uses κόσμος in a negative, dualistic sense, it does not refer to the physical world in which one lives. Although the κόσμος may be distorted into the realm of unbelief, this created earth is the object of God's love (3,16) and the realm in which the light enlightens persons (1,9). So, what does the fourth evangelist mean when he uses this term in a negative way? The world, in these cases, seems to be a symbol representing the realm of unbelief (3,19), the area in which there is total rejection of the truth (cf. 3,21) of God revealed in Jesus. It is used in conjunction with judgement (3,19). It symbolises that way of living which is opposed to God and the divine plan of salvation for mankind. Creation necessitates human dependence upon God. The world symbolises the pretence that human existence can be independent of God. When the world is tied to the negative pole of the Gospel's dualism, it refers to a misunderstanding of who one is and is shrouded in darkness (cf. 3,19).

d) Temporal Opposition

One might expect a third opposition also – the *temporal opposition* between the present world and the world to come. But, in fact, the fourth evangelist nowhere employs the term οὗτος ὁ αἰών, the most usual rendering of the Hebrew הָעוֹלָם הַזֶּה quite common elsewhere in the New Testament, especially in Paul.[417] Its absence in the fourth Gospel is due to a resistance on the evangelist's part to the temporal implications of the term. Whatever the reason, there is no hint of any temporal connotation in the way he uses it. One cannot add the contrast between the two ages to the two spatial oppositions I have pointed out already.

However, I am still faced with some difficulties. Let me grant that there is some truth to the suggestion that the temporal (historical or horizontal) dualism has been transposed into a cosmic (vertical) one in the fourth Gospel.[418] What then is the relationship of this cosmic dualism to the dualism of human self-understanding? One has

---

considered by the Gnostics as an evil deity" (I. Grünwald, *Apocalyptic and Merkavah Mysticism* [Leiden 1980] 111). What distinguishes a Gnostic dualism from all other types is that it is essentially anti-cosmic: that is, its conception includes an unequivocally negative evaluation of the visible world, together with its creator: it ranks as a kingdom of evil and darkness (K. Rudolph, *Gnosis* [Edinburgh 1983] 60). See also S. Pétrement, *Le Dieu séparé: Les Origines du Gnosticisme* (Paris 1984); E. Ruckstuhl, "Das Johannesevangelium und die Gnosis," in: his *Jesus im Horizont der Evangelien* (SBAB 3) (Stuttgart 1988) 311-26; and P. Perkins, *Gnosticism and the New Testament* (Minneapolis 1993).

[417] See Mt. 12,32, where it is explicitly distinguished from 'ὁ αἰών ὁ μέλλων,' the age to come; Mk. 10,30; Lk. 16,8 and 20,34; Rom. 12,2; 1 Cor. 1,20; 2,6.8 and 3,18; 2 Cor. 4,4; and Eph. 1,21. The Pastoral letters prefer 'ὁ νῦν αἰών' (the present age): 1 Tim. 6,14; 2 Tim. 4,10 and Tit. 2,12. For the fourth evangelist's preferred expression 'ὁ κόσμος οὗτος,' see 8,23; 9,39; 11,9; 12,25.31; 13,1; 16,11 and 18,36; and 1 Jn. 4,17.

[418] However, remnants of the temporal division can be found in the fourth Gospel. Part of the reason for saying this is the impression that many references to the historical eschatology are absent in the fourth Gospel. That is, allusions to the end of the present age and the commencement of the age to come are evidently missing in the fourth Gospel. According to Kysar (*Maverick Gospel*, 62-64), the fourth evangelist has 'de-temporalised' the historical dualism of early Christianity and produced a cosmic dualism. On Johannine eschatology, see *ibid.*, 99-106.

the division of persons between those who live authentically as creatures of God (those begotten ἄνωθεν [3,3.7], those begotten of water and Spirit [3,5.8], those who believe [3,15.16.18.36], those who love the light [3,19], those who do what is true [3,21], and those who accept the testimony of the one whom God sends [3,33]), and those who live inauthentically as if they were independent of God (born of the flesh [3,6], those who do not believe [3,18], those who love darkness and hate the light, and do not come to the light [3,19.20], those who do evil [3,19.20], and those who disobey [3,36]).[419]

e) Cosmic or Human Dualism

Is this dualism different from the *cosmic dualism* of the world above and the world below?[420] In my opinion, the cosmic dualism of the fourth Gospel represents another way of stating the *human dualism*. That is, the two different worlds – the world of the human and the world of the divine – are a picture language to say that people must choose to understand themselves either as independent of God or as dependent creatures. In this case, the fourth evangelist would not mean that there are literally two different realms within the cosmos. Rather, those two realms are a symbolic way of expressing his conviction that people must choose either to live under the rule of God (come to the light, do what is true or believe in the Son of God) or try to escape that rule (live in darkness, do what is evil or disobey the Son).

However, I must say that it is difficult to pin point the meaning of 'κόσμος,' because the choice between these two interpretations of the cosmic dualism calls for a basic understanding of how the evangelist used symbols, which I demonstrated in the treatment of the symbol of water. One is wedded to a distinction between literal and symbolic description. But this distinction is a modern one. It is one the fourth evangelist did not know. The first-century Christians did not carefully divide historical description from the interpretation of the meaning of historical events. Picture language and descriptive language are found within the same sentence. All this means that the evangelist might not have made the distinctions I am trying to make in the interpretation of the dualistic symbols of the Gospel. I am of the opinion that the human dualism of the fourth Gospel is continuous with its cosmic dualism. The Gospel makes the point primarily that people are faced with two inescapable possibilities, and that cosmic dualism enters into its language for two reasons. First, it reinforces the importance of the human dualism. Second, the Gospel introduces the cosmic dualism to tie the bipolarity of life to Christology. The fourth evangelist, therefore, tells a story in which the historical, temporal realm is wedded to the cosmic, the other, transhistorical and transtemporal realm. The mystery of transcendence is mixed in with the worldly. The hero of the narrative is both an historic person and a being from the transcendent realm (cf. 3,13.17). The human response to him is both an historical event and an event that has transcendent value.

---

[419] On the subject of good and evil see Stemberger.

[420] Note that the gap between heaven and earth is constantly being bridged, sometimes by theophanies, sometimes by angelic or human messengers, prophets, conceived as sent directly from the heavenly court. Jesus himself was the last of these divine emissaries, entering the world with the God-given task of bringing life (3,15.16. 36 and 10,10), light (8,12 and 12,46) and salvation (3,17; 4,42 and 12,47). Clearest of all, and surprisingly unequivocal, is the assertion that "God so loved the world that he gave his only Son..." (3,16).

β. Life and Death

In the dialogue with Nicodemus, the discourse on regeneration runs into a discourse on 'heavenly things' (3,12), the central point of which is the mission of the Son, who is sent by the Father to be crucified, with the purpose (ἵνα) "that whoever believes in him may not perish but may *have eternal life* (ζωὴ αἰώνιος)"[421] (3,15.16). 3,22-36 describe the final culminating witness of the Baptist when he announces Jesus to be the Messianic Bridegroom (3,29). He concludes his testimony with the words: "whoever believes in the Son has *eternal life* (ζωὴ αἰώνιος)" (3,36a).

'Life' (ζωή) is a favourite theological word of the fourth evangelist.[422] It may be noted that, probably, one of the most conspicuous aspects of word usage in the fourth Gospel is that the wirter consistently attaches the same connotation to the word ζωή. The expression 'ζωὴ αἰώνιος' (eternal life) occurs seventeen times in the fourth Gospel and six times in 1 John. Even without the qualifying adjective αἰώνιος,[423] ζωή in the fourth Gospel does not refer to natural life.[424] Rather ψυχή is used for that life to which death is an end (cf. 13,37 and 15,13).[425] For the fourth evangelist, ζωή consistently means 'eternal life' – a life qualitatively more than and different from the life of fallen man, who is prone to sin and transience. As F.V. Filson has pointed out, the fourth Gospel may be called the Gospel of life,[426] for 20,31 enunciates the chief purpose for which the Gospel has been written: "that you may have life in his name."

a) Dependence on Synoptic Tradition

I have left out the Synoptic Gospels on one side so far, because the polar opposites that I have been considering up to now (κόσμος, light and truth) have relatively little place in them. But life (and implicitly death) is different. The richness of this concept in the Johannine writings is due to the complexity of the traditions it reflects. To begin with, it virtually replaces the proclamation of the kingdom as the object of the Gospel promise; and in the single context in which this does occur – the dialogue with Nicodemus the real topic of discussion is begetting ἄνωθεν (3,3.5) which is to be re-interpreted soon in the fourth evangelist's characteristic fashion as ζωὴ αἰώνιος – a term usually translated as 'eternal life' (3,15.16.36). Where does this term come from and why does the evangelist select it to denote the fruits of the Gospel message?

---

[421] Cf. J. L. Fradua, "Das ewige Leben in den johanneischen Schriften," *IkaZ* 20 (1991) 23-32.

[422] See F.-M. Braun, "La vie d'en haut (Jn. III, 1-15)," *RSPhTh* 40 (1956) 3-24.

[423] Only in 50% of the cases it is used in conjunction with the adjective αἰώνιος and then left out the next time in the one and same verse (cf. 3,36) "without any difference of meaning," as correctly observed by Dodd (*Interpretation*, 144); see esp. J. G. van der Watt, "The Use of αἰώνιος in the Concept ζωὴ αἰώνιος in John's Gospel," *NT* 31 (1989) 217-28.

[424] W. Barclay (*New Testament Words* [Philadelphia 1974] 37) states that "eternal life is nothing less than the life of God himself."

[425] See R. E. Brown, *op. cit.*, 506; see also U. E. Simon, "Eternal Life in the Fourth Gospel," in: F. L. Cross (ed.), *Studies in the Fourth Gospel* (London 1957) 97-109.

[426] F. V. Filson, "The Gospel of Life," in: W. Klassen and G. F. Snyder (eds.), *Current Issues in New Testament Interpretation* (New York 1962) 111-23.

Its immediate source is the Synoptic tradition.[427] Jesus speaks of entering into life and entering into the kingdom of God[428] in a passage where the two expressions are clearly equivalent: "It is better for you to *enter life* maimed than to have two hands and to go to hell... It is better for you to *enter the kingdom of God* with one eye than to have two eyes and to be thrown into hell" (Mk. 9,43.47). Just how close the two concepts are may be seen from Matthew's adaptation of this passage, for he actually replaces Mark's 'kingdom of God' with 'life' (cf. Mt. 18,19). There is also the story of the man anxious to know what to do in order to '*inherit eternal life*' (Mk. 10,17). To his disappointment he is told to get rid of his wealth; whereupon "he was shocked and went away grieving, for he had many possessions" (Mk. 10,22). At this Jesus drove the lesson home to his disciples: "How hard it will be for those who have wealth to *enter the kingdom of God*" (Mk. 10,22f.; cf. Mt. 19,24; and Lk. 18,24).

The passage that points most strongly to the fourth evangelist's dependence upon the Synoptic tradition is this: "those who love their life (τὴν ψυχὴν αὐτοῦ) lose it, and those who hate their life *in this world* (ἐν τῷ κόσμῳ τούτῳ) will keep it for eternal life (εἰς ζωὴν αἰώνιον)" (Jn. 12,25). This is an adaptation of a saying found, with slight variations, in all three Synoptic Gospels: Mt. 10,39 and 16,25; Mk. 8,35; and Lk. 9,24 and 17,33.

b) Dependence on Jewish Eschatology

But the fourth evangelist has made a significant advance by introducing his own special term, ζωὴ αἰώνιος, into the saying. As Dodd remarks, he alone "has given it a form which obviously alludes to the Jewish *antithesis* of the two ages: he who hates his soul בָּעוֹלָם הַזֶּה (in this world/age) will keep it לָעוֹלָם הַבָּא (for the world/age to come) and consequently will possess חַיֵּי הָעוֹלָם הַבָּא (the life of the age to come).[429] If Dodd is right then the fourth evangelist has made two changes, first in distinguishing between ψυχή and ζωή and secondly in selecting the term κόσμος, in which the spatial or local sense predominates (cf. 12,25), rather than αἰών (age), which preserves the temporal meaning of the classical Hebrew עולם.[430] Nevertheless the fourth evangelist continues to attach an eschatological

[427] See M. de Jonge, "The Radical Eschatology of the Fourth Gospel and the Eschatology of the Synoptics. Some Suggestions," in: Denaux, *John and the Synoptics*, 481-87; and the recent study of H. Giesen, *Herrschaft Gottes - heute oder morgen? Zur Heilsbotschaft Jesu und der synoptischen Evangelien* (BU 26) (Regensburg 1995).

[428] Most commentators of the fourth Gospel rightly remark that the fourth evangelist's use of 'the kingdom of God' (3,3.5) reflects contact with earlier Gospel traditions. For a detailed analysis, see Boismard and Lamouille, 118-19; and Lindars, "John and the Synoptic Gospels," 287-94. Having made the remark, they simply affirm that for this evangelist, the kingdom of God is to be identified with eternal life (see e.g. Lagrange, 74; Bernard, I, 101-2; Bultmann, *Gospel*, 152, n. 2; R. H. Lightfoot, *St. John's Gospel. A Commentary* (Oxford 1960) 130-31; and Vellanickal, 208-13), or "the heavenly realm on high to which the divine envoy leads" (Schnackenburg, *op. cit.*, 366-67); see esp. Caragounis, "Kingdom of God," 473-80.

[429] Dodd, *Interpretation*, 146.

[430] Schnackenburg (*op. cit.*, II, 521, n. 5) says of Dodd's suggestion – that in the fourth Gospel 'ζωὴ αἰώνιος' is connected with the Jewish idea of the life of the age to come – that "it can hardly be right," but he offers no argument. In fact, as long ago as 1898 the Aramaic 'לְעָלַם' has been considered to be an abbreviation of 'לְעָלְמָא דְאָתֵי;' see G. Dalman, *Die Worte Jesu mit Berücksichtigung des nachkanonischen jüdischen Schriftums und der aramäischen Sprache* (Leipzig 1898) 121f. The first occurrence of the Hebrew equivalent of ζωὴ αἰώνιος is in Dan. 12,2: "Many of those who sleep in the dust of the earth shall awake, some to everlasting life (לְחַיֵּי עוֹלָם), and some to reproach, to everlasting abhorrence (לְדִרְאוֹן עוֹלָם)." The word 'עולם' is a noun. There are relatively few adjectives in classical Hebrew, and nouns are often employed to qualify a

dimension to 'life,' as is proved by the way in which he opposes it to the traditionally eschatological 'God': "Whoever believes in the Son has ζωὴ αἰώνιος; whoever disobeys the Son will not see life, but must endure God's wrath" (3,36).

The fourth evangelist sees ζωὴ αἰώνιος, then, as a present possession.[431] In the Psalms of Solomon (a work in which, incidentally, the eschatological force of the expression 'kingdom of God' is especially evident) the meaning is different: "But they that fear the Lord shall rise to eternal life (εἰς ζωὴν αἰώνιον) and their life (ζωή) shall be in the light of the Lord and shall never again fail" (Pss. Sol. 3,12). The 'sons of truth' at Qumran are promised both 'abundant peace with long life' and 'eternal joy with life for ever' (בחיינצח), plus 'a crown of glory and a robe of majesty in eternal light' (באור עולמים) (1 QS 4,6-8).[432] The elect in 1 Enoch are to have 'light, joy and peace, and inherit the earth;' once wisdom is given to them 'they will all live' (1 Enoch 5,7-8; cf. Mt. 5,5). In the parables section, too, one is told that "the righteous will be in the light of the sun, and the chosen in the light of eternal life; and there will be no end to the days of their life" (1 Enoch 58,3).

In these passages eternity undoubtedly includes the notion of endlessness, but also (particularly at Qumran) a special quality of life peculiar to the new age. It is this special quality – not endlessness – that is suggested by the fourth evangelist's term ζωὴ αἰώνιος, which might, therefore, be translated 'the life of the new age.' In none of the passages quoted, including those from the Synoptic Gospels, is there any difficulty in thinking of a life that, in the words of Pss. Sol. 3,12 "will never fail" (οὐκ ἐκλείψει ἔτι). But once transferred to this world (and the present age) life has become a symbol, and if one insists on retaining the rendering 'eternal,' which is what αἰώνιος always means in secular Greek, then 'eternal life' can only be a metaphor.[433] The new life enjoyed by the faithful is more than ordinary physical existence:[434] it is the *life of faith*. Christians are no more immune from physical death than other folk.[435] But the benefits that accrue to them from their

---

preceding noun (e.g. 'Holy Spirit,' literally translated from Hebrew, is 'the spirit of holiness' [πνεῦμα ἁγιωσύνης] [cf. Rom. 1,4]). 'עוֹלָם' signifies either the remote past or the distant future; but it can also mean 'perpetuity.' In the latter case it is often hard to know whether this is thought of as never-ending, i.e. eternal, or simply as of indefinite duration. One must let oneself be guided by the context. The Daniel passage appears to imply both *another age* and *for ever*.

[431] A. T. Robertson (*A Grammar of the Greek New Testament in the Light of Historical Research* [Nashville 1934] 879) interprets 'ἔχει ζωὴν αἰώνιον' in Jn. 3,36 as a "descriptive Present." C. Vaughan and V. E. Gideon (*A Greek Grammar of the New Testament* [Nashville 1979] 136) define 'descriptive Present' as "the most common use of the present form for an act in progress. It vividly presents the act as now going on." Roberson understands 'ἔχει ζωὴν αἰώνιον' in 3,36 as: "has it here and now and for eternity." See also R. Kysar, "The Eschatology of the Fourth Gospel – A Correction of Bultmann's Redactional Hypothesis," *Perspective* 13 (1972) 24.

[432] The traditional biblical promise of *long* life is combined remarkably easily with the seemingly very different promise of *eternal* life. The transition is assisted by the ambiguity of 'עוֹלָם' as the notion of indefinite duration slips into that of perpetuity. Did God really, as the English translations of Ps. 21,4 imply, promise the king 'length of days for ever and ever'? For a comparison of 'life' in Johannine writings and the Qumran Scrolls see J. C. Coetzee, "Life (Eternal Life) in John's Writings and the Qumran Scrolls," *Neotest.* 6 (1972) 48-66.

[433] See U. Fischer, *Eschatologie und Jenseitserwartung im hellenistischen Diasporajudentum* (BZNW 44) (Berlin, New York 1978).

[434] It just might occur to an attentive reader of the words 'οὐ μὴ ἀποθάνῃ εἰς τὸν αἰῶνα' (Jn. 11,26) that αἰών, like αἰώνιος, is used metaphorically. But the English ("shall never die") is harder than the Greek.

[435] See D. E. Aune, *The Cultic Setting of the Realized Eschatology in Early Christianity* (NT.S 28) (Trondheim 1972).

acceptance of the message of Jesus are, for the fourth evangelist, best symbolised by ζωή and all that is associated with it; the term αἰώνιος indicates its radical difference from natural life. Once this is understood, it matters little whether the word is taken metaphorically and translated as 'eternal' or given an alternative rendering so as to suggest a different kind of life – 'the life of the new age.'[436] Used as a complementary adjective attached to ζωή, the term αἰώνιος does not describe life, nor does it indicate that this new life differs from ordinary human life. Another term that serves equally well to convey the same idea and found frequently in the Odes of Solomon is 'immortal' or 'deathless' life: "immortal life rose up in the land of the Lord, and it became known to his faithful ones, and was given unsparingly to those who trust in him" (Odes Sol. 15,10; cf. 28,6; 31,7; 38,3 and 40,5). A life that is not subject to death differs from natural life in essence, not just in duration. Conceptually the Odes of Solomon and the fourth Gospel are nowhere closer than in the way they envisage the believer's participation in the life of faith: "All his children will praise the Lord, and they will receive the truth of his faith... We live in the Lord by his grace, and we receive life through his Messiah" (Odes Sol. 41,1.3).

Lying behind the eternal life of the fourth Gospel, therefore, and the immortal life of the Odes of Solomon is not just a profound faith in God as the author of life, but the very different belief that God would ultimately 'swallow up death for ever' (cf. Is. 25,8), a belief that would later find orthodox expression in the prayer of the eighteen benedictions: 'May you be praised, Lord, you who give life to the dead.'[437]

All the eschatological and dualistic implications that could be drawn from such a faith are prominent in a passage from the Testament of Asher (5,2): "death succeeds to life, dishonour to glory, night to day, and darkness to light; but the universe is subject to the day, and darkness to light; and so death is confronted by eternal life (τὸν θάνατον ἡ αἰώνιος ζωὴ ἀναμένει)."[438]

By now it should be clear that the fourth evangelist has two sources for his notion of ζωὴ αἰώνιος: first Jewish eschatology, from which he derives his concept of a life that transcends human life as one knows it; and second the Synoptic tradition, which allows him to replace the preaching of the kingdom by a term more suggestive of the benefits that follow upon the acceptance of the Gospel. In the symbolic structure of the fourth Gospel,[439] for the most part strikingly interlocking and consistent, the concept of life

---

[436] It has been suggested that there is something of the same idea at Qumran, especially in the hymnic conclusion of the Community Rule (1QS 10,9-11,22) and in parts of the Thanksgiving Scroll: 1QH 3,19.36; 11,13-35 and 15. The first to argue this was H.-W. Kuhn (*Enderwartung und gegenwärtiges Heil: Untersuchungen zu den Gemeinden von Qumran, mit einen Anhang über Eschatologie und Gegenwart in der Verkündigung Jesu* [Göttingen 1966]). He has been followed by G. W. E. Nickelsburg (*Resurrection, Immortality and Eternal Life in Intertestamental Judaism* [Cambridge 1972] 152-56); J. J. Collins ("Apocalyptic Eschatology as the Transcendence of Death," *CBQ* 36 [1974] 21-43); and Aune (*op. cit.*, 29-44). All seem to be guilty of misapplying theological categories that simply have no place in the Qumran community. Earlier and better than all these is J. Licht ("The Doctrine of the Thanksgiving Scroll," *IEJ* 6 [1956] 1-15 and 89-101).

[437] Eventually this prayer came to be recited three times a day: *Mishnah Berakoth* 3,3 and 4,1.

[438] See Ashton, *Understanding*, 218.

[439] In an otherwise exhaustive discussion of Johannine symbolism, Culpepper (*Anatomy*, 180-98) fails to include life. It is a notable omission, for life is the symbol around which all the others cluster.

occupies a central place.[440] In fact, all Jesus' great healing miracles carry with them something of the same idea.[441]

It should also be added that life is conceptually very close to salvation, and the proximity both assists and enriches its symbolic significance in the Gospel tradition.[442] Certainly the fourth evangelist evinces little interest in the futuristic eschatology[443] implicit in the doctrine of the resurrection of the dead; nevertheless this is, most probably, the origin of his own concept of the life of the new age. The occasion of the fusion of these two ideas is doubtless the resurrection of Jesus.

Just as salvation is both a present reality and future hope, and the kingdom is both a present reality and a future hope, so also 'eternal life' is both a present reality and a future hope. 'Salvation,' 'redemption,' 'eternal life,' 'the kingdom,' and 'glorification' are all a progressive process and are different names for one phenomenon with present and future dimensions.[444] The terminus *a quo* for glorification is the death and resurrection of Jesus, which becomes effective for the individual when he is begotten ἄνωθεν of water and Spirit.[445]

γ. Salvation and Judgement

a) Ambiguity in Translation

If life is what is promised to those who accept the revelation of Jesus, judgement is what will be the lot of those who do not. In this respect the theme of judgement (κρίσις)[446] is

---

[440] Applied to the water that represents revelation (4,10f. and 7,38), the word 'ζῶν' (living), has a riddling quality, but like 'bread of life' (6,35.48) or 'living bread' (6,51), which have an identical reference, 'living water' is a particularly appropriate term for what the evangelist sees to be the true source of life – 'a spring of water welling up to eternal life' (4,14). In the prophetic 'I am' sayings Jesus is offering life to all prepared to listen to his message (cf. Schweizer, *Ego eimi*). Bread and water, the staple necessities of life, are natural symbols of supernatural life. Wine, in the context of the fruitfulness hoped and prayed for at a wedding-feast (2,1-11), fits easily into the same broad symbolic field, as does the suggestion of begetting ἄνωθεν through water and the Spirit (3,5).

[441] In the first of them Jesus promises the royal official at Capernaum, "Your son will live" (4,50), whilst the second, the healing of the cripple at the pool (Jn. 5), is seen as a fitting occasion for a discourse in which Jesus claims to have been given the power to bestow life. The cure of the blind man symbolises his allegiance to the life that is light; and the most important sign of all, the raising of Lazarus, is the occasion of Jesus' extraordinary claim that he is in person "the resurrection and the life" (11,25).

[442] In the fourth Gospel, told by Jesus that Lazarus is asleep, the disciples reply, "Lord, if he has fallen asleep, he will be all right (εἰ κεκοίμηται σωθήσεται)" (11,12): Lazarus will be cured; he will recover; he will *live*. Here, in the Lazarus episode, last as it is, lies the clearest indication of the likely origins of the fourth evangelist's conception of life. Rising from the dead, Lazarus symbolises – though he does not exemplify – the new life that Jesus has come to bring. The link between this life and resurrection had been noticed already in the great discourse of Jn. 5: "Just as the Father raises the dead and gives them life, so also the Son gives life to whomever he wishes" (5,21).

[443] Cf. W. G. Kümmel, "Ein Jahrhundert Erforschung der Eschatologie," *ThLZ* 107 (1982) 93.

[444] Cf. J. C. Davis, "The Johannine Concept of Eternal Life as a Present Possession," *RestQ* 27 (1984) 167; and J. D. Thompson, *An Analysis of Present and Future in the Eschatology of the Fourth Gospel, and an Examination of the Theological Relationship between the Two* (Ann Arbor 1967).

[445] See I. Broer, "Auferstehung und ewiges Leben im Johannesevangelium," in: I. Broer and J. Werbick (eds.), *"Auf Hoffnung hin sind wir erlöst" (Röm 8,24)* (SBS 128) (Stuttgart 1987) 67-94.

[446] The fourth evangelist uses the verb 'κρίνειν' 19 times, as against 6 times each in Matthew and Luke and none at all in Mark. The only NT book to use the verb more often than the fourth Gospel is Acts, where it is found 21 times. The fourth evangelist also uses the word 'κρίσις' 11 times and 'κρίμα' once. Such statistics show that the idea of judgement interested him more than it did most writers. See Morris, *Gospel*, 205.

simply the obverse of that life. Judgement is also, however, the process of separating the sheep from the goats, the actual sorting out whereby believers and unbelievers are placed on opposite sides of the divide (cf. Mt. 25,32-33). The Greek verb κρίνειν means both 'judge,' with additional connotations of separation, discrimination and condemnation.[447] No English translation can do full justice to this ambiguity, as can be easily perceived by comparing the following two quotations. The first is the most complete statement of the theme found in the fourth Gospel:

> For God so loved the world that he gave his only Son, so that everyone who believes in him may not perish but may have eternal life. Indeed, God did not send the Son into the world to *condemn* (κρίνειν) the world, but in order that the world might be saved through him. Those who believe in him are not *condemned* (κρίνειν); but those who do not believe are *condemned* (κρίνειν) already, because they have not believed in the name of the only Son of God. And this is the *judgement* (κρίσις), that the light has come into the world, and people loved darkness rather than light because their deeds were evil (3,16-19).

In the second, English is forced to use 'judge' instead of 'condemn,' but the Greek word is the same:

> The Father *judges* (κρίνειν) no one but has given all *judgement* (κρίσις) to the Son, so that all may honour the Son just as they honour the Father. Anyone who does not honour the Son does not honour the Father who sent him. Very truly, I tell you, anyone who hears my word and believes him who sent me has eternal life, and does not come under *judgement* (κρίσις), but has passed from death to life (5,22-24).

Just as eternal life is anticipated in the present existence of the believer, so eternal punishment is anticipated in the present of the unbeliever. The fourth evangelist nowhere uses this phrase: unlike the Synoptists, especially Matthew (18,8 and 25,41.46), he reserves the term for the bright side of the divide. Nevertheless, the absolute gulf between the two groups is nowhere more emphatically or eloquently conveyed than in passages dominated by the judgement motif:

> I have come as light into the world, so that everyone who believes in me should not remain in the darkness. I do not *judge* (κρίνειν) anyone who hears my words and does not keep them, for I came not to *judge* (κρίνειν) the world, but to save the world. The one who rejects me and does not receive my word has a *judge* (κρίνειν); on the last day the word that I have spoken will serve as *judge* (κρίνειν) (12,46-48).

For the fourth evangelist, then, darkness is revealed to be darkness by the coming of the light; men discover to belong to the darkness only when they refuse the light or insist, in spite of their blindness, that they are actually sighted: "If you were blind, you would not have sin. But now that you say, 'We see,' your sin remains" (9,41; cf. 15,22). So, from one perspective, the shining of the light is a judgement, in so far as it discloses the true nature of darkness; from the other, it is left to the men of darkness to condemn themselves.

---

[447] F. Büchsel and V. Hentrich, "κρίνω," *TDNT*, III, 938-39.

b) Ethical Dualism

The theme of judgement is the most important single vehicle of the fourth evangelist's *ethical dualism* and the one where all the others culminate and coincide. Despite its subtlety and depth, it is not hard to grasp, except for one point: the extent to which the evangelist retained a properly eschatological belief in the idea of a final judgement on the last day.[448] The fourth evangelist uses the thought of κρίσις to bring out God's loving purpose, and he employs the device of following a negative statement with the corresponding positive: "God did not send the Son into the world to condemn (κρίνειν) the world" (3,17). Elsewhere, however, he says that Jesus did come into the world 'for judgement (κρίμα)' (9,39).[449] The resolution of the paradox demands that one understands salvation as necessarily implying judgement (κρίσις).[450] These are the two sides to the one coin. Jesus came to bring salvation, but the very fact of salvation for *all who believe* implies condemnation (κρίσις) of *all who do not*.[451] Clearly the fourth evangelist sees the whole traditional doctrine of judgement as radically modified in the light of the incarnation. The life and especially the death of Jesus have their effects on the judgement.

The fourth evangelist views judgement not only as one pertaining to the future, but also as a present reality (cf. 3,18). He is convinced that the crucial decision for or against Jesus is made in this world. What people are doing now results in a present preliminary judgement and determines what will happen when they stand before Christ on judgement day.[452] In 3,17 the word 'condemn' is contrasted with 'be saved.' Some people will, in fact, be condemned, and that as the result of Jesus's coming into the world (cf. 3,19). But the purpose of his coming was not this. It was, on the contrary, "in order that the world might be saved through him" (3,17). So the evangelist brings out his positive corresponding to

---

[448] The secondary literature on this vexed question is vast, but does not require to be assessed here since there is virtual unanimity that the fourth evangelist's *primary* understanding of judgement is that it attends acceptance or rejection of the message of Jesus.

[449] See J. Hainz, "'Zur Krisis kam ich in die Welt' (Joh 9,39). Zur Eschatologie im Johannesevangelium," in: H.-J. Klauck (ed.), *Weltgericht und Weltvollendung. Zukunftsbilder im Neuen Testament* (QD 150) (Basel, Freiburg, Wien 1994) 149-63.

[450] The idea in itself is not foreign: throughout prophecy the coming of the kingdom of God is accompanied by the judgement of God over his enemies (cf. also Mt. 3,7f. and parallels), and judgement is part of the fullness of the divine powers of the Son of Man (cf. 5,22.27 and Mt. 25,31ff.). But in the Nicodemus episode everything is viewed from the perspective of the mission of the Son and the descent of the Son of Man from heaven; and these mission and descent have no other purpose, as the evangelist keeps saying (cf. 12,47 and 8,15), than to open a way, in him, for faith and for the world's salvation.

[451] Judgement was a recognised theme in contemporary Jewish thought, but it is the judgement of God, and it is thought of as taking place at the last day. The fourth evangelist modifies both these thoughts. He does, it is true, speak of judging sometimes in much the normal Jewish way (8,50). But it is quite another matter when he says that God has committed all judgement to Christ (5,22.27). He goes on to speak of Christ as judging (5,30 and 8,16.26) or not judging (8,15 and 12,47), and of his word as judging people (12,48). His judgement is just (5,30) and true (8,16). How people will fare in the judgement depends on their relationship to him (5,24 and 3,19).

[452] Because of his presupposition that the Gospel writer was committed to a realised eschatology, Bultmann (*Gospel*, 261) relegates such a futuristic perspective to a later redactor of the Gospel. Realised eschatology is a view that emphasises the present existential nature of both blessing and judgement. It makes the present life the focus of theological thought and rejects future thoughts of heaven and hell as irrelevant mythological constructs of more primitive times. The problem is that it sacrifices the future for the present. Because of criticisms levelled at this view, Dodd (*Interpretation*, 208-11) developed a modified view called 'inaugurated eschatology.' This view continues to emphasise the present but allows an openendedness to the future. The basic problem with this view is its acknowledged vagueness in matters concerning the future.

the negative at the beginning of the verse. Salvation was central to the mission of Jesus, a truth that is brought out also in the Synoptics (Mt. 27,42; Mk. 8,35; and Lk. 19,10).

c) Belief in Jesus Is Central

The evangelist proceeds to bring out the importance of belief. He has said that Jesus died for people, but that does not automatically bring salvation. No one is saved without believing. He asserts this with another example of a favourite construction, the same truth being put both positively and negatively: "those who believe in him are not condemned;" they need not fear judgement. "But those who do not believe are condemned already;" they do not have to wait until the judgement day. Unbelief has shut them up to condemnation. The evangelist goes on to remove all doubts as to why this should be: "because they have *not believed* in the name[453] of the only Son of God" (3,18). The verb 'believe' is repeated thrice in the same verse emphasising its importance.[454] He proceeds further to bring out the enormity of a refusal to believe with his description of Jesus as 'the only Son of God' (3,18), and that "the Father loves the Son and has placed all things in his hands" (3,35). He is, thus, affirming emphatically that Jesus has community of nature with the Father. When people do not believe in such a person they condemn themselves. The coming of Jesus divides people into the saved and the condemned. 3,18 is, therefore, of the utmost importance to understand the paradox that Jesus both came to judge and did not come to judge. His coming gives people the opportunity of salvation and challenges them to a decision. To refuse his gift is to call down judgement on oneself.

The word 'judgement' in 3,19 is misleading; it denotes the process of judging, not the sentence of condemnation.[455] Faced with the light that has come into the world people may prefer the darkness.[456] The evangelist is not saying that God has decreed that people who do such and such things are condemned. It is not God's sentence with which he is concerned here. Rather, he is telling the reader how the process works. People choose the darkness and their condemnation lies in that very fact. They shut themselves up to darkness; they choose to live in darkness; they cut themselves off from the light. Why? "because their deeds were evil" (3,19). Immersed in wrongdoing, they have no wish to be disturbed. They refuse to be shaken out of their comfortable sinfulness. So they reject the

---

[453] Name stands for the whole personality and expresses the whole person. Hence, to believe in the name means to trust the person, to believe in him as he is. It is to believe that God is the God revealed in the Son and to put one's trust in that God. It is more than simple belief. It is not believing that what he says is true, but trusting him as a person. The Greek expression used here is found in the papyri and seems to be linked with the idea of possession ; see J. H. Moulton and G. Milligan (*The Vocabulary of the Greek Testament* [London 1914-1929] 5) on the subject 'ὄνομα.' If the fourth Gospel retains anything of this usage, the expression 'πεπίστευκεν εἰς τὸ ὄνομα' will convey the additional thought that when one believes he/she yields himself/herself up to be possessed by him in whom he/she believes. See also Morris, *Gospel*, 88.

[454] A striking feature of the Nicodemus episode is the degree to which everything is concentrated on the importance of believing. Whereas in 3,3-8 the begetting ἄνωθεν is posed above all else as the indispensable condition for entry into the kingdom of God, in 3,12 and esp. 3,15ff. the crucial importance of believing comes increasingly to the fore. It is clear that the one cannot do without the other: the begetting ἄνωθεν, however much it is a miracle of the Spirit, is not effected without the call to faith and the response of faith. Faith is always the way in which and the means by which the new life comes into being. It is for this reason that all the emphasis falls on believing.

[455] κρίσις, not κρίμα. LSJ (997) gives the meaning of the word as 'separating, distinguishing;' the word can mean 'judgement,' but it is surely the process of judging that is in mind here.

[456] This is one of the fourth evangelist's use of σκότος. He prefers σκοτία (cf. 1,5).

159

light that comes to them and set their love (note the aorist tense ἠγάπησαν) on darkness. Thereby they condemn themselves.

Jn. 3 ends with an emphatic restatement of the fourth evangelist's thesis of 3,18. Believing in the Son issues in ζωὴ αἰώνιος, which contains a present element, but as indicated earlier, does not exclude a future dimension. This sense of the present reality of salvation provides the reader with a wonderful sense of assurance (cf. 1 Jn. 5,9-12). But for the one who disobeys or refuses to believe (ἀπειθῶν) the Son, the result is that such a person will not see (ὄψεται) life or experience God's gift of salvation. Instead, the anger or wrath (ὀργὴ) of God continues or remains (μένει) upon that person. In interpreting 3,36 there is a crucial perspective that must be enunciated. For the fourth evangelist people cannot straddle the fence with God. Indeed, without a positive decision of believing the Son, people do not stand a chance of comprehending or experiencing ζωὴ αἰώνιος. They are and continue to be under the anger or condemnation of God (cf. 3,36).[457]

d) Eschatology

At this point it is necessary to insert a parenthesis on the meaning of this elusive term 'eschatology,' often used as a substitute for thought.[458] In a lucid and penetrating discussion on the modes of prophecy J. Barton allows two meanings of *eschatology*: one in which it refers to the belief that the world, as it is known, will soon come to an end, the other refers to belief in "an end or goal which will one day arrive and the path toward which passes through various distinct phases or epochs."[459] He is concerned to stress "a really crucial difference in mentality between what we may call *imminent* and *non-imminent* eschatology."[460] The text chosen for my study is eschatological in the first sense, but the word properly refers to the *future*, 'the last days,' whether or not the end is expected very soon – within the lifetime, say, of the writer and his readers. In fact, it is often very difficult to tell from any particular description of the events of the last days just how soon the evangelist expects them to occur.

---

[457] The anger or wrath of God is the way the biblical writers expressed God's intolerance of evil or sin (cf. Rom. 1,18). The kingdom of God will not tolerate within it any form of sin (cf. Rev. 21,7-8.27 and 22,15). Sin must be dealt with or else a sinner has no chance of entering God's domain of heaven. The term ἀπειθέω here is operative for the whole human race. The means God provided to overcome the existing state of condemnation is for people to believe the son. Failure to do so is not become condemned; it is to continue (μένει) in condemnation. For a discussion of the anger or wrath of God, see H. Schonweiss and H. C. Hahn, "Anger, Wrath," *NIDNT*, I, 105-13.

[458] For detailed studies on Johannine eschatology, see J. Frey, *Die johanneische Eschatologie. Band I: Ihre Probleme im Spiegel der Forschung seit Reimarus* (WUNT 96) (Tübingen 1997) esp. 267; 276; 322; 324; 417-18 and 446; and his *Das johanneische Zeitverständnis*; P. W. Meyer, *The Eschatology of the Fourth Gospel: A Study in Early Christian Re-interpretation* (New York 1995); and P. Ricca, *Die Eschatologie des vierten Evangeliums* (Frankfurt, Zürich 1966).

[459] J. Barton, *Oracles of God: Perceptions of Ancient Prophecy in Israel after the Exile* (London 1986) 218.

[460] *Ibid.* 219. See also J. T. Carroll, "Present and Future in Fourth Gospel 'Eschatology'," *BTB* 19 (1989) 63-69; see also J. Blank, "Die Gegenwartseschatologie des Johannesevangeliums," in: K. Schubert (ed.), *Vom Messias zum Christus. Die Fülle der Zeit in religionsgeschichtlicher und theologischer Sicht* (Basel, Freiburg, Wien 1964) 279-310.

The fourth evangelist's idea of judgement is unmistakably rooted in traditional Jewish eschatology,[461] specifically in the idea that the righteous and the wicked are to be definitively separated on the last day. For the most part the fourth evangelist effectively de-eschatologises judgement by making it the immediate consequence of an option for or against Jesus in the lifetime of each individual.[462] Naturally even those writers most committed to the inevitability of a final judgement have their own view about the respective identity of the wicked and the righteous. Although the judgement affects all mankind, it is the circumstances and behaviour of the writer's own contemporaries that provide him with a paradigm of the moral gulf dividing the wicked from the good. This is illustrated with striking clarity in Matthew's parable of the sheep and the goats. The place that people will occupy in the life to come is entirely determined by moral decisions made in the present life. The fourth evangelist differs from Matthew in two important respects: in the first place he pulls the actual act of judgement back into the *present*; in the second place he reduces Matthew's rich variety of moral options (feeding the hungry, clothing the naked, etc.) to one: the act of *faith*. The latter modification is not without precedent: "Those who are ashamed of me and of my words in this adulterous and sinful generation, of them the Son of Man will also be ashamed when he comes in the glory of his Father with the holy angels" (Mk. 8,38).[463]

In spite of these parallels to other New Testament writings, the central position of the judgement motif in the fourth Gospel marks it out as the most dualistic of the four Gospels, and the closest in spirit to numerous sectarian works,[464] composed in roughly the

---

[461] See W. Bittner, "Geschichte und Eschatologie im Johannesevangelium," in: H. Stadelmann (ed.), *Glaube und Geschichte. Heilsgeschehen als Thema der Theologie* (Gießen 1986) 154-80; see also M.-É. Boismard, "L'évolution du thème eschatologique dans les traditions johanniques," *RB* 68 (1961) 507-24; and the detailed discussion on this subject in Klauck, *Weltgericht und Weltvollendung*.

[462] See Blank, *Krisis*; and J. Wanke, "Die Zukunft des Glaubenden. Theologische Erwägungen zur johanneischen Eschatologie," *ThGl* 71 (1981) 127-39.

[463] Indeed the idea is so fundamental to the faith of the early Christians that it comes as no surprise to find it in a wide variety of NT authors: cf. Mt. 10,33; Lk. 12,9 and 19,26; Rom. 10,9-11; 2 Tim. 2,12 and 1 Jn. 2,28.

[464] Shortly after the discovery of the Dead Sea Scrolls, when many of the most important documents were still unpublished, K. G. Kuhn ("Die in Palästina gefundenen hebräischen Texte und das Neue Testament," *ZTK* 47 [1950] 203) wrote excitedly that the background of the fourth Gospel had been recovered at last. Subsequently there has been a wide divergence of scholarly opinions, ranging from enthusiastic acceptance of Kuhn's views (cf. Charlesworth, *John and Qumran*) to contemptuous dismissal (cf. H. M. Teeple, "Qumran and the Origin of the Fourth Gospel," *NT* 4 [1960] 6-25). One scholar who took an early interest in the Scrolls was R. E. Brown ("The Qumran Scrolls and the Johannine Gospel and Epistles," *CBQ* 17 [1955] 571), but from the outset he showed himself much more cautious than Kuhn. While admitting that the argument for interrelatedness between the Johannine writings and the Qumran Library is indeed strong, the resemblances for him do *not* seem to indicate immediate relationship. A very similar point of view was put forward by Schnackenburg (*op. cit.*, I, 134). Writing much later Becker (*Johannes*, 175-79) has an alternative suggestion. He, too, is very much aware of the affinities between the dualism of the Scrolls and the *Testaments of the Twelve Patriarchs* on the one hand and of the fourth Gospel on the other, but he accounts for these rather differently. He believes that the Johannine Community was thinking along dualistic lines before being joined by the evangelist himself, but that it was originally non-dualistic. After a non-dualistic phase the Johannine Community must have come under the influence of a dualism close to that of Qumran. In any case one must presuppose a receptivity for such a dualism on the part of the community. In my opinion, where did these ideas come from if not from the evangelist himself? Charlesworth ("Critical Comparison," 104), in what is, probably, the most thorough examination to date of the parallels between the fourth Gospel and the 'theological' section of the Community Rule, concludes that "John, probably, borrowed some of his dualistic terminology and mythology from 1 QS 3,13-4,26." There is no obvious

same period, that are dominated by a sense of the moral division between the good and the wicked.[465] The Qumran War Scroll, which identifies the enemies of the community as the *Kittim*, that is the Romans, alludes to a battle that is about to be joined.[466] It is concerned with the last days. It follows that judgement is essentially an eschatological concept: *of its very nature it is God's last act, His ultimate verdict upon the human race.*

According to Bultmann, as is well known, the remnants of futuristic belief that persist in the fourth Gospel are the work of 'the ecclesiastical redactor.'[467] But at least one of the passages in question (11,25f.) resists source analysis[468] and there is a simpler explanation available. The fourth evangelist may have been converted from what Barton calls an "imminent" eschatological belief to "a non-imminent" one.[469] In other words, he may have continued to pay lip-service to the idea of a future judgement, but no longer with any sense of urgency.[470] In my opinion, however, what seems to be important for the evangelist is to highlight the sending of Jesus.

viii. Reader and Point of View

In this segment (3,14-18), the reader is asked once again to wrestle with a puzzling and ambiguous expression. Along with ἄνωθεν and πνεῦμα, ὑψόω is another hurdle. The Son of Man will be 'lifted up' in a way comparable to Moses' lifting up of the bronze serpent in the wilderness (3,14). The reader will not find all the answers so early in the narrative, but is now provided with basic truths about the way in which God will be revealed in Jesus (3,14-15). He/she is not totally unprepared for Jesus' words in 3,13-15. The implied reader knows already of the conflict between light and darkness that does not overcome the light (1,5); he/she knows that Jesus will be rejected by 'his own' (1,11), has heard of some future 'hour of Jesus' which has not yet come (2,4), and has had the first hints of a conflict between Jesus and 'the Jews' (2,18-20). But that is all the reader knows. Along with the

---

advantage, it seems to me, in any theory of indirect influence. I believe, that the fourth evangelist retained the pattern of thinking with which he was, probably, familiar from an early age, may be from childhood. In relation to the resemblances and differences in Messianic expectations, see N. A. Dahl, "Eschatology and History in the Light of the Dead Sea Scrolls," in: J. M. Robinson (ed.), *The Future of our Religious Past: Essays in Honour of Rudolf Bultmann* (London 1971) 9-28.

[465] See C. Rowland, *The Open Heaven: A Study of Apocalyptic in Judaism and Early Christianity* (London 1982), 133-36; and B. Chilton (ed.), *Kingdom of God in the Teaching of Jesus* (London 1984). The latter has a good bibliography.

[466] See G. Vermes, *The Dead Sea Scrolls in English* (London 1987) 103f.; and H. Shanks, *The Mystery and Meaning of the Dead Sea Scrolls* (New York 1999).

[467] Bultmann, *Gospel*, 138f. It is odd, not to say astonishing, that in this long section, devoted exclusively to the Johannine understanding of 'eschatological existence,' Bultmann (*Theology*, II, 75-92) totally ignores the concept of life. See also his, "Die Eschatologie des Johannesevangeliums," in: his *Glauben und Verstehen. Gesammelte Aufsätze* (Tübingen, ⁴1961) I, 134-52. For a detailed critique of Bultmann see Frey, *Die johanneische Eschatologie*, I, 86-157; and L. van Hartingsveld, *Die Eschatologie des Johannesevangeliums. Eine Auseinandersetzung mit Rudolf Bultmann* (Assen 1962).

[468] Dodd (*Interpretation*, 144ff.; 320-28 and 364ff.), in his careful study of the relevant passages, suggests that the evangelist is deliberately juxtaposing two contrasting eschatologies: "Whether the gift of life is conceived as a present and continuing possession ('he who is alive and has faith in me will never die') or as a recovery of life after death of the body and the end of the world ('even if he dies he will come to life'), the thing that matters is that life is the gift of God – and Christ's gift to men, we know, is himself (6,51)."

[469] Barton, 218-19.

[470] Cf. J. Gnilka, "Der historische Jesus als der gegenwärtige Christus im Johannesevangelium," *BiLe* 7 (1966) 270; see also his, "Zur Christologie des Johannesevangeliums," in: W. Kasper (ed.), *Christologische Schwerpunkte* (Düsseldorf 1980) 92-107.

other ambiguous terms of the passage, the reader is left to suspend his judgement concerning the sense of ὑψόω until further reading. But the puzzling word occasions another recollection from his/her reading experience: "Destroy this temple, and in three days I will raise it up" (2,19). 'Raise up,' 'ascend,' and 'lift up' – could these enigmatic sayings illumine the earlier one or the earlier one these?

The reader is confident that Jesus speaks of himself with the title Son of Man. He/she understands that 'ascending' and 'lifting up' correspond to one another in their verbal image of spatial movement.[471] The reader knows that he/she is working with spatial imagery for something else, but has no other clue as to the meaning of the ὑψόω.[472] From it the reader might conclude that Jesus anticipates his glorification, and he/she recalls the use of βασιλεία τοῦ θεοῦ by Jesus at this juncture.

3,15 shakes the reader with the seriousness of the matter at hand. The reader's puzzlement is increased by the further affirmation that belief in a God made known through the gift of a Son in a 'lifting up' will bring life (3,15). The immediate context of the 'lifting up' (3,13-15) still remains strange for the reader to grasp some initial understanding of the magnitude of God's loving Gift of the Son. The saving love of God stands behind the mystery of the lifting up of the Son. God has 'given' (3,16) the Son, 'sent' (3,17) him to bring the possibility of eternal life and the salvation of the world.[473] At this stage the reader feels, perhaps, the strenuous demands of these fifteen verses – stretched by obscure references, exhausted by the pace of the discussion, and confused by its movement. But the reader must take seriously the claim that something vital is at stake.

Another feature to be noticed in this segment is that images are stacked. The reader is systematically lead to quest the resolution of the earlier image in the next. Hence, ἄνωθεν birth to enter into the kingdom of God *leads to* a birth out of water and Spirit;[474] this further *leads to* spirit like wind, which again *leads to* the Son of Man being lifted up. The strategy of the author is to pile image upon image, letting each illumine and each conceal the others. Image is superimposed on image. The Spirit appears to be the key to the image of the ἄνωθεν birth. But Spirit is only understandable in the context of the event of the crucifixion-exaltation of the Son of Man. There is no resolution of the images, no explanation of the parable. But there is a direction for the reader's contemplation of these mysteries. Ultimately, the passage suggests that all the previous images must be considered in the light of the crucifixion-glorification and witnessing the communion of heaven and earth in that event. From a theological perspective, the author has placed the cross at the apex of the images of the passage and of the dialogue of entering the kingdom of God.

---

[471] See A. Reinhartz (*The Word in the World: The Cosmological Tale in the Fourth Gospel* [Atlanta 1992] esp. 19; 33 and 43) who understands the language of vertical spatial movement in this and other discourses as evidence of the "cosmological tale" of the Gospel. The reader is, thus, unknowingly immersed in a cosmic narrative.

[472] Moloney (*Belief in the Word*, 117) argues that the reader is expected to grasp the double meaning of 'ὑψόω' in 3,14-15, even though the event may be a puzzle.

[473] According to Lindars (*Gospel*, 147-48), it is this passage that supports more than any other Bultmann's theory of adaptation from pre-Gnostic source. The reader is, therefore, encountering now a language very typical of later Gnostic thought: the Son speaks of what he has seen (3,11); the revelation of earthly and heavenly things (3,12); the descent of the Son (3,13); the 'lifting up' of the Son of Man (3,14); and the Father sends the Son to save the world (3,16-17).

[474] See R. Bergmeier, "Gottesherrschaft, Taufe und Geist," *ZNW* 86 (1995) 53-73.

From a literary perspective, the author has tantalised the reader at this point with the grand climax of the entire narrative, *viz.*, the crucifixion-glorification.

The reader notices that the narrative to this point has been carefully set within a Jewish world, and all the responses to Jesus have come from Jews. At this juncture the universal saving will of God is made manifest to the reader: "God so loved the *world*" (3,16); "God sent the Son into the *world* ... in order that the *world* might be saved through him" (3,17). This recalls the prologue (1,10-13) and prepares the reader for a narrative dedicated to the Samaritans and Gentiles (4,1-54).

c. 3,19-21

Finally, in 3,19-21, the background and significance of the belief and unbelief mentioned in 3,18 are further elucidated. By means of reference to the theme of light and darkness previously introduced in the prologue (1,4-11), the concluding three verses of this pericope expand one's understanding of 'those who do not accept' (1,11) and 'those who are condemned'(cf. 3,18). Here, the idea is expanded by the clear indication that 'what one does reflects what one is.'[475]

i. Synonymous and Compound Parallel Structure

Just as the segment 3,14-18, the segment 3,19-21, too, forms a parallelism of the compound formula $ab//a^1b^1//a^2b^2$:

a [19abc]And this is the judgement, that the *light* has come into the world, and people loved
    darkness rather than *light*
        b [19d] because their *deeds* were evil.
a¹ [20abc]For all who do evil hate the *light* and do not come to the *light*,
        b¹ [20d] so that their *deeds* may not be exposed.
a² [21ab]But those who do what is true come to the *light*,
        b² [21cd] so that it may be clearly seen that their *deeds* have been done in God.

The parallelism of the elements a, a¹ and a² is based on the recurrence of the term 'light'[476] while the elements b, b¹ and b² rest on the term 'deeds.' The parallelism between 3,19 and 3,20, *viz.*, $ab//a^1b^1$ entertains a synonymous rapport because of their negative value, *viz.*, 'loving the darkness,' 'hating the light,' 'not coming to the light,' and 'evil deeds.' The last two elements of the parallelism, *viz.*, a²b² entertains an antithetic relation with the first two elements ($ab//a^1b^1$) of the compound parallelism as will also be demonstrated in the argumentative narrative structure; it deals with people who *come* to the *light* and whose *deeds* have been *done in God*.

In fact, the element '**ab**' introduces a definition of judgement in two parts: 1) *a statement of fact*: "the light has come into the world, and people loved darkness rather than light" (**a** – 3,19bc); 2) *a justification*: "their deeds were evil" (**b** – 3,19d). The elements of

---

[475] For community ethical implications see Rensberger, 59-61.

[476] In my opinion, one cannot forget that, for the fourth evangelist, Jesus himself is the true light and life (cf. 1,4.9; 8,12; 9,5; 11,25; 12,46 and 14,6). Moreover, it is as much as he is Logos (cf. 1,1-4.9), Son and revealer of the Father (cf. 1,14.18) that Jesus is the light of the world. It is his word that gives life and reveals the Father (cf. 5,24.25; 6,63.68; 8,43.47; 10,27-28; 12,46-47 and 14,9-10.24). The light can, therefore, designate both the person of Jesus as well as the revelation he brings for the salvation of the world. Through the revelation he brings as light, he is the way, the truth and the life; without him no one can go to the Father (cf. 14,6).

this definition are then paraphrased in an antithetical parallelism ($a^1b^1//a^2b^2$) in 3,20-21. The unilateral statement on the preference of darkness by people is deepened and nuanced by the antithetical dyad 'doing evil' (3,20a) and 'doing what is true' (3,21a), and the dyad 'hating the light and not coming to the light' (3,20bc) as opposed to 'coming to the light' (3,21b). The second element, dealing with the 'evil deeds,' is equally well paraphrased in the form of an antithetical parallelism, *viz.*, the proposition "so that their deeds may not be exposed" (3,20d) which is opposed to the final proposition "so that it may be clearly seen that their deeds have been done in God" (3,21cd).

ii. Argumentative Narrative Structure

This segment is marked by the repetition of the following antithetical and dualistic terms: light-darkness, loving-hating, coming-not coming, doing what is true-doing evil, deeds done in God-evil deeds, and may be clearly seen-may not be exposed. In this segment (3,19-21) I observe the following argumentative narrative structure:

3,19   Action – Reaction - Reason
      19a   Introductory statement ("This is the judgement")
      19b   Divine action – "*light has come* into the world"
      19c   Human reaction – choice of the people ("*loved* darkness rather than light")
      19d   Reason (γὰρ) – "their *deeds* were <u>evil</u>."
3,20   Elucidation (γὰρ; ἵνα) of the reason *per negationem*:
      20a   Reaction – *doing* evil (cf. 19d)
      20bc   Reason – because (γὰρ) they <u>*hate the light*</u> (cf. 3,19c) (*per negationem*)
                 and <u>*do not come*</u> to the light (cf. 3,19b) (*per negationem*)[477]
      20d   Explanation of the reason (ἵνα) – "<u>*non exposition*</u> of *deeds*" (cf. 3,19d.20a)
3,21   Elucidation of the reason in *positive* terms:
      21ab   Reaction – *doing* what is <u>true</u>[478] (antithesis of 3,20a; cf. 3,19d)
                 coming to the light (antithesis of 3,19c.20bc)
      21cd   Reason (ἵνα; ὅτι) – *deeds* <u>*may be seen*</u> (antithesis of 3,20d)
                 deeds done in God (antithesis of 3,19d)

The beginning of 3,19, "And this is the judgement," means something like: 'and this is the reason.' Despite the contrary intention of God, the coming of the Son has turned into a judgement for unbelievers; that is, people have not been able to bear the light of his coming, which arose over darkness and, therefore, have turned away from him.[479] *Darkness, hating,* and *doing evil* together are set against *light*,[480] *loving, doing what is true.* Here, those who side the way of darkness are, for the evangelist, children of the devil, 'the ruler (ἄρχων) of the world' (cf. 8,44 and 12,31). The world hated Jesus and continues to do so, not merely because of some intellectual reason, but because the deeds of world-oriented

---

[477] The assertion 'loving darkness' in 3,19c is repeated in 3,20b *per negationem* as 'hating the light;' and the 'coming of the light' referring to Jesus in 3,19b is negated by the 'not coming to the light' of the people in 3,20c.

[478] 'Doing what is true' (3,21) is the antithetical expression of 'doing evil' (cf. 3,19d.20a). The explanation of the reason in 3,20d also implicitly refers to the deeds being evil as people fear their deeds being exposed.

[479] Taken strictly, the content of the clause falls into two parts, which of course have to be taken as a unity. The judgement does not consist in the coming of the light as such.

[480] The contrast between light and darkness is somewhat akin to the ethical dualism in the Dead Sea Scrolls, where a distinction is made between the sons of light and the sons of darkness (cf. 1 QS 3-4).

people are evil (cf. 7,7; and Col. 1,21). In the nature of the case, the evangelist's concern is not just with evil deeds but with people. But in 3,20-21 the emphasis, in connection with the image of the light, is on the deeds. When the light appears, people become manifest, first of all, in their *deeds*. Let me go into further details of this argumentative narrative structure.

α. Εἰς τὸν κόσμον

This prepositional phrase conveys a rather specific meaning. Of the seventeen times it is used, ten occur with the verb ἔρχομαι (1,9; 3,19; 6,14; 9,39; 11,27; 12,46; 16,28; 18,37 etc.), and five with the verb ἀποστέλλω (3,17; 10,36; 17,18, etc.). 'Coming εἰς τὸν κόσμον' is predicated only of Jesus or the predicted Messiah in the fourth Gospel. Thus, from the text alone one suspects that 'coming εἰς τὸν κόσμον' is a technical term for the Messianic or prophetic mission. That fits in well with the familiar Johannine theme of descending/ ascending Christology which is supported also by 16,28, where the descent is specifically παρὰ τοῦ πατρός. Likewise 'being sent εἰς τὸν κόσμον' refers specifically to Jesus' mission received from the Father.[481] In the Johannine corpus there are a handful of themes treated by the author in which κόσμος shares the focal interest. Κόσμος figures directly or indirectly in Johannine soteriology at least thirteen times; that is, the word κόσμος actually appears in all texts but is associated with the verb σώζω only twice (3,17 and 12,47) and with the noun σωτήρ three times (4,42; and 1 Jn. 4,9.14). Thus, Jesus is the Saviour of the world who takes away its sin(s) (1,29; and 1 Jn. 2,2). God's salvific will for the world prompted him to give His only Son to the world so that it might be saved (3,16-17 and 12,47), might know (14,30 and 17,23), and might believe (17,21). The same interest is reflected in Jesus' comments on the bread he gives for the life of the world (6,33.51). Six instances connect the κόσμος with the concept of judgement. Judgement of the world (9,39) or of its ruler (16,8.11) is one of the purposes of the descent of Jesus (coming εἰς τὸν κόσμον), even though there is indication that this is not the intent either of God (3,17) or of Jesus (12,47). There are six instances where the κόσμος is associated with light - φῶς. In five of the six uses the text stresses that Jesus has come as the light of the world (1,9; 3,19; 8,12; 9,5 and 13,46).[482]

β. **Meaning of Γάρ**

The phrase "ἦν γὰρ αὐτῶν πονηρὰ τὰ ἔργα" (3,19d) seems to pose some difficulties. If one attributes to the conjunction 'γάρ' its habitual causal meaning, the freedom of choice of the people is considerably restricted as their decision – faced with the light – would depend on their evil deeds done before the coming of the light.[483] In other words, their evil deeds are the radical cause of unbelief. Such an explanation would rest, in fact, on the

---

[481] Only in 17,18, the mission is transmitted to the disciples: "As you have sent me εἰς τὸν κόσμον, so I have sent them εἰς τὸν κόσμον." Only on two occasions in the Johannine corpus this prepositional phrase 'εἰς τὸν κόσμον' is used otherwise: once with 'λαλῶ' (8,26) and once with 'ἐγεννήθη' (16,21) in connection with a child being brought 'εἰς τὸν κόσμον;' see Cassem, 83-84.

[482] *Ibid.* 86.

[483] Barrett (182) notes that the distinction between the two groups of people in 3,20-21 existed before their confrontation with the light; there does not seem to be a question of transformation of 'those do evil' into 'those who do what is true.' He traces the background for it in the OT doctrine of election.

moral interpretation of the 'evil deeds,' leading to an understanding of them as manifestations of the corrupt and sinful nature of man.[484] But such a moral conception is more Pauline than Johannine[485] and hence, in my opinion, not acceptable.[486]

Taking inspiration from Bauer that, in some cases, the conjunction 'γὰρ' can play the role of 'δέ' – which serves to introduce a development or a continuation of the precedent idea[487] – I would like to translate 3,19cd as: 'And people loved darkness rather than light; *in fact*, their deeds were evil.' 3,19d does not, therefore, express the *cause* of unbelief, but a concrete *manifestation* of it; that is, the preference of the people for darkness is clearly *seen* in their evil deeds. In other words, the unbelief of the people (3,18) is rooted in their choice of darkness (3,19c) and is manifested concretely by their evil deeds (3,19d).[488] Moreover, the evil deed is the unbelief itself – the fact of not believing in Jesus, the Son sent by the Father. The 'evil deeds' (3,19d) can also be compared antithetically to the 'deeds done in truth and in God' (3,21), that is, believing in Jesus, the one sent by the Father (cf. 6,28-29). Such an interpretation of the evil deeds is more in conformity with the Johannine notion of deeds. The close connection between doing and being – *viz.*, between doing good or evil and the nature of a person – is an important Johannine theological concept, because believing is not merely a matter of mental affirmation but of life commitment. Between the moment of decision for Jesus and the outcome of perfect faith, there should be a process of progressive interiorisation of the word of Jesus.

γ. Antithetical Parallelism

The following verses (3,20-21) are organised in an antithetic parallel pattern whose parts of correspondence paraphrase the elements of 3,19cd.

---

[484] Bultmann (*Gospel*, 158-59) tries to reconcile the impact of the present decision with the previous actions pretending to avoid predestination. According to him, coming to the light shows the true nature (hidden) of man. It is based on the decision either for or against Jesus that the past deeds are judged as 'evil' or as 'done in God.' Such an interpretation is not convincing as a causal relationship is established between the past works and the present decision. For a discussion on predestination in the fourth Gospel, see also D. A. Carson, *Predestination and Responsibility: Elements of Tension-Theology in the Fourth Gospel against Jewish Background* (Cambridge 1975); and G. Röhser, *Prädestination und Verstockung. Untersuchungen zu ihrer Struktur in der biblisch-jüdischen, paulinischen und johanneischen Theologie* (TANZ 14) (Basel, Tübingen 1994) 201.

[485] Cf. A. Vanhoye, "Notre foi, œuvre divine, d'après le quatrième évangile," *NRT* 86 (1964) 347-49. See also Léon-Dufour, *Lecture*, I, 313-14, who recalls Rom. 3,27f. and 4,2.6; and Gal. 2,16 and 3,2.5.10-12.

[486] If doing 'what is evil' or 'what is true' preceded the decision of faith, it must be accepted that truth could refer to an anterior revelation about Jesus, and evil/sin could be considered as being independent and anterior to the decision faced with the coming of the light/Jesus. This does not correspond to the Johannine thinking (cf. 8,24; 15,21-25 and 16,8-9). Both – 'practice of truth' and 'coming to the light' – belong to the same process of faith.

[487] Bauer (*Wörterbuch*, 302) describes the usage as "*anknüpfend und fortführend*." See also M. Zerwick and M. Grosvenor (*A Grammatical Analysis of the Greek New Testament* [Rome 1974] 473) who give the following examples: Lk. 1,15; 12,58 (cf. Mt. 5,25); and 14,28; Acts 2,34; 4,34a; 8,39; 13,27; 15,28; 16,37 and 23,11; Rom. 1,18; 2,25; 4,3.9; 5,6; 12,3 and 14,5; 1 Cor. 10,1; 2 Cor. 1,12; 10,12 and 11,5; Gal. 1,11 and 5,13; and 1 Tim. 2,5.

[488] De la Potterie ("de revelatione," 276-77) says, in the same sense, that the evil deeds do not refer to the deeds that are morally evil and causing disbelief, but to the disbelief itself; they are almost identical with the disbelief in its diverse manifestations. See also Blank, *Krisis*, 101; Léon-Dufour, *op. cit.*, 314. 3,19d does not express the cause, but the result – the effect of 3,19c.

<table>
<tr>
<td>²⁰ For all who do evil hate the light and do X
not come to the light,</td>
<td>²¹ But those who do what is true come to the light,</td>
</tr>
<tr>
<td>so that <u>their deeds</u> may not be exposed.</td>
<td>X so that it may be clearly seen that <u>their deeds</u> have been done in God.</td>
</tr>
</table>

First of all, I would say that the conjunction γὰρ which introduces 3,20-21 takes the same meaning of 'γὰρ' as explained above in 3,19d; that is, it is not a question of causal explanation, but an exposition more developed of 3,19cd. The antithetical bipartite construction of 3,20 and 3,21 interprets and elucidates the statement made in 3,19cd and gives it the maximum amplitude.

δ. 'Doing Evil' and 'Doing What Is True'

The upper part mentions that "all who do evil... do not come to the light" (3,20ac) and conversely "those who do what is true come to the light" (3,21ab). What do these expressions 'do evil' and 'do what is true' mean, and how to situate them chronologically in relation to the 'coming' or 'not coming to the light' respectively (3,21b and 3,20c)? Because of the antithetic parallelism which connects the expression 'do evil' (φαῦλα πράσσων) with 'do what is true' (ποιῶν τὴν ἀλήθειαν),[489] one must notice the antithetical correspondence of one to the other. De la Potterie exposes well that in Judaism the notion of *truth* is close to that of the *Law*.[490] Thus, 'doing what is true' does not only mean 'practising what is right and just.' To this simple moral meaning a new dimension is added, *viz.*, practising justice in observing the Law. In my opinion, the fourth evangelist takes up this identification of the 'truth' with the 'Law' but substitutes it with the idea of revelation (the new Law) brought by Jesus and 're-interprets' the expression 'doing what is true' as not a mere conformity of one's acts to the revelation, but as accepting and interiorising this revelation progressively.

Moreover, in 3,20d the words 'their deeds' (τὰ ἔργα αὐτοῦ) are used to qualify the term 'evil' (φαῦλα). It is evident that these expressions recall the phrase: "because *their deeds* were *evil*" (ἦν γὰρ αὐτῶν πονηρὰ τὰ ἔργα −3,19d). One can, therefore, presume that 'φαῦλα' (3,20a) refers back to "πονηρὰ τὰ ἔργα" (3,19d). If, therefore, the *evil deeds* are the concrete manifestation of the preference of the people for darkness (cf. 3,19c) and their refusal to believe, the expression 'do evil' (3,20a) must also refer to the refusal of the people to believe, and even a persisting refusal.[491]

I would, therefore, say that 'doing evil' and 'doing what is true' refer respectively to the unbelief and belief as interior attitudes of man before Jesus who has come as light

---

[489] The expression 'ποιῶν τὴν ἀλήθειαν' recalls the Hebrew 'עשׂה אמת,' which indicates in Neh. 9,33 the faithfulness of God to His covenant; in 2 Chr. 31,20, it indicates the 'right and faithful' behaviour of king Hezekiah concerning the prescriptions of the Law. Taking inspiration from these usages, I must say that 'doing what is true' means 'proving one's faithfulness' and 'acting with truth and justice.' Cf. Bultmann, *Gospel*, 157; and his article "ἀλήθεια," *TDNT*, I, 242.

[490] De la Potterie, *La vérité*, 479-83.

[491] R. E. Brown (*Gospel*, I, 149) calls it a radical evil. The present participle indicates that, here, it is not a question of an occasional sinner but someone who obstinately refuses the light.

into the world.[492] The faith of those who do what is true is manifested exteriorly only in the effective coming to Jesus, the light – a coming that is concretised in the whole process of acceptance, interiorisation and appropriation of the truth about Jesus.[493]

ε. **Moral Issue?**

The expression 'ὁ φαῦλα πράσσων' (less frequent in the NT) appears again in 5,29; Rom. 9,11; 2 Cor. 5,10; and James 6,16. In Rom. 9,11 and 2 Cor. 5,10 there is opposition between 'doing good' (ἀγαθὸν) and 'doing evil' (φαῦλον). The same opposition is found in Jn. 5,29: "οἱ τὰ ἀγαθὰ ποιήσαντες ... οἱ δὲ τὰ φαῦλα πράξαντες." Moreover, as the context clearly indicates, the evangelist does not apply these terms to the moral behaviour of the believer. Because of the evident parallelism between 5,22-24 and 5,27-29, 'one who does good,' is the one 'who honours the Son as he honours the Father' (5,23) or, in other words, it is 'the one who hears my word and believes in Him who sent me' (5,24). From this, it is clear that the 'one who does evil' is the one who does not honour the Son, does not hear his word, and does not believe in him. It is also important to note that 3,16-21 and 5,19-30 have many other themes in common: judgement, sending of the Son by the Father, attainment of eternal life, etc. In this context it is probable that the expressions "ποιῶν τὴν ἀλήθειαν" (3,21) and "τὰ ἀγαθὰ ποιήσαντες" (5,29) are synonymous, as each of them is opposed to the same contrary expression "τὰ φαῦλα πράξαντες" (3,20 and 5,29). As 'doing good' is equivalent to 'honouring the Son as the Father' (that is, recognising in him the one sent by the Father), 'hearing his word,' 'believing the one sent' and 'doing what is true' must be synonymous or at least belong to the same process of faith.

One may still ask whether, in this way, everything – belief or unbelief, being saved or being condemned – is not reduced merely to the 'moral issue' of 'doing evil' or 'doing what is true.' But, after all that has been said about the descent of the Son of Man and being begotten ἄνωθεν as a begetting of the Spirit, that can hardly be the conclusion or intent. The repeated and emphatic mention of 'deeds' in this segment (3,19-21) is not due to the idea that, in the end, it is one's deeds and not his/her faith that is decisive for entry into the kingdom of God; it is based rather on the idea that *truth* is practical, that something must be done, and that what most deeply motivates a person becomes cognisable in his/her *deeds* (cf. Mt. 7,16ff.). Accordingly, that is what the light/Jesus brings into the open – whether as evil and worthless or as true and 'done in God' (3,21). The antithesis is posed in such absolute terms, because the light in view here is the light of the Word, which was, in the beginning, with God and was God, and because "in him was life and the life was the light of all people" (1,4). What light and darkness, life and non-life, evil/worthlessness and doing what is true are, therefore, is determined by whether or not one knows and accepts the light (cf. 1,4-5.9ff.). 'Because their deeds were evil' extends, therefore, beyond a merely moral judgement. It concerns the nature of the darkness of life outside God and of the evil deeds done outside God.

---

[492] Cf. F. Grob, *Faire l'œuvre de Dieu. Christologie et éthique dans l'Évangile de Jean* (EHPhR 68) (Paris 1986) 23-28.

[493] Cf. de la Potterie, *La vérité*, 515.

ζ. 'Loving Darkness More than the *Light*' and 'Coming to the *Light*'

Now, the antithesis of 'do evil,' *viz.*, 'do what is true' (3,21a) literally means 'act in such a way that truth comes into being,'[494] *truth* being that which is trustworthy, genuine, and non-deceptive. One who so acts 'comes to the light;' and here one has to question whether this statement refers to experience in general or specifically to the coming of the Son of God as light. 3,18 gives a hint in favour of the latter in the categories of belief. I must say that it is in *doing what is true* that people come to the light, that is, express their belief "in the name of the only Son of God" (3,18). Furthermore, it also clearly arises from 6,35 that 'coming to Jesus' is synonymous with 'believing in Jesus.' In 3,21, 'coming to the light' can, thus, signify the final and complete outcome of faith in Jesus, the light of the world[495] cf. 8,12; 9,5 and 12,46). To come to this light, one must 'do what is true,' that is, open oneself to the revelation of the Son.[496]

Moreover, the lower part of the antithetical correspondence between 3,20d and 3,21cd   places in parallel relation these two final propositions which also depend on the antithetical statements 'coming' and 'not coming to the light' (3,21b and 3,20c) respectively. On the one hand, light has a symbolic and allegoric meaning. The fact that evildoers are averse to the light is repeated in 3,20abc as a kind of rule of experience. Everyone who occupies himself/herself in doing[497] worthless and reprehensible things *hates the light* (3,20b). That person does not come to the light so that his/her deeds will not be exposed in its true nature, and unmasked as evil and worthless.[498] On the other hand, the light being Jesus himself (cf. 8,12; 9,5 and 12,46) and the revelation he brings, 'coming to the light' means believing in Jesus and accepting his words, because he speaks the words of God (cf. 3,34) and his deeds are done in God (cf. 3,21).

Now, let me try to seek an explanation for the statement 'coming to the light' in the context of Jesus' encounter with Nicodemus. In 2,23, it was said that "many believed in his name because they saw the signs that he was doing." One of them, a Pharisee and ruler of the Jews, Nicodemus, *came* to Jesus *by night* (3,1-2). The qualification of Nicodemus' *coming* as taking place *at night* is not unimportant, because it is recalled at his third and last appearance in 19,39. In his gesture and movement of 'coming to Jesus,' he is 'coming to the light,' that is, he 'moves in belief toward Jesus;' but I must, perhaps, also see in this *nightly coming* of Nicodemus to Jesus (3,2) a hint at the people's *preference for darkness* (3,19c). If Nicodemus is afraid of being recognised as a believer and comes to Jesus by

---

[494] Cf. A. Schlatter, *Das Evangelium nach Johannes. Ausgelegt für Bibelleser* (EzNT 3) (Berlin 1962) 101.

[495] See E. Achtemeier, "Jesus Christ, the Light of the world. The Biblical Understanding of Light and Darkness," *Interp.* 17 (1963) 439-49.

[496] Cf. de la Potterie, *La vérité*, 518; also for Blank (*Krisis*, 107), 'doing what is true' means: the faith by which man relishes the liberating truth which is offered to him to do what is true according to him. Such an appropriation of the truth – revealed by Jesus – is done with the help of the Paraclete who will teach all things and will remind all that Jesus has said (14,26). He will lead the believers into the whole truth (16,13) – the truth that comes from Jesus (16,14).

[497] Note the present participle - πράσσων.

[498] Light belongs to the day which robbers and other criminals hate for fear of being discovered. Inversely, it is looked forward to by those who have nothing to hide. See Schnackenburg, *op. cit.*, 406. Cf. Job 24,13-17 and 38,12f.; cf. Is. 29,15; Jer. 49,9; and Ps. 11,2 and 91,5; see also J. Riedl, *Das Heilswerk Jesu nach Johannes* (FTSt 93) (Basel, Freiburg, Wien 1973) 329.

night, he 'loves darkness more than light,' because he loved 'human glory more than the glory that comes from God' (12,43).[499]

η. ' Ἐλεγχθῇ' and 'Φανερωθῇ'

One thing now remains to be made clear; that is, the rapport between 'coming and not coming to the light' and the 'manifestation of their deeds' (3,20d.21c). In 3,20 it is said that "all who do evil hate the light and do not come to the light *so that their deeds may not be exposed*" (ἵνα μὴ ἐλεγχθῇ τὰ ἔργα αὐτοῦ), while in 3,21cd one reads: "*so that it may be clearly seen* (ἵνα φανερωθῇ αὐτοῦ) that *their deeds* have been done in God." Majority of the scholars have noticed the synonymy between the verbs 'ἐλεγχθῇ' and 'φανερωθῇ.'[500]

The idea is not that he who does what is true comes to the light to bring his deeds as much as possible into public view – to show them off as it were – but to make them cognisable as having been 'done in God' (that is, in communion with Him and in keeping with His will) and, thus, to identify himself in his deepest intentions. The fact that in the conflict between truth and error, uprightness and deception, reality and illusion one person shuns the light and another is attracted to the light is not just a matter of psychology or of a good or bad conscience. At its root, it is a matter of 'being' of God or not of God, that is, of the devil (8,4; and 1 Jn. 2,21).

Finally, all these do not mean, that the light which came with the sending of God's Son into the world has no other purpose than to unmask the difference between the two kinds of people. It undeniably has this effect. Still, it is the *descent* of the Son of Man and the *incarnation* of the Word that should banish from one's mind any notion that this effect is what is primarily meant. The light that comes into the world and penetrates it, however true it may be that it absolutely unmasks the darkness and everything that is done outside of God, has no other aim than to attract the world to the light of God's love, in order that everyone who believes in the Son should not perish in darkness (cf. 8,12).

iii. Emphasis through Repetition and Re-interpretation through Variation of Imagery[501]

It is evident that 3,19 is found to be in immediate continuity with 3,18 from where the theme of condemnation is picked up. In fact, one could even say that the whole of 3,19-21 must be read as an immediate prolongation of 3,16-18 (see the diagram on the next page):

---

[499] See my further explanation after a couple of pages in comparison with 12,37-48.

[500] Cf. Bultmann, *Gospel*, 157, n. 6; and Barrett, 182. Schnackenburg (*op. cit.*) adds that in the LXX the verb 'ἐλέγχειν' – which translates often 'יכח' – can take a 'forensic' meaning; it refers to the fact of bringing the impious to the court of justice for their crimes. One finds the same verb in 8,46 to indicate the impossibility of finding sin in Jesus. Cf. Eph. 5,11.13 where the two verbs appear together: the works of darkness must be unveiled so that they are exposed to the light. For a detailed analysis of the verbs, see de la Potterie, *La vérité*, I, 404-6.

[501] See J. A. du Rand, "Repetitions and Variations – Experiencing the Power of the Gospel of John as Literary Symphony," *Neotest.* 30 (1996) 59-70; and L. Morris, "Variation – A Feature of the Johannine Style," in: his *Studies in the Fourth Gospel*, 293-319. For a detailed exposition of this narrative technique see and B. F. Kawin, *Telling it Again and Again: Repetition in Literature and Film* (Ithaca 1972). Moreover, the study of I. de la Potterie ("Structure du Prologue de Saint Jean," *NTS* 30 [1984] 354-81) gives an idea of the way in which these repetitions involve order, complexity and delicacy.

³,¹⁶⁻¹⁷ God *gave/send* his only <u>Son</u> *to the world* // ³,¹⁸ᵃᵇ *Those who believe...*<u>not condemned</u> // ¹⁸ᶜᵈᵉ but *those who do not believe* <u>are</u> <u>condemned</u> already ...	³,¹⁹ᵇ The <u>light</u> has *come into the world* ³,²¹ *Those who do what is true* <u>come</u> <u>to the light</u>... ³,²⁰ *All who do evil...*<u>do not come to</u> <u>the light</u>...

The gift/sending of the Son into the world is paraphrased in terms of the coming of the light into the world,[502] and the antithetic couple 'those who believe' and 'those who do not believe' of 3,18 is also reformulated in 3,20-21 using the antithetical expressions 'coming to the light' and 'not coming to the light'[503] respectively. One can, moreover, notice that the judgement announced for those who do not believe is re-interpreted in terms of the people's preference for darkness rather than light (cf. 3,19c.20b).

The purpose of this reformulation of 3,16-18 in antithetical, dualistic and apocalyptic categories is to bring to light the definitive eschatological event of the Son of Man coming into the world. The introduction in 3,19a: "this is the judgement" proves well that the expression "condemned already" (3,18) refers to the definitive eschatological judgement,[504] taking place in the event of 'the light coming into the world' (3,19b). The use of perfect 'ἐλήλυθεν' (3,19b) indicates that the coming of the light in Jesus is valid for the entire time to come; that is, no other judgement will come to substitute the one that took place at the historical coming of the light.

Furthermore, 3,19-21 are strongly reminiscent of 1,9-13. The 'not knowing' and 'non-acceptance' of 1,9-11 are re-interpreted here: people have loved darkness *more*[505] than the light (3,19c). The reason is that "their deeds were evil" (3,19d) (see the diagram on the next page):

The coming of the light into the world provokes judgement as men preferred darkness to the light. In both texts, it is the question of the *coming of the light into the world* (1,9 and 3,19ab) as well as the *rejection of that light* by the world/people (1,10c-11 and 3,19c). Moreover, according to 1,9-13, the world ought to have recognised the light – because 'he (the light) was in the world' (1,10a) and 'the world was created through him' (1,10b) – and accepted to be enlightened (saved) by him. In 3,19c, it is, therefore, absurd that people preferred darkness to the light. The world 'not knowing or accepting' the light (1,10c-11) is repeated in 3,19c as choosing darkness which is diametrically opposed to light. 3,19d-21 elaborate and explain the reason for such a choice and the consequences that follow. Those who do not receive Jesus and believe in his name (1,12 and 3,15.18) are

---

[502] The same association is made in the prologue between the terms 'light,' 'Logos,' and '(only) Son;' comp. 1,19 and 1,14.18; see also 11,27. On the correspondence between 'the coming of the Son' and 'the coming of the light,' see Blank, *Krisis*, 99; and Ruckstuhl, "Abstieg," 340; see especially M. Morgen, "La venue de la Lumière dans le quatrième évangile," in: R. Kuntzman (ed.), *Ce Dieu qui vient: Études sur l'Ancien et le Nouveau Testament offertes au Professeur Bernard Renaud à l'occasion de son soixante-cinquième anniversaire* (LeDiv 159) (Paris 1995) 307-23.

[503] The parallelism between 'believing in the Son' and 'coming to the light' is supported by the Johannine synonymy between 'believing in Jesus' and 'coming to Jesus;' comp. 3,35-36 and 6,35c; 6,44-45 and 6,47; 6,64 and 6,65; 7,37 and 7,38; See also Schnackenburg, *op. cit.*, 407; de la Potterie, "de revelatione," 276-77; and his *La vérité*, 487.

[504] Cf. Blank, *Krisis*, 96; and de la Potterie, *La vérité*, 496.

[505] Μᾶλλον refers not to a relative choice but to an absolute choice.

re-interpreted in 3,20 as those who do evil, hate the light and do not come to the light; and the 'children of God' (1,12) and those born of God (1,13) are re-interpreted using the imagery of light, truth and deeds as "those who *do* what is *true*" (3,21a), those who "come to the *light*" (3,21b), and those whose "*deeds* have been done in God" (3,21d).

[1,9] The *true light*, which enlightens everyone, was *coming into the world*.[506] [10ab] He was in the world, and the world came into being through him;	[3,19ab] And this is the judgement, that the *light has come into the world,*
[10c] yet *the world did not know him.* [11] He came to what was his own, and *his own people did not accept him.*	[19cd] and *people loved darkness rather than light* because their deeds were evil.
[12] But to all *who received him, who believed in his name*, he gave power to <u>become children of God</u>, [13] who were <u>born</u>, not of blood or of the will of the flesh or of the will of man, but <u>of God</u>.	[20] For all *who do evil hate the light and do not come to the light,* so that their deeds may not be exposed. [21] But those *who do what is true* <u>come to the light</u>, so that it may be clearly seen that their <u>deeds have been done in God.</u>

The same idea of *light coming into the world* and people 'loving darkness more than light' is repeated or reappears later on the lips of Jesus in 12,46-48 (see the diagram below):[507]

[3,19ab] And this is the <u>judgement</u>, that *the light has come into the world,*	[12,46a] I have *come as light into the world,*
[19cd] and people *loved darkness* rather than light because their deeds were evil.	[46bc] so that everyone who believes in me should not *remain in the darkness.* [43] for they *loved human glory more* than the glory that comes from God.....
[20] For all <u>*who do evil hate the light* and *do not come to the light*</u>, so that their deeds may not be exposed. [21] But *those who do what is true come to the light,* so that it may be clearly seen that their deeds have been done in God.	[47] I do not judge *anyone who hears my words* and <u>*does not keep them*</u>, for I came not to <u>judge</u> the world, but to <u>save</u> the world. [48] The <u>*one who rejects me and does not receive my word*</u> has a <u>judge</u>; on the last day the word that I have spoken will serve as <u>judge</u>.

---

[506] 'The coming of the *light* into the world' mentioned in 1,9 is re-interpreted as incarnation in 1,14 using the imagery of *Word* and *flesh*: "And the *Word* became *flesh* and lived among us."

[507] 'Believing in Jesus is believing in the one who sent him; seeing Jesus is seeing his sender' (cf. 12,44-45). According to 3,16-17.34-35, it is clear that the relation sender-sent corresponds to the relation God (Father)-Son. Hence, both texts contains the same juridical terminology of the Son-sent and the dualistic-apocalyptic terminology of light-darkness. Comp. 9,3-5 and 9,39-41. I find that the evangelist uses the terminology of *light* when he wants to stress the eschatological dimension of the coming of the Son; the sending of the Son into the world realises the eschatological event of salvation/judgement traditionally awaited at the end of times.

In fact, the construction 'love...more than' (ἀγαπάω... μᾶλλον... ἤ [ἤπερ]...) is found only in 3,19 and 12,43 in the NT. As Son/light come into the world, Jesus brings the revelation, and he 'speaks the words of God' (cf. 3,34), because he himself is the Word who is with God from the beginning (1,1). Rejecting the light is also rejecting the word of life (cf. 6,63.68); it is excluding oneself from salvation. The same Word will judge on the last day, that is, because of their rejection of this Word that people will be condemned. The theme of judgement (3,19a) is repeated oftener in 12,47 and as opposed to salvation. Soteriology is again linked with Christology as it is dependent on 'hearing,' 'keeping' (12,47) and 'receiving' (12,48) the words of Jesus (Logos) who speaks the words of God (cf. 3,34). In other words, "those who do what is true" and "come to the light" (3,21) are re-interpreted here, using the imagery of *Logos*, as those who *hear/receive* (cf. 12,47.48) the *words* of Jesus and *keep* them (12,47); and the statement "all who do evil hate the light and do not come to the light"[508] (3,20) is re-interpreted using the same imagery of *Logos* in antithetical terms ('reject *me*' and 'does not receive my *word*') in 12,48.

Moreover, the statement "although he had performed so many signs in their presence, they did not believe in him" (12,37) and the following statement "nevertheless many, even of the authorities, believed in him. But because of the Pharisees they did not confess it, for fear that they would be put out of the synagogue" (12,42) recall 2,23-3,2. Hearing Jesus' word and not keeping it is synonymous with beginning to believe in Jesus without wanting to confess (like Nicodemus); it is synonymous with coming at night (3,2), preferring darkness to light (3,19c) and remaining in darkness (12,46c). Those who hear the word of Jesus but do not keep it (12,47) – those who do not receive his words and end up in rejecting Jesus – will, inevitably, be judged by the word of Jesus (12,48). The desire to remain in darkness – not confessing their faith – attracts condemnation as they 'love human glory more than the glory that comes from God' (12,43).

Nicodemus 'preferred darkness to the light,' because he preferred human glory to the glory the comes from God. Jesus makes him finally understand that those who do what is true come to the light, that is, those who open themselves to the revelation – those who hear his words and begin to believe – must continue until the complete appropriation of this revelation, that is, keep the word and confess their full faith. They have nothing to fear, for their deeds are done in God; they love the glory that comes from God and not that of men. Nicodemus who began to believe must choose between darkness and light, between human glory and glory that comes from God.

iv. Implicit Commentary – Irony

If 3,16-18 present a brief portrait of God, 3,19-21 present a frank, realistic and decisive portrait of humanity. The verdict (κρίσις) in 3,19 is that people *loved* darkness (σκότος) rather than light (φῶς). Here, there is irony in the fact that people *loved* darkness. The word for *love* is the same as in 3,16 (God's love – ἀγαπάω). People love darkness, because their evil deeds can remain hidden rather than be exposed. But God loves humanity so that it may come to the light and be saved.

---

[508] Cf. Borgen, *Logos Was the True Light.*

v. Dualistic Symbols

α. Light and Darkness

a) Symbol of Revelation

Light is used eminently as a *symbol of revelation* in the fourth Gospel. It is commonly associated with intellectual clarity as well as lordship and divinity. P. E. Wheelwright observes that "of all archetypal symbols there is, probably, none more wide-spread and more immediately understandable than light, as symbolising certain mental and spiritual qualities."[509] Where there is light there is life and the perception of life. The conflict of light and darkness evokes a universal and primordial response. These symbols are used universally in religious discourse and had deep roots both in Hellenism and Judaism, where light was a common symbol for the Law.[510]

Light is a natural phenomenon that lends itself to symbolism. In the OT life was associated with sunlight, while the realm of death was depicted as gloom and darkness (cf. Job 10,21 and 30,26; and Pss. 39,19 and 143,3).[511] Many of the NT usages of the terms light and darkness refer, simply, to physical phenomena; in the fourth Gospel they are used symbolically[512] and in a dualistic contrast. The importance of this archetypal symbol 'light and darkness' (day and night) is evident from the outset. In the prologue the Logos is identified with the *light of revelation* that shines in the darkness; "but the darkness did not overcome it" (1,5). It is an amazing statement, setting out the fundamental opposition to God's revelatory plan in the strongest possible terms. And the sense of conflict is intensified a few verses later, where the hostility is taken up by the world; "and the world did not know him" (1,10). Darkness is virtually identified with the world (the human adversaries of the Logos – cf. 3,19) and this identification is what establishes the basic symbolic pattern of the Gospel. The opposition, therefore, does have a certain cosmic dimension – the light is encompassed by darkness – but the light is the *light of revelation* and is not distinct from the Logos even in his human form. There is no question of light succeeding darkness here. The *light of revelation* accompanies the existence of the human race ("the light has come into the world" – 3,19); indeed it is "the life of men" (1,4) and the present tense in 1,5 φαίνει (shines), which has puzzled many commentators, does not include the bright start of a new age, but a continuous illumination that finally flames out in the incarnation of the Logos.[513]

b) Connection Between Testimony and Judgement

The next time the symbol appears, its significance is expanded to make explicit the *connection between testimony and judgement*: "And this is the judgement, that the light has come into the world, and people loved darkness rather than light" (3,19). Eschatological expectations are thereby fused into present realities and the basis for the acceptance and

---

[509] P. E. Wheelwright, *Metaphor and Reality* (Bloomington, London 1962)116.

[510] See Dodd, *Interpretation*, 201-5; Stemberger, 25-49; and Painter "Johannine Symbols," 26-41.

[511] In the OT light and darkness remain only as 'poetic symbols.' See R. E. Brown, *op. cit.*, 515.

[512] See the detailed exposition of Schwankl, esp. 148-85; see also C. Hélou, *Symbole et langage dans les écrits johanniques: lumière-ténèbres* (Paris 1980).

[513] See J. Ashton, "The Transformation of Wisdom: A Study of the Prologue of John's Gospel," *NTS* 32 (1986) 161-86.

rejection of Jesus is explored. Those who reject Jesus do so, because their works are evil and the light exposes their inherent bent toward evil; they love the darkness (3,20). The one who does the truth, on the other hand, comes to the light with the result that it discloses that his works are of God (3,21). These verses increase the symbol's power. Light is not only the revelation of the *Logos*; it reveals the nature of all who come in contact with it, and the judgement upon each person is determined by his/her response to it. Light shines in darkness. It reveals; it also exposes. The subordinate image of the lamp symbolises the role of the Baptist and the superiority of Jesus. John the Baptist was not the light but a burning and shining lamp (5,35; cf. 1,8), that must fade away (cf. 3,24.30).[514]

c) Rejection of Light

The identification of the symbol with Jesus is complete when Jesus later announces: "I am the light of the world" (8,12 and 1,9).[515] Sin is shown to reside not in the blindness of the one who has not been confronted by the light but in the blindness of those who have *seen the light and rejected it*. They have chosen to live in darkness, because they love it (3,19; cf. Jn. 9). Jn. 9 also confirms the symbolic use of day and night as subordinate symbols which evoke the core symbols, light and darkness (cf. 9,4-5 and 11,9-10). Retrospectively, or upon re-reading, 'night' functions as an index to the character of Nicodemus (3,2), the Jews (9,4 and 11,10) and Judas (13,30).[516]

Later in the Gospel the same idea is taken up in one of the famous 'I am' sayings:[517] "I am the light of the world; he who follows me will not walk in darkness, but will have the light of life" (8,12). The decisive feature is not the universality but the dualism; for without the revelation the world is in darkness. This is true up to a point, for the fourth evangelist's view of the world is often negative and pessimistic. In spite of the coming of the light into the world, the world (people) preferred darkness to light, because they hated the light and did not want to come to the light lest their evil deeds should be exposed (3,19-20).

There is little doubt that in speaking of "those who do what is true" (ὁ...ποιῶν τὴν ἀλήθειαν) and of "deeds done in God" (τὰ ἔργα...ἐν θεῷ...εἰργασμένα – 3,21) the evangelist must be understood as speaking of those whose actions are in harmony with and a reflection of the character of the light which now shines in the midst of men.[518] By contrast, in 3,20 "all who do evil" (πᾶς...ὁ φαῦλα πράσσων) are clearly people whose deeds are consonant with the darkness and, hence, they both hate and shun the light.

---

[514] Note the task of the Baptist as a witness to Jesus – 'the light come into the world' – 3,19); cf. 3,27.36; see J. Becker, *Johannes der Täufer und Jesus von Nazareth* (BSt 63) (Neukirchen-Vluyn 1972).

[515] Boismard ("L'évolution," 508) observes strong parallelism between 3,16-19 and 12,46-48. He contends that they are not two different discourse, but two different editions (Jn. 3 being in the third person whereas Jn. 12 in the first).

[516] Cf. N. R. Peterson, *The Gospel of John and the Sociology of Light: Language and Characterisation in the Fourth Gospel* (Trinity 1993).

[517] See the detailed work of P. B. Harner, *The "I am" of the Fourth Gospel* (FB.B 26) (Philadelphia 1970).

[518] It is worth noting that in the only other place in the Johannine literature where the expression doing 'what is true' occurs (1 Jn. 1,6) the context is likewise dealing with light and darkness and with practical, godly behaviour (cf. 1 Jn. 1,5-10). Cf. Klauck, *Der erste Johannesbrief*, 81-85; and on 'doing what is true' see his explanation from Greek and Hebrew on p. 89.

d) Those Begotten ἄνωθεν Come to Light

It seems virtually inescapable that the persons described in 3,21 must be perceived as begotten ἄνωθεν already.[519] The picture offered by the fourth Gospel is one of a light shining in the darkness and attracting men by its radiance. Drawn to the source of light they come to attach themselves to it, extending and magnifying it and thereby limiting still further the domain of darkness: "While you have the light," Jesus tells his followers, "believe in the light, so that you may become children of light" (12,36). In 3,21 Jesus shows the way to come to the light; it is by doing what is true, because such deeds are done in God.

e) Moral Dualism

The members of the Johannine Community originally belonged to a Jewish group. Their leaders' initial indifference to Jesus' message had developed into open hostility. Accordingly, what looks like and has often been interpreted as a cosmological dualism is really a *moral dualism*:[520] The good (in this case those who accept the revelation of Jesus) versus the wicked (those who reject the revelation – 'the Jews' or 'the world'). "Coming to the light" (3,20-21) is interpreted as the act of faith.[521] This is supported by the repetition of the term 'ἔργα' (thrice – cf. 3,19-21), the emphasis on 'doing' (πράσσω and ποιέω) and the antithetical word-pairs: loving-hating, and what is true-evil.

f) Evidence in Sectarian Literature

This polarisation – regularly accompanied and supported by the dualistic symbols of light and darkness – is very common in the sectarian literature of that period. Just how easy it is to pass from an apparently cosmic dualism to a moral dualism may be seen from a rabbinic comment on the first page of Genesis: "And God divided the light from the darkness, that is the works of the righteous from the works of the wicked, 'and God called the light Day' this refers to the works of the righteous; 'and darkness he called Night;' this is the works of the wicked" (Gen. Rab. 3,8).[522] A similar moral dualism pervades all through the OT, especially the Psalms.

♦ Qumran

The division of mankind into good and bad becomes more noticeable and more extreme in the writings of the Second Temple era that emanate from circles outside the establishment. Characteristic is the separation of the wicked from the righteous at the end of time[523] (cf. Mt. 25,32-33). In view of Israel's profound and pervasive sense of divine election one might expect the wicked to be identified with the Gentiles. This happens quite frequently,

---

[519] Wescott (57) speaks as if he understood the verse to refer to Christians. I think it is a fitting conclusion to the encounter with Nicodemus who came to Jesus by night seeking enlightenment from Jesus, who concludes his discourse with the symbol of light. See also Z. C. Hodges, "Problem Passages in the Gospel of John. Part 4: Coming to the Light – John 3:20-21," *BS* 135 (1978) 317; and Meinertz, 404.

[520] See F. Mußner, *ZΩH. Die Anschauung vom "Leben" im vierten Evangelium unter Berücksichtigung der Johannesbriefe* (MThS.H 5) (München 1952) 166.

[521] Y. Ibuki, *Die Wahrheit im Johannesevangelium* (BBB 39) (Bonn 1972) 344.

[522] As cited in Odeberg, 140; cf. 2 Enoch 30,14f.; Barn. 18,1-2.

[523] To be discussed in the subsequent dualistic symbol of 'Judgement'.

the Qumran War Scroll being a particularly clear example (cf. also Pss. Sol. 3,3-8 and 15,4-13; and 1 Enoch 90,18). The designation 'righteous' is also quite commonly reserved for the members of the writer's own sect; in that case the wicked are either their special enemies or even conceivably the rest of the human race. The so called Epistle of Enoch (1 Enoch 91-108), written, probably, toward the beginning of the second-century, labours the point with insistence from beginning to end: "And the righteous man will rise from sleep...and he will live in goodness and righteousness and will walk in eternal light. And sins will be destroyed in darkness for ever and from that day will never be seen" (1 Enoch 92,3-5). The conclusion is similar: "And they will see those who were born in darkness thrown into darkness, while the righteous shine. And the sinners will cry out as they see them shining, but they themselves will go where the days and times have been written down for them" (1 Enoch 108,14-15).[524]

From the writings at Qumran one knows that light and darkness have become two moral principles engaged in struggle for domination over mankind. Much of the literature on the Dead Sea Scrolls discuss dualism between light and darkness, good and evil, life and death, and their relation to the fourth Gospel.[525] One senses in these passages vindictiveness as well as hope; the writers know already who the righteous are and who the impious. The threat of divine punishment is not employed here as it would be done later in the Christian circle (cf. Jn. 3,19.36 which speak of *judgement* and *God's wrath*). Rather what one has here is a way of assuring the members of the writer's own sect that in spite of all appearances they are really on the winning side. The struggle between the forces of good (light) and the forces of evil (darkness) can have only one outcome: the good will prevail.[526] So Jesus, too, says of the evil 'ruler of this world' that 'he has no power over him' (14,30). While at Qumran the acceptance of the Law separated the sons of light and the sons of darkness, for the fourth evangelist it is the acceptance (coming to the light, loving the light, doing what is true – 3,19-21) or rejection of Jesus (loving darkness, hating light, doing evil – 3,19-21) in faith that is decisive.[527] In the Qumran Scrolls there is a rigid and hopeless determinism. The men of darkness belong to the spirit of error (falsehood). Their fate deprives them of any power of choice. But the fourth evangelist is concerned with meaningful choice, not blind fate. "People loved darkness rather than light" (3,19). It

---

[524] D. Hill ("Dikaioi as a Quasi-Technical Term," *NTS* 11 [1964/65] 296-302) traces the use of the term in Matthew back to 1 Enoch, e.g. 11,1 and 82,4.

[525] For a comparison of dualisms in the fourth Gospel and Qumran, see Charlesworth, "Critical Comparison," 76-106; he rejects the argument of some scholars that there are major differences in the dualism of the various scrolls. He strongly contends that 1 QS 3,13ff. is a key to understanding the dualism of Qumran. See also M. Abegg, Jr., P. Flint and E. Ulrich, *The Dead Sea Scrolls Bible: The Oldest Known Bible Translated for the First Time into English* (New York 1999); and E. Ulrich, *The Dead Sea Scrolls and the Origins of the Bible* (Winona Lake 1999).

[526] See the recent volume of J. A. Fitzmyer (*The Dead Sea Scrolls and Christian Origins* [Grand Rapids 2000]), a collection of twelve studies on the Dead Sea Scrolls, including a new essay on Qumran Messianism; G. Vermes, *An Introduction to the Complete Dead Sea Scrolls* (Philadelphia 2000); and L. Schiffman and J. VanderKam (eds.), *The Encyclopedia of the Dead Sea Scrolls*, 2 Vols. (Oxford 2000) featuring 450 articles by an international community of scholars.

[527] R. E. Brown ("The Qumran Scrolls," 417) contends that when one turns to the 'sons of light' in the fourth Gospel, he/she finds a distance from Qumran. As one would expect, some good men are attracted to the light of Christ. Yet it is not 'good deeds' (3,20) that constitute one a son of light; it is faith in Christ, the light of the world (12,36.46).

was not forced on them; they themselves chose darkness; and in that lies their condemnation (cf. 3,18).

β. Truth and Falsehood

Less picturesque than the opposition between light and darkness, but closely associated with it, is the dualistic contrast between truth and falsehood (cf. 3,21.33). There is distinction between a Hebrew and a Greek concept of truth. In the Hebrew OT, אֱמֶת is related to the root אמן meaning 'to be firm and solid;' and, thus, אֱמֶת is the essential solidity of a thing, or that which makes it trustworthy and reliable. When one attempts to learn the meaning of truth in the fourth Gospel, he/she finds variations of the same kind. The Logos was "full of grace and truth," and "grace and truth came through Jesus Christ" (1,14.17). Truth is something one can *do* (3,21).[528] The true worshippers will worship the Father in spirit and truth (4,23f.). The Baptist had borne witness to the truth (5,33; cf. 3,27-36).[529] The attachment of the second witness of the Baptist to 3,19-21 makes sense as he is the one *par excellence* who 'does what is true.'[530]

a) Moral Dualism

God is absolutely true in the sense of being worthy of confidence and of being faithful to His promises. It is in this sense "whoever has accepted his testimony has certified this, that God is *true*" (3,33) is to be understood. However, words are true if they are solidly founded. A man's life is true if it is faithful to God's ways. Thus, there is a *moral element* in the Hebrew concept of 'truth.' It is in this sense "those who do what is true come to light, so that it may be clearly seen that their deeds have been done in God" (3,21) is to be interpreted.[531] The dualism expressed in 3,19-21 divides the whole of mankind into two groups who are qualified as either doing 'what is *true*'[532] (3,21) or doing '*evil*'[533] (3,20). The criteria for such a division is their *deeds* (works). Anyone who habitually performs the actions that can be described as true comes to the light. The deeds of such a person are not those that must be reproved. They are done 'in God,'[534] and the light will make this clear to

---

[528] On 'doing what is true' see the explanation from Greek and Hebrew in M. Zerwick, "Veritatem facere. Ioh. 3,21; 1 Ioh. 1,6," *VD* 18 (1938) 338-41 and 373-77. On the use of the term 'truth' in the fourth Gospel see also P. Mourlon-Beernaert, "La vérité au sens biblique: approche de saint Jean," *LV* 46 (1991) 287-300; the two-volume dissertation of de la Potterie, *La vérité*; and his, "The Truth in Saint John," in: Ashton, *Interpretation*, 67-82; Klauck, *Der erste Johannesbrief*, 89; R. E. Brown, *Gospel*, I, 499; and Dodd, *Interpretation*, 170f.

[529] Some more references to truth in the fourth Gospel are: 8,31-46; 14,6.17; 15,26; 16,7.13; 17,17-19 and 18,37.38; see also W. Grundmann, *Der Zeuge der Wahrheit. Grundzüge der Christologie des Johannesevangeliums* (Berlin 1985).

[530] Cf. J.-F. Collange, "'Faire la vérité:' Considérations éthiques sur Jean 3,21," *RHPhR* 62 (1982) 416.

[531] Cf. Mußner, *ZΩH*, 166; see also Böcher, *Dualismus*, 99.

[532] One generally speaks of 'telling the truth.' It may be that the evangelist's choice of verb here is partially due to the need for a contrast with 'doing evil' (3,20). Against this is the fact that the Greek verbs are different: πράσσων in 3,20 and ποιῶν in 3,21. But there are *actions* that are true as well as *words*. See Morris, *Gospel*, 208.

[533] One who does evil is not an occasional sinner, but one who "*practices* wickedness;" see R. E. Brown, *op. cit.*, 149.

[534] The expression 'ὅτι ἐν θεῷ ἐστιν εἰργασμένα' (3,21) puts the emphasis on 'in God.' The perfect participle may point to the permanence of such works.

all. The evangelist does not, of course, mean that some people by nature do what is right. He is not teaching salvation by works or by nature. What is decisive is faith in Jesus.

Moreover, their conduct is one of 'loving' or 'hating' (cf. 3,19-20).[535] The Greek word 'ἀλήθεια' has the basic meaning of non-concealment; it describes what is unveiled. Thus, truth is a fact or a state of affairs insofar as it is seen or expressed; and for the Greek, truth and reality are closely related. Both Dodd and Bultmann maintain that the use of ἀλήθεια in the fourth Gospel is closer to the Greek idea. Bultmann says that ἀλήθεια in the fourth Gospel denotes 'divine reality' and this can be related to Greek dualism.[536] This divine reality is revealed[537] to humans and offers the possibility of life. In Jn. 3 the evangelist has reported the words of Jesus which emphasise that not good works, but begetting ἄνωθεν is the way to God. The person whom the evangelist has in mind here is the one who responds to the Gospel invitation and, therefore, has life in Jesus (cf. 3,15).

b) Comparison with Qumran

The expression 'do what is true' (3,21) has a strong Semitic flavour.[538] The dualism of truth and falsehood is nowhere more fully expressed than in the long passage of the Qumran Community Rule (1 QS 3,13-4,26) which sets out the basic theological beliefs of the group. The parallels between this passage and the fourth Gospel have been fully explored by Charlesworth[539] and are alluded to in every recent commentary. The Covenanters are 'the sons of light' (1QS 1,9; 2,16 and 3,13), guided by 'the prince of lights' (1 QS 3,20) in their struggle against 'the sons of darkness' (1 QS 1,10), who are in their turn supported by "the angel of darkness" (1 QS 3,20f.). The phrase 'do what is true' (Jn. 3,21) is also found in Qumran (1 QS 1,5; 5,3 and 8,2).

c) Truth Related to Revelation and Wisdom

De la Potterie thinks that, in these writings, with different shades of meaning in each, it may be said that 'truth' is at once a theme of revelation and a theme of Wisdom. It denotes the revelation of the mystery of God and His revealed teaching itself, *viz.*, Wisdom. The fourth evangelist's terminology is really derived from this apocalyptic and Wisdom background. It is true that the fourth evangelist does not use the terms 'mystery' or 'Wisdom;' but all his expressions that include the word 'truth' are connected with this tradition.[540] Thus, the formulae 'walk in the truth' (2 Jn. 4; and 3 Jn. 3-4),[541] and 'do what is true' (Jn. 3,21; and 1 Jn. 1,6)[542] are found already elsewhere in the Jewish literature.

---

[535] Cf. Becker, *Johannes*, 176; and his, "Beobachtungen," 79.

[536] R. Bultmann, "ἀλήθεια," *TDNT*, I, 245. See also Dodd, *Interpretation*, 177.

[537] J. Blank ("Der johanneische Wahrheitsbegriff," *BZ* 7 [1963] 164-73) maintains that the essential aspect of *truth* in the fourth Gsopel is that it is associated with the revealer.

[538] See Schnackenburg (*op. cit.*, 40), who refers regularly to the resemblance with Qumran documents.

[539] See Charlesworth, "Critical Comparison," 76-106.

[540] See de la Potterie, "Truth," 69. According to him, the primary influence on the fourth evangelist was Judaism, and not Gnosticism nor Hellenistic thought. See also R. E. Brown, *op. cit.*, 150.

[541] Cf. Jub. 21,2 and 25,10; T. Levi 18,8 (some MSS); 2 Enoch 66,6; 1 QH 16,7. On 2 Jn. 4 and 3 Jn. 3-4, see H.-J. Klauck, *Der zweite und dritte Johannesbrief* (EKK XXIII/2) (Neukirchen-Vluyn, Zürich 1992) 46; and 84-85.

[542] Cf. Jub. 20,9; 30,23 and 36,3; T. Reub. 6,9; T. Iss. 7,5; T. Ben. 10,3; Pss. Sol. 17,17; and 1 QS 1,5; 5,3 and 8,2.

d) Divergence

Though I am forced to recognise an affinity of thought and feeling between the fourth Gospel and the Dead Sea Scrolls, there is also a considerable divergence; there is both a depth and a cleverness in the fourth Gospel that surpasses anything in the Dead Sea Scrolls. Becker compares the extract from the Community Rule with Jn. 3,19-21.[543] In the fourth Gospel the struggle between truth and falsehood is equally bitter and the upshot equally certain. The symbolism of light and truth is exploited to a greater effect in the fourth Gospel than at Qumran, for Jesus is identified not only as the light of the world (8,12) but also as the truth (14,6). For the fourth evangelist the main task of the 'Spirit of truth' will be to recall to his disciples' minds the words of Jesus and to lead them into all truth (14,26 and 16,13).[544]

The purpose of 3,19-21, in my opinion, is not to encourage readers to think they fall into a deterministic category bound up with their intrinsic nature, but to make them see the imminence of their danger, and the fundamentally moral reasons why people hate the light. The antithesis is posed in such absolute terms, because the truth in view here is the Word ("full of grace and truth" – 1,14), which was in the beginning with God and was God, and because "in him was life, and the life was the light of all people" (1,4). What light and darkness, life and death, doing what is true and doing evil are, therefore, is determined by whether or not one knows and comes to the light, *viz.*, believes in Jesus. The evangelist stresses these points in dualistic terminology again and again in the hope that his readers will turn to the 'lifted up' Son of Man with the same simple, desperate, unqualified faith as the Israelites displayed who turned to the bronze serpent in the desert (cf. 3,13-15). Through such a faith alone can anyone experience the begetting ἄνωθεν (3,3-5) and thereby gain ζωὴ αἰώνιος (3,15-16).

vi. Reader and Point of View

The reader, so far, has been provided with adequate data to be aware that the loving gift of the Son for the salvation of the world will raise a basic question. One is called to a decision to accept or refuse the saving revelation of the Father who sent the Son. The narrative-like report of the experience of Nicodemus challenges the reader to recognise that a decision has to be made. Nicodemus may have left confused and hesitant, but the author, through the latter part of the discourse of Jesus aimed at the reader, is able to draw upon the familiar language of the prologue to develop the theme of judgement. Using the symbolic and dualistic language of 'life and death,' 'truth and falsehood,' and 'light and darkness'

---

[543] He qualifies the dualism of this passage, quite wrongly, as "*prädestinationisch-ethisch*" (see his, "Beobachtungen," 71-87). In his commentary (149), he emends this to "*deterministisch-ethisch*." But whatever determinism is present here is self-determinism. This sharply differentiates it from the Community Rule, which does indeed suggest that mankind is divided into good and bad by the prevenient will of its creator. Both passages, however, are embedded in contexts that appear to contradict them. The varied instructions that constitute the bulk of the Community Rule imply the possibility of free, that is undetermined, human decisions. As for the fourth Gospel, the good are generally distinguished from the bad not by their earlier moral choices but by their response to the message of Jesus. To argue, as Becker does, that 3,19-21 is representative of one particular stage of the Johannine Community's dualistic thinking is, according to me, to build a rather tall theory on a very narrow base.

[544] On the relationship of Word and Spirit see I. de la Potterie, "Parole et Esprit dans S. Jean," in: de Jonge, *L'Évangile de Jean*, 177-201.

(cf. 1,4-8 and 3,19-21) – already familiar to the reader – the author presents the importance of decision: a commitment to belief or unbelief, which leads to life or death (3,18). Neither God nor the Son acts as judge. To refuse to believe brings self-condemnation, shown in evil deeds and the presence of the darkness (3,18-19). It depends on the refusal or acceptance *now* of the believer[545] faced with the revelation of God in the Son.

As the reader approaches the conclusion of Jesus' discourse, he/she becomes conscious that one cannot be indifferent. Yet the reader is told that the decisions will be made as a result of a long-standing preparedness to accept the revelation of God (3,20-21). The reader is made to understand that the doing of evil or the doing of good is not the *result* of living in the light. One does evil, because one loves the darkness more and, therefore, chooses it hiding one's own ambiguity in the darkness (3,20). In a parallel fashion, he/she knows that good deeds lead to one's coming to the light. It is not as if one lives in the light and simply continues in the blessedness of such an existence. Living in the light involves a continual doing of good deeds to become more deeply a part of the light, and indeed a part of the ongoing revelation of that light.

The author is directing the narrative to the reader, moving from one example of response to the word of Jesus in Israel (2,13-22) to another (3,1-21).[546] The character of Nicodemus is used as a foil to make Jesus speak to a wider audience. The discourse of Jesus in 3,11-21 is clearly intended for all future readers of the Gospel. Nicodemus, however, with all his social status and religious learning is held captive in the Laws of his tradition. He has to rise above these earthly bindings and become open to the heavenly realities (cf. 3,12). His present situation is depicted to be one of living in darkness as long as he treasured his social status, and feared his fellow Pharisees to commit himself to Jesus and confess his faith in him openly. The recommendation of Jesus is to come to light (cf. 3,19-21).

This section of the Gospel (3,11-21) has been called 'the Johannine Kerygma,'[547] because it depends on the themes provided for the reader already in the prologue and summarises themes that will be developed at a later stage in the narrative: the love of God in the gift of the Son, the judgement which the presence of Jesus brings, and the themes of light and darkness. The reader has been solidly instructed in the story of Nicodemus on the uniqueness of the revelation that Jesus brings and the consequences of accepting or rejecting it.

4. Christological Argumentation of 2,23-3,21

While analysing the narrative and literary structure of the text I observed the chiastic structure:

A   2,23-3,2

B   3,3-10

A[1]   3,11-21

---

[545] The realised eschatology of the fourth Gospel stresses the importance of the response of the believer, not the sovereign action of God. See Blank, *Krisis*, 41-52 and 91-108.

[546] The further reading of the story will eventually reveal to the reader that Nicodemus will make his own journey into faith (cf. 19,38-42). Moloney (*Belief in the Word*, 120) contends that the figure of Nicodemus is used by the fourth evangelist as an example, for the reader, of *partial faith*.

[547] Blank, *Krisis*, 53; see also Neyrey, "John III – A Debate," 124-26.

The central element (3,3-9) of the chiasm serves as the pivot of the structure making the passage flow from one element to the other in the narration of the story. At first sight, it seems rather difficult to perceive the argumentative coherence between the central element and the elements at its both ends. In order to interpret the encounter of Nicodemus one must understand the network of relations among the three elements of the episode itself.

In order to understand this network I have to establish clearly which concept of an element is linked with that of another. It is true that all the concepts of an element are not connected with all the concepts of another element in the literary structure. Within the structure of the episode, there is a central concept that forms the heart, and the secondary concepts which serve to expose this central idea or develop and explain one or the other aspect of it. Let me now determine the central concept of each of the three elements and explain their relation to one another.

In the first element (2,23-3,2) the narrative and structural analysis brought to evidence the theme of 'faith based on seeing the signs' performed by Jesus as the central concept. More precisely, the confession of Nicodemus in 3,2 constitutes the narrative outcome of the whole of the introductory narrative. In the second element (3,3-10) – the dialogue between Jesus and Niocdemus – the central concept lies in the statement of Jesus in 3,3. The question of Niocdemus in 3,4 and the development in 3,5-8 serve only to understand better the initial statement of Jesus. The entire weight of the narrative in the third element – the discourse of Jesus – rests on the central element (3,14-18) of the chiasm:

$$\alpha \quad 3,11\text{-}13$$
$$\beta \quad 3,14\text{-}18$$
$$\alpha^{1} \quad 3,19\text{-}21$$

The two outer elements depend on the central element in the sense that they expose the vital importance of accepting the testimony of Jesus. While the first element shows that one should accept the testimony as it comes from the unique and competent witness regarding heavenly things, the third element states the judgement the refusal of such a testimony brings.

One can, thus, observe at the structural level, a relation between the inadequate confession of Nicodemus, *viz.*, "Teacher who has come from God" (3,2), and the testimony of Jesus about his true origin and identity (Son of Man and Son of God; cf. 3,14-18). At the narrative level, there is a link, first of all, between the confession of Nicodemus in 3,2 and the statement of Jesus about being begotten ἄνωθεν (3,3.5); secondly, between the statement of Jesus (3,3.5) and the content of his testimony (3,14-18).

Let me now analyse the three elements of the episode from the points of view of the network among them and of the logical narrative progression and argumentation. While the structural analysis helps to discern the relational scheme and brings forward the global sense of the text contained in the simple correspondence of the units, the narrative analysis exposes the logical argumentation of the story in moving smoothly from one element to another.

i. The Narrative Link Between 3,2 and 3,14-18

The link between the introductory narrative (2,23-3,2) and the testimony in 3,14-18 is clear enough and many scholars observe that the inadequate faith in the name of Jesus (2,23), of which the traditional Messianic confession of Nicodemus (3,2) is an example, is then corrected in 3,14-18 by true faith in the Son of Man and in the only Son of God.[548] Such an observation does not, however, expose the entire relation between the two elements (A – A^1) of the chiastic structure of the episode.

♦ Σημεῖον

In order to understand the full significance of the correlation, intended by the evangelist, between the confession of Nicodemus (3,2) and the testimony of Jesus (3,14-18), one must have recourse to the theme of σημεῖον.[549] As I have mentioned already, Nicodemus holds on to a traditional interpretation of the signs operated by Jesus and sees in him the presence of God. Such a presence, makes him conclude that Jesus must be a 'God-sent teacher' (διδάσκαλος) like Moses or a prophet, which however, is inadequate because it does not correspond to the true identity of Jesus as exposed in his testimony in 3,14-18.

But σημεῖον evokes faith in those who see as it authenticates the divine mission of Jesus and reveals his glory (cf. 2,11 and 11,4.40).[550] The problem rests in the fact that the witness of a sign can remain at the superficial level of mere wondering (cf. 2,23; 4,48 and 6,2.26) or come to a simple conclusion of seeing in Jesus a prophet (cf. 3,2 and 6,14). That is what Nicodemus does in deducing from the sign the presence of God in Jesus,[551] one comparable to what the prophets were privileged to enjoy. Moreover, it is only through a perception of the glory – hidden in a sign – that one comes to the recognition of the Son of God in Jesus as is exposed in 3,16-18. If Nicodemus had perceived such a revelation of glory, he would have interpreted the presence of God in Jesus not in terms of the one possessed by the prophets – as he did – but would have recognised the deeper relation between Jesus and God.

On the other hand, Nicodemus cannot be blamed for his inadequate faith. Signs reveal only imperfectly the glory of Jesus as the Son sent by God. This explains the fact that signs are indications of a perfect and definitive sign, *viz.*, the elevation of the Son of

---

[548] See Moloney, *Son of Man*, 52-53.67; de la Potterie, "Naître de l'eau," 48; Schnackenburg, *op. cit.*, 357-58; Maneschg, 401; F. Porsch, *Pneuma und Wort: Ein exegetischer Beitrag zur Pneumatologie des Johannesevangeliums* (FTS 16) (Frankfurt 1974) 113; and de Jonge, *Stranger from Heaven*, 38 and 145.

[549] Many scholars have studied the notion of 'sign' in the fourth Gospel. Some of them are: M. M. Thompson "Signs and Faith in the Fourth Gospel," *BBR* 1 (1991) 89-108; Bittner, *Jesu Zeichen*; L. Morris, "The Relation of the Signs and the Discourses in John," in: W. C. Weinrich (ed.), *The New Testament Age. Essays in Honor of Bo Reicke* (Macon 1984) II, 363-72; R. F. Collins, "Cana (Jn. 2,1-12)," 99-142; Nicol, *Semeia in the Fourth Gospel*; S. Hofbeck, *Semeion. Der Begriff des 'Zeichen' im Johannesevangelium unter Berücksichtigung seiner Vorgeschichte* (MüSt 3) (Münsterschwarzach 1970); D. Guthrie, "Importance of Signs in the Fourth Gospel," *VoxEv* 5 (1967) 72-83; P. Riga, "Signs of Glory. The Use of 'sêmeion' in St. John's Gospel," *Interp.* 17 (1963) 402-24; L. Cerfaux, "Les miracles, signes messianiques de Jésus et œvres de Dieu selon l'Évangile de S. Jean," in: his *L'attente du Messie*, 131-38; and J.-P. Charlier, "La notion de signe (sêmeion) dans le quatrième évangile," *RSPhTh* 43 (1959) 434-48.

[550] See L. L. Johns and D. B. Miller, "The Signs as Witnesses in the Fourth Gospel: Re-examining the Evidence," *CBQ* 56 (1994) 519-35.

[551] Signs are manifestations of the power of the Father active in the Son. For the fourth evangelist, the Father dwells in Jesus and accomplishes His work of salvation.

Man (comp. 2,18-22 and 3,14-15). The moment of his elevation is also the hour of his glorification (cf. 12,23.32), and it is precisely at that moment the true identity of Jesus as the Son sent by God as well as his constant union with the Father (cf. 8,28-29) will be definitively revealed. As partial revealers of the glory of the envoy, the signs only anticipate the perfect glorification of the Son of Man on the cross, sign of the Son's return to his eternal glory with the Father. Those who, like the disciples, perceive the glory behind the sign, can take the step to believe in Jesus and follow him (cf. 2,11) till the final and definitive confirmation of his identity and of his union with the Father at his elevation on the cross (cf. 8,28 and 19,35-37).

But Nicodemus did not perceive the real glory of Jesus behind the signs he performed. He could not come out of the clutches of his traditional thinking. What seems to indicate a formal certitude (cf. οἴδαμεν – 3,2) about the identity of Jesus is, in fact, only a manifestation of his ignorance (cf. οὐ γινώσκεις – 3,10). It is the incapability of Nicodemus to perceive the real meaning of the signs that has made it necessary for Jesus to authenticate his testimony (cf. 3,11-13) and to expose the perfect sign (3,14-15). Moreover, the confession of Nicodemus in 3,2 is corrected by Jesus in 3,16-18. If Nicodemus wants a sign attesting the true identity of Jesus, he must await the perfect and definitive sign, *viz.*, the elevation of the Son of Man. All the other signs are partial revelations of the glory of Jesus and the Father with him. These signs serve only to anticipate the definitive sign which will attest the return of Jesus into his eternal glory with the Father, in which the perfect union between the sent-Son and the sender-Father is clearly manifested.

But this announced sign will be realised only in the future. It is in the present encounter that Nicodemus is confronted with the revelation of Jesus, not as a prophet, but as the plenipotentiary Son of God, sent by the Father for the salvation of the world (3,16-18). Nicodemus must make a choice between his certitude (3,2) based on his traditional interpretation of the Scriptures, a tradition going back to Moses (cf. 9,28-29), and the certitude of Jesus (3,11), which presents him also as an interpreter of the Scriptures (cf. the typological reading of 3,14-15). But the authority of such an interpretation is not recognised by the Jews (cf. 7,15.47-49 and 9,29). Although Nicodemus recognises Jesus as a teacher come from God, he does not attribute to Jesus more authority than that of his own as a teacher of Israel. He sees in Jesus a prophetic teacher and comes to verify his knowledge in a discussion. With this background he thinks that Jesus can inspire with a new teaching, but never replace that of Moses; hence, it must rather be evaluated in relation to that of Moses.[552] For Nicodemus, the discussion can only be a simple conflict of interpretations.

It is in this perspective that 3,11-13 are inserted. Even if the perfect sign is still to be announced (3,14-15), Nicodemus must immediately believe in the words of Jesus who identifies himself as the eschatological Son sent by the Father (3,16-18), because his words are not a simple interpretation of a teacher, but true revelation of heavenly things (3,11-12). The word of Jesus are not those of a mere inspired teacher but surpasse even those of Moses, for no one has ascended into heaven to learn the heavenly secrets, not even Moses. The only one who could speak of heavenly things with authority is the one come down

---

[552] Tsuchido, 99.

from heaven, the Son of Man (3,12-13). He alone can testify to what he has seen and heard (3,11). True source of knowledge is not the Mosaic tradition (comp. 3,2 with 3,10) but the revelation of Jesus, the unique witness of heavenly things. Since Nicodemus has not penetrated the true meaning of signs (3,2), he must believe in the envoy (3,16-18) while awaiting the definitive authentication through the sign of the elevation of the Son of Man. For the moment, Nicodemus must believe Jesus on account of his words as the Son of Man and unique revealer competent to speak of heavenly things. If Nicodemus remains on the side of the Jews and refuse the testimony of Jesus (cf. 3,11f-12b), there is no chance of believing in Jesus after seeing the definitive sign (cf. 3,12cd).

Now, the testimony of Jesus in the element 3,14-18 is divided into two parts (3,14-15 and 3,16-18) and is connected by the conjunction 'γὰρ' (3,16a). In my opinion, 3,14-18 not only announce the double-Christological scheme of the fourth Gospel, but also indicate the argumentative function of the scheme of the Son of Man (3,14-15) in relation to that of the 'Son-sent' (3,16-18). That is how the meaning of the conjunction 'γὰρ' is to be understood.

The elevation of the Son of Man is the sign which helps to understand Jesus definitively as the Son of God (cf. 8,28), and it is faith in this Son of God which brings eternal life. (3,16-18; cf. 6,40.57 and 17,3). It is therefore that Jesus could say that the Son of Man must be elevated "that whoever believes in him may have eternal life" (3,15). Obtaining eternal life – produced by the elevation of the Son of Man – is, then, interpreted by the scheme of the Son-sent. The soteriological aspect common to both schemes is developed in the rest of the Gospel. 'When the Son of Man is lifted up into heaven, he will draw all those who believe to himself' (12,32). Once the two schemes are superimposed, the spatial soteriology is re-interpreted in relational terms: to be in the heavenly kingdom of the Son of Man is to participate in the life of communion of the Father and the Son. Moreover, it is faith in the Son-sent that makes one enter into the communion of life with God; and it is the elevation of the Son of Man which creates the access to a definitive faith in the Son-sent. In my opinion, therefore, the Christological scheme of the Son of Man is directed to the parallel Christological scheme of the Son-sent, which is clearly the function of the conjunction 'γὰρ' in 3,16a.

ii. The Narrative Flow from One Element to the Other in A – B – A¹

What comes out clearly from the exposition of the structural link between A and A¹, which transcends the narrative flow and argumentation of the story is that Nicodemus and his colleagues must move from the inadequate faith based on signs to a true faith based on the perfect sign. It is the definitive sign of elevation of the Son of Man that gives true meaning to the signs performed by Jesus; they are anticipated revelations of the eternal glory of the Son-sent; this glory will be fully revealed at the elevation/glorification of the Son of Man. But if one neither believes his words nor the definitive sign he/she will be condemned by his/her own choice (3,19-21). In this perspective, the unit of my study appears to be a catechesis of the evangelist on true faith and the salvation that flows from it.

From the narrative point of view, this movement from A to A¹ is not evident. In fact, it flows argumentatively through the central element (B) containing the dialogue between Jesus and Nicodemus. The element A¹ answers why Nicodemus should correct his faith in Jesus. It is to obtain salvation that he should believe in Jesus. This soteriological aspect appears repeatedly in 3,16-18, but is totally absent in the first element (A). If the mission of the Son consists in bringing salvation to the world, and if one must absolutely believe in the Son to be saved, Nicodemus must correct his conception of faith if he wants to attain the salvation offered by Jesus. It is precisely this theme of salvation that demonstrates the narrative flow of the story from element A to A^1.

At first glance one does not recognise a direct link between the Christological confession of Nicodemus in 3,2 and the soteriological statement of Jesus in 3,3. Scholars have tried to explain this semantic gap differently. Some are of the opinion that the affirmation of Nicodemus in 3,2 implicitly contains a question about attaining salvation to which Jesus answers in 3,3.[553] These scholars generally refer to the question of the rich young man in Mt. 19,16f.; Mk. 10,17f., and Lk. 18,18f. and contend that Jesus understands Nicodemus as being moved by the question which preoccupied all Jews (*viz.*, 'how one could attain salvation') and uses the Synoptic expression 'entering into the kingdom of God.' This view, in my opinion, seems to be too simplistic to be true. Even granted that the fourth evangelist has been inspired by the Synoptic tradition, it is difficult, however, to explain why he has completely avoided any trace of salvation in the first affirmation of Nicodemus.

Some other scholars see that Nicodemus' first intervention is not concerned about attaining salvation but is dealing with a confession of faith in Jesus as a prophetic teacher enjoying divine authority visible in the signs he performs. They read in the soteriological statement of 3,3 a Christological affirmation: the kingdom of God is present in Jesus and is even identical with his person.[554] These scholars, therefore, observe an equivalence between the expressions, 'seeing/entering the kingdom of God' and 'believing in Jesus.'[555] In this perspective, they see an evident argumentative, narrative and thematic flow from 3,2 to 3,3ff.[556] Interpreted this way, one may say that Nicodemus makes an inadequate confession of faith in Jesus; and Jesus tells that Nicodemus cannot attain true faith, *viz.*, true knowledge about the identity of his person, unless he is begotten ἄνωθεν.

Although such an interpretation of 3,3 facilitates an harmonious sequence with 3,2, it does not do justice to the evangelist's text. In fact, 3,3 is a soteriological affirmation of Jesus. Although the expression 'kingdom of God' could be from a tradition prior to that of the fourth evangelist, I notice an equivalent of it in the unit of my study, which definitely belongs to the fourth evangelist, *viz.*, 'seeing life' (3,36d) which is synonymous with 'having eternal life' (3,36b) and parallel to 'seeing the kingdom of God' (3,3c), on condition that one 'believes in the Son' (3,36a) which is parallel to 'being begotten ἄνωθεν' (3,3d). Seen from this perspective, true faith in Jesus must, rather, be linked to 'being begotten ἄνωθεν' (3,3d) than 'seeing the kingdom of God' (3,3c). I shall come back to this theme when the narrative and thematic flow from element 'B' to element 'A^1' will

---

[553] E.g. R. E. Brown, *op. cit.*, 138; Schnackenburg, *op. cit.*, 366; and Lindars, *Gospel*, 150.

[554] See the recent detailed study of W. R. Herzog II, *Jesus, Justice, and the Reign of God: A Ministry of Liberation* (Louisville 1999).

[555] See Traets, 128-30; and de la Potterie, "Jesus et Nicodemus," 198-200.

[556] Cf. de Jonge, *Stranger from Heaven*, 38-39; and M. Michel, 227-36.

be demonstrated. For the moment it is sufficient to note that 3,3 contains a soteriological statement posing the condition to attain salvation.

I have pointed out in the structural analysis that the link between A and A^1 rests on the movement from inadequate confession of faith based on signs (2,23-3,2) to true identity of Jesus (3,16-18) based on the definitive sign of the elevation of the Son of Man (3,11-15). Now, the narrative argumentative flow from 3,2 to 3,3 must, also, be based on this underlying theme of sign in the dialogue (3,3-10). The coherence of the narrative from its movement from 3,2 to 3,3 depends on the relation between signs, faith and salvation.

Based on the OT juridical notion of sign (Cf. Ex. 3,12 and 4,27-31; Jud. 6,17; and 1 Sam. 10,2.7),[557] Nicodemus recognises in Jesus a simple prophetic type teacher. For the fourth evangelist, signs have not only a juridical function, but have, above all, a symbolic function, *viz.*, they reveal the salvation operated by the action of the Son-sent. In other words, signs are symbolic manifestations of the salvation offered by God and realised in the person of his Son-sent. The Cana miracle of wine, the multiplication of loaves, the physical healing, life restored, etc. are such symbolic expressions of the eschatological salvation that the Son embodies in himself. In fact, he himself is the bread of life (6,35. 48), the light of the world (8,12 and 9,5), the resurrection and the life (11,25), the way, the truth and the life (14,6). As visible revelations of the salvific power of God being at work in the mission of Jesus, the signs reveal the perfect union of Jesus with his Father and lead to the recognition of him as the plenipotentiary Son-sent. In this sense, signs are not mere authentication of the divine origin of the mission of the Son, but true revelations of salvation present in the person of the Son-sent. Such manifestations of the glory of the Son-sent are meant to lead to the recognition, in faith, of Jesus to attain salvation.

Moreover, the signs being symbolic anticipations of the perfect sign,[558] cannot but lead to true faith; that is, signs effect fully and immediately what they symbolise. The final and perfect glorification of the Son-sent is the moment when he will definitively accomplish his mission, that is, when he will give the full salvation concentrated in his person, as salvation is attaining union with him and the Father. However, this salvific event itself takes the form of a sign – the lifting up of the Son of Man on the cross is the sign of his being lifted up into heaven, from where he draws all to himself. Consequently, the death of the envoy itself is a sign of his return to the Sender. Once returned to his Father, to his glory, he can offer to all the possibility of participating in that union and glory. It is in this perspective that the condition of faith as being necessary for salvation is to be understood. In fact, as salvation is offered in the form of a sign and the reality it signifies is accessible only through faith, one must necessarily have faith to attain this salvation. Hence, for the fourth evangelist authentic faith and salvation are not possible without the acceptance in faith of the perfect sign of the lifting of the Son of Man.

The argumentation making Nicodemus move from the signs seen (3,2f) to the perfect sign (3,14-15) through the interposed theme of attaining salvation (3,3) is, therefore, perfectly logical. For the fourth evangelist, the question of salvation leads necessarily to the lifting up of the Son of Man, which, as sign, not only accomplishes salvation but also demonstrates the true identity of Jesus. The need of attaining salvation

---

[557] Cf. Cerfaux, 43.

[558] See Maneschg, 425.

serves as the necessary medium in leading Nicodemus from the signs (3,2f) to the perfect sign (3,14-15), and consequently from imperfect faith (3,2) to perfect faith (3,16-18).

Coming to the argumentative narrative flow from the element 'B' to 'A¹', I see that one soteriological statement (3,3) leads to another (3,14-15). Both statements argue in a similar fashion:

Goal/Purpose	Necessary Condition
3,3.5 Seeing/entering the kingdom of God	Being begotten ἄνωθεν of the believer
3,14-15 Having eternal life	Lifting up of the Son of Man and faith of the believer

In both cases the goal is attaining salvation, though expressed in different terms. But in the conditions for reaching the goal of salvation there is a difference between the two. Whereas in 3,3 it seems to depend exclusively on the believer who wishes to attain salvation, in 3,14-15 it depends, basically, on an event totally independent of the believer – 'the Son of Man must be lifted up.' Once this external condition is fulfilled the condition for the believer to attain salvation is posed, *viz.*, he must 'believe in him.' To understand the progressive narrative movement from 3,3 to 3,14-15, it is necessary to demonstrate the relation of 'begetting ἄνωθεν' to faith, on the one hand, and that of 'begetting ἄνωθεν' to 'the lifting up of the Son of Man' on the other.

Although being begotten ἄνωθεν and faith seem to be closely related as conditions for attaining salvation, their mutual rapport is not evident. It is not clear whether faith presupposes being begotten ἄνωθεν or vice versa. Many scholars opt for the first solution.[559] The one who is begotten ἄνωθεν receives true faith and can then recognise in Jesus the Son of God. In this perspective, the salvific process is accomplished in the following manner: begetting ἄνωθεν/of water and Spirit – access to faith – attainment of salvation.

Such a view raises the problem of predestination. In fact, faith does not proceed from a free decision of the person but needs being begotten ἄνωθεν. Thus, only those whom God freely chooses to be begotten ἄνωθεν would have access to faith. This view seems to contradict the universal salvific will of God expressed in 3,16-18. The whole κόσμος is called to participate in the salvation offered by God; only those who refuse to believe in the Son will be condemned.

In my opinion, it is faith that enables being begetting ἄνωθεν. This has been clearly stated already in the prologue (1,12-13):

But to all who *received* him,   -   he gave power to become *children of God*,

(to those) who *believed* in his name, -   who were *born*, not of blood or of the will of the flesh or of the will of man, but *of God...*

---

[559] E.g. Bergmeier, *Glaube als Gabe*, 219; de la Potterie, "Naître de l'eau," 433; Vanhoye, "Notre foi," 337-54; and de Jonge, *Stranger from Heaven*, 38-39. Porsch (*Pneuma und Wort*, 125) identifies being begotten ἄνωθεν with the beginning of faith: "die Geburt von oben...die Geburt zum Glauben wie die Geburt des Glaubens."

It is evident that there is a synonymy to be observed between 'all who received him (λόγος)' and 'who believed in his name,' just as 'become children of God' is synonymous with 'born. ...of God.' 'Receiving the λόγος' evidently precedes 'becoming children of God,' and 'believing' precedes being 'born of God.' Moreover, the believers are those who first receive the revelatory word of Jesus which then leads to being 'born of God.' In other words, the one who begins to believe by receiving the word of Jesus must make his/her way to the cross where he/she will make his definitive choice. He/she who looks at the Son of Man lifted up, receives the Spirit who begets him/her ἄνωθεν and leads him/her to the full truth in the Son-sent.

In the narrative structure of the fourth Gospel, the precedence of faith in relation to being begotten ἄνωθεν is clearly visible. For example, in 2,11 the disciples are said to believe in Jesus after seeing the glory revealed by him. However, the disciples, at that initial moment of access to faith, had not yet been begotten by the Spirit as the Spirit would be given only after the glorification of Jesus (cf. 7,39) on the cross. Theologically, however, access to faith does not depend on being human; on the contrary, it is God who takes the initiative. It is in this sense Jesus says: "No one can come to me unless drawn by the Father who sent me....Everyone who has heard and learned from the Father comes to me" (6,44-45). It is, therefore, to be admitted that God acts in one even before he/she is begotten by the Spirit. I, therefore, notice the following process in sequence: the Father draws one to Jesus which leads to an initial access to faith or coming to Jesus; Then the begetting by the Spirit takes place through the lifting up of the Son of Man which gives true faith that leads to salvation or seeing/entering the kingdom of God.[560] This sequence is also confirmed by the words of Jesus in 17,14: "I have given them your word, and the world has hated them, because they do not belong to the world, just as I do not belong to the world." The disciples who have received the gift of the word of Jesus are hated by the world as they do not belong to the world like Jesus. Hence, receiving the gift of the word means not belonging to the world, but being begotten from above – the same perspective as in 1,12-13.

This leads to the soteriological aspect attached to the Christological scheme of the Son of Man. I observe here the spatial-vertical Christological plan (↑) of the evangelist. To be drawn into the world above (↑), like the Son of Man, the believer must belong to the world above, which takes place in being begotten ἄνωθεν by the Spirit. Such a begetting is inserted between faith (initial reception of the word) and access to salvation (seeing/ entering the kingdom of God ↑).

Thus, the logic behind the narrative is to lead Nicodemus to the perfect sign of the lifting up of the Son of Man which enables the begetting and leads to salvation. But in the argumentative plan the order of the different stages is inverted. In order to attain salvation (see/enter the kingdom of God) the first condition posed is the begetting ἄνωθεν. Once this condition is established (cf. 3,3-8), the argument of the lifting up of the Son of Man is

---

[560] It is to be recognised that true faith in Jesus, the Son sent by the Father, cannot be attained without being begotten ἄνωθεν by the Spirit. In my opinion, a chronological distinction may not be exact; true faith and being begotten ἄνωθεν are two aspects of the same event (see also Porsch, *Pneuma und Wort*, 111). In the narrative sequence, however, being begotten is preceded by an initial access to faith – expressed often in terms of 'coming to Jesus,' 'receiving the word' and so on. The argumentation of the Nicodemus must be placed in such a narrative sequence.

brought in as an answer to the question of Nicodemus about the 'how' of this begetting (3,9): only after the elevation of the Son of Man could he give the Spirit which enables the mysterious begetting ἄνωθεν and gives access, through true faith, to salvation/eternal life.

At the level of the narrative sequence, Jesus opens the dialogue posing 'being begotten ἄνωθεν' as a condition for salvation. But the traditional understanding of Nicodemus considers 'being a descendent of Abraham' (physical and nationalistic) as a condition for salvation. He does not understand that the kingdom of God – that Jesus refers to – is not of this world (cf. 18,36). This false understanding of Nicodemus necessitates Jesus to correct not his misunderstanding but also to correct his notion of salvation. This necessitates the discourse of Jesus (3,11-21).

If the response of Jesus comprised of 3,16-21 alone, it would have been incomplete. In fact, between the doublets being begotten ἄνωθεν–salvation of 3,3.5, and faith–salvation of 3,16-18 there is a missing link. Without this link Nicodemus will not be able to know how he could attain this true faith and how the Spirit that enables being begotten ἄνωθεν can be given and received.

3,11-15 fulfils the function of bridging the gap and establishes a close relationship between faith and begetting ἄνωθεν by the Spirit. On the one hand, faith in the Son-sent, which leads to eternal life, could be attained only with the help of the sign of the lifting up of the Son of Man – sign that definitively attests the identity of Jesus as the Son-sent (cf. 8,24.28-29). There is a 'cause and effect relation' between the sign of the lifting up of the Son of Man and faith in the Son-sent. This relation is literarily supported, on the one hand, by the recurrence of the expression 'have eternal life' in 3,15 and 3,16, and, on the other hand, by the recurrence of 'whoever believes in him' and the causal conjunction 'γὰρ ' (3,16a) connecting 3,14-15 with 3,16ff. In short, in order to have eternal life, one must believe in the Son-sent; and true belief can be attained only in looking at the Son of Man lifted up.

Moreover, it is precisely at the time of the lifting up that the Son of Man gives the Spirit (comp. 7,38-39 with 19,30.34) to those who have been drawn to the cross (cf. 6,44 and 12,32). It is at that moment that the disciples can see the Son of Man lifted up (cf. 19,35-37) and believe in the Son-sent. Again, it is at that moment the Spirit founds the new community of believers enabling them to share in the origin of Jesus (cf. 19,26-28). Thereafter, the disciples are no more of this world just as Jesus is (cf. 17,14.16). Once their mission on earth is accomplished (cf. 17,11.18 and 20,21.23), they will follow Jesus to the Father into his heavenly kingdom (cf. 17,24; 3,3b.5b; 8,21.24 and 12,26.32), because by their being begotten ἄνωθεν of the Spirit (cf. 1,12-13; 3,3.5; 8,23.24; 12,36 and 19,26-27) they belong to the world above.

The testimony of Jesus in 3,14-18 contains, therefore, all the elements of an answer to the question of Nicodemus in 3,9. The pivotal argument rests in the announcement of the sign of the lifting up of the Son of Man. If Nicodemus was to attain salvation he must follow Jesus till the cross, lifted up from where, he will give the Spirit that would enable his being begotten ἄνωθεν. It is at that moment that Nicodemus can see the Son of Man ascending into heaven and the Son-sent returning to his Father.[561]

---

[561] See J. Becker, "Joh 3,1-21 als Reflex johanneischer Schuldiskussion," in: H. Balz and S. Schulz (eds.), *Das Wort und die Wörter. FS Gerhard Friedrich* (Stuttgart 1973) 85-95; and Gaeta, 91-92.

Each of the Christological schemes generate a particular aspect of soteriology. In the Christological scheme of the Son of Man, one has to be begotten ἄνωθεν in order to follow Jesus to where he is – heaven (cf. 8,21-30). On the contrary, in the Christological scheme of the Son-sent, one participates in the communion of life which the Father-sender shares with the Son-sent (cf. 6,38-40.48-51.56-58). It is in the superimposition of the two Christological schemes on the unique event of the cross that the two soteriological perspectives are finally merged. Thus, Jesus tells his disciples that 'in his Father's house there are many dwelling places; he goes to the Father to prepare a place and will return to take them where he is' (cf. 14,1-3). On the other hand, 'Jesus himself is the way, the truth and the life; it is only through him that one reaches the Father, because to know him is to know the Father, and to see him is to see the Father' (cf. 14,4-10). In these texts, salvation is presented, on the one hand, as 'entering the Father's house,' and, on the other hand, as participation in the union of the Father and the Son. In the Nicodemus episode, I find the same superimposition of the two Christological schemes (in the sign of the cross) which lead to the understanding of salvation as a movement, *viz.*, 'entering into the kingdom of God' (3,3.5), and as 'having eternal life' (3,15.16); that is, participation in the life of the Father and the Son.

Conclusion

To conclude my analysis of 3,19-21, let me now try to recall my argumentative conclusions on the structural scheme of the whole of 3,11-21. As demonstrated already, 3,19-21 paraphrase 3,16-18; and the theme of judgement that these verses bring out help clarify 3,11-13. I can, thus, observe a structural rapport between 3,11-13 and 3,19-21. I have pointed out that 3,11-13 lay the foundation for the validity of the witness of Jesus on the 'heavenly things.' Jesus is the only credible and authoritative witness to the heavenly things, because he is the Son of Man come down from heaven; no one else has had access to heaven; he is the only eye-witness of the divine realities on salvation. But one does not receive his testimony, because one *does not believe* when he speaks of the heavenly things.

These verses are essential to understand the salvation/eschatological judgement expressed in 3,19-21. In fact, the notion of light was applied to the Law of Moses in the Jewish religion. The Jews had, therefore, seen this 'light come into the world' (revelation of the Law) for their salvation. In order to eliminate the idea of obtaining eschatological salvation through means other than the true light/Jesus, the evangelist demonstrates in 3,11-13 that the coming of Jesus into the world has a definitive impact on salvation; that is, the authentic revelation of the heavenly things can come only from the Son of Man descended from heaven and not from Moses (Law). Because Jesus is the Son of Man come down from heaven, his words are decisive for *salvation*, and rejecting them is condemning oneself and excluding oneself from salvation; this is the judgement (3,19a). To establish the validity of revelation, the evangelist speaks of the Son of Man and of his heavenly origin; and to refer to the effective communication of this revelation to the people during the earthly mission of Jesus, the evangelist speaks of the Son as μονογενής, as the one *sent* by the Father (3,16) and as the light come into the world (3,19).

B. Literary and Narrative Analysis of 3,22-36

In 3,3-21 Jesus fulfilled prophecies of a 'water and spirit' regeneration, and proved his death to be the ultimate anti-type of the bronze serpent 'lifted up' in the desert. In 3,22-36 he surpasses the Baptist and any baptism or rite of purification he may represent. In my opinion, at least three reasons stand against the view that the juxtaposition of the ἄνωθεν birth story (3,1-21) and the following episode (3,22-36) – the second or the final testimony of the Baptist with its mention of baptism – is a solid evidence that the fourth evangelist understood 'being begotten of water and Spirit' (3,5d) as referring to baptism. First of all, the most natural reading of 'being begotten of water and Spirit' lies elsewhere. Secondly, not baptism but Christology and soteriology are the major themes of both episodes. Baptism is mentioned, in so far as it is associated with the old covenant purification rites (cf. 3,25). Thirdly, if 3,22-36 pictures Jesus as baptising more people than the Baptist, the focus of interest is not on the nature of their baptisms, but on the relative and passing stature of the Baptist compared to that of Jesus who has come from above, because the evangelist, by a parenthetical note in 4,2, will shortly distance Jesus from the actual act of baptising.

The literary analysis of this second episode (3,22-36) does not offer the same results as that of the preceding parallel episode (2,23-3,21). In spite of parallel themes, which I shall demonstrate later in detail at the end of this chapter, there is a break from the preceding scene of Nicodemus. This is marked by an expression often used in the fourth Gospel to indicate a new stage in the narrative: Μετὰ ταῦτα (3,22a). At first sight, the introductory segment (3,22-26) *seems* to remain isolated from the following two segments (3,27-30 and 3,31-36) as far as their vocabulary is concerned. Only the verb 'μαρτυρέω' (3,26.28.32) seems to imply a formal link among all the three segments.

Thematically, there is, however, a common notion between the first two segments, namely the contrast between the two characters – the Baptist and Jesus. It is expressed in their parallel baptismal activities – the dwindling popularity of the Baptist in contrast to Jesus attracting more crowds. The relation of the Baptist to Jesus is then expressed in subordinate terms – all placed on the lips of the Baptist – as the *one sent ahead of the Messiah* (3,28), and as the *friend of the bridegroom* (3,29); and in 3,30 the Baptist expresses the same contrast clearer and stronger in the statement that 'he must *decrease* and Jesus must *increase*.' A more fundamental contrast between the two is evoked in the third segment in the fact that Jesus is 'the one who comes from above' (3,31a.f; cf. 3,13) and who 'is above all' (3,31b.g) while the Baptist is of the earth (3,31cd).

Between the first (3,22-26) and the third (3,31-36) segments, there is an antithetical correspondence between "all are going to him" (3,26g) and "yet no one accepts his testimony" (3,32d), that is, even if all go to Jesus, no one accepts his testimony. This recalls the πολλοὶ who believed in Jesus' name in Jerusalem seeing his signs (2,23), but 'no one' really accepted him, because their faith did not make Jesus trust them (cf. 2,24-25).

Note that the second and the third segments, which contain the testimony of the Baptist couched in the form of an answer to his anxious disciples, are linked formally by the recurrence of the terms: λαμβάνω (3,27.32.33); δίδωμι (3,27.34.35); ἐκ τοῦ οὐρανοῦ (3,27.31); μαρτυρέω/μαρτυρία (3,28.32.33); ἀποστέλλω (3,28.34); and ἀκούω (3,29.32). The synonymous correspondence between 3,27c and 3,35 in the expressions 'given from heaven' and 'the Father gives' is also noteworthy. To say that Jesus cannot receive any disciple unless it is given from heaven is equal to saying that, as Son, Jesus can have only those whom the Father has placed in his hands. The theme of the gift of believers to the Son by the Father is quite frequent in the fourth Gospel (cf. 6,37.39.44.65 and 17,24).

Moreover, the section is full of designations of Jesus. For example, he is designated as the 'bridegroom' (3,29; cf. 2,9 and the betrothal motif in Jn. 4), 'Messiah' (3,28; cf. 1,20.25.41 and 4,25.29), 'Son' (3,36; cf. 3,17), 'the one who comes from above' (3,31a), 'the one who comes from heaven' (3,31f), 'he whom God has sent' (3,34a), one who 'speaks the words of God' (3,34b), 'Son loved by the Father' (3,35a; cf. 3,16ab.18), and 'the one in whose hands all things are placed by the Father' (3,35b).

Finally, it is, perhaps, possible to see in the Baptist the ideal believer in Jesus as 'the bridegroom's friend,' as 'one who stands and hears the bridegroom' (3,29de), 'who rejoices at the bridegroom's voice' (3,29f) as 'one who accepts his testimony' (3,33a) and as 'one who believes in the Son' (3,36a). Moreover, the 'voice of the bridegroom' (3,29a) corresponds to 'the words of God spoken by the one whom God has sent' (3,34ab).

Let me now subject each of the three segments of the second testimony of the Baptist to a thorough narrative and structural analysis from various angles:

1. Literary and Narrative Analysis of 3,22-26

a. Concentric Structure

This segment is organised in the form of a concentric structure a/b/a¹ as shown below:

a   ³,²² After this *Jesus* and **his disciples** went into the <u>Judean countryside,</u> and he spent some time there with them and *baptised*. ²³**John** also *was baptizing* at <u>Aenon near Salim</u> because water was abundant there; and *people kept coming* and were being *baptised*. ²⁴**John**, of course, had not yet been thrown into prison.

b ²⁵ Now a discussion about purification arose between John's disciples and a Jew.

a¹ ²⁶   <u>They</u> (disciples of John) came to **John** and said to him, "Rabbi, *the one who was with you* (Jesus) <u>across the Jordan,</u> *to whom you testified* (Jesus), here *he* (Jesus) *is baptising*, and *all are going to him*.

Thematically, the dyad a-a¹ is evidently formed by the recurrent mention of the baptismal activity of Jesus (3,22c and 26f). The antithesis arises from the transfer of popularity in favour of Jesus: in the element (**a**) people approach (παρεγίνοντο) the Baptist to be baptised while in (**a¹**) it is toward Jesus that they all go (ἔρχονται). One can, perhaps, complete the correspondence of the two elements through the mention of the place where Jesus is and was: in 3,22a Jesus is found in the 'Judean countryside' while in 3,26 there is a reference to a location 'across the Jordan'⁵⁶² where Jesus was with the Baptist earlier (cf. 3,26c). At the centre (**b**) there is the theme of a dispute between the disciples of the Baptist

---

⁵⁶² This recalls "Bethany *across the Jordan* where John was baptising" (1,28). The contention of P. Parker ("Bethany Beyond Jordan," *JBL* 74 [1955] 257-61) translating the adverb 'πέραν' as 'beyond' or 'over against' by comparing 1,28 with 11,1.18 brings difficulties between 3,26 and 10,40. Many commentators are of the opinion that the site must be on the east of Jordan (cf. Barrett, 146; R. E. Brown, *op. cit.*, 44; and Schnackenburg, *op. cit.*, 296).

and a Jew on the subject of purification. I shall prove later that this dispute is not without rapport to the baptismal activities of Jesus and the Baptist in 3,22.26 and 3,23 respectively.

From the point of view of the *characters* involved in this segment, the dyad **a-a**[1] mentions Jesus and the Baptist, each with his disciples, engaged in administering baptism. Of course, the element (**a**[1]) describes Jesus' relationship to the Baptist further in such terms as "the one who was *with you* across the Jordan" (3,26d; cf. 1,28 – this refers, probably, to the time of the baptism of Jesus) and "to whom you testified" (3,26e; cf. 1,29-34). While Jesus and the Baptist are portrayed as being closer to each other, the disciples of the Baptist are portrayed as being anxious about the increasing popularity of Jesus. Besides, in both elements of the dyad, the people/all (3,23c/3,26g) are portrayed as flocking to the Baptist and Jesus respectively. In the central element (**b**) of the concentric structure the main characters, Jesus and the Baptist, are absent as the discussion is about them.

b. Argumentative Narrative Structure

The narrative exposition of the first segment (3,22-26) lays the foundation for the discourse of the Baptist which is presented in the form of a bipartite structure in the subsequent segments (3,27-30 and 3,31-36). In the first segment I observe the following argumentative narrative structure:

3,22-26 Setting of the Scene
3,22   Baptismal activity of Jesus
        22a   Announcement of a new scene (Μετὰ ταῦτα)
        22a   *Movement* (ἦλθεν) of Jesus with his disciples *to the site* of baptism (Judean countryside)
        22b   *Stay* (διέτριβεν) of Jesus with his disciples
        22c   Baptismal *activity* of Jesus (ἐβάπτιζεν)
3,23   Parallel (ἦν δὲ καὶ ὁ Ἰωάννης) baptismal activity of the Baptist
        23a   Baptismal *activity* of the Baptist (βαπτίζων), and the *site* (Aenon near Salim[563])
        23b   *Reason* for the choice of the place (ὅτι) – 'abundance of water there'
        23cd   Reaction of the people: *movement* (παρεγίνοντο) and reception (*activity*) of baptism (ἐβαπτίζοντο)
3,24   Narrator's aside – Justification for the parallel baptismal activities
3,25   Dispute on purification (ζήτησις περὶ καθαρισμοῦ)
3,26   Exposition of the *problem* (πάντες ἔρχονται πρὸς αὐτόν)
        26a   *Movement* (ἦλθον) of the Baptist's disciples toward him
        26b   Speech opening: εἶπαν
        26c   Addressing: Ῥαββι
        26d   Description about Jesus referring to a former *site* (across the Jordan)
        26e   Description about Jesus referring to a former *testimony*

---

[563] For a survey of possible sites see B. Manzano, "Les sources d'Aenon, près de Salim, où Jean baptisait," *TS(F)* 5-6 (1987) 124-30; and R. E. Brown, *op. cit.*, 151. On its Samaritan location see M.-É. Boismard, "Aenon, près de Salem (Jean III,23)," *RB* 80 (1973) 218-22; and J. Murphy-O'Connor, "John the Baptist and Jesus: History and Hypotheses," *NTS* 36 (1990) 363-66. For a symbolic interpretation of the place-name and the scene as a whole see N. Krieger, "Fiktive Orte der Johannes Taufe," *ZNW* 45 (1953/54) 121-23. This is not called for. In my opinion, a Samaritan site for Aenon serves the narrative well. The mention of a Samaritan location is a hint that the focus on Jewish people in Jewish places is coming to an end and opens the way for Jesus' proximate presence in Samaria (cf. 4,4).

(μεμαρτύρηκας) of the Baptist

26f   Baptismal *activity* of Jesus (βαπτίζει)

26g   The actual problem – the *movement* (ἔρχονται) of all toward Jesus

Note that the whole segment (3,22-26) is enclosed by the movement of Jesus with his disciples to the site of baptism (3,22a) and the movement of 'πάντες' toward Jesus – in which the purpose of his movement in 3,22a is fulfilled.

i. Setting of the Scene (3,22-23)

At the narrative level 3,22-23 prepare the setting in presenting the parallel scenes of the baptismal activities of Jesus and the Baptist. The description of the characters, the time, and the place set the scene for the brief narrative that follows. There is no hint in these verses that there is any qualitative difference between the two baptisms. Besides, the verbal forms 'ἐβάπτιζεν' (3,22c) and 'ἐβαπτίζοντο' (3,23d) – both in the imperfect – indicate a repeated action.[564] The verbs 'διέτριβεν' (3,22b) referring to the stay of Jesus for some time at the site of baptism and 'παρεγίνοντο' (3,23c) referring to the continuous coming of the people to the Baptist – both in the imperfect – justify such a prolonged ministry.

ii. Justification for the Parallel Ministry

The parenthetical statement in 3,24 seems to justify the historic possibility of such a parallel ministry.[565] This narrator's aside indicates that the evangelist knew the tradition regarding the imprisonment of the Baptist.[566] It is possible that the fourth evangelist wanted to correct the Synoptic tradition, according to which Jesus had begun his ministry only after the beheading of the Baptist (cf. Mt. 4,12; Mk. 1,14). Even without this narrator's aside (3,24) the narrative continuity of the story seems to flow from 3,23 to 3,25 without any interruption whatsoever. Hence, the fourth evangelist must have had a clear purpose in inserting this historical note against the Synoptic tradition. He seems to take pains to add this apparently unnecessary verse.[567] In my opinion, what is important for the fourth evangelist is not the fact of the parallel baptismal activities or the destiny of the Baptist – transmitted by all the traditions – but that the Baptist be brought into the scene once again to bear witness in favour of Jesus *before* his arrest and death. As I have remarked already, for the fourth evangelist, his interest in the Baptist is primarily theological; the Baptist is essentially a *witness* to Jesus.[568] He is interested in the Baptist only as an historical figure, insofar as he has some bearing on the story of Jesus, as is

---

[564] The form "ἦν...βαπτίζων" (3,23a) could be taken to mean that the Baptist 'remained there and baptised' which corresponds to "διέτριβεν...καὶ ἐβάπτιζεν" (3,22bc). See also R. E. Brown, *op. cit.*

[565] Historically the baptism administered by Jesus would have been parallel to that of the Baptist. See B. Witherington III, "Jesus and the Baptist – Two of a Kind?," in: D. Lull (ed.), *SBL 1988 Seminar Papers* (Atlanta 1988) 225-44.; see also S. Légasse, "Le Baptême administré par Jésus (Jn 3,22-26; 4,1-3) et l'origine du baptême chrétien," *BLE* 78 (1977) 25-29; Murphy-O'Connor, "John the Baptist and Jesus," 367-74; and. X. Léon-Dufour, "'Et là, Jésus baptisait' (Jn 3,22)," in: *Mélanges Eugène Tisserant, Tome I: Écriture Sainte - Ancien Orient* (StT 231) (Vatican 1964) 295-309.

[566] W. Schenk, "Gefangenschaft und Tod des Täufers. Erwägungen zur Chronologie und ihren Konsequenzen," *NTS* 29 (1983) 453-83; Dodd, *Historical Tradition*, 280; Schnackenburg, *op. cit.*, 413; and R. E. Brown, *op. cit.*, 153.

[567] For a discussion see Wilson, 34-41.

[568] Cf. Morris, *Gospel*, 210. For a detailed study see A. Ottilinger, *Vorläufer, Vorbild oder Zeuge? Zum Wandel des Täuferbildes im Johannesevangelium* (ThDiss 45) (St. Ottilien 1991).

shown in the fact that he does not relate what happened to the Baptist after his imprisonment. The Baptist must make a second testimony to substantiate and authenticate juridically the first testimony of Jesus about himself (cf. 3,11-21), because any testiomony has to be authenticated by two witnesses to be juridically binding. Hence, for the fourth evangelist, the arrest of the Baptist could not have preceded this first revelation of Jesus; he, therefore, adds 3,24 in order to make his readers – who were possibly aware of the Synoptic tradition – understand that the Baptist should have made the second testimony before he was thrown into prison.

iii. Ζήτησις περὶ καθαρισμοῦ

After introducing the scene in 3,22-23 and justifying the parallel baptismal activities (3,24), the evangelist brings to the notice of the reader a controversy on the subject of purification (3,25). This verse is placed at the centre of the concentric structure (a/b/a^1), indicating an important element of the story. In the narrative framework, 3,25 furnishes an incident (ζήτησις) that would provoke the movement of the Baptist's disciples toward him in 3,26a, and solicit his response in the rest of the chapter (3,27-36, *viz.*, his second testimony on Jesus). The structural and argumentative perspectives here are remarkably unified. Moreover, from the point of view of the plot development of the story, the controversy raised in 3,25 constitutes the pivot around which the plot moves logically from 3,22-24 to 3,26.[569]

♦ Περὶ καθαρισμοῦ

The ζήτησις of the Baptist's disciples with a Jew,[570] is regarding καθαρισμός.[571] Now, certain questions in the flow of the narrative (3,22-24) remain unanswered: where do the disciples of the Baptist come from suddenly into scene? How do they know that Jesus is baptising in Judea while they are expected to be with their master in Aenon near Salim (Samaria)? And how do they know that 'all are going to Jesus'? In my opinion, the fourth evangelist, in general, does not describe superfluous details which do not contribute to the discussion. Boismard finds an answer to these questions in his interpretation of the Jew, who discusses with the Baptist's disciples, as one who had been to Jesus for baptism, and in the dispute being indirectly about the comparative value of the baptism of Jesus and of the Baptist.[572]

---

[569] The conjunction 'οὖν' (3,25a) indicates a rupture as well as a continuation, simultaneously, of the narrative. F. Blass, R. Debrunner and R. W. Funk (*A Greek Grammar of the New Testament and Other Early Christian Literature* [Chicago 1967] § 451:1) rightly contend that this conjunction should be interpreted loosely as a temporal connective in the continuation or resumption of a narrative.

[570] There is some textual confusion over 'μετὰ Ἰουδαίου' (P^{75} A B K L..). Some manuscripts (P^{66} ℵ Θ f$^{1.13}$...) have 'μετὰ τῶν Ἰουδαίων' which would make excellent sense, but should be rejected precisely because it is the *lectio facilior*. There is also a popular (but unattested) reading of 'μετὰ Ἰησοῦ' which would also make good sense. Schnackenburg (*op. cit.*, 413-14) makes the good suggestion that 'the Jew' may have come from Judea, where Jesus was baptising. In my opinion, this would lead logically into the question of 3,26. The presence of 'the Jew' also retains the narrative focus on the world of Judaism.

[571] Barrett (221) suggests that the discussion, probably, arose from the Baptist's lack of concern in his baptismal ministry to observe the details of Jewish ablutions.

[572] Cf. M.-É. Boismard, "L'ami de l'époux (Jo. III,29)," in: *À la rencontre de Dieu. Mémorial Albert Gelin* (BFCTL 8) (Le Puy 1961) 289.

As such, the term 'καθαρισμός' recalls the Jewish rites of purification prescribed by the Law (cf. 2,6). In the present context καθαρισμός must refer to the purificatory value of baptism.[573] The subject of controversy, therefore, deals with the relative value of the two baptisms in bringing about purification.[574] Besides, the focus on baptism in 3,22-23 and the question posed to the Baptist by his disciples in 3,26 point to baptism. Moreover, comparing the two testimonies of the Baptist, it is interesting to note the connection between the present discussion on purification (3,25) and the function attributed by the Baptist to the Messiah in 1,29.33. I shall demonstrate in Part II that the expressions "who takes away the sin of the world" (1,29) and "who baptises with the Holy Spirit" (1,33) are parallel in meaning. But if the controversy is about baptism, why does the evangelist not employ directly the terms 'περὶ βαπτίσμοῦ'?

The first answer lies in the fact that the dispute is between the disciples of the Baptist and a Jew. For a Jew, though the act of baptising as such, as an exterior sign of conversion, is not a matter of dispute, the purificatory value assigned to it is not free from controversy. The number of rites of purification accompanying the observance of the Law was defended rigorously by the Pharisees (cf. Mk. 7,1-23; and Mt. 15,1-20). Moreover, all that pertains to the Law and the rites of purification was vital for the Jewish religion.

I shall demonstrate in part II that there is perfect correspondence between the two testimonies of the Baptist (1,19-34 and 3,22-36). It is the baptism of the Baptist that provoked the high priests and the Pharisees of Jerusalem to sent a delegation to scrutinise his activities. The fact that the delegation was composed of priests and Levites (cf. 1,19) betrays all the more clearly that it was a question of the baptism of the Baptist being considered as a rite of purification. Now, all that was related to the question of purification came under the domain of the priests and Levites (cf. Lev. 14,1-32). To act as a religious reformer as the Baptist did, viz., instituting a new rite of purification through baptism, one must necessarily be commissioned by God, and must prove his divine authority. That is why the priests and the Levites go straight away to the heart of the problem and ask: "Who are you?" (1,19.22) and "What do you say about yourself?" (1,22). As the Baptist answers that he is neither the Messiah, nor Elijah nor the prophet, that is, none of the figures authorised by God and awaited at the Messianic times, they are forced to ask: "Why then are you baptising?" (1,25).

In my opinion, it is to the question of the identity of the one who baptises that the evangelist wants to lead to through the problem he raises in introducing the terms 'περὶ καθαρισμοῦ' at this juncture. That is, a debate on the purificatory value of baptismal activity must inevitably lead also to the question: 'who is he that is baptising?,' or in other words: 'on what authority does he baptise?' The terms 'περὶ καθαρισμοῦ' indirectly pave

---

[573] See Bultmann, *Gospel*, 168; Schnackenburg, *op. cit.*, 413-14; and Bernard, I, 129. The water practices of the Qumran sectarians were also associated with purification (cf. 1 QS 3,1-9 and 5,13-14). On the complex question of purity at Qumran, see F. García Martínez and J. T. Barrera, *The people of the Dead Sea Scrolls. Their Writings, Beliefs and Practices* (Leiden 1993) 139-57; and F. García Martínez and E. Tigchelaar, *The Dead Sea Scrolls Study Edition*, 2 Vols. (Grand Rapids 1999).

[574] Barrett (184), on the contrary, contends that the purification in the context does not refer to the baptism of Jesus and the Baptist, but alludes to the Jewish purification in general. The purificatory value of baptism is also affirmed in Mt. 3,6.11; Mk. 1,4; and Lk. 3,3.

the way for the planned testimony of the Baptist (3,27-36) to the identity of Jesus and his divine authority.

iv. Exposition of the problem

Certainly the baptism of the Baptist was open to misunderstanding by Jewish observers (cf. 1,25-28 and 3,25). Apparently the dispute with the Jew(s) fostered further reflections among the Baptist's disciples over the durability of their master's ministry, especially in the light of the rising popularity of Jesus. In fact, behind the anxious statement of the Baptist's disciples an implicit question is to be observed: 'How is it that 'πάντες ἔρχονται πρὸς αὐτόν?' (3,26g). The disciples of the Baptist do not seem to understand the parallel activity of Jesus. Such a misunderstanding is further supported by the syntactic structure of the verse. "The one who was with you across the Jordan...here he is baptising" (3,26def). Baptist's disciples see a contradiction between Jesus and their teacher. They wonder as to how one could be 'with the Baptist' on the one hand, and baptise in a competitive manner on the other hand. However, one thing is clear from the correspondence of 3,26 to 3,22-23: the disciples of the Baptist attribute the same value to the baptism of their master and of Jesus. They are only troubled and agitated about the increasing popularity of the new baptiser across the Jordan, and their complaint that 'all[575] are going to Jesus' betrays their uneasiness.[576] Thus, the first segment (3,22-26) ending with this hint of incomprehension of the first testimony of the Baptist on the part of his disciples directly necessitates a second testimony (3,27-36).

It is also interesting to note at this juncture, that there is a link between 'coming to the light' in 3,21 and 'coming to Jesus' in 3,26. Having made Jesus pronounce that "those who do what is true come to the light" (3,21), the evangelist brings in Jesus' baptismal ministry (3,22) and mentions that "all are going to him" (3,26). There is, thus, a continuity at the narrative sequence level between the end of the Nicodemus episode and the second testimony of the Baptist.

c. Characterisation of the Disciples

In the unit of my study, the narrator portrays the disciples of Jesus as associates engaged in baptising along with their master in a Judean countryside (3,22). They accompany Jesus wherever he goes and are his co-workers sharing the task of their master.[577] In the same way the disciples of the Baptist are presented as resolutely engaged in a discussion with a Jew(s) (3,26) definitely defending their Rabbi; they are portrayed as being faithful to him – troubled by the overshadowing of their master in relation to Jesus – by immediately

---

[575] Something of the same idea is reflected obliquely in the later statements that "the one who comes from above is *above all*," (3,31ab) and that the Father has placed 'all things in the hands of His Son' (3,35). Thus, in contrast to the Nicodemus episode, which seemed to be focused primarily on the Jews, this episode evokes the emergence of a community which is universal. See Brodie, *Gospel*, 206.

[576] The statement "all are going to him" (3,26g) counters the indications of the Baptist's successful ministry in 3,23cd: "and people kept coming and were being baptised." The πάντες creates the impression that the Baptist's once-successful mission is falling away dramatically. Πάντες is also an indignant exaggeration, very natural in the circumstances.

[577] See Waldstein, 203-21.

reporting to him about the threat of competition to their master (3,25-26).[578] Unlike the disciples of Jesus they are not baptising, only the Baptist is engaged in a parallel mission of baptism.

In sharp contrast to the Gospel of Mark, where the disciples struggle without much success to discern who Jesus is, in the fourth Gospel they know from the very beginning who Jesus is. Unlike the reader, they have not read the prologue and so are ignorant of Jesus' pre-existence, but other than that both know who Jesus is, both know what others in the story will learn only later. The reader, of course, has the advantage of the help of the narrator.

Moreover, the disciples who behold Jesus' glory in the fourth Gospel are set in distinct contrast to 'the Jews.' Unlike the other Gospels, the fourth calls Jesus' closest associates not 'apostles' but 'disciples,' a term that could be used for all believers. Only later does one learn that they were twelve in number; and a group known as 'the twelve' is mentioned only occasionally (6,67.70.71 and 20,24); the evangelist never gives a list of who they are nor suggests that they should be distinguished from other followers of Jesus. When an individual disciple speaks, it is usually in the first person plural (cf. 1,41.45). The paradigmatic character of the disciples[579] becomes apparent in the way they come to faith. In Jn. 1 the disciples come to faith by hearing about Jesus from someone they knew. It was at the instance of the Baptist two of his disciples leave their master (Andrew and an unknown one) and follow Jesus (cf. 1,37ff.). But there is a hint here to the subordination of the Baptist and the superiority of Jesus (cf. 3,28-30). Through the mediation of Andrew, Peter joins Jesus' company. Jesus calls Philip directly, who, on his turn, wins Nathanael for Jesus. This pattern differs from the other Gospels, which say that Jesus himself called all of his first disciples, but it would be congruent with the experience of a later generation of Christians, who came to faith through the witness of others (cf. 17,20).

The representative character of the disciples' faith is reinforced by repetition of this pattern throughout the Gospel. Those who come to genuine faith do so on the basis of hearing testimony about Jesus or from Jesus.[580] Collectively and individually the disciples are models or representatives with whom readers may identify. They are marked especially

---

[578] According to Acts 18,25 and 19,1-7, there were followers of the Baptist at Ephesus during Paul's ministry there. They could very well have claimed that their leader was the Messiah, especially after his death. There could have been also tensions between the followers of the Baptist and the Johannine Community. See R. L. Webb, *John the Baptiser and Prophet: A Socio-Historical Study* (JSNT.S 62) (Sheffield 1991). Note also the characterisation of John the Baptist in the following pages regarding the hypothesis of the existence of Baptist sects in the first-century. See also R. E. Brown, *op. cit.*, lxvii-lxx; his *The Community of the Beloved Disciple* (New York 1979) 69-71; and R. Schnackenburg, "Das vierte Evangelium und die Johannesjünger," *HJ* 77 (1958) 21-38.

[579] For a detailed study see D. R. Beck; *The Discipleship Paradigm. Readers and Anonymous Characters in the Fourth Gospel* (BibInstS 27) Leiden 1997.

[580] In contrast to the 'many' in 2,23 and Nicodemus (3,2.11) whose response to Jesus was dependent upon the miracles and so failed to understand Jesus, the Samaritan townspeople believed in Jesus because of Jesus' words, even though they saw no miracles (4,39.41). The royal official sought Jesus out because he had heard about him, believed Jesus' promise that his son would live (4,47.50.53). See C. R. Koester, "Hearing, Seeing and Believing in the Gospel of John," *Bib.* 70 (1989) 327-48.

by their recognition of Jesus and belief in his claims. Yet, the disciples are not models of perfect faith, but of positive responses and typical misunderstandings.[581]

The faith of the disciples is at first a faith based on signs (2,11). Their believing is based on seeing (1,36.39.46.51). Others "ἐπίστευσαν εἰς τὸ ὄνομα αὐτοῦ" (2,23), because they saw signs, but Jesus does not entrust himself to them (2,24-25). What is the difference between these and the disciples? Both begin with a faith based on signs, but the disciples show a willingness to *follow* Jesus (1,37-38.40), and they *remember* what Jesus said (2,22). True faith must lead to journeying with Jesus (2,2.12 and 3,22), *remaining* (μένειν)[582] with him (1,39 and 2,12), and *becoming his associates* in his concerns (cf. 3,22 and 4,1-2).

d. Reader and Point of View

For the newspaper-type readers the situation in this chapter could be quite confusing not only because 3,22-36 does not seem to fit the sequence[583] here, but also because the discourse at 3,31-36 seems to cover a set of themes similar to those included in the preceding dialogue with Nicodemus. But the sequence of events in Jn. 3, for the reader, makes extremely good sense theologically.

The reader is informed that Jesus is no longer in Jerusalem, but baptising at a Judean countryside (3,22) and the Baptist at Aenon near Salim (3,23).[584] The shift of Jesus to a place nearer to Samaria is a hint to the reader that the long section devoted to the Jewish response to Jesus is coming to a conclusion. The narrator gives a further hint to the reader that these events took place before the imprisonment of the Baptist (3,24). This narrator's aside and editorial note reminds the reader that the evangelist is fully aware of the historical sequences. Though the reader notices that Jesus does not play an active role in this section, he/she is conscious that the whole scene focuses on the relationship between Jesus and the Baptist – both engaged in a baptismal ministry. In the story narrated so far, the reader is aware, that Jesus and the Baptist are the major characters. The contrast between Jesus and the Baptist is brought into focus by the disciples of the Baptist, who apparently had been engaged in a dispute or argument (ζήτησις) with a Jew(s) over purification or 'ceremonial washing' (καθαρισμός – cf. 2,6 and 3,25). The recognition of the true identity of Jesus by the Baptist on the occasion of his baptism, the testimony of the Baptist concerning the baptism of the Spirit administered by Jesus (cf. 1,33), and the condition of a begotten ἄνωθεν of water and the Spirit to enter into the βασιλεία τοῦ θεοῦ in the previous episode, remind the reader that there is some unresolved problem over the question of the baptism of Jesus and that of the Baptist.

Though the scene (3,25ff.) may be set in Samaria, the reader easily notices that the characters (the Baptist, his disciples, the unnamed Jew(s) disputing on purification with

---

[581] De Jonge (*Stranger from Heaven*, 15) analyses that "the disciples, both in their acceptance and their misunderstandings of Jesus' word, are portrayed as models for future generation believers."

[582] For a detailed discussion see the recent study of K. Scholtissek, *In ihm sein und bleiben. Die Sprache der Immanenz in den johanneischen Schriften* (HBS 21) (Freiburg i. Br. 2000).

[583] The nature of the fourth evangelist's story of Jesus is not a chronological report of the events of Jesus' ministry.

[584] There is growing agreement among scholars that the site is in Samaria. See Manzano, "Les sources d'Aenon," 124-30; Boismard, "Aenon, près de Salem," 219-22; Murphy-O'Connor, "John the Baptist and Jesus," 363-66; and Schnackenburg, *Gospel*, I, 412-13; For a survey of possible sites see the discussion in R. E. Brown, *op. cit.*, 151.

them) in the narrative belong to the Jewish world. Moreover, the disciples of the Baptist address their master with the Jewish title 'Rabbi.'[585] The reader has come across this title already on three occasions: twice in the first days of Jesus, when he was addressed in this way by his first disciples (cf. 1,38.49), and very recently in Nicodemus' addressing of Jesus (3,2). The keen reader is conscious of the use of the title of honour – that has been reserved to Jesus till now – is applied to the Baptist. From the viewpoint of the reader, a parallel is being drawn between Jesus and the Baptist. This is further strengthened as the disciples of the Baptist refer to Jesus as the one who had been with him on the other side of the Jordan and to whom he had borne testimony (3,26). The reader is able to observe that the disciples of the Baptist are obviously concerned to protect the prestige of their teacher, and want their master to counter Jesus' growing popularity by taking some affirmative action on his own behalf.

2. Narrative and Structural Analysis of 3,27-30

Having heard the anxious concern of his disciples, one may expect the Baptist to defend his role, but after 1,6-8.15.19-34 this will not happen, as his only function is to bear witness to Jesus. The Baptist does not respond to his disciples' question concerning baptism;[586] he shifts the discussion to the realm of revelation. In the immediately preceding episode, Jesus instructed Nicodemus on the heavenly origin of what he had to offer and had seen and heard (cf. 3,3.5.7-8.11-12). The readers of the Gospel know what Jesus wants of them – a 'radical rebirth.' They know that he will die for their salvation. They know that those who believe in him have eternal life, and those who do not are condemned already. After making it plain what Jesus stands for, the evangelist returns to the Baptist to show that he bears witness to Jesus once again. Although he is not the anointed one of God the Baptist has been 'sent by God' (1,6) and his testimony to Jesus is in agreement with God's design. The Baptist's witness has an unquestionable authority, but he is not the Messiah.

a. Thematic Parallel Structure

In 3,27-30 one does not find any remarkable formal criterion such as verbal recurrence. However, I can observe a thematic parallel structure of the type ab//a^{1}b^1(see the diagram on the next page):

In the dyad **a-a^1** the parallelism rests on the verbs 'receive' and 'give' which correspond to the verb 'have.' In some sense all the three verbs are related to verbs of possession. On the one hand, the Baptist states the principle according to which a man can 'receive' or 'take' what has been given to him from heaven. On the other hand, he affirms that the one who has (possesses) the bride is the bridegroom. The parallelism implies that the bridegroom possesses the bride, because she has been *given* to him from heaven.

---

[585] The designation of the Baptist by his disciples as 'Rabbi' is, in my opinion, intended by the evangelist to pinpoint the contrast between Jesus and the Baptist, because 3,26 is the only place in the fourth Gospel where the title 'Rabbi' refers to someone other than Jesus (cf. 1,38; 6,25; 9,22; 11,8 as well as 20,16, where the heightened form 'Rabboni' is used after the resurrection).

[586] See the detailed discussion of A. Feuillet, "Le baptême de Jésus commenté par le précurseur. Contribution à l'étude du Christ et de l'Esprit-Saint dans leurs rapports avec l'Église dans le Quatrième Évangile," *NT* 61 (1986) 90-140.

a //	a¹
[3,27] John answered, "No one can *receive* (λαμβάνειν) anything except what has been *given* (δεδομένον) from heaven.	[29ab] He who *has* the bride is the bridegroom
b //	**b¹**
[28] You yourselves are **my** (μοι) witnesses that I said, 'I (εἰμὶ) am not the Messiah, but **I** (εἰμὶ) have been sent ahead of <u>him</u> (ἐκείνου).'	[29 c-g] The friend of the bridegroom, who stands and hears him, rejoices greatly at the bridegroom's voice. For this reason **my** (ἐμὴ) joy has been fulfilled. [30] He (ἐκείνου) must increase, but I (ἐμὲ) must decrease."

The dyad **b-b¹** deals with the relative position of the Baptist to Jesus. The element **(b)** recalls his previous testimony, according to which he is not the Messiah,[587] but the one sent ahead of him. In 3,29c-g the same relative position is expressed in the nuptial categories dear to the Messianic tradition:[588] the Baptist is not the bridegroom but a friend of the bridegroom who stands and hears him, and rejoices at his voice. The statement of 3,30 is applied to the two elements of this dyad **(b-b¹)**: as forerunner he must make place for the Messiah; when the bridegroom appears the friend of the bridegroom is no more the centre of attraction. This dyad is, however, not completely devoid of formal parallels. I find here a repetition of the personal pronoun of the first person to designate the Baptist (μοι ... ἐγω//ἐμὴ ... ἐμὲ) as well as the recalling of the pronoun 'ἐκείνου//ἐκείνον' to designate the Messiah.

b. Argumentative Narrative Structure

Although such a parallelism is, apparently, not strong in its argumentation, a deeper literary analysis seems to bring to the fore a dynamic argumentative complex.

3,27-30 The Baptist's Final Testimony to Jesus – Part I

27a	Speech opening (εἶπεν)
bc	Statement of *a general principle (maxim)* – in terms of 'giving' and 'receiving'
28	*Subordinate relation* of the Baptist to Jesus in rank in Messianic categories: Messiah – precursor
ab	Recalling of a previous testimony
c	Repetition of 1,20d
d	Paraphrasing of 1,23.27
29ab	Statement of *a general principle* – in terms of 'possessing'
c-f	*Subordinate relation* of the Baptist to Jesus in Messianic nuptial categories: Bridegroom – friend of the bridegroom

---

[587] Cf. R. Schnackenburg, "Die Messiasfrage im Johannesevangelium," in: *Neutestamentliche Aufsätze. FS J. Schmid* (Regensburg 1963) 240-64.

[588] The relation between God and his people has been often described in the OT in terms of bridegroom and bride: Hos. 1-2; Jer. 2,2 and Is. 61,10. In the NT Christ takes the place of God and it is he who is considered as the bridegroom of the people of the new covenant; cf. Mt. 22,1-14; Rev. 19,7 and 21,2-10; 2 Cor. 11,2; and Eph. 5,27. See Boismard, "L'ami de l'époux," 291; and R. E. Brown, *op. cit.*, 156. Schnackenburg (*Gospel*, I, 416-17) adds that the evangelist and his Christian readers must have interpreted the 'bride' as the Messianic Community. The primitive church understood the 'bridegroom' in the parable of Mk. 2,19-20 and parallels, as a direct allusion to Jesus, the Messiah.

g   Reasoning (αὔτη οὖν)
30   Concluding statement (therefore) – "He must increase, but I must decrease."

i. A Maxim

In 3,27 the Baptist opens his discourse with the general principle or maxim: "No one can receive anything except what has been given *from heaven*"[589] (cf. 19,11). As such it is extremely broad: God's sovereignty stands hidden behind all human claims, for a human being does not have anything but what he has received (cf. 1 Cor. 4,7). The evangelist sees the hand of the Father in everything. In the immediate context, the Baptist is applying the maxim to the situation brought to his attention by his disciples. His reply is an immediate justification of Jesus' success. Now, there are three ways of understanding this maxim.

♦ Three Interpretations

A first interpretation consists in understanding the terms 'ἄνθρωπος' and 'αὐτῷ' as referring to the believer. In such a case, the fact of 'all going to Jesus' (cf. 3,26g) is 'what has been *given*[590] from heaven.' Faith is a gift from God. The evangelist affirms the same idea in 6,65 by placing the statement on the lips of Jesus: "No one can come to me unless it is granted by the Father" (cf. 6,37.44).[591] In the exegesis of 3,19-21, I have demonstrated already that 'coming to Jesus' and 'believing in Jesus' are synonyms (cf. 6,35). The Baptist, in his response, teaches his disciples not be perturbed by the movement of all toward Jesus, because it is *God who gives faith to the people* and leads them to Jesus.[592] The same idea is reflected in the prologue: 'Whoever *receives* the light (believe in his name) is given power to become children of God'[593] (cf. 1,12).

A second interpretation would consist in applying the terms 'ἄνθρωπος' and 'αὐτῷ' to Jesus. In that case, the believers are to be understood as a gift of the Father to Jesus. Note that the evangelist affirms such an idea, too, in a statement on the lips of Jesus: "Everything that the Father gives me will come to me" (6,37). The believers being envisaged as gift to the Son and his giving them eternal life in turn is quite frequent in the fourth Gospel (cf. 3,25-36; 6,39-40; 10,27-29 and 17,2.9.11.24).[594] In this perspective, the Baptist expresses to his disciples that, if 'all are going to Jesus,' it is because *God has given them as a gift to Jesus.* In both interpretations, it is God who is the prime mover and the centre of action. The principle Jesus revealed to Nicodemus – *viz.,* that it was God who *gave* His Son out of love (3,16) and *sent* him into the world for its salvation (3,17) – is once again testified to by the Baptist whose primary function is to bear witness to Jesus.

---

[589] Note that '*heaven*' is a typical Jewish circumlocution for 'God' to avoid the use of the divine name; cf. Mt. 21,25; Mk. 11,30; and Lk. 15,18.21; see Borchert, 191.

[590] The fourth evangelist uses the verb 'δίδωμι' 76 times, which is more often than any other NT writer. He has an especially interesting number of things the Father gives the Son (cf. 3,35).

[591] Cf. T. E. Pollard, "The Father-Son and God-Believer Relationship according to St. John," in: de Jonge, *L'Évangile de Jean*, 363-68.

[592] The Baptist's reaction stands in vivid contrast to the usual pattern of the world, illustrated well by the attitude of the Pharisees at the entry of Jesus into Jerusalem (12,9). The Pharisees were worried by their loss of prestige; John the Baptist was not.

[593] For a discussion on the communion of the children of God see H. Klein, "Die Gemeinschaft der Gotteskinder. Zur Ekklesiologie der johanneischen Schriften," in: W.-D. Hauschild (ed.), *Kirchengemein-schaft – Anspruch und Wirklichkeit. FS Georg Kretschmar zum 60. Geburtstag* (Stuttgart 1986) 59-67.

[594] Cf. Schnackenburg, *op. cit.,* 415; and Haenchen, I, 210.

Thirdly, the principle that 'one can receive only what God has given him' (3,27bc) is further supported by applying it to the Baptist as well. In fact, as much as the Baptist is on the losing side – considering the number of people going to him for baptism – so much is Jesus on the gaining side as "all are going to him." The Baptist attributes this fact to the divine will in the principle he states in 3,27. It is in his submission to this divine plan that he is able to state in all humility, "he must (δεῖ)[595] increase, but I must decrease"[596] (3,30), meaning all must effectively go to Jesus. He meant what he said. Both he and Jesus were given their roles by heaven (cf. 3,27), and the Baptist was entirely content with his. In my opinion, the intention of the evangelist is to show the reason for Jesus' greater success. But the language he uses is certainly capable of these multiple applications.

ii. Messiah and the 'One Sent Ahead'

Having justified the movement of crowds to Jesus through the statement of a general principle in 3,27, the Baptist then tries to explain his subordinate relation to Jesus in terms of the 'Messiah' and the 'one sent ahead' (3,28). He answers to the recalling of his disciples in 3,26e ("to whom you testified") and invites them to remember his earlier affirmation exactly (as they have not understood it), namely, that he was not the Messiah but the one sent ahead of him (cf. 1,20.23.30).[597] He is appealing to what was well known about his preaching.[598] This recalling of his previous testimony and the repeated mention "I am not the Messiah," in the context, implicitly point to Jesus as the awaited Messiah.

The designation of the Baptist as the one 'sent ahead of the Messiah' recalls the prophecy of Malachi (3,1ff.) which announces the sending of a messenger by God to prepare his coming. In the Synoptic tradition this function of the precursor is realised in his "baptism of repentance for the forgiveness of sins" (Mk. 1,4; cf. parallels). The fourth evangelist re-interprets the purpose of the Baptist's baptism as one meant for the manifestation of the Messiah to Israel (cf. 1,31-34). I have repeated often enough that, for the fourth evangelist, the function of the Baptist as the 'one sent ahead of the Messiah' is to be seen above all in his role as witness to Jesus. The mission of the Baptist as the one sent "to prepare the way of the Lord"[599] is demonstrated further in Messianic nuptial categories in the following verse (3,29).

---

[595] The 'must' is nothing less than the determined will of God. It is not merely advisable, nor is it the way events might happen to turn out. The evangelist sets 'he' and 'I' over against one another in emphatic contrast. They are not cast for identical or even similar roles. It is God's plan that the Messiah *must* continually increase. The Baptist finds his joy, not in grudgingly conceding victory to a superior opponent, but in wholeheartedly embracing God's will, and the supremacy it assigns to God's will. See Fascher, 228-54 for a discussion on 'δεῖ.'

[596] Later calendar makers placed the birth of the Baptist on June 24 (three days after the summer solstice), on the day light noticeably begins to decrease, and the birth of Jesus on Dec. 25 (three days after the winter solstice), the day light noticeably begins to increase. The notion is also suggested by the fact that the Greek verbs here for 'increase' (αὐξάνω) and 'decrease' (ἐλαττόω) are those used for the waxing and waning of light from celestial bodies. See R. E. Brown, *op. cit.*, 153; Bultmann, *Gospel*, 175; and Schnackenburg, *op. cit.*, 417; see also E. Linnemann, "Jesus und der Täufer," in: G. Ebeling, E. Jüngel and G. Schunack (eds.), *FS für Ernst Fuchs* (Tübingen 1973) 225.

[597] Having a true understanding of who one is became for the evangelist a critical issue. As an authentic witness, the Baptist modelled such a perspective by repackaging here his earlier assertion (1,20), namely, "I am not the Messiah" (Ἐγὼ οὐκ εἰμὶ ὁ Χριστός) in a slightly different Greek word order in 3,28.

[598] Note the emphatic use of 'you yourselves' in 3,28a.

[599] Cf. J. Redford, "Preparing the Way: John the Baptist," *CleR* 66 (1981) 193-200.

iii. Bridegroom and Friend of the Bridegroom

Having asserted that he is not the Messiah but the 'one sent ahead,' the Baptist continues to clarify to his disciples by describing his relationship with Jesus in typical Jewish parabolic terms.[600] 3,29ab state the general principle: "he who has the bride is the bridegroom." It is not a definition, but a designation of the bridegroom. The bride belongs to the bridegroom; he is the principal person of the wedding, because 'he has the bride.' He then explains his relationship to Jesus allegorically. The point of comparison is the difference between the bridegroom and the 'friend of the bridegroom.' 3,27 interpreted already the movement of the crowd toward Jesus (3,26) as a gift of God. In the same way, in the movement of the crowd there is an implicit gift of the Messianic bride to Jesus (the eschatological bridegroom) by God. If Jesus has received the bride, he is the bridegroom to whom God gives her. The Baptist being only a friend of the bridegroom cannot receive the bride.[601]

The Baptist's use of nuptial imagery has two sources. The Scriptures often speak of Israel as the bride of God (cf. Is. 62,4-5; Jer. 2,2; Ezek. 16,8 and 23,4; and Hos. 2,21).[602] This is sufficient background for the Baptist to affirm that 'not he but the Messiah is the head of the New Israel.'[603] The image of the 'friend of the bridegroom' is also drawn from the marriage practices of the time. He plays exactly the same role as the 'one sent ahead' (3,28d), because it is he who is responsible for the task of preparing the ceremonies of the marriage and of watching over that everything takes place according to the ancestral customs (e.g. that all the purification rituals are followed). In a precise manner, it is he who is responsible for adorning the bride and leading her to the house of the bridegroom, which is the principal rite of ceremonies.[604] It is this last aspect which is specially taken into consideration here: as friend of the bridegroom, the Baptist must prepare (adorn) the people (the bride) through his baptism of purification and lead them to the Messiah (the bridegroom).[605]

---

[600] B. Lindars, "The Parable of the Best Man (John iii,29)," *NTS* 16 (1969/70) 324-29; Barrett (185); Dodd (*Historical Tradition*, 282); and Schnackenburg (*op. cit.*, 416) consider 3,29 a parable. Bultmann (*Gospel*, 173, n. 6; and his *History of the Synoptic Tradition* [New York 1963] 167f.) and J. Jeremias ("νύμφη," *TDNT*, IV, 1101) see in it a metaphor.

[601] There is good evidence that in ancient Sumerian and Babylonian law the friend of the bridegroom was absolutely prohibited from marrying the bride. The influence of this tradition on the OT period is, probably, to be traced in Jud. 14-15, where even the Philistines recognise Samson's grievance as legitimate. If this perspective, mediated through the OT, descends as far as the Baptist, he is the last who could compete with the bridegroom. See A. van Selms, "The Best Man and the Bridegroom from Sumer to St. John," *JNES* 9 (1950) 75; Boismard, "L'ami de l'époux," 291-92; see also Lindars, "The Parable," 324-29.

[602] See E. Trocmé, "Jean 3,29 et le thème de l'époux dans la tradition pré-évangélique," *RevSR* 69 (1995) 13-18.

[603] The symbol of marriage, of course, has been employed as a striking picture of the relationship between Christ and his Church, and as Schnackenburg (*op. cit.*, 417) correctly observes, has given rise to 'the allegory of the Church as the bride of Christ.' Cf. 2 Cor. 11,2; Eph. 5,25-27.31-32; and Rev. 21,2 and 22,17. For a detailed study see also A. Feuillet, "Les épousailles du Messie: la mère de Jésus et l'Église dans le Quatrième Évangile," *RT* 86 (1986) 257-391 and 536-75. For a helpful discussion see also R. A. Batey, *New Testament Nuptial Imagery* (Leiden 1971) esp. 46-50; and W. Brownlee, "Messianic Motifs of Qumran and the New Testament," *NTS* 3 (1957) 205-6.

[604] For references to marriage customs see Strack-Billerbeck, I, 45-46 and 500-2; and R. de Vaux, *Les institutions de l'Ancien Testament* (Paris ²1967) I, 58-60; cf. also Schnackenburg, *op. cit.*, 416-17.

[605] M. und R. Zimmermann, "Der Freund des Bräutigams (Joh 3,29): Deflorations- oder Christuszeuge?," *ZNW* 90 (1999) 128-29. Strack-Billerbeck (I, 500-4) observes that the Rabbis attributed to Moses the role of

Such an important and honourable task of the friend of the bridegroom cannot but bring joy to him when the ceremonies take place successfully. This is, in fact, the attitude brought out in 3,29c-g. In this parabolic context, the voice of the bridegroom could signify the triumphal cry through which the bridegroom announces to his friends, who stand outside the bridal chamber, that he is married to a virgin bride.[606] But there is also an allegoric meaning to be observed in the mention of the terms 'listening to the voice of the bridegroom' (ἀκούων αὐτοῦ ... τὴν φωνὴν). In the fourth Gospel, the attitude of faith is often expressed as 'hearing the voice of Jesus' (cf. 5,25.28; 10,3.16.27 and 18,37) which is synonymous with 'hearing his word' (cf. 5,24; 7,40; 8,43; 12,47 and 14,24). Besides, while applying this joy of the friend of the bridegroom to himself, the Baptist employs the terms 'ἡ χαρὰ ἡ ἐμὴ πεπλήρωται' (3,29g). All the other Johannine occurrences of the term 'joy' along with the verb πληρόω are regarding the disciples' perfect joy arising out of their communion with Jesus in faith (cf. 15,11; 16,24 and 17,13; and 1 Jn. 1,4). In my opinion, such a use implies an allusion to the joyful reception of the words of Jesus by the Baptist. This interpretation confirms that the Baptist depends on the revelation of Jesus, the unique revealer descended from heaven (cf. 3,13). The Baptist must, first of all, *hear* this revelation, that is, *believe* in it before he could bear witness to it.

Paralleling himself with the friend of the bridegroom who accompanies the bridegroom until such time as he takes possession of his bride, he places himself in a subordinate position of 'standing' (waiting), 'hearing' and 'rejoicing' at the bridegroom's 'voice.' The Baptist demonstrates openness to the word of Jesus even though it means he must soon disappear from the scene. This hearing has taken place and, thus, the Baptist can announce, in the present tense, his joy is now full (πεπλήρωται). This description of the decreasing importance of the Baptist and the increasing centrality of Jesus is then asserted in 3,30 as a divine imperative (δεῖ). This also reflects what happens from this point on in the story.

c. Reader and Point of View

The reader, having read that the authority of Jesus (cf. 1,1-2 and 3,13-14.16-17) and that of the Baptist (cf. 1,6.33) come from God, is aware of the truth about both Jesus and the Baptist, and so understands the indirect answer of the Baptist to his disciples: "No one can receive anything except what has been given from heaven" (3,27). The reader immediately understands that the Baptist is associating himself with the point of view expressed by Jesus in his dialogue with Nicodemus (cf. 3,3.5.7-8.11-12). It is on the basis of what has been received from the only source of authentic revelation, 'from above,' that anyone can

---

the 'friend of the bridegroom' in his mediation between God and Israel at Sinai. Paul attributes this role to himself in 2 Cor. 11,2; cf. Boismard, "L'ami de l'époux," 292-93; and R. E. Brown, *op. cit.*, 152.

[606] According to L. Infante ("L'amico dello sposo. Figura del ministero di Giovanni Battista nel quarto vangelo," *RivBib* 31 [1983] 13-14), the voice refers to the jubilant voice of the bridegroom who recited the solemn prayer of seven blessings as a final act of the nuptial ceremonies. He also notes that the end of this prayer makes an explicit reference to the joyous voice of the bridegroom of the prophecy of Jer. 33,11 having strong eschatological connotations; see also his dissertation at the Pontifical Gregorian University in Rome the following year under the same title. For further interpretations with a little variation see also Schnackenburg, *op. cit.*, 416; and Jeremias, "νύμφη," 1101.

be in a proper relationship with God (3,27).[607] On the basis of this affirmation, the Baptist is able to remind his disciples of his earlier testimony (cf. 1,19-28) that he is not the Messiah, but the one '*sent* ahead of him' (3,28). The reader is aware that there is more to the use of the verb *sent* than the disciples would realise, because he/she has read 1,6: "there was a man *sent* from God, whose name was John" (cf. 1,33). The reader here is taught that, if one is an authentic witness, matters of power, possessions, and calling ought not to be viewed in terms of one's self-made, human achievements but rather in terms of one's grateful and responsible use of what God has given, as exemplified by the Baptist (3,27-28). The principle enunciated for the reader here is that 'a man sent from God' is not self-oriented or self-serving but is one who acknowledges the gift of life from 'heaven.' In fact, his reaction stands in vivid contrast to the usual pattern of the world.

3. Narrative and Structural Analysis of 3,31-36

3,31-36 constitute the second part of the final testimony of the Baptist. The evangelist here concentrates on the theme of revelation (3,31-35), but concludes with the themes of life and judgement in 3,36. Belief results in eternal life but anger and wrath of God are the fruits of a refusal to accept this revelation.

a. Thematic Parallel Structure

I notice here, too, a thematic parallel structure of the type ab//a¹b¹:

a //	a¹
³,³¹ The *one who comes from above* **is above all**; the *one who is of the earth* belongs to the earth and speaks about earthly things. The *one who comes from heaven* **is above all.** ³²ᵃᵇᶜ He **testifies to what he has seen and heard,**	³⁴ *He whom God has sent* **speaks the words of God,** for he gives the Spirit without measure. ³⁵ *The Father loves the Son and has placed all things in his hands.*
b //	b¹
³²ᵈ yet *no one accepts his testimony.* ³³ *Who-ever has accepted his testimony* has certified this, that God is true.	³⁶ *Whoever believes in the Son* has eternal life; *whoever disobeys the Son* will not see life, but must endure God's wrath.

The elements **a-a¹** designate Jesus as the 'one who comes from above/heaven,' (3,31af) and as the one 'whom God has sent' (3,34a) respectively. While the element **(a)** describes Jesus' status and dignity as being 'above all'(3,31bg) because of his heavenly origin, the parallel statement in the element **(a¹)** describes his dignity as God's envoy. It is interesting to note that the designation of Jesus as the 'one who comes from above,' reminds one of the descent of the Son of Man[608] from heaven (3,13), while the designation

---

[607] While many scholars consider this verse as a general statement about the source of ultimate truth applicable to anyone, Becker (*Johannes*, I, 154) applies this verse only to the Baptist.

[608] In 3,13 the 'Son of Man' is further described as 'the one who descended from heaven.' One may, however, raise the question as to why the evangelist does not use the title in 3,31. In my opinion, it is important to note that the evangelist places the title 'Son of Man' always on the lips of Jesus. (It is an added reason supporting the integrity of Jn. 3 and to refute the opinion that 3,31-36 is a continuation of Jesus'

'he whom God has sent' takes one back to the same designation of Jesus in 3,17 in the preceding Nicodemus episode. That is to say, between the parallel elements **(a)** and **(a¹)** one finds the same double-Christological scheme (Son of Man/Son of God) as in 3,14-15 and 3,16-18. Besides, the parallelism between **(a)** and **(a¹)** rests on the revelatory function of Jesus as one who "testifies to what he has seen and heard" (3,32abc) and as one who "speaks (λαλεῖ) the words of God" (3,34b) in contrast to the earthly one who also speaks (λαλεῖ), but about earthly things (3,31cde).

Moreover, the statement on the transcendence of Jesus as the heavenly figure, *viz.*, "ἐπάνω πάντων ἐστίν" (3,31bg), is paralleled by the statement "ὁ πατὴρ ... πάντα δέδωκεν ἐν τῇ χειρὶ αὐτου" (3,35), which explains the reasons for his 'being above all' as he is the beloved Son of the Father who has placed everything in the hands of His Son. This completes the correspondence of the two parallel elements **a-a¹**.

Furthermore, the element **(a)** uses an antithetical parallelism to insist on the heavenly origin and revelatory function of Jesus:

^{3,31ab.fg} The one who comes from above is above all; **X** ^{3,31cd} the one who is of the earth belongs to the earth

^{3,32abc} He testifies to what he has seen and heard   **X** ^{3,31e} and speaks about earthly things (heaven things)

Once again it is interesting to note that the mention of 'earthly and heavenly things' takes one back to the discussion about the same in the Nicodemus episode (cf. 3,12). Moreover, 3,32abc reflect the words of Jesus in 3,11bcde.

The second parallelism (**b-b¹** in the diagram given above) is founded on the synonymous and antithetical expressions 'accepting/not accepting his testimony' (3,33a/ 32d) and 'believing/disobeying the Son' (3,36a/c). Undoubtedly there is a correlation between 'certifying that God is true' (3,33bc) and 'having eternal life' (3,36b) as 'accepting the testimony of Jesus' (3,33a) is synonymous with 'believing in the Son' (3,36a). There are enough parallels of these in the Nicodemus episode.

b. Argumentative Narrative Structure

Essentially, the segment 3,31-36 presents two principal themes, *viz.*, origin and function of Jesus and the reaction of men, which are narrated structurally in four parts of argumentation as shown in the chart below:

3,31-32c Testimony of the "one who comes from above/heaven"
31ab	Heavenly origin and his superior status
cd	Earthly origin of the listener
e	Earthly activity of the listener
fg	Heavenly origin and his superior status (repetition of 31ab – note the chiasm)
32a	His function on earth (testimony)
bc	Whose content is heavenly (what he has seen and heard there)

---

discourse and, therefore, should be transposed to the Nicodemus episode. 3,31-36 must be ascribed to the Baptist and belongs to his second testimony). The Jews in 12,34 only quote the words of Jesus when they use the title 'Son of Man' (3,14; 8,28 and 12,32). The only use, perhaps, on the lips of Stephen is outside the Gospels (Acts 7,56). Even there, Stephen actually refers to the words of Jesus as a judge (cf. Lk. 22,69). For a further discussion see Moloney, *Son of Man*, 66.

32d –33 Reaction of listeners
d   Negative reaction (adversative καί) – non-acceptance of the testimony (a fact)
33a   Positive reaction – acceptance of the testimony
  bc   Result of positive reaction – acquisition of certitude that God is true

34-35 Function of the envoy and the source of his authority
34a   Reasoning (γάρ): God has sent him, and
  b   He speaks the words of God.
  c   Reasoning (γάρ):
  c   He is Spirit-filled, and
35a   Is loved by the Father, and
  b   All things have been placed in his hands by the Father.

36   Goal of testimony
36ab   Positive reaction (belief in the Son) brings eternal life
  cde   Negative reaction (disobedience) brings loss of life and God's wrath
        (A synonymous and antithetic parallelism)

i. Heavenly Origin and Testimony of Jesus

In the first part of his discourse (3,27-30) the Baptist characterised his relation to Jesus in the distinction between the Messiah and the one sent ahead of him, the bridegroom and friend of the bridegroom. In the second part of his discourse (3,31-36) he characterises this distinction further as the "one who comes from above" (3,31abfg) and "one who is of the earth" (3,31cd). However, there is a change of perspective between 3,28-30 and 3,31. While the expression "the one who comes from above" re-interprets the designations of Jesus as the Messiah and bridegroom, the phrase "one who is of the earth" refers, on the one hand, to the Baptist as one who bears witness to Jesus on earth, and, on the other hand, to every human being[609] of 'earthly nature.'[610] In my opinion, the latter makes more sense in the context as I shall demonstrate it from the argumentation of the narrative.

To a great extent, the first part of the Baptist's discourse (3,27-30) still lingers on in the same political Messianic perspective of his first testimony (1,19-34). But already then a transition from this traditional Messianic scheme was announced in Jesus' promise of greater things in connection with the Son of Man (1,50-51). It is precisely this transition that is to be observed once again in passing from the first part of the Baptist's testimony (3,27-30) to the second (3,31-36). In the first, the Baptist recalls his first testimony, of which his disciples were witnesses, but remains in Messianic categories of the one sent ahead of the Messiah and the bridegroom evoking the eschatological Messianic banquet.

---

[609] As the evangelist characterises the Baptist always positively as 'a man sent from God' (1,6), 'a witness to testify to the light' (1,7) and to the truth (5,33), in my opinion, it cannot refer to the Baptist (cf. also 1,19-28 and 3,27-30). See Schnackenburg (*op. cit.*, 382); and R. E. Brown (*op. cit.*, 160-61). Bultmann (*Gospel*, 162) and Beutler (*Martyria*, 316) giving a generic meaning to the article 'ὁ' in 3,31c supports my view further. Some other authors (Boismard and Lamouille, 119; and Blank, *Krisis*, 66) see here a contrast between the Baptist and Nicodemus which, in my opinion, is not clear. There is not an exclusive reference either to the Baptist or to Nicodemus.

[610] One may note here an allusion to 3,6. The word 'γῆ' does not imply an opposition to God as it is the case with the term κόσμος in the dualistic use of the evangelist. The use of 'γῆς' here refers to the simple contrast with 'ἄνωθεν' (3,31a) and 'ἐκ τοῦ οὐρανοῦ' (3,31f). For a discussion see Barrett, 187; Boismard and Lamouille, 119; R. E. Brown, *op. cit.*, 157; Bultmann, *op. cit.*; and Schnackenburg, *op. cit.*

But the revelation of Jesus in the Nicodemus episode (3,11-21) has exploded this Messianic scheme. The evangelist must, therefore, make the Baptist bear witness to the true nature of Jesus and, thus, bring to completion his mission of witnessing. In relation to Jesus, the fundamental distinction is no more Messiah and forerunner, but Son of Man and humanity. If Jesus must increase and the Baptist must decrease, it is not just because Jesus is the Messiah, but because he is also *the Son of Man*;[611] and the Son of Man is essentially a transcendent and heavenly figure, *who is above all*.[612] It is this affirmation that opens the second part of the Baptist's discourse in the form of an antithetical parallelism (3,31).

The argumentation of the narrative structure is self-explanatory as is easily observable from the scheme given above. It is also easy to recognise here the same perspective of authentication of the testimony found in 3,11-13. It is surprising to notice that commentators, who observe a parallelism between 3,11-13 and 3,31-32, have not clearly brought forth the contrast. There is a clear contrast to be observed between "the one who is of the earth and speaks of earthly things" and "the one who comes from above and testifies to what he has seen and heard." The one who comes from heaven is the unique, an authentic witness and is authorised to speak of heavenly things. All others, Moses, Elijah, the prophets, and the Baptist could speak only of earthly things as they had never ascended into heaven to learn the heavenly secrets. Only Jesus, the Son of Man, can speak of what he has seen (cf. 1,18; 3,11 and 8,32) and heard[613] (cf. 8,26.40 and 15,15) in heaven. Hence, he is a qualified and trustworthy witness.

ii. Reaction of Listeners

α. Either Non-acceptance of Testimony

The conjunction 'καὶ' in 3,32d has an adversative value (yet). Jesus is the only witness of the things seen and heard in heaven, "*yet* no one accepts his testimony." In the narrative sequence, there seems to be a contradiction between this statement and the anxiety expressed by the Baptist's disciples, *viz.*, "all are going to him" (3,26g). The laying of the accent on the movement of the people toward Jesus (as the possessor of the bride) has to be

---

[611] The fourth evangelist often uses the expression 'Son of Man' to correct the traditional Messianic understanding of Jesus (cf. 1,49 with 1,50-51; 3,2 with 3,14; 3,28-30 with 3,31-32; 9,17.22.33 with 9,35; 12,13.15 with 12,23; and 12,34a with 12,34bc). It is, perhaps, to break with the Messianic perspective of 3,28-30 that the evangelist uses the participle 'ἐρχόμενος' in 3,31af instead of 'καταβάς' as in 3,13. It is to be noted that the Messiah is designated in the Synoptic tradition as 'ὁ ἐρχόμενος' (cf. Mt. 11,3; 21,9 and 23,39; Mk. 11,9; Lk. 7,19-20; 13,35 and 19,38) which are adopted by the fourth evangelist in the same sense in Jn. 1,15.27; 11,27 and 12,13; See R. E. Brown, *op. cit.*; and Barrett, 187. In the fourth Gospel the nominal phrase 'ὁ ἄνωθεν ἐρχόμενος/ὁ ἐκ τοῦ οὐρανοῦ ἐρχόμενος' (3,31) could be understood as being in opposition with 'ὁ ὀπίσω μου ἐρχόμενος' (1,15.27), which is attributed to the Baptist and, thus, clearly signify a passing from a Christology of the traditional Messianic plan to a Christology of the Son of Man.

[612] The terms 'ἐπάνω πάντων' express the transcendence of the one who has come from above/heaven. This is similar to the expression 'ὁ ὢν ἐπί πάντων' (Rom. 9,5) applied to Christ or God depending on the punctuation; In Eph. 4,6 it refers, however, clearly to God. In this sense the one who comes from above/heaven is equal to God in his relation to the world; cf. R. E. Brown, *op. cit.*, 158; and Bultmann, *op. cit.*, 16-62.

[613] 'Ὁράω' and 'ἀκούω' are typical verbs referring to the authentication of testimony. An eyewitness is the ideal witness. That is why in the OT (cf. Gen. 31,50; Lev. 5,1; Job 29,11; and Jer. 32,12) testimony is often connected with "seeing." Cf. Beutler, *Martyria*, 317. 'Seeing' is related to 'knowing' when it is the result of 'seeing' (cf. 3,11). Having been in heaven (cf. 3,13.31), Jesus had the opportunity to see and hear and, therefore, he is juridically qualified to bear witness.

seen as an argument of the evangelist in support of his designation of Jesus as the Messiah and the Messianic bridegroom, in the first part of the second testimony of the Baptist (3,27-30) dealing with a Christology in traditional Messianic categories.

The categorical affirmation of 3,32d, however, recalls the words of Jesus to Nicodemus in 3,11f: "καὶ τὴν μαρτυρίαν ἡμῶν οὐ λαμβάνετε." But the second testimony of the Baptist in 3,32d brings in a universal character (cf. οὐδείς)[614] echoing the affirmation of the prologue: "He came to what was his own, and his own people did not accept him" (1,11).[615] Moreover, this reminds one of the polemic context of the confrontation between Jesus and the Jews in particular, as well as Jesus and the world in general as in the Nicodemus episode (cf. 3,16-21).

β. Or Acceptance of Testimony

However, there is hope of some accepting the testimony[616] (especially the Baptist and disciples of Jesus), because "whoever has accepted his testimony has certified this, that God is true" (3,33). As in 3,11-12, the negative generalisation admits certain exceptions. Here, the Baptist is arguing from his own experience to convince the listeners and move them to a positive decision. The verb σφραγίζειν is used in the sense of 'confirming' and 'attesting.' In fact, to understand this verse, one must consider 6,27 which contains the only other Johannine mention of the verb σφραγίζειν. This verse states that 'the Son of Man will give the food that endures for eternal life, for it is on him that God the Father has set His seal.' It deals with an official recognition in the form of a seal which authenticates a document.[617] Accepting the testimony is equated with attesting that God is true, which in turn is a confession of faith in Jesus, His envoy. This leads to 3,36ab where this confession of faith in the Son brings in a soteriological result.

If God has attested Jesus as the Son of Man, accepting the testimony of Jesus is recognising the divine attestation, because he says and does only what God says and does (cf. 5,19-30; 6,37-40 and 8,29); conversely, refusing the testimony is denying the fidelity and truthfulness of God, making Him a liar (cf. 12,44-50 and 1 Jn. 5,10). The Baptist is arguing his case already here with his audience, and he knows that the case for the defence must be powerful if it is to be accepted, when so many have rejected such a testimony before. In his mind it is not just his veracity or that of Jesus which is on the line, but that of

---

[614] The use of 'οὐδείς' in 3,32d is to be understood as a literary hyperbole to emphasise the world's tragic rejection of the envoy. It must not be pressed literally to suggest that no one responded. In the next breath (3,33) following the statement of universal rejection, there is the typical Johannine contrast with those who accept the divine messenger's testimony. This contrast is clearly a mirror image of the initial one made in the prologue (cf. 1,11-12) as explained above.

[615] On this verse read K. Scholtissek, "'Er kam in sein Eigentum – und die Eigenen nahmen ihn nicht auf' (Joh 1,11). Jesus – Mittler und Ort rettender vita communis in Gott nach dem Johannesevangelium," *GuL* 72 (1999) 436-51.

[616] However, even among the crowds who were going to Jesus (cf. 3,26d) some will not accept (cf. 6,60-61.64.66). That some will accept his testimony has been hinted at already in 1,12 in contrast to 1,11: "But to all who received him, who believed in his name, he gave power to become children of God." Comp. also 12,37 with 12,42.

[617] Cf. R. E. Brown (*op. cit.*, 158) and Barrett (189) refer to the *seal* as indicating approval on a legal document. See also Bultmann (*Gospel*, 163). In my opinion, it is a metaphor used by the evangelist from the existing customs of the time to interpret the attestation and confirmation of the authentic authority of God's envoy in His Son.

God, for it is God who has sent the Son, God who speaks in and through Jesus, and God who has given Jesus the Spirit without measure.

iii. Function of the Envoy and the Source of His Authority

3,34 brings in a change in the narrative. There is a passing from the scheme of the apocalyptic Son of Man to the scheme of God's envoy. It is similar to the passing (movement) that took place already from 3,11-15 to 3,16-21. In both cases, the transition is introduced by the conjunction 'γὰρ' (cf. 3,16a and 3,34a). There is a logical consequence between the two schemes.

3,34ab presents Jesus as the revealer of God as he speaks His words. Jesus asserts the same in 14,10 and adds that his revelation is the work of his Father who dwells in him. When the envoy pronounces God's words, which are spirit and life (cf. 6,63) containing eternal life (cf. 6,68), it is God Himself who is at work in and through His envoy. Moreover, Jesus interprets the work of God as evoking faith in his listeners to believe in His envoy (cf. 6,29).[618] Furthermore, it is in doing the will of his Father that Jesus completes his work (cf. 4,34), and the will of the Father is that whoever sees the Son and believes in him may have eternal life (cf. 6,39-40). Hence, the purpose of the Father in leading people to believe in His envoy is soteriological. Thus, a close connection is established between the revelatory function of God's envoy and his salvific mission. No doubt, the testimony of the Baptist in 3,34 is a repetition of the Christological and soteriological scheme of Jesus revealed in 3,16-17.

3,34c gives the reason (cf. γὰρ) for God's envoy being able to speak the words of God as his being filled (ἐκ μέτρου) with the Spirit.[619] In this statement neither the subject of the verb 'give' nor the receiver of the gift is specified. Hence, there is a possibility of interpreting it as God giving the Spirit without measure to His envoy[620] or the envoy giving the Spirit in abundance to the believers.[621]

I shall try to find an answer to the ambiguity by referring to the first testimony of the Baptist where he attests that the Spirit descended from heaven and remained on Jesus (cf. 1,32). The following verse (1,33) presents Jesus as possessor of the Spirit and hence, as one having the capacity to baptise with the Spirit, namely to give the Spirit to the believers. Moreover, all along the fourth Gospel Jesus is presented as the one who pours the Spirit. This theme, in fact, encloses the Gospel through the inclusive correspondence between 1,32-34, dealing with the function of the Messiah giving the Spirit, and 20,22, where Jesus

---

[618] This throws further light on the statement of the Baptist that "No one can receive anything except what has been given from heaven" (3,27bc).

[619] The Holy Spirit who rested on the prophets did so according to the measure of each prophet's assignment (cf. *Leviticus Rabbah* 15,2). Not so to Jesus: to him God gives the Spirit without limit. John the Baptist had testified already that he had seen the Spirit descending on Jesus (1,32-33) in fulfilment of Isaiah's prophecy (Is. 11,2; 42,1 and 61,1). See Carson, *Gospel*, 213; Barrett, 189; and R. E. Brown, *op. cit.* See also the detailed discussion of H.-C. Kammler, "Jesus Christus und der Geistparaklet. Eine Studie zur johanneischen Verhältnisbestimmung von Pneumatologie und Christologie," in: Hofius and Kammler, *Johannesstudien*, 87-190.

[620] Barrett, Bultmann, Dodd, Lindars, Loisy, Schnackenburg and van den Bussche are of this opinion.

[621] R. E. Brown, I. de la Potterie ("L'Esprit Saint dans l'Évangile de Jean," *NTS* 28 [1972] 448f.), Lagrange and Porsch are of this opinion. For a summary see O. Hofius, "'Er gibt den Geist ohne Maß' Joh 3,34b," *ZNW* 90 (1999) 131-34; see also J. Golub, "...non enim ad mensuram dat Spiritum (Jo 3,34b)," *VD* 43 (1965) 62-70.

breathes the Spirit on his disciples in view of their soteriological mission (forgiveness of sins – 20,23).

Moreover, in my opinion, in the context of 3,34-36, the accent seems to lie rather on the possession of the Spirit as the basis for the mission of the one sent. In 3,16-17, the evangelist evoked the mission of the one sent. He must now demonstrate the competence of the one sent to accomplish his mission. The envoy has not just received his mandate from his Father, but has also the indwelling and supportive power of the Spirit[622] to bring his mission to a successful completion. I am convinced, in both episodes, the role of the trinity in the salvation of the world is subtly brought out.[623] While in the Nicodemus episode the Son sent by the Father for the salvation of mankind demands that one has to be begotten of water and the Spirit to attain it, the second testimony of the Baptist insists on the Spirit-filled nature of the Son in fulfilling the will of his Father to lead mankind to eternal life. One more detail that is to be observed in both episodes is that it is the *love of the Father* which is the driving force: it is the love of the Father who takes the initiative to send His only begotten Son (3,16-17); and it is the same love of the Father (3,35a) that fills him with the Spirit (3,34c) empowering him to accomplish his soteriological mission.

Another argument in favour of my opinion is to be picked up from the parallelism between 3,31-32a and 3,34 (cf. **a-a**^{1} in the diagram above). The first element (**a**) deals with the testimony about the heavenly things 'seen and heard' (3,32abc), and the authenticity of this testimony depends on the heavenly origin and the transcendent nature of the witness (3,31ab.fg). In the same way, the element (**a**^{1}) deals with the envoy speaking the words of God (3,34ab), the needed capacity being given by the Father who fills him with the Spirit (3,34c), because the envoy is His unique and authorised mouth piece.[624]

In my opinion, the decisive argument remains, however, in the narrative and syntactic structure of 3,34-35. In fact, 3,34ab states the revelatory mission of the one sent while the rest of the verse (34c) is introduced by a causal conjunction 'γὰρ' which extends its content up to 3,35 in the narrative flow of the argument. In fact, it is the whole of 3,34c-35 which exposes the authority that endorses and supports the mission of the one sent. Moreover, in 3,35 it is said that the one sent is God's beloved Son in whose hands[625] all authority to accomplish his mission has been placed. The verb 'δίδωσιν' of 3,34c is formally repeated in 35b (δέδωκεν). Therefore, the subject in both cases is clearly the Father.

---

[622] The same process is followed by Jesus in sending his disciples: "'As the Father has sent me, so I send you.' When he had said this, he breathed on them and said to them, 'Receive the Holy Spirit.'" (cf. 20,21-22). For a detailed discussion see Bühner.

[623] On the trinitarian aspect see the detailed commentary of R. G. Gruenler, *The Trinity in the Gospel of John. A Thematic Commentary on the Fourth Gospel* (Grand Rapids 1986).

[624] Cf. Bruce, 97.

[625] The expression 'placing in the hand' is a Semitic expression referring to the transfer of power and authority (cf. Is. 47,6; and Dan. 2,38); cf. Barrett, 190; Schnackenburg, *op. cit.*, 388; Boismard and Lamouille, 124; and Bultmann, *Gospel*, 166. The fourth evangelist often speaks of the special gifts of the Father to the Son as power and authority: judgement (5,22.27); life (5,26); glory (17,22). It is also interesting to note that all these gifts are related to the soteriological mission of the Son.

iv. Goal of Testimony

Finally, 3,36 demonstrates the soteriological impact of the mission of the one sent. I notice a synonymous parallelism in the positive reaction (belief in the Son) bringing about a positive result (eternal life), and the negative reaction (disobedience) producing a negative result (loss of life and God's wrath[626]). Moreover, there is an antithetical parallelism between the positive (3,36ab) and negative reactions and results (3,36cde) as they are diametrically opposed to each other.

Just as in 3,18, one has either to believe and receive eternal life/be not condemned, or not believe/disobey and not see life/be condemned/endure God's wrath. There is only an either or in both episodes. Since Jesus is the eschatological envoy of the Father, belief in him brings forth eternal life immediately as the verb 'ἔχει' (3,36b) in the present tense indicates. The one who believes, therefore, possesses *from now* on eternal life and has passed already from death to life (cf. 5,24). On the contrary, the one who "disobeys[627] will not see life, but must endure the wrath of God" (3,36de). The expression 'seeing life' is a Johannine equivalent of 'seeing/entering the kingdom of God' (cf. 3,3.5) and expresses salvation.[628] The wrath of God refers normally to the eschatological judgement[629] of God awaited on the last day. Here the verb 'μένειν' is in the present, which proves the present reality of salvation providing the reader a wonderful sense of assurance (cf. 1 Jn. 5,9-12).

I have pointed out already (in the diagram above) the parallelism between 3,32d-33 and 36: the acceptance/non-acceptance of the testimony of the Son of Man corresponds to the belief/refusal to believe in the Son in the Christological scheme of the envoy. One difference is, however, remarkable: in 32d-33 there is no mention of the soteriological aspect in connection with the acceptance of the testimony. In fact, one can notice that the same absence characterises 3,11-13 which are parallel to 3,31-33. In the scheme of the Son of Man, the only mention of salvation in Jn. 3 is found in 3,15 and does not depend directly on the acceptance of the testimony but on the elevation of the Son of Man (cf. 3,14). On the contrary, in 3,34-36 the statement of the revelatory mission of the envoy in 3,34 leads to a soteriological affirmation in 3,36. In my opinion, this divergence can only be explained by a deeper study of the double-Christological scheme and its respective function within the Johannine argumentation. I shall deal with it in a separate chapter on the parallel narrative Christology.

c. Characterisation of the Baptist

A keen observation of the conclusion of the discourse with Nicodemus will reveal that the renewed focus on the Baptist (3,22ff.) is hardly a coincidence. Of all the figures in the Gospel (except Jesus) none is a better reflection of 'the truth' than the Baptist. Indeed,

---

[626] The anger or wrath of God is the way biblical writers expressed God's intolerance of evil or sin (cf. Rom. 1,18). The kingdom of God will not tolerate within it any form of sin (cf. Rev. 21,7-8,27 and 22,15). For a discussion of the anger or wrath of God see Schonweiss and Hahn, 105-13.

[627] The word 'disobey' must be understood as the opposite of 'believing.' Those who disobey are those who refuse to believe. Cf. Barrett, 190; Brown, *op. cit.*, 158; and Bultmann, *op. cit.*

[628] It is an equivalent of the expression 'having eternal life' (3,36b). The antithesis of 'seeing life' is 'seeing death' (8,51).

[629] Cf. Mt. 3,7; Lk. 3,7 and 21,23; Rom. 2,5-8; and Eph. 5,6.

nothing is more natural for the reader than to regard him as the one who both 'does what is true'[630] and whose 'deeds are done in God' (3,21).

In Jn. 3,22ff. the Baptist is once again, and for the last time, brought on stage to testify to Jesus. His portrait, here, is very compact. He is first represented as being both a witness, who in some way represents the old preparatory order, and as being in tension with the Jews (cf. 3,24-26). Then, there is the image of the bridegroom in 3,29. Though the Baptist's testimony here may be brief, "it involves a dense synthesising of diverse components"[631] and reveals a lot about his character. As usual the implied author has eyes only for the point he is making, namely, the relationship in ministry and dignity between Jesus and the Baptist.

The Baptist appears more frequently and has a more carefully qualified role than any of the other minor characters in the fourth Gospel. Apart from brief references to the Baptist in Jn. 5,33 and Jn. 10,40-41 all of the material about the Baptist is found in Jn. 1 and Jn. 3.[632] In accordance with the fourth evangelist's outlook, the Baptist is not seen in strictly historical terms. He is never called a prophet and there is no reference to his dress or diet (cf. Mk. 1,6; 6,15 and 9,13). He explicitly denies that he is *the* prophet (cf. 1,21). In the fourth Gospel Jesus is the protagonist and most of the other characters are ficelles. This observation is quite important for understanding the literary architecture of the fourth Gospel.

Prior to the Baptist's imprisonment (cf. 3,24), he and Jesus are portrayed as carrying on parallel baptising missions. However, Jesus and his disciples are making more disciples than the Baptist (3,26; cf. 4,1). But what is of special interest in connection with 3,21 is that, in 3,22-30, the Baptist takes his stand clearly and unequivocally for the Messianic claims of Jesus. He has an opportunity not to do so. For as an outcome of a debate on purification in which the disciples of the Baptist are engaged (3,25), these disciples come to their teacher with an apparent complaint about the growing popularity of Jesus, expressing concern over the ministry of their own teacher being eclipsed by that of Jesus; they seem to see in Jesus a rival to their master. But the Baptist is not chagrined at all; rather he is filled with joy, because these developments conform to his true testimony. The Baptist's answer to his worried disciples is in every way admirable. First, he reminds them of a broad religious principle 'providence governs all:' "No one can receive anything except what has been given from heaven" (3,27). He, then, humbly repeats the essential distinction he has made before: "You yourselves are my witnesses that I said, 'I am not the Messiah, but I have been sent ahead of him'"(3,28).

In fact, the gathering of the disciples is tied with Jesus' encounter with the Baptist in a way that is unique to the fourth Gospel, for only here does the Baptist send his own disciples over to Jesus; once he has borne his witness, he directs his followers to Jesus (cf. 1,35-36.40 and 3,25ff.), so that he may decrease in significance while Jesus increases.[633] In

---

[630] See Collange, 416 and 422.

[631] Brodie, *Quest for the Origin*, 118.

[632] See R. E. Brown, "Three Quotations from John the Baptist in the Gospel of John," *CBQ* 22 (1960) 292-98.

[633] For historical reasons for such a characterisation of the Baptist see R. E. Brown, *Gospel*, I, lxvii-lxx; and Schnackenburg, "Johannesjünger," 21-38.

his representational value in the fourth Gospel, he is a model of what his followers should do. In contrast to both the individual disciples and most of the other minor characters, the Baptist has no deficiencies in his faith. He is a model witness, because it is *given* to him to perceive who Jesus is.

The evangelist characterises the Baptist to the reader as one whose 'deeds' (cf. 3,19-21) – ministry and witness – are as far removed as possible from the kind of self-serving opportunism that marked the Pharisaic circle from which Nicodemus comes. Instead, the Baptist is distinctly 'doing what is true,' even at personal cost to himself – and thus, it becomes clear that 'his deeds are done in God' (cf. 3,21). Instead of attempting to recover a declining prominence on the religious scene, he utters one of the noblest statements in Scripture about the unique superiority and prerogatives of the Son of God. The essence of his attitude is beautifully expressed in his humble assertion: "he must increase, but I must decrease" (3,30).

The terminology about the Baptist is rather abstract and especially legal. From the outset he is introduced as a witness to Jesus, a man sent from God (1,6-8.15) [634] to tell the truth about Jesus (5,33.35 and 10,41). That is the sole significance of his work. His mission is to testify to the light (1,7). In its nominal and verbal forms, the word 'witness' (testimony/testify) is used repeatedly to define the Baptist's role. In the fourth Gospel a witness is conceived as one who tells what he has seen and heard (cf. 3,11.32 and 19,35). This pattern is applied also to the Baptist; what happened at the baptism of Jesus is understood as a revelation given to the Baptist, under the experience of which he could say: "I myself have seen and have testified that this is the Son of God" (1,34; cf. 1,32-33). As a witness, the Baptist is simply the *voice* announcing the coming of Jesus as the Lord, Son of God (1,23.34), and who takes away the sin of the world (1,29.36) during his baptising mission (1,30.33). [635] He is not only the voice; he finds joy and fulfilment in his relation to Jesus as "the friend of the bridegroom, who stands and hears [636] him, rejoices greatly at the bridegroom's *voice*" (3,29).

A careful reading of the opening scene of the Gospel reveals that up to 1,35, the Baptist has had the dominant role in the narrative and has described himself in active terms as "a voice crying in the wilderness" (1,23) and as one who "came baptising" (1,31). By comparison, Jesus has been mute and only begins to speak and take a major role in the story after 1,35. However, in the Baptist's final appearance in the story (3,22-36), where the author allows him to speak again, he finally admits that his is the passive role. He says that he is now standing [637] and listening (cf. 3,29). The picture of the Baptist in the fourth

---

[634] See M. D. Hooker, "John the Baptist and the Johannine Prologue," *NTS* 16 (1970) 354-58.

[635] See C. Payot, "L'interprétation johannique du ministère de Jean-Baptiste (Jean I)," *FV* 68 (1969) 21-37.

[636] For Moloney (*Belief in the Word*, 127; and *John*, 107), the Baptist displays here a radical openness to the word of Jesus. R. E. Brown (*op. cit.*, 531) describes this reply of the Baptist as "the reaction of those who believe in Jesus, even without seeing the signs;" see also Painter, *John*, 83-85.

[637] The verb 'ἵστημι' is used only three times in the first three chapters (1,26.35 and 3,29), and only rarely in the subsequent narrative. In its first two usages, the Baptist and the narrator were describing Jesus' and the Baptist's respective spatial positions in the narrative world at a very mundane level. But when the Baptist picks up and repeats the word in 3,29d, he uses it in a metaphorical context. This interplay between narration and direct speech reminds me of the way I see them used in the prologue, where the Baptist picks up the narrator's major verbs and repeats them in a riddle-like formula. In Jn. 1 the Baptist was confirming in direct

Gospel is very clearly focused, and it may be summed up in one of the Gospel's pointed statements: "he was not the light, but came to bear *witness* to the light" (1,8).

Since Jesus is the light, he *ranks* before the Baptist and must increase in stature, while the Baptist must decrease (3,29-30; cf. 1,15); he is the self-effacing witness to Christ. In contrast to Nicodemus, who does not deserve the title 'teacher of Israel,' Israel is invited to associate itself with the Baptist in his declaring that the Messiah "comes after me" but "ranks ahead of me because he was before me" (1,15). He is misunderstood if he is taken to have any greatness of his own (cf. 1,19-27 and 3,25-30). He is not the Christ and he does no signs (10,41).[638] Unlike Mark, the fourth evangelist does not describe Jesus as being baptised[639] or tempted; such ideas would not fit well with the exalted picture of Jesus as descending from God (cf. 3,13ff.). Instead the baptism account is so rewritten that it exalts Jesus above the Baptist (1,30-34), and the picture of a temptation or trial is adapted to become the trial-like[640] questioning of the Baptist (1,19-27).

However, the interest of the evangelist for the figure of the Baptist seems to be purely functional. His person has no autonomous narrative consistence. He is brought into the drama only to turn the attention to Jesus. In fact, the evangelist cannot leave to the Baptist the job of exposing the heart of his Christology,[641] because it belongs to the domain of 'heavenly things' (3,12) that Jesus alone can reveal, being the unique revealer come down from heaven (cf. 3,13).

But with the first testimony, used to introduce Jesus to Israel, the Baptist has not yet fulfilled the essential function which the fourth Gospel attributes to him, that is, to authenticate juridically in front of 'the Jews' the Christological claim of Jesus. Only after Jesus had revealed his true identity and the soteriological implication of his mission, it becomes necessary that the Baptist reappears and exercises his role of juridical witness taking into account the words of Jesus. It is the agreement of these two testimonies that

---

speech what the narrator had said about him (cf. 1,7-8). Here now, for a second time, the Baptist picks up the narrator's 'earthy' term and endows it with special meaning. In so doing, his own role in the story is brought to a conclusion, and his theological relationship to Jesus is reconfirmed to the reader. Alter (182) speaking of the role of direct speech in ancient Hebrew narrative describes that phrases or whole sentences first stated by the narrator do not reveal their full significance until they are repeated, whether fully or with distortions, in direct speech by one or more of the characters. See also U. Eco, *The Role of the Reader: Explorations in the Semiotics of Texts* (Bloomington 1979) 26.

[638] E. Bammel ("The Baptist in Early Christian Tradition," *NTS* 18 [1971] 112; and his, "John Did No Miracle: John 10:41," in: C. F. D. Moule [ed.], *Miracles: Cambridge Studies in their Philosophy and History* [London 1965] 179-202) observes that "Jesus' miracle-working activity differentiates him from the Baptist." See also D. M. Smith, "Johannine Christianity: Some Reflections on its Character and Delineation," *NTS* 21 (1975) 246; see also his *Johannine Christianity: Essays on its Setting, Sources and Theology* (Columbia 1984).

[639] Jesus had likely been baptised by the Baptist even as the Gospel witnesses assert. Interestingly, the fourth Gospel does not report this baptism directly, and in Matthew the Baptist at first demurs from baptising Jesus, suggesting that he himself needed to be baptised by Jesus (Mt. 3,14). This actual relationship makes the fourth Gospel's attempt to get the priorities straight quite intelligible and understandable.

[640] Cf. A. T. Lincoln, "Trials, Plots and the Narrative of the Fourth Gospel," *JSNT* 56 (1994) 3-30.

[641] In fact, the Baptist needs to be equipped with knowledge about Jesus, without, however, having a share in the exclusive knowledge coming from Jesus. The evangelist, therefore, adapts the Synoptic tradition: the Baptist did not know Jesus (cf. 1,31.33; comp. Mt. 3,13-14) and the descent of the Spirit upon Jesus becomes a pure sign of God addressed to the Baptist to designate Jesus as the one to be revealed to Israel (cf. 1,33-34; Mt. 3,16-17; Mk. 1,11; and Lk. 3,21-22). Except the consciousness of his mission, the Baptist is found in a situation just like the people and shares their Messianic concept.

will serve as the valid juridical argument in conformity with the principle of the OT.[642] It is precisely for this that the evangelist has placed the encounter with Nicodemus (2,23-3,21) parallel to the second testimony of John the Baptist (3,22-36) in the structural unity of the third chapter.

i. Brautführer[643]

Furthermore, the witness underlines the difference between himself and Jesus with a figure of speech that would have been very clear to his hearers. The *best man* is the trusted friend of the bridegroom[644] who prepares for the marriage ceremony;[645] any rival approach to the bride on his part would be unthinkable. The characterisation of himself as the friend of the bridegroom (שושבין) is an apt portrayal of the one who prepares the way of another.[646] The fourth evangelist's recourse to the figure of the Baptist – in his designation as witness and friend of the bridegroom – has only one purpose of leading Israel to believe in Jesus through his testimony, except that his function as witness in Jn. 1 is re-interpreted in Jn. 3 in nuptial categories. The friend of the bridegroom must take care that everything at the marriage happens according to the customs and tradition, especially those concerning the ritual norms of purification (cf. 3,25). Hence, there is a link between the two testimonies of the Baptist. The bride, who is not actually mentioned, is the people in general, the Messianic community,[647] to whom the message of Jesus is addressed. At one level Jesus himself is the bridegroom. But at a deeper level the bridegroom is God, for whose kingdom Jesus seeks to win the outcast. For in biblical tradition Israel is God's bride (Is. 13,4f.; and Hos. 2,16). The Baptist is sent before Jesus into Samaria[648] to prepare the conversion of the

---

[642] There should be at least two witnesses, according to the Jewish tradition, to authenticate a case (cf. Deut. 17,6 and 1915). It is essentially the role of the Baptist in the confrontation between Jesus and the Jews (cf. 5,31ff. and 10,40-42). According to *Mishnah*, a person cannot bear witness to himself (cf. *Ketuboth* 2,9).The witness of the Baptist is to satisfy this condition of convincing the Jews. For Létourneau (*Jésus*, 84-85) without such a confrontation the Baptist is not necessary for the fourth Gospel ("johanniquement inutile"); because Jesus does not need the witness of men (cf. 5,34 and 2,25). The testimony of Jesus in itself is valid as he knows whence he comes and whither he goes (cf. 8,14). If Jesus calls for the witness of the Baptist it is only with the hope of making the Jews believe and, thus, be saved (cf. 5,34). See Beutler, *Martyria*, 339-61.

[643] The German term '*Brautführer*' expresses more clearly the function of the bridegroom's friend.

[644] Commentators give little attention to the culminating importance of 3,29-30 in the narrative; Infante (12-14) sees it as crucial.

[645] See Batey, 46-50.

[646] Barrett, 186.

[647] Cf. Batey, 49; see also M. Stowasser, *Johannes der Täufer im vierten Evangelium. Eine Untersuchung zu seiner Bedeutung für die johanneische Gemeinde* (ÖBS 12) (Klosterneuburg 1992) 190. At the background is the OT theme of the spiritual marriage between God and his people (cf. Hos. 1-2; Jer. 2,2; and Is. 61,10) which the NT applies to the relation between Christ and the people of the new covenant (cf. Mt. 22,1-14; 2 Cor. 11,2; Eph. 5,27; and Rev. 19,7 and 21,2.10). The task of the Baptist, therefore, was to prepare the New Covenant between Christ and the Church, just as Moses did in the perspective of the marriage between God and his people during the covenant made at Sinai.

[648] Boismard ("L'ami de l'époux," 295) rightly observes that there exists a close theological link between the encounter of Jesus with the Samaritan woman and the Samaritans of Sychar preceded by the baptismal activity of the Baptist at Aenon near Salim. In the story of the fourth Gospel Jesus meets the woman at Jacob's well in Samaria, that is, ancient Israel. Jesus has been identified already at Cana as the true bridegroom who supplied the superior wine for the wedding feast (2,9-10) and by the Baptist as the true bridegroom to whom God has given the New Israel as bride (3,27-30).

Samaritans – the new bride – which culminates in their acceptance of Jesus as the true 'Saviour of the world.' (4,42).

ii. Baptist-Sects?

Now, the emphasis that the Baptist's allegiance and subordination to Jesus are seen as evidence for the existence of discrete groups of the Baptist's followers in the late first-century and the Christians' efforts to convert them to Jesus as the awaited Messiah.[649] Moreover, if the prologue, the key to the Gospel, makes an unfavourable contrast between Jesus and the Baptist, such an unfavourable contrast means that the Gospel as a whole wants to put the Baptist in his place – a purpose which is best explained by the idea that when the evangelist was wirting, followers of the Baptist were making undue claims for their master and so were causing a problem.[650]

In the nature of the case, it is virtually impossible to prove the non-existence of such sectarians.[651] In my opinion, nothing of the kind follows from the prologue. As a close analysis of the prologue indicates, the Baptist is depicted as embodying the tradition of the ancient prophets – he is a positive witness, someone who cheers when Jesus finally enters the scene (cf. 3,29). To speak of an unfavourable contrast between Jesus and the Baptist is to inject polemic where there is none. The difference between Jesus and the Baptist as found in the prologue – a difference which is real – is fully accounted for by bearing in mind the difference between prophecy and its fulfilment. No further theory is necessary, still less, one that invents a whole social group.

What is true of the prologue is true also of those other texts which are sometimes mentioned as reflecting the existence of Baptist sectarians. Texts which tell what the Baptist is not (not the light, not the Messiah, not the bridegroom, etc.: 1,8-15.19-24.30; 3,28-30 and 10,41), and texts which show his disciples asking anxious questions about the

---

[649] See E. Trocmé, "Jean-Baptiste dans le quatrième évangile," *RHPhR* 60 (1980) 136.

[650] Cf. H. Lichtenberger, "Täufergemeinden und frühchristliche Täuferpolemik im letzten Drittel des 1. Jahrhunderts," *ZThK* 84 (1987) 36-57. In order to find a statement in which a disciple of the Baptist really does exalt his matter over Jesus, one has to move to the third-century author Pseudo-Clement (one of several Pseudo-Clements). This writer describes a fictitious meeting held at Caesarea between Peter and Clement of Rome, in the course of which Peter tells how "one of the John's disciples used to affirm that it was John who was the Christ, not Jesus" (*Recognitiones*, 1:60; cf. 1:54); see B. Rehm (ed.), *Die Pseudoklementinen, II, Rekognitionen* (GCS 51) (Berlin 1965) 42. The statement indeed is clear, but as R. E. Brown (*Community*, 70) remarks, "there are problems about this reference." One problem is that the original Greek has been lost, and the two ancient translations, Latin and Syriac, vary considerably, particularly in these passages involving the Baptist. Such a phenomenon suggests that what is being reflected in the Baptist passages is not a fixed text, still less an ancient fixed tradition, but a theology which, even at the time of translation, is in motion and under development. Cf. R. E. Brown, *Gospel*, I, lxviii. The detailed study of Pseudo-Clement is complex and inconclusive. Rather than trying to build on such shaky grounds and shifting sands, it seems more reasonable to be guided by a text which is solid and pertinent, the fourth Gospel itself. When that is examined, and when due account is taken of its theological dimension, the theory concerning the Baptist and the late first-century Baptist sectarians appear to be without foundation.

[651] On this controversy see K. Backhaus, *Die 'Jüngerkreise' des Täufers Johannes. Eine Studie zu den religionsgeschichtlichen Ursprüngen des Christentums* (PaThSt 19) (München, Paderborn, Wien, Zürich 1991); his, "Täuferkreise als Gegenspieler jenseits des Textes. Überlegungen zu einer kriteriologischen Verlegenheit," in: J. Hainz (ed.), *Dokumentation des Symposions 'Methodenstreit zum Johannesevangelium' vom 29. und 30. Juni 1990 in Kelkheim* (Darmstadt 1991) 16-44; J. Ernst, "War Jesus ein Schüler Johannes des Täufers?," in: Frankemölle and Kertelge, *Vom Urchristentum zu Jesus*, 13-33; and O. Cullmann, *Der johanneische Kreis. Sein Platz im Spätjudentum, in der Jüngerschaft Jesu und im Urchristentum. Zum Ursprung des Johannesevangeliums* (Tübingen 1975).

increasing appeal and popularity of Jesus (3,26-30; cf. also Mt. 11,2-19; and Lk. 7,18-35) – all of these passages, while telling what the Baptist is not, also tell positively what he is (he is not the light, but he is a witness; he is not the Messiah, but he is a voice like that of Isaiah; he is not the bridegroom, but he is the bridegroom's friend).[652] They are further variations of the relationship between prophecy and its fulfilment. These are anxious questions, including a suggestion of some tension that is appropriate, for the transition from the old order to the new required a tense combination of continuity and breakthrough. The tension in question turns out in the last analysis to be a variation of the tension which is found in the Sermon on the Mount, when Jesus speaks of the relationship between the old and the new: "I did not come to destroy but to fulfil..." (Mt. 5,17.21). Such is the implication of the texts dealing with the Baptist; the tension fits within a larger unity. Never in the four Gospels does the Baptiser utter a word of resentment concerning Jesus; and once he has explained the continuity to his disciples, nor do they. The matter is resolved; the old and new despite their differences complement one another.

What is essential is that the tension, such as it is, is theological. It does not require that its elements be projected onto opposing sociological groups. Let me consider Acts 18,24-19,7. This speaks of some people, particularly Apollos, who had received only the baptism of the Baptist. I do not find any undue exaltation of the Baptiser, still less any lack of enthusiasm for Jesus. On the contrary, Apollos reflects all that is best in the Baptist: he embodies the Scriptures and he teaches about Jesus (Acts 18,24-25; and again in 18,28). When these Baptist-related people hear of the baptism of Jesus they accept, and there is no hint of resistance or delay. On the contrary, 'hearing, they were baptised...;' and even as Paul laid his hands on them, the Holy Spirit came down (Acts 19,5-6). Hence, on the basis of an account, which is so thoroughly positive, it is not reasonable to build a hypothesis which is negative. What emerges overall is that if one is to use the NT as a basis for speaking of the existence of unresponsive Baptist sectarians, one first has to project into the text an antagonism which is not there, and then take the further step of converting the antagonism into a late first-century social group.

Nevertheless, I must say that more attention is paid to the Baptist in the fourth Gospel than in any of the others. The concern to keep the identity of the Baptist in proper perspective must be understood as arising from the implied author's concentration upon the true and proper confession of Jesus as Messiah and Son of God. The Baptist becomes the first human witness to him.

Furthermore, just as the characterisation of the disciples is paired in Jn. 2 and placed in contrast with that of 'the Jews,' the character of the Baptist is paired in Jn. 3 with that of Nicodemus, 'a leader of the Jews,' and one's character is portrayed in contrast to the other. Though both hold the title *Rabbi* (cf. 3,10.26) – both are teachers within Judaism, both are men of power and influence, and both are challenged by the coming of Jesus – Nicodemus is not presented with his pupils, whereas the Baptist is surrounded by his faithful disciples (cf. 3,26). The contrast is personal and, on a deeper level, symbolic.[653] Nicodemus is described as belonging to a particular group in the society – ἄνθρωπος ἐκ

---

[652] See Rinke, *Kerygma und Autopsie*, 86-87.

[653] D. A. Lee, *Symbolic Narratives of the Fourth Gospel. The Interplay of Form and Meaning* (JSNT.S 95) (Sheffield 1994) 58.

τῶν Φαρισαίων, whereas the Baptist is portrayed as a partyless man called John (1,6). Nicodemus holds the worldly title ἄρχων τῶν Ἰουδαίων, whereas the Baptist's titles – 'a man sent from God' (1,6), 'witness to the light' (1,7-8), and 'friend of the bridegroom' (3,29) – are heavenly and are to be seen only in relation to Jesus. Nicodemus has no courage to openly confess his faith and follow Jesus, whereas the Baptist boldly, openly and cheerfully bears witness to Jesus in spite of the hostile cross-examination at the Jordan by an investigating committee of priests and Levites from Jerusalem (1,19-25), and the tricky instigation of his disciples by a Jew(s) (cf. 3,25); he would even suffer imprisonment and death for his witnessing mission (cf. 3,24). In contrast to Nicodemus, he is the prototype of those chosen and dedicated ones who give up all for Christ, and who, in this world, get little or nothing in return. The sublime phenomenon is unintelligible to the fervent fulfilment-of-personality seekers like Nicodemus and the leaders of the Jews.

Finally, the Baptist is also employed as a character symbol who is to be contrasted directly with Jesus. Jesus is the long awaited Messiah; he is the witness (1,7-8). Jesus is the Light (1,4.5,7-9), he is the lamp (5,35). Jesus is the Word (1,14); he is the voice (1,23). Jesus baptises with the Holy Spirit; he baptises with water (1,33). Jesus is the bridegroom; he is the friend of the bridegroom (3,29). To miss this contrast in characterisation is to miss the theology of the Gospel enunciated through vivid contrasts.

d. Reader and Point of View

For the reader the Baptist is portrayed as a person laying himself open to all that comes 'from above.' A series of previously used images is repeated to emphasise Jesus' superiority over the Baptist. From the immediate context, the narrator is explaining why Jesus must increase: he alone is from above (ἄνωθεν) and from heaven, and is, therefore, above all (3,31). The Greek term 'ἄνωθεν' immediately recalls 3,3: begetting from above can be experienced only by faith in the one who comes from above. By contrast, all others are from the *earth* (γῆ). The term 'γῆ,' unlike 'κόσμος,' betrays nothing of sinfulness but only of finitude and limitation. In the immediate context, the Baptist must decrease (3,30), because he is from the earth: he called people to repentance and to baptism in water, but he could not reveal heavenly things, nor could he offer a begetting from above, the long-promised renewal from water and the Spirit (3,5). Thus, although he was sent from God (1,6) he, too, fits into the restriction of 3,13: only the Son of Man can speak with supreme authority of heavenly things, for he alone testifies to what he has seen and heard in the heavenly sphere.

He has testified to what he has seen and heard, but no one accepts his testimony (3,32). The completely negative implication of this statement is immediately softened in the following verse (3,33): "Whoever has accepted his testimony has certified this, that God is true." The singular can make the reader associate it with the Baptist, whose ability to receive Jesus is a gift from heaven. The reader can also understand that in contrast to the bountiful but limited number of the Jewish purification jars (2,6), the one sent from God "does not give the Spirit by measure" (3,34). This introduction of the theme of 'giving the Spirit' completes the contrast with the Baptist which he himself began in 1,26 and continued in 1,34 with the theme of Jesus baptising with the Holy Spirit.

For the reader it becomes clear that 'the Jews' and Nicodemus must be judged as being 'of the earth' (3,31). Failure to accept the testimony of Jesus has marked much of the narrative from 2,12-3,30, even though he has revealed what he has heard (3,32; cf. 3,11).[654] The risk of such rejection is made clear in the narrator's insistence that one who accepts Jesus' revelation of God is attesting to the ultimate truth. As the reader come to the end of this section he/she finds a reflection showing interest in 'the word' (cf. 3,34). It is also from this perspective the reader is expected to understand the figure of the Baptist as the friend of the bridegroom, who stands and *hears* him (his word), rejoices greatly at the bridegroom's *voice* (his word) (3,29).

Finally, the reader is drawn into the narrative and invited to respond.[655] Reader response, however, is not effected through the faith of the leading character, but rather in the challenge to move beyond Nicodemus' indecision. It is the witness of the Baptist which enables the reader to realise the full meaning of an appropriate faith response. The Baptist's faith opens the way for the reader to succeed where Nicodemus – at least in this narrative – has failed.

4. Christological Argumentation of 3,22-36

All along this episode I notice a thematic progression between the false understanding about the identity of the person of Jesus by the Baptist's disciples (cf. 3,26) and the witnessing exposition of his true identity by the Baptist (cf. 3,27-36). The detection of the Christological argument of this episode consists in understanding the argumentative and narrative flow from one segment to the other, *viz.*, from 3,22-26 to 3,27-30 and to 3,31-36.

3,22-26 introduces the story and paves the way for the bipartite Christological discourse of the Baptist (3,28-30 and 3,31-36). On the one hand, there is a natural flow of narration and argumentation from 3,26 to 3,27. On the other hand, 3,27 contains a general principle which is developed in the subsequent bipartite segments. I shall demonstrate the flow of the narrative from 3,26 to 3,28-30 as well as from 3,26 to 3,31-36 through the intermediary verse 27.

As I have mentioned already, the baptismal activity of a person leads naturally to the question of his identity or his divine authority as baptism had a purificatory function. The Baptist is left with only two choices – either to confirm the divine authority of Jesus or to deny it.[656] To make his disciples understand, the Baptist states a general principle at first (3,27). I have explained the various possible interpretations of this maxim in the above pages.

In the first part of the Baptist's testimonial discourse (3,28-30), the maxim of 3,27 serves to interpret the movement of the crowds toward Jesus in relation to the Baptist. The argumentative flow from 3,26 to 3,28 is established by the formal recurrence of the verb 'μεμαρτύρηκας' (3,26) and 'μαρτυρεῖτε' (3,28). The disciples recall to the mind of their master his testimony about Jesus (3,26) and the Baptist, on his turn, recalls what he had

---

[654] Schnackenburg (*op. cit.*, 384) points out that the καί in 3,11f and 3,32d is adversative. Jesus reveals from direct access to God, *but* this is rejected.

[655] See the enlightening study of P. B. Harner, *Relation Analysis of the Fourth Gospel: A Study in Reader-Response Criticism* (Lewiston 1993).

[656] See the work of G. Barth, *Die Taufe in frühchristlicher Zeit* (BThSt 4) (Neukirchen-Vluyn 1981).

testified earlier (3,28cd; cf. 1,6.15.20.23.27.30.33). Having recalled the distinction between him and Jesus, he begins to interpret the movement of crowds toward Jesus.

He, then, moves from the distinction 'Messiah'-'one sent ahead of him' to the distinction 'bridegroom-friend of the bridegroom' (3,29). The last two figures stand in relation to the bride, but with a fundamental difference that the bride does not belong to the friend of the bridegroom. He can only prepare and lead her to the bridegroom; she never comes back to the friend of the bridegroom. Consequently, if the bride (people) goes to Jesus (3,26g) and if "no one can receive anything except what has been given from heaven" (3,27bc), Jesus is the bridegroom whom God has given the bride. It is divine will that the all go to Jesus and the disciples have, therefore, no reason to be anxious about it. The movement of people toward Jesus must (δεῖ) continue till all the disciples of the Baptist and all the people go to Jesus (cf. 3,30).

Till now, the movement of the people toward Jesus has been interpreted as a fulfilment of the divine will (3,27) and, thus, Jesus could be identified as the bridegroom. The actual movement of people toward Jesus confirms the former statements of the Baptist: "this is the Son of God" (1,34), *viz.*, "one who baptises with the Holy Spirit" (1,33), and "the Lamb of God who takes away the sin of the world" (1,29; cf. 1,36). But what is the necessity of this second testimony?

The function of 2,23-3,36 is to introduce the true Christological scheme of the Gospel as against the traditional Messianic categories. As the Baptist is the authorised witness of Jesus before Israel, it is his duty to present them their Messiah (cf. 1,31). However, the true identity of Jesus can be revealed only by himself, the unique and competent revealer regarding heavenly things (cf. 3,11-13). Before this self revelation of Jesus, the Baptist could not but depend on the traditional concept of the Messiah; that is why he affirms that he did not know the Messiah (1,31) and needs a divine sign to recognise him (cf. 1,32-34). But once the true identity of Jesus has been revealed, the Baptist must once again testify to the truthfulness of this self-revelation of Jesus. That is the reason for the parallel juxtaposition of these two episodes (2,23-3,21//3,22-36).

Although his disciples must see in 'all going to Jesus' a confirmation of their master's earlier testimony, they must now understand that this movement toward Jesus – the Son-sent – is the only way to salvation. To demonstrate this, the general principle of 3,27 is elaborated with a soteriological perspective in the second part of the Baptist's discourse (3,31-36).

In 3,31-36, the Baptist makes his disciples move from their observation of all going to Jesus, to understanding the soteriological goal of the movement, *viz.*, "whoever believes in the Son has eternal life" (3,36). To take his disciples to this end, the Baptist re-interprets the principle he stated in 3,27 in Christological categories of the Son-sent (3,34-35). That 'the Father loves His Son and has placed everything in his hands' indicates that he has full authority and power (cf. 5,19-30) to accomplish his mission of saving the world, *viz.*, giving eternal life to the believer (cf. 6,16-18). Hence, it is only evident and natural that all go to Jesus (3,26); it is necessary for them to go to Jesus and believe in him in order to have eternal life.

However, the principle of 3,27 is not only a Christological statement demonstrating the transfer of divine authority and power to Jesus in view of his mission. As its primary purpose is to interpret the movement of all toward Jesus, its application in the Christological scheme of the Son-sent, is, above all, for a soteriological purpose. People, who belong to God as his creatures are given to His Son-sent so that he could give them eternal life (cf. 6,39; 10,28-29 and 17,1-2). So understood, 3,27 seems to be the condition for obtaining salvation in the scheme of the Son-sent. To have eternal life one *must go to* the Son and believe in him (3,36). However, to go to the Son, one *must be drawn by* the Father (cf. 6,44) or, in other words, they must be given by God to Jesus (3,27). Just as the intervention of God is necessary for being begotten ἄνωθεν (3,3) in the Christological scheme of the Son of Man, the offer of salvation, too, needs divine intervention. To obtain the salvation offered by God and realised through His Son, the people must make the radical choice of believing in His envoy. Interpreting the general principle of 3,27 in the Christological categories of the Son-sent (3,34-36), the Baptist drives home the point that Jesus is not a competitor, but the plenipotentiary Son sent by the Father for the salvation of the world.

Till now I demonstrated the argumentation that connects the incomprehension of the Baptist's disciples (3,26) and the witness of the Baptist about Jesus as the Son-sent through the intermediary principle stated in 3,27, but without taking into account 3,31-33. 3,31-33 operate the transition of the narrative from the Messianic scheme (3,28-30) to the Christological scheme of the Son-sent. The triple occurrence of the term 'witness' (μεμαρτύρηκας – 3,26; μαρτυρεῖτε – 3,28; μαρτυρεῖ – 3,32) establishes a formal structural link between the three segments of the Baptist episode. The repetition of the verb 'witness' by the Baptist reminds his disciples of his first testimony. This recalling of his earlier witness is necessary as the remark of his disciples in 3,26 betrays that they have not understood it rightly. If they had rightly understood they would not be surprised at the fact that all go to Jesus. The Baptist had clearly said that he was not the Messiah.

The third occurrence of the verb 'witness' in 3,32 is different from the first two, in the sense, that it recalls not the first testimony of the Baptist, but the first testimony of Jesus in the Nicodemus episode (3,11-13 and 3,14-18). As it is clear in 3,31-32, the Baptist, being of the earth, is of earthly nature and, therefore, can speak only of earthly things. All the others like Moses (cf. 3,13) and the Baptist (1,31-34) received their knowledge about heavenly things from above. Just as at the first testimony, the Baptist needed a divine revelation now, too, in order to testify to Jesus as the Son sent by God. This time the source of the divine revelation is the word of Jesus himself; and he is trustworthy as he (Son of Man) has come down from heaven which makes him a competent witness to heavenly things.

Moreover, the testimony of Jesus about heavenly things are about the identity and the mission of the Son-sent as well as faith as the necessary response to attain salvation. These are the elements that the Baptist recalls in his second testimony (3,34-36). That is why the Baptist says that "whoever has accepted his testimony has certified this, that God is true" (3,33). As explained already, 'God is true' means that, as sender, He is faithful and does not abandon His obedient envoy and remains in perfect union with him (cf. 8,26-29). Accepting the testimony of Jesus, the Son of Man, is recognising him as the plenipotentiary (cf. 3,35b) Son sent by God. The connection between 3,33 and 3,34-36 is once again supported by the causal conjunction 'γὰρ' just as in the transition from 3,15 to 3,16 in the previous episode.

Thus, the argumentation of the Baptist in 3,31-33 is similar to the one employed by Jesus in 3,11-13. Since Jesus alone is the competent witness to heavenly things one must accept his revelation about his identity and mission. The traditional Messianic concept (1,19-51 and 3,28-30), rooted in the OT must be corrected as the authority of Jesus is superior to all other witnesses. I do not insert any conclusion to this part here to avoid repetion as it will be done in the general conclusion.

Chapter 4

PLOT

Plot is an interpretation of the story from the evangelist's point of view.[1] Characterisation and plot are the means used in every narrative to accomplish this task of interpretation. Analysis of plot and characterisation is indispensable to comprehend the unique design of the entire Gospel as well as that of its individual pericopes or episodes. What is true of characterisation of the fourth evangelist is equally true of his creation of a plot for his Gospel. The essential element of plot is "the dynamic shaping force of the narrative discourse"[2] or "the structure of its actions, as these are ordered and rendered toward achieving particular emotional and artistic effects."[3] The material the fourth evangelist, received from various traditions, had a shape already. Yet, he fashioned these materials into a coherent whole. Every event in the narrative has a definite meaning, because it is part of a story having a conclusion. The evangelist, therefore, went through a process of selecting, shaping and systematising the information he had at hand in order to establish an internal coherence – sequence of events involving progression and causality – and to convey the message of the story.

As actions occurring after the beginning are the result or the natural consequence of what preceded, plot, inevitably, is connected with time and causality. To Stibbe's definition of plot as "the organisation of events into a coherent unity characterised by a causal[4] and temporal logic,"[5] I would like to add the *structural aspect* to complement and complete it. Let me now explore each of these three features in 2,23-3,36 in reference to the Gospel.

A.   The Causal Aspect of Plot

Some comments about tragedy might help to understand causality better. In an ideal tragedy there is a beginning, a central point and a culmination or end. The whole action must ascend toward the central point in an orderly sequence, and from it descend again in an equally ordered sequence to the end.[6] Based on this one observes five acts in a tragedy: there is the beginning, the development toward the central point, the central point itself, the development toward the end, and the end.[7]

Although the fourth Gospel is not a tragedy, this framework does help one to see something of the causality of the plot of the Gospel. After a dramatic prologue and introduction, the narrative of the Gospel is established in *the beginning*. The first stage is described in Jn. 2-4, where Jesus begins his public ministry with a journey from Cana in

---

[1] See J. A. du Rand, "Plot and Point of View in the Gospel of John," in: J. H. Petzer and P. J. Hartin (eds.), *A South African Perspective on the New Testament. FS B. M. Metzger* (Leiden 1986) 149-69.

[2] P. Brooks, *Reading for the Plot* (London ²1992) 13; see also U. C. von Wahlde, "Literary Structure and Theological Argument in Three Discourses with the Jews in the Fourth Gospel," *JBL* 103 (1984) 575-84.

[3] Abrams, 127.

[4] E. M. Forster (*Aspects of the Novel* [New York 1962] 87) gives the following simple example to illustrate causality: "The king died, and then the queen died" is a story. "The king died, and then the queen died of grief" is a plot. The time-sequence is preserved, but the sense of causality overshadows it.

[5] M. W. G. Stibbe, *John's Gospel* (London, New York 1994) 34.

[6] F. R. M. Hitchcock, "Is the Fourth Gospel a Drama?," in: Stibbe, *Gospel of John as Literature*, 16.

[7] Cf. *Ibid.*

Galilee (2,1-11) to Jerusalem through Samaria, and then back to Cana again (4,46-54). Here the character and mission of Jesus is firmly established in the mind of the reader.[8]

The second stage of the plot is *the development toward the central point*. This is done in Jn. 5-10, where conflict begins to emerge. Here the *enemy of God* comes to the fore, in the form of the Jewish hierarchy in Jerusalem. They plot to kill Jesus from 5,18 onwards, and make every attempt to arrest or stone him as he performs his ministry of teaching and healing.

The third stage of the plot is described in Jn. 11-12. This is the *central point* of the story. The raising of Lazarus is the seventh miracle performed by Jesus in the Gospel. Since seven is the perfect number in Judaism, the raising of Lazarus in 11,1-44 needs to be seen as the climactic miracle. Indeed, it is the most dramatic, lengthy and provocative narrative of all the miracles. It is this event which precipitates Jesus' downfall (11,45-53). It is from this point that the Sanhedrin plotted to put an end to his life (11,53).

The fourth stage of the plot is the *development toward the end*. This is described in Jn. 13-19, where Jesus bids farewell to his followers and is crucified. These seven chapters of the narrative cover the last twenty-four hours of Jesus' life from Thursday evening to Friday evening in the Passover week. Here Jesus prepares for and experiences the fate which the Sanhedrin had planned for him in stage three.

The fifth and final stage of the plot is Jn. 20, the resurrection of Jesus. This is the *end* of the story, with Jn. 21 functioning as an epilogue. It is here that the disciples meet the risen Jesus, and it is here that the recognition scene occurs. This takes place when Thomas looks at the risen Jesus and says, "My Lord and my God" (20,28). This Christological confession forms the climactic denouement in the plot of the Gospel.

It has been noted by commentators that each unit of the fourth Gospel contains the essence of the entire Gospel in a micro form. The study of form criticism and the history of traditions has helped to detect this phenomenon. This does not mean that each and every pericope of the Gospel contains the gist of salvation history, nor does each episode of the Gospel accommodate the complete message of Jesus. But I contend that each pericope of the Gospel embodies within itself some components of his central message. In particular, I legitimately claim that the narrative of the encounter between Jesus and Nicodemus contains the core of the Gospel message in a nutshell.

Applying it to the unit of my study I observe immediately that 2,23-25 plays the first stage of *the beginning* where Jesus' presence and mission brings an apparent success of leading many to believe in him seeing the signs he performed. The second stage of *development toward the centre* is seen in the supernatural knowledge of Jesus capable of reading through the hearts of many, whose faith is insufficient, and so in his not trusting them and their representatives (Nicodemus, the Pharisees). A conflict with 'the Jews' is implicit here. In Jn. 3 Jesus does not meet real opposition. The narrator gives the reader further guidance in understanding the meaning of acceptable faith and the consequence of

---

[8] See F. F. Segovia, "The Journey(s) of the Word of God: A Reading of the Plot of the Fourth Gospel," *Semeia* 53 (1991) 23-54.

believing or not believing.[9] In fact the plot of the whole Gospel is propelled by conflict between belief and unbelief as responses to Jesus.[10] Trying to define dramatic monologue, R. Ingarden says that a conversation aims at influencing the person who listens to the words. "The speech addressed to a character is a form of action on the part of the speaker."[11] It has importance for the events in the play only if it actually brings about a genuine advance in the action of the play. In his encounter with Nicodemus, Jesus begins to make an impression on a representative of Jewish leadership. At the same time, the evangelist clarifies that the real conflict is not between Jesus and 'the Jews' or their official leadership but between Jesus and those who refuse to accept his revelation. Unbelief is the real *opponent*. It is described in images such as flesh, world, earthly things, and darkness which are opposed to Spirit.

The *central point* (third stage) and the next stage of *development toward the end* are to be found in the motif of the descent and ascent of the Son of Man and his being lifted up (3,13-14) definitely alluding to Jesus' crucifixion and glorification. The task of Jesus is to *reveal the Father* by bearing witness to the truth and *take away the sin* of the world. For the fourth evangelist the two seem to be related. The revelation of the Father seems to be the distinctive contribution of Jesus' role of taking away sin. Jn. 16,8-9 characterise the sin of the world as unbelief. Sin is taken away when one recognises the *Logos*; and this recognition comes only to those who believe. Both facets of Jesus' task culminate at his death. The cross is his glorification; it reveals his glory for all to see. The more Jesus announces his redemptive mission the more clearly his identity is revealed and the more intense the hostility toward him becomes. The hostility in turn dramatises the radical difference between those who believe and those who do not. The fifth stage or *the end* is expressed in many verses of the Nicodemus pericope dealing with the necessity of belief in the Son of God for life (cf. 3,15-21).

The same pattern of five stages is to be observed in the following episode (3,22-36) as well. The first stage of *the beginning* is to be found in the narrator's note of Jesus' baptismal ministry parallel to that of the Baptist attracting many (3,22-23). The second stage of *development toward the centre* is to be noted in the subtle hint of a conflict provoked by a Jew(s) that leads the disciples of the Baptist to an apparent opposition against Jesus as he attracted more crowds than their own master (3,25-26). The third and the fourth stages are to be perceived in the testimony of the Baptist to Jesus as the Messiah (3,28), the bridegroom (3,29), the one come from above (3,31), and the one whom God has sent (3,34), though there is no explicit hint at the death of Jesus. One could, perhaps, notice a very faint hint at it in 3,32 speaking about the rejection of his testimony. *The end* is to be observed in the reference to the necessity of belief in the Son for life (3,36). Though, like the reference to Jesus' hour in Jn. 2,4, the death and glorification of Jesus are left unexplained, through the plot of Jn. 3, the evangelist is showing that Jesus' influence widens and his followers increase. Finally, plot development in the fourth Gospel is, in my

---

[9] On the representation of various types of faith in the first section of the fourth Gospel, see F.-J. Moloney, "From Cana to Cana (Jn. 2:1-4:54) and the Fourth Evangelist's Concept of Correct (and Incorrect) Faith," *Sal.* 40 (1978) 817-43. See also Hodges, "Untrustworthy Believers," 139-52.

[10] The centrality of this conflict is confirmed by the fact that almost half of the occurrences of the verb "πιστεύω" in the NT are found in the fourth Gospel (98 out of 239). See Painter, *Witness and Theologian*, 77.

[11] R. Ingarden, *Das literarische Kunstwerk* (Tübingen 1960) 408-9.

opinion, a matter of how Jesus' identity comes to be recognised and how it fails to be recognised.

Conscious plotting of the narrative is more obvious in the fourth Gospel than in the Synoptics. The fourth Gospel has a different order of events. For example, Jesus moves back and forth between Judea and Galilee. The confrontation in the Temple at Jerusalem is his first public act while in the Synoptics it is his final provocation. The dialogues in the fourth Gospel are more contrived and less realistic compared to those of the Synoptics.[12] The dialogues are often impelled by misunderstanding, inept questions, and double meaning which I have pointed out already. The same themes recur repetitively. The great deal of repetition in the fourth Gospel only shows that the evangelist is trying to drive his point home.[13] Images, terms, themes, signs, confrontations over the Law and Jesus' identity, presence at feasts in Jerusalem, and dialogues with followers and *opponents* are repeated all through the fourth Gospel. All these features point unmistakably to the careful crafting of a unified sequence and a logic of causality.

B. The Temporal Aspect of Plot

There is also a clear sense of temporality. Aristotle observes order, amplitude, unity, and probable and necessary connection as the components of plot in a narrative. Order requires that plot has a beginning, a middle, and an end in the temporal unity of a story.[14] This is what I find in the fourth Gospel. The events of the story are given temporal unity by the threefold mention of Passover. In the fourth Gospel three such festivals are mentioned: 2,13; 6,4 and 13,1.[15] Moreover, the narrator describes three times that the ὥρα "has not yet come" (2,4; 7,30 and 8,20), and with the third Passover there is the triple mention that the promised ὥρα "has come" (12,23; 13,1 and 17,1). This image of the ὥρα is used on a number of occasions to remind the reader that there is a temporal horizon[16] which functions as the goal of Jesus' work. The ὥρα is the time for Jesus "to be lifted up on the cross" (3,14), to leave this world and return to the Father. It is also the time of Jesus' glorification. The reader is led to anticipate the arrival of the hour.[17]

As far as causality and temporality are concerned, the unit of my study, like the Gospel, contains discernible order and direction in its plot. Seen as a whole, the story of the fourth evangelist contains a kind of Passover plot in which events follow one another and move toward that climactic ὥρα in which Jesus is crucified, precisely the moment when the Passover lambs were being slaughtered in the Temple. There is no explicit

---

[12] Wilder, 48; and H. W. Frei, *The Eclipse of Biblical Narrative: A Study in Eighteenth and Nineteenth-Century Hermeneutics* (London, New Haven 1974) 16.

[13] On this point of repetition see J. A. du Rand, "Repetitions and Variations – Experiencing the Power of the Gospel of John as Literary Symphony," *Neotest.* 30 (1996) 59-70; and W. A. Beardslee, *Literary Criticism of the New Testament* (Philadelphia 1970) 25. See also Painter, *Witness and Theologian*, 11.

[14] Aristotle's *Poetics* 1450b-1451b, in: D. A. Russel and M. Winterbottem (eds.), *Ancient Literary Criticism: the Principal Texts in New Translations* (Oxford 1972).

[15] There has been considerable discussion over their significance for the theology and the structure of the fourth Gospel. E.g. Schnackenburg, *Gospel*, I, 1-2; and Léon-Dufour, *Lecuture*, I, 31-32 and 252-53. R. E. Brown (*Gospel*, I, cxxxix) rightly sees the three Passovers as "setting for a particular narrative."

[16] See R. Kieffer, "L'espace et le temps dans l'évangile de Jean," *NTS* 31 (1985) 404.

[17] Cf. G. R. O'Day, "'I Have Overcome the World' (Jon 16:33): Narrative Time in John 13-17," *Semeia* 53 (1991) 158.

mention of the hour in the unit of my study, but the crux of the pericope is the necessity of belief in the Son for life (3,15f.36); however, there is an implicit reference to that life giving hour as the hour when Jesus will be 'lifted up' on the cross (cf. 3,14-15).

C. The Structural Aspect of Plot[18]

Having looked at the causal and temporal aspects of the fourth evangelist's plotting of events, let me now turn to the structural dimension of the same. For this I need to use the insights of structuralism – an ideology committed to exposing deep structures in all aspects of life. The most helpful approach for exposing the structural character of the fourth Gospel's plot is the method of deep structure analysis, commonly referred to as *actantial* analysis, proposed by A. J. Greimas. In this approach, exegesis consists in mapping a given biblical story against Greimas' universal structure of narrative possibilities. Essentially his argument is that all stories can be reduced to a deep narrative structure, a kind of trans-cultural and universal grammar of story telling. In the form of a diagram, Stibbe presents it as follows:

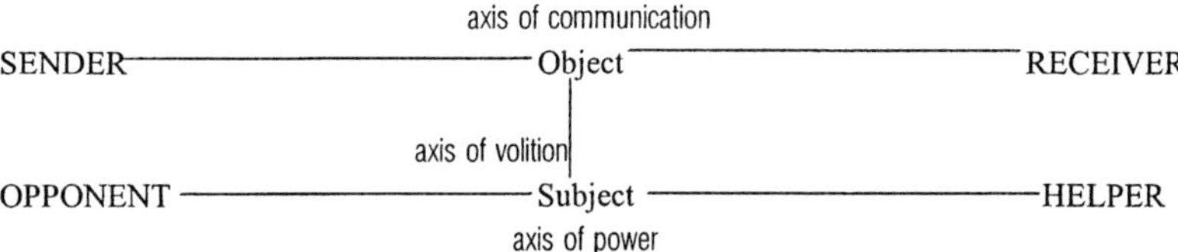

This deep structure has three axes: an *axis of communication*, an *axis of volition* and an *axis of power*. These three axes are basic plot functions. The axis of communication is the commission; someone tells someone else to undertake a task. The axis of volition is the quest; the hero undertakes to do a particular task or fulfil a particular mission. The axis of power is the conflict experienced by this hero from *helpers* and *opponents*.

These three axes have four character-types or *actants* associated with them. The first is the *sender* (Father). He gives a commission to the second actant, the *receiver* (Jesus) through a third actant, the *subject* (Jesus), who comes into conflict with the fourth actant, the *opponent*. However, he receives assistance from the fifth actant, the *helper*. Throughout all of this, the *subject* is involved in a quest, and the quest itself is the *object*. Curiously, the *receiver* is identical with the *subject*.

Stibbe, in my opinion, has confused in this actantial model the *receiver* – to whom the *object* comes – with the *subject* who receives the mandate for action. Thus, he makes Jesus both the *receiver* – instead of the Jews/the world (the addressees of Jesus' dialogues and discourses) – and the *subject*. In my opinion, in what Stibbe sees as the central plot statement (Jn. 3,16),[19] it should be observed that it is the world and believers within it who are the *receivers* of the *object*. In addition, it is not only the language of 'sending' but also

---

[18] This part is based on A. J. Greimas, *Sémantique Structurale* (Paris 1966); Stibbe, *Storyteller*, 30-46; his *John's Gospel*, 38-53; his, "'Return to Sender' A Structuralist Approach to John's Gospel," in: Ashton, *Interpretation*, 261-78; and his, "Structuralism," in: R. J. Coggins and J. L. Houlden (eds.), *A Dictionary of Biblical Interpretation* (London, Philadelphia 1990) 650-55.

[19] Stibbe, "'Return to Sender'," 193.

that of 'receiving' (cf. 3,11.27)[20] that makes the fourth Gospel so appropriate for an actantial analysis. When this is recognised, confirmation is provided for the identification of the *receiver* as the world, represented primarily by the Jews.

When I apply this kind of actantial model to the plot of the fourth Gospel, and to my unit of study in particular, I begin to see its usefulness for narrative exegesis. God the Father is clearly the *sender* figure in the plot of the fourth Gospel. The verb *send* is used extensively throughout the fourth Gospel. Note that the verb ἀποστέλλειν (cf. 3,17.28.34), is used twenty-eight times and πέμπειν thirty-two times. Moreover, it is God the Father who is most often the subject of these verbs; in fact the fourth evangelist characterises God as the *sending Father*. Father's commission is attested by the repeated description of Jesus as *the one sent* by the Father (cf. 3,17.34).[21] The *receiver* is the world (3,16.17.19) or Israel.

The commission which the Father gives to Jesus is an ἔργον or a task. Though there is no scene in which this ἔργον (work) is explicitly described, Jesus does speak of "the works that the Father has given me to complete" (5,36 and 4,34).[22] In the unit of my study this work is described as *saving the world* (cf. 3,17) and giving *eternal life* (3,16). The fulfilment of this ἔργον is achieved by Jesus on the cross as described in Jesus' words "it is finished" (19,30). Thus, the cross becomes the place from which Jesus will be 'lifted up' (cf. 3,14), that is, accomplish his work and return to the *sender*. The axis of communication consists of a commission by the Sending Father through the *subject* (Jesus) to the Receiving world. The *object* of this commission is the ἔργον given by the Father for Jesus to accomplish.[23] These observations help to present the first aspect of the fourth evangelist's plot as given below:

axis of communication

SENDER	Object	RECEIVER
(*Father*)	(ἔργον - ζωή)	(*World*)

Let me now move on to the axis of volition. Here, I am faced with the issue of the quest in the story of the fourth Gospel. The *subject* of this quest is Jesus, and the *object* is to bring ζωή αἰώνιος (eternal life) to those who believe in him (*receiver*), as is clear from

---

[20] The verb λαμβάνω is used 19 times and παραλαμβάνω once for receiving some aspect of the *object* such as Jesus himself, his words or the Spirit, and on each of these occasions it is the world or Israel and those within them who constitute the intended *receiver*. Only once, in 10,18, is λαμβάνω employed for the mandate or command Jesus receives from the Father. The dominant pattern is set by the language of the prologue, where the true light comes into the world, comes to what was his own, and his own people did not receive him (1,9-11). Yet there are those who do receive him, who in fact receive from his fullness, grace upon grace (1,12.16). Other passages which illustrate clearly this pattern are 13,20 with its fourfold use of λαμβάνω – "Amen , amen, I tell you, whoever receives one whom I send receives me; and whoever receives me receives him who sent me" – and 14,17 with its talk of "the spirit of truth, whom the world cannot receive."

[21] On twenty-four occasions, πέμπειν is used in the phrase *the one who sent me*, and on seventeen occasions ἀποστέλλειν is used of the sending of Jesus by the Father. The fourth evangelist is, thus, presenting Jesus as the focus of an *emissary Christology* (see Bühner), and in narrative terms as the *receiver* of the *sender*'s commission; see also Waldstein, 203-21; and F. Agnew, "On the Origin of the Term Apostolos," *CBQ* 38 (1976) 49-53.

[22] The concept of the hour of Jesus refers to the time-limit prescribed to accomplish this work.

[23] There is no text in the fourth Gospel in which this commission is explicitly given. It is presupposed throughout. The axis or channel of communication between the *sender* and the *receiver* is kept open throughout the narrative (cf. 3,16-17.34-35; 5,19.30; 11,41-42; 12,28 and 17,1).

3,16: "... so that everyone who believes in him may not perish but may have eternal life." Here, I notice that the ἔργον given by the Father to Jesus is concretised as giving ζωή[24] αἰώνιος to the believers (the children of God). I find a confirmation of the same quest in the words of Jesus: "I came that they may have life, and have it abundantly" (10,10), as well as in the words of the narrator at the end of the Gospel: "These are written....that ....you may have life in his name" (20,31). In fact Jesus describes his ministry as doing "the will of him who sent me and to complete his work" (4,34). Thus, the axis of volition can be shown as follows:

SENDER	Object	RECEIVER
(*Father*)	(*ζωή*)	(*World*)
	axis of volition |	
	Subject	
	(*Jesus*)	

The third axis is the axis of power. In the development of plot in the story of fourth Gospel, one often comes across 'the Jews,' the Pharisees (cf. 3,1), and the 'world' (cf. 3,16.17.19) as *opponents* of Jesus resisting his desire to fulfil his quest. In the unit of my study those who occupy the opponent pole of the axis of power are further described as 'those who do not believe in the name of the only Son of God' (3,18), 'love darkness' (3,19), 'do evil and hate the light' (3,20), and 'disobey the Son' (3,36).

I am now left with the *helper* figure. In the plot function of the narrative of the fourth Gospel neither the Baptist, nor the disciples, nor the Holy Spirit, not even the Father[25] is depicted as a *helper* to Jesus in his mission. The fourth evangelist has intentionally portrayed Jesus as a man without obvious *helpers*. He wants to evoke superhuman and solitary heroism in the characterisation of Jesus, who achieves his goal against all odds.[26]

As D. Brewer describes that "the relationship of the narrative is primarily to the message about the *hero*, only secondarily to actual events... the message then shapes the telling of the events."[27] Coming back to the diagram, I can now add the axis of power and see the plot of the Nicodemus pericope as follows:

---

[24] Already in the prologue the narrator says of Jesus: "in him was life" (1,3). The noun ζωή recurs thirty-six times in John as against sixteen times in the Synoptics.

[25] Though the relationship between the Son and the Father is one of unanimity and the Son only does what he sees the Father doing, the fourth evangelist carefully avoids giving the impression of Jesus receiving divine assistance in his task. Jesus' prayers in the fourth Gospel are not petitionary in character. He never cries for help. For example, in 11,41-42 he prays to the Father before raising Lazarus. He is doing so not because he needs the Father's help, but because he wants the crowd to hear what he is praying. In 12,27, though Jesus is in anxiety, he does not throw himself at the mercy of God as in Lk. 24,42. He prays rather: "Father glorify your name" (12,28). See also Jn. 17 and 18,1.

[26] This emerges with particular power in the passion narrative (18-19). For example, in contrast to the Synoptics, Jesus goes out to greet Judas and the arresting party (18,4), he confidently embraces the cup which the Father has given him (18,11); he has no need for angels in the garden. And he carries his cross alone to Golgotha (19,16); he has no need for Simon of Cyrene at Golgotha. Thus, Jesus is portrayed as a hero who has no need of *helpers*.

[27] D. Brewer, "The Gospels and the Laws of Folktale: A Centenary Lecture, 14 June 1978," *Folklore* 90 (1979) 45.

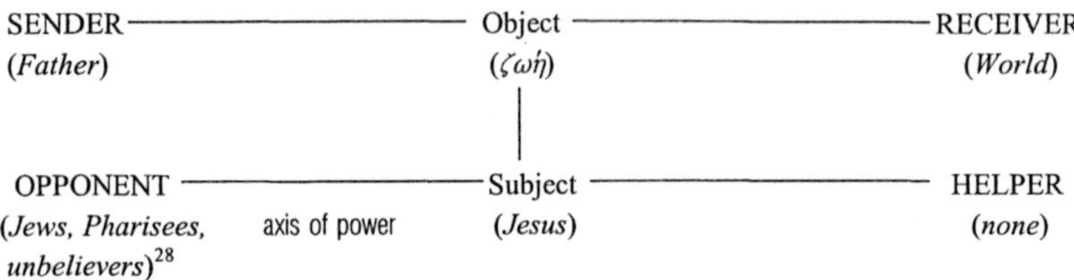

This actantial model is helpful in revealing the deep structure of the fourth Gospel's plot. The story of the fourth evangelist subverts this structure as far as the portrayal of the *opponents* and *helpers* of Jesus are concerned, in the sense that, paradoxically, the *opponents* play the role of the *helpers*, too. It was the purpose of the *sender* that the 'Son of Man must be lifted up' in order that people may have eternal life and the world may be saved (cf. 3,14-17). The narrator has taken pains to formulate it carefully: "This was to fulfil what the scripture says" (19,24.36.37). In theological terminology, the antagonists of Jesus therefore contribute to the predetermined will of God. In narrative terminology, the antagonists of Jesus are both *opponents* and *helpers*. In fact, Jesus' enemies[29] help him to fulfil his commission. Indeed, without them, he could not have completed his work. The moment of Jesus' apparent failure (in terms of his quest) is therefore ironically the moment of his great triumph. Conversely, for 'the Jews,' the moment of their apparent triumph is ironically the moment of their greatest failure. The ironic triumph of Jesus' *opponents* is in fact the awesome fulfilment of his mission. Jesus' "end comes as expected, but not in the manner expected."[30] Thus, the 'lifting up of the Son of Man' (3,14) refers to the death and glorification of Jesus simultaneously. The cross is, in reality, Jesus' triumphal exit – return to his *sender*.

Let me now apply the same actantial structure to the narrative episodes of the *story of John the Baptist* (1,1-37 and 3,22-36). I find here some interesting similarities with the plot of 3,1-21. The story of the Baptist, as portrayed in Jn. 1 and Jn. 3, shines in a revealing light when exposed to an actantial approach. Let me begin with the axis of communication. It is interesting to note that the Baptist, like Jesus, is "a man sent from God" (1,6). Obviously the *sender* is God the Father, the *receiver* is his listeners (Jews, his disciples, those who came to him for baptism).

As far as the axis of volition is concerned, the Baptist is the *subject* and the *object* of his quest is to bear witness to Jesus. As the narrator explains, "he came as a witness to testify to the light" (1,7). In fulfilling this mission of his, he has to face an *opponent*. Here I have the axis of power. He is challenged by the enquiry commission sent by the Jews in Jerusalem. These envoys are priests, Levites and Pharisees. The Baptist is subjected to an

---

[28] As far as the unit of my study is concerned, the Jews and the Pharisees are not yet explicitly portrayed as *opponents* of Jesus. They are presented as unbelievers as shown above. Nicodemus is one of them, more so he is a leader of the Jews and belong to the party of the Pharisees. At this stage he is still a representative of the unbelievers.

[29] It is they who seek to arrest and kill Jesus (Jn. 5). It is they who formally decide to have him put to death (Jn. 11). It is they who acquire the service of Judas and Pilate in the arrest and execution of Jesus. In a certain sense Jesus depends upon the actions of his antagonists in order for his salvific death to occur; see Stibbe, "Return to Sender," 269-70.

[30] F. Kermode, *The Sense of an Ending: Studies in the Theory of Fiction* (London, New York 1967) 53.

informal trial (1,19-28).[31] The opposition he faces is a forewarning and foretaste of what awaits Jesus. He, too, will be subjected to many interrogations.

It is interesting to note that the Baptist, too, has no obvious *helper* in his mission. His disciples are not described as assisting him in any way (e.g. comp. 3,22 with 3,23), nor is there any obvious reference to God helping him at any point. Like Jesus, the Baptist stands alone. His is a solitary voice crying in the wilderness (1,23).

What I have, therefore, in the narrative of the Baptist is a rehearsal and an anticipation of the story of Jesus. The deep structure of the plot of the Baptist's story has resonance with the deep structure of the plot of Jesus' story.[32] Greimas' actantial approach, thus, helps to confirm the point made by Dodd that "each episode...contains in itself, implicitly, the whole of the Gospel."[33]

So what happens to the Baptist echoes with the story of Jesus. Both are 'sent from God' and in that sense *receivers*. Both stand alone against an array of antagonists (indeed, the same *opponents*) and are unaided by *helpers*. Both are subjected to interrogations and trials by the Jewish authorities in Jerusalem.[34] In terms of the deep plot-structure of the Baptist story, I see that something of the plot of the Gospel as a whole is being imitated in the story of the Baptist. The structural similarities between the stories of the Baptist and of Jesus imply that followers of Jesus can expect their own story of discipleship to follow a similar pattern. Their story will have a structural similarity with the story of Jesus. In this respect, the fourth evangelist's work with plot sequences has a pastoral purpose.[35]

D. Plot - An Elaboration of the Prologue in Action?

As I have pointed out, the beginning, end, repeated material, tasks of the characters, and nature of the conflicts – all provide clues to the plot of the Gospel. The plot, evidently, revolves around Jesus' fulfilment of his mission to reveal the Father and authorise the children of God (τέκνα θεοῦ). In fact, the prologue provides clues to the plot of the entire Gospel.[36] The prologue also establishes the antithetical norms which will be in conflict throughout the narrative: light and darkness (1,6 and 3,19-21), belief and unbelief (1,11-12 and 3,15-16.18.36), grace and truth, and the Law (1,14.16-17 and 3,21.33). The whole Gospel is seen as an elaboration of the prologue. The prologue, would, probably, never be convincing to the reader were it not for the rest of the narrative. Plot is inherent in the concept of the protagonist (Jesus), but the concept is not realised in the narrative until this character is expressed through action.

Crane classifies plots in three categories: plots of action involving a change in the protagonist's situation, plots of character implying a change in his moral character, and

---

[31] See Lincoln, 6.

[32] See R. A. Culpepper, "The Plot of John's Story of Jesus," *Interp.* 49 (1995) 347-58.

[33] Dodd, *Interpretation*, 384.

[34] Cf. Lincoln, 12-14.

[35] However, these insights concerning the structural aspects of the fourth evangelist's plot are not supposed to imply that the evangelist is playing a subtle game with narrative techniques. In any event, it would be difficult to argue that the evangelist was entirely conscious of the interpretation offered here. What I can say is that the evangelist's construction of both macro and micro-plot sequences is not to be regarded merely as an aesthetic adornment. Rather, it is geared to help the reader who comes to faith and decides to follow in the footsteps of Jesus.

[36] Cf. R. A. Culpepper, "The Pivot of John's Prologue," *NTS* 27 (1980) 1-31.

plots of thought suggesting a change in his thoughts or feelings.[37] The affective power of plot is produced by the hopes and fears, desires and expectations it imposes on the reader as it unfolds the change from beginning to end. By the end of the story the reader has been led to a particular emotional or volitional response: catharsis, satisfaction, outrage, anxiety, or belief.[38] I have demonstrated this already under characterisation how each character in the unit of my study is carefully portrayed to evoke a response in favour of Jesus.

Hence, the plot of the fourth Gospel is a *plot of action*[39] in the sense that Jesus achieves his goal while his fortune apparently changes for the worse. Not only is Jesus' identity progressively revealed by the repetitive signs, dialogues and discourses and the progressive enhancement of metaphorical and symbolic images, but, as shown above already, each episode has essentially the same plot as the story of the whole. The story is repeated over and over. Individual episodes seem almost convey the message of the whole; at least they suggest or recall it for those who know the story. The prologue gives each of these episodes an ironic background in that the reader has been taken already into the confidence of the narrator and knows who Jesus is.[40] Thus, the plot of the fourth Gospel uses a literary dynamic pushing the reader to embrace the point of view of the evangelist, that is, the confession that Jesus is "the Christ, the Son of God" (20,31). The ignorance and blindness of 'the Jews,' the misunderstanding of a leader of the Jews and a teacher of Israel, the apparent jealousy of the disciples of the Baptist faced with the increasing popularity of Jesus, the witness of the Baptist and his subordination to Jesus – all give to the plot of the story a continuing dramatic force,[41] ties the various episodes together and maintains the tension as various characters accept or reject Jesus.

E. An Admiration Plot

N. Friedman, extending Crane's system of three plot types, suggests six types of classification within each type. One of them is the *admiration plot*.[42] The πολλοί flock to Jesus because they are attracted by a sense of admiration for Jesus on seeing his miraculous signs (2,23). One notices Nicodemus approaching Jesus with sentiments of admiration: "Rabbi, we know that you are a teacher who has come from God; for no one can do these signs that you do apart from the presence of God" (3,2). Nicodemus also belongs to the nobility of the Jewish teachers, but fails to understand Jesus. Risking his reputation and under fear of being noticed by his fellow Pharisees, Nicodemus approaches Jesus, though he disappears from the scene without notice which evokes the readers' sympathy and disappointment. The protagonist's (Jesus') nobility of character, honour and reputation is enhanced by such a visit.

---

[37] R. S. Crane, "The Concept of Plot," in: R. Scholes (ed.), *Approaches to the Novel* (San Francisco 1966) 239.

[38] N. Friedman, "Forms of the Plot," in: P. Stevic (ed.), *The Theory of the Novel* (New York 1967) 154-55.

[39] Cf. Lincoln, 3-30.

[40] The reader is, therefore, in a privileged position and is made to feel superior to the characters Jesus confronts, because in contrast to them he/she knows that Jesus is the incarnate *Logos*.

[41] T. Onuki ("Zur Literatursoziologischen Analyse des Johannesevangeliums – Auf dem Wege zur Methodenintegration," *AJBI* 8 [1982] 186-87) considers the fourth Gospel as *"dreiaktiges Schauspiel."*

[42] The other five are: a) the action plot, b) the pathetic plot, c) the tragic plot, d) the punitive plot, e) the sentimental plot; see Friedman, 160.

In the same way, the complaint of the disciples of the Baptist that "all are going to Jesus" (3,26) implying increase in the popularity and importance of Jesus, the Baptist's expression of joy on hearing it, his calling himself as a 'friend of the bridegroom' (3,29), and his wish that Jesus should increase and he himself should decrease (3,30) indicating the superiority of Jesus – all suit well with the admiration plot. The final response of the readers should be respect and admiration for a man outdoing himself and the expectations of others concerning what a man is normally capable of.

Conclusion

The conversation with Nicodemus, like each succeeding sign, dialogue, and discourse, introduces new images and gives a richer texture to the Gospel's interpretation of Jesus. Thus, the plot of the fourth Gospel is interwoven with a progressive unveiling of the identity of Jesus, involving signs and conflicts, dialogues and discourses, and short allusive references to his end, almost in every episode. In his plot the evangelist uses the various episodes skilfully to enrich the texture of the whole.

The constitutive features of a plot are present in 2,23-3,36. I shall demonstrate in Part II how Jn. 3 is interwoven into the network of the Gospel in its section (1,19-4,54) and, thus, has its meaningful place in the story proving *sequence or order*. The second feature, *causality*, contributes to the unity of the Gospel story. The affective power of a narrative, however, is the most important feature of its plot. Jesus is shown as confronting and conversing with a wide variety of individuals and groups in everyday situations (at a wedding, at the Temple, at a feast, in the night at his lodge, at a well, at a pool, etc.). The plot of each episode, especially that of 2,23-3,36, is structured in such a way as to enclose the reader – who is faced with the conflict between belief and unbelief – into the company of faith. In fact, the plot of the Nicodemus pericope and of the Baptist's episode, like the whole Gospel, is controlled by thematic development and a strategy to convince and draw the readers to believing in Jesus. The affective power of the plot pushes the reader toward a response to Jesus. In short, the purpose of plot in 2,23-3,36 is Christocentric.

Chapter 5

NARRATOR AND POINT OF VIEW

In the fourth Gospel as a whole and in the unit of my study in particular, one is aware of being told a story, and is conscious of a narrating voice. The narrator is the voice of the omniscient[1] author. The same narrator and the same voice speaks throughout. His voice is always in the third person. He stands outside the action, and has a privileged view and understanding of the words and works of Jesus. He is capable of reading into the mind of Jesus who 'knew all people' (2,24) and 'knew what was in everyone' (2,25; cf. 4,1; 5,6; 6,6.15.61.64 and 11,33.38). He serves as the competent and authoritative interpreter of Jesus' words. Thus, the narrator appears to be a character who is both transcendent and immanent to the narrative. Within the narrative, it is he who provides temporal[2] and spatial[3] co-ordinates, introduces characters (cf. 2,23 and 3,1.22-26), indicates who is speaking (cf. 3,2-5.9-10.26-27), interprets words and works, describes, explains, addresses, announces, etc. Everywhere the narrator works, obviously, to get round the reader to the point of view or ideological position he holds;[4] that is the enlightened post-resurrectional (cf. 2,22 and 12,16) understanding of Jesus as the Messiah, the Son of Man and the Son sent by the Father. Moreover, his view is influenced by OT Scripture[5] (3,14 → Num. 21,8f. and 3,16 → Gen. 22,1-19) and the Spirit (3,5-6.8; cf. 14,26). And it is this understanding which supports the narrator's rhetorical strategy expressed in 20,31.

B. Uspensky identifies five planes in which the narrator's point of view may be expressed: the psychological (internal and external to the characters), the spatial (location of the narrator), the temporal (the time of the narrator), the ideological (evaluative norms),

---

[1] Omniscient is not to be understood as divine.

[2] Besides the mention of the Passover festival and the past tense of the verbs there is only one time marker, νυκτός (3,2), which would need to be interpreted together with all the time markers of the fourth Gospel. Yet, it is clear that this is a secondary time-frame that remains largely undefined, so much so the reader still belongs to it. In fact, in 3,1-6, there is no future which closes the time of the pronouncement. In 3,12 the future is the time when people will believe, when they will be taught heavenly things, a time which apparently is still future for the reader. Note also the reference to the imprisonment of the Baptist (3,24) as a future event still to take place (a prolepsis).

[3] The space is mentioned as Jerusalem in the case of the Nicodemus pericope, and as the Judean country side, Aenon near Salim, prison and across the Jordan in the Baptist episode. Besides, Patte (17) observes a fourfold space constructed: i) A space 'near Jesus' where verbal exchanges take place. It is, thus, a verbal space, but not in the sense that it is created verbally. He calls it 'euphorie space' since Jesus is described as 'performing signs' and as having God 'with him.' ii) A space 'away from Jesus,' the space where Nicodemus was among the Pharisees. iii) A space 'with God,' the space from which Jesus comes (3,2), identified as 'heaven' or 'above' in 3,13.27.31. iv) a space, 'kingdom' that one can 'see' (3,3) and 'enter' (3,5), which is related to 'water and the Spirit.' v) The 'mother's womb' (3,4) is a space of the 'flesh' (3,6), opposed to the space of the spirit (the kingdom). The concrete spaces (away from Jesus with the Pharisees, the 'mother's womb,' and the flesh) are called 'dysphorie.' The euphorie spaces are verbal, in relation with the divine and spiritual. Both the temporal (again) and the spatial (from above) meaning of the word ἄνωθεν must be accepted if one is to see the kingdom of God; see Barrett, 205; and Moloney, *Belief in the Word*, 110.

[4] Duke (*Irony*, 156) speaks of the narrator of the fourth Gospel "winking" at the reader; and Staley (*Print's First Kiss*, 95-97) remarks of the narrator as "victimising" the reader.

[5] See M. J. J. Menken, *Old Testament Quotations in the Fourth Gospel: Studies in Textual Form* (Kok Pharos 1996); Marrs; and Westermann.

and the phraseological (speech patterns).[6] I shall adopt these five aspects to analyse the point of view of the narrator in the unit of my study.

A. Psychological Point of View

As one reads the text, the voice of the narrator introduces the narrative world of the text: its characters (in the unit of my study - the Jews, the many, Nicodemus, the disciples, those who went for baptism, the Baptist), values and norms (e.g. "no one can do these signs that you do *apart* from the presence of God" – 3,2fgh; "no one can receive anything except what has been given from heaven" – 3,27bc), conflicts (cf. between believers and unbelievers, Spirit and flesh, light and darkness, heavenly and earthly things, knowledge and ignorance, life and judgement, salvation and condemnation), and events (cf. 2,23-25 and 3,22-27) which constitute the plot of the story. The narrator conveys the author's perspective (cf. 3,16-21.31.36) to the reader and sends signals which establish expectations, distance and intimacy, and powerfully affect the reader's sense of identification and involvement (cf. 3,18f.36). The narrator's claims and norms of the story charm, move, and challenge the reader to believe that the story, its narrative world, and its central character (Jesus) reveal something profoundly true about the real world in which the reader lives.

Comments by the narrator are distributed throughout the narrative and generally serve as introductions (2,23-25 and 3,22-25) or conclusions – to scenes or sections – or as transitional and explanatory notes. Moreover, the authority of the narrator is elevated by the fact that he knows everything relevant for the story. For example, in 2,23-25 the narrator speaks directly to the reader in a commentary on the quality of a faith based on *seeing* the signs of Jesus.[7] Strangely, the story has not reported the signs in Jerusalem, and these signs upset the numbering of a first and a second miracle at Cana (2,11 and 4,54), but the ongoing narrative takes it for granted that they happened. Moreover, the initial reaction of the Jews (2,20) would seem to discourage such a mass movement of believers toward Jesus. However, the reader must accept the word of the narrator.[8]

The narrator, at times, manifests only limited insight into the story, or supplies privileged information which no ordinary observer of the action would have (cf. 3,24), in which case the narrator is, to a certain extent, omniscient. Through the narrator, the reader knows more than any of the characters who interact with Jesus in the story. The narrator recalls past events, has had time to reflect and puzzle things out *post factum* and so is able to reconstruct the internal state of the people, imagining what they must have experienced. For example, the narrator knows that, in the beginning, the Word was with God and knows what is going to happen in the story before it actually takes place (e.g. the death of Jesus on the cross and the imprisonment of the Baptist – cf. 3,14.24). He informs the reader that Jesus knew all things (2,24-25); he discloses what Jesus was thinking, and is able to interpret Jesus' thoughts and emotions; he knows what Jesus meant by what he said (3,14; cf. 4,1; 5,6; 6,6.15.61.64; 11,5.33.38 and 13,1.11.21), tells that people were attracted by

---

[6] Cf. B. Uspensky, *A Poetics of Composition. The Structure of the Artistic Text and Typology of a Compositional Form* (Berkeley, Los Angeles 1973) 6.

[7] The narrative "slows down" as the narrator speaks directly to the reader; see Genette, *Nouveau discours*, 22-25.

[8] Genette (*Narrative Discourse*, 34-47) calls it a sort of Johannine "anachrony." See the apt remarks of Schnackenburg, *Gospel*, I, 342.

Jesus (2,23 and 3,26); he is aware that some individuals, like Nicodemus, wanted to meet him and discuss with him, and some others were disturbed that many were flocking to Jesus (e.g. the Jewish authorities, the disciples of the Baptist – 3,25-26).

Not only Jesus, but some of the characters like Nicodemus, the Baptist, the disciples (cf. 2,11.17.22; 3,2-9; 4,27; 12,16; 13,28.29; 20,9 and 21,4), the Samaritan woman, the royal official (cf. 4,53) Joseph of Arimathea (cf. 19,38), and others are open to the narrator. But the narrator does not make profound or lengthy scrutiny of these characters. Most of the comments are artistically or rhetorically motivated; they involve disclosures which establish characters and explain responses.[9] For example, Nicodemus, though a learned man, is presented as one not capable of understanding the words of Jesus. The narrator is aware of the anxiety of the disciples of the Baptist on seeing the new baptiser (Jesus) attracting the crowds of their master (3,26). He knows that their master, the Baptist, must soon disappear from the scene through imprisonment and death, and make place for Jesus, who is greater than him (3,24.30). In general, the inside views are brief but credible in the light of the narrator's retrospective point of view.

B. Spatial Point of View

It is difficult to locate where the narrator usually stands. He does not define his geographical position. The Greek verb ἔρχεσται, which is used frequently in the fourth Gospel and may mean either *to come* or *to go*, is ambiguous. However, the repeated use of ἐκεῖ and ἐκεῖθεν, which mean *there* and *from here* respectively gives me a clue. Ἐκεῖ occurs twenty-two times and ἐκεῖθεν twice in the fourth Gospel. Ἐκεῖ occurs twice in the unit of my study referring to: Judea (3,22b) and Aenon near Salim (3,23b). Though some of these references are determined by narrative factors, other than distance from the narrator, I observe a significant pattern in the fourth Gospel. Both the references, mentioned above, are part of the narrative. In contrast, *here* (ὧδε) occurs only five times (cf. 6,9.25; 11,21.32 and 20,27), and all of them are in dialogues. I can, therefore, conclude that, for the narrator, everywhere means *there* and nowhere refers to *here*.[10] This gives the impression that the narrator stands at some distance from the locations mentioned in the narrative.[11] But the location of the narrator does not necessarily provide any clue to the location of the evangelist. However, and the fourth evangelist does not seem to fix his narrator in any specific place.

By telling the reader what no historical person could know (e.g. conversations where only two persons – like Jesus and Nicodemus, Jesus and his disciples, the Baptist and his disciples or two groups of persons – like the Jews and the disciples of the Baptist – were present), the narrator exposes the story to the question of how anyone could know these things. He generally assumes the position of one who observes Jesus and those who converse with him, but one who is also free to interpret their minds when necessary. The narrator, in his omnipresence, does not limit himself to the position of Jesus' partners in

---

[9] Cf. Lee, 54-55.

[10] Culpepper, *Anatomy*, 27.

[11] F. F. Segovia, "The Significance of Social Location in Reading John's Story," *Interp.* 49 (1995) 370-78.

conversation. The narrator never refers to himself and the disciples as 'we.' His third person references to them serve to place them at a distance. However, the narrative gives the impression that the narrator is a part of the group around Jesus, because much of it deals with events that occurred within that group. In short, the story is presented by a narrator who is an omniscient observer.

C. Temporal Point of View

The narrator in the fourth Gospel describes the ministry of Jesus from the standpoint of his death and resurrection, as well as his cosmic role, and therefore with full knowledge of his theological significance. Though the same narrator and the same voice speaks throughout the fourth Gospel, one can discern and distinguish at least three temporal perspectives merging in it. The revelation of God in Jesus is first presented in a cosmic, eternal dimension in the prologue. Yet, the entire Gospel is written, and could only have been written, from the standpoint of a distinctly Christian and *post-resurrection* perspective. But as reader, I feel, I should make note also of the historical perspective of this highly theological Gospel.

The last perspective has, however, two dimensions: the evident one of the earthly, historical Jesus, but also the no less important historical dimension of the Johannine Community, represented by Jesus' disciples. Thus, the historical and post-resurrection perspectives actually coalesce. Jesus, who was historically real, is now truly known only in the light of his death and resurrection and in the struggle of the community of his followers. That is, the struggle of the Johannine Community or the Christian Church with its enemies is a continuation or extension of the conflict in which Jesus ultimately laid down his life (3,14ff.; cf. 15,18-19 and 17,14). But as he was with God in the beginning (1,1), so he is and will be with God always (3,13-14.35; cf. 14,1-3 and 17,24).

In general, the description of Jesus' ministry by the fourth evangelist is similar to that of the Synoptics: Jesus gathers disciples, works wonders, teaches, involves in conflicts with opponents, and is finally condemned to death and is crucified. But the way in which the fourth evangelist describes and nuances these activities and events is distinctive of his narrative style and theology.[12] However, one does not find the transfiguration scene in the fourth Gospel because throughout this Gospel Jesus appears transfigured. This transfigured Jesus is, after all, the incarnate Word of God (1,1), *eternally* loved by the Father (3,35), in whose hands the Father has placed all things (3,35); he has descended from heaven (cf. 3,13.17), and is sent by the Father (3,16-17.34); he speaks the words of God (3,34), and gives the Spirit (3,34). The prologue, especially the communication of the narrator that "the Word became flesh and dwelt among us" (1,14), prepares the reader for the portrayal of Jesus and his ministry.[13] In fact the implied author identifies Jesus not only with the Word of God and calls him God's Son (3,16-18.35.36), but says that he is himself God (20,29; cf. 1,1.18).[14] By identifying Jesus not only with the purpose and mission of God,

---

[12] See O'Day, "Narrative Mode," 668.

[13] See J. L. Staley, "The Structure of John's Prologue: Its Implications for the Gospel's Narrative Structure," *CBQ* 48 (1986) 250-53.

[14] By contrast, in the Synoptic gospels, Jesus' teaching is concrete and time-bound. See R. T. Fortna, *The Fourth Gospel and its Predecessor: From Narrative source to Present Gospel* (Edinburgh, Philadelphia 1989) 2.

but with his own being, the fourth evangelist goes a step beyond the other Gospels. Yet, he does not allow the man Jesus, that is, his humanity, to fall out of sight. Nevertheless, his purpose is not, simply, to present or advocate Jesus' humanity, but to argue that in this man God was uniquely present.

The narrator's voice seems to replace that of Jesus in 3,16 where the point of view is retrospective: the one speaking talks in the *past* of a God who *loved* and who *gave* (3,16). Since the previous verses (3,14-15) have been about the *lifting up* of the Son of Man on the cross, the supreme and divine act of love referred to in 3,16 must be the death of Jesus. At this point the narrator can observe matters from the point of view of *eternity*.[15] Looking back at Jesus' life on earth after his resurrection, the narrator takes the reader into the bosom of the Father in order to reveal the divine initiative and purpose in the giving of the only begotten Son of God.

The fundamental revelation which the narrator gives to the reader in 3,16-21 concerns the nature of God and the nature of humanity. Indeed, the narrator's words highlight the fundamental aspects of the God-humanity dualism:

> 3,16-18   The nature of God – love for the *world*
>
> 3,19-21   The nature of humanity – love for the *world*

In 3,16-18, the narrator reveals heavenly secrets about God's nature. Having taken the reader deeper into the identity and mission of the Spirit and the Son in 3,1-15, the narrator now takes him/her deep into the mystery of God the Father. There is, therefore, a progression in the fourth evangelist's storytelling from revelation about the Spirit (3,5-8), to revelation about the Son (3,13-15), and to revelation about the Father (3,16-21). The narrator, thus, leads the reader into the very heart of the *eternal* and Triune God.

This retrospective point of view of the narrator is illustrated by such proleplic statements as "the Son of man must be lifted up" (3,14), or "John, of course, had not yet been thrown into prison" (3,24), or "for the Spirit was not yet given because Jesus had not yet been glorified" (7,39). More, specifically, the narrator tells the story of Jesus' ministry from the *temporal perspective of a group*, which advocates belief in Jesus after his resurrection. The narrator, therefore, speaks from some point in the *future* within the narrative world, and interprets Jesus as no contemporary observer would have been able to do. The reference to what the disciples did not know at that time but discovered after Jesus' resurrection (cf. 2,22; 12,16; 13,7 and 20,9) suggests that the perspective of the believing community – say the Johannine Community – is presented as absolutely necessary for a proper understanding of Jesus. By employing the device of *narrator* who speaks retrospectively, the author shows that he is not attempting to write *history* without interpreting it.

There is yet one more factor to consider regarding his temporal point of view. While the story is told retrospectively, there are occasional departures from this perspective which take the reader from *narrative time* into *story time*. These are often signalled by the use of verbs in the present tense (*historical present*) in the narration. The imperfect tense is a half step between the aorist (or simple past tense) and the present tense, in that it causes the reader to see past action in progress.[16] A survey of the early

---

[15] Kieffer, "L'espace et le temps," 399-401.

[16] Uspensky, 74-75.

chapters of the fourth Gospel reveals a fairly well defined pattern in the appearance of historical presents. Whenever the narrator is providing a transition from one scene to another, his normal mode is the aorist or imperfect tense[17] (e.g. ἐπίστευσαν, ἐποίει, ἐπίστευεν – 2,23-25; and ἦλθεν – 3,22).

In a broad sense, the narrator in the fourth Gospel, who reflects the perspective of the author, tells the story from a point of view which, in its retrospection, is informed by memory, interpretation of Scripture, blending of traditions with the post-resurrection experience of the early Church, consciousness of the presence of the Spirit, a reading of the glory of the risen Christ back into the days of his ministry, and a sharp awareness of the history and the struggles of the Johannine Community. But with this observation one has moved into the narrator's ideological or evaluative point of view.

D. Ideological Point of View

The most important function of the narrator in the fourth Gospel is bound up in his ideological or evaluative point of view.[18] No narrator can be absolutely impartial; inevitably a narrator, especially an omniscient, omnipresent, omni-communicative and intrusive one, will prejudice the reader toward or away from certain characters, assertions, claims, or events and their implications. More than that, no story can be meaningful unless the readers are introduced to its value system or provided with some way of relating it to their own.[19] Besides, I do not find any evidence that the narrator in the unit of my study attempts to maintain any neutrality toward his story; his function is to facilitate communication of the implied author's ideological or evaluative system to the reader. That is, one must believe in Jesus and be begotten from above in order to have eternal life (3,3-21.35-36; cf. 20,31). There is only an *either or*: belief or unbelief, eternal life or judgement (God's wrath), Salvation or condemnation, doing what is true and coming to light or doing what is evil and remaining in darkness.

E. Relationship Between Jesus and Narrator

The narrator in the fourth Gospel knows who Jesus is and what he knows. They both know *all things*. For example, the pre-historical *analepses*[20] such as "the Father loves the Son and has placed all things in his hands" (3,35; cf. 6,38 and 8,28) are closely tied to the functions of the Father and the identity of Jesus. Their importance may be that they convey Jesus' special knowledge concerning his identity, origin, and mission. The narrator shares this knowledge with the reader, and in the story of Jesus attempts to convey it to others.

---

[17] Uspensky (71) compares this particular kind of narrative construction to a slide show, where the individual slides are linked together sequentially to form a plot. When a slide is shown, narrative time stops; in the intervals between the slides, narrative time is accelerated and moves very rapidly. For a detailed discussion on the fourth evangelist's understanding of time see Frey, *Das johanneische Zeitverständnis*. See also Kieffer, "L'espace et le temps," 404; H. Saxby, "The Time-Scheme in the Gospel of John," *ET* 104 (1992) 9-13; and J. E. Bruns, "The Use of Time in the Fourth Gospel," *NTS* 13 (1967) 285-90.

[18] Uspensky, 8.

[19] Cf. W. C. Booth, *The Rhetoric of Fiction* (Chicago 1983) 112.

[20] A survey of the external analepses in the fourth Gospel reveals that they fall into two distinct categories, which can be called 'historical' and 'pre-historical,' though the Gospel itself does not make this distinction. The historical analepses recall moments in the history of Israel. The pre-historical analepses refer to events which did not occur in human history but in the relationship between Father and Son in the identifiable past of the incarnate Logos.

The author presents the narrator as the one who understands Jesus' words even when the learned Nicodemus, the Scribes and Pharisees, the Jewish authorities, and the disciples do not. The narrator speaks in the third person, as one outside the action, and thereby provides the effect of the voice of an observer.

The importance of the narrator's role as interpreter becomes obvious when one skips the narration and reads only the dialogue. Without the narration, the dialogue loses most of its significance. The narrator serves as the authoritative interpreter of Jesus' words. Often enough the narrator's interpretation of the meaning of an event is carried over into the dialogue (e.g. comp. 2,23-25 with 3,1-21, and 3,22-26 with 3,27-36). Because of the similarity in Jesus' and the narrator's speech patterns, and because of the narrator's influence on dialogue, it is difficult to tell when Jesus or the Baptist stops speaking in Jn. 3, and when or if the narrator speaks. The identity of the speaker in 3,13-21 and 3,31-36 is a well known problem. The author often allows characters to fade from the narrative without notice, but does not normally change speakers without telling the reader. The temporal perspective, terminology, and content of 3,13-21.31-36 vary in appropriateness for Jesus, the Baptist and the narrator. It appears to be a classic instance of the blending of the narrator with Jesus' voice. There are numerous parallels between these verses. There is also a change of temporal point of view in verses 13 and 14. The imposition of one time on another, one voice on another, requires the reader to hear Jesus speaking to the reader's time through the narrator. When it is not possible to decide whether the words are a character's or the narrator's, according to S. Chatman, "it doesn't matter who says or thinks this; it is appropriate to both character and narrator."[21] The ambiguity may strengthen the bond between the two, make the reader trust still more the narrator's authority. Perhaps, I should speak of neutralisation or unification, rather than ambiguity. Such statements, in my opinion, imply that character and narrator are so close, in such sympathy, that it is, at times, unimportant to whom I assign the statement.

Conclusion

The overall effect of the similarity between the narrator's and Jesus' points of view, the relationship between narration and the narrator's influence on dialogue and discourse, and the blending of voices in the unit of my study point to a complex relationship between Jesus and the narrator. Both narrator and character, of course, can be vehicles for the implied author's ideology. In the unit of my study, it appears as if the narrator is adopting Jesus' point of view ideologically and phraseologically. Actually, the author, who was informed by the tradition handed down within the Johannine Community, fashioned the character (Jesus) as he wrote and interpreted Jesus through both his dialogue and the narrator's interpretative comments. It is, therefore, not a matter of the narrator's speech being conformed to that of Jesus, but of both reflecting the author's speech patterns and expressing his ideological point of view. The harmony between Jesus and the narrator is a result of the author's expression of his point of view through both his central character (Jesus) and the narrator. His narrative is a quasi-secretive act of communication between narrator and reader. The 'narrator-figure' is important in the appreciation of my unit of study. Any true analysis of the narrative of this unit must, therefore, include *narrator and*

---

[21] Chatman, 206.

point of view in its programme, and must evaluate the extent to which the aim of 20,31 – the persuasiveness of the Gospel's narrative Christology – is achieved.

Chapter 6

NARRATIVE CHRISTOLOGY IN PARALLEL EPISODES

Literary and narrative analysis remains futile if it does not lead to a correct interpretation and deeper understanding of a text. However, such an analysis alone is not sufficient for the interpretation of a text, nor does it lead automatically to a fuller meaning of the text. Nevertheless, in my opinion, it is the basic and fundamental tool as it helps to infer the organisation of ideas and articulation of the content of the unit under study. My objective in the following pages is, therefore, to explore and expose the true Christological scheme emerging as a result of my literary and narrative analysis.

The observation that I have made already about my unit of study is that it forms a bipartite parallel structure (2,23-3,21//3,22-36). I Shall indicate the presence of a similar bipartite division of the preceding and following units in the first section of the Gospel in Part II. Though, many scholars have observed already the bipartite parallel relation in 2,23-3,36, the difference in my analysis is that I have divided the tripartite segments of each of the sub-units differently and have demonstrated and substantiated the rightfulness of the same in detail in chapter 3. Now I must explore and establish the reason for the juxtaposition of the Nicodemus episode and the second testimony of the Baptist. This will be answered partially in my study of the context and network of the first section (1,19-4,54) in Part II. In fact, the parallelism between Jn. 1,19-34 and Jn. 3,22-36 brings out clearly the function of the Baptist as the witness of Jesus to Israel. At the beginning of the Gospel, the Baptist's role was to introduce Jesus to Israel as its traditionally awaited Messiah. However, for the fourth evangelist and the Johannine community, the person and the mission of Jesus surpass this traditional Jewish Messianic scheme.[1] On the one hand, because of his heavenly origin and the heavenly content of his revelation, he is the only competent person to reveal the true identity of his person and his saving mission. The implied author makes Jesus fulfil this requirement in the story of Nicodemus. Jesus is not a mere "teacher who has come from God" (3,2de), but the "Son of Man descended from heaven" (3,13) who is to be 'lifted up' (3,14); he is the only beloved Son of God sent for the salvation of the world (cf. 3,16-21). On the other hand, the Baptist – whose role being that of a witness to Israel – legally speaking, must come again in order to authenticate Jesus' revelation about his origin, identity and mission.[2] In my opinion, that is what one can infer from the juxtaposition of the second testimony of the Baptist through the literary medium of a parallel structure between 2,23-3,21 and 3,22-36 and the inclusive structure between 1,19-34 and 3,22-36 (to be demonstrated in Part II). Besides, there is narrative sequence with Jn. 4 where Jesus widens his universal saving mission among the non-Jews (Samaritans – cf. 4,1-42) and gentiles (cf. 4,43-54), as announced in 3,16ff. Note also the

---

[1] Cf. W. Horbury, "The Messianic Associations of 'the Son of Man'," *JTS* 36 (1985) 34-55; see also G. Reim, "Jesus as God in the Fourth Gospel: The Old Testament Background," *NTS* 30 (1984) 158-60; and M. Hengel, *Der Sohn Gottes. Die Entstehung der Christologie und die jüdisch-hellenistische Religions-geschichte* (Tübingen 1975).

[2] Later in the Gospel, the Father himself testifies to the sending of Jesus (cf. 5,36-37 and 8,18); and what Jesus says is true as 'he knows whence he comes and whither he goes' (cf. 8,14); he does not need the testimony of the Baptist or anyone else (cf. 5,33-34). The witness of the Baptist is needed only to fulfil the Jewish legal requirement of a double witness for a testimony to be valid and acceptable.

fact that Christology and soteriology are inseparably intertwined in the fourth Gospel. Moreover, the nuptial symbolism of the section (wedding at Cana, the Baptist being the friend of the bridegroom, and the motif of marriage in Jn. 4) suits well to envisage the Baptist's activity at Aenon near Salim as preparing the bride to meet Jesus, the eschatological bridegroom (to be demonstrated in Part II).

A. Parallel Scene Settings (2,23-3,2 and 3,22-26)

In the previous chapters I analysed the narrative and structural patterns of both episodes dividing them into three segment each. Guided by the general semantic orientation attained through this analysis let us now try to observe closely the details of the parallelism and try to plunge a little deeper in order to understand its content and its Christological scheme.

The first two parallel segments (2,23-3,2//3,22-26) – dealing with a report that establishes the narrative setting – introduce the Christological issue in question; the rest of the segments in both episodes serve to elaborate the same scheme. Thus, the first two parallel segments contain the Christological orientation of the unit. The first segment of Nicodemus episode narrates the reaction of many to the signs performed by Jesus, and introduces Nicodemus as one among the many who were attracted by Jesus and confessed that Jesus must be a 'teacher come from God.' Nicodemus' statement creates the necessary semantic opening for the story to advance, in the sense, the Christological question of the divine origin and identity of Jesus has been introduced on the lips of Nicodemus at the narrative summit (3,2) of the report or scene-setting of the episode, awaiting correction and development by Jesus himself in the narrative that follows, in the forms of dialogue and discourse.

The parallel report (3,22-26) in the Baptist-episode has also a Christological orientation. Here, it is the baptismal activity of Jesus attracting crowds that evokes the Christological question on the part of the Baptist's disciples. Though the context is the parallel baptismal activities of Jesus and the Baptist, the actual discussion is on the administers of baptism, indirectly leading to an enquiry about the true identity of Jesus. It is craftily couched in a story form where Jesus' superiority over the Baptist is hinted at.

The same pattern is clearer in the enquiry of the delegation from Jerusalem in 1,19-28 (as I shall demonstrate in Part II). After the Baptist had denied that he was neither the Messiah nor Elijah nor the prophet (cf. 1,19-23), the delegation from Jerusalem asked him why, then, he was baptising (1,25). In fact, what follows demonstrates well that the question about the baptismal activity (1,24-27) is basically a question about the identity of the baptiser. The anxiety of the Baptist's disciples can be resolved only through an answer to their question raised, indirectly, about the identity of Jesus in the narrative summit (3,26) of the report or scene-setting of the episode. The Christological question about the true origin, identity and mission of Jesus is what the implied author develops on the lips of the Baptist in the forms of dialogue (though the Baptist's disciples do not intervene anymore) and discourse.

As I have pointed out above, the respective narrative summits (3,2 and 3,26) – which lead to the narrative progression – link the two parallel segments thematically. This is further supported by the formal verbal correspondence between these two verses:

οὗτος *ἦλθεν πρὸς αὐτὸν νυκτὸς καὶ εἶπεν αὐτῷ, 'Ραββί, ...* (3,2)
καὶ *ἦλθον πρὸς τὸν Ἰωάννην καὶ εἶπαν αὐτῷ, 'Ραββί, ...* (3,26)

Nicodemus addressing Jesus as 'Rabbi' and the disciples of the Baptist addressing their master with the same title 'Rabbi,' indirectly, hint at Jesus, the real 'Rabbi,' who is the subject of discussion in the subsequent segments of each of the episodes of the story. Thus, these two summit verses serve as a pedestal and create the point of departure for the parallel progression of the story in both episodes.

B. Parallel Answers to Questions (3,3-10 and 3,27-30)

The actual dialogue with Nicodemus begins in 3,3 concluding with his 'not-knowing' (οὐ γινώσκεις – 3,10). The questions of Nicodemus (cf. 3,4.9) are essentially rhetoric and meant to advance the dialogue. The thematic heart of the segment is found certainly in the two interventions of Jesus in 3,3 and 3,5-8 which revolve around the central theme of being begotten *ἄνωθεν/of water and the Spirit* as a necessary condition for (eternal life/ salvation) *seeing/entering* the kingdom of God.

But this passage remains in isolation in relation with the rest of the Gospel as it is the only place where salvation is explained using the image of the kingdom of God that one must *see* or *enter into* with the preconditions of ἄνωθεν/water and Spirit birth. Salvation is usually explained as obtaining *eternal life* with *faith* as precondition. A probable interpretation has to be found in the inclusion between 3,3c and 3,36b. The evangelist re-interprets the traditional theme of seeing/entering the kingdom of God with that of eternal life. This is not new to the evangelist. As I had explained already in the analysis of the unit (cf. chapter 3), he often reinterprets his ideas using the technique of variation of imagery. Moreover, a quick glance at the prologue will throw light to understand them as synonyms: "But to all who received him, who believed in his name, he gave power to become children of God, who were born, not of blood or of the will of the flesh or of the will of man, but of God" (1,12-13). That is, on the one hand, faith in Jesus is a condition to become children of God; on the other hand, there is a further explanation of 'becoming children of God' through the distinction made between 'born of God' and 'physical birth' similar to the 'Spirit-birth' and 'flesh-birth' in 3,6.

This makes me observe three phases in the process of salvation: 1) faith, 2) becoming children of God which is synonymous with born ἄνωθεν/of God/of water and the Spirit and 3) seeing/entering the kingdom of God which is synonymous with having eternal life. It is interesting to notice that, in the dialogue with Nicodemus (3,3-10), the aspect of faith as the first phase is absent. This answers the question why Nicodemus does not understand the begetting ἄνωθεν; because he lacks faith. This missing element of faith becomes the object of discussion in the discourse (revelation) of Jesus about his heavenly origin, identity and soteriological mission (3,11-21). Thus, the narrative logically leads to the next stage in the episode.

Now, what is the central theme of correspondence between the dialogue with Nicodemus and the first part of the Baptist's discourse[3] (3,27-30). First of all, 3,3 and 3,27

---

[3] Strictly speaking 3,27-30 cannot be called a dialogue as there is no intervention of the Baptist's disciples in it; however, as the Baptist's discourse here answers, indirectly, to the question raised by his disciples, in my opinion, it can still be considered, in a remote sense, as a dialogue.

respectively contain basically the same statement which is further explained in the rest of the verses of each of the parallel segments, *viz.*, 3,4-10 and 3,28-30:

3a ἀπεκρίθη Ἰησοῦς καὶ εἶπεν αὐτῷ, b Ἀμὴν ἀμὴν λέγω σοι, c *ἐὰν μή* τις γεννηθῇ <u>ἄνωθεν</u>, d *οὐ δύναται* <u>ἰδεῖν</u> τὴν βασιλείαν τοῦ θεοῦ.	27a ἀπεκρίθη Ἰωάννης καὶ εἶπεν, b *Οὐ δύναται* ἄνθρωπος <u>λαμβάνειν</u> οὐδὲν c *ἐν ἐὰν μὴ* ᾖ <u>δεδομένον</u> αὐτῷ ἐκ τοῦ οὐρανοῦ.

In my opinion, these verses correspond to each other not only at the syntactic structural level (cf. οὐ δύναται ... ἐὰν μή), but also at the thematic level. In fact, there is a relation between 'being begotten ἄνωθεν' and the 'gift of the believers to Jesus' by the Father. Though I have not yet defined the two principal Christological schemes I can, however, affirm that both statements express, in their respective fields, the entrance of believers into a salvific relationship with Jesus.

It is also to be noticed that 3,3 is situated in the vertical cosmic axis (heaven-earth – ↓↑) corresponding to the Son of Man (cf. 3,13-14). At this stage I must to turn to a later part of the Gospel for further light to understand this axis. In 8,21-24 Jesus tells 'the Jews' that they cannot follow him where he is going to and will die in their sins, if they do not *believe* in him (8,21.24), for they are *from below* and he is *from above*; and they are *of this world* and he is *not of this world* (8,23). *Faith* leading to salvation must bring about a radical change; like Jesus, one cannot belong to this world anymore (must be from above) which is more explicit in the case of Jesus' disciples: "I have given them your word, and the world has hated them because they do not *belong to the world*, just as I do not belong to the world (17,14). Here, the *word* given by Jesus is to be understood as *faith*; and the needed change of the world one belongs to is what is expressed in 3,3 in terms of being begotten ἄνωθεν in order to see/enter into the kingdom of God.

The same theme of soteriology is expressed in 3,27 in legal and horizontal categories of the Christological scheme of the Son-sent (envoy). In this scheme, the coming toward Jesus for salvation (horizontal movement →) is interpreted in legal terms of giving and receiving; this corresponds to the gift of the Father to his Son-sent, his legal representative. Again we have to refer to a later part of the Gospel to understand it better; e.g. to the words of Jesus in 17,6: "I have made your name known to those whom *you gave me* from the world. They were yours, and *you gave them to me*, and they have kept your word," and in 17,9: "I am not asking on behalf of the world, but on behalf of those whom *you gave me*, because they are yours." This 'receiving' of the disciples by the Son-sent reflects the soteriological aspect (3,27; cf. 3,34-36).

This is the central element of correlation between the two segments introduced by the two verses 3,3 and 3,27: In the scheme of the Christology of the Son of Man, salvation comes from acquiring a new identity by being begotten ἄνωθεν, which one can attain through faith. In the scheme of the Christology of the Son-sent, salvation is depicted as communion of life with Jesus; but it is God who *moves* the believers towards Jesus and *gives* them to him so that they may be saved. It is important to note that Christology is inseparably intertwined with soteriology in both episodes.

C. Jesus' Revelation and the Baptist's Testimony (3,11-21 and 3,31-36)

The third segment places the discourse of Jesus (3,11-21) in parallel with the second part
of the discourse of the Baptist (3,31-36) which is a testimony to authenticate the revelation
of Jesus about his heavenly origin, identity and soteriological mission in 3,11-21. In the
structural analysis of 3,11-21 I discussed already the following chiastic structure:

$$\begin{array}{ll} \text{A} & 3,11\text{-}13 \\ \quad \text{B} & 3,14\text{-}15 \\ \quad \text{B}^1 & 3,16\text{-}18 \\ \text{A}^1 & 3,19\text{-}21 \end{array}$$

The elements A-A^1 deal with Jesus' revelation as the unique witness of heavenly things –
being the Son of Man descended from heaven ($\downarrow$)/light come into the world($\downarrow$) – and the
non-acceptance of his testimony/loving darkness rather than light.

The central elements B-B^1 demonstrate the Christological scheme (3,14.16a.17a),
and its soteriological purpose and impact on the world (3,15.16cde.17bc-18). The
Christology of both episodes revolves around the two designations of Jesus as the **Son of
Man** who descended ($\downarrow$) from heaven and must be lifted up (re-ascend into heaven – $\uparrow$),
and the **Son of God** sent into the world ($\downarrow$) out of love for the salvation ($\rightarrow$) of the world.
These two titles of Jesus contain the heart of the Christology of the fourth Gospel.[4] Eternal
life (salvation) depends on faith in this envoy of God. The choice is either belief or
unbelief, acceptance of light or preference for darkness, and the result is either salvation or
condemnation, eternal life or death. At this juncture it is necessary to treat a little more in
detail the two designations of Jesus as the 'Son of Man' and 'Son of God' for a better
evaluation of the Christological scheme of the fourth Gospel.

Now, the same Christological scheme is to be observed in the second part of the
Baptist's discourse (testimony): 3,31-32c designate Jesus as the 'one who comes from
above/heaven' and thus as the unique witness of heavenly things, as well as the 'one whom
God loves and has sent' (3,35a.34a) corresponding to the designation of Jesus as Son of
Man and Son of God respectively.[5] The soteriological purpose and impact of 3,11-21 are
also repeated in 3,36, in the second testimony of the Baptist, as depending on the choice
between *belief* and *disobedience* (disbelief) resulting in *eternal life* or *not seeing life*
(*God's wrath*) respectively.

The essential point of the correlation between the two segments is, no doubt, their
common Christological scheme of the double designation of Jesus as the Son of Man and
Son of God. In both segments, it is interesting to observe that, in the Christological scheme
of the Son of Man, its function is to present Jesus as an authentic witness and, therefore, to
insist on the importance of accepting his testimony.[6] There is no direct mention of the
soteriological impact of the testimony in both episodes. Though in 3,15 salvation is

---

[4] See the detailed study of F. Hahn, *Christologische Hoheitstitel. Ihre Geschichte im frühen Christentum*
(FRLANT 83) (Göttingen 1963) esp. 22 and 29.

[5] On this subject see R. H. Fuller, "Lower and Higher Christology in the Fourth Gospel," in: R. T. Fortna
and B. R. Gaventa (eds.), *The Conversation Continues. Studies in Paul and John. In Honour of J. Louis
Martyn* (Nashville 1990) 357-65.

[6] For a detailed discussion see R. Rhea, *The Johannine Son of Man* (AThANT 76) (Zürich 1990).

presented as flowing from faith in the Son of Man, this statement is not directly related to his testimony but to the elevation of the Son of Man.

Moreover, we can notice in both segments a movement from the Christological scheme of the Son of Man to that of the Son-sent (envoy/Son of God) introduced in the use of the causal conjunction 'γὰρ' (cf. 3,16a.34a). This indicates that the Christological scheme of the descent from heaven (3,31-32) as well as the elevation of the Son of Man (3,14-15) must be logically oriented to the Christological scheme of the Son of God. Thus, the fourth evangelist seems to follow a double-Christological scheme of descending and ascending for the purpose of the soteriological mission. This necessitates a short and separate analysis of the two titles – Son of God and Son of Man.

1. Son of Man[7]

Among the many puzzles presented by the fourth Gospel one of the most intriguing is the paradoxical contrast between the titles 'Son of God' and 'Son of Man.' 'Son of Man' points to a figure whose true home is heaven, who is invested by God with an authority no ordinary human being would dare to claim. Why this should be so is a question whose answer revolves upon the interpretation of a single text – the famous vision of Daniel 7,13-14.[8] Somehow or other a move was made from this 'a man-like figure'[9] (for the Aramaic term[10] meant no more than this) to the Son of Man. Whether Jesus ever thought of himself or referred to himself as the mysterious personage who appears in Daniel's dream is not a question that need concern us here.[11] The term 'Son of Man,' as used in the fourth Gospel, also implies some sort of heavenly status is evident.[12]

It is widely agreed that the Son of Man sayings as a whole contain some of the fourth evangelist's most profound and individual reflections on the role of the person of Jesus. So the question what he understands by the term – in the context – is more important than the identification of the sources he used.

Though the number of texts, in which the allusion to the Son of Man is underlined, is relatively small (thirteen in all),[13] Schnackenburg believes that they form a consistent

---

[7] See esp. the detailed evaluation of D. Burkett, *The Son of Man Debate: A History and Evaluation* (MSSNTS 107) (Cambridge 2000).

[8] See M. Girard, "Le semblant de fils d'homme de Daniel 7, un personnage du monde d'en haut: approche structurelle," *ScEs* 35 (1983) 265-93; A. Deissler, "Der 'Menschensohn' und 'das Volk der Heiligen des Höchsten' in Dan 7," in: Pesch and Schnackenburg, *Jesus und der Menschensohn*, 81-91; and G. F. Hasel, "The Identity of 'The Saints of the Most High' in Daniel 7," *Bib.* 56 (1975) 173-92.

[9] See M. Casey, "The Corporate Interpretation of 'One like a Son of Man' (Dan 7,13) at the Time of Jesus," *NT* 18 (1976) 167-80; and R. Bauckham, "The Son of Man: 'A Man in my Position' or 'Someone'," *JSNT* 23 (1985) 23-33.

[10] Cf. M. Casey, "General, Generic and Indefinite. The Use of the Term 'Son of Man' in Aramaic Sources and in the Teaching of Jesus," *JSNT* 29 (1987) 21-56.

[11] There has been a clash between Lindars (*Jesus Son of Man*) and M. Black (*An Aramaic Approach to the Gospels and Acts* [Third Edition with an Appendix on the Son of Man by Geza Vermes] [Oxford ³1967]). For a survey see J. R. Donohue, "Recent Studies on the Origin of the 'Son of Man' in the Gospels," *CBQ* 48 (1986) 484-98; see also W. Bittner, "Gott-Menschensohn-Davidssohn. Eine Untersuchung zur Traditionsgeschichte von Daniel 7,13f.," *FZPhTh* 32 (1985) 343-72.

[12] Cf. M. M. Pazdan, *The Son of Man. A Metaphor for Jesus in the Fourth Gospel* (ZSNT) (Collegeville 1991).

[13] 1,51; 3,13; 3,14; 5,27; 6,27; 6,53; 6,62; 8,28; 9,35-38; 12,23; 12,34e; 12,34f. and 13,31-32.

and well-knit whole[14] while Loader considers them as a cluster.[15] Martyn views that the fourth evangelist employed the Son of Man motif as a complement and corrective to the identification of Jesus as Mosaic prophet-Messiah.[16] The latter title, he observes, has never been allowed to occupy the centre of the stage for long: it is always replaced soon afterwards by another motif: Furthermore, this other motif always has to do with the Son of Man.[17] Martyn, however, holds the view that the titles 'Son of Man' and 'Son of God' have become interchangeable for the fourth evangelist.[18] This, in my observation, is a careless and unacceptable opinion.

It is hard to specify any features common to all thirteen Son of Man sayings[19] apart from the title itself. What one can say at most is that the reader's attention is continually being directed to one particular aspect of Jesus' self-revelation. The title embodies the theme of Jesus' heavenly origin and destiny, and does so often enough, to be significant in terms of his descent and (more frequently) ascent (cf. 3,13 and 6,62).[20] It, therefore, adds to the Messiahship and sonship, albeit indirectly, the notion of pre-existence. What it does not convey, paradoxically, is either humanity[21] (which mostly rests upon the Messianic titles) or any suggestion of sonship (differing in this respect from the title 'Son,' which

---

[14] Schnackenburg, *Gospel*, I, 532; and his, "Der Menschensohn im Johannesevangelium," *NTS* 11 (1964/65) 123-37; see also Lindars, *Jesus Son of Man*, 155; and J. Coppens, "Le Fils de l'homme dans l'évangile johannique," *EThL* 52 (1976) 28-81.

[15] W. Loader, "The Central Structure of the Johannine Christology," *NTS* 30 (1984) 188-216.

[16] See the detailed studies of J. Coppens, *Le messianisme et sa relève prophétique. Les anticipations vétéro testamentaires. Leur accomplissement en Jésus* (Gembloux 1974); and his *La relève apocalyptique du messianisme royal, Vol. II: Le Fils de l'homme vétéro et intertestamentaire* (BEThL 61) (Louvain 1983).

[17] Martyn, *History and Theology*, 134, the single exception being the Samaritan episode in Jn. 4. There, appropriately, the movement is from the Mosaic Taheb to the Jewish Messiah as the Saviour of the world; see also the detailed studies of V. Hampel, *Menschensohn und historischer Jesus. Ein Rätselwort als Schlüssel zum messianischen Selbstverständnis Jesu* (Neukirchen-Vluyn 1990).

[18] *Ibid.*, n. 193. This he believes to have been demonstrated by Schulz (*Untersuchungen*, 127; 132-33; 136-37 and 141-42). In fact Schulz is concerned with the *Son* theme (not Son of God), which he believes to be rooted in the apocalyptic vision of the Son of Man; see also the discussions of R. Leivestad, "Exit the Apocalyptic Son of Man," *NTS* 18 (1971/72) 234-67; and B. Lindars, "Re-Enter the Apocalyptic Son of Man," *NTS* 22 (1975) 52-72. E. D. Freed ("The Son of Man in the Fourth Gospel," *JBL* 86 [1967] 403) is even more emphatic than Martyn. He contends that 'Son of Man' is only a variation for at least two other titles, namely the 'Son of God' and the 'Son.' There is no separate Son of Man Christology in the fourth Gospel. This view, in my view, is a simplistic solution and is false. See also S. Kim, *"The 'Son of Man'" as the Son of God* (WUNT 30) (Tübingen 1983) 5.

[19] Cf. P. Borgen, "The Son of Man Sayings in John 3.13,14," in: his *Logos was the True Light and Other Essays on the Gospel of John* (Trondheim 1983) 133-48.

[20] In the fourth Gospel the ascent cannot be completely detached from the descent. For parallels in Mandaean writings for the pattern of the descent/ascent of a heavenly messenger see Meeks, *Prophet-King*, 297.

[21] Against this view see Moloney (*Son of Man*, 213) who asserts that there is a concentration on the human figure of Jesus in the use of 'the Son of Man;' it is a title which is entirely dependent upon the incarnation. The Son of Man reveals the truth to men because he is man – because of the incarnation. Moloney's error is to take the Christology of the incarnate Logos as a kind of axiom from which everything else derives. Equally misguided is Dodd's (*Interpretation*, 244) view that for the fourth evangelist the Son of Man is the ἀληθινός ἄνθρωπος, the real or archetypal Man, or the Platonic Idea of Man. M. Pamment ("The Son of Man in the Fourth Gospel," *JTS* 36 [1985] 56-66), too, has a similar view when he says that it is misleading to label 'Son of Man' a 'Christological term' since, unlike 'Son of God,' it does not seek to distinguish Jesus' unique nature or function, but defines the attributes of humanity which all men should exemplify.

points directly to Jesus' relationship with God). Nor is the Son of Man ever said to be *sent*.[22]

♦ Three Assertions

In looking at the thirteen Son of Man passages, we find that they, first of all, deal with the Son of Man on earth, who *is present* and *can be perceived* as such (cf. 1,51 and 9,35-38); his future coming is not addressed as it is done in the Synoptics. One could at most hold that according to the perfect tense in 3,13a *he is already in heaven*. But the aorist in 3,13b (ὁ καταβάς) leads again to his *historical coming* and the sentence, "no one has ascended into heaven," discourages the idea that anyone has ascended to heaven, as was actually the case with the Son of Man. This ascension is announced in 6,62 (cf. also 20,17).

The second assertion concerns the lifting up (3,14; 8,28 and 12,34e) and *glorification* of the Son of Man[23] (12,23 and 13,31-32). The two – being lifted up and being glorified – are closely connected but are distinguished with regard to the death on the cross and the resurrection and return home to the Father. For the fourth evangelist this is associated with Jesus' 'hour,' toward which Jesus' entire work moves. One cannot understand the Son of Man if one does not keep in mind his destiny in Jesus' 'hour' (see the treatment in Part II).

The third assertion is clearly *soteriological*. The Son of Man is a salvific figure. He must be lifted up on the cross, so that everyone who believes in him may have eternal life (3,14). He gives the food that endures to eternal life (6,27), his flesh and blood, with which he feeds the believers so that they may have eternal life (6,53).

In the figure of the Son of Man various ideas come together; it is a weaving of adopted and further developed concepts, which, however, have an essential meaning for the fourth evangelist's picture of Jesus. Because of the curious mode of expression and its overall view, the statements of the Son of Man are much discussed,[24] and there is rich literature on this group of concepts, into which I cannot go further at this point.

2. Son of God[25]

The 'only Son of God' (3,16.18) is the briefest and the most pregnant expression for Jesus in the fourth Gospel.[26] The aim of the fourth evangelist in writing his Gospel is to lead his readers to confess that "Jesus is the Messiah, the Son of God" (20,31; cf. the addition in

---

[22] See the discussion of W. G. Kümmel, *Jesus der Menschensohn?* (Stuttgart, Wiesbaden 1984).

[23] See Y. Ibuki, "Die Doxa des Gesandten. Studie zur johanneischen Christologie," *AJBI* 14 (1988) 38-81; and Hurst and Wright, *Glory of Christ*.

[24] See esp. A. Vögtle, *Die "Gerechtenfrage" des Menschensohnproblems. Bilanz und Perspektive* (aD 152) (Freiburg i. Br. 1994).

[25] In the fourth Gospel God is called 'Father' 120 times and Jesus is called '(the) Son'/'Son of God' 27 times. The correlation Father-Son suggests itself. The full title 'Son of God' is found primarily in confession like-formulas (1,39.49 and 20,31; cf. also 1 Jn. 4,15; 5 and 2 Jn. 3). While 'Son of God' is associated with 'the Father' only twice (5,25 and 10,36), 'the Son' which is found 18 times (as against only three times in the Synoptics and once in Paul), is virtually always correlated with the idea of God as Father (e.g. 3,16.17.35). The intimacy between the Father and the Son is thereby emphasised. The Son does only what the Father wants him to do; he is thus a true revelation of God. See the recent study of J. van Bruggen, *Jesus and the Son of God: The Gospel Narrative as Message* (Grand Rapids 1999).

[26] Jesus' designation of himself as 'the Son' when speaking of his relationship to God is typically Johannine.

11,27: "who comes into the world). He has this baptismal confession also in view when he speaks of 'faith' in the *name* of the 'Son of God' (3,18.36). Part of faith is the deliberate saying of Jesus' *name* as a confession and a testimony (cf. 1 Jn. 4,15 and 5,5).

The title 'Son of God' is clearly fundamental in the fourth evangelist's *Christology*, and is used to express a number of basic convictions about Jesus.[27] First of all, it expresses the metaphysical or essential relationship between Jesus and his Father.[28] The Father and Son belong inseparably to each other (cf. Jn. 1,18 and 5,23). He is God's 'only' Son (3,16b.18e), a term which expresses the special love between the Father and Jesus (cf. 3,35). 'The Son' stands in such close relationship with 'the Father' that one has to include all those far more numerous passages in which the Jesus of the fourth Gospel speaks of 'the Father' or 'my Father.'[29] The 'Father-son relationship' is the key to the understanding of Jesus as portrayed by the fourth evangelist, and of his words and actions as interpreted by him. It is a deliberately chosen theological expression to interpret the coming and work of Jesus in the light of faith. The Johannine Jesus does indeed speak of himself as the 'Son of God' (3,18; 5,25; 10,36 and 11,4), and with the same meaning as when he says 'the Son;' Schnackenburg argues that the title 'Son of God' has a different *Sitz im Leben* (e.g. confessional formula – cf. 1,34; 1,49; 11,27 and 20,31) from the absolute use of 'the Son,' which is reserved to Jesus alone.[30]

For the fourth evangelist, the God who sent the Son is none other than the Father. The subject in the passage about the sending of the only Son (3,16ff.) is not 'Father' but 'God'. Jesus, however, speaks often enough of 'the Father who sent me' or simply of 'him who sent me.' Surveying the Christological discourse and the second testimony of the Baptist in Jn. 3, *viz.*, i) the sending of the Son into the word (3,16ff.), ii) the love of the Father for the Son (3,35; cf. 5,20) and iii) the offer of slavation to the believers in the Son (3,16ff.; cf. 6,40), one finds that all the essential aspects of Jesus' revealing and saving work come out in them: his mission into the world, his revealing activity in the world, his doing of works, 'signs,' which manifest his life-giving power, and finally his way into glory. The uniqueness of Jesus' mission and the saving significance of his words and deeds are expressed through the uniqueness of his relation to God, that is his Son-relationship.

Secondly, he mediates between God and men. Everything that he spoke and made known upon earth was done as part of God's commission to mediate salvation, eternal life to all men. He was *given/sent* by the Father in order that men might be *saved* (3,16ff.). The title 'Son' expresses above all the fact that Jesus is the *Saviour* (3,16-17). For the fourth evangelist, Jesus is the saviour particularly because of his metaphysical relationship with God (cf. 11,41; 12,27 and 17,1).[31] Moreover, the *sending* of Jesus is a firm foundation for his doctrine of *salvation* (3,17). The statement about his being sent has its explicit purpose in showing Jesus' status as Son.[32] The Christology of the Son-sent is essentially the

---

[27] See Rinke, *Kerygma und Autopsie*, 149-60.

[24] E. Schweizer ("υἱός," *TDNT*, VIII, 388) rightly warns that the Johannine use of the 'Son of God' idea "carries with it the risk of a purely metaphysical conception."

[29] There are more than fifty such passages, and eight include the formal expression 'the Father who sent me.'

[30] Schnackenburg, *Gospel*, II, 173; and Hahn, *Christolgische Hoheitstitel*, 319ff.

[31] See Dodd, *Interpretation*, 250-62; and Schnackenburg, *Gospel*, II, 172-83.

[32] Rengstorf, "ἀποστέλλω (πέμπω)," 445.

doctrine of salvation for believers, i.e. not a doctrine about Jesus in isolation, but taking in the human race with Jesus as God's envoy revealing and mediating salvation. The title 'son of God' is continually used by the fourth evangelist in the context of a dynamic of a salvation which is at once the will of God (the Father) and the task of the Son. The Christological scheme of the fourth evangelist was not chiefly concerned with statements about the metaphysical being of the Son, his relationship to the Father within the Trinity, his pre-existence, etc.;[33] he places in the foreground the *functional* character of his Christological scheme of the Son-sent (Son of God), the theme of revelation and salvation which it articulates.

Summary

To summarise my observations briefly, the analysis of the logical and argumentative narrative structure and the various literary patterns like the chiastic, synonymous and antithetical parallel structures have helped me to demonstrate the integrity of the unit (2,23-3,36), its rightful place in the narrative context and sequence of the story and the purpose of the juxtaposition of the two diptych like episodes (2,23-3,21 and 3,22-36) with common and parallel elements in their corresponding parallel segments. I have observed three main moments in the narrative progression of the story in both episodes. The first two, the scene setting segments, introduce the search for the true identity of Jesus through the description of people flocking to him because of his signs (2,23-3,2) and because of the popularity of his baptismal activity (3,22-26) respectively. The second, narrated in the form of an answer to the questions raised by Nicodemus, presents the person and the activity of Jesus in the context of salvation (seeing/entering the kingdom of God) coming from above (ἄνωθεν birth). In the parallel episode (3,27-30), the Baptist answers his disciples by presenting the attraction of crowds by Jesus as salvation offered from above (3,27). The third segments contain the key to salvation (begetting ἄνωθεν/coming to Jesus). It is the acceptance of testimony through faith in Jesus as the Son of Man lifted up into heaven and as the Son of God sent into the world.

Son of God and Son of Man stand immediately beside each other. The sending of the Son of God into the world (3,16-18) is made more precise in that he is the Son of Man come down from heaven, who must be 'lifted up' (3,13-14) just as Moses did in the wilderness. The believers receive the gift of life from the Son, but more precisely, in such a way that they have life in the exalted Son of Man (3,15).

---

[33] F.-J. Moloney ("The Johannine Son of God," *Sal.* 38 [1976] 71) rightly asserts that the fourth evangelist was not primarily interested in Jesus' nature. He contends that both the metaphysical and docetic interpretation of the concept of 'Son of God' in the fourth Gospel miss the evangelist's use of the title; cf. *ibid.*, 72.

PART II

LITERARY DESIGN AND NETWORK OF 1,19-4,54

Any exegetical study, I feel, is incomplete if it does not take into account that an episode or pericope is woven into a certain web or network of structures in a section of the Gospel and that there is continuity and flow in the narration. A message communicated in a text, I am sure, is also dependent on the *way* it is expressed. As the *how* of communication is the first element through which the text reaches the reader, the structure of the text confronts him/her first and supports the meaning it conveys. My aim in this Part, therefore, is to explore *how* the author narrates the story of Jesus, besides *what* he narrates, to bring its readers to a point of decision[1] (cf. 20,30-31).

Therefore, a detailed consideration of the context of a story is an indispensable part of narrative exegesis. No episode in a Gospel like the fourth is to be studied in isolation. It is part of the plot of the whole Gospel and must therefore be placed within the overall flow of the evolving drama. Reading through the entire document, constructing an outline, and consulting the outlines given in commentaries and other works can aid in determining the general structure and style of the larger work and the compositional techniques employed in its production. Examining a passage in relation to its larger literary context leaves open the possibility that the author sought carefully to construct the document as a whole in order to achieve maximum effect.

It is normal that one tries to understand the meaning of a word in the context of its sentence, a sentence in its paragraph, a paragraph in its chapter, a chapter in its section, a section in its part, and a part in the context of the book or document. Like all written documents, the fourth Gospel is a meaningful arrangement of language intended to communicate a message. Smith and Spaller are right in their observation that the exegesis of any text must take into account its position and role in the document of which it is a part and the attempt to analyse a text of the fourth Gospel without considering its structure is doomed to failure.[2] There can be little doubt that the account of the ministry of Jesus in the fourth Gospel exhibits a very careful organisation.

Having subjected 2,23-3,36, as a literary unit, to a thorough literary and narrative analysis in Part I, I shall now, in Part II, demonstrate the narrative flow and continuity of the unit of my study in the context of its section (1,19-4,54) and skim the Christology emerging from its narrative structure in order to expose the Christological scheme of 2,23-3,36.

---

[1] Cf. Zumstein, "L'Évangile johannique," 217-32. A. Wind ("Destination and Purpose of the Gospel of John," *NT* 14 [1972] 30) summarises the variety of purposes of the fourth Gospel and gives also a fairly elaborate list of scholars agreeing or disagreeing with those purposes.

Chapter 1

DIVISION OF 1,19-4,54

A. General Division of the Gospel

Dodd finds carefully planned theological themes in the fourth Gospel and is of the opinion that it must be interpreted as it is, as if the present order is intended by the evangelist.[3] On the contrary, in his review of Dodd's *The Interpretation of the Fourth Gospel*, Bultmann contends that he cannot convince himself of any structure in the fourth Gospel as it stands.[4] There is no consensus among scholars about the division of the fourth Gospel into parts and sections, as well as the criteria used to do so. There is general agreement among many scholars in separating the prologue (1,1-18) and the epilogue or appendix (21,1-25) from the narrative of the Gospel because of their particular style. The contentions of de la Potterie and Brodie that the prologue, too, forms a clear unity with the narrative of the Gospel as a whole,[5] I feel, are not acceptable because of the sublimity of poetry and uniqueness of vocabulary. Moreover, the prologue gives a gist of the entire Gospel in a nutshell and thus remains an introduction to the whole document.

Barrett, Gnilka, Haenchen, Hoskyns, Howard-Brook, Lindars, Marrow, Marsh, and Sanders among others leave the Gospel in its present order and do not attempt to make major divisions. Dodd observes that the Gospel is divided at the end of chapter 12 "virtually into two books."[6] Based on this assumption, he proposes the division of the Gospel into the 'Book of Signs' (2,1-12,50) and the 'Book of the Passion' (13,1-20,31). Most modern scholars consider the division of the fourth Gospel in two main parts,[7] *viz.*, the 'Book[8] of Signs'[9] (1,19-12,50) and the 'Book of Glory'[10] (13,1-20,31) besides the prologue and the epilogue. I believe it is evident that the Gospel naturally divides itself at the end of chapter 12, and this division corresponds to that which is made in all the Gospels before the beginning of the Passion-narrative.

Although Mlakuzhyil also maintains that there are two major parts of the fourth Gospel, he differs slightly from the other scholars in the bipartite division of the Gospel into 'Book of Signs' and 'Book of Glory.' He defines 2,1-12,50 as the 'Book of Jesus'

---

[2] D. M. Smith, *John* (Philadelphia 1976) 11; and C. Spaller, "Strukturale Überlegungen zu biblisch-exegetischem Arbeiten," *PzB* 7 (1998) 1-16.

[3] Dodd, *Interpretation*, 289.

[4] R. Bultmann, "The Interpretation of the Fourth Gospel," *NTS* 1 (1954/55) 86. His view, according to me, is an exaggeration. See also D. M. Smith, *The Composition and Order of the Fourth Gospel. Bultmann's Literary Theory* (YPR 10) (London, New Haven 1965); and D. E. Orton, *The Composition of John's Gospel: Selected Studies from Novum Testamentum* (Leiden 1998).

[5] De la Potterie, "Structura primae partis," 131; and Brodie, *Gospel*, 133.

[6] Dodd, *op. cit.*, 289.

[7] E.g. See Bultmann, *Gospel*, 457; Schnackenburg, I, 5-6; and II, v-vi and 1-9. Mollat, 35-36; Léon-Dufour, *Lecture*, I, 423-33; and Beasley-Murray, *John*, xci-xcii; see also Morris, Borchert, and Ridderbos.

[8] The term 'Book' is not to be understood as a complete work but only as 'a major division of a literary work' (*Webster's New Collegiate Dictionary*, 127). Ancient authors used to divide their works into 'books' in the above sense.

[9] R. E. Brown, *Gospel*, Vol. 1; and Moloney, *John*, 23.

[10] R. E. Brown, *op. cit.*, Vol. 2; and Moloney, *op. cit.*, 24.

Signs' and prefers to designate 11,1-20,29 as the Book of Jesus' Hour.[11] Thus, chapters 11 and 12 overlap; he explains it as being caused by the bridge-section (11,1-12,50) which concludes the first part and introduces the second simultaneously. This observation is true also of smaller sections and episodes.

The unit of my study is situated in the first part (1,19-12,50) dealing with the public life of Jesus and is interwoven with his signs and preaching. As it is difficult to establish an objective criterion for the subdivisions of this first part, there have been a variety of proposals. There are the various themes treated in the sections, diverse patterns, and the multiple literary and narrative techniques used. It only confirms how profoundly deep and eminently rich the fourth Gospel is. Now, where does 2,23-3,36 fit into this Book of Signs (1,19-12,50)?

B. Division of 1,19-4,54

Relying on a variety of criteria – thematic,[12] structural,[13] symbolic,[14] dramatic[15] and narrative[16] – many scholars have proposed different structures to the first section (1,19-4,54) of the first part of the Gospel – the book of signs – containing 2,23-3,36.

---

[11] Mlakuzhyil, 154 and 162.

[12] A vast majority of the commentators of the fourth Gospel proposes a thematic structure to each section of the Gospel. Létourneau (*Jésus*, 30-31) presents them in a chart summarising the diverse treatment of various scholars showing also well their differences. His presentation is helpful to have a bird's eye view of their positions.

[13] E.g. P. Defourney ("Au sujet de la composition du quatrième évangile," *Collectanea Mechliniensa* 11 [1937] 359-67) structures the fourth Gospel based on the literary-chronological expressions Μετὰ τοῦτο (2,12) and Μετὰ ταῦτα (3,22; 5,1; 6,1; 7,1 and 21,1). He, thus, divides the whole Gospel (excluding the prologue) into seven episodes (episodic structure). The section 1,19-4,54 contains three episodes: 1,19-2,11; 2,12-3,21 and 3,22-4,54. But his proposal is not acceptable as the expressions Μετὰ τοῦτο and Μετὰ ταῦτα occur in many other places (e.g. 5,14; 11,7.11; 19,28 and 19,38). I feel that Defourney seems to be under the spell of the magic number seven. E. C. Webster ("Pattern in the Fourth Gospel," in: D. J. A. Clines, D. M. Gunn and A. J. Hauser [eds.], *Art and Meaning: Rhetoric in Biblical Literature* [Sheffield 1982] 230) contends that the fourth "Gospel as a literary whole is meticulously constructed on the basis of symmetrical design and balanced units." He observes a chiastic structure in the whole Gospel. According to him there are five *Christological statements* which are linked to one another chiastically (cf. *ibid.*, 249-50). For a parallel structure (1,19-3,21//3,22-4,54) see Gourgues, *Pour que vous croyiez*, 73-100; and Létourneau (*Jésus*, 57ff.), who also proposes a parallel structure of 1,19-4,54, rightly argues that the enumeration of the two Cana signs has eclipsed the observation of a more important structural correspondence in the section, *viz.*, the one between the two testimonies of the Baptist in 1,19-34 and 3,22-36. C. H. Talbert ("Artistry and Theology: An Analysis of the Architecture of John 1,19-5,47," *CBQ* 32 [1970] 341-66) finds in 1,19-5,47 a chiastic structure of the pattern ABCD//D^{1}C^{1}B^{1}A^1 with the theme of testimony at its centre. He ignores completely the important link between the two testimonies of the Baptist (1,19-34 and 3,22-36), and between the two signs at Cana (2,1-11 and 4,43-54). Hence, I feel, his structure is baseless. Mlakuzhyil (199), who also offers a chiastic structure (ABC//C^{1}B^{1}A^1) for the section 2,1-4,54, clearly points out the correspondence between the two signs at Cana (2,1-11 and 4,43-54). Unfortunately, he does not search to show the thematic dimension of the formal links where the foundation of the parallelism lies, and the valuable link between the two testimonies of the Baptist is simply ignored. Nicholson (45-48) observes a concentric structure (ABCDC^{1}B^{1}A^1) in 2,1-4,54. This section, according to him, comprises of typical encounters with and faith-responses to Jesus. It is clearly encompassed by the two signs at Cana. His attention to the second testimony of the Baptist by placing it at the eye of the structure is noteworthy. Finally, P. F. Ellis (14-15 and 29) has published a structural commentary on the whole Gospel. He structures each of the sections as well as units concentrically in the same pattern of ABCB^{1}A^1. He treats 1,19-4,3 as a section. For several reasons I find his argumentation very weak and unacceptable.

[14] E.g. for seven-fold divisions see J. Goettmann (*Saint Jean. Évangile de la Nouvelle Genèse* [Paris 1982]); M.-É. Boismard, "L'évangile à quatre dimensions," *LV(B)* 1 (1951) 99; Boismard and Lamouille, 38-39; V. Pasquetto, *Da Gesù al Padre. Introduzione alla lettura esegetico-spirituale del vangelo di Giovanni*

261

1. 1,19-51

Most commentators divide this section of the first four chapters into two main sub-sections (1,19-51 and 2,1-4,54). However, as the diagram below shows, there is difference of opinion among scholars about the attachment of the wedding at Cana (2,1-11±12) to the first or second sub-section. I do not intend to treat here the opinion of each individual author but summarise briefly the reason behind their position.

Group A	Group B	Group C
1,19-51	1,19-51 ± 2,1- 11(12)	1,19-2,11(12)
Beasley-Murray, Blank, Borchert, Bultmann, Carson, de la Potterie, Dodd, Hoskyns, Létourneau, Lohmeyer, Malina & Rohrbaugh, Mateos and Barreto, Moloney, Morris, O'Day, Ridderbos, Sloyan, Stibbe, and van den Bussche,	Braun R. E. Brown, and Mlakuzhyil	Westcott, Loisy, Bernard, Lagrange, Strachan, Lightfoot, Schnackenburg, Barrett, Léon-Dufour, Becker, Boismard, Tenney, Mollat, Witherington, Painter, L'Éplattenier, Schenke, and Korting

For the scholars of Group A, Jn. 1 plays an introductory role – the prologue (1,1-18) to the whole Gospel, and the rest of the chapter (1,19-51) to the first part of the Gospel (Book of signs).[17]

Now, the *chronological indications* appearing in 1,29.35.43 ('the next day') and 2,1 ('the third day') make a number of authors (Group C) consider 1,19-2,11±12 as one literary unit forming an inaugural week of the ministry of Jesus.[18] Some of the scholars see in this week an allusion to the first week of Creation (Gen. 1,1-2,3) because of the use of the term ἀρχὴν (Jn. 2,11; cf. Gen. 1,1); the seven days of Jn. 1 and 2 are an echo of the seven days of Creation, and so see a 'New Creation' in the coming of Jesus, the Messiah.[19]

(Rome 1983) 107-9 and 159-60; E. Lohmeyer, "Über Aufbau und Gliederung des vierten Evangeliums," *ZNW* 27 (1928) 11-36; and M. Rissi, "Der Aufbau des vierten Evangeliums," *NTS* 29 (1983) 52.

[15] See Schenke, *Johanneskommentar* (14) observes three scenes (which he calls 'Bild') in the first section (19-2,12; 2,13-3,21 and 3,22-4,54) on the geographical basis. See also his *Johannesevangelium*.

[16] E.g. Culpepper, *Anatomy*; and Stibbe, *John*.

[17] Cf. Morris, *Gospel*, viii; Blank, *Johannes*, 63; Carson, *Gospel*, 141; Ridderbos, 6; Beasley-Murray, *John*, xci and 18; G. S. Sloyan, *John* (IBC) (Atlanta 1988) 30; J. Mateos and J. Barreto, *El Evangelio de Juan. Analisis Lingüistico y Comentario Exegetico* (Madrid 1979) 13-17; Lohmeyer, 11-36; and Dodd, *Historical Tradition*, 248-49.

[18] There is difference of opinion among authors with regard to the purpose of the fourth evangelist in introducing these chronological notes. Cf. Bernard, I, 33-34; Strachan, 121. Haenchen (I, 152) contends that the chronological notes are used only to indicate the beginning of a new scene. In the same way, van den Bussche (116-17) thinks that the chronological indications are only a literary technique to knit the unit together. Moreover there is no mention of the rest of the days to form a whole week of seven days. R. E. Brown (*Gospel*, I, cxlii and 106) warns against a passion for finding sevens. M.-É. Boismard (*Du Baptême à Cana [Jean 1,1-2,11]* [LeDiv 18] [Paris 1956] 14ff.) without evidence introduces a day between 1,46 and 47; see also his, "L'évangile à quatre dimensions," *LV(B)* 1 (1951) 99 and 105-13; and Boismard and Lamouille, 38-39. For Léon-Dufour (*Lecture*, I, 150) the arguments based on chronological indications are insufficient. See also B. Olsson, *Structure and Meaning in the Fourth Gospel. A Text-Linguistic Analysis of John 2:1-11 and 4:1-42* (CB.NT 6) (Lund 1974) 102-4 and 276.

[19] M. Girard ("La structure heptapartite de quatrième évangile," *SR* 5 [1975/76] 350-59) proposes a seven-week structure to the fourth Gospel corresponding to the seven-day Creation story of Gen. 1,1-2,4a. According to this proposition, the first day of Creation (Gen. 1,2-5) corresponds to the first week of the ministry of Jesus or of the new Creation (Jn. 1,19-2,12), and the second day of Creation (Gen. 1,6-8)

Some others observe a formal link between 1,50-51 and 2,11 in the fact that the promise made to Nathanael in 1,50-51 – "You will see greater things than these" – comes to a sort of fulfilment in 2,11,[20] and the almost private character of the event at Cana fits in well with the introductory character of 1,19-51.

The idea of the inaugural week has attracted some scholars to hold an *ambivalent position* reconciling a two-type division (Group B). F.-M. Braun – though advocates a thematic division of 2,1-4,42 – recognises that 2,1-11 forms part of the first days of Jesus (1,19-2,11).[21] R. E. Brown and Mlakuzhyil consider 2,1-11 as a pericope having a double function of closing the first part and opening the second.[22] I would say that divisions between literary units are not impenetrable brick walls.[23]

Based on these diverse views, it appears sensible to me to hold, for the time being, that the actual story begins in 1,19. Up to 1,51 the story is limited to the account of preparations – the testimony of the Baptist as a result of which his disciples join the company of Jesus (1,35ff.), and Peter, Philip, and Nathanael are called (1,41-51) – leading to Jesus' public ministry to be narrated in the following chapters. "You will see" (1,50-51) constitutes the climax of the motif that governs the coming of the disciples to Jesus in this entire pericope (1,35-51). Though 1,19-51 as a whole clearly forms a unit, the difficulty persists as to whether this section concludes with the promise made to Nathanael (1,50-51) or with the first revelation of the glory of Jesus and the faith of his disciples in 2,1-11.

2. Cana to Cana (2,1-4,54)

A good number of scholars who affirm the introductory character of 1,19-51 identify 2,1-4,54 as a distinct section in Jesus' ministry presenting the inauguration of his public ministry with signs, words and encounters.[24] Several features of 2,1-11 also separate this miracle story from 1,19-51. First of all, there is a change of place: In 1,43 Jesus decides to

---

parallels the week of the first Passover (Jn. 2,13-4,54) organised after the formula ABCDE//E'D'C'B'A'. See also Saxby, 9-13; L. P. Trudinger, "The Seven Days of the New Creation in St. John's Gospel: Some Further Reflections," *EvQ* 44 (1972) 154-58; Reinhartz, *Word in the World*; T. Barosse, "The Seven Days of the New Creation in St. John's Gospel," *CBQ* 21 (1959) 507-16; and Westcott, I, xlii-xliii and 16. Against the use of 'days,' see Léon-Dufour, *Lecture*, I, 150-51; B. Lindars and P. Borgen, "The Place of the Old Testament in the Formation of New Testament Theology: Prolegomena and Response," *NTS* 23 (1976/77) 64-65; and Schnackenburg, *Gospel* I, 297; 308 and 313.

[20] Cf. Lightfoot, 92-93; J. N. Suggit, "John 2,1-11: The Sign of Greater Things to Come," *Neotest.* 21 (1987) 141-58; Becker, *Johannes*, 8 and 104-42; Léon-Dufour, *op. cit.*; H.-J. Kuhn, *Christologie und Wunder. Untersuchungen zu Joh 1,35-51* (BU 18) (Regensburg 1988) 153-59; and Painter, "Quest and Rejection Stories," 20-23; see also C. R. Koester, "Messianic Exegesis and the Call of Nathanael (John 1:45-51)," *JSNT* 39 (1990) 23-34; J. H. Neyrey, "The Jacob Allusions in John 1:51," *CBQ* 44 (1982) 586-89; and G. Korting, *Die esoterische Struktur des Johannesevangeliums* (BU 25) (Regensburg 1994) I, 142.

[21] F.-M. Braun, *Les grandes traditions d'Israël et l'accord des écritures selon le quatrième évangile* (Paris 1964) II, 99.

[22] R. E. Brown, *op. cit.*, cxl-cxliii. For a summary of this phenomenon of *bridge pericopes* and *bridge verses* in the fourth Gospel see Mlakuzhyil, 146-54. Moloney (*Belief in the Word*, 59) also acknowledges 2,1-12 as a bridge pericope belonging to both sub-sections, but prefers to attach it to the Cana cycle.

[23] E.g. Wilckens (*Evangelium*, 36-62) and Brodie hold rather unique views. Wilckens sees 1,19-2,22 as forming a literary unit on the basis of the beginnings, namely the first testimony of the Baptist, the first disciples, the first sign and the beginning of the way of the cross (in the cleansing of the Temple); Brodie (*Gospel*, xii and 129ff.), on the other hand, divides the whole Gospel into a three year period and assigns 1,1-2,22 to the first year of the public life of Jesus, 2,23-6 comprise the second year, and the rest, the third year.

[24] Cf. Carson, *Gospel*, 166ff.; see also Malina and Rohrbaugh, 65ff.; and B. Prete, "Vangelo di Giovanni," in: *Il Messaggio della Salvezza*, VIII (Torino [4]1978) 797-870.

go to Galilee, and in 2,1 he is there. Along with the disciples of Jesus (2,2) new characters enter the story, the mother of Jesus (2,1) and several participants at the wedding feast: servants (2,5), the steward (2,8), the bridegroom (2,9), Jesus' disciples (2,11). There is a change in literary form as the account shifts from the initial response of the Jews and the first disciples to the Baptist and Jesus (1,19-51) to a *sign* story (2,1-11).

Many scholars name this sub-section 'from Cana to Cana'[25] or call it 'the Cana Cycle,'[26] because it begins and ends with a *sign* each at Cana, and describes a journey from Cana to Cana. They argue that the wedding at Cana (2,1-11) forms an *inclusion* with 4,43-54 and would, thus, favour 2,1-4,54 as a sub-section. In both Cana signs there is a 'request-rebuke-response' sequence.[27] As S. Temple points out, the two Cana signs are the only signs in the fourth Gospel which do not lead immediately to a discourse. After each Cana sign Jesus goes up to Jerusalem and the Temple,[28] and many scholars who attempt to reconstruct the signs source link 2,12 with 4,46-54.[29] Besides, the wedding at Cana is specifically enumerated by the evangelist as the first of *signs*[30] and, thus, indicates the beginning of the revelation of the *glory* of Jesus which is one of the main themes of the second sub-section (2,1-4,54) as a whole. Hence, the wedding at Cana seems to fit in better to a beginning rather than to a conclusion of a sub-section.[31]

---

[25] Cf. R. E. Brown, *op. cit.*; Moloney, "From Cana to Cana," 817-43; and his *John*, 63; Ridderbos, 97; G. Segalla, *Giovanni. Versione, Introduzione, Note* (NVB) (Rome 1976) 130-37; and Pasquetto, 107-9.

[26] Cf. Borchert, 151ff.

[27] See C. H. Giblin, "Suggestion, Negative Response and Positive Action in St. John's Portrayal of Jesus (John 2.1-11; 4.46-54; 7.2-14; 11.1-44)," *NTS* 26 (1979/80) 197-211. Bauer (*Johannesevangelium*, 78) notices the following presentation of the narratives in parallel: "Die Geschichte baut sich übrigens ganz auf wie das erste Kanawunder 2,1-12: Bitte, schroffe Abweisung, Fortdauer des Vertrauens, Erhörung." Moloney (*John*, 70 and 158; and his *Belief in the Word*, 90 and 189-90) points out the same pattern of: "problem-request-rebuke-reaction-consequence" in both signs; see also R. E. Brown, *op. cit.*, esp. 194-98; and Bultmann, *Gospel*, 115.

[28] S. Temple, "The Two Signs in the Fourth Gospel," *JBL* 81 (1962) 170.

[29] E.g. Bultmann, *op. cit.*, 205-6; Fortna, *Fourth Gospel and its Predecessor*, 58-65.

[30] Cf. R. F. Collins, "Cana (Jn. 2,1-12) – The First of his Signs or the Key to his Signs?," *IThQ* 47 (1980) 99-142. Contrary to this view, G. R. O'Day (*The Gospel of John* [NIntB 9] [Nashville 1995] 508) argues that the Cana signs are not a unit in themselves, but only part of the first cycle of Jesus' ministry which establishes a tension between the manifestation of Jesus' glory (2,1-11) and the rejection of that glory (5,9-47); the second cycle (6,1-10-42), too, follows the same pattern with the difference that the hostility, in the second cycle, increases and the conflict intensifies. See also R. Kysar, *John* (ACNT) (Minneapolis 1986) 22-23. Their observations, though partially correct from a particular point of view, do not take all the pericopes of 2,1-4,54 and their themes seriously into consideration in postulating their structure; hence, according to me, their thematic structure remains a dubious one.

[31] Cf. Stibbe, *John*, 43. Lightfoot (12) and Braun (*Les grandes traditions d'Israël*, II, 96), too, consider 2,12-4,54 as a unit having the theme of the *new order* against the background of the *old*. Though their observation of the old being substituted by the new is praiseworthy, their contention does not give 3,22-36 its rightful place; hence, I feel, is wanting in its argument. See also Barrett, 12; 190-91. A few other scholars see the theme of the life giving word in 4,43-54 coupling with the healing of the paralytic in 5,1-18, and depict Jesus as the mediator of life; e.g. Beasley-Murray, *John*, 67. Such is the view of exegetes as varied as Bultmann, *op.cit.*, 203; Hoskyns, 249; A. Feuillet, "La signification théologique du second miracle de Cana (Jo. IV.46-54)," *RSR* 48 (1960) 62-75. But, in my opinion, the fourth evangelist is not primarily concerned with telling a miracle story about restoration to life. At the centre of this account stands an encounter between an official and Jesus, where the miracle of restoration to life is the result of an encounter in which the official believes in the word of Jesus. The author's main focus is not the miracle itself. There are obvious indications that the author wants the reader to link the two Cana miracles. As Loisy (194) remarks: "Il n'y a pas à se demander pourquoi Jésus revient à Cana, mais pourquoi l'évangeliste l'y ramène." The narrator reminds the reader that Jesus "came again (πάλιν) to Cana in Galilee" (4,46). There is a repetition of the place,

Conclusion

The section 2,1-4,54 is interwoven with a variety of repeated themes. Its multi-faceted dimensions do not simply allow one to put it under one single pattern. The declaration of purpose, the progress of action, the chronological and geographical (Galilee, Judea and Samaria) divisions indicate clearly that the author has an extensive knowledge of the career of Jesus, and that his arrangement of the narrative is both intelligent and purposeful. However, one notices among scholars a general hesitation between 2,1 and 2,12/13 as the initial mark, and between 4,42 and 4,54 as the final mark.

First of all, one can say that it is difficult to challenge the strong formal correlation between the two sings at Cana. At the same time, one should not come to a hasty conclusion of linking a pericope always with what precedes. The rule of thumb should be: the structure that is less contestable is the one which is supported by the most number of significant literary and narrative characteristics. Secondly, the correlation between 2,1-22 and 4,1-54 under the themes of living water, wedding motif, purification and Temple cult, faith, etc. must be unveiled to take up a further and deeper study of the context, insertion and the literary unity of Jn. 3. Thirdly, it should be remarked that only a few authors have shown interest in the function of the second testimony of the Baptist (3,22-36) in the fourth Gospel. Among those who have proposed structural and narrative patterns many have ignored this pericope, considering it as embarrassing and bypassed it stressing solely the encounter with Nicodemus (3,1-21 and 31-36). One has to try convincingly to bring the Baptist back to his place in 3,22-36. I shall, in the next chapter, establish the perimeters of the units and sub-units of 1,19-4,54.

---

accompanied by the expression 'πάλιν.' The narrator then reminds the reader: "where he had changed the water into wine" (4,46). As he concludes the story of the second miracle at Cana, the narrator once more recalls the earlier miracle at Cana: "Now this was the second (πάλιν δεύτερον) sign that Jesus did after coming from Judea to Galilee (4,54).

Chapter 2

PERIMETERS OF UNITS AND SUB-UNITS

A unit is a network of interrelated sub-units and segments whose meaning can be determined only through relating them to the whole. Most of the commentaries on the fourth Gospel have followed primarily a thematic plan in exploring and exegeting the various sections, units and pericopes. Such a treatment alone does not lead to a satisfactory solution to trace the intention of the evangelist in organising the material the way he has done it. One has to proceed further and explore the formal relationship between the various units and sub-units of the text. The most efficacious criterion to discern the structure of a section is the accumulation of the formal compositional indications as there are many combinations possible between the recurring themes in the fourth Gospel.

In order to do it effectively, one must, first of all, determine the perimeters of the sub-sections, units and sub-units of 1,19-4,54 and, then, search for the structural correlations among them applying literary and narrative methods. My scope in this chapter is, therefore, to determine the limits of each of the units and sub-units using some of the literary characteristics found in them.

A. 1,19-51

The first unit of the section, *viz.*, 1,19-51, dealing with the testimony of the Baptist and the coming of the first disciples to Jesus forms a literary unit. A careful consideration of the *narrative structure* reveals that the unit is marked by a series of days, indicated by the narrator: 'the next day' (Τῇ ἐπαύριον – 1,29), 'the next day again' (Τῇ ἐπαύριον πάλιν – 1,35), 'the next day' (Τῇ ἐπαύριον – 1,43) The four segments (1,19-28; 29-34; 35-42 and 43-51)[1] of this unit are, thus, well knit together through the systematic repetition of this chronological indication at the beginning of every segment. The steady progression of *days* features both 'story time' and 'plotted time.'[2] Therefore, 1,19-51 narrates a story about a *succession of events* that took place over a period of four days.

In 1,19 the curtain raises and in the first days several *dramatis personae* (characters): the Baptist, Judeans, priests and Levites from Jerusalem are introduced to the reader. The prologue prepares for this narrative. One observes a *prolepsis*[3] (flash-forward) in 1,7-8. Here, the narrator makes three statements (*tripartite structure*) about the Baptist. first, that he himself is not the light (1,8a); second, that he came to testify to the light (1,7ab and 8b); and third, that through his testimony all people might believe (1,7c). In

---

[1] Many scholars subdivide this unit in this way using the chronological indication of 'the next day;' e.g. cf. Moloney, *John*, 51-57; and Stibbe, *John*, 31-42.

[2] 'Story time' reports events systematically in their correct temporal sequence as the story unfolds. In 1,19-51 the story time is the succession of events over four successive days. 'Plotted time' breaks into the logic of the temporal sequence and points the reader either backward (*analepsis*) or forward (*prolepsis*) to some past or future moment relevant to the story which, however, does not form part of the regular succession of events being reported. For a detailed study on this subject see Genette, *Narrative Discourse*, 33-85. See also S. Rimmon-Kenan, *Narrative Fiction: Contemporary Poetics* (London 1983) 43-58; Culpepper, *Anatomy*, 63-70; and A. Reinhartz, "Jesus as Prophet: Predictive Prolepses in the Fourth Gospel," *JSNT* 36 (1989) 3-16.

[3] *Prolepsis* is a literary device marking the anticipation of events occurring later on in the Gospel. They are references to events which have not yet occurred at the point in the narrative at which they are foretold (e.g. 2,19-22 and 3,14.24).

1,19-51, too, there are three narratives fulfilling the same three expectations in succession. First, in 1,19-28, the Baptist insists that he is not the light ('I am not the Messiah, Elijah nor the prophet'); second, in 1,29-34, he testifies to the light ("Here is the lamb of God!"); third, in 1,35-51, one sees people (disciples) coming to faith in Jesus as a result of his testimony. Note the use of the word πιστεύεις in 1,50. There is also a link between the prologue and the subsequent narrative indicated by the first word in the narrative, 'and' (1,19).[4]

Another noteworthy device is the narrator's language of *movement*. In 1,29 the Baptist sees Jesus approaching him (ἐρχόμενον πρὸς αὐτόν), exactly the same way as Nathanael's movement towards Jesus in 1,47 (ἐρχόμενον πρὸς αὐτὸν). In 1,36 the Baptist sees Jesus walking by (περιπατοῦντι); in 1,38 Jesus sees the disciples following him (ἀκολουθοῦντας. The verbs of movement have symbolic overtones of coming into faith and discipleship. There is also a chain of movements of persons – one from the Baptist to Jesus, Jesus to Andrew and Andrew to Peter (1,19-34), and the other from Jesus to Philip and Philip to Nathanael. The movement culminates again in Jesus as Nathanael comes to Jesus; this reveals the centrality of the figure of Jesus (1,35-51).

A further literary technique that contributes to the sense of meaningful history is the narrator's use of the *historic present tense*. 1,19 begins with a present tense: "Καὶ αὕτη ἐστὶν ἡ μαρτυρία τοῦ Ἰωάννου" and 1,51 ends also with a present tense: "καὶ λέγει αὐτῷ.....λέγω ὑμῖν..." Again in 1,29 "the next day the Baptist *sees* (βλέπει) Jesus..."; and in 1,45 Philip *finds* (εὑρίσκει) Nathanael and *says* (λέγει):[5] "we have found him..." Furthermore, 'λέγω/λέγει' appears often in the present tense throughout the unit.[6]

An added indication that supports the consideration of 1,19-51 as a literary unit is the concentration of the principal *titles* attributed to Jesus in the rest of the fourth Gospel: Christ (1,19.25.41), Elijah (1,21), Prophet (1,21.25), Lamb of God (1,29.36), Son of God (1,34.49), 'Rabbi' (1,38. 49), Messiah (1,41), 'of whom Moses in the law and also the prophets wrote' (1,45), King of Israel (1,49) and Son of Man (1,51). Besides, one cannot fail to observe the constant mention of the *themes* of 'seeing': βλέπω (1,29), θεωρέω (1,32.38), ἐμβλέπω (1,36.42), ὁράω (1,33.34.36.39.46.47.48.50.51)[7] and 'following'[8] (ἠκολούθησαν – 1,37; ἀκολουθοῦντας – 1,38; ἀκολουθησάντων – 1,40; ἀκολούθει – 1,43). Moreover, one notices a *gradual revelation of the identity of Jesus* in this unit. At the beginning, the statements of the Baptist leading to the identity of Jesus are vague: "Among you stands one whom you do not know, the one who is coming after me" (1,26-27); then, at a second level, he identifies Jesus as 'the Lamb of God' (1,29) and as 'the one who baptises with the Holy Spirit' (1,33); it is then followed by the true and clear identity of Jesus as the 'Son of God' – at the end of the first sub-section (1,34). One notices here a

---

[4] Note that this 'and' appearing in RSV is left out in NRSV.

[5] This brings the past into the reader's present and implies a purposeful continuity of mission.

[6] Cf. 1,21.29.36 etc. This technique helps to reduce the effects of the transition from orality to textuality in the Gospel's composition. By having characters speaking in the present tense, the evangelist recreates the living aspect of oral storytelling – a speech characteristic.

[7] Cf. Létourneau, *Jésus*, 50; see also Léon-Dufour, *Lecture*, I, 185-87.

[8] The theme of discipleship is important in the story of the fourth Gospel. Connected with it is the idea of following. The fact that this verb is used in this sense four times in seven verses (1,37-43) indicates that the narrator is initiating a major theme in this unit; see Koester, "Hearing," 331.

tripartite arrangement in the above mentioned triple identification of Jesus by the Baptist and observes the repetition of the same in the segment (1,35-42): 'Lamb of God' (1,36), 'Rabbi' (1,38) and 'Messiah' (1,41). A particularly important aspect of the storytelling – the tendency to provide explanatory parentheses – occurs here *three* times: "which translated means Teacher" (1,38), "which is translated Anointed" (1,41), and "which is translated Peter" (1,42).[9] Besides, there are also *three* references to 'the next day' in 1,19-51. In addition to these, the fourth evangelist's marked tendency to structure material in *tripartite* patterns is visible in the three confessions about Jesus in 1,43-51 – one by Philip: "about whom Moses in the law and also the prophets wrote" (1,45); and the two by Nathanael: "Rabbi, you are the Son of God! You are the King of Israel!" (1,49).

1. 1,19-34

Having ascertained the literary unity of 1,19-51, let me take into consideration the bipartite sub-units and establish the flow of the narrative from one to the other. First of all 1,19-34, forming the first two segments (1,19-28 and 29-34), are controlled and encompassed by an *inclusion* formed by the mention of the words 'testimony' (1,19) and 'testify' (1,32.34) at the two extremities of the sub-unit. This testimony of the Baptist is described as taking place on *two days* (1,19-28 and 29-34), separated by the mention of 'the next day' in 1,29. On the first day, the testimony is provoked by the enquiry commission from the home of Law, Jerusalem. The Baptist stands in front of the authorities from Jerusalem. On the second day, he testifies to the true identity of Jesus. What the evangelist describes has having happened on these two days can be considered as a sort of *itinerary* of discovery of the Baptist. In both segments of this sub-unit there is a double negation on the part of the Baptist. In 1,20-21 he *denies twice* with a resounding 'I am not' (οὐκ εἰμι).[10] In 1,31.33, too, he *asserts twice*: "I myself did not know him" (κἀγὼ οὐκ ᾔδειν αὐτόν).

2. 1,35-51

In this sub-unit five new characters are introduced into the story: Andrew, an unknown disciple and Simon in 1,35-42, Philip and Nathanael in 43-51. This is marked by an *inclusion* through the mention of 'Rabbi' in 1,38 and 1,49. The text is again enclosed by *two major declarations*, first that of the Baptist: "Here is the Lamb of God" (1,36) and second that of Jesus announcing the mystery of 'the Son of Man' (1,51). Just as in the preceding segments (1,19-28 and 29-34) the sequence is again distributed on *two days* (1,35-42 and 43-1)[11] one leading to the other.

---

[9] There are many of these asides in the fourth Gospel (cf. 2,9.22; 4,2.9.25; 6.59.64.71; 7,5.39; 8,27; 9,7; 10,6; 11,2.18.51; 12,6.16; 13,11; 18,10.14.40; 19,13.14.17.31.35-36.42; 20,9.16.30-31 and 21,7.14.19.23.24-25). On at least four occasions (9,7; 19,13.17 and 20,16) these asides contain Greek translations of Hebrew or Aramaic terms. This is the function of the three parentheses in 1,38.41 and 42. Evidently there were Greeks in the author's original readership. P. F. Ellis (30) observes a concentric structure knitting this unit together, but the segments of the units, according to him, have different perimeters. I find it not convincing as he places Simon at the centre of the unit, which is evidently not the central theme. For various possibilities of chiasms in this section on 1,19-22; 19-28; 19-36; 29-36; 37-44; 37-51 and 45-51 see Howard-Brook, 62-75.

[10] The reader is being remotely prepared for the one who alone can claim 'I am he' (Ἐγὼ εἰμι); cf. E. D. Freed, "*Ego eimi* in John 1,20 and 4,25," *CBQ* 41 (1979) 288-89; and Hoskyns, 174.

[11] Malina and Rohrbaugh (296) demonstrate the literary unity of each of the segments 1,35-42 and 1,43-51 through chiastic structures.

In 1,43 one is on the fourth day where a turning point in the narrative occurs. No longer do the disciples find Jesus, but he actively finds and calls Philip.[12] The theme of the *movement* returns, as Jesus decides to go to Galilee (1,43). It is on a journey that he finds and calls Philip to follow. For the first time in the narrative a disciple of Jesus is the result of *Jesus' initiative*. Moreover, the plot of the Nathanael narrative (1,43-51)[13] is similar to that of the preceding one (1,35-42) suggesting that they are linked to one another. Both share the same formal characteristics of a *call story*.

I am convinced that the fourth evangelist has carefully arranged his material in the first unit in an artistic manner using techniques of rhetorical repetition which go back and forth. Besides, the narrative moves the story forward at every level of the episode. There is an aesthetic relation and crafty network established between the different segments of the unit. The narrative of 1,19-51 is, no doubt, marked by indications of the real author's careful organisation of the material.

B. 2,1-22

1. 2,1-11

Compared with what preceded there is a marked change of setting at the beginning of this unit. The perimeters of this pericope do not pose much of a problem as it is well enclosed by the mention of the geographical detail 'in Cana of Galilee' in 1,1 and 1,11. The scene suddenly changes into that of a wedding and banquet involving a change in characters (the mother of Jesus, his disciples, the servants, the steward and the bridegroom), vocabulary (jars, water, draw, fill, wine) and theme. The language is no more that of testimony (absence of the verbs *testify* or *see* and the titles of Jesus), nor that of the quest of the disciples (absence of verbs *hear, search, follow, find* etc.). The introduction of the miracles of Jesus, described as *signs* indicates a new beginning. For the first time in the Gospel, the narrator speaks of σημεῖον[14] of Jesus (cf. 2,11).

Besides, the opening words of the Cana narrative – "on the third day" (τῇ ἡμέρᾳ τῇ τρίτῃ) – have symbolic resonance. Following the suggestions of A. M. Serra, Olsson, in a very extensive monograph on Jn. 2,1-11, attempts to understand the entire story against what he calls the "Sinai Screen."[15] He bases this link on various expressions and phrases in 2,1-11 that occur more or less in the same form in Exodus, which also could go in favour of considering the Cana sign of wine as a literary unit. Moreover, I observe the following ring composition demonstrating the literary unity of this pericope:

---

[12] The text here has some difficulty, as the verb 'decided to go' has no subject. But the verb 'said' has Jesus as its subject. One can thus suppose that the narrator intends Jesus to be the subject throughout, as he takes the initiative to find and call. See L. Schenke "Die literarische Entstehungsgeschichte von Joh 1,19-51," *BN* 46 (1989) 30.

[13] Regarding the literary unity of 1,43-51 see S. Schreiber, "Die Jüngerberufungsszene Joh 1,43-51 als literarische Einheit," *SNTU* 23 (1998) 5-28, esp. 21-24: the narrative structure; see also F. Hahn, "Die Jüngerberufung John 1,35-51," in: J. Gnilka (ed.), *Neues Testament und Kirche: Für Rudolf Schnackenburg* (Freiburg 1974) 172-73.

[14] This Johannine term always includes two aspects: 1. *Demonstrative:* the sign elicits the faith of the disciples in Jesus; 2. *Expressive:* it manifests the glory of the one who performs it; cf. Léon-Dufour, *op. cit.*, 209.

[15] Olsson, 102-9.

A	1-2	Introduction	Cana, a wedding, disciples present.
B	3-4	Dialogue	Mother's request and Jesus' rebuke ("Woman, what concern is that to you and to me? My hour has not yet come").
C	5-8	Miracle	Mother's confidence, Jesus changes water into wine.
B[1]	9-10	Dialogue	Steward's surprise and rebuke ("Everyone serves the good wine first, and then the inferior wine after the guests have become drunk. But you have kept the good wine until now").
A[1]	11	Conclusion	Cana, first sign, disciples believe.

The Cana scene is central. Within the fourth Gospel as a whole it represents a considerable development. It indicates, more clearly than any of the preceding episodes, that the ministry of Jesus has become quite public. It also indicates explicitly that his disciples have come to believe in him. Thus it represents a dramatic advance in the narrative, besides forming a unit by itself. The present shape of 2,1-11 reveals the real author's careful selection and ordering of the material.

2. 2,12-22

Analysing a plot in the fourth Gospel, one cannot fail to observe a very careful arrangement with a beginning, middle and an end. Stibbe considers that the Passover feasts are important in the creation of a sense of plot in the fourth Gospel.[16] This episode is the first of the references to the Passover in the fourth Gospel. While the Cana episode suggests a "joie de vivre,"[17] the Temple scene speaks of limitation, tension and death. The cleansing of the Temple, therefore, is quite different in mood from the Cana scene. Yet the continuity between the two scenes is not broken. For instance, the Cana scene's faint references to Jesus' death and resurrection (the third day, the hour, *doxa*) are echoed in clearer references to Jesus' death and resurrection (three days, destroy and raise up). The idea of *sign* appears in a varied form (cf. 2,11 and 2,18). The emphasis on the disciples is maintained. Both episodes explore the theme of the replacement of the old order of worship with a new one centred on Jesus: He replaces the water of Jewish purification with the new wine of the kingdom in 2,1-11 and the Temple in Jerusalem with the new one of his body in 2,12-22.

The task of establishing the perimeters of this pericope is not as easy as that of the preceding ones because there is the absence of an inclusion linking the initial and final marks of the story. However, one can fix the beginning of the pericope in 2,12-13 thanks to the chronological indication found there.[18] In fact the evangelist is accustomed to

---

[16] Stibbe, *John*, 49. R. E. Brown, *Gospel*, I, cxxxix rightly sees the three Passovers as "setting for a particular narrative." See also Schnackenburg, *Gospel*, I, 1-2; and Léon-Dufour, *op. cit.*, 31-32, 252-53.

[17] Cf. Brodie, *Gospel*, 172.

[18] The Capernaum verse (2,12) has been seen by commentators in diverse ways. Some regard it as pertaining to the Cana episode (cf. Lindars, *Gospel*, 132). Others, some of whom group it with the Cana scene, regard it as some kind of free-floating element – a transition or interlude (cf. Westcott, I, 39; Lagrange, 62-64; Barrett, 194; R. E. Brown, *op. cit.*, 112-13; H. Strathmann, *Das Evangelium nach Johannes* [NTD 4] [Göttingen ⁹1959] 58; Morris, *Gospel*, 186-88; Schulz, *Johannes*, 47; and Haenchen, I, 175). Mlakuzhyil (191-93) considers it as a bridge-verse. Yet others group it with the Temple episode (cf. Loisy, 146-47; Hoskyns, 192; Lightfoot, 111; Schnackenburg, *op. cit.*, 342-43; and J. N. Sanders, *The Gospel according to Saint John* [HNTC] [New York 1968] 115). Discussion on this puzzlingly placed verse is frequently dominated by issues of history and background, particularly by comparison with the synoptic references to a Capernaum ministry (cf. Mk. 1,21-2,12 and parallels). In examining its place within the text, in my opinion, it is necessary to look at the text itself, for it is there, rather than in the background, that the

indicating the beginning of a unit through a chronological syntagm or phrase as in 1,29.35.43; 2,1; 3,22, etc. Moreover, one notices a complete change of scene, place and characters. One *goes down* to Capernaum and then *up* to Jerusalem, on the occasion of a Passover, and are in the presence of Jews. The text concerning the Temple episode begins, not with Jesus' ascent (ἀνέβη) to Jerusalem (2,13), but with the preceding verse – his descent (κατέβη) to Capernaum (2,12). It may appear strange that the account of a simple incident, the cleansing of the Temple, should reach back, so to say, to include the descent to Capernaum. But the incident is not simple. It recalls the death and resurrection of Jesus in 2,22.

One of the clues is the balance between "he descended" (to Capernaum) and "he ascended" (to Jerusalem). The two phrases seem to be carefully linked, making the *going down* as an introduction to the *going up*. A further clue consists of the balance between the opening reference to his mother: "He went down to Capernaum *with his mother....*" (2,12) and the closing reference to his disciples ("*his disciples....*believed" – 2,22). At Cana 'mother' and 'disciples' were related. In other words, if the Capernaum verse is read as a part of the Temple episode, there is a double balance – first between its two opening verses (2,12 and 2,13), and then between its two enclosing verses (2,12 and 2,22).

I notice here the following carefully constructed ring composition revolving around the hint at Jesus' death and resurrection and the true Temple affirming the arguments exposed above:

A	2,12-13	Presence of disciples, descent to Capernaum and ascent to Jerusalem
B	2,14-16	Post-resurrectional remembrance of the *prophetic action* at Temple
C	2,17	Narrator's aside or comment – *prolepsis* of Jesus' passion and death
D	2,18	Question of the Jews – about a sign
E	2,19	**Answer of Jesus – sign of the new Temple of his body – his descent and ascent** – *prolepsis* of Jesus' resurrection
D¹	2,20	Question of the Jews – about the Jerusalem Temple
C¹	2,21	Narrator's aside or comment – *prolepsis* of Jesus' passion and death
B¹	2,-22a	Post-resurrectional remembrance of the *divine action*
A¹	2,22b	Belief of the disciples in the scripture and the words of Jesus about his resurrection (ascent) after his death (descent)

Moreover, the narratives of the first miracle at Cana (2,1-11) and the purification of the Temple (2,12-22) are shaped in an identical fashion having a diptych relation: a setting, verbal exchange, action and a final comment of the narrator on the scene. The only major difference between the shape of the two narratives is that at Cana the exchange of words between the mother of Jesus and her son took place *before* the action; but in Jerusalem the action leads to the exchange of words. Note also the Cana episode beginning with the mention of "on the third day" (2,1) and the Temple episode concluding with a repetition of it in a varied form ("after he was raised from the dead" – 2,22). Having analysed the unit 2,23-3,36 in detail in Part I, let me move on to the next.

---

necessary clues appear to be present. And these clues – literary details – indicate that the verse belongs to the Temple episode.

C. 4,1-54

1. 4,1-42

The episode of the Samaritan woman has various *dramatis personae*. 4,1-6 is considered an introduction.[19] In my opinion, 4,1-4 is a transition summary; and 4,5-6 speaks of time (noon) and place (Sychar). The narrator moves Jesus away from Judea, on a journey to Galilee through Samaria. The story forms a *three-fold scene* (4,7-15; 16-26 and 27-42).

The first two scenes form a diptych of revelation parallel to each other in their narrative design (4,7-15//4,16-26). One of the striking features of both episodes is that the dialogue in each of the diptych has three interventions (a *tripartite structure*) each of Jesus (4,7b; 10 and 13-14) and of the Samaritan woman (4,9; 11-12 and 15). The first three concerning thirst, water and life occur in the first part of the conversation (4,7-15).[20] The next set of three verbal exchanges occur in the second scene (4,16-26) which deals with the woman's history and true worship (cf. Jesus speaks thrice: 4,16; 17b-18 and 21-24; and the woman speaks thrice:4,17a; 19-20 and 25).

The last episode (4,27-42), too, has a diptych scene (4,31-38 and 39-42), but with a variation of intermission (4,27-30) containing an interlude ("ἐν τῷ μεταξὺ..." – 4,31).[21] Thus in the last section of the episode one scene enfolds another. In the first scene (4,31-38) there is a dialogue between Jesus and his disciples on food, Father's work and harvest. Another event is taking place simultaneously. The Samaritan woman is describing her experience to all in the city and they are on their way to Jesus at the well. The disciples are told to lift up their eyes to see the advent of the Samaritans – described symbolically as fields ripe for the harvest (4,35). In the final encounter between Jesus and the Samaritans (3,39-42) there is no further setting.

Moreover, all these sub-units are encompassed by verbal inclusions: In the dialogue on living water, note the use of the verb 'to draw' in 4,7 (ἀντλῆσαι) and 4,15 (ἀντλεῖν). Besides, Jesus initiates a dialogue with the Samaritan woman using an imperative in 4,7 (δός μοι)[22] and 4,16 (ὕπαγε φώνησον).[23] In the dialogue on the true Lord, the same function

---

[19] The introduction to this narrative contains a number of literary and historical problems, but once the scene is set, Jesus encounters a Samaritan woman. Some critics have 4,1-4 as the introduction, making 4,5-6 part of the encounter. See e.g. Léon-Dufour, *op. cit.*, 342-43. Olsson (134) demonstrates how an interweaving of 4,1-4 and 4,5-6 form a unified introduction.

[20] These themes disappear completely in 4,16-26, where the issues concern the identity of the person of Jesus (prophet or Messiah?) and true worship. Most commentators see this, but not all regard it as important. Beasley-Murray (*John*, 61) has the first stage of Jesus' encounter with the Samaritan woman run to 4,18; Olsson (193-208) sees no break at 4,15 and shows the unity of 4,7-26; but many scholars consider 4,15 as the climax to the first section of the narrative; e.g. Dodd, *Interpretation*, 311; and Okure, 79 and 92. C. Hudry-Clergeon ("De Judée en Galilée: Étude de Jean 4:1-45," *NRTh* 103 [1981] 819) calls 4,16 a "changement brusque."

[21] Lindars (*op. cit.*, 193) sees here the employment of a Markan "sandwich" construction (the practice of enfolding one incident within another); e.g. the woman with the flow of blood within the account of the raising of the daughter of Jairus (Mk. 5,21-43). G. R. O'Day (*Revelation in the Fourth Gospel: Narrative Mode and Theological Claim* [Philadelphia 1986] 53) points out that 4,27-30 is "a 'narrative hinge' that serves to end the first dialogue and to provide a context out of which a second dialogue can operate." Moloney (*Belief in the Word*, 147) observes a parallelism between 4,7-15 and 4,16-30.

[22] Cf. O'Day, *Revelation*, 52-53. At the end of this sub-unit (4,15), too, the same δός μοι is placed on the lips of the Samaritan woman forming an inclusion.

has turned into a synonymous repetition of the terms "ὸν ἄνδρα σου" and "σου ἀνήρ" in 4,16 and 4,18. One can attribute a role of inclusion to the titles 'prophet' (4,19) and 'Messiah' (4,25) which are found at the extremities of the dialogue on true cult. The final sub-unit (4,27-42) is enclosed by the expressions "μετὰ γυναικὸς ἐλάλει" (4,27) and "τῆ τε γυναικὶ ἔλεγον" (4,42).

In 4,7-26 there is, perhaps, an inclusion in the similarity of the syntagms "τίς ἐστιν ὁ λέγων σοι" (4,10) and "Εγώ εἰμι, ὁ λαλῶν σοι" (4,26), although 4,10 is not at the beginning of the sub-unit. A final inclusion between the introduction (4,1-6) and the conclusion (4,38-42) speaks in favour of the literary unity of 4,1-42: The correlation between the two extremities is strongly established by the recurrence of the verb κοπιάω in perfect form in 4,6 and 4,38; this verb is otherwise absent in the rest of the Gospel. The inclusion is completed by the repetition of the temporal phrase Ὡς οὖν (4,1 and 4,40), the verb ἀκούω (4,1 and 4,42) and the comparative degree of πολύς (4,1 and 4,41). Besides, the verbs γινώσκω (4,1) and οἶδα (4,42) are similar.

The following concentric structure, I believe, is also a proof for the literary unity of this episode:

A	4,7-9	The Samaritan woman comes to Jesus
B	4,10-15	Dialogue on living water
C	4,16-26	Dialogue on true worship
B¹	4,27-38	Dialogue on spiritual food
A¹	4,39-42	The Samaritan townsfolk come to Jesus

2. 4,43-54

This pericope, describing the second visit of Jesus to Galilee, can be divided into two segments – one playing a transitional-redactional role and dealing with the welcome of the Galileans (4,43-45) and the other having a narrative character centred on the healing of the royal official's son (4,46-54). The inclusion in the first sub-unit is found in the mentioning of the departure for Galilee: "He *went* (ἐξῆλθεν) from that place to *Galilee*" (4,43) and in 4,45 he is there: "When he *came* (ἦλθεν) to *Galilee*..."

The same geographical details constitute an inclusion for the segment 4,46-54. Thus the words "...he came again to Cana in *Galilee*" in 4,46 correspond to those in 4,54: "...after coming from Judea to *Galilee*." Besides, the pericope is also enclosed by the verbs of *movement* (a departure and an arrival) in 4,43 and 4,54 respectively: "He *went* (ἐξῆλθεν) from that place to Galilee" (4,43) and ".. after *coming* (ἐλθὼν) from Judea to Galilee" (4,54).

As far as the shape of the narrative and sequence of events are concerned, there is flow and continuity in the narrative 4,46-54 with the immediately preceding encounter between Jesus and the Samaritans (4,39-42), even though both narratives deal with two different settings and events. The Samaritans come to Jesus on the word of the woman (4,39) and present a request to Jesus, to which he responds positively (4,40). His presence leads them to believe in his word (4,41-42). Similarly, the royal official goes to Jesus

---

[23] This command to go and call her *husband* (lord) and the words of Jesus at the end of this sub-unit (4,26: "I am he, the one who is speaking to you"), seen against the screen of the Messianic nuptials, correspond to each other. This can also remotely serve as a clue to enclose this sub-unit.

because he has heard about him from the Galileans (4,47). He, then, requests Jesus to go down and heal his son (4,49); and Jesus responds positively: "Go; your son will live" (4,50). This results in the belief of the official and his household (4,54). Even the rare phrase "πάντα ὅσα ἐποίησα" (4,29.39) – which is found twice at the end of the Samaria story but not found elsewhere in the Gospel – recurs with a minor variation in the introduction to the story of the royal official: "...the Galileans welcomed him, since they had seen all that he had done..." (πάντα... ὅσα ἐποίησεν – 4,45). While the story of the Capernaum official has its own newness and integrity, it is described in such a way that it constitutes a carefully crafted progression of the preceding narrative.

Conclusion

With the aid of literary indicators for a reliable division of the text and specific details suggesting transition from one scene to the next, I have established the perimeters of the units and sub-units, episodes and pericopes of 1,19-4,54 containing 2,23-3,36. The foregoing study has demonstrated the artistic and careful narrative structure of various episodes. This paves the way for my next step, in the following chapter, of exploring the structural and narrative correlation (web and network) involved in holding the section together and unearth the Christological scheme behind the narrative structure employing the methods of literary and narrative criticism.

Chapter 3

LITERARY AND NARRATIVE CORRELATION BETWEEN THE UNITS AND THE UNDERLYING NARRATIVE CHRISTOLOGY

In attempting to understand a particular text, an exegete should seek to see the text within the interweaving context and structure (plan/design) of the section and its units, sub-units and segments. As Marsh notices "the discourse with Nicodemus is very skilfully placed" in the context of the Gospel.[1] To tie together the different units and sub-units of material and to give structural outline to his work, the evangelist could have used various literary techniques[2] explained already in my introduction. Several factors in a text may indicate the use and incorporation of sources. Among these are changes in literary style, shifts in vocabulary, breaks in continuity of thought or presentation, the presence of secondary linking and connecting statements, change in theological and other points of view, duplications of material, clearly defined and isolatable sub-units, and chronological, geographical, factual or other inconsistencies.

Questions of literary function one should ask are: How does the particular passage function with respect to its immediate and larger context? Is it transitional, that is, does it serve as a literary bridge from one unit or sub-unit to another? Is it climactic, that is, does it serve as the culmination of several episodes or scenes immediately preceding it? Is it illustrative, that is, does it function to illustrate an earlier assertion? Is it extrinsic to the larger literary unit, that is, does it not fit at all into the literary context? What holds the narrative together? What has the author done to make this an engaging and readable story?

Asking such questions as these, I shall now seek to relate 2,23-3,36 to its larger literary context by establishing connections within the text. Doing so is an important aspect of exegesis because clues to interpreting a passage often lie also outside the passage in its larger literary setting. Hence, my goal in this chapter is to study how 2,23-3,36 is intertwined with the other units of its section. I shall demonstrate it by taking two units or sub-units at a time and comparing them under the aspects of genre, context, characterisation, narrator and point of view, symbolism, literary devices and themes.

A. Narrative Continuity and Correlation Between 1,19-51 and 2,23-3,36

1. Between 1,19-34 and 3,22-36

a. Genre

As far as the genre of these two episodes are concerned, both contain elements of dialogue, involve baptismal activity, controversy, interrogation, investigation and testimony. The meeting between the Baptist and the enquiry commission from Jerusalem is no ordinary confrontation. As Bultmann and Brown have indicated, it is something more – a trial scene.[3] The Baptist is being forced to give an account of himself, and, as in a trail scene, to

---

[1] Marsh, *Saint John*, 173.

[2] See Ruckstuhl and Dschulnigg, 63-162.

[3] See Bultmann, *Gospel*, 86; and R. E. Brown, *Gospel*, I, 45. On the question of genre see R. Guelich, "The Gospel Genre," in: P. Stuhlmacher (ed.), *Das Evangelium und die Evangelien. Vorträge vom Tübinger*

bear witness. In his second testimony he stands in front of his disciples to clarify the relation between him and Jesus.

b. Narrator and Point of View

The narrator's function in both scenes is largely informational. In the first case, he provides us with details about the Jews in Jerusalem and the enquirers (1,19), the openness of the Baptist's testimony (1,20), who is speaking (1,21-22), the source of Baptist's quotation (1,23), the identity of the questioners (1,24), and the location of the event (1,28). In the second scene, the narrator describes the baptismal activities of Jesus and the Baptist (3,22c.23a), the location of the event (Judean countryside and Aenon near Salim), and the movement of people (3,22-23); he hints at the future destiny of the Baptist (3,24), and at the dispute between a Jew(s) and the disciples on purification (3,25). Since a large part of the pericope, in both cases, is in direct speech, the role of the narrator largely merges into the background.

c. Characterisation

Though a number of characters appear in both sub-units (the Baptist and his disciples, Jews, priests and Levites, Pharisees, Jesus and his disciples), the focal character, apparently, is the Baptist. These are the rare occasions in the fourth Gospel when Jesus is physically absent.[4] However, the reader knows that Jesus is the subject of the questioning that is taking place. He may not be present in person, but he is still the centre of the reader's attention.[5] Another important character in both episodes is the Spirit (cf. 1,32-33 and 3,34).[6] In both episodes the Baptist is portrayed as a faithful and humble witness. He does not feel threatened by the questioning of the Jews, the priests and Levites in the first scene, nor is he perturbed, in the second episode, by the anxiety expressed by his disciples that all were going to Jesus. The Baptist is found calm and composed in both scenes.[7]

d. Narrative Echo Effects

These two narratives give us an opportunity to highlight a literary device frequently used in the fourth Gospel which revels in echo effects. One part of the story resonates with the other through repetition of key words. 3,22-30 echoes 1,19-34 in may ways. In 3,28, the Baptist recalls his testimony made in 1,19: "I am not (οὐκ εἰμι) the Messiah." He describes his role as the one *sent* (3,28); it is an echo of the prologue: "A man *sent* from God, whose

---

Symposium 1982 (WUNT 28) (Tübingen 1983) 181-209; C. H. Talbert, *What is a Gospel? The Genre of the Canonical Gospels* (Philadelphia 1977); D. Aune, "The Problem of Genre of the Gospels: A Critique of C. H. Talbert's 'What Is a Gospel?'" in: R. France and D. Wenham (eds.), *Gospel Perspectives: Studies in History and Tradition in the Four Gospels* (Sheffield 1981) 9-60; and R. H. Gundry, "Recent Investigations into the Literary Genre 'Gospel,'" in: R. Longenecker and M. Tenney (eds.), *New Dimensions in New Testament Study* (Grand Rapids 1974) 97-114.

[4] In 1,29 Jesus appears overtly for the first time on the stage of the story and quickly passes by.

[5] Jesus is at the centre of things in the Baptist's allusions to "the Lord" (1,23), "one whom you do not know" (1,26), and "one who comes after me" (1,27). Jesus is the character who emerges *in medias res*. In terms of narrative focus, he emerges always in the middle, the centre of things. In terms of plot, he emerges in the middle of his life-story (there are no infancy narratives in the fourth Gospel).

[6] On the one hand, the Baptist saw the Spirit descending and resting on Jesus (1,32); on the other hand, he affirms that God *gives* the Spirit without measure to whom He has sent (3,34).

[7] I have analysed his character in detail already in Part I.

name was John" (1,6) and repeated in 1,33: "one who *sent*[8] me to baptise." In 3,28, The Baptist claims that he has been *sent ahead of* the Messiah; this echoes 1,23 where the Baptist describes himself as the one *preparing the way* of the Lord. The Baptist's humble declaration that he *must decrease* while Jesus *must increase* (3,30) echoes 1,30 where the Baptist points to Jesus as the superior one who *"ranks ahead of me because he was before me."* Moreover, the anxiety of the Baptist's disciples (triggered by a dispute with a Jew) that all are going to Jesus (3,26) has an *echo* in the implicit anxiety of the Jews in Jerusalem sending the enquiry commission to the Baptist who was attracting crowds (1,19ff.). The narrator, thus, wants clearly to link the first and the last appearances of the Baptist using *echo effects.*

e. Themes

As already mentioned above, both scenes (1,19-34 and 3,22-36) revolve around the central theme of the *testimony* of the Baptist. Besides, the theme of baptism with *water* in 1,26.31.33 reappears in 3,23 where the narrator speaks of the plentiful supplies of water for the Baptist's ministry. Both the Baptist (1,25.26.28.31.33 and 3,23) and Jesus (3,23.26) are referred to as being engaged in baptising, raising a discussion about purification[9] (3,25; cf. 1,25-26).

f. Symbolism

There is also a relation between the *role of the Baptist* as reflected in the two scenes of testimony. In 1,31 he declares that the reason for his baptismal activity is *to reveal* (φανερωθῇ)[10] to Israel the Lamb of God who takes away the sin of the world (cf. 1,29). In the second scene he presents himself as *'the friend of the bridegroom'* (3,29). As I have pointed out already, one of the important functions of the bridegroom's friend was to make sure that the bride underwent all the purification ceremonies as per law and lead her to the bridegroom. This correspondence, therefore, is very significant as the baptism of the Baptist had a value of purification (cf. 3,25). Having waited for the purification (through baptism) of the bride (Israel, the disciples), he now leads her to the bridegroom (cf. 1,35-37). In 1,31 Jesus (the bridegroom) is revealed to Israel (the bride). As per the relation between the Messianic nuptials and the 'hidden Messiah,' the Messiah must remain unknown until he is introduced. He must be led to his bride. This theme will find echoes in the other units, too, as we shall see in the following pages.

g. Verbal Parallels

Besides, there are verbal similarities (less significant) in the two episodes which also tie them together. The recurrence of the verbs 'see' (βλέπω, εἶδον, ὁράω) and 'testify' (μαρτυρέω – 1,34 and 3,32) in both episodes indicate, too, a close relationship between the

---

[8] Note the theme of *sending* in the narrative; ἀποστέλλω is used in 1,19.24 and πέμπω in 1,22. These refer to the sending of the enquiry commission from Jerusalem.

[9] The Synoptics clearly present the Baptist's baptism as one of repentance and forgiveness of sins (Mt. 3,11; Mk. 1,4; and Lk. 3,3).

[10] The verb φανερόω is found nine times in the fourth Gospel and connotes an emergence from concealment and obscurity. This word is again linked to the central plot motif of the elusiveness of Christ. Jesus is concealed from human understanding until he sovereignly chooses to reveal himself.

two scenes. Besides, the faithfulness of the Baptist is suggested by the use of the word 'stand': he is "the friend of the bridegroom, who *stands* (ἑστηκὼς) and hears him, rejoices greatly at the bridegroom's voice" (3,29). The first scene, too, portrays the Baptist as *standing* (εἱστήκει) in relation to Jesus (cf. 1,35). His role as *witness* is indicated by a number of details in both episodes, especially in the occurrence of the words (testimony, testify and witness) μαρτυρία (1,19) and μεμαρτύρηκα (1,34) μεμαρτύρηκας (3,26) μαρτυρεῖτε (3,28) μαρτυρεῖ, μαρτυρίαν (3,32.33). While 1,32 is a flash-back (analepsis) on the baptism of Jesus,[11] 3,24 is a flash-forward (prolepsis) on the martyrdom of the Baptist.

2. Between 1,19-34 and 2,23-3,21

The first testimony of the Baptist (1,19-34) is not solely linked to 3,22-36. There are a number of thematic and verbal correspondences between it and the Nicodemus episode.

a. Characterisation

First of all, we have the delegation of *Jews*, priests and Levites from *Jerusalem* (1,19) sent from among the *Pharisees*[12] (cf. 1,24). Turning to the scene of Nicodemus, we meet in 3,1 a *Pharisee* (of Jerusalem), a leader of the *Jews*, who comes to Jesus to find out his true identity. The plural 'we know' (3,2) placed on the lips of Nicodemus suggests that he is representing a group, and gives him an official character which stresses the correspondence with 1,19.24. Besides, the motive of Nicodemus in coming to Jesus is almost similar to that of the delegation sent from Jerusalem to the Baptist (1,19-25), *viz.*, *to ascertain* Jesus' identity and *to enquire* about his work – performance of signs (cf. 3,2). Secondly, the Baptist identifies Jesus as "the Lamb of God who *takes away the sin of the world*" (1,29) and as the 'Son of God'[13] (1,34). In the dialogue between Jesus and Nicodemus, the identity and mission of Jesus is reinterpreted in *Christological and soteriological terms* – 'Son of Man descended from heaven' and 'Son sent by God into the world to *save it*' (cf. 3,13-17).

b. Themes

The theme of *elusive Christ*[14] is evident in both episodes. In 1,26, though Jesus is not visibly present in the scene, his mysterious and elusive presence is felt in the Baptist's

---

[11] The baptism of Jesus is not described directly in the fourth Gospel, but is referred to as a past event. Because the elusiveness of Jesus in the fourth evangelist's story requires that there should be no open heaven except at 12,28. Even there the voice from heaven proves elusive to the majority.

[12] Pharisees are mentioned 19 times in the fourth Gospel and are synonymous with the Jewish authorities.

[13] There is a remarkable alternative reading for 'Son of God' (ὁ υἱὸς τοῦ θεοῦ) as 'the Chosen one of God' (ὁ ἐκλεκτός τοῦ θεοῦ – cf. P⁵ and ℵ*). It would be easy for a scribe to alter this to ὁ υἱὸς τοῦ θεοῦ, which is a common description of Jesus in the Gospel, whereas ὁ ἐκλεκτός τοῦ θεοῦ would be unique. This reading is favoured by Sanders and R. E. Brown. Lightfoot thinks it is probable. Lindars is uncertain and Haenchen actually rejects it. Barrett seems to favour it. According to J. Jeremias (*Theology of the New Testament* [London 1971] 53-55), in the second century, the idea that Jesus was a man chosen to be the Messiah was regarded as an Ebionite heresy. This would explain why it was replaced in many manuscripts by ὁ υἱὸς τοῦ θεοῦ. There is a long debate among the exegetes regarding the choice between 'the chosen one of God' and 'the Son of God.' See esp. Braun, *Les grandes traditions d'Israël*, II, 71-73. Because of the strong recurrence of the title 'Son of God,' I prefer it. However, whether the title 'chosen one of God' or 'Son of God' that is placed on the lips of the Baptist here, all the Messianic titles of the first chapter are inadequate and will be corrected in Jn. 3 exposing the true identity of Jesus as 'Son of Man' and 'Son of God.'

[14] Cf. Stibbe, "Elusive Christ," 20-39.

rather obscure remark that "among you stands one whom you do not know." On the contrary, in the Nicodemus pericope, Jesus is physically present, but proves to be elusive – a concealing revealer; he is portrayed as the revealer of heaven's secrets (cf. 3,12), speaks in puns, *double meaning* and metaphors, and discloses truths about the elusiveness of the Spirit by comparing him with the wind that blows where it will (3,8).[15]

One cannot ignore the parallel relationship between 1,33 and 3,5-8 on the theme of *baptism in the Spirit* . In the first scene, Jesus is portrayed as the one who baptises with the Holy Spirit (cf. 1,33), and in the second, it is the question of being begotten by the Spirit (3,5.6.8). Note also the recurrence of the terms Spirit (πνεῦμα) in 1,32.33 and the spirit (πνεύματος) in 3,5; πνεύματος and πνεῦμα in 3,6; πνεῦμα and πνεύματος in 3,8; and πνεῦμα in 3,34.

c. Literary Device

One cannot miss the *antithetical parallelism* and *irony* between, "among you stands one whom *you do not know*" (1,26), and "but Jesus on his part would not entrust himself to them, because *he knew all people*" (2,24). In the same tone, Jesus lays bare the incompetence of Nicodemus who pretends to know who Jesus is (cf. 3,2c): "Are you a teacher of Israel, and yet you *do not understand* these things?" (3,10). Nicodemus confesses that Jesus is from God (cf. 3,2), yet he does not know the full import of what he is confessing.

d. Verbal Parallels

The detection of some verbal recurrences, purely formal, may also help complete the list: the nouns 'μαρτυρία' in 1,19 and 3,11,[16] 'φωνή' in 1,23 and 3,8, and the verb 'φανερωθῇ' in 1,31 and 3,21.

3. Between 1,35-51 and 2,23-3,36

a. Characterisation

The protagonist of the fourth Gospel introduced in 1,26 as one standing mysteriously and elusively among the Pharisees, and is merely seen coming towards the Baptist (cf. 1,29) turns now and utters his first words to two disciples (cf. 1,38). At last the elusive Christ speaks to those who seek him. In the same way Jesus speaks to Nicodemus who seeks clarity about his identity. The Baptist, after confessing Jesus as 'the Lamb of God' in 1,36, disappears from the scene and the narrator's focus shifts to Jesus. The minor characters, then, serve as foils for Jesus' words and works. Similarly Nicodemus apparently disappears after 3,10 and there seems to be a monologue where Jesus reveals his identity and mission in the following verses.

---

[15] What is interesting about Jesus' portrayal of the Spirit in 3,8 is his elusiveness. No one knows whence it comes or whither it goes. This indicates the identity between Jesus and the Spirit. Both are elusive.

[16] Cf. Note also the verbal forms of 'testify' – μεμαρτύρηκα (1,34), μαρτυρήσῃ (2,25) and μαρτυροῦμεν (3,11).

b. Themes

The reference to Jesus' supernatural *knowledge* (γινώσκειν) about Nathanel's guilelessness (cf. 1,48) is picked up both by Nicodemus' οἴδαμεν (3,2) and by Jesus' οἴδαμεν in 3,11. Jesus points to Nicodemus' lack of knowledge (οὐκ οἶδας) about the movements of God's Spirit (3,8). Nicodemus' ignorance and Jesus' divine knowledge grow more obvious as the story unfolds.

There is also a strong link between the confession of Nathanael (1,49) and the promise of Jesus to him (1,50-51), and the Christological part of 3,13-18. Nathanael's acknowledgement of Jesus as the 'Son of God' and 'King of Israel' does not transcend the nationalistic and traditional concept of the Messiah. Similarly, the recognition of Jesus by Nicodemus as a teacher come from God and having God with him (3,2) is restricted to the concept of the prophetic Messiah and so falls short of the Christology of the fourth evangelist. Jesus promises to Nathanael that 'he would see greater things and see heaven opened and the angels of God ascending and descending upon the Son of Man' (1,50-51). Jesus, in the same way, leads Nicodemus to understand that he is the 'Son of Man'[17] who must ascend into heaven, since he has descended from there (3,13-15). Moreover, it is evident that the title, 'Son of God,' confessed by Nathanael is reinterpreted by Jesus in 3,16-18: He is not the awaited Messiah of the popular tradition, but the only begotten Son of God sent for the salvation of the world.[18] Moreover, all the titles accumulated in Jn. 1,19-51 have their structure in the titles 'Son of Man' and 'Son of God' found in Jn. 3.[19] There is no more adequate faith for the fourth evangelist than confessing Jesus as the 'Son of Man' and the 'Son of God.' Note also the recurrences of the word 'πιστεύω' (1,50 and 3,12.15.16.18.36).

This study of the recurrences and formal similarities between 1,19-51 and 2,23-3,36 in the foregoing pages demonstrates the presence of a strong parallel structure between the two units. Now, the reason for the insertion of Jn. 2 between these two chapters is to be sought in the Christological scheme underlying the evangelist's narrative structure.

4. Narrative Christology

1,19-51 together with 2,23-3,36 is an excellent example of narrative Christology – Christological belief expressed through the medium of story. In these two chapters there is a synthesis of the Christology and soteriology of the whole Gospel.[20] It appears as though the fourth evangelist wants to set up mile stones already at the beginning of his Gospel to guide his readers to understand his portrayal of Jesus.

---

[17] It is very important to note that the title 'Son of Man' appears only in 1,51 and 3,13-14 in the whole section 1,19-4,54. Hence, this observation is another added reason for the correspondence between 1,19-51 and 2,23-3,36. In 1,51 Jesus had spoken of the *descent and ascent* of the angels *upon the Son of Man*. But in 3,13-14 it is *the Son of Man himself* who descends from and ascends into heaven. He is the one who mediates the binary opposition of above and below, earth and heaven.

[18] Note well again that the title 'Son of God' is found in the first section only in 1,34.49 and 3,18. The term 'Son' appears in 3,16.17.35.36.

[19] J. Guillet, "À propos des titres de Jésus: Christ, Fils de l'homme, Fils de Dieu," in: *À la rencontre de Dieu*, 309-17.

[20] Neyrey ("John III – A Debate," 118-23) has shown that 3,1-10 treats Johannine epistemology, 3,11-17 Christology, and 3,18-21 judgement. For a detailed discussion on the soteriological aspect see Rodriguez Ruiz.

The Christology of the prologue is, now, being acted out in the story of Jesus. The narrator faces the challenge of disclosing the divine reality concealed in Jesus' humanity.[21] He wants to show that the man Jesus is also the 'Messiah and the Son of God'[22] (cf. 20,31). He selects a group of persons and depicts their behaviour and physical surroundings. Through positive examples he directs the reader toward his goal, *viz.*, 1) one must believe 2) that Jesus is the Messiah, the Son of God 3) to have life (cf. 20,30-31). This is closely linked to the Christological scheme of Jn. 1 and 3 which betray the same plan, *viz.*, 1) the coming of the first disciples in *faith* to Jesus (cf. 1,35-51),[23] 2) revelation of the true *identity* of Jesus (cf. 1,19-34.51; 3,13-15 and 31-35), and 3) its inseparable *soteriological component* (cf. 3,16-21.36).

The narrative portion of the Gospel begins with a Jewish delegation from Jerusalem enquiring about the identity of the Baptist and his authority to baptise. It is set within the context of Jewish discussions about the coming of the Messiah.[24] It is the Baptist himself who introduces the Messianic question (1,20). A widespread representation of Judaism (priests, Levites, Jews and Pharisees) suspects that the Baptist must be part of its vision of Messianic times.[25] Jesus is disclosed as the fulfilment of Jewish Messianic expectations. These expectations are listed twice and include questions about the Messiah, Elijah, and the prophet[26] (1,20-21.25). Moreover, the interrogation takes place at Bethany, east of Jordan (1,28), a location appropriate for either of these figures to appear.[27] The Baptist refuses to claim the role of the Messiah, Elijah or the prophet like Moses, and points

---

[21] He presents all the aspects of Jesus' identity – the human, the Messianic, and the divine – without negating anyone of them. Comprehension of who Jesus is does not simply entail recognition of his divinity; it involves reflection on the interplay between several genuine facets of his identity. Jesus is a man, but not only a man; he is prophet and Messiah, but not only prophet and Messiah; he is divine, but not only divine. Even at the end of the Gospel, the evangelist states that the man Jesus is also the Christ and the divine Son of God (20,31). Each facet has its own integrity; the disclosure of his divinity is given through his humanity and is interpreted in the light of the traditions of Israel. See de Jonge, *Stranger from Heaven*, 49-116; Ashton, *Understanding*, 238-79. Bultmann (*Gospel*, 63) rightly comments that God's glory is not to be seen along side Jesus' flesh nor through his flesh as through a window; it is to be seen in the flesh and nowhere else. "The revelation is present in a peculiar hiddenness."

[22] See J. H. Charlesworth, "From Messianology to Christology: Problems and Prospects," in: his (ed.), *The Messiah. Developments in Earliest Judaism and Christianity* (Minneapolis 1992) 4-6 and 33-35; and L. Morris, *Jesus is the Christ. Studies in the Theology of John* (Grand Rapids 1989).

[23] See K. Scholtissek, "'Rabbi, wo wohnst du?' (Joh 1,38). Die mystagogische Christologie des Johannesevangeliums (am Beispiel der Jüngerberufungen 1,35-51). Mit Johannes das Evangelien entdecken (3+4)," *BiLi* 68 (1995) 223-31.

[24] See J. J. M. Roberts, "The Old Testament's Contribution to Messianic Expectations," in: Charlesworth, *Messiah*, 39-51; and J. Howton, "The Son of God in the Fourth Gospel," *NTS* 10 (1963/64) 227-37.

[25] Cf. R. A. Horsley, "'Messianic' Figures and Movements in First-Century Palestine," in: Charlesworth, *Messiah*, 281.

[26] The Scriptures said that Elijah was to return before the great and terrible day of the Lord (Mal. 4,5-6) and that God would raise up for Israel another prophet like Moses (Deut. 18,15-18). See F. Manns, *L'Évangile de Jean à la lumière du Judaïsme* (SBFA 333) (Jerusalem 1991).

[27] Bethany lies apparently on the plains opposite Jericho. It was from there that Elijah was swept up into heaven by a whirlwind and his successor Elisha received a share of the prophet's spirit and parted the waters of the Jordan on his return (2 Kings 2,9-15); cf. 'the spirit and power of Elijah' in Lk. 1,17. Moses, too, was endowed with a special spirit from God in order to lead Israel until he died and was buried on Mount Nebo overlooking the area around Bethany. His role was assumed by his spirit-filled successor, Joshua, who parted the waters of the Jordan when he crossed (Deut. 34,1.9; and Josh. 3,7-13). On the association of Elijah and Moses with Bethany, see C. Kopp, *The Holy Places of the Gospels* (New York 1963) 113-29.

instead to Jesus, who appears at Bethany and fulfils all these roles.[28] The Baptist flatly denies that he is 'the Messiah,' – a title, readers know, is reserved to Jesus alone (1,17).

The Baptist, furthermore, warns that there is one among them 'whom they do not know' (1,26). The author is directing the warning also to the reader, who could associate the Baptist with the Messianic expectations of the Jews.[29] As long as the search for the Messiah continues within the traditional Jewish categories and expectations, he will be among them, but they will not be able to know him (cf. 1,26). The inability to know the one who stands among them is the result of their inability to transcend their own Messianic schemes.[30] The narrator is thus shaping the Messianic understanding of the reader. Jesus himself is not yet brought into the scene, but the reader's attention is systematically directed away from the Baptist[31] to "the one among you whom you do not know" (1,26).

The Baptist's ministry provides a context in which Jesus' divinity is to be made known. He bears witness that Jesus was before him (1,30). The reader knows already from the prologue that Jesus is the Son of God (cf. 1,14.18). The story is being told in the light of the prologue. But the characters in the story – who have not read the prologue – are not aware of the true identity of Jesus. The reader alone knows the Baptist's witness to Christological truths which are essential for a correct understanding of Jesus.

In 1,29 Jesus makes his first remote appearance in the narrative but says or does nothing. For the fourth evangelist the Baptist is a *witness*. The reader in the narrative is informed that the Baptist's mission is to reveal Jesus to Israel (1,31). Here, the author jumps out of 'story time' and enters into 'plotted time' and through *analepsis* makes the

---

[28] Although Jesus is not called Elijah or the prophet, he performed works reminiscent of the miracles of these prophets during his ministry, and the evangelist gives readers no reason to think that an Elijah or Moses come to life again would appear alongside Jesus. See R. A. Horsley and J. S. Hanson, *Bandits, Prophets, and Messiahs: Popular Movements in the Time of Jesus* (Philadelphia ²1999) 164-67. Like those earlier figures, Jesus bore the Spirit of God; but unlike them, he bore it permanently. It was an abiding presence. The Spirit remained (μένειν) on Jesus, a word that regularly indicates a continuing relationship (cf. 8,31 and 15,4-10). See Scholtissek, *In ihm sein und bleiben*.

[29] Some argue that the fourth evangelist knew a group of persons who believed that the Baptist was the Messiah. Hence, the argument here is a polemic against those persons. This is possible, for it does seem that the Baptist attracted a group of followers (cf. 1,35 and 3,25-26). They could very well have claimed that their leader was the Messiah, especially after his death. According to Acts 18,25 and 19,1-7, there were followers of the Baptist at Ephesus during Paul's ministry there. See Lichtenberger, 36-57. For surveys of texts on the Baptist and his ministry see Webb; and J. Ernst, *Johannes der Täufer: Interpretation – Geschichte – Wirkungsgeschichte* (BZNW 53) (Berlin, New York 1989).

[30] See K. Scholtissek, "'Mitten unter euch steht der, den ihr nicht kennt' (Joh 1,26). Die Messias-Regel des Täufers als johanneische Sinnlinie – aufgezeigt am Beispiel der relecture der Jüngerberufungen in der Begegnung zwischen Maria von Magdala und Jesus," *MThZ* 48 (1997) 103-21.

[31] Before I go to treat the series of Christological titles in Jn. 1, I must note another issue present in this passage. Along with these titles there is a persistent theme of the relationship between Jesus and the Baptist. In the course of the narrative describing the witness of the Baptist to Christ, three points are made with regard to the relationship: First of all, Jesus is greater than the Baptist. We are told this not once but twice. The Baptist is not worthy enough to untie the thong of his sandal (1,27), for Jesus ranks far ahead of the Baptist (1,30). Secondly, Baptist claims, "he was before me" (1,30). Given the theme of the pre-existence of Jesus in the Gospel (cf. 8,58, as well as the prologue), it is clear that the evangelist here has the Baptist witnessing to the pre-existence of Jesus. Thirdly, the baptism of the Baptist is with water. Jesus baptises with the Holy Spirit (1,33). To this one should add the assertion of the prologue that the Baptist was not the light but only a witness to the light (1,8). The evangelist seems to correct certain exaggerated claims made about the Baptist while incorporating him firmly into the narrative as a *witness* to Jesus. He portrays Jesus as belonging to an entirely different category. To make it carry the greatest possible weight, the evangelist puts it on the lips of the Baptist himself.

Baptist recall the event of Jesus' baptism that lead him to understand Jesus as "the Lamb of God who takes away the sin of the world" (1,29), "the one who baptises with the Holy Spirit" (1,33),[32] and "the Son of God"[33] (1,34). The reader is challenged to go beyond what he knows and understands. The Baptist bears witness to Jesus in a way that seems to transcend Jewish Messianic expectations. Not even the Baptist would have recognised Jesus apart from revelation. The water he used for baptism did provide the context for such a divine revelation. The agent of revelation was the Spirit (1,33). Through the repeated reference to Jesus as the Lamb of God (1,29.36) by the Baptist, the narrator is, perhaps, indicating that comprehending the significance of Jesus' sacrificial death is basic to understanding his identity.

Now, how to understand these three titles placed on the lips of the Baptist in Jn. 1? Have they also been used in the traditional Messianic connotation? The concentric structure of the pericope (1,29-34), as proposed by M. Roberge,[34] may throw some light (see the diagram below).

It demonstrates clearly that the titles 'Lamb of God' in **A** and 'Son of God' in **A**[1] correspond to each other and must be interpreted together. This correspondence is supported by the recurrence of the formula of designation οὗτός ἐστιν and the synonymy of the verbs βλέπει and ἑώρακα. The correlation between B and B[1] is seen in the repetition of the phrases: "I myself did not know him" (κἀγὼ οὐκ ᾔδειν αὐτόν) and "baptising with water" (βαπτίζειν ἐν ὕδατι). The hinge of the argument is that the vision (τεθέαμαι) of the Spirit descending on Jesus gives to the sight (βλέπει) of the Baptist a depth (ἑώρακα) to understand the mystery of the person of Jesus. He could, therefore, testify that he is really the "Lamb of God who takes away the sin of the world," that is, the 'Son of God who baptises with the Holy Spirit.'[35]

A (1,29-30) Designation and function of the Messiah

> Τῇ ἐπαύριον *βλέπει* τὸν Ἰησοῦν ἐρχόμενον πρὸς αὐτόν καὶ λέγει, Ἴδε ὁ *ἀμνὸς τοῦ θεοῦ ὁ αἴρων τὴν ἁμαρτίαν τοῦ κόσμου.* οὗτός ἐστιν ὑπὲρ οὗ ἐγὼ εἶπον, Ὀπίσω μου ἔρχεται ἀνὴρ ὃς ἔμπροσθέν μου γέγονεν, ὅτι πρῶτός μου ἦν.

---

[32] The descent of the Spirit marked Jesus as God's anointed. Israel's first king, Saul, bore the Spirit for a time before it was given to David, his successor (1 Sam. 10,10 and 16,13-14), and the Messianic heir to David's throne was also expected to bear the Spirit. One of the most important Messianic passages in Isaiah – the book mentioned in Jn. 1,23 – said that the shoot would come forth from the stump of Jesse and that "the Spirit of the Lord shall rest upon him" (Is. 11,2). A similar idea appears later in Isaiah, where God promises to put His Spirit upon His anointed one (61,1), and it is also found in other Jewish sources of the period. Cf. R. E. Brown, *op. cit.*, 66; Porsch, *Pneuma und Wort*, 23-26; Burge, 55-59; and Bittner, *Jesu Zeichen*, 139-43.

[33] It is not clear if the full Johannine idea of Jesus as the Son of God is implied here, or whether the Baptist is confessing that Jesus fulfils Israel's expectations of a Messianic 'son of God.' Moloney (*Belief in the Word*, 66) is of the opinion that the Baptist points to Jesus as the Son of God in the full Johannine sense. Jewish speculation of a Messianic 'son of God' has its roots in 2 Sam. 7,14 and Ps. 2,7. For a comprehensive treatment see B. J. Byrne, *'Sons of God – Seed of Abraham:' A Study of the Idea of the Sonship of God of All Christians in Paul against the Jewish Background* (Rome 1979) 9-78; esp. 16-18 and 59-62.

[34] M. Roberge, "Structures littéraires et christologie dan le IVᵉ évangile. Jean 1,29-34," in: R. Laflamme and M. Gervais (eds.), *Le Christ, hier, aujourd'hui et demain* (Québec 1976) 467-77. Ashton (*Understanding*, 258) finds a chiastic balance between the titles *Lamb of God* and *Son of God* on the lips of the Baptist. He contends that the phrase "who takes away the sin of the world" (1,29) is a later addition.

[35] See also the structural propositions of Menken, *Numerical Literary Techniques*, 51-57; and Talbert, "Artistry and Theology," 364.

B (1,31)   Role of the Baptist
κἀγὼ οὐκ ᾔδειν αὐτόν, ἀλλ' ἵνα φανερωθῇ τῷ Ἰσραὴλ διὰ τοῦτο ἦλθον ἐγὼ ἐν ὕδατι βαπτίζων.

C (1,32)   Testimony of the Baptist
Καὶ ἐμαρτύρησεν Ἰωάννης λέγων ὅτι Τεθέαμαι τὸ πνεῦμα καταβαῖνον ὡς περιστερὰν ἐξ οὐρανοῦ καὶ ἔμεινεν ἐπ' αὐτόν.

B¹ (1,33abc) Role of the Baptist
κἀγὼ οὐκ ᾔδειν αὐτόν, ἀλλ' ὁ πέμψας με βαπτίζειν ἐν ὕδατι ἐκεῖνός μοι εἶπεν, Ἐφ' ὃν ἂν ἴδῃς τὸ πνεῦμα καταβαῖνον καὶ μένον ἐπ' αὐτόν,

A¹ (1,33d-34) Designation and function of the Messiah
οὗτός ἐστιν ὁ βαπτίζων ἐν πνεύματι ἁγίῳ.
κἀγὼ ἑώρακα, καὶ μεμαρτύρηκα ὅτι οὗτός ἐστιν ὁ υἱός τοῦ θεοῦ.

The first element confirming the Messianic connotation of these two titles comes from 1,31-33c which exposes the role of the baptism administered by the Baptist as well as his testimony on the descent of the Spirit. His mission proceeds from God who sent him to baptise with water in order to reveal the Messiah to Israel. The necessity for a revelation of the Messiah is rooted in the Jewish doctrine on the awaiting for the Messiah, according to which the Messiah will remain hidden until the day of his revelation (cf. Jn. 7,27).[36] The Baptist did not understand Jesus as the Messiah until he saw the sign from heaven (cf. 1,33). A second element of confirmation is to be found in the designation of Jesus as "the one who baptises with the Holy Spirit"[37] (1,33) which means that Jesus is the agent of God's own power.[38] In my opinion, in this opening section of the narrative, the symbol of water is associated with the Spirit and the revelation of several interrelated facets of Jesus' identity.

Now, what is the correlation between the titles 'Lamb of God who takes away the sin of the world' and 'Son of God?' The structural correspondence between these two titles brings a new element, perhaps decisive, in the interpretation of the expression 'Lamb of God who takes away the sin of the world.' Dodd, Boismard and Bittner suggest that the use of the term ἀμνὸς refers to the Servant of Yahweh.[39] It seems most probable that it has a direct reference to Isaiah 53,4-7. In 53,7 the LXX reads: πρόβατον ἐπὶ σφαγὴν ἤχθη καὶ

---

[36] Cf. Dodd, *Historical Tradition*, 290-92; R. E. Brown, *op. cit.*, 53; Lindars, *Gospel*, 293; J. C. O'Neil, "The Silence of Jesus," *NTS* 15 (1969) 153-67; and M. M. Thompson, *The Humanity of Jesus in the Fourth Gospel* (Philadelphia 1988) 19.

[37] Outpouring of the Spirit has been foretold by the prophets as one of the signs of the Messianic times (cf. Is. 32,15-18 and 44,3-5; Ezek. 36,25-29; and Joel 3,1-2). There is hardly any doubt that Jesus is the Messiah. According to Létourneau (*Jésus*, 75), the evangelist superimposes two OT traditions at this point. In the Isaiah tradition (Is. 11; 42 and 61) it is the Messiah himself who receives the Spirit from God to be able to teach the Law, justice and the knowledge of God. On the contrary, according to the tradition represented by Ezek. 36-37; Joel 3,1ff.; and Zech. 12,9-13,1 it is on the people of Israel that God will send His Spirit. Both the traditions are united in the fourth Gospel in presenting Jesus as the Messiah who is not only filled with the Spirit but also dispenses it.

[38] The Spirit was God's own gift, which was given to Jesus and through Jesus, the one who had come from above and made it possible for people to be born from above (3,3-5.31.35). When Jesus finally gave the Spirit to his disciples after his resurrection, he breathed it into them, just as God breathed the breath or 'spirit' of life into Adam at the dawn of creation (20,22). See Schnackenburg, *Gospel*, I, 305. A number of biblical texts used images of water to speak of the day when God would send His Spirit to enliven the people of Israel (cf. Joel 2,28-29; and Ezek. 36,25-27).

[39] Dodd, *Interpretation*, 235-36; Boismard and Lamouille, 91-92; and Bittner, *Jesu Zeichen*, 245-46.

ὡς ἀμνὸς ἐναντίον τοῦ κείροντος αὐτὸν ἄφωνος ("like a lamb that is led to the slaughter, and like a sheep that before its shearers is silent..."). In 53,4 we meet the phrase: οὗτος τὰς ἁμαρτίας ἡμῶν φέρει ("he has borne our infirmities"). If we put these quotations together we get in fact the lamb who takes away sins.

Now, the difficulty lies in the explanation of the words 'who takes away the sin of the world.' The fourth evangelist does not attribute in the rest of his Gospel an expiatory sacrificial value to the death of Jesus. One therefore wonders in what sense the evangelist could affirm that Jesus 'takes away the sin of the world.' Boismard and Lamouille observe that it is not said that Jesus 'carries' (φέρειν – cf. Is. 53,4) the sins of the world, but he 'takes away' or 'removes' (αἴρειν cf. 1 Jn. 3,5) meaning an abolition and not an expiation of sins.[40] To put an end to sin was a function of the Jewish Messiah without any link to the idea of a redemptive death.[41] The concentric structure of Roberge for Jn. 1,29-34 cited above gives us a hint to understand that the function of the Messiah as one 'who takes away the sin of the world' is to be reinterpreted in terms of 'one who baptises with the Holy Spirit.' Jesus is, therefore, a dispenser of the Spirit rather than the Messiah who takes away the sin of the world (Ezek. 36,25.27.29.33). Hence, there is no objection in understanding the title 'Lamb of God' as a Messianic designation for Jesus.

Moreover, according to Is. 11,1-2 and 61,1 the Messiah is the anointed one and would descend from the Davidic dynasty.[42] In this perspective, the designation of Jesus as the Lamb of God possessing the Spirit can well refer to the Servant of the book of Isaiah conceived as a Messianic figure. But this reference to the Servant does not exhaust the meaning of the title 'Lamb of God' in Jn. 1,29. In the apocalyptic tradition, lamb is often used as a symbol for the Messiah, who is considered to be the chief of God's flock, that is as King of Israel (cf. Rev. 6,16; 7,17; 14,1-5 and 17,14). Moreover, the whole context shows that the evangelist understands 'Lamb of God' as a synonym for Messiah (comp. 1,41 with 1,36). Dodd suggests that there is a virtual equivalence between the titles 'Lamb of God' and 'King of Israel.'[43]

Finally, we might observe that Is. 42,9 reads: "See, the former things have come to pass, and new things I now declare." This appropriately fits the Baptist's utterances: he has told us that Jesus existed long before he was born (cf. 1,30); and he now announces the future redemptive activity of the one who was before him. The reason for the evangelist in placing on the lips of the Baptist the divine utterance, according to Hanson, is to enhance the role of the Baptist as witness rather than baptiser.[44] The Baptist's allusion to Jesus' pre-existence shows that the title 'Son of God' conveys a sense of divinity as well as Messiahship.

---

[40] Boismard and Lamouille, 91.

[41] Is. 60,21; Jer. 50,20; Ezek. 11,19-20 and 36,25-27; Zech. 13,1; and Mal. 3,3-4. Cf. Braun, *Les grandes traditions d'Israël*, II, 79.

[42] See S. Talmon, "The Concept of Māšîaḥ and Messianism in Early Judaism," in: Charlesworth, *Messiah*, 91 and also 87-90.

[43] Cf. Dodd, *Interpretation*, 238.

[44] The Synoptic accounts do not say who heard the voice. In the Christological scheme of the fourth Gospel Jesus did not need to hear a voice in order to reassure him. He already knows who he is and what he must do. This puts the Baptist also into the category of prophets, which is exactly where the fourth evangelist wants him to be. He is using the Baptist for his own Christological scheme. See A. T. Hanson, 35-36.

However, the Christology of Jn. 1 has not come to an end with the Baptist's proclamation. As the story moves on, basic affirmations about Jesus are made by those who first follow him. But their response falls short even of the earlier Messianic speculations raised of the Baptist by the delegation of Jews from Jerusalem (1,19-28). The narrator makes clear to the reader that the ex-disciples of the Baptist, in addressing Jesus as 'Rabbi,'[45] have failed to grasp their ex-master's indication that Jesus is the Lamb of God (1,36). Calling Jesus as *Rabbi* was appropriate, but it did not exhaust his identity. Finding his brother Simon, Andrew makes the confession of faith: "We have found the Messiah" (1,41).[46] There is a development from Rabbi to Messiah. 'The Jews' and the disciples have worked within categories they could understand. They accept Jesus against their own historical, cultural and religious background.[47] But Jesus' response to them has been full of promise: "What are you looking for?" (1,38); "Come and see" (1,39); "You are to be called *Cephas*" (1,42). It may appear that the disciples are on their way to finding Jesus.[48]

Philip, called by Jesus to follow him, meets Nathanael and claims that he has found him "of whom Moses in the Law and also the prophets wrote" (1,45). This echoes Andrew's Messianic confession and so falls short of the full truth about Jesus. The reader knows from the prologue that Jesus is not simply the fulfilment of the OT promises.[49] He is more. Even the confession of Nathanael – in the juxtaposition of the two titles "Rabbi, you are the Son of God! You are the King of Israel!" (1,49) – is still bound by his own culture, history and religion, *viz.,* the fulfilment of Jewish Messianic hopes. The title 'King of Israel' connects Jesus with expectations concerning the appearance of a royal Messiah who would lead the people of Israel. On the lips of Nathanael, the title 'Son of God' is, in an important sense, Messianic. The Scriptures said that the heir to David's throne would be a 'son' of God, and Nathanael's confession associates Jesus with these promises.[50] Passages

---

[45] *'Rabbis'* do not wander. They have a home where they sit and teach, gathering students. This is the meaning of "where are you staying?" (1,36). Jesus is often identified as a 'Rabbi' or 'teacher' in the fourth Gospel, and Jesus accepts these titles. The Gospel refers to teaching as a primary form of activity during the central part of Jesus' public ministry. He taught in the synagogue at Capernaum and the Temple at Jerusalem (6,59; 7,14.28 and 8,20; cf. 13,13 and 18,19-20).

[46] See Rinke, *Kerygma und Autopsie*, 85-86.

[47] The narrative of the fourth Gospel is marked by a rhetoric of persuasion. It does not allow the Johannine Community to settle for a Christology that is congenial, a Christology based on the first century Jewish Messianic hopes.

[48] The people Jesus encounters play a vital supporting role in the narrative. Culpepper (*Anatomy*, 104) calls them "the prism which breaks up the pure light of Jesus' remote epiphany into colours the readers can see." See also R. F. Collins, "Representative Figures," 26-46 and 118-32.

[49] The infant Church looked constantly to the OT for its witness to Jesus, but that is not enough for the fourth evangelist. See Menken, *Old Testament Quotations*.

[50] See Ashton, *Understanding*, 260-62. The text also provides more subtle clues to his Messiahship. The comment of Jesus that he saw Nathanael under a fig tree is an allusion to Zech. 3,10: "On that day, says the Lord of hosts, you shall invite each other to come under your vine and fig tree." Although several OT texts envision a future era of peace when people will sit securely under their vines and fig trees (cf. 1 Kings 4,25; Mic. 4,4; and 1 Macc. 14,12), only the Zechariah passage speaks of one man calling another under a vine and fig tree. According to Zech. 3,8 the act of one man calling another under a vine and fig tree was to mark the arrival of the 'branch,' who was widely understood to be the Davidic Messiah. Jewish writings of this period show that people understood that this Messianic Branch was foretold by Moses in the Law (Gen. 49,10) and in the Prophets (Jer. 23,6 and 33,16; and Zech. 3,8 and 6,12-13), just as Philip had said in Jn. 1,45. These same texts identified the Messianic Branch as the heir of David, who would be considered Son of God and King of Israel – the Messianic titles used by Nathanael in 1,49. For complete discussion on this subject see Koester, "Messianic Exegesis," 23-34.

like 2 Sam. 7,14 and Ps. 2,2.6-7 speak of the anointed heir to Davidic throne as God's 'son,' and Jewish sources use the language of sonship for the Messiah.[51] The title 'Son of God/Chosen One' is exceptionally useful for the evangelist because it could present Jesus as the fulfilment[52] of Jewish Messianic expectations while allowing for an expanded understanding of Messiahship that would include Jesus' heavenly origin.

The disciples, then, are promised a greater sight as the narrator again reaches outside story time and enters plotted time: "You will see greater things than these" (1,50).[53] The future tense of the plotted time forces the reader to conclude that the events of the story time need to be transcended. The promise of Jesus indicates that the 'now' of Nathanael's faith (1,50) is to be transcended by a 'not yet' in the experience of all the disciples (1,51).[54] There is an important balance in the carefully organised narrative. It is not only a question of the gradual revelation of who Jesus is,[55] but also a summon to the disciples to a deeper response in faith (cf. 20,31). At this situation one does not understand why the evangelist has tried to gather in the first chapter the majority of the Christological titles attributed to Jesus.[56] He has done so, perhaps, to throw them back in a better light in favour of his Christology of the Son of Man in 1,51. This would be the logical conclusion if the evangelist shows interest for the designation of Jesus only as the Son of Man. On the

---

[51] Used in an adoptive rather than a metaphysical sense; see Ashton, *Understanding*, 260-62. Cf. *1 Enoch* 48,5.10, which connects the titles Chosen One and Messiah, and 49,1-3, which connects the Chosen One with Is. 11,2. See also G. W. E. Nickelsburg, *Jewish Literature between the Bible and the Mishna* (Philadelphia 1981) 217-18; and M. Black, "The Messianism of the Parables of Enoch: Their Date and Contributions to Christological origins," in: Charlesworth, *Messiah*, 145-68.

[52] D. A. Carson and H. G. Williamson ([eds.], *It is Written: Scripture Citing Scripture* [Cambridge 1988] 245-64; see esp. 254-56) note how often Jesus not only fulfils OT themes but actually replaces them. According to them, the fourth evangelist does not treat the OT with scorn or rejection; they view it with reverence, treating it as the given of revelation that anticipates the new revelation occurring in Jesus. Contrary to this Theobald (288) holds that the fourth evangelist in 1,51 is teaching that Jesus, not Bethel, is the place where heaven is opened and communication with God is set up. But it cannot be true that the fourth evangelist is trying to discredit the old, least of all that he is trying to discredit Scripture. See also J. C. VanderKam, "Righteous One, Messiah, Chosen One, and the Son of Man in 1 Enoch 37-71," in: Charlesworth, *Messiah*, 169-91.

[53] Many scholars see 1,49 as the original ending of the chapter and claim that 1,50-51 has been added to the text. E.g. Fortna, *Gospel of Signs*, 179-80; Boismard, *Du Baptême à Cana*, 105; H.-J. Kuhn, *Christologie und Wunder*, 153-59; R. E. Brown, *op. cit.*, 88, and Neyrey, "Jacob Allusions," 586-89. Whatever has been the prehistory of 1,19-51, it is clear that Nathanael has confessed his faith only in terms of Jewish Messianic expectations. Note the remarks of Hahn ("Jüngerberufung," 189); Barrett (185-86); and Schnackenburg (*op. cit.*, 317-19). Pancaro (*Law in the Fourth Gospel*, 288-304) claims that 'Son of God' here has the full Johannine Christological meaning.

[54] This is the meaning of the words of Jesus, prolonging the promise of the plotted time in 1,51: "Amen, amen I tell you, you will see heaven opened and the angels of God ascending and descending upon the Son of Man." See Moloney, *Son of Man*, 23-41. The use of the 'double-amen' found only in the fourth Gospel (26 times), tells the reader that he is about to encounter a significant statement which is intimately linked with what went before. Cf. Bernard, I, 67; and B. Lindars, *Behind the Fourth Gospel* (SCC 3) (London 1971) 52-54. Shifting from his discussion with Nathanael ('you' singular in 1,50 and 'him' in 1,51a), Jesus now addresses a wider group of disciples ('you' plural in 1,51b). In doing this the narrator has Jesus reach out of the immediate situation of the 'you' of Nathanael to the various disciples who came to him and with their limited expressions of faith, and to the reader. The reader is part of the second person plural. All are promised: "You will see." The view of the Jews and the disciples needs to be surpassed. There is need for a greater faith, so that the "greater things" of 1,50 may be seen.

[55] The fourth evangelist is not primarily concerned with presenting an account of how Jesus called his first disciples. He is more interested in presenting a true account of who Jesus really is. See A. T. Hanson, 38.

[56] See M. Hengel, "Christological Titles in Early Christianity," in: Charlesworth, *Messiah*, 425-48.

contrary, his interest seems to lie principally on the designation of Jesus as the 'Son' and 'Son of God.' In fact these two titles are used by the Baptist to designate Jesus as the one sent by the Father with a mission to save the world.

The title 'Son of Man' is used in various ways outside the fourth Gospel. The meaning of the title in the fourth Gospel is established by its use in this literary context, where the Son of Man[57] is the link between heaven and earth. This sense continues to be apparent throughout the Gospel, where the Son of Man himself is said to descend from and re-ascend into heaven (cf. 3,13 and 6,62). Perhaps, it is the only one not used in the traditional (political/royal) Messianic sense in Jn. 1. It is to be observed that Jesus, at the end of this Messianic chapter, announces something greater, more fundamental on his person than the simple Messianic identity. From the beginning, Nathanael, the other disciples and the reader are warned that they should go beyond the simple acknowledgement of Jesus as the traditional Jewish Messiah.

2,23-3,36 structurally hangs on 1,19-51. Jn. 2 serves as a foot-rest to make a leap from 1,19-51 to 2,23-3,36. The quest for the identity of Jesus continues among the crowds (2,23-25) and on the part of 'Jews' in the person of Nicodemus (3,1ff.), who perceive Jesus "through the lens of their own preconceptions."[58] We find here the first Christological discourse of Jesus (3,11-21). For the first time, the key elements of the fourth evangelist's Christology are exposed in discourse form which will be developed in the rest of the Gospel. "By the end of the discourse their nocturnal meeting becomes a microcosm of the encounter between Jesus and the world"[59] (cf. Jn. 3,17; 4,22.42 and 12,47). It is a synthesis which gives the essential parameters to define the Christological scheme of the whole Gospel. 2,23-3,36 is, in fact, the turning point in the opening section of the Gospel. It corrects the traditional notion of the Messiah of Jn. 1 and helps to understand the real person and true mission of Jesus. In fact the Christological elements of Jn. 3 become the criteria to judge the Christological understanding of the first disciples (1,35-2,11), the Jews (2,12-22), Nicodemus (3,1-10), the Samaritan woman and the Samaritans (4,1-42), and the royal official (4,43-54). When one recognises the synthetic nature of this first section (1,19-4,54) and its introductory and summary function to the whole Gospel, he/she can easily observe that 2,23-3,36 forms the key to the Christological and soteriological interpretation of the entire Gospel.

According to me, Jn. 3 seems to exercise a counter weight to balance the Messianic tendency of Jn. 1 in affirming the heavenly origin of the Messiah. Jesus cannot be purely and simply assimilated into the concept of the traditional Jewish concept of the Messiah as he has 'come down from heaven.' Now, the purpose of the observation of the parallels between Jn. 1 and Jn. 3 is also to clarify the positions of the Baptist and Jesus as well as the value of their testimonies. We notice strict correlations in form and content in the fourth evangelist's portrayal of the Baptist. His role as forerunner (1,19-34) and friend of the bridegroom (3,29) is to be found basically in his testimony, as the prologue clearly states: "He came as a 'witness' to testify to the light, so that all might believe through him"

---

[57] See F. H. Borsch, "Further Reflections on 'The Son of Man:' The Origins and Development of the Title," in: Charlesworth, *Messiah*, 130-44.

[58] Koester, *Symbolism*, 46.

[59] *Ibid.*, 47.

(1,7). The Johannine recourse to the figure of the Baptist – in his designation as witness and friend of the bridegroom – has only one purpose of leading Israel to belief in Jesus through his testimony. The function of the Baptist as witness in Jn. 1 is reinterpreted in Jn. 3 in nuptial categories – as 'friend of the bridegroom' whose task is to prepare the marriage ceremony and lead the bride to the house of the bridegroom. In particular, he must take care that everything happens according to the customs and tradition, especially those concerning the ritual norms of purification.[60] Hence, there is an inclusive link between the two testimonies of the Baptist.

Moreover, the interest of the evangelist for the figure of the Baptist seems to be purely functional. His person has no autonomous narrative consistence. He is brought into the drama only to turn the attention to Jesus. In fact, the evangelist cannot leave to the Baptist the job of exposing the heart of the fourth evangelist's Christology, because it belongs to the domain of 'heavenly things' (3,12) that Jesus alone can reveal, being the unique revealer come down from heaven (cf. 3,13).[61]

But with the first testimony, used to introduce Jesus to Israel, the Baptist has not yet fulfilled the essential function which the fourth Gospel attributes to him, that is, to authenticate juridically in front of 'the Jews' the Christological claim of Jesus. Only after Jesus had revealed his true identity and the soteriological implication of his mission, it becomes necessary that the Baptist reappears and exercises his role of juridical witness taking into account the words of Jesus. It is precisely for this reason that the evangelist has placed the encounter with Nicodemus (2,23-3,21) parallel to the second testimony of the Baptist (3,22-36) in the structural unity of Jn. 3. The main themes 're-treated' by the Baptist are the heavenly origin of Jesus (3,31; cf. 3,13), his function as the unique revealer (3,32; cf. 3,11-13), his identity as the Son of God (3,34-35; cf. 3,16-17), as well as the soteriological impact of the faith on the Son (3,36 cf. 3,16.18-21). It is, therefore, for the Baptist essentially a question of juridical authentication of the Christological claim of Jesus, in conformity with the principle of non-acceptance of a single witness in the Jewish tradition.

Now, in order to understand the heart of the fourth evangelist's Christology, one should try to understand what the fourth evangelist says about Jesus as Son of Man, Son of God[62] or Son, and his relationship with the Father. Just as there is a concentration of the Messianic titles in Jn. 1 on the lips of the Baptist and the first disciples, there is a concentration of the corrected notions of Christology on the lips of Jesus himself in Jn. 3.

---

[60] At the background is the OT theme of the spiritual marriage between God and His people (cf. Hos. 1-2; Jer. 2,2; and Is. 61,10) which the NT applies to the relation between Christ and the people of the new covenant (cf. Mt. 22,1-14; 2 Cor. 11,2; Eph. 5,27; and Rev. 19,7 and 21,2.10). The task of the Baptist therefore was to prepare the New Covenant between Christ and the Church, just as Moses did in the perspective of the marriage between God and His people during the covenant made at Sinai.

[61] In fact the Baptist needs to be equipped with knowledge about Jesus, without however having a share in the exclusive knowledge coming from Jesus. The evangelist, therefore, adapts the Synoptic tradition: The Baptist did not know Jesus (Jn. 1,31.33; comp. Mt. 3,13-14) and the descent of the Spirit upon Jesus becomes a pure sign of God addressed to the Baptist to designate Jesus as the one to be revealed to Israel (Jn. 1,33-34; Mt. 3,16-17; Mk. 1,11; and Lk. 3,21-22). Except the consciousness of his mission, the Baptist is found in a situation just like the people and shares their Messianic concept.

[62] Cf. 1,34.49; 3,18; 5,25; 11,4.27; 19,7 and 20,31. For passages on Father-Son relationship see: 3,16-17.31-35; 4,34; 5,19-23.37; 6,29.38.40-46; 7,16.28-29; 8,16.36-38.42.54; 10,17.30-38; 12,45-49; 14,9-11.20.28; 16,5.28 and 17,8.11-24.

We find nine such assertions in Jn. 3 which are further developed in the rest of the Gospel later. I just enumerating them here as I have treated it in Part I in detail already.

First of all, *Jesus is the Son of Man*.[63] Already at the beginning of his Gospel the evangelist wants his readers to understand that the man Jesus of Nazareth is indeed this mysterious Son of Man (3,13; cf. 1,51). *Secondly*, his home is in the heavenly realm with God. Jn. 3,13-15 is the simplest statement of this idea. The Son of Man originates in that heavenly home, descends into the human world, and will once again ascend after the completion of his task (3,13; cf. 6,62 and 16,28). He does not belong to this world. His origin is elsewhere – it is divine. He appears mysteriously from nowhere, lingers among people for a time, and then departs. Hence, there is a great deal of discussion in the fourth Gospel about the origin of Jesus. The descent and ascent themes are good examples of the way in which the evangelist represents Nicodemus and the crowd totally misunderstanding the words of Jesus. The origin of the Messiah was an important credential for Jewish thought in the first century, and the evangelist uses that concern to make the point repeatedly that the Son of Man has no worldly origin. *Thirdly*, the idea that the *Son has been sent by the Father* is associated with his heavenly origin and destination. The passages that express this idea are numerous to examine (just to mention a few: 3,34; 4,34; 8,26; 9,4 and 17,3). The Son is sent forth into the world. As one sent and commissioned by the Father, he speaks for the Father as he carries His authority, represents Him and acts on His behalf. A sort of *agency Christology* figures prominently in the Christology of the fourth Gospel. This agent is none other than the Son of Man.

The *fourth* assertion is related to the ascent of the Son of Man into heaven (3,13). The sayings relevant to this ascent are of two kinds. The first are those in which Jesus is made to speak of his glorification. He claims that his death is his glorification (cf. 12,23). The *fifth* assertion made about the Son of Man and the Father-Son relationship is this: The functions of the Son are the functions of the Father. For example, the Son judges on behalf of the Father (3,18; cf. 5,22.27). He is the giver of life or eternal life (3,15; cf. 6,27.53). Father's work is the work of the Son, which leads us to a *sixth* point: The Son carries the full authority of the Father. That is, the authority of the divine realm resides in the Son (3,31.36).

Moreover, the Father and Son are represented as one, yet with distinct individuality. This is the *seventh* point. The Father loves the Son (3,34) which supposes a relationship and implies individuality.[64] The *eighth* assertion is simpler. The evangelist calls Jesus the 'only Son' (3,16.18; cf. 1,18). The Greek word μονογενὴς (translated as 'only' in the

---

[63] Kysar (*Maverick Gospel*, 40) notices that "the unembellished Son title may well be a fourth evangelist's synthesis of the content and associations of both the longer Son designations" (Son of Man and Son of God). Son is the designation that dominates the names for Jesus in the fourth Gospel. The title 'Son of Man' appears 13 times in all (1,51; 3,13.14; 5,27; 6,27.53.62; 8,28; 9,35; 12,23.34 x twice and 13,31) in the fourth Gospel.

[64] The Son also obeys the Father (4,34) implying individuality. On the other hand, there is a series of passages that speak of an identity between the two (10,30.38 and 17,1.22; cf. 5,19). The fourth evangelist claims that the Father and Son are one in being and action. At any rate, he leaves the reader with a profound paradox. The Son is one with the Father but not identical. He is divine, yet he is in a sense subordinate to God. The evangelist seems to be struggling to define the relationship of the founder of his faith to God.

NRSV) means 'one of its kind.'[65] *Finally*, it is obvious that the fourth evangelist wants the reader to get one message loud and clear: To believe in the Son is to have eternal life/salvation (3,15-17.36). In other words, to respond to Jesus, the Son, is to respond to God, the Father (cf. 5,23). What the evangelist does in the rest of the Gospel is an elaboration of this basic exposition of his Christological scheme.

B. Narrative Continuity and Correlation Between 2,1-22 and 4,1-54

This is not a comprehensive and exhaustive study of all the correlations between the two units. This is meant only to facilitate a better understanding of the narrative Christology couched in story form in the first section of the Gospel. Just as in the case of the previous units, these two units also consist of four principal sub-units, *viz.*, 2,1-11; 2,12-22; 4,1-42 and 4,43-54 which entertain various correlations among them. To proceed with clarity, we shall search for corresponding elements of each of the sub-unit of 2,1-22 with those of 4,1-54.

1. Between 2,1-11 and 4,1-42

There is hardly any detailed study that has tried to expose the correlation between the wedding at Cana and the encounter of Jesus with the Samaritan woman. Many scholars have explored the relation between the two Cana signs.[66]

a. Characterisation

From the point of view of characters, only in the wedding at Cana and in the narrative of the encounter with the Samaritan woman, one comes across two women in this section – the mother of Jesus[67] and the Samaritan woman[68] – and, hence, the recurrence of the word γυνή (2,4 and 4,7.9.10) which establishes a formal link between the pericopes.

The Cana miracle is performed unobtrusively. It is depicted as the secret work of a hidden and elusive Messiah. Jesus' true identity remains undisclosed.[69] That is one of the reasons why the narrator does not bring the wedding guests (2,10) to acknowledge Jesus; neither the wedding couple nor the steward come in direct contact with Jesus.[70] On the other hand, in the Samaria episode Jesus reveals – though his language is still elusive – his identity as the Messiah (cf. 4,26). The people of Sychar, too, acknowledge him as "the true

---

[65] While the evangelist does not make extensive use of this adjective, it seems important that the meaning of Son is qualified with it on these two or three occasions. Possibly the qualification means to suggest the absolute distinction between the sonship of Jesus and any ideas of humans as sons of God (since they may be 'children of God,' 1,12). The sonship of the Son of Man, Jesus, is absolutely unique. The evangelist again might be responding to Jewish charges that the Jesus whom Christians call Messiah is at best an angel. Not so, responds the evangelist. He is God unique.

[66] Only Gourges (*Pour que vous croyiez*, 78-82) has tried to compare the 2,1-3,21 with 4,1-54 based on the geographical scheme of the self-revelation of Jesus at Cana, Jerusalem, Samaria and again at Cana.

[67] Note that she is not called Mary by the narrator, and she is addressed by Jesus as 'woman' (γυνή).

[68] See A. Fehribach, *The Women in the Life of the Bridegroom: A Feminist Historical-Literary Analysis of the Female Characters in the Fourth Gospel* (Collegeville 1998).

[69] Cf. J. Becker, "Wunder und Christologie. Zum literarkritischen und christologischen Problem der Wunder im Johannesevangelium," *NTS* 16 (1969/70) 130-48.

[70] The author's strange introduction of the bridegroom at 2,9-10 will be clarified in 3,29. While speaking to the bridegroom, ironically, the steward is speaking to the one who provided the wine, and thus Jesus is present throughout the whole narrative. See Scholtissek, "Ironie und Rollenwechsel," 242.

Saviour of the world" (4,42).[71] At Cana there is an implicit revelation of Jesus as God in the motif of giving – in giving wine abundantly (cf. 2,6.7). To the Samaritan woman Jesus says that he is the one who can give this gift of living water[72] (cf. 4,10.14), suggesting an implicit equation of himself with God.

Along side these indications of Jesus' divinity, there are also signs of his humanity. Jesus accepts an invitation to be guest at the wedding in Cana (cf. 2,2); takes time to participate in a social function like any other man. Similarly the narrator in Jn. 4 does not hide the human side of Jesus, that he was tired (κεκοπιακὼς) of his journey, needed rest and so sat down at a well (4,6); he was thirsty and so asked for a drink (4,7); he was hungry and so his disciples went to the city to buy food (4,8). Jesus is presented as a real, human saviour in both episodes.[73]

b. Literary Genre

In the case of the wedding at Cana, no doubt, it is a wedding scene involving a dialogue. In Jn. 4, even if the wedding character is less apparent, considering the dynamic of the text, it is equally well present. 4,4-42 focuses on a dialogue and an evolving relationship between Jesus and a woman. Jesus' encounter with the woman follows the literary conventions of a specific type-scene, that of the encounter with the betrothed at a well. In Jewish literature such meetings are betrothal scenes. The fundamental plot ingredients of the betrothal type-scenes according to Alter are:

1. The betrothal scene must take place when the future bridegroom has journeyed to a foreign land.
2. There he encounters a girl or girls at a well;
3. Someone, either the man or the girl, then draws water from the well;
4. Afterward the girl or girls rush home to bring the news of the stranger's arrival;
5. Finally, a betrothal is concluded between the stranger and the girl, in the majority of instances, only after he has been invited to a meal.[74]

Examples of this type-scenes may be found in the stories of Isaac and Rebekah (Gen. 24,11-30), Jacob and Rachel (Gen. 29,1-14), and Moses and Zipporah (Ex. 2,15-22). Boismard and Lamouille enlist the various similarities between the two episodes.[75] Let me consider only the case of Isaac briefly. In both narratives, the encounter takes place outside the town, near a well (cf. Gen. 24,11; and Jn. 4,5.8); and the man asks for a drink from the

---

[71] Cf. C. R. Koester, "'The Saviour of the World' (John 4,42)," *JBL* 109 (1990) 665-80.

[72] The image of *water* as spiritual gift was widespread in ancient religions. Cf. Bauer, *Johannesevangelium*, 68-69; and Bernard, I, 140-42. The discussion on the meaning of 'the gift of God' and its relationship to 'living water' is never ending. For a survey see Okure, 96-97. The main question is: Does it refer to Jesus himself or the gift of the Spirit? F.-M. Braun ("Avoir soif et boire [Jn 4,10-14 and 7,37-39]," in: A. Descamps and A. de Halleux [eds.], *Mélanges Bibliques en hommage au R. P. Béda Rigaux* [Gembloux 1970] 249-51) is in favour of the Spirit. For Olsson (212-18) it is the revelation of Jesus giving life through the action of the Spirit. C. R. Koester (*Symbolism*, 168) argues that "the giver and the gift must be understood together."

[73] See M. M. Thompson, *Humanity of Jesus*.

[74] Cf. Alter, 52.

[75] Boismard and Lamouille, 136-37; see also M. Girard, "Jesus en Samarie (Jean 4,1-42): Analyse des structures stylistiques et du processus de symbolisation," *EeT(O)* 17 (1986) 303; P. Dagonet, *Selon Saint Jean: Une Femme de Samarie* (Paris 1979) 47-53; and C. M. Carmichael, "Marriage and the Samaritan Woman," *NTS* 26 (1979/80) 332-46.

woman who comes out of the town to draw water (cf. Gen. 24,17.45; and Jn. 4,7). In the story of Isaac (Gen. 24,28-30), after the encounter, Rebekah runs home to announce the incident (οὕτως λελάληκέν μοι ὁ ἄνθρωπος – Gen. 24,30); Laban, her brother, then runs to the man at the well. One finds the same movement in Jn. 4,28-30. The Samaritan woman leaves her water jar and goes back to the city and narrates to the people what Jesus told her (ὃς εἶπέν μοι πάντα ὅσα ἐποίησα – Jn. 4,29), which provokes the Samaritans to come out of their city and go to Jesus at the well. While in the Genesis story the encounter concludes with a request on the part of the mother and the brother of Rebekah that she be allowed to remain a few more days (ten days) with them (cf. Gen. 24,55), in Jn. 4,40 it is Jesus who is asked by the Samaritans to stay with them. We can also notice a few more traits common to both narratives. In both accounts it is water drawn also for the animals (Gen. 24,19 and Jn. 4,12), there is a mention and a discussion of worship respectively (Gen. 24,26 and Jn. 4,20-24), and a refusal to eat until the mission is accomplished (Gen. 24,33 and Jn. 4,31-34). This pattern is visible in the episode of the Samaritan woman. Jesus is the bridegroom (cf. 3,29) and here he is portrayed as travelling into the foreign land of Samaria (4,4). He meets a Samaritan woman who comes to the well. This woman draws water from the well. Jesus speaks to her, and she runs home to tell the people of Sychar that a stranger has arrived who could be the Messiah.

If the crucial elements of the meal and betrothal are absent, it is not because they have been forgotten, but because they appear in another form. Instead of the ordinary meal there is a kind of spiritual meal. When the disciples buy food and offer it to Jesus, he replies: "My food is to do the will of him who sent me and to complete his work" (cf. 4,8.31-34). In other words, the idea of a meal is replaced by an insistence on the priority of the spiritual – God's will. And the idea of a betrothal has been replaced by a spiritual betrothal. The woman, as the text implies, comes to believe, and so do the people whom she in some way represents. The text does not say explicitly that Jesus was involved in any process of betrothal, but at the end of the scene at the well, exactly where the type-scene would usually require the actual betrothal, the story tells that the believers invited Jesus to stay with them; and he did so for two days. It is in this idea of abiding with the believers, that the reality of betrothal finds new expression. Thus, what was suggested at Cana becomes somewhat clearer: Jesus communicates a presence which is better than wedding wine.

c. Symbolism

The pericope of the wedding at Cana has certain other elements common to the rest of the episode of the Samaritan woman, which will only add to stressing the strong correlation already established. For example, the recurrence of the word ὑδρία (water jar) is not insignificant (2,6.7 and 4,28), as these are the only occasions where they occur in the whole of the NT. That the ὑδρία were *six* in number at the wedding in Cana (cf. 2,6) also suggests a symbolic meaning with the *six* men of the Samaritan woman (cf. 4,18). The choice of the number *six* at the Cana wedding is probably a further hint to the implied reader that the Jewish world represented by this ritual lacks the perfection[76] of the number *seven*.

Besides, the immediate context of the pericope, *viz.*, that of the encounter near a well structured after the episode of Gen. 24, cannot but imply a parallel to the wedding at Cana. In the OT the relation between God and His people is often compared to that of a relation between husband and wife. The Samaritan woman had six men – six false gods – a number indicating imperfection and incompleteness. She is at the point of discovering her seventh husband/Lord.[77] Since *seven* is the perfect number in Judaism, the implicit commentary must be that Jesus is the man whom she has been waiting for, the man in whose presence she will find wholeness (σωτηρία – 4,22). All these linking similarities, beyond doubt, bear witness to the close parallelism between the two pericopes.

Moreover, the marital symbolism in 2,1-11 (the arrival of the eschatological wedding) and in 3,29 (the Baptist as the best man and Jesus as the Messianic bridegroom) places precisely this kind of expectation in the mind of the reader. The surprise, of course, is the fact that this bride is a Samaritan and not a Jew. The eschatological wedding between Yahweh and His people is, therefore, not narrowly nationalistic as was anticipated by the Jews. Jesus is the Saviour of the *world* (4,42; cf. 3,16-17), not just the Saviour of the Jewish people.

Furthermore, the role of the mother of Jesus at the Cana wedding is crucial to the logic of the narrative. There have been many symbolic interpretations of the figure of the woman, the mother of Jesus, found only here and at the foot of the cross (19,25-27) and in close connection with *'the hour'* of Jesus (cf. 2,4 – 'my hour').[78] The encounter with the Samaritan woman took place *at* (death-evoking) *noon* (4,6). It is unlikely, historically speaking, that the woman would come to the well 'about the sixth *hour*,' in other words, about noon. "Such a chore was done in the morning and evening."[79] But it makes theological sense. It was at such an hour that Jesus was condemned to death: "When Pilate heard... he brought Jesus outside and sat on the judge's bench....; and it was about *noon*" (19,13-14). In other words the scene is deliberately being related to the crucifixion. The entire Samaria episode is governed by a literary convention: If the exhaustion of Jesus

---

[76] Perfection is also suggested by the abundance (cf. 2,6) and quality (cf. 2,10) of the wine. The quality of the water that Jesus would give to the Samaritan woman is also superior ('living water'), cf. 4,14.

[77] It is important to observe that the Samaritan woman addresses Jesus three times using the term Κύριε (4,11.15.19) which is an equivalent of *ba'al*, but also used for Yahweh in the OT. Against the screen of Gen. 24, it is interesting to note that Jesus is the husband and the servant simultaneously. As husband (cf. 3,29) he is the new Isaac, the seventh husband/*ba'al*, God of the Samaritan woman. He also plays the role so the servant, Eliezer, in leading the Samaritan woman (the bride) to her true *ba'al*/Κύριε, while introducing her to true worship (cf. 4,20-26). For the symbolism of seventh husband, see Girard, "Jesus en Samarie," 301-4.

[78] This is the first reference to a theme that will grow as the Gospel story unfolds. The 'hour' will be the moment of Jesus' violent end (cf. 7,4.30; 8,20 and 12,27) but, strangely, also the moment of his glorification (cf. 12,23 and 13,31), through which he will return to his Father (cf. 13,1.32 and 17,5). Jesus says that his hour "has not yet come" (2,4). The miracle at Cana is not 'the hour,' which is 'not yet' (cf. 7,4.30 and 8,20). For a survey, cf. R. E. Brown, *op. cit.*, 99; see also A. Vanhoye, "Interrogation johannique et l'exégèse de Cana," *Bib.* 55 (1974) 157-77; and R. F. Collins, "Cana," 79-95. The implied reader does not know this; he cannot reach outside story time. He has been made aware of a plotted time in the future. On the theology of the last hour see H. Balz, "Johanneische Theologie und Ethik im Licht der 'letzten Stunde'," in: W. Schrage (ed.), *Studien zum Text und zur Ethik des neuen Testaments. FS zum 80. Geburtstag von Heinrich Greeven* (BZNW 47) (Berlin, New York 1986) 35-56.

[79] R. E. Brown, *op. cit.*, 169.

(tired, thirsty, hungry – cf. 4,6-8)[80] alludes to his final giving way to the disciples, then it is appropriate that the *hour* also should allude to that final process. Furthermore, since Jesus, in speaking to the woman, will be referring in various ways to the giving of the Spirit (cf. 4,23.24), and since the giving of the Spirit is associated with Jesus' death and glorification, it is appropriate, that there is an evoking of that final *hour*.

Finally, the wine which is so abundant is given at Cana "on the third day" (2,1); in other words, on a day which, within the context of the early church, cannot but evoke the resurrection.[81] That the wine is also associated with Jesus' 'hour' and his 'glory' means that it is an outflow of the final 'hour' when Jesus will be glorified, when he will pass from this world to the Father.[82] The reader meets, for the first time, the typical indication of the fourth evangelist's unique eschatological perspective: "The hour is coming, and is now here" (4,23). As at Cana it is an hour which, in one sense has *not yet come*, but in another sense is *already present* and effective (cf. 2,4-10). This tension, between the 'not yet' and the 'already,' has been described that "the eschatological reign of God was (already) present and operative in the ministry of Jesus, but in a provisional way."[83]

d. Verbal Parallelism

A familiar theme of the fourth Gospel, *viz.*, the 'whence,' 'source' or 'origin'[84] also occurs in these sub-units: In the wedding at Cana, the steward does not know where the wine came from (cf. 2,9).[85] In Jn. 4 the Samaritan woman asks Jesus *ironically*: "Where do you get that living water?" (cf. 4,11). Further, the steward of the wedding feast "called the bridegroom" (φωνεῖ τὸν νυμφίον ὁ ἀρχιτρίκλινος – 2,9) has a similarity in Jesus telling the Samaritan woman to go and call her husband (Ὕπαγε φώνησον τὸν ἄνδρα σου – 4,16). On the one hand, Jesus gives the Messianic wine drawn from water, and on the other hand, he gives the living water for eternal life. The recurrence of the verb 'to draw' (ἀντλέω) is also important (cf. 2,8.9 and 4,7.15), as it appears only here in the whole of the NT. Note also the recurrence of the terms 'water' (ὕδωρ –2,7.9 and 4,7.10.11.13.14.15)   and 'become' (γεγενημένον – 2,9 and γενήσεται – 4,14). One should also observe that in 2,9 it is the question of water *turned into* wine (τὸ ὕδωρ οἶνον γεγενημένον). It is very similar to the idea in 4,14: "The water that I will give will *become* in them a spring of water gushing up to eternal life (τὸ ὕδωρ... γενήσεται ἐν αὐτῷ πηγὴ ὕδατος ἁλλομένου...)." We can also observe a formal similarity in the remark of the mother of Jesus in 2,3: "They have no wine" (οἶνον οὐκ ἔχουσιν), and that of the Samaritan woman in 4,11: "You have no bucket" (οὔτε ἄντλημα ἔχεις). Finally, it is interesting to observe in both cases – the wine brought to be tasted (ἐγεύσατο – 2,9) and the food brought by the disciples to be eaten

---

[80] Lightfoot (121-22) sees a number of hints in 4,1-15 that point toward the passion: Jesus' weariness (cf. 19,1-2), his desire for water (19,28), and the 'sixth hour' (19,14). See also Hudry-Clergeon, 821-23.

[81] It is likely that 'on the third day' had become a very frequently used expression in Greek pre-Synoptic tradition for dating the resurrection of Jesus in the early Church; cf. also Lindars, *Gospel*, 124.

[82] Cf. Schnackenburg, *op. cit.*, 329-31.

[83] R. E. Brown, *op. cit.*, cxvii. At the time Jesus is speaking to the woman the Spirit has not yet been given – not fully and formally.

[84] The 'whence' (πόθεν and ποῦ) is used in the fourth Gospel to enquire about the origin of persons or things. See 1,38 (ποῦ μένεις); 4,11; 7,27-28; 8,14; 9,29-30 and 19,9.

[85] As Gnilka (*Johannesevangelium*, 23) puts it: "Das Woher der Gabe ist wie das Woher des Gebers ein verborgenes" (comp. 4,11 and 19,9).

(φαγεῖν – 4,33) – the recurrence of the verb φέρω in aorist form in 2,8 (ἤνεγκαν) and 4,33 (ἤνεγκεν). All these above mentioned observations of formal indications betray a strong narrative link between the two episodes.

2. Between 2,12-22 and 4,1-42

a. Themes

Many scholars of the fourth Gospel have noticed the presence of corresponding links between the scenes of cleansing the *Temple* at Jerusalem (2,12-22) and the conversation between Jesus and the Samaritan woman on true *worship* (4,19-26). In both episodes there is a discussion about worship and the place of worship. The terms used for 'Temple' (ναὸς) in 2,19-21 and 'mountain' (ὄρος) in 4,20-21 are analogous, in the sense that mountains are the privileged places for erecting sanctuaries; and the Samaritans consider it the place of their worship. While referring to the love life of the Samaritan woman (4,16-18), the conversation suddenly turns to worship (4,19-24). In 2,1-22 the episode of cleansing the Temple evoking true worship is preceded by the wedding at Cana. Love life and worship are, therefore, connected. Note also the mention of six waters jars at Cana meant for ritual purification referring to cult and worship (2,6). Whatever may be psychological motives suggested for these changes – for instance, the woman's wish to change the subject[86] – the present text has considerable theological coherence. Love and worship touch the core of the human heart. On both topics the woman makes a partial statement; and in both cases Jesus cuts through the camouflage with amusing irony and considerable deference ("you are right..." – 4,17; "woman, believe me..." – 4,21), and clarifies the true state of things: her love life is in disorder and the worship of her people is empty ("you worship what you do not know" – 4,22). And it is to this interwoven disorder, this confused spiritual plight, that Jesus responds: "The hour is coming, and is now here" (4,23). The hour in question is that of Jesus' death and resurrection as already explained above (cf. 3,14).

There is also a parallelism to be observed in Jesus' reference to the Temple of Jerusalem as his *Father*'s house (τὸν οἶκον τοῦ πατρός μου – 2,16) and the instruction to the Samaritan woman regarding worship to be rendered to the *Father* in spirit and truth (4,23). But the theme of *father* has already been subtly and ironically introduced earlier in this narrative. In 4,12 the woman spoke of Jacob's gift of water to his *sons*; in 4,20 she again challenged Jesus to better the *fathers* who worshipped in Gerizim. Such notions of father are now eclipsed by Jesus' words on God as Father[87] (4,23; cf. 3,35 and the references to the *Son* in the Nicodemus episode). Thus, in cryptic and proleptic language, Jesus lays bare before the woman the richness of life in the Spirit and in the presence of the Father.[88]

---

[86] J. Bligh ("Jesus in Samaria," *HeyJ* 3 [1962] 335-36) feels that there is sufficient evidence in the text for the claim that she has marital designs on Jesus; on the contrary, Okure (108-10) suggests that it is her way of trying to bring the discussion to a close.

[87] See Bernard, I, 147; Schnackenburg, *op. cit.*, 436-37; and Léon-Dufour, *Lecture*, I, 368-71.

[88] The term 'Father' is used rather indirectly, and the primary emphasis, as Duke (*Irony*, 101-3) suggests, is on a process of betrothal; but this indirect reference to the 'Father' is given three times (4,21-23), and the eagerness of the Father to meet the woman and her people is underlined by the final references: "for the Father seeks such as these to worship him" (4,23). Thus Jesus reveals to the woman, on the one hand, the disorientation of herself and her people, and, on the other, the nearness of a parental spouse like God who offers spiritual integration.

In Jerusalem, Jesus speaks of his resurrection as a sign accrediting his action of cleansing the Temple. It is hardly an accident that this happens at the approach of the Passover (2,13), the time of the year when Jesus will eventually die, or that the scene goes on to allude to his death and resurrection.[89] For it is particularly death and the prospect of death which bring out the full reality of affiliation with the divine. His resurrected (glorified) body will be the new location of true worship, the new Temple (περὶ τοῦ ναοῦ τοῦ σώματος αὐτου – 2,21) replacing the old (ὁ ναὸς οὗτος – cf. 2,20-21).[90] Just like the Jews, the Samaritans, too, are attached to their place of worship. Hence, she corners Jesus with a tricky question: 'Is it on our mountain (Gerizim) or at Jerusalem that one should worship?' In a similar manner, as in Jn. 2, Jesus answers that true worship is to be rendered neither on this mountain nor at Jerusalem, but "in spirit and truth" (cf. 4,23-24).[91] The most obvious clue for a parallel between the two episodes is that the word 'Temple' refers to a body (cf. 2, 21). The body in question is the risen body of Jesus; and there is an implication that the Jewish Temple is to be replaced (4,21.23) by the risen Jesus – the Spirit filled Jesus – as a centre of worship. Putting the two episodes together, the apparently restricted incident in 2,12-22 has a universal dimension – it involves dimly the perspective of a time when the narrowly based worship of the Jerusalem Temple will be replaced by a centre of worship which is open to all (cf. 4,24).

Finally, the confession of *faith* of the disciples *in Jesus and in his word* at the end of the Cana and Temple episodes (2,11 and 22 respectively) correspond to the *faith* of the Samaritans *in Jesus and in his word* (4,39 and 41 respectively). This also strengthens the link between the two units 2,1-22 and 4,1-42.

b. Literary Devices

Jesus addresses the Jews in direct speech (cf. 2,19). They reject his words. They throw his words back at him, refusing to take a leap beyond the categories of the stones of their Temple building. Not only do they *misunderstand* Jesus' shift from a Temple building (τῷ ἱερῷ) – through his reference to that building as his Father's house (ὁ οἶκος) – to a different Temple (ὁ ναός), but they also reject the words he offers as his authority: "and in three days I will raise it up" (2,19). The narrator reports the response of the Jews, placing on their lips the same words of Jesus suggesting a *mockery*. The sign Jesus offered was: "Destroy this Temple *and in three days I will raise it up*" (2,19). The Jews reply: "It has taken forty-six years to build this Temple, *and you, will raise it up in three days?*" (2,20). In an insolent use of the personal pronoun '*you*' they make a mocking question of the

---

[89] Many scholars point out that the verbs used for 'destroy' (λύω) and 'raise up' (ἐγείρω) can be applied equally well to the tearing down and reconstruction of a building, or the destruction and resurrection of the body of Jesus. See e.g. Schnackenburg, *op. cit.*, 349.

[90] Regarding the new Temple see R. H. Hiers, "Purification of the Temple: Preparation for the Kingdom of God," *JBL* 90 (1971) 82-90.

[91] In 4,21 and 23 Jesus says twice "the hour is coming" when the worship will change to one "in spirit and truth." In the fourth Gospel, 'the hour' refers, first of all, to the elevation on the cross, to the moment of the death and glorification of Jesus. This mention of 'the hour' in connection with the change of place of worship is directly linked to the mention of the resurrection in 2,13-22 in relation to the new Temple. With regard to the expression 'worship in spirit and truth,' it presupposes the gift of the Spirit after the glorification of Jesus. Cf. O. Betz, "'To Worship in Spirit and in Truth:' Reflections on John 4:20-26," in: A. Finkel and L. Frizzel (eds.), *Standing Before God: Studies on Prayer in Scriptures and in Tradition with Essays in Honour of John M. Österreicher* (New York 1981) 53-72.

words of Jesus. We notice a parallel situation of *mockery and misunderstanding* in the conversation between Jesus and the Samaritan woman on the living water. To the offer of living water (4,10) on the part of Jesus, the woman mockingly poses a question that strikes the reader. Given the depth of the well and Jesus not having a bucket in hand to drop into the well, she logically asks: "πόθεν οὖν ἔχεις τὸ ὕδωρ τὸ ζῶν" (4,11).[92] In the mockery of the Jews in 2,20 there is the same logic of physical impossibility on the part of Jesus to raise the Temple up in three days.

3. Between 2,1-11 and 4,43-54

Most of the scholars have noticed the link between these two pericopes, especially because of the enumeration of the two signs at Cana in 2,11 as the first and 4,46.54 as the second. The circle of his first missionary itinerary is now complete (from Cana to Jerusalem, Jerusalem to Judea, Judea to Samaria, and from Samaria back to Cana). In both cases Jesus arrives in Galilee 'on the third day' (cf. 2,1; "When the two days were over" – 4,43").

a. Characterisation

The narrative focus is upon an encounter between Jesus and his mother in the first Cana sign, and between Jesus and the royal official in the second. By naming the mother of Jesus first in the list of characters, the narrator forewarns the reader of her importance for the following scene. She is even listed before Jesus. Her role is crucial to the logic of the narrative. Just as it is the mother of Jesus who provokes the miracle and shows perfect faith in her son, the royal official, too, is portrayed as one with great faith requesting Jesus to heal his son.

The characterisation of Jesus in both episodes is complex. In the first scene, he shows reluctance to the request of his mother saying, "Woman, what concern is that to you and to me?" (2,4), though her request is finally heeded to. To the request of the royal official the reaction of Jesus is the same: "Unless you see signs and wonders you will not believe"[93] (4,48); and the result at the end here, too, is positive.

Besides, the appearance of the slaves (οἱ δοῦλοι) in 4,51 reminds us of the servants (διακόνοι) in 2,5. It is not insignificant that the news about the son living is brought by the δοῦλοι, who like the διακόνοι at the wedding feast (2,5-9) had been closest to the miracle and, who, in some way, had known of it ahead of their master and took the water turned into wine to the steward (2,8). Given the deliberateness with which the second Cana miracle is related to the first, the reference to the servants/slaves evokes the earlier

---

[92] Note also the parallelism already observed in the use of πόθεν.

[93] However, it is important to note that this statement is not a critique of the official. Even though the statement is addressed at him (πρὸς αὐτόν – 4,48), the actual addresses are the Galileans in general, not the official in particular. The verbs seeing (ἴδητε) and believing (πιστεύσητε) are used in second person plural. Thus Jesus' polemical outburst against faith based on signs and wonders (cf. 2,23-25) is not a heartless condemnation of the anxious father before him, but of a social group who persist in pestering him for faith evoking miracles. For a discussion on this verse see G. van Belle, "Jn 4,48 et la foi du centurion," *EThL* 61 (1985)167-69. See also R. Schnackenburg, "Zur Traditionsgeschichte von Joh 4,46-54," *BZ* (1964) 64-67. Bittner (*Jesu Zeichen*, 128-34) eliminates Jesus' rebuke and claims that sentences with Ἐὰν μὴ....οὐ μὴ are proverbial, and he thus translates 4,48 as a positive statement: "Wenn ihr nicht Zeichen und Wunder seht, werdet ihr nicht glauben." This strains the grammar and misses the parallel with 2,4.

emphasis on the servants' responsiveness to Jesus' word. They have been reported as obedient recipients of the word of Jesus on two occasions (2,7.8). Thus the renewal of life depends on response to Jesus' word. To some degree of course, the royal official himself had responded already, and it was precisely his initial responsiveness which was crucial to the renewal of life. But now, as he realises what the word has done, and as the presence of the servants evokes a more complete attentiveness, his own responsiveness increases: "So he himself believed, along with his whole household" (4,53).

b. Structure

Considering the literary design of both miracles there is unanimity among the scholars about the identical structure of both scenes.[94] Moreover, at the end of the wedding at Cana, "the Passover of the Jews was near, and Jesus went up to Jerusalem" (2,13). It is then followed by an action (cleansing of the Temple) leading to a conflict with the Jews (2,12-22). The same strategy is noticed after the healing of the royal official's son: "After this there was a festival of the Jews, and Jesus went up to Jerusalem" (5,1). It is then followed by an action (healing on a Sabbath – 5,2-9) leading to a conflict with the Jews (5,10ff.). Besides, these are the only two signs that do not lead to a discourse immediately after.

c. Literary Devices

First of all, neither of the stories tells us how the miracle is accomplished. The event of the miracle is told only parenthetically.[95] Both stories represent a *culmination*. The first Cana miracle comes at the end of a week-long drama – primarily a culmination of time (temporal plot); the second comes at the end of Jesus' journey[96] to Judea (cf. 4,54) – a culmination primarily of space (spatial plot). To some small degree, the first Cana miracle completes a journey, the journey to Galilee which is referred to in the preceding episode concerning the call of Philip (1,43). And, to some extent, the second Cana miracle completes an elapse of time (temporal plot) – the two days which Jesus had spent with the Samaritans at Sychar (4,40.43). The (secondary) time element of the second Cana miracle – insofar as it speaks of two days and suggests that Jesus arrived in Galilee on the third day – corresponds to the (primary) time element of the first Cana miracle ('on the third day' and 'my hour'– 2,1.4). And the (secondary) journey element of the first Cana miracle, insofar as it suggests a journey to Galilee, corresponds to some of the (primary) journey elements of the second Cana miracle – the journey which, having ultimately begun in Jerusalem, went from Judea to Galilee. Thus what is primary in one finds a precise

---

[94] Moloney, *John*, 70 and 158; Moloncy, *Belief in the Word*, 90 and 190; Bauer, *Johannesevangelium*, 78; Giblin, "Suggestion, Negative Response," 197-211; R. E. Brown, *op. cit.*, 194; and Malina and Rohrbaugh, 68; see also P. Geoltrain, "Les noces à Cana: Jean 2,1-12: Analyse des structures narratives," *FV* 73 (1974) 83-90.

[95] Olsson, 58.

[96] To add to the journey element of the second Cana miracle, in the latter part of the story (4,51-54), the setting moves from Cana to the Cana-Capernaum road, consisting of a meeting even more explicit than the first, a coming together of complementary journeys. The royal official had come from Capernaum to meet the journeying Jesus. Now, as he himself is journeying back home, his servants come to meet him to say that his son lives.

secondary *balance* in the other. This balance describes a *complementarity* between the texts, a complementarity which is both complex and coherent.

d. Themes

It is also interesting to observe that the word *sign* is used in different senses. First of all, in a positive sense, as something which is not the basis of *faith*, but which, after faith is established, plays a secondary and confirming role. Thus 'the beginning of signs' at the wedding feast was a confirming sign for those who already believed – for the disciples were already his followers (unlike those in 2,23-25 and Nicodemus whose faith depended on signs). And the 'second sign' likewise was not the basis for the royal official's faith; it was rather something which confirmed it.[97] Other themes will be treated later under narrative Christology.

4. Between 2,12-22 and 4,43-54

a. Context

There is a link, though less substantial, established between the two pericopes. In 2,13 it is said: "The *Passover* of the Jews was near, and Jesus went up to *Jerusalem*." This visit of Jesus to Jerusalem is explicitly recalled in 4,45: "...the Galileans welcomed him, since they had seen all that he had done *in Jerusalem at the festival*."

b. Themes

A major link connecting 2,22 and 4,50 is the theme of *faith in the word* of Jesus . Note the formal recurrence of the terms 'believing' and 'the word of Jesus' in both cases where it is the question of *faith* evoked by the *word of Jesus* and not faith evoked by seeing signs:

2,22: "...ἐμνήσθησαν οἱ μαθηταὶ αὐτοῦ ὅτι τοῦτο ἔλεγεν, καὶ ἐπίστευσαν <u>τῇ γραφῇ καὶ τῷ λόγῳ</u> ὃν εἶπεν ὁ 'ιησοῦς.

4,50: "ἐπίστευσεν ὁ ἄνθρωπος <u>τῷ λόγῳ</u> ὃν εἶπεν αὐτῷ ὁ 'ιησοῦς..."

Besides, there is a similarity, though insignificant, in the faith expressed in Jesus in 2,22 and 4,53. In both scenes it is a *group of believers* – the *disciples* of Jesus in the first case, the royal official and his *whole household* in the latter one.

Moreover, strong formal links hold these two pericopes together. The most important one is the parallelism between 2,18 and 4,48. On the one hand, the Jews of Jerusalem ask Jesus for a *sign* authorising his action at the Temple: "What sign can you show us for doing this?" (2,18); on the other hand, Jesus rebukes the Galileans[98] for not believing before seeing signs: "Unless you see signs and wonders you will not believe" (4,48). In fact, considering the context, these words of Jesus to the royal official appear to be out of place: Moreover, this Galilean will believe without even seeing. The *rebuke* of Jesus seems to fit in well at 2,18. We can imagine that the reason for inserting this rebuke in 4,48 could be to insist on the theme of *faith and signs* and thus establish a link to the pericope of the Temple cleansing. Then, the two phrases 'in three days' (ἐν τρισὶν

---

[97] The same sense apparently applies to the famous phrase "ταῦτα δὲ γέγραπται ἵνα πιστεύ[σ]ητε" (20,30-31). The signs are not to initiate belief, but to strengthen it. Cf. Schnackenburg, *Gospel*, III, 338; and R. E. Brown, *op. cit.*, II, 1056.

[98] Jesus using the plural in addressing the royal official: you (pl.) see (ἴδητε) and you (pl.) believe (ποτεύσητε) in 4,48 indicates that he is referring to the Galileans (cf. also 4,45).

ἡμέραις) in 2,19-20 and 'when the two days were over' (Μετὰ δὲ τὰς δύο ἡμέρας) in 4,43 connect the two stories referring to the theme of the resurrection of Jesus.

c. Implicit Commentary

As I have mentioned above already, in 2,12 it is said that: "Jesus went down to Capernaum" (κατέβη εἰς Καφαρναοὺμ). The same expression occurs in 4,46-47 where the royal official requests Jesus to descend (καταβῇ – 4,47) to Capernaum to heal his son. There is a subtle and nuanced use of the verbs καταβαίνω and ἀναβαίνω in the fourth Gospel. As we seen in Jn. 3 already, these verbs are used to portray the ascent and descent of Jesus. However, the narrator also uses these verbs at strategic points to describe Jesus' geographical movements (cf. 2,13; 11,55; 12,50 and 20,17 near the point of Jesus' return to the Father). The latter references are used as reminders of the main plot of the Gospel, which has to do with the descent and ascent of Jesus. The royal official's request for Jesus' καταβαίνω[99] to Capernaum helps to keep the over all ascent and descent shaped plot of the fourth Gospel in the mind of the reader. All these above mentioned correlations illustrate powerfully the close structural link between these two pericopes.

5. Narrative Christology

The Christology of these two chapters – closely linked to one another through several elements shown above – is to be found in the typical examples of the reaction of individuals and groups to Jesus. The wedding at Cana is "a *symbolic narrative* with many allusive meanings."[100] It is a traditional symbol of the Messianic times and the Messianic fullness in Israel (see esp. Hos. 2,19-20; Is. 25,6-8; Jer. 2,2; and Song of Songs). The narrator, through the symbol of marriage, introduces the breakthrough, in time, of the new covenant between the Messiah and the people of the new covenant (represented by Mary and the disciples). The motif of 'abundance of wine' often occurs in prophecy as a characteristic of the glory of the coming kingdom of God (cf. Is. 25,6 and 55,1-3; Amos 9,13.14; Jer. 31,12ff.; and Prov. 9,5b; cf. Gen. 49,11). In Jesus' own preaching 'new wine' is the symbol of the time of salvation that has come and is still to come (cf. Mk. 2,22; and Lk. 22,18.30). This is the first meaning of the pericope as it flows from its structural position. Many commentators acknowledge the Messianic meaning of this episode.[101]

There are two more references to the Messianic era in this episode: In 2,6 we have a reference to the *quantity* (abundance) and in 2,10 to the superior *quality* of the new wine. These two remarks indicate the superiority of the new covenant (over the old and imperfect cf. 6 jars) inaugurated by the Messiah. Wine is also a symbol for the revelation of God,

---

[99] The verb "to descend" is never applied to Jesus as Son or as Son of God in the fourth Gospel, but only as Son of Man (3,13). The Son of Man is the one who comes down from heaven and who must ascend back through the cross. It is this passing through the cross that makes the meeting point of the two principal Christological schemes of the Gospel.

[100] Olsson, 114. My italics.

[101] Against this eschatological interpretation E. Linnemann ("Die Hochzeit zu Kana und Dionysos," *NTS* 20 [1974] 411) advances the objection that in Jewish eschatology the abundance of wine is never the result of a miracle performed by the Messiah but is described as a marvellous natural growth. In my opinion, this is not acceptable as it is based on a very literal view of what the NT considers the fulfilment of prophecy and of Jewish future expectation. In the multiplication of the loaves in Jn. 6, for example, the audience acknowledges that Jesus is the prophet and the Messianic king (cf. 6,14 and 7,31).

first in the OT through Law and wisdom, then in the NT through Jesus, the Messiah.[102] All that has been promised by God and held out in prospect in a profusion of images and concepts is now fulfilled in Jesus.

The episode of cleaning the Temple (2,12-22) forms the companion piece to the miracle at Cana. If the transformation of water at Cana in to wine identified Jesus' death as the new means of purification, the disruption of trade in the Temple anticipated the time when atonement and cleansing would be effected through his passion and resurrection. It has also Messianic connotations.[103] God alone or His Messiah has the authority to execute such an action upsetting the central institution of the Jewish religion.[104] 'The Jews,' therefore, demand for a sign from Jesus to prove his divine authority and thus his Messianic credentials.[105] The exchange of words between Jesus and 'the Jews' reveals that his action cannot be fully comprehended within the framework of traditional Messianic expectations. That is why they find Jesus' words incomprehensible.

It is significant that in both pericopes the mention of the faith of the disciples is pushed to the end of the episodes (2,11.22), and in both stories the disciples play a very passive role (spectators). However, such a double insistence on the faith of the disciples indicates that the major theme of this bipartite scene is directly related to the promise (greater things, ascent and descent, Son of Man) made in 1,50-51. Already in 1,50-51

---

[102] Cf. Boismard and Lamouille, 104-5. For Olsson (107ff.) wine does not function as an eschatological symbol but (in the light of the "Sinai Screen") stands for the Law, which is now replaced by something new.

[103] The Jews who witnessed the incident posed a question that focussed attention on the issue of Jesus' identity or authority rather than on the meaning of his action or his motivation for doing it. The author had said earlier that 'the Jews' in Jerusalem were looking for the Messiah, Elija, or the prophet to appear (cf. 1,19-21). Therefore, we should assume that 'the Jews' in Jerusalem Temple (2,20) were also looking for an eschatological figure.

[104] According to C. A. Evans ("Jesus' Action in the Temple: Cleansing or Portent of Destruction?," *CBQ* 51 [1989] 237-70) the Jewish tradition awaited that the Messiah would restore Jerusalem and its Temple (cf. Jer. 7; Ezek. 40-43; Sir. 36,18f.; Hag. 2,7ff.; Zech. 2,5-9; and Mal. 1-3). There was the hope of a new Temple in the place of the Herodian Temple. According to various sources a new and glorious Temple would be erected in Jerusalem in the new age of salvation. Some texts did not identify the builder of the Temple (e.g. Tob. 13,10), and others anticipated that God would establish it (1 Enoch 90,29). Tob. 14,5 suggests that people might rebuild the sanctuary. On the complex relationship of Jesus' actions to contemporary Jewish expectations, see J. K. Riches, "Apocalyptic – Strangely Relevant," in: W. Horbury (ed.), *Templum Amicitiae: Essays on the Second Temple Presented to Ernst Bammel* (JSNT.S 48) (Sheffield 1991) 237-63. Still other texts expected the Messiah to raise the new structure. According to 2 Sam. 7,12-13, the heir to David's throne would build Israel's house of worship; and Zech. 6,12 said that the Temple would be built by the Davidic 'branch.' The Targums on Zech. 6,12 and Is. 53,5 refer to the Messiah as builder of the Temple. The *fourteenth benediction*, which became an important feature of Jewish worship, associated the rebuilding of the Temple with the advent of the Messiah. See D. Juel, *Messiah and Temple. The Trial of Jesus in the Gospel of Mark* (SBL.DS 31) (Missoula 1977) 169-209. This relation between the coming of the Messiah and the reconstruction of the Temple must have existed in the first century. The same seems to be implied in the question of the high priest in Mk. 14,61: When the false witnesses recall the words of Jesus on the reconstruction of the Temple, he asks Jesus if he was the Messiah. We can, therefore, conclude that the cleansing of the Temple can be understood in the sense of presenting Jesus to be the Messiah; see also E. P. Sanders, *Jesus and Judaism* (Philadelphia 1985) 62-63; R. E. Brown, *op. cit.*, I, 121-22; and Schnackenburg, *op. cit.*, I, 350.

[105] In the Synoptic tradition the episode of cleansing the Temple is followed by the Jews questioning the authority of Jesus (cf. Mt. 21,1-13.23; Mk. 11,15-17. 27-28; and Lk. 19,45-46 and 20,1-2). Having taken the pericope out of its context, the fourth evangelist brings in the Jews asking him for a sign – a traditional Jewish way of attesting the divine authority of one's mission (cf. Ex. 3,12.19-20; and Deut. 13,1-6 and 18,18-22). For details see I. Dunderberg, *Johannes und die Synoptiker. Studien zu Joh 1-9* (AASF.DHL 69) (Helsinki 1994).

Nathanael has been warned that his restricted Messianic faith would be toppled by a greater sign than that of the mysterious knowledge of Jesus.[106] In both episodes a reference to the cross is rubbing shoulders with the Messianic faith of the disciples. In fact the vision of the Son of Man promised by Jesus hints at the event of the cross – the sign *par excellence*. The first sign at Cana is considered as a manifestation of Jesus' *glory* (cf. 2,11).[107] In the fourth Gospel, the supreme revelation of the glory of Jesus is the event on the cross, where the work of the Father is accomplished (cf. 7,4-5; 12,23 and 17,1-2). The glory revealed at Cana, therefore, can only be an anticipation of the glory of Jesus on the cross.[108] The words of Jesus: "My hour has not yet come" (2,4) must also be interpreted in this sense, besides the narrator's introduction "on the third day" (2,1). The episode of the Temple, of course, refers clearly to the death and resurrection as a sign *par excellence*.[109]

Let me now pass on to the episodes of the Samaritan woman and the royal official (4,1-54). In Jn. 2 the point of departure was the traditional Jewish Messianism. There was the constant falling back on the cross, presented as the sign *par excellence* putting an end to the Jewish traditional, cultural and religious Messianic awaiting.[110] Just like the Jews, the Samaritans are taught here to surpass the limits of their cultural and religious traditions to have access to the benefits of salvation. Couched in story form Jesus is revealed gradually, in the course of the narrative of Jn. 4,[111] as one greater than Jacob (4,12), more than a prophet (4,19) and as one transcending the category of the Messiah of the Samaritans (4,25).[112] Jesus is the one sent by the Father whose mission is salvation (4,34ff.); he is the true "saviour of the world" (4,42). Just like the disciples (but contrary to

---

[106] See C. C. Caragounis, *The Son of Man. Vision and Interpretation* (WUNT 38) Tübingen 1986.

[107] See M. S. Collins, "The question of Doxa: A Socio-literary Reading of the Wedding at Cana," *BTB* 25 (1995) 100-9; and M. Pamment, "The Meaning of *Doxa* in the Fourth Gospel," *ZNW* 74 (1983) 12-16.

[108] From the beginning of the Cana wedding episode there is a hidden reference to the resurrection of Jesus in the mention of 'the third day' (cf. Jn. 19,31 and 20,1). See Thüsing, 94.

[109] The Temple in Jerusalem was the place where God made His name or glory dwell. Although God's presence was not confined to the Temple, it was generally understood that the sanctuary was, in some sense, Israel's tabernacle in the wilderness (Ex. 40,34) and the Temple that Solomon had built (1 Kings 8,10-11). The prophet Ezekiel said that the glory of God had left the first Temple at the time of the Babylonian exile, but he envisioned its return at the time of Israel's restoration (Ezek. 10,18-19; 11,22-23 and 43,1-5). Jesus' promise of a new Temple suggests that God's glory would be manifested, not in a building, but in a person, as it had been at Cana. See G. I. Davies, "The Presence of God in the Second Temple," in: Horbury, *Templum Amicitiae*, 32-36. Moreover, in the Synoptic tradition, to the Jews who ask for a sign, only the sign of Jona – the resurrection of Jesus (cf. Mt. 12,38-40 and 16,1-4; and Lk. 11,16. 29-32) – is given. Hence, Jn. 2 concludes with the announcement of the definitive sign, the cross as the theological moment of uniting the death and resurrection of Christ. The main arguments in favour of the fourth evangelist's conception of the cross as a sign are: The response of Jesus to the Jews asking for a sign (cf. 2,18-22); the use of the verb σημαίνων in connection with the elevation (cf. Jn. 12,32-33); the typology of Jn. 3,14-15 based on Num. 21,8-9 speaking about the bronze serpent set up on a 'pole/sign.' Cf. M. Girard, "La composition structurelle des sept 'signes' dans le quatrième évangile," *SR* 9 (1980) 315-24.

[110] In fact the cross will reveal that Jesus is the Son of Man and the eschatological Son sent by the Father and that the salvation offered by him will transcend the simple nationalistic preoccupations.

[111] See P. J. Cahil, "Narrative Art in John IV," *RSB* 2 (1982) 41-48.

[112] While the Jews awaited a royal/political Messiah who will lead to the establishment of a kingdom, the Samaritans had the concept of a Messiah, the *Ta'eb*, who would announce everything and reveal the truth (cf. Deut. 18,18-22). See J. Bowman, "Samaritan Studies I: The Fourth Gospel and the Samaritans," *BJRL* 40 (1958) 299; Lagrange, 115; and Schnackenburg, *op. cit.*, 441; see also F. Dexinger, *Der Taheb. Ein "messianischer" Heilsbringer der Samaritaner* (Salzburg 1986).

the Jews), the Samaritans are lead from their Messianic faith (4,29.39; cf. 2,11) to the implicit post-resurrectional belief in Jesus (4,41-42; cf. 2,22).

In these two parallel chapters, the transition from the traditional concept of the Messiah to the Christology of the fourth evangelist is exposed thematically through the replacement of traditional institutions. The crucified and risen Jesus would be a unifying symbol for God's people, as the Temple had been for the Jews before.[113] When Jesus halted trade in the Temple, he alluded to a portion of Scripture that envisioned all nations worshipping in Jerusalem (Zech. 14,16.21; cf. Jn. 2,16). In his crucified and risen body the promise was fulfilled; he became a sanctuary that transcended and replaced other places of worship (cf. 4,21) and endured beyond the destruction of the Jerusalem Temple (cf. 11,48) to unite the community of those called to worship in spirit and truth (cf. 4,24).

Just as the wine given by Jesus at the Cana wedding substituted the water meant for Jewish traditional ritual purification (cf. 2,6), the water given by the Patriarch Jacob is replaced by the living water of revelation (4,12-15)[114] promised by Jesus. In the same way, as pointed out already the wedding at Cana symbolised the inauguration of the new covenant – the eschatological marriage between Jesus and the people of the new Covenant. The same nuptial symbolism is suggested by the encounter with the Samaritan woman (and the Samaritan people). The soteriological link is made through the confession of faith in Jesus, the true 'saviour of the world.' The same themes also connect the episode of the Temple (2,12-22) with the dialogue on cult (4,20-26): Both national cults, centred on the Temple of Jerusalem and the sanctuary on Mount Gerizim respectively, will be replaced by the worship of the Father in spirit and in truth (4,21-24).[115]

There are a number of common themes in these two chapters, especially the surpassing of the traditional awaiting on the Messiah and that of the replacement of their respective institutions. However, there seems to be a fundamental difference as far as the soteriological aspect is concerned. In Jn. 2, although the sign of wine as well as that of the

---

[113] Reverence for the Jerusalem Temple helped to give a distinctive identity to Jews scattered across the Greco-Roman world and into Babylonia. Devout Jews prayed in the direction of the sanctuary (1 Kings 8,48; and Dan. 6,19) and sometimes prayed at the times sacrifices were offered (Jud. 9,1). When possible, they made pilgrimages or sent delegations to the festivals there. See S. Safrai and M. Stern, *The Jewish People in the First Century. Historical Geography, Political History, Social, Cultural and Religious Life and Institutions*, (Assen 1974) I, 117-215; and J. Neusner (ed.), *Judaism and their Messiahs at the Turn of the Christian Era* (Cambridge, New York 1987).

[114] Commentators are divided in their opinion with regard to the meaning of 'living water.' It can refer to a revelation brought by Jesus which corresponds to the use of water in the OT as symbol of Law, of the Word of God and of Wisdom which make man live in harmony with the will of God (Sir. 24,21ff. and 30ff.; Prov. 13,14 and 18,4; Wis. 9,17-18; and Is. 55,1-3 and 58,11; cf. Boismard, 139-40). Living water can also symbolise the Spirit as it is expressed in 7,37-39. In fact, one may think that living water indicates these two realities in a rapport not of opposition but of succession: the gift of the word of God is followed by the gift of the Spirit when Jesus will be glorified and return to the Father. This double reference to the word and the Spirit by the theme of living water is well known in the Jewish tradition, especially in connection with the traditions on the 'wells.' On this subject see A. Jaubert, "La symbolique du puits de Jacob (Jean 4,12)," in: H. de Lubac (ed.), *L'homme devant Dieu. Mélanges* (Lyon 1963) 63-73; his, "Symbolique de l'eau et connaissance de Dieu," *FV* 64 (1965) 455-63; and his, "Les images d'eau vive dans le judaïsme contemporain du IVe évangile," in: his *Approches de l'évangile de Jean* (Paris 1976) 140-46.

[115] The reader meets for the first time, the typical Johannine indication of his unique eschatological perspective: "the hour is coming, and is now here" (4,23). What Jesus is about to announce is eschatological, but one need not wait till the end of time for its availability: it is present because Jesus is present. See Barrett, 237. Beasley-Murray, *John*, 62 puts it well: the expression "brackets future and present without eliminating either."

Temple refer clearly to the elevation and glorification of Jesus on the cross as a decisive moment of Christological event, there is no mention of the salvific effect of that event as yet. On the contrary, Jn. 4 refers constantly to the eternal life produced by the living water (cf. 4,14), resulting in the harvest (cf. 4,36), and giving life to the royal official's son (cf. 4,50.51.53). This stress suits well to the confession of the Samaritans who acknowledge in Jesus the true "saviour of the world" (4,42).

Now, this soteriological perspective must be understood in connection with the mention of the 'hour' and the 'Father's work' (cf. 4,21.23.34.52.53). In 4,34 Jesus reveals to his disciples that his food is to do the will of Him who sent him and to complete His work.[116] The moment of accomplishment of this work on the cross is evoked by the theme of the 'hour' of Jesus.[117] It is the seventh hour, the perfect hour when the officer could hear the words of Jesus: "Your son will live" (4,53; cf. 4,50-52). It is finally the hour of the gift of the Spirit (cf. 19,30), the moment when the disciples will hear Jesus speaking openly about the Father (cf. 16,25). With the arrival of the 'hour' arrives also the 'worship in spirit and truth' (4,21.23), the time of the harvest[118] of fruits for eternal life (cf. 4,36).[119]

There is also a link between the demand for a sign on the part of 'the Jews' in Jerusalem (2,18) and the rebuke of Jesus against faith based on signs in 4,48 which betray the intention of the author to link the two pericopes structurally. The Jews asked Jesus for a sign to show his Messianic identity and to prove the divine origin of his mission (cf. 2,18). In reply Jesus gave the sign of the cross, his death and resurrection (cf. 2,19.21). For the fourth Gospel, the elevation on the cross is the meeting point of Christology and soteriology. It is the moment of perfect revelation of Jesus and of the total gift of salvation. Jn. 4, therefore, brings in this dimension of soteriology. The cross is the place *par excellence* of the gift of life, a reality which is anticipated in the healing of the official's son. Moreover, in 2,22 it is affirmed that the disciples "believed the scripture and the word that Jesus had spoken." In the same way, in 4,50, the royal official "believed the word that Jesus spoke to him." The literary and narrative correlation between the episode of the Temple and that of the healing of the royal official's son reveals more.[120] This reference to

---

[116] The will of the Father is that Jesus raises up all those He has given him and gives eternal life to those who see and believe him (cf. 6,39-40). That is the work of the Father entrusted to the Son. And it is on the cross that Jesus accomplishes fully the work of the Father (cf. 17,4 and 19,30).

[117] It is also the moment of his glorification (cf. 12,23.27 and 17,1), of his return to the Father (cf. 13,1). It is also the hour of salvation, the hour when the dead will raise hearing the voice of the Son of God (cf. 5,25.28).

[118] The hour of glorification of the Son of Man is the moment when, elevated from the earth, he will draw all men to himself (cf. 12,23.32). The narrative arrangement of 4,21.23 and 35 reveals a close link between the hour and the time of harvest. In 4,21.23 we read that "the hour is coming, and is now here," which corresponds to "then comes the harvest....the fields are ripe for harvesting (now)" (4,35). The harvest of fruits gathered is to be understood as the gathering of worshippers in spirit and truth.

[119] In the whole of the episode of the Samaritan woman only in 4,14 and 4,36 eternal life is mentioned establishing a relation between living water and harvest. In fact it is on the cross that Jesus gives living water (revelation and Spirit) in full for eternal life (cf. 7,37-39 and 19,30.34). It is also from the cross that Jesus will draw all men to himself (cf. 12,32) in a perfect harvest – total and unique – for eternal life (cf. 4,36). The cross is therefore the meeting point of the gift of Jesus and of the welcome of the believers, as it is indicated in 7,37-38: the believer comes towards Jesus to drink from the spring of living water which flows from his side.

[120] Note the critical position of the evangelist with regard to faith based on signs (cf. 2,23-25 and 4,48). Although Jesus had performed many signs before the Jews, they did not believe in him (cf. 12,37). In fact,

the faith in the word of Jesus indicates that the sign of the cross must be understood in connection with his word. The signs can lead to true faith only through the simultaneous acceptance of the revelatory word of Jesus. This must be all the more true of the perfect sign of the cross: it is Jesus himself who will unfold the real meaning at the elevation of the Son of Man to the place where he was before (cf. 3,13-14 and 6,62) and at his return to the Father (cf. 8,21-29 and 13,1).

C. Narrative Continuity and Correlation Between 1,19-51 and 2,1-22

1. Flow and Gradualness

Here, we try to establish literary indicators which suggest a transition from one scene to the next. Apart from the coherence that is to be expected in any well-told account, the description of the successive days and the Temple-cleansing contains a strong emphasis on narrative continuity. As the story moves forward, earlier phrases reappear in varied form, and it is through this process of *repetition and variation*[121] that the narrative is forged into a unity. One of the basic features of repetition in the fourth Gospel is that it is carefully graded. The text moves slowly from suggestion or intimation to a narrative which is more and more explicit. For example, with regard to the disciples, the evangelist first gives suggestions or implications of belief (when Andrew calls Simon, and when Philip calls Nathanael) and then gives three belief statements which are not only explicit but increasingly elaborate (cf. 1,50 and 2,11.22). And by referring to the 'third day, 'hour' 'glory,' and 'destruction of the Temple' Jesus' coming death and resurrection are hinted at.

Just as the announcement of greater things in 1,51 is a secret, there is an element of secrecy or mystery in 2,1-11. Unlike the servants, the steward does not know the source of the wine, and as he calls the bridegroom to express his surprise, the focus again shifts – this time from the wine to the secret, and to the timing of the secret – "you have kept the good wine *until now*" (2,10). These two ideas, *time and secrecy*, are not peripheral to the basic drama. Rather they are important aspects of what the drama is all about – the process of revelation. Revelation – the unveiling of the secret – must await a particular time. When the mother of Jesus says, "Do whatever he tells you..." (2,5) a sense of waiting and expectation – a sense of pregnant time – is created. This corresponds to some of the most basic elements of these two chapters. Moreover, the fact that the wine is given 'on the third day' is also associated with Jesus' 'hour' and with his 'glory;' this means that it is an outflow of that final hour when Jesus will be glorified, when he will pass from this world to the Father (cf. 13,1 and 17,1).

Furthermore, the wine in question has to do with togetherness, the ultimate togetherness of Jesus with his Father. As Schnackenburg indicates, it is no accident that the miracle of the wine is preceded by a picture of exuberant two-way communication with God – angels ascending and descending upon the Son of Man (1,51).[122] Nor is it an

---

the evangelist will make us understand that the cross is not a sign which only signifies a wonder and a visible manifestation (cf. 4,48); it is also a sign which cannot be rightly interpreted without having recourse to the word of Jesus.

[121] See K. R. R. Gros Louis, *Literary Interpretations of Biblical Narratives II* (Nashville 1982) 58; Culpepper, *Anatomy*, 74 and 200; Alter, 88-113; and Sternberg, 365-440.

[122] Schnackenburg, *op. cit.*, 338. According to Brodie (*Gospel*, 173) the idea that togetherness (being in communion with someone) is like drinking wine, is not unique to the Gospel.

accident that it is set in a context which evokes intimacy. In other words, the wine is presented in the context of a wedding, which in various ways suggests intimate two-way communication. It is a union which may indeed take an extra dimension with death, but it is already present. In the Cana scene there is a highlighting of the idea of revelation – the fact that at Cana Christ's power brings into the world a revelation of glory. It is necessary, however, to complement that emphasis by another one which is equally important. It is through the confidence of the mother of Jesus and in the attentive servants and disciples that the miracle happens. It is through their grasping of his word and of its meaning – in other words through their response – that the revelation is fulfilled. Their attitude is one of contemplative alertness, and it is through that attitude and disposition of heart and mind, that the wine flows – there is revelation.

Though there are a lot of parallels in themes and literary devices we do not go into such details here as the scope of my study is finally restricted to 2,23-3,36. Moreover, it involves a lot of repetition of what has already been exposed in the correlation of 1,19-51 with 2,23-3,36, and 2,1-22 with 4,1-54. We shall, therefore, explore only the Christological development observed in these units that might help to understand the unit of my study better.

2. Narrative Christology

As D. M. Smith rightly describes, "the Gospel of John is a story, a narrative of Jesus' ministry."[123] The fourth evangelist, according to him, portrays the character of Jesus in such a manner that "Jesus continuously talks about Christology, often in debate with opponents."[124] Now, what is the purpose of the fourth evangelist in placing the episode of the cleansing of the Temple at the beginning of Jesus' public life unlike in the Synoptics?

The delegation of priests and Levites sent by the Jews of Jerusalem suspected that the Baptist could be a part of their vision of the Messianic times. They came to survey on the person of the Baptist because of the baptism he was administering and questioned his authority to administer such a baptism. Indirectly they demanded for a demonstration of the divine origin of his mission in order that his authority may be recognised. If the Baptist were the Messiah, Elijah or the prophet, his action would be justified (1,19-21). They listened to the negative witness of the Baptist;[125] the reader was part of that audience.

A similar theme concludes Jn. 2. One should probably assume that 'the Jews' in the Jerusalem Temple (2,20) were also looking for an eschatological figure. They demanded for a sign from Jesus to attest his authority allowing him to drive the traders away from the Temple. God alone or His Messiah could execute such an action disrupting the central institution of the Jewish religion. Jesus must, therefore, attest with a sign, to prove his divine authority and thus his Messianic identity.[126] These two interventions of the Jews at the beginning and end of these two chapters form a sort of inclusion and knit them together.

---

[123] D. M. Smith, *The Theology of the Gospel of John* (Cambridge 1995) 20.

[124] *Ibid.*, 86.

[125] Cf. Rinke, *Kerygma und Autopsie*, 84-85.

[126] See the detailed study of M. D. Hooker, *The Signs of a Prophet: The Prophetic Actions of Jesus* (Minneapolis 1997).

From the testimony of the Baptist we know that the primary purpose of his testimony is to reveal Jesus, the Son of God, to Israel (cf. 1,31.34). The Baptist is not the Messiah, nor Elijah, nor the prophet; he has been sent by God before the Messiah (cf. 1,6-8; 1,21.25 and 3,28). One cannot miss to observe in Jn. 1-2 a fulfilment of Mal. 3,1:[127] "See, I am *sending my messenger to prepare the way before me*, and the Lord whom you seek *will suddenly come to his temple*. The messenger of the covenant in whom you delight – indeed, he is coming, says the Lord of hosts." The Baptist is to be considered the messenger sent by God to prepare the eschatological arrival of the Messiah before he himself would come into his Temple for the purification of the cult on the day of Judgement. His special function consists in designating Jesus as the Messiah who will baptise with the Holy Spirit, and lead the people to him. Thanks to the testimony of the Baptist, a first group of disciples join Jesus – a movement that culminates in the revelation of the glory of Jesus at the Cana wedding (2,11); through the faith of the disciples, the Messianic community is constituted. Revealed and recognised as the Messiah, Jesus enters into the Temple to execute the renewal awaited and foretold by the prophet.[128] In this perspective the fourth evangelist has placed the episode of the cleansing of the Temple at the beginning of the ministry of Jesus which fulfils what has been foretold by Malachi. This prophecy helps to clarify the diptych relationship suggested by Jn. 1-2 and interpret Jesus' cleansing of the Temple. In Jesus God Himself has come into His Temple; he is "the Lord whom you seek" and "the messenger of the covenant in whom you delight" (Mal. 3,1b).

In Jn. 1 the evangelist has accumulated most of the Christological titles placed on the lips of the Baptist and the first disciples. We have already exposed the Messianic colouring of those titles. Seen against this back-drop of the prophecy of Malachi, the episodes of the wedding at Cana and the cleansing of the Temple are also clothed with such a Messianic character. In the first chapter the list of Messianic titles culminate in the confession of Jesus as "the Son of God and King of Israel" (1,49). The juxtaposition of these two titles lay bare the direct and full designation of Jesus as the Messiah. There is a certain continuity between the designation of Jesus by Nathanael as "Son of God and King of Israel" and the revelation of Jesus as the Messiah in the Cana wedding narrative.[129]

---

[127] Cf. Loader, *Christology*, 40; and Létourneau, *Jésus*, 93-96 is of the opinion that this prophecy gives the reason for the position and structure of these two chapters in the fourth Gospel.

[128] See Giblet, "Prophétisme," 85-130.

[129] The text couples the proclamation of Jesus' Messiahship (by the disciples) with the miracle of the wine without explicitly stating how they are related. Readers themselves must forge the link between the disciples' testimony and the miracle at Cana. Philip's confession directs attention to the Law and the Prophets. Readers familiar with the Scriptures would probably have known that one of the Law's most important Messianic passages said that a ruler would come from the tribe of Judah to command the obedience of the peoples: "The scepter shall not depart from Judah, nor the ruler's staff from between his feet, until tribute comes to him; and the obedience of the peoples is his. Binding his foal to the vine and his donkey's colt to the choice vine, he washes his garments in wine and his robe in the blood of grapes; his eyes are darker than wine, and his teeth whiter than milk" (Gen. 49,10-12). Several of the prophetic writings looked for a new outpouring of divine favour upon Israel, saying that on that day "the mountains shall drip sweet wine, and all the hills shall flow with it" (Amos 9,13; cf. Joel 3,18; and Is. 25,6). By the late first century, Jewish tradition associated this lavish outpouring of wine with the advent of the Messiah. See M. Hengel, "The Interpretation of the Wine Miracle at Cana: John 2:1-11," in: Hurst and Wright, *Glory of Christ*, 101; see also 83-112; and R. E. Brown, *op. cit.*, 105. Note also the eschatological and Messianic connotation of the wedding at Cana already treated above.

Here, in the first revelation of the glory of Jesus (2,1-11), a new summit is reached.[130] But if we consider that both chapters together constitute the fulfilment of the prophecy of Malachi, it is only with the cleansing of the Temple that the Messianic progression reaches its highest summit. In driving away the traders from the Temple, Jesus announces cryptically the restoration of this central institution and the inauguration of the new worship awaited at the definitive coming of the Messianic era.

I must, however, remember the fact that the story of Jesus' coming to the Temple (2,12-22) refers proleptically to the death and resurrection of Jesus. Ps. 69,9[131] quoted analeptically in 2,17 announces the death of Jesus and indicates a link between the Messianic act of Jesus in the Temple and his death that it hints at.[132] The Temple that Jesus is going to raise up in three days is his resurrected body (cf. 2,20-22). Therefore, for the fourth evangelist, the prophecy of Malachi – which links the coming of the Lord into His Temple, the judgement and the purification of worship – finds its fulfilment in the death and resurrection of Jesus. The restoration or purification that Jesus executes in the Temple[133] is, therefore, only an anticipation of the true and eschatological restoration to take place at the time of the 'lifting up of the Son of Man.'

Moreover, the intention of this episode is to present Jesus as the true Temple, the house of God. A. T. Hanson finds a link between these two chapters, in the sense that there is a transition from 1,51 to 2,17 – a transition from Messiah as place of God's presence to Messiah as the *house of God*.[134] For Smith 1,51 evokes Gen. 28,12, where in Jacob's dream at *Bethel* angels ascend and descend upon the ladder into heaven, or as it is

---

[130] The narrator has used the present tense of the verb καὶ λέγει αὐτῷ (1,51) to report direct speech of Jesus that reaches outside story time into the plotted time of a promised future sight of the Son of Man. Jesus accepted Messianic titles from his disciples but intimated that his identity was not confined to Jewish expectations. Before going to Cana he told them they would see heaven opened, and the angels of God ascending and descending upon the Son of Man (1,51). People might expect the Messiah to enjoy the kind of honour or glory normally granted to a ruler, but readers were to be told that Jesus' glory was of another order: It was 'the glory as of a father's only son' (1,14). This comment together with Jesus' promise about the heaven opening, enables readers to see the sign as a demonstration of Jesus' divinity as well as his Messiahship. There were, perhaps, some precedents for this in the Scriptures, which associated the outpouring of wine with God's own presence among His people (Joel 3,17-18; and Is. 25,6); yet such ideas go well beyond traditional Messianic expectations. The Davidic Messiah is associated with the manifestation of God's glory, but it is not apparent that the glory is manifested in his person. The promise to Nathanael of 'greater things' in 1,50 is to a certain degree fulfilled in the revelation of his glory (2,11). See Lütgehetmann, 292; see also 293-316 for the Christological meaning of the pericope.

[131] It is a Psalm of the righteous sufferer; the very next line is quoted by Paul in Rom. 15,3 to refer to Christ's vicarious suffering.

[132] This word contains a reference to the death of Jesus, because it is the Jews who are supposed to destroy the Temple.

[133] The function of sacrifice, which was integral to the Jerusalem Temple, is fulfilled and replaced by Jesus. The animals and birds mentioned in 2,14 were prescribed by the Levitical code for sacrifices used for atonement and purification (Lev. 1,13-17). By temporarily disrupting the trade necessary for sacrifice, Jesus foreshadowed the permanent cessation of sacrificial worship in Jerusalem and its replacement by his own death. His action took place during the feast of Passover, when lambs were slain to commemorate Israel's deliverance from death and slavery; Jesus would be crucified at Passover two years later as "the lamb of God who takes away the sin of the world" (1,29). The water-baptism of preparation administered by the and the water jars meant for purification (2,6), the sacrifices at the Temple for atonement and purification also knit the two chapters together.

[134] Cf. A. T. Hanson, 43-44.

possible to construe from the Hebrew, upon Jacob (Israel) himself.[135] Besides, in 2,16 (οἶκος ἐμπορίου) there is also a reference to Zech. 14,21: "And there shall no longer be traders in the house of the Lord of hosts on that day." In my opinion, the evangelist seems to stress the continuing importance of the scripture to understand Jesus. The revelation in Jesus harks back to and recapitulates the revelation of God to Israel. Moreover, revelation, that is, God's self-manifestation in Jesus, is precisely the theme of the fourth evangelist. Hence, once again, the theme of revelation is sounded as Jesus makes his epiphany at the Temple in Jerusalem, the place of revelation. It is *Bethel*, the house of God, where God reveals Himself to His people. Maillet agrees with Léon-Dufour's conclusion in his Dictionary of the NT: *"la maison de Dieu es maintenant la terre; c'est la maison qu'habite Jésus."*[136] So the angels who are to be found on the ladder are going from one house of God (the Father) to another (the Son).

The fourth evangelist introduces Jesus beginning his public ministry with two symbolic actions that are juxtaposed in Jn. 2. In many ways the two actions are different. One is a miracle and the other not. One is festive and the other violent. At Cana Jesus' mother and disciples responded favourably to him, but at Jerusalem the crowd reacted with scepticism and unreliable belief. Yet both episodes include conversation that help disclose the significance of these actions, and both utilise Jewish institutions to reveal something about who Jesus is: The water at Cana is contained in jars used for Jewish purification rites, and the Jerusalem Temple is the central Jewish sanctuary. Both foreshadow the passion, directing the readers to reflect on their significance in the light of Jesus' death and resurrection.

Moreover, as already explained above, the two episodes of Jn. 2 are connected in the use of the word σημεῖον (2,11.18). Hence, the Cana miracle was the beginning of Jesus' signs and the second looks forward to the last and the greatest of the signs – the 'lifting up of the Son of Man.' The absence of a discourse attached to the Cana miracle may to some extent be accounted for. The evangelist does not offer a discourse, but an incident which, when seen in the light of the cross and resurrection, explains the true meaning of all the signs. It is as if the evangelist is indicating in his extremely subtle manner the true meaning of all the signs just after he has described the first sign. They all point to the nature of the Messiah, whose true function can be understood only after his elevation and glorification.[137] At the end of these two chapters the evangelist wants to show to the reader that death and resurrection of Jesus is *the* sign surpassing the Messianic awaiting and is *the* reality toward which the entire Christology of his Gospel is oriented.[138]

---

[135] *Bethel* in Hebrew means 'house of God,' and in the Genesis story Jacob exclaims after his dream: "This is none other than the house of God, and this is the gate of heaven" (Gen. 28,17). See D. M. Smith, *Theology*, 24; see also Neyrey, "Jacob Allusions," 586-605; Moloney, *Son of Man*, 23-41; and C. C. Rowland, "John 1.51, Jewish Apocalyptic and Targumic Tradition," *NTS* 30 (1984) 498-507.

[136] H. Maillet, "'Au-Dessous' ou 'Sur'? (Jean 1/51)," *ÉTR* 59 (1984) 210-11.

[137] All the Gospels, as well as the rest of the New Testament, take Jesus to be the awaited Messiah. No Gospel makes the element of fulfilment more explicit than the fourth. Perhaps the fourth evangelist recognised most clearly that the crucifixion of Jesus spelled the end of any traditional Messianic conception.

[138] Thus 2,18-22 prepares the way for the development of the Christological exposition in the following chapters. In fact, the theme of signs will be taken up immediately in 2,23-3,2 and of the cross in 3,11ff.

D. Narrative Continuity and Correlation Between 2,23-3,36 and 4,1-54

The fourth Gospel depicts encounters between Jesus and many people. Often the individuals are paired in the narrative, which provides opportunities to assess their character through comparison and contrast.[139] The first pair consists of Nicodemus and the Samaritan woman – two figures whose representative significance is highly developed in these two chapters.

1. Between 2,23-3,36 and 4,1-42

a. Characterisation

The story of Nicodemus and that of the Samaritan woman are set in marked contrast to one another:

The Story of Nicodemus (3,1-15)	*The Story of the Samaritan woman (4,1-42)*
takes place in Jerusalem	takes place in Samaria
the context is the city	the context is the countryside
happens at night	happens at noon
focuses on a man	focuses on a woman
the man is a Jew	the woman is a Samaritan
the man is socially respectable	the woman has a history of immorality
Nicodemus initiates the dialogue	Jesus initiates the dialogue
Nicodemus descends into misunderstanding	the woman comes to faith
Nicodemus fails to see Jesus as the world's Saviour (3,16)	the woman and her village see Jesus as the Saviour of the world (4,42)[140]

There are a lot of other similarities between the two characters:[141] The preparedness of the Samaritan woman to accept Jesus as a prophet (4,19) and possibly as the Messiah (4,25.29) echoes the response of Nicodemus in 3,1-12. He was prepared to accept that Jesus was a 'Rabbi,' a teacher from God who did great signs and who had God with him (3,2). The ideas of Nicodemus are earthbound as the dialogue between him and Jesus reveals sufficiently well the contrasts between: born of flesh and born of the Spirit (3,6), born of water and born of the Spirit (3,5), born from below and born from above (cf. 3.3.7), earthly things and heavenly things   eternal life/kingdom of God[142] (3,12; cf. 3,5.15-16f.), darkness and light (3,19-21), salvation and condemnation (3,17-18). Similarly, the words of the Samaritan woman add to her earth-bound atmosphere: She is engrossed by the practicalities of the well – the need for a bucket, its depth, the fact that it had been used once not only by Jacob himself but also to provide water for his sons and cattle, and her own need to come and draw (4,11-12.15b). She is also focussed on a form of 'flesh' – on short-term marriages and affairs with men (4,18).

---

[139] On the use of juxtaposition in the Gospel see Koester, "Hearing," 327-48.

[140] Stibbe, *John*, 62. See also C. M. Conway, *Men and Women in the Fourth Gospel: Gender and Johannine Charcterization* (SBL.DS 167) (Missoula 1999); M. Pazdan, "Nicodemus and the Samaritan Woman: Contrasting Models of Discipleship," *BTB* 17 (1987) 145-48; and M. J. Selvidge, "Nicodemus and the woman with Five Husbands," *Pro* 2 (1982) 63-75.

[141] Cf. W. Munro, "The Pharisee and the Samaritan in John: Polar or Parallel?," *CBQ* 57 (1995) 710-28.

[142] Most commentators affirm that the 'kingdom of God' in the fourth Gospel is to be identified with 'eternal life' or 'the heavenly realm of God on high to which the divine envoy leads.' Cf. Schnackenburg, *op. cit.*, 366-67.

Yet it is within this situation that Jesus speaks to both. Starting from the things most on their minds he leads them to an awareness of higher things and to a desire to communicate that awareness to others. Both of them fall into *misunderstanding* (cf. 3,4.9 and 4,11) and *irony* (3,10 and 4,12). Both show some knowledge of tradition (cf. 3,2).[143] That the Samaritan woman has knowledge of tradition concerning Jacob (4,12), Jerusalem (4,20) and a Messiah (4,25), and shows openness and perceptiveness. The man who came to Jesus by night and the woman who came to draw water end up by receiving a whole new revelation (cf. 3,13-21 and 4,10.13-15.21-24.26). Just as the conversation with Nicodemus suggested the possibility of an ascent to God, so also here; but in a more developed and down-to-earth form the episode of the Samaritan woman suggests a form of ascent – "the drama of a soul struggling to rise from the things of this world to believe in Jesus."[144] While Nicodemus leaves silently without leaving any trace of his reaction, the Samaritan woman becomes, for the whole people, an instrument leading to salvation.

Interwoven with the story of the woman is that of the disciples. The disciples had to be removed from the scene, so that Jesus could have his conversation with the Samaritan woman (4,8). Their presence would have rendered Jesus' revelation of himself to the non-Jewish world impossible, for "Jews do not share things in common with Samaritans" (4,9). But in many ways they are like her – intent on the practicalities of life (on buying food), and with little understanding of Jesus (they call him 'Rabbi' – 4,31). But when Jesus has a conversation with them, as he did with the woman, they, too, emerge as evangelisers (cf. 4,31-38).

b. Themes

An examination of the text (2,23-4,54) shows the idea of *'coming'* (ἔρχομαι) to Jesus, mentioned explicitly: The coming to Jesus of Nicodemus (3,2) is parallel to that of the Samaritan woman (4,7), and the coming of 'all' to baptism (3,26) is similar to that of the Samaritans coming to Jesus (4,40). Taken together, these references build a sense of concerted movement of people coming toward Jesus from all sides as individuals and in groups. The idea of Jesus' *staying* with the Samaritans in Sychar (4,40) represents the process of betrothal and finds confirmation in the context. The preceding scene (3,22-36) gives interrelated images of Jesus staying with the disciples (3,22),[145] a whole people

---

[143] Out of his knowledge Nicodemus is prepared to accept Jesus as a teacher from God and as a prophet. He even goes so far as to say that no one could do these signs unless God was with him, a dignity reserved for the great figures of Israel. LXX Ex. 3,12 applies this title to Moses. In Jer. 1,8 the prophet is told that Yahweh is 'with him.' Bernard (I, 101) claims that this phrase "expressed the general belief of Judaism" about great Israelites. See also Barrett, 205.

[144] R. E. Brown, *op. cit.*, 178. See also J. E. Botha, *Jesus and the Samaritan Woman: A Speech Act Reading of John 4:1-42* (NT.S 65) (New York 1991).

[145] Thus, what was suggested at Cana becomes somewhat clearer: Jesus communicates a presence which is better than wedding wine. But there is also a difference to be noted. Jesus' hesitancy in Jerusalem, his sudden caution (2,23-25), implied an element of withdrawal. Even when he was with his disciples, precisely when he was described as baptising (3,22), his togetherness with them was described as 'sojourning' (διατρίβω), in other words, as a process of just passing through, living like an alien, living on limited time (cf. also 11,54). In 4,40 the verb used is 'remaining' (μένω) (cf. also 1,38.39). Cf. Moloney, *Belief in the Word*, 173; see also the recent work of Scholtissek, *In ihm sein und bleiben*; and J. Heise, *Bleiben - Menein in den Johanneischen Schriften* (HUTh 8) (Tübingen 1967).

('all') coming to Jesus (3,26), and of his *relationship* to the disciples/people as that of a groom to a bride (3,29).

The act of *worshipping* is described by the use of the verb προσκυνεῖν. It implies the act of bending or prostrating oneself in the direction of the one worshipped.[146] The expression 'in spirit and *truth*' (4,24) finds its parallel where Nicodemus is told that those who are begotten ἄνωθεν of water and *spirit* (3,3-5) come to the light and do *what is true* (3,21).

Although the narrative to this point has been carefully set within the Jewish world, and all the responses to Jesus have come from the Jews, the *universal saving will of God* is made explicit in 3,16-17: "God so loved the *world* that he *gave* his only Son so that *everyone* who believes in him may not perish but may have eternal life... God did not send the Son into the *world* to condemn the *world*, but in order that the *world* might be saved through him." This recalls the prologue (1,10-13) and prepares the reader for a narrative dedicated to the Samaritans and a Gentile. Moreover, a loving God who *gives* His Son to save the *world* is echoed in 'the *gift* of God' (4,10)[147] – promised by Jesus to the Samaritan woman. Jesus himself is the gift of God (1,14.16-17). He makes God known (1,18) and thus offers the possibility of eternal life to those who are begotten ἄνωθεν of water and spirit (3,5).

c. Literary Device

Besides, in all these four episodes, there is an *introduction/report*: Just as the coming of Nicodemus, as already mentioned, is introduced by the brief account of Jesus' Jerusalem ministry – the reaction to his signs and his knowledge of the human person (2,23-25) – the coming of the Samaritan woman, too, is introduced by an enigmatic picture of various administrators (Jesus and the disciples) of baptism and by a cryptic reference (through the image of exhaustion – 4,6) to the ultimate departure of Jesus (4,1-6). In the same way the account of people coming to the Baptist and Jesus is introduced by a picture of the baptismal ministries (of Jesus and the Baptist) and by a reference to the impending demise (through imprisonment) of the Baptist (3,22-24).[148]

d. Verbal Parallels

The reader is not surprised by the title 'saviour' (σωτήρ – 4,42) on the lips of the Samaritans,[149] as he has already learned from the reliable witness of Jesus himself that "God did not send the Son into the world to condemn the world, but in order that the world might be *saved* through him" (ἵνα σωθῇ ὁ κόσμος δι' αὐτοῦ – 3,17).

---

[146] In this context, where holy mountains and their sanctuaries are being excluded, true worship is the orientation of oneself toward the Father Himself in such a way that He becomes the imperative of one's life. See H. Greeven, "προσκυνέω," *TDNT*, VI, 760-61; see also Okure, 116.

[147] Okure (98) summarises the meaning of 'the gift of God' as 'something which is inseparably linked with the person of Jesus, and belongs to the order of revelation and proclamation.' See also L. Blomberg, "The Globalisation of Biblical Interpretation: A Test Case – John 3-4," *BBR* 5 (1995) 1-15.

[148] Note also the coming of the royal official to Jesus (4,47) being introduced by a summary of the Galileans' reactions to Jesus – a reaction which is explicitly connected with Jesus' earlier brief ministry in Jerusalem (4,43-45; cf. 2,23-25).

[149] See Barrett, 243: "The Samaritans speak the language of Johannine Christology."

The Baptist describes himself at his final appearance as the friend of the bridegroom who "stands and hears (ἀκούων) him" (3,29). The Samaritans, having had the experience of the presence of Jesus come to faith in Jesus saying "we believe, for we have heard (ἀκηκόαμεν) for ourselves" (4,42). Only on the basis of their hearing they claim "to know (οἴδαμεν) that this is indeed the saviour of the world" (4,42). The reader recalls that Nicodemus also 'knew' about Jesus (3,2), but his knowledge came from his own traditions and expectations. But the knowledge of the Samaritans comes from their hearing. The knowledge of Jesus (γινώσκω – 2,24.25) and that of Nicodemus (οἶδα – 3,2.8) at the beginning of the chapter and the knowledge of the Samaritan woman, of the Samaritans (οἶδα – 4,10.22.25.32.42), and of the royal official (γινώσκω – 4,53) at the end of the episodes suggest a type of inclusion.

2. Between 2,23-3,36 and 4,43-54

a. Characterisation

In both narratives an individual, belonging to the group indicated earlier, approaches Jesus: in 3,2 ("ἦλθεν πρὸς αὐτὸν") and in 4,47 ("ἀπῆλθεν πρὸς αὐτὸν"). In 2,23-25 many in Jerusalem believed in his name because they saw the signs he was doing. One of them, a Pharisee, named Nicodemus comes to Jesus (3,2), probably with good intentions, but his response does not show anything more than the faith expressed in 2,23-25. At the end of his encounter with Jesus there is no mention about his confession of faith in Jesus or in his words. On the contrary, in 4,45-54 the Galileans welcome Jesus[150] and one of them, the royal official of Capernaum, comes to him; his response at the end is one of total belief along with his whole household.

b. Verbal Parallels

Many factors confirm the close relation between the two narratives: First of all, the parallelism between the introductory verses of both narratives, *viz.*, 2,23-25 and 4,43-45. The remark of the narrator: "... the Galileans *welcomed him, since they had seen all that he had done in Jerusalem at the festival*" (4,45) echoes the narrator's notice: "When he was *in Jerusalem* during the Passover festival, many believed in his name *because they saw the signs that he was doing*" (2,23). Moreover, the recurrence of the verb 'testify' (μαρτυρέω) in 2,25 and 4,44 is to be noted.

c. Themes

Faith in Jesus provoked by *signs seen* is the important relation coupling the two pericopes. Nicodemus confesses, at the beginning of his encounter, that Jesus is a teacher come from God. This confession of Nicodemus, a Pharisee, rests on the signs performed by Jesus which demonstrate his relation with God. Even though *seeing signs* may turn the audience towards the right direction of relating with God, it does not necessarily lead to right

---

[150] This is the only place in the fourth Gospel where the verb 'welcome' (δέχομαι – 4,45) occurs in the fourth Gospel. In the Synoptics the verb is used in most cases to describe the welcome of Jesus (cf. Mt. 10,40-41; 18,5; Mk. 9,37; and Lk. 9,48), of the disciples (cf. Mt. 10,14.40; Mk. 6,11; and Lk. 9,5 and 10,8.10) or of the Kingdom (cf. Mk. 10,15; and Lk. 18,17). The term has been used in most cases very positively and hence, we can take it for granted that in this case the welcome contains an aspect of faith taking into account the context in which it is found.

understanding of Jesus and true faith (comp. 3,2 with 20,30-31). That is why Jesus is very sceptical about the faith generated solely by signs (cf. 2,23-24).[151] Having heard that Jesus had arrived at Cana in Galilee, a royal official comes from Capernaum to request Jesus to go down to Capernaum and heal his son before he dies (cf. 4,46-47). Jesus answers him: "Unless you see signs and wonders you will not believe" (4,48). This verse is very important to interpret the episode, because it contains the true meaning of the story. Without 4,48, the narrative will be a simple miracle story placing the stress on the power of Jesus and on the faith of the royal official. But the response provoked by Jesus makes us observe carefully the fact that the royal official believed without seeing.[152] Hence, the purpose of 4,48 is to present us an example of perfect faith, not generated by seeing signs.

Fortna indicates that 4,48 "conflicts sharply with the context."[153] At one level this is true, but the fact that a text appears to conflict with its context does not necessarily mean that it is a redactional insertion. What needs to be asked is not whether the text involves *conflict* but whether the conflict has any meaning in the context. In this case, the conflict has meaning; it is a way of indicating that the process of believing (the focus of the episode) is conflictual. In other words, believing is not a smooth development, one that follows the normal flow of feelings and logic. On the contrary, it cuts across one's accustomed patterns. In the encounter with Nicodemus Jesus did not respond to the orderly thoughts of Nicodemus in the same way. He challenges the now-confused Nicodemus to enter a new realm of thought and reality (3,3-4). In the episode involving the Baptist and his disciples there is conflict or disruption of another kind – the dispute with the old Jewish order (3,25-27). And when the Samaritan woman enters, she finds Jesus' words to be extremely perplexing – at odds with her established expectations and perceptions (cf. 4,9.11-12). The association of faith with conflict or disruption is part of the pattern of the fourth Gospel.

The word *sign* is also used in a negative way; it is used as a basis for superficial faith – of those in Jerusalem (2,23-24), including Nicodemus (3,2). The warning of Jesus in 4,48 is to be seen from this perspective. It is never said of the Galileans or of the royal official that they had a signs-induced superficial faith. In fact, the description of the Galileans' reaction to what Jesus had done in Jerusalem omits the two crucial words 'signs' and 'faith' (cf. 4,45). The effect of Jesus' actions on them was not superficial faith, but a welcoming attitude, a predisposition to faith. And the royal official manifests the same pre-disposition. Though Jesus' warning to the Galileans (cf. 4,48), however much it may echo the reaction of Jesus in Jerusalem (cf. 2,23), brings out the contrast between the two.

Ultimately the contrast between the two kinds of signs is part of a larger contrast or tension – the contrast between the geographical poles of this entire section of the Gospel, between Jerusalem at one end and Galilee at the other (2,23-4,54). Jerusalem seems to evoke Jerusalem-based Judaism. Galilee however, evokes the world of the Gentiles. It is a

---

[151] Cf. H. von Lips, "Anthropologie und Wunder im Johannesevangelium. Die Wunder Jesu im Johannesevangelium im Unterschied zu den synoptischen Evangelien auf dem Hintergrund johanneischen Menschenverständnisses," *EvTh* 50 (1990) 296-311.

[152] Cf. Moloney, *John*, 153-56; and his *Belief in the Word*, 184-89.

[153] Fortna, *Fourth Gospel and its Predecessor*, 64.

tension which is reflected in various ways in which the narrative, with more and more transparency, moves slowly but steadily from Jerusalem to Galilee. While his fatherland rejected Jesus, the Galileans welcomed him.[154] And it is precisely at the opposite poles of the text (2,23 and 4,54) that one finds the contrasting references to "τὰ σημεῖα" and the "δεύτερον σημεῖον."

A soteriological theme, too, links the two pericopes. In Jn. 3 the reader is told that the Son of Man is the one who has descended from heaven (καταβάς – 3,13) and that he must be raised up so that whoever believes in him may have eternal life (3,15). The same theme is repeated in 3,16, that God gave His only Son, so that everyone who believes in him may have *eternal life*. The same is insisted upon again in 3,17: "God sent his Son into the world in order that the world might be saved through him." This is echoed in 4,46-54. The narrative is structured in such a way that all the important elements are repeated twice or even thrice. The request of the royal official asking Jesus *to go down* to heal his son before he dies is repeated twice (4,47 and 49). The verbs 'to descend' and 'to die' are explicitly repeated: Jesus has to *descend* in order that the son *may not die* (may be healed or saved). The life giving word of Jesus, "Your son will live" is, on the other hand, repeated thrice (4,50.51.53), laying the accent on the life given to the son.[155] Finally, the response of faith is also repeated twice (4,50.53) and the term '*hour*' occurs thrice (cf. 4,52-53).[156] The royal official believes, not just because Jesus gave life at the seventh hour, but all the more that he will give Life at *his Hour* (when he is lifted up on the cross).

Other themes echoing in both the chapters are '*father* and *life*.' 4,46-54 is a powerful father-son story.[157] It is carefully integrated with the narrative as a whole. Its emphasis on life builds on the theme of life which was announced in Jn. 3 (cf. 3,15-16.36) and developed in Jn. 4 particularly in the discussion on 'living water' (life giving water) (4,10-15). In addition, the father-son emphasis brings to the fore a motif which has been presented in various ways from the beginning of the Gospel (cf. 1,14.18 and 3,16.36 and the father motif in 4,21-23).

One observes also a dissimilarity of relation between the two pericopes in 3,12 and 4,50. In the former, Jesus addresses his listeners: "If I have told you about earthly things and you *do not believe*, how can you believe if I tell you about heavenly things?" Hence, the question is *not believing* in *things told by Jesus*. In 4,50 one hears exactly the opposite: "The man believed the word that Jesus spoke to him..." Here, it is the question of *believing* in the *word spoken by Jesus*.

---

[154] See the edition of S. Freyne, *Galilee and Gospel: Collected Essays* (Tübingen 1999).

[155] In 4,47 the royal official begs Jesus to come down and *heal* (ἰάομαι) his son. But in 4,50.51.53 Jesus says, "your son will *live*" (ζάω). In the Synoptics, in the apparently similar stories, the verb used is (ἰάομαι – Mt. 8,13; ὑγιαίνω – Lk. 7,10). The fourth evangelist has used this verb consciously to stress the theme of his Gospel, *viz.*, those who believe in the Son of God may have eternal life (cf. 3,15-17 and 20,31). It reminds the reader of the allusions to Jesus as the giver of life (3,16.36 and 4,14). Often it is the question of the hour of Jesus (ἡ ὥρα μου – 2,4 and 13,1), the hour of his elevation/glorification on the cross (cf. 4,21.23; 5,25.28; 12,23.27 and 17,1). The healing of the official's son at the seventh hour – perfect hour – anticipates the gift of eternal life at the hour when Jesus will be elevated. See also Létourneau, *Jésus*, 71.

[156] For the fourth evangelist the 'hour' is a theologically important theme. For a detailed study see A. Dauer, *Johannes und Lukas. Untersuchungen zu den johanneisch-lukanischen Parallelperikopen Joh 4,46/Lk 7,1-10 – Joh 12,1-8/Lk 7,36-50; 10,38-42 – Joh 20,19/Lk 24,36-49* (FzB 50) (Würzburg 1984).

[157] He is introduced first as a 'royal officer' (4,46.49), then as a 'man' (4,50), and finally as a 'father' (4,53). The father-son relationship is the key to understand the Johannine Jesus.

All these various correlations clearly link the two narratives with one another. The purpose of exposing the inclusive nature of this relation is not only to establish the literary unity of these two pericopes, but also to indicate the probable major thematic orientation. The two important related themes are: 'faith and signs' and 'the saving or life-giving aspect of the person and mission of Jesus.' The leading clue to the structure must probably be searched with this background in mind.

3. Narrative Christology

The beauty of the narrative in Jn. 3-4 is that it is centred on people who seem to be preoccupied with such daily chores as drawing water and buying food, yet it is precisely among these people and through their chores that the evangelist unfolds his Christology. As Lindars remarks, "Jesus is presented as maintaining the Jewish case against the Samaritans, at the same time as asserting that both Jewish and Samaritan aspirations are alike fulfilled in his person."[158]

We notice continuity as well as development in the exposition of Christology in the narrative through encounters, dialogues and monologues. There is structural and narrative sequence. We have already observed the structural dependence of 2,23-3,26 on 1,19-51. Here we find the narrative sequence of Jn. 3-4 still in thematic continuity with 2,1-22. The word *sign* (2,11.18.23; 3,2 and 4,48.54), the movement of *ascent* and *descent* (1,32-33.51; 2,12; 3,13 and 4,47.49), and the *hour* (2,4 and 4,21.23.52.53), *noon* (4,6), *third day* (2,1), *three days* (2,19.20), *after two days* (4,43), and seventh hour (4,52) – all closely associated with the *sign* and occurring in all the four chapters – are used by the evangelist to keep the narrative alive; at the same time, the reconsideration of the theme of signs in the course of the narrative leads also to a gradual unfolding and deepening of new perspectives on Christology.

Jesus' encounter with the Jewish authorities at the Temple in Jerusalem (2,18-22) makes clear that the death and resurrection of Christ is the *only and perfect sign* given to the Jews as confirmation of his identity and Messianic authority. Signs as attestation of divine origin is effectively taken up by Nicodemus in 3,2. But the signs performed by Jesus remain insufficient to generate true faith if they are not seen as orientations towards the sign of the cross from which the gift of life flows. To the Jews and to Nicodemus Jesus gives the elevation of the Son of Man on the cross (cf. 3,14) as the definitive sign leading to the revelation of Jesus as the Son sent by the Father (3,16-18; cf. 4,26). Believing is looking at the Son of Man who ascends into heaven and Son of God who returns to the Father.

Salvation as the mission of Jesus is the new aspect brought into Jn. 3-4. This theme has already been slightly touched at in 1,29 when the Baptist designates Jesus as 'the Lamb of God *who takes away the sin of the world.*' This aspect is developed in 3,14-18.36. Eternal life is given to those who believe in the Son of Man raised onto the cross (3,14-15) and in the Son of God who has been sent into the world for its salvation (3,16-18.36).

The evangelist does not, however, abandon the reader to a simple theoretical exposition on the identity of Jesus and his saving mission. The Christological designations must be followed by the revelation of Jesus. After the Messianic designation of Jesus (cf.

---

[158] Lindars, *Gospel,* 176.

Jn. 1,19-51), the first disciples were witnesses of two actions of Jesus, *viz.*, sign of wine at Cana and the cleansing of the Temple in Jerusalem (Jn. 2), which revealed the fulfilment of the Messianic expectations (cf. Mal. 3,1ff.), but left already a hint of their surpassing nature in the person of Jesus. In Jn. 3 Jesus is designated explicitly as the Son of Man and Son (of God) sent by the Father; his saving mission, then, becomes evident in the Samaritan and Galilean episodes (4,1-42 and 4,43-54). In the first episode, the Son sent by the Father reveals himself to the Samaritan woman as the one who gives living water for eternal life (cf. 4,14), makes the Father known (cf. 4,23-24), and will proclaim all things (cf. 4,25-26). Such a revelation leads to the confession of Jesus as the true "Saviour of the world" (4,42). This recognition of the Son sent from above as the only Saviour of the world (cf. 3,16-17) is demonstrated by a sign which anticipates as well as symbolises the final gift of life (cf. 4,50.51.53). The narrative thus has a thematic continuity which has an inseparable trail of the soteriological dimension of the mission of Jesus:[159] one passes from the exposition of salvation attached to the person of Jesus (cf. 3,14-18) to the recognition of him in faith (cf. 4,39-42), and then to its anticipated realisation in the narration of a sign (cf. 4,49-54).

In this soteriological perspective, the formal link between the episodes of Nicodemus (2,23-3,21) and the royal official (4,43-54) is also important. One cannot miss in these two episodes the recurrence of the same theme. While 3,11-21 is a discourse on revelation, 4,46-54 is a concrete example of faith in story form. The second sign at Cana is a concrete soteriological application (in anticipation) of the gift of life offered on the cross. In fact, it is at the seventh hour that Jesus tells the royal official: "Your son will live" (cf. 4,50.52-53); this 'perfect hour' is the hour of Jesus, the hour of elevation/glorification of the Son of Man (cf. 12,23), the moment when the Son-sent returns to the Father (cf. 12,32) for life eternal (cf. 5,25.28-29). This saving aspect of the elevation of the Son of Man and the fulfilment of the mission of the Son on the cross have just been announced in 3,14-18. The descent and ascent of the Son of Man (3,13-15) and the sending and returning of the Son (3,16-18) – both of which have eternal life as their goal – are also symbolised in the request of the official that Jesus *descends*[160] to Capernaum (4,47.49; cf. 2,12) to give life to his son. This evident diptych relation between these two episodes confirms the fundamental Christological exposition of the fourth Gospel, *viz.,* that Jesus is the Son of

---

[159] A. Link (*"Was redest du mit ihr?" Eine Studie zur Exegese-, Radaktions- und Theologiegeschichte von Joh 4,1-42* [BU 24] [Regensburg 1992] 361) speaks of soteriology being at the service of Christology in the fourth Gospel.

[160] Létourneau, *Jésus*, 98 feels that the evangelist is careful to avoid all direct connections between the verb 'descend' and the mention of the town of origin, and this for the three occurrences of the verb (4,47.49.51). We know from 4,46-47 that Jesus is at Cana in Galilee and that the officer comes to him from Capernaum. The *whence* of those who descend are not indicated and the verb is used only absolutely. On the other hand, it is interesting to note that the movement of the officer from Capernaum towards Cana in 4,47 is expressed by the verb, ἀπέρχομαι while the movement requested of Jesus (from Cana towards Capernaum) is expressed by the verb καταβαίνω (4,47.49). But it is strange that the same movement of the slaves from Capernaum towards Cana (exactly like the officer) is described using the verb καταβαίνω. In fact, the verb 'descend' must be applied to the opposite direction. I think it is intentionally done by the author as he wants theologically to link the verb 'descend' with the verb 'live' because the slaves descended saying: "ὁ παῖς αὐτοῦ ζῇ" (4,51). Here and in Jn. 3, the verb 'to descend' has a soteriological purpose.

Man come down and the Son (of God) sent by the Father for the salvation of the world[161] – the gift of eternal life.

A further element, which may not be insignificant, is the geographical displacement of Jesus in these two chapters. Jesus journeys from Jerusalem (2,23-3,21) to Judea (3,22-4,3), then through Samaria (4,4-42) to Galilee (4,43-54). Having given a proleptic hint to the death and resurrection of Jesus in his sign given to the Jews at the Temple (2,19), the narrator now treats in advance and in a micro-structure the post-resurrectional mission of the disciples as expressed in Acts 1,8: "You will be my witnesses in Jerusalem, in all Judea and Samaria, and to the ends of the earth."[162] In Jn. 3-4 the evangelist makes Jesus undertake in advance the same itinerary. The result of the anticipated missionary journey brings the harvest of the Samaritans who readily acknowledge Jesus as the *true Saviour of the world*. This echoes the Christological and soteriological theme of Jn. 3. In my opinion, one notices the theoretical exposition of the theme in Jn. 3 being enacted in a story form in Jn. 4.

The role of the Baptist was to prepare the way of the Lord as foretold in Mal. 3,1. His function in Jn. 3 is further interpreted, using the nuptial imagery, as the 'friend of the bridegroom' (3,29), whose task is to prepare for the wedding and lead the bride (Israel) to the home of the bridegroom.[163] In his first testimony he leads the disciples to Jesus (cf. 1,35ff.) which resulted in the Messianic nuptials (2,1-11). In the same way, the Baptist is sent before Jesus into Samaria to prepare the conversion of the Samaritans[164] – the new bride – which culminates in their acceptance of Jesus as the true "Saviour of the world." (4,42).

Conclusion

In the biblical narrative there is an elaborately integrated system of repetitions – some dependent on the actual recurrence of individual phonemes, words, or short phrases, others
linked to the actions, images, and themes that are part of the world of the narrative. In a written narrative there is scope for various forms of repetition and, as a number of authors have shown, repetition forms an integral part of biblical storytelling. The two kinds of repetition – the verbal or material, and the more dramatic or conceptual – are somewhat different in their effect, but they are often used together to reinforce each other and to

---

[161] The Son comes down from heaven (alone), calls through word and deed to a saving faith, opens the only door for men to God, and ascends back to the Father (but takes all those who believe in him). Link (357-58) speaks of a "Sendungs- und Herrlichkeitschristologie."

[162] The missionary itinerary of the disciples, according to the fourth evangelist is modelled on that of Jesus and is seen as a continuation and prolongation of the same (cf. 17,18 and 20,21). The royal official being a pagan (it was also the case in the case of the centurion in the similar Synoptic stories – Mt. 8,5-13; and Lk. 7,1-10) one can consider the mission as reaching beyond the boundaries of Judea and Samaria to the ends of the earth.

[163] We have already discussed the literary genre of the Samaritan episode against Gen. 24 as the back-drop. The mission of the servant of Isaac was facilitated by an angel of God sent to prepare the hearts (cf. Gen. 24,7). We can compare the role of the Baptist as 'friend of the bridegroom' to that of the angel in the OT. See the two articles of Boismard, "Aenon, près de Salem," 218-29; and his, "L'ami de l'époux," 289-95.

[164] See also the discussion of E. D. Freed, "Did John Write his Gospel Partly to Win the Samaritan Converts," *NT* 12 (1970) 241-56; M. Pamment, "Is There Convincing Evidence of Samaritan Influence on the Fourth Gospel?" *ZNW* 73 (1982) 221-30; A. F. Segal, "Conversion and Messianism: Outline for a New Approach," in: Charlesworth, *Messiah*, 322-23; and Köstenberger, *Missions of Jesus*.

produce a concerted whole. Both kinds of repetitions are found in 1,19-4,54. To some extent I have drawn the attention to the presence of these repetitions in the parallels between units, sub-units and segments.

Besides, an important linear development of the narrative, controlled by Jesus' movements, is noticed. He moves from Galilee to Jerusalem, into the Judean country side, and back to Galilee via Samaria. The reader follows this journey, reported in a series of episodes that are linked by closely matched literary shapes. The shape of 2,1-11 is repeated in 2,12-22, and that of 3,1-21 is repeated in 3,22-36. The shape of 4,7-15 is repeated in 4,16-30, and that of 4,39-42 returns in 4,43-54. This literary technique insures the ongoing reading process that introduces the reader to the fundamental question of the Gospel emerging across these stories. Jesus is the unique revelation of God (cf. 3,13-14.31-35), the unique Son of the Father (2,16 and 4,34), the perfection of the former gift of the Law (cf. 2,6-7.11 and 4,10-14), the revelation of the δόξα (2,11), and the one who creates a new situation of freedom where people judge themselves by accepting or refusing what Jesus reveals (3,18-21.36). The time has come for God to make known that salvation is available to all people, in all places (4,20-24.42). Jesus initiates a mission in response to the will of the Father, and he draws his disciples into it (4,31-38). God is Spirit, and true life is lived in the Spirit (3,6-8 and 4,24) after a ritual entry into a new community, a place where God reigns (3,3-5). The death of Jesus will not be the outrageous slaying of a failed Messiah but the 'lifting up' of the Son of Man (3,14). Much of this is beyond the understanding of the disciples, but the time will come – after the death and resurrection of Jesus – when they will understand the word of Jesus and believe (cf. 2,19-22). The reader is now instructed in some of the most important beliefs. What has been said in the prologue is being proclaimed and acted out in the story of Jesus in a narrative form (1,19-4,54).

It is also important to note the phenomenon of *gradualness*, because only when one takes it into account that the continuity between texts can be followed. At every repetition there is an additional aspect which draws the reader to a better understanding of the person of Jesus. Just to give an example, it seems that the 'third day' and 'hour' are just casually mentioned in 2,1 and 2,4. In the following episode, in the mention of the 'three days,' 'destruction' and 'raising up,' (2,19-21) the meaning becomes clearer and deeper. It is further elaborated in the imagery of the serpent (3,14), and that of ascent and descent in the following chapters (cf. 3,13). The sixth hour ('noon' – 4,6) evoking the elevation of Jesus on the cross – the life-giving and saving act – gradually becomes the seventh hour (4,53) – the perfect hour – in the next scene when the son of the royal official receives life. The gradual revelation of Jesus to the Samaritan woman is portrayed with utmost care in the gradation of the words used by her to address Jesus: 'you, a Jew' (4,9); 'sir' (4,11.15.); 'prophet' (4,19); and 'Messiah' (4,29); the evangelist finally places on the lips of the Samaritans the true identity of Jesus 'Saviour of the world' (4,42) – a repetition of the revelation of Jesus to Nicodemus (cf. 3,16-17.36). In the character portrayal of the *royal official*, too, there is a *gradualness* that he is then spoken of as a *man* and finally as a *father*. To the belief evoked by a *sign* in 2,11 another element of belief in the *word* (2,22 and 4,41.50) is added to complement it. One can say that the fourth evangelist is a competent author who knew how to use literary techniques to drive home his concept of Christology.

What we find as strikingly remarkable is the Christological bearing of the unit of my study (2,23-3,36) for the whole Gospel. It is a reminder given to the reader already at the beginning of the Gospel to instruct him of the fact that any confession of Jesus that does not recognise his identity as the Son of Man and as Son of God is insufficient. Jesus is the 'Son of Man *descend*ed from heaven' and the 'Son (of God) sent by the Father' *for the salvation of the world*, and this Son of Man must *ascend*. These two aspects are the keys to open the treasure house and understand the heart of the fourth evangelist's Christology coupled with its soteriology – the origin, identity and mission of Jesus. This pattern of a complementary and parallel schemes of Christology, rubbing shoulders with each other, is gradually unveiled in the rest of the Gospel. The Christology of the fourth Gospel is presented in a *U-shaped narrative form* (having vertical [descent and ascent], and horizontal [mission] dimensions): The Son of Man has descended from heaven (the Son is sent by the Father into the world).[165] His mission is to offer (through words and deeds) salvation – eternal life – to all men.[166] This mission is achieved *par excellence* in the ascending (lifting up/glorification)[167] of the Son of Man. Hence, a Christology that is inseparably intertwined with soteriology[168] appears to be the scheme of the fourth Gospel.

The fourth evangelist develops this Christology in the first section through a narrative that is complex in its character. Its pattern is gradually introduced through the narrative of the first two chapters, theoretically exposed through encounter and discourse in the third chapter, and demonstrated in short in the fourth chapter. The purpose of the Gospel (20,31) – "These are written so that you may come to believe that Jesus is the Messiah, the Son of God, and that through believing you may have life in his name" – has been enacted in the first four chapters in a dramatic and summary manner, in the revelation of Jesus as the Son of God and Son of Man, and in the portrayal of the faith of his disciples (Jews), Samaritans and Gentiles in the Saviour of the world.

---

[165] In the fourth Gospel we do not have the infancy narratives. The prologue straight away starts with the divine origin of the Son. This Son is introduced in the narrative – in the words (titles) of the disciples, in Messianic categories, which Jesus do not deny. The evangelist makes Jesus correct their conceptions about him and leads them to surpass those traditional Messianic categories – revealing through signs and words his glory – to understand his true identity and mission (cf. 1,50-51 and 2,11).

[166] We have enough of proof of this in words in 3,15-17.21.36 and 4,14.36.42, and in deeds (In the case of the Samaritans and the healing of the royal official's son there is an anticipation as well as a demonstration of this salvation).

[167] "When I am lifted up from the earth, I will draw all people to myself" (12,32; cf. 3,14 and 8,28). The purpose of this being *lifted up* is soteriological.

[168] The whole purpose of the Gospel according to the evangelist is soteriological: Through believing in the Messiah, the Son of God, one my have life (20,31). The goal of faith is life (soteriology).

GENERAL CONCLUSION

Being a literary and narrative exegesis, in the introductory chapter, I clarified my methodology and explained briefly the literary devices and narrative techniques that help understand a biblical passage as it is. I began the exegetical analysis in chapter 1 (Part I) by determining the perimeters of the unit chosen for my study and pointing out its bipartite division into two sub-units (2,23-3,32 and 3,22-36) and the division of each of them into tripartite segments. I, then, expressed briefly my arguments for the rejection of dislocation theories and assumed the integrity of the text as demanded by my methodology. I also took for granted that the speaker in 3,31-36 is the Baptist promising, of course, to clarify and substantiate the same in the course of my dissertation. Chapter 2 dealt with a short summary of the results of the past research. It was observed that most scholars notice a parallel bipartite structure (2,23-3,21//3,22-36) but vary considerably in the further sub-division of the pericopes into segments.

Informed and enlightened by the disparity of results and encouraged by the richness and complexity hidden in the simplicity of the text, I undertook the detailed and elaborate treatment of the text from the literary and narrative perspectives (cf. chapter 3). My main search in Part I has been to detect the thematic orientation of the text and to analyse the Christological and soteriological scheme underlying it. This I did by analysing the argumentative narrative structure of each segment and by discovering the parallel structure in the narration of the two episodes. The parallel and narrative structure (revolving around Christology and soteriology) *found on the following two pages* summarily presents the structure emerging out of my literary and narrative analysis of the two episodes.

Besides, I gave a special attention to their insertion in the structural network through the spectrum of characters and implicit commentary conveyed through double meaning, misunderstanding, irony, symbolism, dualism and other literary and narrative devices. Hence, at every stage, I demonstrated how the evangelist seeks to reveal *characters*, narrate events, describe situations, exhibit motives in a consistent way and aim at making his story a coherent whole, where every character and every situation is bound up with the rest that this character at this situation cannot but act in this way and one cannot imagine him/her acting otherwise. I have also shown how the fourth evangelist has, like every historian, selected, simplified, schematised, omitted and added from his source the materials which he thought were important and formed the events into a story with a *plot* to drive his point of Christology and soteriology home (cf. 20,31). Moreover, I have clearly shown that the plot of 2,23-3,36 – like the whole Gospel – is Christocentric as it is aimed at convincing and attracting the reader, through affective power, to respond to Jesus and believe in him (cf. chapter 4).

Furthermore, I analysed the unit of my study and other units from various points of view of narrative criticism and exposed the *artistry* of the Gospel story. One of the things which has been omitted by narrative critics is a careful consideration of the relation between theological purpose and narrative form. Sometimes narrative critics have been guilty of implying an art-for-art's sake mentality on the part of the evangelist. Therefore, all along I have been careful to show how narrative qualities are used by the fourth evangelist to persuade the *reader* to accept the truthfulness of his Christological credo. The

Parallel Narrative Structure

| 2,23-3,21 | // | 3,22-36 |

2,23-3,2: Introduction/Report (Scene-setting)

2,23a: Specification of place and time (Jerusalem; Passover)

23d: Activity of Jesus: doing signs
23b: Reaction of people – belief in Jesus
23c: Reasoning – *seeing* Jesus' signs
24a: Reaction of Jesus – 'non-trust'
24a-25: Reasoning – 'he knew all'
Popularity of Jesus (*many* believed in Jesus-23b;
Jesus knew *all* people-24b; knew what was in *everyone*-25d)
3,1: Introduction of Jesus' dialogue partner: (Nicodemus)
2c: Addressing: 'Rabbi'
2de: Subject of discussion – origin and identity of Jesus

2fg: Reasoning – performance of sings

3,3-10: Dialogue between Jesus and Nicodemus:

3a: "Jesus answered..."
b: Double-amen formula of authority
c: Necessity of salvation (seeing the kingdom of God)
d: Condition: 'being begotten ἄνωθεν'
4: Question of Nicodemus about 're-birth' (salvation)
5-10: Clarification of Jesus about 'being begotten ἄνωθεν'
5b: On his own authority (double-amen formula)
5c: 'Seeing' clarified as 'entering' the kingdom of God

3,22-26: Introduction/Report (Scene-setting)

3,22a.23a: Specification of place and time (Judean countryside;
Aenon near Salim; Μετὰ ταῦτα)
22b;26f: Activity of Jesus – baptism
23a: Activity of the Baptist - baptism
23bc: Reasoning – coming of people and abundance of water
23cd: Reaction of people – reception of baptism
26g: Popularity of Jesus ('all are going to him')
24: Primacy of Jesus (hint at the Baptist's destiny)

25: Introduction of Baptist's dialogue partners (disciples)
26c: Addressing: 'Rabbi'
26de: Subject of discussion (Jesus: associate of the Baptist
across the Jordan and to whom he bore witness)
26fg: Reasoning: Jesus' baptism and 'all going to him'

3,27-30: Dialogue between the Baptist and his disciples

27a: "John answered..."
No such formula of authority (subordinate to Jesus)
b: Salvation (being drawn to Jesus)
c: Condition: given from heaven (ἐκ τοῦ οὐρανοῦ)
26de: *Implied question* of the disciples about Jesus' identity
28-30: Clarification of the Baptist about his relationship to Jesus
28ab: Recalls his former testimony (cf. 1,19-30) as his authority
28cd: Clarification: 'not Messiah,' but 'one sent ahead of him'

5d: 'Being begotten ἄνωθεν' further clarified as being begotten of water and Spirit; and through the parable of the wind
◆ The dialogue is on the *theme of salvation* (3,3-9)

7c: There is a necessity (δεῖ) to be begotten ἄνωθεν (for salvation)

10bc: Ironic retort of Jesus to Nicodemus

3,11-21: Discourse of Jesus (Revelation of his identity and Mission)

11a: Jesus speaks on his own authority (double-amen formula)

Reasons for his authority:
bc: i) He *knows* what she *speaks*
de: ii) Has *seen* what he *testifies* to
12: Jesus speaks of earthly and heavenly things
13f.: Jesus is the Son of Man descended from heaven
16-18: Jesus is the Son of God, sent by the Father for the world's salvation
19b: He is the light come into the world

15ab ⎤
16cde ⎥ Belief in the Son results in eternal life (salvation)
18ab ⎦
18cd ⎤ Non-believers are condemned
19c ⎥ Lovers of darkness are judged
20a ⎦ Evil doers do not come to the light

29: Further clarification of relationship using nuptial imagery

◆ The 'bride' standing for (the Samaritans – Jn. 4; Israel in line with the OT; and the world/humanity – 3,16-17; cf. 4,42) the *theme of salvation* is implicit.

30: There is a necessity (δεῖ) that Jesus increases (for salvation)

28ab: Slight reproach of his disciples on the part of the Baptist

3,31-36: Discourse of Baptist (Second Testimony about Jesus)

Absence of such a formula of authority (being a witness has no authority of his own)
Reasons for Jesus' superiority:
32ab: He *testifies* to what he has *seen*
c: He *testifies* to what he has *heard*
31c-e Baptist being of the earth speaks about earthly things
31ab.fg: Witness to the heavenly origin and superiority of Jesus
35a: Jesus is the Son whom the Father loves
34a: He has been sent by the Father
34b: Speaks God's words
34c: Gives the Spirit
35b: Has the authority of the Father

36ab: Believers in the Son have eternal life (salvation)

36cde: Those who disobey will not see life, but God's wrath

narrative of the fourth Gospel is a rhetorical phenomenon carefully engineered to reinforce a particular theological understanding of Jesus in the minds of its readers. My literary and narrative exegesis interestingly exposes how the fourth Gospel – in which Jesus is a literary character – can make him known to readers more profoundly than he, as a person, could have been known by his contemporaries. The advantages of a narrative appreciation, like the one I have done, is that it reclaims the final form of the text as a narrative unity, helps one to see how the evangelist's portrait of Jesus is communicated to the reader and enables him/her to examine the significance and persuasiveness of his *narrative Christology*.

My task in this dissertation has been not theoretical but exegetical, hermeneutical, and self-reflective. The application of *reader-response criticism* to the unit of my study has helped to understand its compositional integrity which is attained by the analysis of its *language*. The author takes the *reader* by the hand to lead him/her on from one thought to another by means of something like catch-words. Establishing such a repertoire of terms focuses the reader's attention and formulates a *theme*. Using them to lead the reader on, the author provides transitional bridges and holds the reader's mind tightly to the reading as the story progresses. I must say that the text exists so that the reader may fill it, and the reader exists so that the text may fill him/her.

Thus, I have demonstrated that the Nicodemus story furnishes an excellent example of a *quest narrative* meant to relate to those who are religious seekers. While the dialogue with Nicodemus slows down the action, it intensifies conflict and characterisation and provides space for thematic development. My study has demonstrated how a more synchronic, formalist, reader-oriented, narratological approach offers a way to hover closely over the text itself and breathe new life into it. I have displayed that the analysis of biblical texts are narratives, which could draw back together into one loaf the fragmentary crumbs of texts left over after the historical methodologies had departed and that they are to be seen also as 'mirrors' and not only as 'windows' to the past and interpreted as unified wholes. Besides, my study proves how analysis of the affective and persuasive aspects of story-worlds help bridge the growing gap between the academician studying the text as artifact and the layperson reading it as article of faith.

I have also exposed that Jesus in the narrative is portrayed as a static character; he does not change, but only emerges more clearly through his signs, encounters, conflicts, and discourses as the narrative progresses. The implied author uses *narrator* as a vehicle to convince the reader of his Christological argumentation by making the narrator adopt Jesus' point of view ideologically and phraseologically. The narrator's point of view is a quasi-secretive act of communication of the evangelist to persuade the reader of his narrative Christology (cf. chapter 5). In short, Jesus is what the Gospel narrative exists for; it exists to reveal him.

The detection of the use of *double meaning*, a refinement of the technique the fourth evangelist uses to develop the historical interpretative elements of his theology, has enabled me to notice that words of the text are carefully chosen and that they bring new depth of meaning to the text. Besides, an extensive use of the narrative technique of *misunderstanding* is particularly visible in the story of Nicodemus. There can be no doubt that understanding, misunderstanding and not understanding are important themes for the fourth evangelist. He has, therefore, done the most with it because he chose to write a Gospel about a man whose ministry happened '*einmalig,*' and whose death radically altered the understanding of his followers. His purpose in writing was to foster belief "that Jesus is the Messiah, the Son of God" (20,31).

Moreover, being a master of *irony*, the implied author makes the silent communication between narrator and reader fascinating through irony for his Christological purpose. Irony is used in the unit of my study to lead the reader into that dimension of truth about Jesus – that he is the true teacher and the expected Messiah, which Nicodemus and the Baptist's disciples seem to miss, but the reader, in fact, can grasp.

Furthermore, understanding of the *symbols* is an index to the position and movement of the characters. Symbols point to the central conflict in the Gospel, the conflict between that which is 'from above' and that which is 'from below.' Primarily the conflict is between Jesus who is 'from above' and those who cannot and will not recognise his identity. The fourth evangelist, therefore, calls his readers to affirm the fulfilment of the Jewish heritage in Jesus as well as the divinity of the one 'from above,' who is not this 'worldly' or 'earthly' (cf. 3,31).

Added to these, I have also demonstrated how the fourth evangelist uses *dualistic symbols* to tie the bipolarity of life to Christology. I must say that the evangelist has dualism in his bones. He tells a story in which the historical, temporal realm is wedded to the cosmic, the other, trans-historical, and trans-temporal realm. The mystery of transcendence is mixed in with the worldly. Jesus, the hero of the narrative, is both a historic person and a being from the transcendent realm (cf. 3,13.17). The human response to him is both an historical event and an event that has transcendent value. Consequently, one of the additional features of the story of the fourth evangelist is that time is both historical and beyond history. What light and darkness, life and death, doing what is true and doing evil are, therefore, is determined by whether or not one knows and comes to 'the light.' The evangelist stresses these points in dualistic terminology in the hope that his readers will turn to the 'lifted up' Son of Man with the same simple, desperate and unqualified faith which the Israelites displayed when they turned to the bronze serpent in the desert (cf. 3,13-15). By such faith alone can anyone experience the begetting ἄνωθεν (3,3-5) and thereby gain ζωὴ αἰώνιος (3,15-16). Just as salvation/kingdom is both a present reality and a future hope, so also 'eternal life' is both a present reality and a future hope. 'Salvation,' 'kingdom,' 'eternal life,' and 'glorification' – all indicate a progressive process and are different names for one phenomenon with present and future dimensions. The terminus *a quo* for glorification is the death of Jesus ('lifting up of the Son of Man'), which becomes effective for the individual when he/she is begotten ἄνωθεν of water and Spirit. By virtually abandoning the term 'kingdom of God' (3,3.5) in favour of the term 'eternal life' (3,15.16.36) and by insisting that the divine judgement is effectively enacted in the earthly life of every individual, the evangelist is simply drawing out the most important implications of the Christian message. All this has obvious Christological implications. Clearly the fourth evangelist has a high view of Jesus' person. His teaching on judgement is yet another way in which he brings out the Messiaship of Jesus – his great central aim.

Though I cannot repeat all the thematic implications of the literary and narrative structure of the unit of my study, I must say that the main contribution is the establishment of its *double Christological scheme*. I can, thus, observe how Jn. 2,23-3,21 act as a summary exposition of the Christology that is developed in the rest of the Gospel.

By the inclusive structure between 1,19-51 and 2,23-3,36, the evangelist alerts the reader about the insufficiency of the traditional Jewish Messianic confession (1,19-51) and presents the key statements which govern his correct Christological conception (2,23-3,36 – cf. Part II). One of the major purposes of the fourth Gospel was to present a corrective view of Jesus. The disciples did not understand Jesus or his words during his ministry (cf. 12,16 and 13,7).

I began this process of unearthing the double and parallel Christological scheme underlying the unit of my study by analysing the literary and narrative structure of the text and by dividing each episode into three segments. I, thus, brought to light the presence of a diptych structure (2,23-3,21//3,22-36) as well as a tripartite and parallel one (2,23-3,2// 3,22-26; 3,3-10//3,27-30; and 3,11-21//3,31-36). In the first episode (2,23-3,21), the dynamic of the narrative shows Jesus making Nicodemus move from his inadequate confession (3,2) to the knowledge of the true identity of Jesus as the Son-sent (3,16-18). In the second episode (3,22-36) the dynamic of the narrative revolves around the person of the Baptist, who makes his disciples move from a false understanding of the activity of Jesus (3,26) to a correct knowledge of his origin, identity and mission (3,34-36). In both episodes the interlocutors of a 'Rabbi' are brought progressively from an inadequate conception of the person of Jesus (cf. 3,2//3,26) to an unveiling of the true identity of Jesus as the Son-sent (cf. 3,16-18//3,34-36). Moreover, I have exposed that in both episodes the point of departure is an initial activity of Jesus falsely interpreted by his interlocutors. In the first episode, it is the false interpretation of the signs performed by Jesus (and therefore of his identity) that makes the evangelist place on the lips of Jesus the soteriological statement of 3,3, leads to the announcement of the perfect sign (3,14-15), and reveals the true identity of Jesus (3,16-18). In the second episode, the point of departure resides in the false understanding of the baptismal activity of Jesus (by the Baptist's disciples) attracting more crowds (hence, a question about the person of Jesus); this false interpretation is rectified having recourse to the argumentation of the general principal having a soteriological implication (3,27) and leading to a recognition of Jesus as the Son sent by the Father.

Thus, I detect a double Christology elaborated around the two titles 'Son of Man' and 'Son of God' which are inseparably intertwined with *soteriology*. In the unit chosen for my study the organising concept seems to be the theme of belief in Jesus as the 'Son of Man come down from heaven and lifted up' and as the 'Son of God sent by the Father for the *salvation* of the world.' I have also recognised two soteriological conceptions which flow from these two Christological schemes. In the Christological scheme of the Son of God – resting on the juridical principle of the unity between the Sender and the Sent salvation – is expressed in terms of participation in the communion of life of the Father and the Son; on the other hand, in the apocalyptic and ascent-descent scheme of the Son of Man (U-shaped Christology), salvation consists in the ability to enter into the (heavenly) kingdom of God by being begotten ἄνωθεν of water and the Spirit.

Moreover, the argumentative function of these parallel Christological schemes is to be found in their juxtaposition. The narrator of the fourth Gospel views Jesus and his ministry from the twin perspectives of his 'whence' and his 'whither' (cf. 3,8ef), his origin as the Son of God sent and his destiny as the Son of Man lifted up/exalted. Only when these two perspectives are taken together can Jesus be rightly understood. This stereoscopic perspective conditions not only what the narrator says but the Gospel's entire characterisation of Jesus.

Then, I continued my study, in Part II, with a brief and intensive exploration of the insertion of 2,23-3,36 in the narrative and structural *network* of its section (1,19-4,54) in story of the fourth Gospel. I plunged into this section to unearth anew its thematic, literary and narrative patterns and to demonstrate the evangelist's meaningful insertion and organisation of 2,23-3,36 into the plot of his story by subjecting it to a thorough literary and narrative analysis. This study was a revealing disclosure and an eye opener to me. It enabled me to unearth the *major correlations* in the first section of the Gospel, especially the long forgotten and neglected one between the two testimonies of the Baptist (1,19-34 and 3,22-36) and the most evident one between the two miracles at Cana (2,1-11 and 4,43-54) observed already by most of the scholars of the fourth Gospel. The parallelism between the two testimonies of the Baptist constitutes the fundamental element of correlation in the first block (1,19-3,36), while the two Cana miracles having an identical literary design encompass the second block (2,1-4,54) structurally and aesthetically (see the diagrams below).

I have demonstrated the evangelist's purpose in bringing the Baptist into the story a second time (cf. 1,19-51 and 3,22-36) besides exposing the presence of a large number of *formal and secondary links* that hold the section together as a *continuous and meaningful story* skilfully establishing the purpose of the Gospel, *viz.*, faith in Jesus (Son of Man and Son of God) for eternal life – Christology and soteriology (cf. 20,31). My brief literary and narrative analysis of each unit, sub-unit and segment has unearthed a number of parallel elements (ignored by many scholars or casually remarked only by a few) between units (1,19-51 and 2,23-3,36; 2,1-22 and 4,1-54; 1,19-51 and 2,1-22; 2,23-3,36 and 4,1-54) and established the *smooth transition of the narration* from sub-unit to sub-unit and unit to unit through the intentional and rhetoric style of repetition, re-treatment and variation of key themes, hook-words (e.g. testimony, greater things/glory, third day/hour/destruction/ death and resurrection/lifting up/sign, descent/ascent, Son of Man/Son of God/Son, earthly/ heavenly, above/below, flesh/Spirit, purification/Temple/worship, wedding/bridegroom/ husband, kingdom of God/eternal life/saviour/salvation, worship, etc.), symbols (water and light), purposeful gradation, careful characterisation and skilful plot. This study helped me draw the hermeneutical conclusions in the form of narrative Christology in chapter 3 of Part II.

Besides, just as I observed a bipartite structure and a diptych relation between the sub-units of every unit (*viz.,* 1,19-34 and 1,35-51; 2,1-11 and 2,12-22; 2,23-3,21 and 3,22-36 and 4,1-42 and 4,43-54), I also detected a diptych relation in the whole section between the two blocks (1,19-3,36 and 2,1-4,54). The diagrams given below explain *schematically* the careful and artistic structural web or network woven by the evangelist.

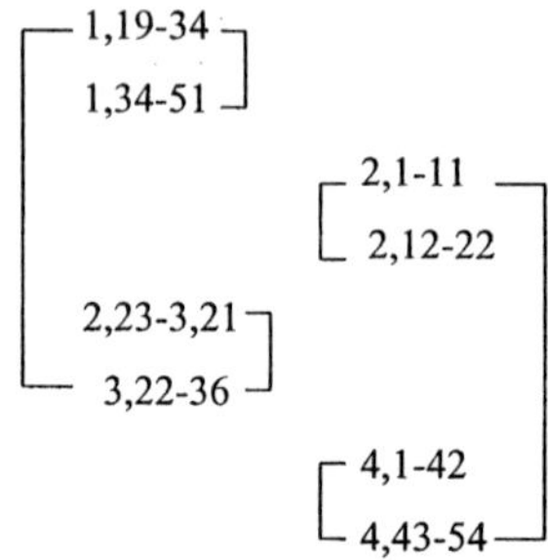

First of all, the left and the right wings are clearly held together by the device of inclusion at the extremities, *viz.*, between 1,19-34 and 3,22-36 in the two testimonies of the Bapitst, and between 2,1-11 and 4,43-54 in the geographical (Cana in Galilee), numerical (first and second), and structural (suggestion-negative response-positive action) and inclusive nature of the two miracles performed by Jesus at Cana. If ones considers the narrative of 1,19-4,54 as a *chain*, each unit and sub-unit of it serves as a necessary *tooth* holding the chain of the story together. In this way, 2,1-22 acts as a tooth fitting into the chain between 1,19-51 and 2,23-3,36; and 2,23-3,36 while forming, on the one hand, the chain with 1,19-51 serves, simultaneously, as the tooth that fits into the chain between 2,1-22 and 4,1-54 as shown in the diagram below:

| 1,19-51 |
| 2,1-22 |
| 2,23-3,36 |
| 4,1-54 |

Moreover, there is smooth transition of the narrative from segment to segment, sub-unit to sub-unit, unit to unit and sub-section to sub-section. On the one hand, the sub-units 1,19-34 and 1,35-51 describe two different episodes, *viz.*, enquiry and testimony of the Baptist, and the following of the first disciples respectively, each taking place in a duration of two days; the second episode, on the other hand, is a consequence of the first. Jesus is introduced by the Baptist in the first and, as a result, is followed by the disciples in the second. There is a concentration of inadequate *Messianic titles attributed to Jesus* distributed in the two sub-units. While the important title 'Son of God' is placed on the lips of the Baptist and Nathanael, the title 'Son of Man' appears on the lips of Jesus (1,51). The unit culminates in the promise of 'greater things' (1,50) and a hint at it in the dualistic symbol of ascent and descent which will be repeated with variation in the following units (cf. 2,12.13; 3,13.14; and 4,47.49).

The second unit (2,1-22) narrates two different symbolic actions of Jesus revealing his Messianic character and evoking the faith of his disciples. While in the mention of the 'third day' (cf. 2,1) there is a chronological continuation of the story with what preceded, in the performance of the Cana *sign* revealing his 'glory' (cf. 2,11) and in the revelation of the greatest of *signs* (cross/resurrection/ascent – cf. 2,19-22) there is a hint at and a partial fulfilment of the promise made in 1,50-51. Thus, there is perfect plot in the transition of the story from the first to the second unit.

The third unit, the unit chosen for my study, pairing 2,23-3,21 and 3,22-36 and presented under a parallel narrative structure, is the *pivotal unit* of the section as it exposes the fourth evangelist's *heart of Christology* that is inseparably *intertwined with a soteriology* that breaks all cultural and ethnical barriers and embraces the whole world (cf. 3,16-17; comp. 4,42). While the first sub-unit (2,23-3,21) is a self-revelation of the origin, identity and mission of Jesus, the second (3,22-36) is to be seen as a juridical necessity to *authenticate* the words of Jesus by a second witness of the Baptist whose principal role in the fourth Gospel is to bear witness to Jesus. Moreover, in this unit there is thematic development of and narrative continuity with the previous unit. After the performance of a sign at Cana and the announcement of the greatest of signs at the Temple in Jerusalem, crowds are attracted by Jesus who, however, do not understand his true identity. Hence, the discourse of Jesus, in the course of a dialogue, revealing his true identity becomes necessary. The fourth evangelist, thus, portrays Jesus as revealing himself only gradually and in stages. Jesus himself admits in 5,31 his testimony is not true if he testifies about himself. Hence, in order to conform to the Jewish Law he has to depend on other witnesses. The testimony of Jesus is sealed by the testimony of the Baptist. The purpose of bringing the Baptist into the scene a second time (as two witnesses are necessary according to the Jewish Law) is to authenticate the words of Jesus (the Messiah) about his origin, identity and mission (which have been the focus of the enquiry commission from Jerusalem and of the dispute with the Jews at the Temple). This requirement is fulfilled by the episode (3,22-36) which encloses the first three chapters of the Gospel.

The fourth unit pairing 4,1-42 and 4,43-54, on the one hand, is an immediate demonstration as well as a foretaste of the results brought by the soteriological mission of Jesus announced in 3,16-17. The *universal saving mission* of Jesus having drawn in Jews (the mother of Jesus, the Baptist and the disciples) first, embraces now the non-Jews (Samaritans) and the gentiles. There is a transition from insufficient and partial faith evoked by the signs of Jesus (cf. 2,23-25; comp. 4,49) to perfect faith in the words of Jesus (cf. 4,42.50). Moreover, the nuptial motif contained in the sign at Cana, the role of the Baptist as the friend of the bridegroom and the betrothal motif hidden in the episode of the Samaritan woman run like a thread unifying the plot of the story in the section. In the same way, the motif of purification (cf. 2,6 and 3,25), Temple (2,14-21) and cult (4,19-26) are also unifying elements knitting the story together. I do not go into details mentioning all the elements of correlation as I have done it already in a comprehensive manner in Part II.

Furthermore, I brought to notice an important *formal relation* between the story of the wedding at Cana (2,1-11) and the dialogue with the Samaritan woman on the subject of living water and husbands (4,7-15 and 4,16-19), pointed out the correlation between the purification of the temple (2,12-22) and the discussion on the place of the eschatological cult (4,20-26). I think that the establishment of this narrative and structural network, integrating a vast majority of formal links, demonstrating its integral structure, purposeful plot, and careful selection of episodes skilfully woven into an uninterrupted story constitutes a step ahead in the research of the fourth Gospel. As I have pointed out more than once, the key to understanding the meaning of a pericope or episode is to be sought, often, in its context. Moreover, being a literary and narrative exegesis, Part II forms an indispensable section of my dissertation. This, in my opinion, sufficiently justifies the rather elaborate treatment in Part II.

However, *integrity, unity and coherence* are not to be found primarily in plot development or in the progression of action from scene to scene. Instead, they are to be observed in the effect achieved through *thematic development*. The real accent of my contribution is not to be found in the formal narrative and structural design but at the thematic level supported by this structure. Themes are the basic ideas of narratives, and their function is to give internal shape and completeness to a sequence of episodes. In other words, themes are organising narrative concepts. In fact, in accordance with my methodology, the establishment of the structure is only the first step to the hermeneutical interpretation of the text. The configuration of the structural network must, then, help interpret the meaning of the semantic correlation generated by it.

Besides, in this process of exposing the double Christological scheme I have been able to demonstrate also the literary unity and integrity of 2,23-3,36 and the coherent narrative and argumentative structure of each of its segments. In fact, I have to underline that the insertion of the second testimony of the Baptist (3,22-36) is in its *rightful place*, and the Christological argumentation in both episodes has a coherent and identical structure and narrative sequence, clearing all doubts about the *speakers* of 3,11-21 and 3,31-36 and shattering all the past theories and hypotheses about *dislocations and transpositions*. I have contended that the evangelist had doubled the testimony of the Baptist because of his exclusive function in the fourth Gospel as a witness to Jesus. In fact, this doubling was motivated by two reasons: on the one hand, Jesus alone could reveal his true origin, identity and mission being the unique and competent witness concerning heavenly matters. On the other hand, the Baptist had to play his role, till the end, as a witness to the world (whose principal representatives are 'the Jews') that opposed Jesus. Therefore, it is necessary that the Baptist returns to the bar to authenticate the revelation of Jesus, that is, his self-revelation as Son of Man and Son-sent. It is in this perspective that one understands well the parallelism between the episodes 1,19-34 and 3,22-36, and between 2,23-3,21 and 3,22-36.

My aim has not been merely to establish the literary structure of these units, but above all to bring to evidence the narrative argumentation that is supported by the structure. In fact, the originality of my work is to show the juxtaposition of the narrative and structural *design* in the interpretation of the units. In my opinion, one must understand the text both from the literary and structural organisation (of the text) points of view and from the narrative display (argumentation employed in the organisation of the material). It is by the superimposition of these two dimensions, as I have demonstrated in Part I and Part II, that the meaning of the text is clarified.

I think, in the light of the results arrived at by this study, new avenues have been opened to explore further. For example, a study of the other titles such as Prophet, Messiah, Lamb of God, King of Israel, Shepherd, etc. could be explored to see how they fit into this scheme of the double and parallel narrative Christology of Jn. 3. Other sections of the Gospel could also be subjected to a similar literary and narrative analysis to verify the chain like narrative found in the first and the Christological scheme underlying it. One could, perhaps, study the influence of this double Christology on the Johannine community. However, my literary and narrative exegesis has been an attempt to understand the fourth Gospel from within rather than to explain it from without, and the double Christological scheme is not to be seen as a water-tight compartment but as one complementing the other.

ABBREVIATIONS

Except for the following abbreviations all the rest are as found in S. M. Schwertner, *IATG².*
International Glossary of Abbreviations for Theology and Related Subjects, Berlin ²1992.

BAGD	Bauer, W., Arndt, W. F. and Gingrich, F. W., *A Greek-English Lexicon of the New Testament and Other Early Christian Literature* (2nd ed. rev. and augm. by Gingrich, F. W. and Danker, F. W.) Chicago 1979.
BBE	The Bible in Basic English (1949/64)
BBR	Bulletin for Biblical Research
BibA	Bibliographical Aids
BibInt	Biblical Interpretation
BibIntS	Biblical Interpretation Series
BPP	La Bible, Porte-Parole
BSU	Bulletin of the Seikei University
BTS	Bibeltheologische Schwerpunkte
CI	Critical Inquiry
CPC	Collection de Philologie Classique
DBY	The Darby Bible (1884/1890)
EDNT	Balz, H. and Schneider, G. (eds.), *Exegetical Dictionary of the New Testament*, 3 Vols., Grand Rapids ²1994.
GBSNT	Guides to Biblical Scholarship, New Testament Series
HBS	Herders biblische Studien/Herder's Biblical Studies
HNTC	Harper's New Testament Commentary
HSL	Herald Scriptural Library
IBC	Interpretation Biblical Commentary
IVPNTC	InterVarsity Press New Testament Commentaries
KST	Kohlhammer Studienbücher Theologie
LSJ	Liddell, H. and Scott, R., *A Greek-English Lexicon* (rev. and augm. throughout by Jones, H. S. with a rev. Supplement) Oxford ⁹1996.
LT	Literature and Theology
NAC	New American Commentary
NAS	New American Standard Bible (1977)
NASB	New American Standard Bible (1995)
NJBC	Brown, R. E., Fitzmyer, J.A. and Murphy, R. E. (eds.), *The New Jerome Biblical Commentary*, Engelwood Cliffs 1989.
NKJV	New King James Version (1982)
NRSV	New Revised Standard Version
NTR	New Testament Readings
PD	Parole de Dieu
Pro	Proceedings
ProC	Proclamation Commentaries
PzB	Protokolle zur Bibel
RNBC	Readings: A New Biblical Commentary
RNS	Recherches Nouvelle Série
RNT	Reading the New Testament Series
RSB	Religious Studies Bulletin
RT	Ricerche Teologiche
RWB	Revised 1833 Webster Update (1995)
SNTI	Studies in New Testament Interpretation
SPS	Sacra Pagina Series
SzR	Schriften zur Religionserkenntnis

TrinJ	Trinity Journal
WBC	Word Biblical Commentary
WEB	The Webster Bible (1833)
WPC	Westminster Pelican Commentaries
YBCC	Year Book of Comparative Criticism
YLT	Young's Literal Translation (1862/1898)
ZSNT	Zacchaeus Studies: New Testament

BIBLIOGRAPHY

A. Texts and Translation used here (unless stated otherwise) are:

Elliger, K. and Rudolph, K. (eds.), *Biblia Hebraica Stuttgartensia*, Stuttgart 1983.

Aland, K., Black, M., Martini, C. M., Metzger, B. M. and Wirkgren, A. (eds.), *Novum Testamentum Graece*, Stuttgart [27]1993.

The New Revised Standard Version, Oxford 1989.

B. Bibliography and Surveys of Studies on the Fourth Gospel

Becker, J., "Aus der Literatur zum Johannesevangelium (1978-1980)," *ThR* 47 (1982) 279-301 and 305-47.

——, "Das Johannesevangelium im Streit der Methoden (1980-1984)," *ThR* 51 (1986) 1-78.

Beutler, J., "Literarische Gattungen im Johannesevangelium. Ein Forschungsbericht 1919-1980," *ANRW* II.25.3 (1985) 2506-68.

——, "Methoden und Probleme heutiger Johannesforschung," in: his *Studien zu den johanneischen Schriften* (SBAB 25) Stuttgart 1998, 191-214.

Dubois, J., "Chronique johannique," *ETR* 51 (1976) 373-81.

Espinosa, R. R. and Léon, D. M., *Bibliografía Joánica: Evangelio, Cartas y Apocalipsis, 1960-1986*, Madrid 1990.

Haenchen, E., "Aus der Literatur zum Johannesevangelium," *ThR* 23 (1955) 295-335.

——, *John*, Vol. 2 (Hermeneia) Philadelphia 1984, 254-346.

Hainz, J. (ed.), *Dokumentation des Symposions 'Methodenstreit zum Johannesevangelium' vom 29. und 30. Juni 1990 in Kelkheim*, Darmstadt 1991.

Howard, W. F., *The Fourth Gospel in Recent Criticism and Interpretation*, London [4]1955.

Koester, C. R., "R. E. Brown and J. L. Martyn: Johannine Studies in Retrospect," *BTB* 21 (1991) 51-55.

Kümmel, W.G., *Das Neue Testament im 20. Jahrhundert: Ein Forschungsbericht* (SBS 50) Stuttgart 1970.

Kysar, R., *The Fourth Evangelist and His Gospel: An Examination of Contemporary Scholarship*, Minneapolis 1975 (covering 1955-1975).

——, "The Fourth Gospel: A Report on Recent Research," *ANRW* II.25.3 (1985) 2391-480 (covering upto 1977).

——, "The Gospel of John in Current Research," *RStR* 9 (1983) 314-23 (covering upto 1983).

Langevin, P.-É., *Bibliographie Biblique, Biblical Bibliography, Biblische Bibliographie, Bibliografia Biblica, Bibliografica Biblica I (1930-1970)* Québec 1972, 336-72; *II (1930-1975)* Québec 1978, 731-81; and *III (1930-1983)* Québec 1985, 925-68.

Lémonon, J. P., "Chronique johannique (1981-1992)," *LV(L)* 41 (1992) 95-104.

Léon-Dufour, X., "Bulletin de littératur johannique," *RSR* 69 (1980) 271-316.

——, "Bulletin d'exégèse du NT. l'évangile de Jean," *RSR* 82 (1994) 227-50.

Malatesta, E., *St. John's Gospel 1920-1965. A Cumulative and Classified Bibliography of Books and Periodical Literature on the Fourth Gospel* (AnBib 32) Rome 1967.

Menken, M. J. J., "The Christology of the Fourth Gospel: A Survey of Recent Research," in: de Boer, M. C. (ed.), *From Jesus to John. Essays on Jesus and New Testament Christology in Honour of Marinus de Jonge* (JSNT.S 84) Sheffield 1993, 292-320.

Mills, W. E., *Bibliographies for Biblical Research*, Lewiston 1995.

Morgen, M., "La littérature johannique," *RSR* 84 (1996) 277-303.

Onuki, T., "Zur literatur-soziologischen Analyse des Johannesevangeliums. Auf dem Wege zur Methodenintegration," *AJBI* 8 (1982) 162-216.

Schmithals, W., *Johannesevangelium und Johannesbriefe. Forschungsgeschichte und Analyse* (BZNW 64) Berlin, New York 1992.

Schnackenburg, R., "Entwicklung und Stand der johanneischen Forschung seit 1955," in: de Jonge, M. (ed.), *L'Évangile de Jean. Sources, rédaction, théologie* (BEThL 44) Gembloux, Leuven 1977, 19-44.

Schnelle, U., "Perspektiven der Johannesexegese," *SNTU* 15 (1990) 59-72.

Scholtissek, K., "Johannes auslegen I. Forschungsgeschichtliche und methodische Reflexionen," *SNTU* 24 (1999) 35-84.

———, "Johannine Studies. A survey of Recent Research with Special Regard to German Contributions," *CRBS* 6 (1998) 227-59.

———, "Neue Wege in der Johannesauslegung. Ein Forschungsbericht I," *ThGl* 89 (1999) 263-95.

Sloyan, G. S., *What are They Saying about John?*, New York 1991 (covering 1970-1990).

Smith, D. M., *John among the Gospels: The Relationship in Twentieth-Century Research*, Minneapolis1992.

Thyen, H., "Aus der Literatur zum Johannesevangelium," *ThR* 39 (1974) 1-69 and 222-52; 40 (1975) 298-330; 42 (1977) 211-70; 43 (1978) 328-59; and 44 (1979) 97-134.

Untergaßmair, F. G., "Das Johannesevangelium. Ein Bericht über neuere Literatur aus der Johannesforschung," *ThRv* 90 (1994) 91-108.

van Belle, G., *Johannine Bibliography 1966-1985: A Cumulative Bibliography on the Fourth Gospel* (BEThL 82) Leuven 1988.

Wagner, G., *An Exegetical Bibliography on the Gospel of John* (BibA 8) Rüschlikon, Zürich 1975.

———, *An Exegetical Bibliography of the New Testament. John and 1, 2, 3 John*, Macon 1987.

C. Reference Works

Abbott, E. A., *Johannine Vocabulary*, London 1905.

Abrahams, I., *Studies in Pharisaism and the Gospels*, Vol. 2, Cambridge 1924.

Abrams, M. H., *A Glossary of Literary Terms*, New York [4]1981.

Aland, K. (ed.), *Synopsis Graeca Quattuor Evangeliorum*, Stuttgart [13]1990.

Balz, H. and Schneider, G. (eds.), *Exegetical Dictionary of the New Testament*, 3 Vols., Grand Rapids [2]1994.

Bauer, W., *Griechisch-Deutsches Wörterbuch zu den Schriften des Neuen Testaments und der übrigen urchristlichen Literatur*, Berlin, New York [5]1971.

———, Arndt, W. F. and Gingrich, F. W., *A Greek English Lexicon of the New Testament and Other Early Christian Literature* (2nd ed. rev. and augm. by Gingrich, F.W. and and Danker, F. W.) Chicago 1979.

Beyer, K., *Semitische Syntax im Neuen Testament* (StUNT I/1) Göttingen 1968.

Black, M., *An Aramaic Approach to the Gospels and Acts*, Oxford [3]1967.

Blass, F., Debrunner, R. and Funk, R. W., *A Greek Grammar of the New Testament and Other Early Christian Literature* (rev. and trans. by Funk, R. W.) Chicago 1967.

Brown, C. (ed.), *The New International Dictionary of New Testament Theology*, 4 Vols., Grand Rapids 1986.

Brown, F., Driver, S. R. and Briggs, C. A., *A Hebrew and English Lexicon of the Old Testament with an Appendix Containing the Biblical Aramaic*, Oxford 1907.

Brown, R. E., Fitzmyer, J.A. and Murphy, R. E. (eds.), *The New Jerome Biblical Commentary*, Engelwood Cliffs 1989.

Coggins, R. J. and Houlden, J. L. (eds.), *A Dictionary of Biblical Interpretation*, London, Philadelphia 1990.

Daube, D., *The New Testament and the Rabbinic Judaism*, London 1956.

Freedman, D. N. et al. (eds.), *The Anchor Bible Dictionary*, 6 Vols., New York 1992.
García Martínez, F. and Tigchelaar, E., *The Dead Sea Scrolls Study Edition*, 2 Vols., Grand Rapids 1999.
Hays, J. (ed.), *Dictionary of Biblical Interpretation*, 2 Vols., Nashville 1998.
Holtzmann, O., *Das Neue Testament nach dem Stuttgarter griechischen Text übersetzt und erklärt*, Gießen 1926.
Humbert, J., *Syntaxe grecque* (CPC II) Paris 1954.
Kittel, G. and Friedrich, G. (eds.), *Theological Dictionary of the New Testament*, 10 Vols., Grand Rapids 1995.
Lauterbach, J.(ed. and trans.), *Mekilta de Rabbi Ishmael*, 3 Vols., Philadelphia 1961.
Liddell, H. and Scott, R., *A Greek-English Lexicon* (rev. and augm. throughout by Jones, H. S. with a rev. Supplement) Oxford [9]1996.
Lightfoot, J., *A Commentary on the New Testament from the Talmud and Hebraica. Matthew – 1 Corinthians*, Vol. 4, New York 1997.
McKim, D. K. (ed.), *Westminster Dictionary of Theological Terms*, Westminster 1996.
Metzger, B. M., *A Textual Commentary on the Greek New Testament*, London, New York 1971.
Morgenthaler, R., *Statistik des Neutestamentlichen Wortschatzes*, Zürich [2]1982.
Morrison, C., *An Analytical Concordance to the Revised Standard Version of the New Testament*, Philadelphia 1979.
Moulten, H. K. (ed.), *The Analytical Greek Lexicon Revised*, Grand Rapids 1990.
Moulton, J. H., Howard, W. F. and Turner, N., *A Grammar of New Testament Greek*, 4 Vols., Edinburgh 1909-1976.
—— and Milligan, G., *The Vocabulary of the Greek Testament*, London 1914-1929.
Muller, R. A., *Dictionary of Latin and Greek Theological Terms*, Grand Rapids 1985.
Robertson, A. T., *A Grammar of the Greek New Testament in the Light of Historical Research*, Nashville 1934.
Rogers, C. L., Jr. and Rogers, C. L., III, *The New Linguistic and Exegetical Key to the Greek New Testament*, Grand Rapids 1998.
Schiffman, L. and VanderKam, J. C. (eds.), *The Encyclopedia of the Dead Sea Scrolls*, 2 Vols., Oxford 2000.
Silva, M., *Biblical Words and Their Meaning. An Introduction to Lexical Semantics*, Grand Rapids 1994.
Strack, H. L. and Billerbeck, P., *Kommentar zum Neuen Testament aus Talmud und Midrasch. Band 2: Das Evangelium nach Markus, Lukas und Johannes und die Apostelgeschichte erläutert aus Talmud und Midrasch*, München [8]1983.
Vaughan, C. and Gideon, V. E., *A Greek Grammar of the New Testament*, Nashville 1979.
Zerwick, M., *Biblical Greek Illustrated by Examples*, Rome 1963.
—— and Grosvenor, M., *A Grammatical Analysis of the Greek New Testament*, Rome 1974.

D. Commentaries on the Fourth Gospel

Barrett, C. K., *The Gospel according to St. John*, London [2]1978.
Bauer, W., *Das Johannesevangelium erklärt* (HNT 6) Tübingen [3]1933.
Beasley-Murray, G. R., *John* (WBC 36) Waco 1987.
Becker, J., *Das Evangelium nach Johannes*, 2 Vols. (ÖTBK 4/1-2) Gütersloh, Würzburg [3]1991.
Bernard, J. H., *A Critical and Exegetical Commentary on the Gospel according to St. John*, 2 Vols. (ICC) Edinburgh [6]1962.
Blank, J., *Das Evangelium nach Johannes*, 3 Vols. (GSL.NT 4/1-3) Düsseldorf 1981.
Boice, J. M., *The Gospel of John. An Expositional Commentary, Vol. 1: John1,1-4,54*,

Grand Rapids 1975.

Boismard, M.-É. and Lamouille, A., *L'Évangile de Jean* (*Synopse des quatres évangiles en français,* Vol.3) Paris 1977.

Borchert, G. L., *John 1-11* (NAC 25A) Nashville 1996.

Braun, F.-M., *Commentaire de l'Évangile selon Saint Jean*, in: Pirot, L. and Clamer, A. (eds.), *Les Saints Évangiles. S. Luc; S. Jean* (La Sainte Bible 10) Paris 1935.

Brodie, T. L., *The Gospel according to John. A Literary and Theological Commentary*, New York, Oxford 1993.

Brown, R. E., T*he Gospel according to John*, 2 Vols. (AncB 29/29a) Garden City 1966/70.

Bruce, F. F., *The Gospel of John: Introduction, Exposition and Notes*, Grand Rapids 1994.

Büchsel, F. , *Das Evangelium nach Johannes* (NTD 4) Göttingen [5]1949.

Bultmann, R., *Das Evangelium des Johannes* (KEK 2) Göttingen [21]1986.

———— , *The Gospel of John. A Commentary*, Oxford, Philadelphia 1971.

Calloud, J. and Genuyt, F., *L'Évangile de Jean (I): Lecture sémiotique des chapitres 1 à 6*, Lyon 1989.

Carson, D. A., *The Gospel according to John*, Grand Rapids 1991.

Culpepper, R. A. (ed.), *The Gospel and Letters of John*, Nashville 1998.

de la Potterie, I., "L'Evangelo di San Giovanni," in: Rinandi, G and de Benedetti, P. (eds.), *Introduzione al Nuovo Testamento*, Brescia 1971.

Delebecque, E., *Évangile de Jean. Texte Traduit et Annoté* (CRB 23) Paris 1987.

Dodd, C. H., *The Interpretation of the Fourth Gospel*, Cambridge 1954.

Ellis, P.F., *The Genius of John. A Compositional-Critical Commentary on the Fourth Gospel*, Collegeville 1984.

Flanagan, N. M., *The Gospel according to John and the Johannine Epistles* (CBC 4) Collegeville 1984.

Gnilka, J., *Das Johannesevangelium* (NEB 4) Würzburg [4]1993.

Godet, F. L., *Commentary on the Gospel of John,* 2 Vols., Grand Rapids 1969.

Goettmann, J., *Saint Jean. Évangile de la Nouvelle Genèse*, Paris 1982.

Grayston, K., *The Gospel of John* (NC) Philadelphia 1990.

Gruenler, R. G., *The Trinity in the Gospel of John. A Thematic Commentary on the Fourth Gospel*, Grand Rapids 1986.

Haenchen, E., *John*, 2 Vols. (Hermeneia) Philadelphia 1984.

Holtzmann, H. J., *Evangelium des Johannes* (HC 4.1) Tübingen [3]1908.

Hoskyns, E. C., *The Fourth Gospel*, London [2]1947.

Howard-Brook, W., *Becoming Children of God. John's Gospel and Radical Discipleship*, New York 1994.

Hunter, A. M., *The Gospel according to John* (CNEB) Cambridge 1965.

Keil, G., *Das Johannesevangelium. Ein philosophischer und theologischer Kommentar*, Göttingen 1996.

Kreyenbühl, J., *Das Evangelium der Wahrheit*, Berlin 1900.

Kysar, R., *John* (ACNT) Minneapolis 1986.

Lagrange, M.-J., *Évangile selon saint Jean* (EtB) Paris 1964.

Léon-Dufour, X., *Lecture de l'Évangile selon Jean*, 4 Vols. (PD) Paris 1988/'90/'93/'96.

L'Éplattenier, C., *L'Évangile de Jean* (BPP) Geneva 1993.

Lightfoot, R. H., *St. John's Gospel. A Commentary*, Oxford 1960.

Lindars, B., *The Gospel of John* (NCB) Grand Rapids [2]1981.

Loisy, A., *Le quatrième Évangile. Les Épîtres dites de Jean*, Paris 1921.

Maier, G., *Johannesevangelium,* Part I (EdC.B 6) Neuhausen, Stuttgart 1984.

Malina, B. J. and Rohrbaugh, R.L., *Social-Science Commentary on the Gospel of John*, Minneapolis 1998.

Manns, F., *L'Évangile de Jean à la lumière du Judaisme* (SBFA 33) Jerusalem 1991.

Marrow, S. B., *The Gospel of John. A Reading*, New York 1995.

Marsh, J., *The Gospel of John* (PGC) Baltimore 1978.

———, *Saint John* (WPC) Philadelphia 1977.

Mastin, B. A. and Sanders, J. N., *A Commentary on the Gospel according to St. John* (BNTC) London 1968.

Mateos, J. and Barreto, J., *El Evangelio de Juan. Analisis Lingüistico y Comentario Exegetico*, Madrid 1979.

Michaels, J. R., *John* (NIBC 4) Peabody 1989.

Molla, C. F., *Le quatrième Évangile*, Geneva 1977.

Mollat, D., *L'Évangile selon saint Jean* (BiJer) Paris ³1973.

Moloney, F.-J., *Belief in the Word. Reading John 1-4*, Minneapolis 1993.

———, *Signs and Shadows. Reading John 5-12*, Minneapolis 1996.

———, *Glory not Dishonor. Reading John 13-20 (21)*, Minneapolis 1998.

———, *The Gospel of John* (SPS 4) Collegeville 1998.

Morris, L., *The Gospel according to John* (rev. ed.) (NIC) Grand Rapids 1995.

O'Day, G. R., "The Gospel of John," (NIntB 9) Nashville 1995, 491-865.

Odeberg, H., *The Fourth Gospel. Interpreted in its Relation to Contemporaneous Religious Currents in Palestine and the Hellenistic-Oriental World*, Amsterdam 1968.

Pasquetto, V., *Da Gesù al Padre. Introduzione alla lettura esegetico-spirituale del vangelo di Giovanni*, Rome 1983.

Perkins, P., *The Gospel according to St. John. A Theological Commentary* (HSL) Chicago 1978.

Porsch, F., *Johannesevangelium* (SKK.NT 4) Stuttgart 1988.

Prete, B., "Vangelo di Giovanni," in: *Il Messaggio della Salvezza*, VIII, Torino ⁴1978, 797-870.

Ridderbos, H., *The Gospel of John. A Theological Commentary*, Cambridge, Grand Rapids 1997.

Sanders, J. N., *The Gospel according to Saint John* (HNTC) New York 1968.

Sanford, J. A., *Mystical Christianity. A Psychological Commentary on the Gospel of John*, 1997.

Schenke, L., *Johanneskommentar*, Düsseldorf 1998.

Schlatter, A., *Der Evangelist Johannes, wie er spricht, denkt und glaubt. Ein Kommentar zum vierten Evangelium*, Stuttgart ³1960.

———, *Das Evangelium nach Johannes. Ausgelegt für Bibelleser* (EzNT 3) Berlin 1962.

Schnackenburg, R., *The Gospel according to St. John*, 3 Vols., London, New York 1980-82.

———, *Das Johannesevangelium. Vierter Teil. Ergänzende Auslegungen und Exkurse* (HThK IV/4) Basel, Freiburg, Wien 1984.

Schneider, J., *Das Evangelium nach Johannes* (ThHK Sonderband) Berlin1976.

Schulz, S., *Das Evangelium nach Johannes* (NTD 4) Göttingen ¹⁵1983.

Segalla, G., *Giovanni. Versione, Introduzione, Note* (NVB) Rome 1976.

Sloyan, G., *John* (IBC) Atlanta 1988.

Smith, D. M., *John* (ProC) Philadelphia ²1986.

———, *John*, Nashville 1999.

Stibbe, M. W. G., *John* (RNBC) Sheffield 1993.

Strachan, R. H., *The Fourth Gospel. Its Significance and Environment*, London ³1960.

Strathmann, H., *Das Evangelium nach Johannes* (NTD 4) Göttingen ⁹1959.

Talbert, C. H., *Reading John. A Literary and Theological Commentary on the Fourth Gospel and the Johannine Epistles* (RNTS) London 1992.

Tasker, R. V. G., *The Gospel according to St. John. An Introduction and Commentary* (TNTC) London 1960.

Tenney, M. C., *John: The Gospel of Belief. An Analytic Study of the Text*, Grand Rapids 1988.

van den Bussche, H., *Jean. Commentaire de l'Évangile Spirituel*, Bruges 1967.

Voigt, G., *Licht – Liebe – Leben. Das Evangelium nach Johannes* (BTS 6) Göttingen 1991.

Westcott, B. F., *The Gospel according to Saint John: The Greek Text with Introduction and Notes*, 2 Vols., London ²1908.

Whitacre, R. A., *John* (IVPNTC 4) Downers Grove 1999.

Wikenhauser, A., *Das Evangelium nach Johannes* (RNT 4) Regensburg ³1961.

Wilckens, U., *Das Evangelium nach Johannes* (NTD 4) Göttingen ¹⁷1998.

Wiles, M. F., *The Spiritual Gospel. The Interpretation of the Fourth Gospel in the Early Church*, Cambridge 1960.

Witherington, B., *John's Wisdom. A Commentary on the Fourth Gospel*, Louisville 1995.

Zahn, T., *Das Evangelium des Johannes* (KNT 4) Leipzig ⁶1921.

Zevini, G., *Commentaire spirituel de l'Évangile de Jean*, Montréal, Paris 1995.

E. Other Literature

Abegg, M., Jr., Flint, P. and Ulrich, E., *The Dead Sea Scrolls Bible: The Oldest Known Bible Translated for the First Time into English*, New York 1999.

Achtemeier, E., "Jesus Christ, the Light of the world. The Biblical Understanding of Light and Darkness," *Interp.* 17 (1963) 439-49.

Agnew, F., "On the Origin of the Term *Apostolos*," *CBQ* 38 (1976) 49-53.

Agrelo, S., "A Propositio de Jn 3,1-3," *Anton.* 60 (1985) 233-39.

Alter, R., *The Art of Biblical Narrative*, New York 1981.

Anderson, P. N., *The Christology of the Fourth Gospel. Its Unity and Disunity in the Light of John 6* (WUNT 78) Tübingen 1996.

Appold, M. L., *The Oneness Motif in the Fourth Gospel. Motif Analysis and Exegetical Probe into the Theology of John* (WUNT II/1) Tübingen 1976.

Ashton, J., "The Identity and Function of the ΙΟΥΔΑΙΟΙ in the Fourth Gospel," *NT* 27 (1985) 40-75.

—— (ed.), *The Interpretation of John* (SNTI) Edinburgh ²1997.

——, *Studying John. Approaches to the Fourth Gospel*, Oxford 1994.

——, "The Transformation of Wisdom: A Study of the Prologue of John's Gospel," *NTS* 32 (1986) 161-86.

——, *Understanding the Fourth Gospel*, Oxford 1993.

Aune, D. E., *The Cultic Setting of the Realized Eschatology in Early Christianity* (NT.S 28) Trondheim 1972.

——, "The Problem of Genre of the Gospels: A Critique of C. H. Talbert's 'What Is a Gospel?', " in: France, R. and Wenham, D. (eds.), *Gospel Perspectives: Studies in History and Tradition in the Four Gospels*, Sheffield 1981, 9-60.

Auwers, J.-M., "La nuit de Nicodème (Jean 3,2; 19,39) ou l'ombre du langage," *RB* 97 (1990) 481-503.

Backhaus, K., *Die 'Jüngerkreise' des Täufers Johannes. Eine Studie zu den religionsge-schichtlichen Ursprüngen des Christentums* (PaThSt 19) München, Paderborn, Wien, Zürich 1991.

——, "Täuferkreise als Gegenspieler jenseits des Textes. Überlegungen zu einer kriterio-logischen Verlegenheit," in: Hainz, J. (ed.), *Dokumentation des Symposions 'Methodenstreit zum Johannesevangelium' vom 29. und 30. Juni 1990 in Kelkheim*, Darmstadt 1991, 16-44.

Balz, H., "Johanneische Theologie und Ethik im Licht der 'letzten Stunde'," in: Schrage, W. (ed.), *Studien zum Text und zur Ethik des neuen Testaments. FS zum 80. Geburtstag von Heinrich Greeven* (BZNW 47) Berlin, New York 1986, 35-56.

Bammel, E., "The Baptist in Early Christian Tradition," *NTS* 18 (1971) 95-128.

———, "John Did No Miracle: John 10:41," in: Moule, C. F. D. (ed.), *Miracles: Cambridge Studies in their Philosophy and History*, London 1965, 179-202.

Barclay, W., *New Testament Words*, Philadelphia 1974.

Barosse, T., "The Seven Days of the New Creation in St. John's Gospel," *CBQ* 21 (1959) 507-16.

Barth, G., *Die Taufe in frühchristlicher Zeit* (BThSt 4) Neukirchen-Vluyn 1981.

Barton, J., *Oracles of God: Perceptions of Ancient Prophecy in Israel after the Exile*, London 1986.

Bassler, J. M., "Mixed Signals: Nicodemus in the Fourth Gospel," *JBL* 108 (1989) 635-46.

Batey, R. A., *New Testament Nuptial Imagery*, Leiden 1971.

Bauckham, R., "Nicodemus and the Gurion Family," *JThS* 47 (1996) 1-37.

———, "The Son of Man: 'A Man in my Position' or 'Someone'," *JSNT* 23 (1985) 23-33.

Baum-Bodenbender, R., *Hoheit in Niedrigkeit. Johanneische Christologie im Prozeß Jesu vor Pilatus (Joh 18,28-19,16a)* (FzB 49) Würzburg 1984.

Baumgarten, J., Chazon, E. G. and Pinnick, A. (eds.), *The Damascus Document: A Centennial of Discovery. Proceedings of the third International Symposium of the Orion Centre for the Study of the Dead Sea Scrolls and Associated Literature, 4-8 February, 1998*, Leiden 1999.

Bayens, P. J., *'Begotten of Water and Spirit' (John 3:5): Baptism in the Johannine Tradition* (DissA Marquette) Milwaukee 1993.

Beardslee, W., *Literary Criticism of the New Testament*, Philadelphia 1970.

Beasley-Murray, G. R., *Baptism in the New Testament*, Grand Rapids 1981.

———, "John 3,3.5: Baptism, Spirit and the Kingdom," *ET* 97 (1985/86) 167-70.

Beauvery, R., "Accueillir le dessein d'amour que de Dieu révélé en Jésus (Jean 3,14-21)," *EeV* 80 (1970) 113-16.

———, "Jésus élevé attire tous les hommes à lui (Jean 12,20-33)," *EeV* 80 (1970) 117-19.

Beck, D. R., *The Discipleship Paradigm. Readers and Anonymous Characters in the Fourth Gospel* (BibIntS 27) Leiden 1997.

Becker, J., "Beobachtungen zum Dualismus im Johannesevangelium," *ZNW* 65 (1974) 71-87.

———, "Ich bin die Auferstehung und das Leben. Eine Skizze der johanneischen Christologie," *ThZ* 39 (1983) 136-51.

———, "Joh 3,1-21 als Reflex johanneischer Schuldiskussion," in: Balz, H. and Schulz, S. (eds.), *Das Wort und die Wörter. FS Gerhard Friedrich*, Stuttgart 1973, 85-95.

———, *Johannes der Täufer und Jesus von Nazareth* (BSt 63) Neukirchen-Vluyn 1972.

———, "Wunder und Christologie. Zum literarkritischen und christologischen Problem der Wunder im Johannesevangelium," *NTS* 16 (1969/70) 130-48.

Belleville, L., "'Born of Water and Spirit:' John 3:5," *TrinJ* 1 (1980) 125-41.

Berger, K., *Die Amen Worte Jesu. Eine Untersuchung zum Problem der Legitimation in apokalyptischer Rede* (BZNW 39) Berlin, New York 1970.

———, *Im Anfang war Johannes. Datierung und Theologie des vierten Evangeliums*, Stuttgart 1997.

———, *Die Auferstehung des Propheten und die Erhöhung des Menschensohnes. Traditionsgeschichtliche Untersuchungen zur Deutung des Geschickes Jesu in frühchristlichen Texten* (StUNT 13) Göttingen 1976.

———, "Zum traditionsgeschichtlichen Hintergrund christologischer Hoheitstitel," *NTS* 17 (1970/71) 391-425.

Bergmeier, R., *Glaube als Gabe nach Johannes. Religions- und theologiegeschichtliche Studien zum prädestinatianischen Dualismus im vierten Evangelium* (BWANT 112) Stuttgart 1980.

———, "Gottesherrschaft, Taufe und Geist," *ZNW* 86 (1995) 53-73.

Bertram, G., "ὕψος," *TDNT*, VIII, 602-20.

Betz, O., *Jesus. Der Messias Israels* (WUNT 42) Tübingen 1987.

———, "'To Worship in Spirit and in Truth:' Reflections on John 4:20-26," in: Finkel, A. and Frizzel, L. (eds.), *Standing Before God: Studies on Prayer in Scriptures and in Tradition with Essays in Honour of John M. Österreicher*, New York 1981, 53-72.

Beutler, J., "Johannesevangelium und Rhetorikkritik. Zu einem neueren Buch," in: his *Studien zu den johanneischen Schriften* (SBAB 25) Stuttgart 1998, 233-46.

———, *Martyria. Traditionsgeschichtliche Untersuchungen zum Zeugnisthema bei Johannes* (FTS 10) Frankfurt 1972.

———, "So sehr hat Gott die Welt geliebt (Joh 3,16). Zum Heilsuniversalismus im Johannesevangelium," *GuL* 66 (1993) 418-28.

———, *Studien zu den johanneischen Schriften* (SBAB 25) Stuttgart 1998.

Bishop, E. F. F., "'The Authorised Teacher of the Israel of God' Jn. 3:10," *BiTr* 7 (1956) 81-83.

Bishop, J., "Encounters in the New Testament," in: Gros, L. and Kenneth, R. R. (eds.), *Literary Interpretations of Biblical Narratives*, Vol. 2, Nashville 1982, 285-94.

Bittner, W., "Geschichte und Eschatologie im Johannesevangelium," in: Stadelmann, H. (ed.), *Glaube und Geschichte. Heilsgeschehen als Thema der Theologie*, Gießen 1986, 154-80.

———, "Gott-Menschensohn-Davidssohn. Eine Untersuchung zur Traditionsgeschichte von Daniel 7,13f.," *FZPhTh* 32 (1985) 343-72.

———, *Jesu Zeichen im Johannesevangelium. Die Messiaserkenntnis im Johannesevangelium vor ihrem jüdischen Hintergrund* (WUNT II/26) Tübingen 1987.

Black, D. A., "The Text of John 3.13," *GTJ* 6 (1985) 49-66.

Black, M., "The Messianism of the Parables of Enoch: Their Date and Contributions to Christological origins," in: Charlesworth, J. H. (ed.), *The Messiah. Developments in Earliest Judaism and Christianity*, Minneapolis 1992, 145-68.

Blank, J., "Die Gegenwartseschatologie des Johannesevangeliums," in: Schubert, K. (ed.), *Vom Messias zum Christus. Die Fülle der Zeit in religionsgeschichtlicher und theologischer Sicht*, Basel, Freiburg, Wien 1964, 279-310.

———, "Der johanneische Wahrheitsbegriff," *BZ* 7 (1963) 164-73.

———, *Krisis. Untersuchungen zur johanneischen Christologie und Eschatologie*, Freiburg 1964.

———, "Die Sendung des Sohnes. Zur christologischen Bedeutung des Gleichnisses von den bösen Winzern Mk 12,1-12," in: Gnilka, J. (ed.), *Neues Testament und Kirche: Für Rudolf Schnackenburg*, Freiburg 1974, 11-41.

Bligh, J., "Four Studies in St. John, II: Nicodemus," *HeyJ* 8 (1967) 40-51.

———, "Jesus in Samaria," *HeyJ* 3 (1962) 329-46.

Blomberg, C. L., "The Globalisation of Biblical Interpretation: A Test Case - John 3-4," *BBR* 5 (1995) 1-15.

Böcher, O., *Der johanneische Dualismus im Zusammenhang des nachbiblischen Judentums*, Gütersloh 1965.

———, "Ὕδωρ," *NIDNT*, III, 988-91.

———, "Wasser und Geist," in: Böcher, O. and Haacker, K. (eds.), *Verborum Veritas. FS Gustav Stählin zum 70. Geburtstag*, Wuppertal 1970, 197-209.

Boers, H., "Narrative Criticism, Historical Criticism, and the Gospel of John," *JSNT* 47 (1992) 35-48.

Boismard, M.-É., "Aenon, près de Salem (Jean III,23)," *RB* 80 (1973) 218-29.

———, "L'ami de l'époux (Jo. III,29)," in: *À la rencontre de Dieu. Mémorial Albert Gelin* (BFCTL 8) Le Puy 1961, 289-95.

————, *Du Baptême à Cana (Jean 1,19-2,211)* (LeDiv 18) Paris 1956.

————, "L'évangile à quatre dimensions," *LV(B)* 1 (1951) 94-114.

————, "L'évolution du thème eschatologique dans les traditions johanniques," *RB* 68 (1961) 507-24.

————, *Moïse ou Jésus. Essai de christologie johannique* (BEThL 84) Leuven 1988.

————, "Rapports entre foi et miracles dans l'évangile de Jean," *EThL* 58 (1982) 357-64.

Bonvin, B., "Nicodème ou l'invitation à renaître. Jn 3,1-21," *NV* 64 (1989) 68-71.

Booth, W.C., *The Rhetoric of Fiction*, Chicago 1983.

————, *A Rhetoric of Irony*, Chicago 1974.

Borgen, P., "God's Agent in the Fourth Gospel," in: Neussner, J. (ed.), *Religions in Antiquity. Essays in Memory of E. R. Goodenough* (SHR 14) Leiden 1968, 137-48.

———— (ed.), *Logos Was the True Light and Other Essays on the Gospel of John*, Trondheim 1983.

————, "Some Jewish Exegetical Traditions as Background for Son of Man Sayings in John's Gospel (Jn 3, 13-14 and context)," in: de Jonge, M. (ed.), *L'Évangile de Jean. Sources, rédaction, théologie* (BEThL 44) Gembloux, Leuven 1977, 243-58.

————, "The Son of Man Saying in John 3.13,14," in: Borgen, P. (ed.), *Logos was the True Light and Other Essays on the Gospel of John*, Trondheim 1983, 133-48.

Borsch, F. H., "Further Reflections on 'The Son of Man:' The Origins and Development of the Title," in: Charlesworth, J. H. (ed.), The *Messiah. Developments in Earliest Judaism and Christianity*, Minneapolis 1992, 130-44.

Botha, J. E., "The Case of Johannine Irony Reopened I: The Problematic Current Situation," *Neotest.* 25 (1991) 209-20.

————, *Jesus and the Samaritan Woman: A Speech Act Reading of John 4:1-42* (NT.S 65) New York 1991.

Bowman, J., "Samaritan Studies I: The Fourth Gospel and the Samaritans," *BJRL* 40 (1958) 298-327.

Boyd, W. J. P., "Ascension according to John," *TLon* 70 (1967) 207-11.

Brandenburg, H., *Das Nachtgespräch. Jesus und Nikodemus*, Gladbeck 1961.

Braun, F.-M., "Le don de Dieu et l'initiation chrétienne (Jn. 2-4)," *NRTh* 86 (1964) 1025-48.

————, *Jean le théologien et son Évangile dans l'Église ancienne*, Paris 1959; Vol. 2: *Les grandes traditions d'Israël et l'accord des écritures selon le quatrième évangile*, Paris 1964; Vol. 3: Part 1: *Le mystère de Jésus-Christ*, Paris 1966, Part 2: *Le Christ, notre Seigneur, hier, aujourd'hui, toujours*, Paris 1972.

————, "Le péché du monde selon saint Jean," *RThom* 65 (1965) 181-201.

————, "Le sacrifice d'Isaac dans le quatrième évangile d'après le Targum," *NRTh* 101 (1979) 481-97.

————, "La vie d'en haut (Jn. III, 1-15)," *RSPhTh* 40 (1956) 3-24.

Brewer, D., "The Gospels and the Laws of Folktale: A Centenary Lecture, 14 June 1978," *Folklore* 90 (1979) 37-52.

Brodie, T. L., *The Quest for the Origin of John's Gospel. A Source-Oriented Approach*, Oxford 1993.

Broer, I., "Auferstehung und ewiges Leben im Johannesevangelium," in: Broer, I. and Werbick, J. (eds.), *"Auf Hoffnung hin sind wir erlöst" (Röm 8,24)* (SBS 128) Stuttgart 1987, 67-94.

Brooks, P., *Reading for the Plot*, London ²1992.

Brown, R. E., *The Community of the Beloved Disciple. The Life, Loves, and Hates of an Individual Church in New Testament Times*, New York 1979.

————, "Hermeneutics," *NJBC* (1990) 71.

————, "The Qumrân Scrolls and the Johannine Gospel and Epistles," *CBQ* 17 (1955) 405-

18 and 559-61.

——, "Three Quotations from John the Baptist in the Gospel of John," *CBQ* 22 (1960) 292-98.

Brownlee, W., "Messianic Motifs of Qumran and the New Testament," *NTS* 3 (1957) 195-210

Brumlik, M., "Johannes: Das judenfeindliche Evangelium," *KuI* 4 (1989) 102-13.

Bruns, J. E., "The Use of Time in the Fourth Gospel," *NTS* 13 (1967) 285-90.

Büchsel, F. and Hentrich, V., "κρίνω," *TDNT*, III, 921-54.

Buetubela, B., "Jn 3,8: L'esprit saint ou le vent naturel?," *RAT* 4 (1980) 55-64.

Bühler, P. and Habermacher, J.-F. (eds.), *La narration. Quand le récit devient communication* (LiTh 12) Geneva 1998.

Bühner, J.-A., *Der Gesandte und sein Weg im 4. Evangelium. Die kultur- und religionsgeschichtlichen Grundlagen der johanneischen Sendungschristologie sowie ihre traditionsgeschichtliche Entwicklung* (WUNT II/2) Tübingen 1977.

Bull, K.-M., *Gemeinde zwischen Integration und Abgrenzung. Ein Beitrag zur Frage nach dem Ort der johanneischen Gemeinde(n) in der Geschichte des Urchristentums* (BET 24) Bern, New York, Paris 1992.

Bultmann, R., "ἀλήθεια," *TDNT*, I, 232-51.

——, "Die Eschatologie des Johannesevangeliums," in: Bultmann, R., *Glauben und Verstehen. Gesammelte Aufsätze*, Vol. 1, Tübingen ⁴1961, 134-52.

——, *History of the Synoptic Tradition*, New York 1963.

——, "The Interpretation of the Fourth Gospel," *NTS* 1 (1954/55) 77-91.

——, *Theology of the New Testament*, 2 Vols., London 1955.

Burge, G. M., *The Anointed Community. The Holy Spirit in the Johannine Tradition*, Grand Rapids 1987.

Burkett, D., *The Son of Man Debate: A History and Evaluation* (MSSNTS 107) Cambridge 2000.

——, *The Son of the Man in the Gospel of John* (JSNT.S 56) Sheffield 1991.

Burns, R. J., "Jesus and the Bronze Serpent," *BiTod* 28 (1990) 84-89.

Byrne, B. J., *'Sons of God – Seed of Abraham:' A Study of the Idea of the Sonship of God of All Christians in Paul against the Jewish Background*, Rome 1979.

Cahil, P. J., "Narrative Art in John IV," *RSB* 2 (1982) 41-48.

Calloud, J., "Toward a Structural Analysis of the Gospel of Mark," *Semeia* 16 (1980) 133-65.

Cambe, M., "Jésus baptise et cesse de baptiser en Judée (Jean 3/22-4/3)," *ETR* 53 (1978) 98-102.

Cantwell, L., "The Quest for the Historical Nicodemus," *RelSt* 16 (1980) 481-86.

Caragounis, C. C., "The Kingdom of God in John and the Synoptics: Realized or Potential Eschatology?," in: Denaux, A. (ed.), *John and the Synoptics* (BEThL 101) Leuven 1992, 473-80.

——, *The Son of Man. Vision and Interpretation* (WUNT 38) Tübingen 1986.

Carmichael, C. M., "Marriage and the Samaritan Woman," *NTS* 26 (1979/80) 332-46.

Caron, G., "Exploring a Religious Dimension: The Johannine Jews," *SR* 24 (1995) 159-71.

——, "The Lifting Up of the Human One and the Johannine Jews," *EeT(O)* 26 (1995) 319-29.

Carroll, J. T., "Present and Future in Fourth Gospel 'Eschatology'," *BTB* 19 (1989) 63-69.

Carson, D. A., *Predestination and Responsibility: Elements of Tension-Theology in the Fourth Gospel against Jewish Background*, Cambridge 1975.

——, "Understanding Misunderstandings in the Fourth Gospel," *TynB* 33 (1982) 59-91.

—— and Williamson, H. G. (eds.), *It is Written: Scripture Citing Scripture*, Cambridge 1988.

Casey, M., "The Corporate Interpretation of 'One like a Son of Man' (Dan 7,13) at the Time of Jesus," *NT* 18 (1976) 167-80.

———, "General, Generic and Indefinite. The Use of the Term 'Son of Man' in Aramaic Sources and in the Teaching of Jesus," *JSNT* 29 (1987) 21-56.

Cassem, N. H., "A Grammatical and Contextual Inventory of the Use of κόσμος in the Johannine Corpus with some Implications for a Johannine Cosmic Theology," *NTS* 19 (1972/ 73) 81-91.

Cerfaux, L., "Les miracles, signes messianiques de Jésus et œvres de Dieu selon l'Évangile de S. Jean," in: Cerfaux, L. (ed.), *L'attente du Messie*, Bruges 1958, 131-38.

Charbonneau, A., "Jésus en croix (Jn 19,16b-42); Jésus élévé (3,14ff.; 8,28f.; 12,31ff.)," *ScEs* 45 (1993) 5-23 and 161-80.

Charlesworth, J. H., "A Critical Comparison of the Dualism in 1 QS 3:13-14:26 and the 'Dualism' Contained in the Gospel of John," in: his *John and Qumran*, London 1972, 76-106.

———, "From Messianology to Christology: Problems and Prospects," in: his (ed.), *The Messiah. Developments in Earliest Judaism and Christianity*, Minneapolis 1992, 3-35.

——— (ed.), *John and Qumran*, London 1972.

——— (ed.), *The Old Testament Pseudepigrapha*, Garden City 1983.

Charlier, J.-P., "La notion de signe (sêmeion) dans le quatrième évangile," *RSPhTh* 43 (1959) 434-48.

Chatman, S., *Story and Discourse. Narrative Structure in Fiction and Film*, Ithaca 1978.

Chevallier, M. A., *Souffle de Dieu. Le Saint-Esprit dans le Nouveau Testament* (PoTh 54) Paris 1990.

Childs, B. S., *The New Testament as Canon*, Philadelphia 1985.

Chilton, B. (ed.), *Kingdom of God in the Teaching of Jesus*, London 1984.

Clavier, H., "L'ironie dans le quatrième évangile," in: Aland, A. (ed.), *Studia Evangelica I* (TU 73) Berlin 1959, 261-76.

Coetzee, J. C., "Life (Eternal Life) in John's Writings and the Qumran Scrolls," *Neotest.* 6 (1972) 48-66.

Cohen, S., "The Political Background of the Words of Amos," *HUCA* 36 (1965) 153-60.

Collange, J.-F., "Faire la vérité: Considérations éthiques sur Jean 3,21," *RHPhR* 62 (1982) 415-23.

Collins, J. J., "Apocalyptic Eschatology as the Transcendence of Death," *CBQ* 36 (1974) 21-43.

Collins, M. S., "The Question of Doxa: A Socio-literary Reading of the Wedding at Cana," *BTB* 25 (1995) 100-9.

Collins, R. F., "Cana (Jn. 2,1-12) – The First of his Signs or the Key to his Signs?," *IThQ* 47 (1980) 99-142.

———, "Jesus' Conversation with Nicodemus," *BiTod* 93 (1977) 1409-19.

———, "The Representative Figures in the Fourth Gospel," *DR* 94 (1976) 26-46 and 118-32.

———, *These Things Have Been Written. Studies on the Fourth Gospel* (LThPM 2) Louvain, Grand Rapids 1990.

Conway, C. M., *Men and Women in the Fourth Gospel: Gender and Johannine Charcterization* (SBL.DS 167) Missoula 1999.

Conzelmann, H., *Grundriß der Theologie des Neuen Testaments* (UTB 1446) Tübingen ⁶1997.

——— and Lindemann, A., *Interpreting the New Testament: An Introduction to the Principles and methods of N. T. Exegesis*, Peabody 1999.

Coppens, J., "Le Fils de l'homme dans l'évangile johannique," *EThL* 52 (1976) 28-81.

———, "Le prophète eschatologique. L'annonce de sa venue. Les relecture," *EThL* 49 (1973) 5-35.

———, *Le messianisme et sa relève prophétique. Les anticipations vétérotestamentaires. Leur accomplissement en Jésus*, Gembloux 1974.

———, *La relève apocalyptique du messianisme royal, Tome II: Le Fils de l'homme vété-ro et intertestamentaire* (BEThL 61) Louvain 1983.

Cosgrove, C. H., "The Place where Jesus is: Allusions to Baptism and the Eucharist in the Fourth Gospel," *NTS* 35 (1989) 522-39.

Cotterell, F. P., "The Nicodemus Conversation: A Fresh Appraisal," *ET* 96 (1984/85) 237-42.

Counet, P. and Chatelion, J. E., *John, a Post-Modern Gospel: Introduction to Deconstructive Exegesis Applied to the Fourth Gospel*, Leiden 2000.

Craffert, P. F., "Relationships between Social-Scientific, Literary and Rhetorical Interpretation of Texts," *BTB* 26 (1996) 45-55.

Crane, R. S., "The Concept of Plot," in: Scholes, R. (ed.), *Approaches to the Novel*, San Francisco 1966, 233-43.

Culler, J. D., *Structuralist Poetics: Structuralism, Linguistics and the Study of Literature*, Ithaca 1975.

Cullmann, O., *The Christology of the New Testament*, London ²1963.

———, *Heil als Geschichte*, Tübingen 1965.

———, "Der johanneische Gebrauch doppeldeutiger Ausdrücke als Schlüssel zum Verständnis des vierten Evangeliums," in: Cullmann, O. (ed.), *Vorträge und Aufsätze 1925-62*, Zürich 1966, 176-86.

———, *Der johanneische Kreis. Sein Platz im Spätjudentum, in der Jüngerschaft Jesu und im Urchristentum. Zum Ursprung des Johannesevangeliums*, Tübingen 1975.

Culpepper, R. A., *Anatomy of the Fourth Gospel. A Study in Literary Design*, Philadelphia 1983.

——— and Black, C. C. (eds.), *Exploring the Gospel of John: In Honour of D. Moody Smith*, Westminster 1996.

——— (ed.), *Johannine Literature*, Sheffield 2000.

———, *The Johannine School. An Evaluation of the Johannine School Hypothesis Based on an Investigation of the Nature of Ancient Schools* (SBL.DS 26) Missoula 1975.

———, "The Pivot of John's Prologue," *NTS* 27 (1980) 1-31.

———, "The Plot of John's Story of Jesus," *Interp.* 49 (1995) 347-58.

———, "Reading Johannine Irony," in: Culpepper, R. A. and Black, C. C. (eds.), *Exploring the Gospel of John. In Honour of D. Moody Smith*, Louisville, Westminster 1996, 194-207.

———, "Story and History in the Gospels," *RExp* 81 (1984) 467-78.

Dagonet, P., *Selon Saint Jean: Une Femme de Samarie*, Paris 1979.

Dahl, N. A., "Eschatology and History in the Light of the Dead Sea Scrolls," in: Robinson, J. M. (ed.), *The Future of Our Religious Past: Essays in Honour of Rudolf Bultmann*, London 1971, 9-28.

Dahms, J. V., "The Johannine Use of Monogenes Reconsidered," *NTS* 29 (1983) 222-32.

Dahood, M., "Chiasmus," *Interpreter's Dictionary of the Bible*, 5 Vols., Nashville 1976.

Dalman, G., *Die Worte Jesu mit Berücksichtigung des nachkanonischen jüdischen Schrifttums und der aramäischen Sprache*, Leipzig 1898.

Dauer, A., *Johannes und Lukas. Untersuchungen zu den johanneisch-lukanischen Parallelperikopen Joh 4,46/Lk 7,1-10 – Joh 12,1-8/Lk 7,36-50; 10,38-42 – Joh 20,19/Lk 24,36-49* (FzB 50) Würzburg 1984.

———, "Schichten im Johannesevangelium als Anzeichen von Entwicklungen in der (den) johanneischen Gemeinde(n) nach G. Richter. Darstellung und Kritik," in: Hierold,

A. E., Eid, V., Escribano-Alberca, I., Fuchs, O. and Glatzel, N. (eds.), *Die Kraft der Hoffnung. Gemeinde und Evangelium. FS J. Schneider*, Bamberg 1986, 62-83.

Davies, G. I., "The Presence of God in the Second Temple," in: Horbury, W. (ed.), *Templum Amicitiae: Essays on the Second Temple Presented to Ernst Bammel* (JSNT.S 48) Sheffield 1991, 32-36.

Davies, M., *Rhetoric and Reference in the Fourth Gospel* (JSNT.S 69) Sheffield 1992.

Davis, J. C., "The Johannine Concept of Eternal Life as a Present Possession," *RestQ* 27 (1984) 161-69.

de Boer, M. C. (ed.), *From Jesus to John. Essays on Jesus and New Testament Christology. FS M. de Jonge* (JSNT.S 84) Sheffield 1993.

——, "Jesus the Baptiser: 1 John 5:5-8 and the Gospel of John," *JBL* 107 (1988) 87-106.

——, *Johannine Perspectives on the Death of Jesus*, Pharos 1996.

——, "Narrative Criticism, Historical Criticism, and the Gospel of John," in: Ashton, J. (ed.), *The Interpretation of John*, Edinburgh ²1997, 301-14.

Deissler, A., "Der 'Menschensohn' und 'das Volk der Heiligen des Höchsten' in Dan 7," in: Pesch, R. and Schnackenburg, R. (eds.), *Jesus und der Menschensohn. FS A. Vögtle*, Freiburg 1975, 81-91.

de Jonge, M., "The Conflict between Jesus and the Jews, and the Radical Christology of the Fourth Gospel," *PRSt* 20 (1993) 341-55.

—— (ed.), *L'évangile de Jean. Sources, rédaction, théologie* (BEThL 44) Leuven 1977.

——, *Jesus: Stranger from Heaven and Son of God. Jesus Christ and the Christians in Johannine Perspective* (SBibSt) Missoula 1977.

——, "Jewish Expectations about the 'Messiah' according to the Fourth Gospel," *NTS* 19 (1972) 246-70.

——, "Nicodemus and Jesus: Some Observations on Misunderstanding and Understanding in the Fourth Gospel," *BJRL* 53 (1971) 337-59.

——, "The Radical Eschatology of the Fourth Gospel and the Eschatology of the Synoptics. Some Suggestions," in: Denaux, A. (ed.), *John and the Synoptics* (BEThL 101) Leuven 1992, 481-87.

Dekker, C., "Grundschrift und Redaktion im Johannesevangelium," *NTS* 13 (1966) 66-80.

de la Potterie, I., "Ad dialogum Jesu cum Nicodemo (2,23-3,21). Analysis litteraria," *VD* 47 (1969) 141-50.

——, "L'Esprit Saint dans l'Évangile de Jean," *NTS* 28 (1972) 448-51.

——, "L'evangelo di san Giovanni," in: Rinaldi, G. and Benedetti, P. (eds.), *Introduzione al Nuovo Testamento*, Brescia 1971.

——, "Jesus et Nicodemus: de necessitate generationis ex Spiritu (Jo 3,1-10)," *VD* 47 (1969) 193-214.

——, "Jesus et Niocodemus: de revelatione Jesu et vera fide in eum (Jo 3,11-21)," *VD* 47 (1969) 257-83.

——, "'Naître de l'eau et naître de l'Esprit'. Le texte baptismal de Jn 3,5," *ScEc* 14 (1962) 417-43.

——, "Parole et Esprit dans S. Jean," in: de Jonge, M. (ed.), *L'Évangile de Jean. Sources, Sources, rédaction, théologie* (BEThL 44) Gembloux, Leuven 1977, 177-201.

——, "Structura primae partis Evangelii Johannis (capita III et IV)," *VD* 47 (1969) 130-40.

——, "Structure du Prologue de Saint Jean," *NTS* 30 (1984) 354-81.

——, "The Truth in Saint John," in: J. Ashton (ed.), *The Interpretation of John*, London 1997, 67-82.

——, *La vérité dan S. Jean*, 2 Vols. (AnBib 73/74) Rome 1977.

de Mello, A., "Von Neuem geboren. Eine Symbolmeditation über Joh 3,3," in: Soares-Prabhu, G. M. (ed.), *Wir werden bei ihm wohnen. Das Johannesevangelium in indi-*

scher Deutung (TDW 6) Basel, Freiburg, Wien 1984, 124-28.

Denaux, A., "The Q-Logion Mt 11,27/Lk 10,22 and the Gospel of John," in: Denaux, A. (ed.), *John and the Synoptics* (BEThL 101) Leuven 1992, 163-99.

den Heyer, C. J., *Jesus and the Doctrine of the Atonement: Biblical Notes on a Controversial Topic*, Minneapolis 1998.

Derrett, J. D. M., "The Bronze Serpent," *EstB* 49 (1991) 311-29.

Detweiler, R. and Robbins, V. K., "From New Criticism to Post-structuralism: Twentieth-Century Hermeneutics," in: Prickett, S. (ed.), *Reading the Text: Biblical Criticism and Literary Theory*, Cambridge 1991, 225-80.

de Vaux, R., *Les institutions de l'Ancien Testament*, Vol. 1, Paris ²1967, 58-60.

Dexinger, F., *Der Taheb. Ein "messianischer" Heilsbringer der Samaritaner*, Salzburg 1986.

Dobbs-Allsopp, F. W., "Rethinking Historical Criticism," *BibInt* 7 (1998) 235-71.

Dodd, C. H., *Historical Tradition in the Fourth Gospel*, Cambridge 1963.

Doignon, J., L'esprit souffle où il veut (Jn III,8) dans la plus ancienne tradition patristique latine," *RSPhTh* 62 (1978) 345-59.

Donahue, J. R., "Recent Studies on the Origin of the 'Son of Man' in the Gospels," *CBQ* 48 (1986) 484-98.

Dowell, T. M., "Jews and Christians in Conflict: Why the Fourth Gospel Changed the Synoptic Tradition," *LouvSt* 15 (1990) 19-37.

Dschulnigg, P., " Nikodemus im Johannesevangelium," *SNTU* 24 (1999) 103-18.

Duke, P. D., *Irony in the Fourth Gospel*, Atlanta 1985.

Dunderberg, I., *Johannes und die Synoptiker. Studien zu Joh 1-9* (AASF.DHL 69) Helsinki 1994.

Dunn, J. D. G., *Baptism in the Holy Spirit. A Re-examination of the New Testament Teaching on the Gift of the Spirit in relation to Pentacostalism Today*, London 1970.

—— (ed.), *Jews and Christians. The Parting of the Ways A. D. 70 to 135* (WUNT 66) Tübingen ²1999.

du Plessis, I. J., "Integrating Historical and Literary Study: Luke as a Case Study," Paper read at 1995 SNTS meeting.

du Rand, J. A., "The Characterization of Jesus as Depicted in the Narrative of the Fourth Gospel," *Neotest.* 19 (1985) 18-36.

——, "Plot and Point of View in the Gospel of John," in: Petzer, J. H. and Hartin, P. J. (eds.), *A South African Perspective on the New Testament. FS B. M. Metzger*, Leiden 1986, 149-69.

——, "Repetitions and Variations – Experiencing the Power of the Gospel of John as Literary Symphony," *Neotest.* 30 (1996) 59-70.

Eckert, F., *Das Schweigen des Nikodemus. 49 Wortmeldungen eines Grenzgängers*, Basel, Freiburg, Wien 1990.

Eco, U., *The Role of the Reader: Explorations in the Semiotics of Texts*, Bloomington 1979.

Eisler, R., *The Enigma of the Fourth Gospel*, London 1938.

Elliot, J. H., *What is Social-Scientific Criticism?* (GBSNT) Minneapolis 1993.

Ellis, E. E., *Christ and the Future in New Testament History*, Leiden 1999.

Empson, W., *Seven Types of Ambiguity*, New York 1966.

Ernst, J., *Johannes. Ein theologisches Portrait*, Düsseldorf 1991.

——, *Johannes der Täufer. Interpretation – Geschichte – Wirkungsgeschichte* (BZNW 53) Berlin, New York 1989.

——, "War Jesus ein Schüler Johannes des Täufers," in: Frankemölle, H. and Kertelge, K. (eds.), *Vom Urchristentum zu Jesus, FS J. Gnilka*, Basel, Freiburg, Wien 1989, 13-33.

Evans, C. A., "Jesus' Action in the Temple: Cleansing or Portent of Destruction?," *CBQ* 51 (1989) 237-70.

Ewert, D., "Born of the Spirit. John 3:1-8," in: Brunk, G. R. (ed.), *Encounter with the Holy Spirit*, Scottdale 1972, 16-25.

Farmer, W. R. (ed.), *Anti-Judaism and the Gospels*, Minneapolis 1999.

Fascher, E., "Theologische Beobachtungen zu δεῖ," in: *Neutestamentliche Studien für R. Bultmann* (BZNW 21) Berlin 1957, 228-54.

Fehribach, A., *The Women in the Life of the Bridegroom: A Feminist Historical-Literary Analysis of the Female Characters in the Fourth Gospel*, Collegeville 1998.

Festugière, A.-J., *Observations stylistiques sur l'évangile de S. Jean* (EeC 84) Paris 1974.

Feuillet, A., "Le baptême de Jésus commenté par le précurseur. Contribution à l'étude du Christ et de l'Esprit-Saint dans leurs rapports avec l'Église dans le Quatrième Évangile," *NT* 61 (1986) 90-140.

———, "Les épousailles du Messie: la mère de Jésus et l'Église dans le Quatrième Évangile," *RThom* 86 (1986) 257-391 and 536-75.

———, *Le mystére de l'amour divin dans la théologie johannique*, Paris 1972.

———, "La signification théologique du second miracle de Cana (Jo. IV. 46-54)," *RSR* 48 (1960) 62-75.

Filson, F. V., "The Gospel of Life," in: Klassen, W. and Snyder, G. F. (eds.), *Current Issues in New Testament Interpretation*, New York 1962, 111-23.

Finkel, A. and Frizzel, L. (eds.), *Standing Before God: Studies on Prayer in Scriptures and in Tradition with Essays in Honour of John M. Österreicher*, New York 1981.

Fischer, U., *Eschatologie und Jenseitserwartung im hellenistischen Diasporajudentum* (BZNW 44) Berlin, New York 1978.

Fitzmyer, J. A., *The Dead Sea Scrolls and Christian Origins*, Grand Rapids 2000.

Flanagan, N. M., "The Gospel of John as Drama," *BiTod* 19 (1981) 264-70.

Fohrer, G, "σῴζω and σωτηρία in the Old Testament," *TDNT*, VII, 970-80.

Forestell, J. T., *The Word of the Cross. Salvation as Revelation in the Fourth Gospel* (AnBib 57) Rome 1974.

Forster, E. M., *Aspects of the Novel*, New York 1962.

Fortna, R.T., *The Fourth Gospel and its Predecessor. From Narrative Source to Present Gospel*, Edinburgh, Philadelphia 1989.

———, *The Gospel of Signs. A Reconstruction of the Narrative Source Underlying the Fourth Gospel* (MSSNTS 11) Cambridge 1970.

Fowler, R. M., "Born of Water and the Spirit (Jn 3:5)," *ET* 83 (1970/71) 159.

———, *Let the Reader Understand: Reader-Response Criticism and the Gospel of Mark*, Minneapolis 1991.

Fradua, J. L., "Das ewige Leben in den johanneischen Schriften," *IKaZ* 20 (1991) 23-32.

Freed, E. D., "Did John Write his Gospel Partly to Win Samaritan Converts?," *NT* 12 (1970) 241-56.

———, "*Ego eimi* in John 1,20 and 4,25," *CBQ* 41 (1979) 288-91.

———, "The Son of Man in the Fourth Gospel," *JBL* 86 (1967) 402-9.

Frei, H. W., *The Eclipse of Biblical Narrative: A Study in Eighteenth and Nineteenth Century Hermeneutics*, London, New Haven 1974.

Frey, J., *Die johanneische Eschatologie. Band I: Ihre Probleme im Spiegel der Forschung seit Reimarus* (WUNT 96) Tübingen 1997.

———, *Die johanneische Eschatologie. Band II: Das johanneische Zeitverständnis* (WUNT 110) Tübingen 1998.

———, "'Wie Mose die Schlange in der Wüste erhöht hat...' Zur frühchristlichen Deutung der 'ehernen Schlange' und ihrer christologischen Rezeption in Johannes 3,14f.," in: Hengel, M. and Lohr, H. (eds.), *Schriftauslegung im antiken Judentum und im*

Urchristentum (WUNT 73) Tübingen 1994, 153-205.

Freyne, S., *Galilee and Gospel: Collected Essays* (Tübingen 1999).

Friedman, N., "Forms of the Plot," in: Stevic, P. (ed.), *The Theory of the Novel,* New York 1967, 145-66.

Fuller, R. H., "Lower and Higher Christology in the Fourth Gospel," in: Fortna, R. T. and Gaventa, B. R. (eds.), *The Conversation Continues. Studies in Paul and John. In Honour of J. Louis Martyn*, Nashville 1990, 357-65.

———, "New Testament Roots to the Theotokos," *MarSt* 29 (1978) 46-64.

Fyre, N., *Anatomy of Criticism*, Princeton 1971.

———, *The Great Code. The Bible and Literature*, London, New York 1981.

Gabriel, A., "Faith and Rebirth in the Fourth Gospel," *BiBh* 16 (1990) 205-15.

Gaeta, G., *Il dialogo con Nicodemo. Per l'interpretazione del capitolo terzo dell'evangelo di Giovanni* (StBi 26) Brescia 1974.

Gaffney, J., "Believing and Knowing in the Fourth Gospel," *TS* 26 (1965) 215-41.

Gander, G., "Jean III,22 à IV,3 parle-t-il d'un baptême administré par Jésus?," *RTP* 36 (1948) 133-37.

García Martínez, F. and Barrera, J. T., *The People of the Dead Sea Scrolls. Their Writings, Beliefs and Practices*, Leiden 1993.

Genette, G., *Narrative Discourse: An Essay in Method*, Ithaca, New York 1980.

———, *Nouveau discours de récit*, Paris 1983.

Geoltrain, P., "Les noces à Cana: Jean 2,1-12: Analyse des structures narratives," *FV* 73 (1974) 83-90.

Giblet, J., "Prophétisme et attente d'un Messie Prophète dans l'ancien Judaïsme," in: Cerfaux, L. (ed.), *L'attente du Messie* (RechBib 1) Bruges 1954, 85-130.

Giblin, C. H., "Suggestion, Negative Response and Positive Action in St. John's Portrayal of Jesus," *NTS* 26 (1979/80) 197-211.

Giesen, H., *Herrschaft Gottes – heute oder morgen? Zur Heilsbotschaft Jesu und der synoptischen Evangelien* (BU 26) Regensburg 1995.

Girard, M., "La composition structurelle des sept 'signes' dans le quatrième évangile," *SR* 9 (1980) 315-24.

———, "Jésus en Samarie (Jean 4,1-42): Analyse des structures stylistiques et du processus de symbolisation," *EeT(O)* 17 (1986) 275-310.

———, *Les Psaumes. Analyse structurelle et interpretation, Tome I, 1-50*, Montréal, Paris 1984.

———, "Le semblant de fils d'homme de Daniel 7, un personnage du monde d'en haut: approche structurelle," *ScEs* 35 (1983) 265-93.

———, "La structure heptapartite de quatrième évangile," *SR* 5 (1975/76) 350-59.

Glasson, T. F., *Moses in the Fourth Gospel* (SBT 40) London 1963.

Gnilka, J., "Zur Christologie des Johannesevangeliums," in: Kasper, W. (ed.), *Christologische Schwerpunkte*, Düsseldorf 1980, 92-107.

———, "Der historische Jesus als der gegenwärtige Christus im Johannesevangelium," *BiLe* 7 (1966) 270-78.

Goergen, D. J., *Jesus, Son of God, Son of Mary, Immanuel* (ThJS 4) Collegeville 1995.

Golub, J., "...non enim ad mensuram dat Spiritum (Jo 3,34b)," *VD* 43 (1965) 62-70.

Goppelt, L., "Taufe und neues Leben nach Joh 3 und Röm 6," *SOrth* 4 (1970) 51-53; and 5 (1970) 36-41.

Görg, M., "Vom Wehen des Pneuma," *BN* 66 (1993) 5-9.

Goulder, M. D., "Nicodemus," *SJTh* 44 (1991) 153-68.

Gourgues, M., "Notes critiques: Sur la structure et la Christologie de Jean 3. Approche et apport d'un ouvrage récent," *ScEs* 46 (1994) 221-27.

———, *Pour que vous croyiez. Pistes d'exploration de l'évangile de Jean* (Initiations) Paris

1982.

———, "Section christologique et section eucharistique en Jean VI: une proposition," *RB* 88 (1981) 515-31.

Graf, J., "Nikodemus (Joh 3,1-21)," *ThQ* 132 (1952) 62-86.

Gräßer, E., "Die antijüdische Polemik im Johannesevangelium," *NTS* 11 (1964/65) 74-90.

———, "Die Juden als Teufelssöhne in Johannes 8,37-47," in: Eckert, W. (ed.), *Antijudaismus im Neuen Testament? Exegetische und systematische Beiträge* (ACJD 2) München 1967, 157-70.

Grayston, K., "Who Misunderstands the Johannine Misunderstandings?," *ScrB* 20 (1989) 9-15.

Greeven, H., "προσκυνέω," *TDNT*, VI, 760-61.

Greiner, A., "Le serpent d'Airain et le Crucifié. Quelques réflexions relatives à deux textes bibliques conjoints," *PosLuth* 34 (1986) 22-27.

Gremias, A. J., *Semantique structurale*, Paris 1966.

Grese, W. C., "'Unless One is Born Again:' The Use of a Heavenly Journey in John 3," *JBL* 107 (1988) 677-93.

Grigsby, B. H., "The Cross as an Expiatory Sacrifice in the Fourth Gospel," *JSNT* 15 (1982) 51-80.

Grob, F., *Faire l'œuvre de Dieu. Christologie et éthique dans l'Évangile de Jean* (EHPhR 68) Paris 1986.

Gros Louis, K. R. R., *Literary Interpretations of Biblical Narratives II*, Nashville 1982.

Grossouw, W., "La glorification du Christ dans le quatrième évangile," in: *L'évangile de Jean. Études et problèmes*, Paris 1958, 131-45.

Grundmann, W., "δει," *TDNT*, II, 21-25.

———, *Der Zeuge der Wahrheit. Grundzüge der Christologie des Johannesevangeliums*, Berlin 1985.

Grünwald, I., *Apocalyptic and Merkavah Mysticism*, Leiden 1980.

Guelich, R., "The Gospel Genre," in: Stuhlmacher, P. (ed.), *Das Evangelium und die Evangelien. Vorträge vom Tübinger Symposium 1982* (WUNT 28) Tübingen 1983, 181-209.

Guillet, J., "À propos des titres de Jésus: Christ, Fils de l'homme, Fils de Dieu," in: *À la rencontre de Dieu. Mémorial Albert Giblin* (BFCTL 8) Le Puy 1961, 309-17.

Gundry, R. H., "Recent Investigations into the Literary Genre 'Gospel,'" in: Longenecker, R. and Tenney, M. (eds.), *New Dimensions in New Testament Study*, Grand Rapids 1974, 97-114.

——— and Howell, R. W., "The Sense and Syntax of John 3.14-17 with Special Reference to the Use of οὕτως ...... ὥστε in John 3:16," *NT* 41 (1999) 24-39.

Guthrie, D., "Importance of Signs in the Fourth Gospel," *VoxEv* 5 (1967) 72-83.

Haacker, K., *Die Stiftung des Heils. Untersuchungen zur Struktur der johanneischen Theologie* (AzTh 47) Stuttgart 1972.

Hahn, F., *Christologische Hoheitstitel. Ihre Geschichte im frühen Christentum* (FRLANT 83) Göttingen 1963.

———, "Das Glaubensverständnis im Johannesevangelium," in: Gräßer, E. and Merk, O. (eds.), *Glaube und Eschatologie. FS Werner Georg Kümmel zum 80. Geburtstag*, Tübingen 1985, 51-69.

———, "Die Jüngerberufung Joh 1,25-51," in: Gnilka, J. (ed.), *Neues Testament und Kirche: Für Rudolf Schnackenburg*, Freiburg 1974.

Hainz, J., "'Zur Krisis kam ich in die Welt' (Joh 9,39). Zur Eschatologie im Johannesevangelium," in: Klauck, H.-J. (ed.), *Weltgericht und Weltvollendung. Zukunftsbilder im Neuen Testament* (QD 150) Basel, Freiburg, Wien 1994, 149-63.

Hamerton-Kelly, R. G., *Pre-existence, Wisdom, and the Son of Man. A Study of the Idea of*

Pre-existence in the New Testament (MSSNTS 21) Cambridge 1973.

Hammer, P. L., "Baptism with Water and the Spirit," *ThLS* 8 (1965) 35-43.

Hampel, V., *Menschensohn und historischer Jesus. Ein Rätselwort als Schlüssel zum messianischen Selbstverständnis Jesu*, Neukirchen-Vluyn 1990.

Hanhart, K., "The Structure of John I 35 - IV 54," in: *Studies in John. Presented to J. N. Sevenster on the Occasion of his Seventieth-Birthday* (NT.S 24) Leiden1970, 22-46.

Hanson, A. T., *The Prophetic Gospel. A Study of John and the Old Testament*, Edinburgh 1991.

Hare, D. R. A., *The Son of Man Tradition*, Minneapolis 1990.

Harner, P. B., *The "I am" of the Fourth Gospel* (FB.B 26) Philadelphia 1970.

——, *Relation Analysis of the Fourth Gospel: A Study in Reader-Response Criticism*, Lewiston 1993.

Harrington, D. J., "Sociological Concepts and the Early Church: A Decade of Research," *TS* 41 (1980) 181-90.

Harris, M. J., "Prepositions and Theology in the Greek New Testament," *NIDNT*, III, 1171-1215.

Harsh, P. W., *A Handbook of Classical Drama*, Palo Alto 1944.

Hartin, P. J., "A Community in Crisis. The Christology of the Johannine Community as the Point at Issue," *Neotest.* 19 (1985) 37-49.

Harvey, A. E., "Christ as Agent," in: Hurst, L. D. and Wright, N. T. (eds.), *The Glory of Christ in the New Testament*, Oxford 1987, 239-50.

Hasel, G. F., "The Identity of 'The Saints of the Most High' in Daniel 7," *Bib.* 56 (1975) 173-92.

Hasitschka, M., "Sozialgeschichtliche Anmerkungen zum Johannesevangelium," *PzB* 1 (1992) 59-67.

Hasler, V., *Amen: Redaktionsgeschichtliche Untersuchung zur Einführungsformel der Herrenworte "Wahrlich, ich sage euch"*, Stuttgart, Zürich 1969.

——, "Glauben und Erkennen im Johannesevangelium. Strukturale und hermeneutische Überlegungen," *EvTh* 50 (1990) 279-96.

Hatina, T. R., "Intertextuality and Historical Criticism in New Testament Studies: Is There a Relationship?," *BibInt* 7 (1999) 28-43.

Hawkin, D. J., *The Johannine World: Reflections on the Theology of the Fourth Gospel and Contemporary Society*, Albany 1996.

Hays, J. H. and Holladay, C. R., *Biblical Exegesis. A Beginner's Handbook*, Atlanta 1987.

Heer, J., "Johanneische Botschaft (VI). Der Offenbarer und Nikodemus (Jo 3,1-12)," *SuS* 32 (1967) 435-49.

Hegermann, H., "Er kam in sein Eigentum. Zur Bedeutung des Erdenwirkens Jesu im vierten Evangelium," in: Lohse, E., Schaller, B. and Burchard, C. (eds.), *Der Ruf Jesu und die Antwort der Gemeinde. Exegetische Untersuchungen. FS Joachim Jeremias zum 70. Geburtstag,*Göttingen 1970, 112-31.

Heise, J., *Bleiben - Menein in den Johanneischen Schriften* (HUTh 8) Tübingen 1967.

Hélou, C., *Symbole et langage dans les écrits johanniques: lumière-ténèbres*, Paris 1980.

Hemelsoet, B., "L'Ensevelissement selon saint Jean," in: *Studies in John. Presented to J. N. Sevenster on the Occasion of his Seventieth-Birthday* (NT.S 24) (Leiden 1970) 47-65.

Hengel, M., "Christological Titles in Early Christianity," in: Charlesworth, J. H. (ed.), *The Messiah. Developments in Earliest Judaism and Christianity*, Minneapolis 1992, 425-48.

——, "The Interpretation of the Wine Miracle at Cana: John 2:1-11," in: Hurst, L. D. and Wright, N. T. (eds.), *The Glory of Christ in the New Testament Studies in Christology in Memory of George Bradford Caird*, Oxford 1987, 83-112.

——— , "Jesus als messianischer Lehrer der Weisheit und die Anfänge der Christologie," in: *Sagesse et Religion. Colloque de Strasbourg, Octobre 1976*, Paris 1979, 148-88.

——— , *Der Sohn Gottes. Die Entstehung der Christologie und die jüdisch-hellenistische Religionsgeschichte*, Tübingen 1975.

——— , *Studies in Christology*, Edinburgh 1998.

Henning, J. S., "Realized Eschatology: A Study of John's Gospel and Gestalt Therapy," *BiTod* 68 (1973) 1332-34.

Herzog, W. R., II, *Jesus, Justice, and the Reign of God: A Ministry of Liberation*, Louisville 1999.

Hiers, R. H., "Purification of the Temple: Preparation for the Kingdom of God," *JBL* 90 (1971) 82-90.

Higgins, A. J. B., *The Son of Man in the Teaching of Jesus* (MSSNTS 39) Cambridge 1980.

Hill, D., "Dikaioi as a Quasi-Technical Term," *NTS* 11 (1964/65) 296-302

Hinderer, W., "Theory, Conception, and Interpretation of the Symbol," in: Strelka, J. (ed.), *Perspectives in Literary Symbolism* (YBCC 1) University Park 1968.

Hitchcock, F. R. M., "Is the Fourth Gospel a Drama?," in: Stibbe, M. W. G. (ed.), *The Gospel of John as Literature. An Anthology of Twentieth-Century Perspectives*, Köln, Leiden, New York 1993, 15-24.

Hodges, Z. C., "Problem Passages in the Gospel of John. Part 2: Untrustworthy Believers - John 2:23-25," *BS* 135 (1978) 139-52.

——— , "Problem Passages in the Gospel of John. Part 3: Water and Spirit – John 3,5," *BS* 135 (1978) 206-20.

——— , "Problem Passages in the Gospel of John. Part 4: Coming to the Light – John 3:20-21," *BS* 135 (1978) 314-22.

Hofbeck, S., *Semeion. Der Begriff des 'Zeichen' im Johannesevangelium unter Berücksichtigung seiner Vorgeschichte* (MüSt 3) Münsterschwarzach 1970.

Hofius, O., "Das Wunder der Wiedergeburt. Jesu Gespräch mit Nicodemus. Jn. 3,1-21," in: Hofius, O. and Kammler, H.-C. (eds.), *Johannesstudien: Untersuchungen zur Theologie des vierten Evangeliums* (WUNT 88) Tübingen 1996, 33-80.

——— , "'Er gibt den Geist ohne Maß' Joh 3,34b," *ZNW* 90 (1999)131-34.

Hollis, H., "The Root of the Johannine Pun – 'ΥΨΩΘΗΝΑΙ," *NTS* 36 (1989) 475-78.

Holmberg, B., *Sociology and the New Testament. An Appraisal*, Philadelphia 1990.

Hooker, M. D., "John the Baptist and the Johannine Prologue," *NTS* 16 (1970) 354-58.

——— , *The Signs of a Prophet: The Prophetic Actions of Jesus*, Minneapolis 1997.

Höppl, B., *Das Nachtgespräch mit Nikodemus. Urtext, Übersetzungen, Kommentar und Meditationen zum Johannesevangelium Kapitel 3,1-21*, Münsing 1983.

Horbury, W., "The Messianic Associations of 'the Son of Man'," *JTS* 36 (1985) 34-55.

Horrell, D. G. (ed.), *Social-Scientific Approaches to New Testament Interpretation*, Edinburgh 1999.

Horsley, R. A., "'Messianic' Figures and Movements in First-Century Palestine," in: Charlesworth, J. H. (ed.), *The Messiah. Developments in Earliest Judaism and Christianity*, Minneapolis 1992, 276-95.

——— and Hanson, J. S., *Bandits, Prophets, and Messiahs: Popular Movements in the Time of Jesus*, Philadelphia ²1999.

Horst, U., "Heilsverlangen und Wiedergeburt. Zu Joh 3:1-12," *AnzKG* 88 (1979) 408.

Howton, J., "The Son of God in the Fourth Gospel," *NTS* 10 (1963/64) 227-37.

Hoyt, H. A., "The Explanation of the New Birth," *GrJ* 8 (1967) 14-21.

Hudry-Clergeon, C., "De Judée en Galilée: Étude de Jean 4:1-45," *NRTh* 103 (1981) 818-30.

Huffmon, H. B, Spina, F. A. and A. Green, A. R. W. (eds.), *The Quest for the Kingdom of*

God: Studies in Honour of George E. Mendenhall, Winona Lake 1983.

Hull, W. E., *Love in Four Dimensions: John 3:16. Divine Love in Human Life*, Nashville 1982.

Hurst, L. D. and Wright, N. T. (eds.), *The Glory of Christ in the New Testament. Studies in Christology*, Oxford 1987.

Ibuki, Y., "Die Doxa des Gesandten. Studie zur johanneischen Christologie," *AJBI* 14 (1988) 38-81.

——, "Καὶ τὴν φωνὴν αὐτοῦ ἀκούεις - Gedankenaufbau und Hintergrund des 3. Kapitels des Johannesevangeliums," *BSU* 14 (1978) 9-33.

——, "Über den johanneischen Kosmosbegriff," *BSU* 18 (1981) 27-55.

——, "Viele glaubten an ihn - Auseinandersetzung mit dem Glauben im Johannesevangelium," *AJBI* 9 (1983) 128-83.

——, *Die Wahrheit im Johannesevangelium* (BBB 39) Bonn 1972.

Infante, L., "L'amico dello sposo. Figura del ministero di Giovanni Battista nel quarto vangelo," *RivBib* 31 (1983) 3-19.

Ingarden, R., *Das literarische Kunstwerk*, Tübingen 1960.

James, H., "The Art of Fiction," in: Edel, L. (ed.), *Henry James: Selected Fiction*, New York 1953, 585-609.

Jaubert, A., "Les images d'eau vives dans le judaïsme contemporain du IVe évangile," in: Jaubert, A. (ed.), *Approches de l'évangile de Jean*, Paris 1976, 140-46.

——, "Symbolique de l'eau et connaissance de Dieu," *FV* 64 (1965) 455-63.

——, "La symbolique du puits de Jacob (Jean 4,12)," in: de Lubac, H. (ed.), *L'homme devant Dieu. Mélanges*, Lyon 1963, 63-73.

Jefferson, A., "Russian Formalism," in: Jefferson, A. and Robey, D. (eds.), *Modern Literary Theory. A Comparative Introduction*, Totowa 1982, 16-37.

Jeremias, J., "νύμφη," *TDNT*, IV, 1099-1106.

——, "πολλοί," *TDNT*, VI, 536.

——, *Theology of the New Testament*, London 1971.

Johns, L. L. and Miller, D. B., "The Signs as Witnesses in the Fourth Gospel: Reexamining the Evidence," *CBQ* 56 (1994) 519-35.

Johnston, G., "*Ecce Homo*! Irony in the Christology of the Fourth Evangelist," in: Hurst, L. D. and Wright, N. T. (eds.), *The Glory of Christ in the New Testament. Studies in Christology*, Oxford 1987, 125-50.

Johnston, R. E. C., *From an Author-Oriented to a Text-Oriented Hermeneutic: Implications of Paul Ricoeur's Hermeneutical Theory for the Interpretation of the New Testament*, Leuven 1977.

—— and Henry, P., *New Directions in New Testament Study*, Philadelphia 1979.

Jones, L. P., *The Symbol of Water in the Gospel of John* (JSNT.S 145) Sheffield 1997.

Joubert, S. J., "A Bone of Contention in Recent Scholarship: The 'birkat ha-mimim' and the Separation of Church and Synagogue in the First-Century A. D.," *Neotest.* 27 (1993) 351-63.

Juel, D., *Messiah and Temple. The Trial of Jesus in the Gospel of Mark* (SBL.DS 31) Missoula 1977, 169-209.

Kaestli, J. D., Poffet, J.-M. and Zumstein, J. (eds.), *La communauté johannique et son histoire. La trajectoire de l'évangile de Jean aux deux premiers siècles* (MB) Geneva 1990.

Kamlah, E., "πνεῦμα," *NIDNT*, III, 689-93.

Kammler, H.-C., "Jesus Christus und der Geistparaklet. Eine Studie zur johanneischen Verhältnisbestimmung von Pneumatologie und Christologie," in: Hofius, O. and Kammler, H.-C. (eds.), *Johannesstudien: Untersuchungen zur Theologie des vierten Evangeliums* (WUNT 88) Tübingen 1996, 87-190.

Kanagaraj, J., *'Mysticism' in the Gospel of John: An Inquiry into its Background* (JSNT.S 158) Sheffield 1998.

Karrer, M., *Jesus Christus im Neuen Testament* (NTD Ergänzungsreihe 11) Göttingen 1998.

Katz, S. T., "Issues in the Separation of Judaism and Christianity after 70 C.E.: A Reconsideration," *JBL* 103 (1984) 43-76.

Kawin, B. F., *Telling it Again and Again: Repetition in Literature and Film*, Ithaca 1972.

Kee, H. C., *Knowing the Truth. A Sociological Approach to New Testament Interpretation*, Minneapolis 1989.

—— and L. H. Cohic (eds.), *Evolution of the Synagogue: Problems and Progress*, Minneapolis 1999.

Kelber, W. H., *The Oral and Written Gospel. The Hermeneutics of Speaking and Writing in the Synoptic Tradition, Mark, Paul and Q*, Philadelphia 1983.

Kemper, F., "Zur literarischen Gestalt des Johannesevangeliums," *ThZ* 43 (1987) 247-64.

Kennedy, G. A., *New Testament Interpretation Through Rhetorical Criticism*, Chapel Hill, London 1984.

Kermode, F., *The Genesis of Secrecy: On the Interpretation of Narrative*, Cambridge 1979.

——, *The Sense of an Ending: Studies in the Theory of Fiction*, London, New York 1967.

Kieffer, R., "L'espace et le temps dans l'évangile de Jean," *NTS* 31 (1985) 393-409.

——, *Le monde symbolique de saint Jean* (LeDiv 137) Paris 1989.

Kim, S., *'The Son of Man' as the Son of God* (WUNT 30) Tübingen 1983.

King, J. S., "Nicodemus and the Pharisees," *ET* 98 (1986/87) 45.

Kingsbury, J. D. (ed.), *Gospel Interpretation: Narrative-Critical and Social-Scientific Approaches*, Minneapolis 1999.

Klaiber, W., "Der irdische und der himmlische Zeuge. Eine Auslegung von Joh 3,22-36," *NTS* 36 (1990) 205-33.

Klappert, B., "βασιλεία," *NIDNT*, II, 372-89.

Klauck, H.-J., *Die antike Briefliteratur und das Neue Testament* (UTB 2022) München, Paderborn, Wien, Zürich 1998.

——, *Der erste Johannesbrief* (EKK XXIII/1) Neukirchen-Vluyn, Zürich 1991.

——, "Gemeinde ohne Amt? Erfahrungen mit der Kirche in den johanneischen Schriften," *BZ* 29 (1985) 193-220.

—— (ed.), *Weltgericht und Weltvollendung. Zukunftsbilder im Neuen Testament* (QD 150) Basel, Freiburg, Wien 1994.

——, *Der zweite und dritte Johannesbrief* (EKK XXIII/2) Neukirchen-Vluyn, Zürich 1992.

Klein, H., "Die Gemeinschaft der Gotteskinder. Zur Ekklesiologie der johanneischen Schriften," in: Hauschild, W.-D. (ed.), *Kirchengemeinschaft – Anspruch und Wirklichkeit. FS Georg Kretschmar zum 60. Geburtstag*, Stuttgart 1986, 59-67.

Knight, G. A. F., *Christ the Centre*, Grand Rapids 1999.

Koester, C. R., "Hearing, Seeing, and Believing in the Gospel of John," *Bib.* 70 (1989) 327-48.

——, "Messianic Exegesis and the Call of Nathanael (John 1:45-51)," *JSNT* 39 (1990) 23-34.

——, "'The Saviour of the World' (John 4,42)," *JBL* 109 (1990) 665-80.

——, *Symbolism in the Fourth Gospel. Meaning, Mystery, Community*, Minneapolis 1995.

Kohler, H., *Kreuz und Menschwerdung im Johannesevangelium. Ein exegetisch-hermeneutischer Versuch zur johanneischen Kreuzestheologie* (AThANT 72) Zürich 1987.

Kopp, C., *The Holy Places of the Gospels*, New York 1963.

Korting, G., *Die esoterische Struktur des Johannesevangeliums*, 2 Vols. (BU 25) Regensburg 1994.

Köstenberger, A. J., *Encountering John: The Gospel in Historical, Literary, and Theological Perspective* (EBS) Grand Rapids 1999.

———, *The Missions of Jesus and the Disciples according to the Fourth Gospel: With Implications for the Fourth Gospel's Purpose and the Mission of the Contemporary Church*, Grand Rapids 1998.

Kramer, W., *Christos Kyrios Gottessohn. Untersuchungen zu Gebrauch und Bedeutung der christologischen Bezeichnungen bei Paulus und den vorpaulinischen Gemeinden* (AThANT 44) Zürich 1963.

Krieger, N. "Fiktive Orte der Johannes Taufe," *ZNW* 45 (1953/54) 121-23.

Kuhn, H.-J., *Christologie und Wunder. Untersuchungen zu Joh 1,35-51* (BU 18) Regensburg 1988.

Kuhn, H.-W., *Enderwartung und gegenwärtiges Heil: Untersuchungen zu den Gemeinden von Qumran, mit einen Anhang über Eschatologie und Gegenwart in der Verkündigung Jesu*, Göttingen 1966.

Kuhn, K. G., "Die in Palästina gefundenen hebräischen Texte und das Neue Testament," *ZTK* 47 (1950) 192-211.

Kümmel, W. G., *Jesus der Menschensohn?*, Stuttgart, Wiesbaden 1984.

Kuschel, K.-J., *Geboren vor aller Zeit? Der Streit um Christi Ursprung*, München 1990.

Kuzenzama, K. P. M., "La conception johannique de la 'montée-descente' du Fils de l'Homme. Étude sémantique," *RAT* 1 (1977) 207-18.

Kysar, R., "The Eschatology of the Fourth Gospel – A Correction of Bultmann's Redactional Hypothesis," *Perspective* 13 (1972) 23-33.

———, *The Fourth Evangelist and His Gospel*, Minneapolis 1975.

———, *John. The Maverick Gospel*, Louisville, Westminster 1993.

———, "The Making of Metaphor: Another Reading of John 3.1-15," in: Segovia, F. F. (ed.), *'What is John?' Readers and Readings of the Fourth Gospel*, Atlanta 1996, 21-41.

———, *John's Story of Jesus*, Philadelphia 1984.

Lattke, M., *Einheit im Wort. Die spezifische Bedeutung von 'ἀγάπη,' 'ἀγαπᾶν' und 'φιλεῖν' im Johannesevangelium* (StANT 41) München 1975.

Le Déaut, R. (ed.), *Targum du pentateuque III Nombres* (SC 261) Paris 1979.

Lee, D. A., *The Symbolic Narratives of the Fourth Gospel. The Interplay of Form and Meaning* (JSNT.S 95) Sheffield 1994.

Légasse, S., "Le Baptême administré par Jésus (Jn 3,22-26; 4,1-3) et l'origine du baptême chrétien," *BLE* 78 (1977) 3-30.

Leidig, E., *Jesu Gespräch mit der Samaritanerin und weitere Gespräche im Johannesevangelium* (ThDiss 15) Basel 1979.

Leivestad, R., "Exit the Apocalyptic Son of Man," *NTS* 18 (1971/72) 234-67.

Léon-Dufour, X., "'Et là, Jésus baptisait' (Jn 3,22)," in: *Mélanges Eugène Tisserant, Tome I: Écriture Sainte - Ancien Orient* (StT 231) Vatican 1964, 295-309.

———, "Toward a Symbolic Reading of the Fourth Gospel," *NTS* 27 (1980/81) 439-56.

———, "Trois chiasmes johanniques," *NTS* (1960/61) 249-55.

Leroy, H., "Das johanneische Mißverständnis als literarische Form," *BiLe* 9 (1968) 196-207.

———, *Rätsel und Mißverständnis. Ein Beitrag zur Formgeschichte des Johannesevangeliums* (BBB 30) Bonn 1968.

Létourneau, P., "La gloire de Jésus: Gloire et glorification dans le IV. Évangile," *LTP* 51 (1995) 551-72.

———, *Jésus fils de l'homme et fils de Dieu. Jean 2,23-3,36 et la double christologie johannique* (RNS 27) Montréal, Paris 1992.

Licht, J., "The Doctrine of the Thanksgiving Scroll," *IEJ* 6 (1956) 1-15 and 89-101.

Lichtenberger, H., "Täufergemeinden und frühchristliche Täuferpolemik im letzten Drittel des 1. Jahrhunderts," *ZThK* 84 (1987) 36-57.

Lincoln, A. T., "Trials, Plots and the Narrative of the Fourth Gospel," *JSNT* 56 (1994) 3-30.

Lindars, B., *Behind the Fourth Gospel* (SCC 3) London 1971.

——, *Jesus Son of Man. A Fresh Examination of the Son of Man Sayings in the Gospels in the Light of Recent Research*, London 1983; Grand Rapids 1984.

——, "John and the Synoptic Gospels: A Test Case," *GrJ* 27 (1980/81) 287-94.

——, "The Parable of the Best Man (John iii,29)," *NTS* 16 (1969/70) 324-29.

——, "Re-Enter the Apocalyptic Son of Man," *NTS* 22 (1975) 52-72.

—— and Borgen, P., "The Place of the Old Testament in the Formation of New Testament Theology: Prolegomena and Response," *NTS* 23 (1976/77) 59-66.

Link, A., *'Was redest du mit ihr?' Eine Studie zur Exegese-, Redaktions- und Theologiegeschichte von Joh 4, 1-42* (BU 24) Regensburg 1992.

Linnemann, E., "Die Hochzeit zu Kana und Dionysos," *NTS* 20 (1974) 408-18.

——, "Jesus und der Täufer," in: Ebeling, G., Jüngel, E. and Schunack, G. (eds.), *FS für Ernst Fuchs*, Tübingen 1973, 219-36.

Loader, W., "The Central Structure of the Johannine Christology," *NTS* 30 (1984) 188-216.

——, *The Christology of the Fourth Gospel. Structure and Issues* (BET 23) Frankfurt ²1992.

Loewen, J. A., "The 'World' in John's Gospel through West African Eyes," *BiTr* 34 (1983) 407-13.

Lohmeyer, E., "Über Aufbau und Gliederung des vierten Evangeliums," *ZNW* 27 (1928) 11-36.

Lohse, E., "Wort und Sakrament im Johannesevangelium," *NTS* 7 (1960/61) 116-25.

Lowe, M., "Who were the Ἰουδαῖοι?," *NT* 18 (1976) 101-30.

Lütgehetmann, W., *Die Hochzeit von Kana (Joh 2,1-11). Zu Ursprung und Deutung einer Wundererzählung im Rahmen johanneische Redaktionsgeschichte* (BU 20) Regensburg 1990.

Mack, B. L., *Rhetoric and the New Testament* (GBSNT) Minneapolis 1990.

MacRae, G. W., "Theology and Irony in the Fourth Gospel," in: Stibbe, M. W. G. (ed.), *The Gospel of John as Literature. An Anthology of Twentieth-Century Perspectives*, Köln, Leiden, New York 1993, 103-13.

Maier, J., *Jüdische Auseinandersetzung mit dem Christentum in der Antike* (EdF 177) Darmstadt 1982.

Maillet, H., "'Au-Dessous' ou 'Sur'? (Jean 1/51)," *ÉTR* 59 (1984) 207-13.

Malbon, E., "Texts and Contexts. Interpreting the Disciples in Mark," *Semeia* 62 (1993) 81-102.

Maneschg, H., *Die Erzählung von der ehernen Schlange (Num 21,4-9) in der Auslegung der frühen jüdischen Literatur. Eine traditionsgeschichtliche Studie* (EHS.T 157) Bern, Frankfurt 1981.

Manns, F., *L'Évangile de Jean à la lumière du Judaïsme* (SBFA 33) Jerusalem 1991.

——, "Les mots à double entente. Antécédents et fonction herméneutique d'un procédé johannique," *SBFLA* 38 (1988) 39-57.

——, "Nicodème ou la nécessité de renaître de l'Esprit," *TS(F)* 3 (1990) 107-10.

Mannucci, V., "Amour de Dieu et foi de l'homme (Jn 3,14-21)," *ASeign* 17 (1970) 40-50.

Manzano, B., "Les sources d'Aenon, près de Salim, où Jean baptisait," *TS(F)* 5/6 (1987) 124-30.

Marguerat, D., "Raconter Dieu. L'évangile comme narration historique," in: Bühler, P. and

Habermacher, J.-F. (eds.), *La narration. Quand le récit devient communication* (LiTh 12) Geneva 1998, 104-5.

Marrs, R. R., "John 3,14-15. The Raised Serpent in the Wilderness: The Johannine Use of an Old Testament Account," in: Priest, J. E. (ed.), *Johannine Studies. FS F. Pack*, Malibu 1989, 132-47.

Martyn, J. L., "Glimpses into the History of the Johannine Community. From its Origin through the Period of its Life in which the Fourth Gospel was Composed," in: de Jonge, M. (ed.), *L'Évangile de Jean. Sources, rédaction, théologie* (BEThL 44) Leuven 1977, 149-75.

——, *History and Theology in the Fourth Gospel*, Nashville ²1979.

Matera, F. J., *New Testament Christology*, Louisville 1999.

——, "The Plot of Matthew's Gospel," *CBQ* 49 (1987) 233-53.

Mattill, A. J., "Johannine Communities Behind the Fourth Gospel: Georg Richter's Analysis," *TS* 38 (1977) 294-315.

McKnight, E. V. and Malbon, E. S. (eds.), *The New Literary Criticism and the New Testament*, Minneapolis 1994.

McLeod, D., *The Person of Christ*, Downers Grove 1999.

McNamara, M., "The Ascension and Exaltation of Christ in the Fourth Gospel," *Scrip.* 19 (1967) 65-73.

Mealand, D. L., "The Christology of the Fourth Gospel," *SJTh* 31 (1978) 449-67.

Meeks, W. A., "The Divine Agent and His Counterfeit in Philo and the Fourth Gospel," in: Fiorenza, E. S. (ed.), *Aspects of Religious Propaganda in Judaism and Early Christianity*, Notre Dame 1976, 43-67.

——, "The Man from Heaven in Johannine Sectarianism," in: Ashton, J. (ed.), *The Interpretation of John*, Edinburgh ²1997, 169-205.

——, *The Prophet-King: Moses Traditions and the Johannine Christology* (NT.S 14) Leiden 1967.

Mees, M., "Das 3. Kapitel des Johannesevangeliums in frühchristlicher Sicht," *Laur.* 27 (1986) 121-37.

——, "Erhöhung und Verherrlichung Jesu im Johannesevangelium nach dem Zeugnis neutestamentlicher Papyri," *BZ* 18 (1974) 32-44.

Meinertz, M., "Die 'Nacht' im Johannesevangelium," *ThQ* 133 (1953) 400-7.

Mendner, S., "Nikodemus," *JBL* 77 (1958) 293-323.

Menken, M. J. J., "The Christology of the Fourth Gospel: A Survey of Recent Research," in: M. C. de Boer (ed.), *From Jesus to John. Essays on Jesus and New Testament Christology. FS M. de Jonge* (JSNT.S 84) (Sheffield 1993)

——, *Numerical Literary Techniques in John. The Fourth Evangelist's Use of Numbers of Words and Syllables* (NT.S 55) Leiden 1985.

——, *Old Testament Quotations in the Fourth Gospel: Studies in Textual Form*, Kok Pharos 1996.

Mercer, C., "Ἀποστέλλειν and Πέμπειν in John," *NTS* 36 (1990) 619-24.

Merklein, H., "Gott und Welt. Eine exemplarische Interpretation von Joh 2,23-3,21; 12,20-36 zur theologischen Bestimmung des johanneischen Dualismus," in: Söding, T. (ed.), *Der lebendige Gott. Studien zur Theologie des Neuen Testaments. FS für Wilhelm Thüsing zum 75. Geburtstag* (NTA 31) Münster 1996, 287-305.

Meyer, B. F., "The Challenges of Text and Reader to the Historical-Critical Method," in: Beuken, W., Freyne, S. and Weiler, A. (eds.), *The Bible and its Readers*, Piladelphia 1991, 3-12.

Meyer, P. W., *The Eschatology of the Fourth Gospel: A Study in Early Christian Re-interpretation*, New York 1995.

Meyer, R., "καθαρός," *TDNT,* III, 418-23.

Meynet, R., *L'analyse rhétorique: une nouvelle méthode pour comprendre la Bible. Textes fondateurs et Exposé systématique*, Paris 1989.

Michel, M., "Nicodème ou le non-lieu de la vérité," *RevSR* 55 (1981) 227-36.

Michel, O., "Der aufsteigende und der herabsteigende Gesandte," in: Weinrich, W. C. (ed.), *The New Testament Age. Essays in Honor of Bo Reicke*, Vol. 2., Macon 1984, 335-61.

Miles, J. A., "Radical Editing.... and.... Willed Confusion," in: Halpern, B. and Levenson, J. D. (eds.), *Traditions in Transformation*, Winona Lake 1981, 9-31.

Miller, D. G., "John 3:1-21," *Interp.* 35 (1981) 174-79.

Minear, P. S., *John, the Martyr's Gospel*, New York 1984.

Miranda, J. P., *Die Sendung Jesu im Vierten Evangelium. Religions- und theologiege-schichtliche Untersuchungen zu den Sendungsformeln* (SBS 87) Stuttgart 1977.

Mlakuzhyil, G., *The Christocentric Literary Structure of the Fourth Gospel* (AnBib 117) Rome 1987.

Moloney, F.-J., "From Cana to Cana (Jn. 2:1-4:54) and the Fourth Evangelist's Concept of Correct (and Incorrect) Faith," *Sal.* 40 (1978) 817-43.

———, "The Johannine Son of God," *Sal.* 38 (1976) 71-86.

———, *The Johannine Son of Man* (BSRel 14) Rome ²1978.

———, "When is John talking about Sacraments?," *ABR* 30 (1982) 10-33.

———, "Who is 'The Reader' in the Fourth Gospel?," in: Ashton, J. (ed.), *The Interpretation of John*, Edinburgh ²1997, 219-33.

Moore, R. R., *Soteriology and Structure. A Study of the Relation Between the Soteriology and Present Literary Structure of the Fourth Gospel*, Altanta 1982.

Moore, S. D., *Literary Criticism and the Gospels. The Theoretical Challenge*, London, New Haven 1989.

———, "Rifts in (a reading of) the Fourth Gospel, or: Does Johannine Irony Still Collapse in a Reading that Draws Attention to Itself?," *Neotest.* 23 (1989) 5-17.

Moore, S. R., "'Mirror, Mirror.....:' Lacanian Reflections on Malbon's Mark," *Semeia* 62 (1993) 165-71.

Morgen, M., "Le Fils de l'homme élevé en vue de la vie éternelle (Jn 3,14-15 éclairé par diverses traditions juives)," *RevSR* 68 (1994) 5-17.

———, *À fin que le monde soit sauvé. Jésus révèle sa mission de salut dans l'évangile de Jean* (LeDiv 154) Paris 1993.

———, "Jean 3 et les évangiles synoptiques," in: Denaux, A. (ed.), *John and the Synoptics* (BEThL 101) Leuven 1992, 514-22.

———, "Les traditions sapientielles à l'arrière-plan de Jn 3," in: Trublet, J. (ed.), *La Sagesse biblique de l'Ancien au Nouveau Testament* (LeDiv 160) Paris 1995, 385-412.

———, "La venue de la Lumière dans le quatrième évangile," in: Kuntzman, R. (ed.), *Ce Dieu qui vient: Études sur l'Ancien et le Nouveau Testament offertes au Professeur Bernard Renaud à l'occasion de son soixante-cinquième anniversaire* (LeDiv 159) Paris 1995, 307-23.

Morris, L., *Jesus is the Christ. Studies in the Theology of John*, Grand Rapids 1989.

———, "Love in the Fourth Gospel," in: Cook, J. I. (ed.), *Saved by Hope. Richard C. Oudersluys FS*, Grand Rapids 1978, 27-43.

———, "The Relation of the Signs and the Discourses in John," in: Weinrich, W. C. (ed.), *The New Testament Age. Essays in Honor of Bo Reicke*, Vol. 2, Macon 1984, 363-72.

———, *Studies in the Fourth Gospel*, Grand Rapids 1969.

———, *Testaments of Love*, Grand Rapids 1981.

———, "Variation – A Feature of the Johannine Style," in: his *Studies in the Fourth*

Gospel, Grand Rapids 1969, 293-319.

Moser, F., "Mißverständnis und Ironie in der johanneischen Argumentation und ihr Gebrauch in der heutigen pfarramtlichen Praxis," in: Rose, M. (ed.), *Johannesstudien. Interdisziplinäre Zugänge zum Johannesevangelium. Freundesgabe der Theologischen Fakultät der Universität Neuchâtel für Jean Zumstein,* Zürich 1991,47-73.

Motyer, S., *Your Father the Devil? A New Approach to John and the Jews,* Exeter 1997.

Mourlon-Beernaert, P., "Nicodème et les croyants. Trois méthodes de lecture (Jn 3)," *Tel* 42 (1985) 11-20.

――, "La vérité au sens biblique: approche de saint Jean," *LV* 46 (1991) 287-300.

Mowry, L., "The Dead Sea Scrolls and the Background for the Gospel of John," *BA* 17 (1954) 78-97.

Muecke, D. C., *The Compass of Irony,* London 1969.

――, *Irony* (The Critical Idiom 13) London 1970.

Müller, T., *Das Heilsgeschehen im Johannesevangelium. Eine exegetische Studie,* Frankfurt, Zürich 1958.

Müller, U. B., *Die Geschichte der Christologie in der johanneischen Gemeinde* (SBS 77) Stuttgart 1975.

Munro, W., "The Pharisee and the Samaritan in John: Polar or Parallel?," *CBQ* 57 (1995) 710-28.

Murphy-O'Connor, J., "John the Baptist and Jesus: History and Hypotheses," *NTS* 36 (1990) 359-74.

Mußner, F., "Die 'semantische Achse' des Johannesevangeliums. Ein Versuch," in: Frankemölle, H. and Kertelge, K. (eds.), *Vom Urchristentum zu Jesus, FS J. Gnilka,* Basel, Freiburg, Wien 1989, 246-55.

――, *"ZΩH." Die Anschauung vom "Leben" im vierten Evangelium unter Berücksichtigung der Johannesbriefe* (MThS.H 5) München 1952.

Neusner, J. (ed.), *Judaism and their Messiahs at the Turn of the Christian Era,* Cambridge, New York 1987.

Newheart, M. W., "Toward a Pyscho-literary Reading of the Fourth Gospel," in: Segovia, F. F. (ed.), *'What is John?' Reader and Readings of the Fourth Gospel,* Atlanta 1996, 43-58.

Newman , B. M., Jr., "Some Observations Regarding the Argument, Structure and Literary Characteristics of the Gospel of John," *BiTr* 26 (1975) 234-39.

Neyrey, J. H., *An Ideology of Revolt. John's Christology in Social-Science Perspective,* Philadelphia 1988.

――, "John III - A Debate over Johannine Epistemology and Christology," *NT* 23 (1981) 115-27.

――, "The Jacob Allusions in John 1:51," *CBQ* 44 (1982) 586-605.

Nicholson, G. C., *Death as Departure: The Johannine Descent-Ascent Schema* (SBL.DS 63) Chico 1983.

Nickelsburg, G. W. E., *Jewish Literature between the Bible and the Mishna,* Philadelphia 1981.

――, *Resurrection, Immortality and Eternal Life in Intertestamental Judaism,* Cambridge 1972.

Nicol, W., *The Semeia in the Fourth Gospel. Tradition and Redaction* (NT.S 32) Leiden 1972.

Nissen, J., "Rebirth and Community. A Spiritual and Social Reading of John 3,1-21," in: Bilde, P., Nielsen, H. K. and Sorensen, J. P. (eds.), *Apocryphon Severini. FS Sören Giversen,* Aarhus 1993, 121-39.

―― and Pedersen, S. (eds.), *New Readings in John: Literary and Theological Perspectives - Essays from the Scandinavian Conference on the Fourth Gospel in Aarhus*

1997 (JSNT.S 182) Sheffield 1999.

O'Day, G. R., "'I Have Overcome the World' (Jon 16:33): Narrative Time in John 13-17," *Semeia* 53 (1991) 153-66.

——, "Narrative Mode and Theological Claim: A Study in the Fourth Gospel," *JBL* 105 (1986) 657-68.

——, *Revelation in the Fourth Gospel: Narrative Mode and Theological Claim*, Philadelphia 1986.

Oehler, W., *Das Johannesevangelium. Eine Missionsschrift für die Welt*, Gütersloh 1936.

——, *Zum Missionscharakter des Johannesevangeliums*, Gütersloh 1941.

Okure, T., *The Johannine Approach to Mission: A Contextual Study of John 4:1-42* (WUNT II/32) Tübingen 1988.

Olsson, B., *Structure and Meaning in the Fourth Gospel: A Text-Linguistic Analysis of John 2,1-11 and 4,1-42* (CB.NT 6) Lund 1974.

O'Neill, J. C., "The Jews in the Fourth Gospel," *IBSt* 18 (1996) 58-74.

——, "The Silence of Jesus," *NTS* 15 (1969) 153-67.

Ong, W. J., *Rhetoric, Romance and Technology*, Ithaca, London 1971.

Onuki, T., *Gemeinde und Welt im Johannesevangelium. Ein Beitrag zur Frage nach der theologischen und pragmatischen Funktion des johanneischen "Dualismus"* (WMANT 56) Neukirchen-Vluyn 1984.

Opeke, A., "λούω," *TDNT*, IV, 295-307,

Orton, D. E., *The Composition of John's Gospel: Selected Studies from Novum Testamentum*, Leiden 1998.

Osburn, C. D., "Some Exegetical Observations on John 3:5-8," *RestQ* 31 (1989) 129-38.

Osiek, C., "The New Handmaid. The Bible and the Social Sciences," *TS* 50 (1989) 260-78.

Østenstad, G., "The Structure of the Fourth Gospel: Can it be Defined Objectively?," *StTh* 45 (1991) 33-55.

Ottilinger, A., *Vorläufer, Vorbild oder Zeuge? Zum Wandel des Täuferbildes im Johannesevangelium* (ThDiss 45) St. Ottilien 1991.

Painter, J., "Johannine Symbols: A Case Study in Epistemology," *JTSA* 27 (1979) 26-41.

——, "Quest and Rejection Stories in John," *JSNT* 36 (1989) 17-46.

——, "Quest Stories in John 1-4," *JSNT* 41 (1991) 33-70.

——, *John: Witness and Theologian*, London 1975.

Pamment, M., "Is There Convincing Evidence of Samaritan Influence on the Fourth Gospel?," *ZNW* 73 (1982) 221-30.

——, "John 3:5: 'Unless One is Born of Water and the Spirit, He Cannot Enter the Kingdom of God'," *NT* 25 (1983) 189-90.

——, "The Meaning of *Doxa* in the Fourth Gospel," *ZNW* 74 (1983) 12-16.

——, "The Son of Man in the Fourth Gospel," *JTS* 36 (1985) 56-66.

Pancaro, S., *The Law in the Fourth Gospel. The Torah and the Gospel, Moses and Jesus, Judaism and Christianity according to John* (NT.S 42) Leiden 1975.

——, "A Statistical Approach to the Concept of Time and Eschatology in the Fourth Gospel," *Bib.* 50 (1969) 511-24.

Pangritz, A., "Der 'maskierte Christus.' Nikodemismus und Antinikodemismus in der italienischen Reformation," *EvTh* 54 (1994) 8-22.

Panimolle, S. A., *Il Dono della Legge e la Grazia della Verità. Gv. 1,17*, Rome 1973.

Parker, P., "Bethany Beyond Jordan," *JBL* 74 (1955) 257-61.

Patte, D., "Jesus' Pronouncement about Entering the Kingdom Like a Child: A Structural Exegesis," *Semeia* 29 (1983) 3-42.

Payot, C., "L'interprétation johannique du ministère de Jean-Baptiste (Jean I)," *FV* 68 (1969) 21-37.

Pazdan, M. M., "Nicodemus and the Samaritan Woman: Contrasting Models of Discipleship," *BTB* 17 (1987) 145-48.

——, *The Son of Man. A Metaphor for Jesus in the Fourth Gospel* (ZSNT) Collegeville 1991.

Pendrick, G., "ΜΟΝΟΓΕΝΗΣ," *NTS* 41 (1995) 587-600.

Perkins, P., *Gnosticism and the New Testament*, Minneapolis 1993.

Perrin, N., *Jesus and the Language of the Kingdom*, Philadelphia 1976.

Pesch, R. and Schnackenburg, R. (eds.), *Jesus und der Menschensohn. FS Anton Vögtle*, Basel, Freiburg, Wien 1975.

Peterson, N. R., *The Gospel of John and the Sociology of Light: Language and Characterisation in the Fourth Gospel*, Trinity 1993.

Pollard, T. E., "The Father-Son and God-Believer Relationship according to St. John," in: de Jonge, M. (ed.), *L'Évangile de Jean* (BEThL 44) Gembloux 1977, 363-68.

——, *Johannine Christology and the Early Church* (MSSNTS 13) Cambridge 1970.

Porsch, F., *Pneuma und Wort. Ein exegetischer Beitrag zur Pneumatologie des Johannesevangeliums* (FTS 16) Frankfurt 1974.

Powell, M. A., *What is Narrative Criticism. A New Approach to the Bible*, London 1993.

Pratscher, W., "Die Juden im Johannesevangelium," *BiLi* 59 (1986) 177-85.

Prior, J. G., *The Historical Critical Method in Catholic Exegesis*, Rome 1999.

Pryor, J. W., "John 3. 3,5. A Study in the Relation of John's Gospel to the Synoptic Tradition," *JSNT* 41 (1991) 71-95.

——, "The Johannine Son of Man and the Descent-Ascent Motif," *JETS* 34 (1991) 341-51.

Rau, C., *Struktur und Rhythmus im Johannesevangelium* (SzR) Stuttgart 1972.

Rebell, W., *Gemeinde als Gegenwelt. Zur soziologischen und didaktischen Funktion des Johannesevangeliums* (BET 20) Bern, Frankfurt, New York, Paris 1987.

Redford, J., "Preparing the Way: John the Baptist," *CleR* 66 (1981) 193-200.

Rehm, B. (ed.), *Die Pseudoklementinen, II, Rekognitionen* (GCS 51) Berlin 1965.

Reim, G., "Jesus as God in the Fourth Gospel: The Old Testament Background," *NTS* 30 (1984) 158-60.

——, *Studien zum alttestamentlichen Hintergrund des Johannesevangeliums* (MSSNTS 22) Cambridge 1974.

——, "Targum und Johannesevangelium," *BZ* 27 (1983) 1-13.

——, "Zur Lokalisierung der johanneischen Gemeinde," *BZ* 32 (1988) 72-86.

Rein, M., *Die Heilung des Blindgeborenen (Joh 9). Tradition und Redaktion* (WUNT II/73) Tübingen 1995.

Reinhartz, A., "Great Expectations. A Reader-Oriented Approach to Johannine Christology and Eschatology," *LT* 3 (1989) 61-76.

——, "Jesus as Prophet: Predictive Prolepses in the Fourth Gospel," *JSNT* 36 (1989) 3-16.

——, *The Word in the World: The Cosmological Tale in the Fourth Gospel* (SBLMS 45) Atlanta 1992.

Reinmuth, E., "Nikodemus," *ZdZ* 39 (1985) 53-54.

Rengstorf, K. H., "ἀποστέλλω," *TDNT*, I, 398-447.

——, "διδάσκαλος," *TDNT*, II, 148-65.

Renner, G. L., *The Life-World of the Johannine Community: An Investigation of the Social Dynamics which Resulted in the Composition of the Fourth Gospel*, Boston 1982.

Rensberger, D. K., *Johannine Faith and Liberating Community*, Philadelphia 1988.

Resseguie, J., "John 9: A Literary-Critical Analysis," in: Stibbe, M. W. G. (ed.), *The Gospel of John as Literature. An Anthology of Twentieth-Century Perspectives*, Köln, Leiden, New York 1993, 115-22.

Rhea, R., *The Johannine Son of Man* (AThANT 76) Zürich 1990.

Rhoads, D., "Narrative Criticism and the Gospel of Mark," *JAAR* 50 (1982) 411-34.

Ricca, P., *Die Eschatologie des vierten Evangeliums*, Frankfurt, Zürich 1966.

Richard, E., "Expressions of Double Meaning and their Function in the Gospel of John," *NTS* 31 (1985) 96-112.

Riches, J. K., "Apocalyptic – Strangely Relevant," in: Horbury, W. (ed.), *Templum Amicitiae: Essays on the Second Temple Presented to Ernst Bammel* (JSNT.S 48) Sheffield 1991, 237-63.

Richter, G., "Präsentische und futuristische Eschatologie im vierten Evangelium," in: Fielder, P. and Zeller, D. (eds.), *Gegenwart und kommendes Reich. Schülergabe A. Vöglte zum 65. Geburtstag* (SBB) Stuttgart 1975, 117-52.

———, *Studien zum Johannesevangelium*, Hainz, J. (ed.) (BU 13) Regensburg 1977.

———, "Zum sogenannten Tauftext Joh 3,5," *MThZ* 26 (1975) 101-25.

Ricoeur, P., *Interpretation Theory: Discourse and Surplus of Meaning*, Fort Worth 1976.

———, *Time and Narrative*, Chicago 1984.

Riedl, H., *Zeichen und Herrlichkeit. Die christologische Relevanz der Semeiaquelle in den Kanawundern Joh 2,1-11 und Joh 4,46-54* (RSTh 51) Frankfurt 1997.

Riedl, J., *Das Heilswerk Jesu nach Johannes* (FTSt 93) Basel, Freiburg, Wien 1973.

———, "Wenn ihr den Menschensohn erhöht habt, werdet ihr erkennen (Joh 8,28)," in: Pesch, R. and Schnackenburg, R. (eds.), *Jesus und der Menschensohn. FS Anton Vögtle*, Basel, Freiburg, Wien 1975, 355-70.

Riesenfeld, H., "Zu den johanneischen ἵνα-Sätzen," *StTh* 19 (1965) 213-20.

Riesner, R., *Jesus als Lehrer. Eine Untersuchung zum Ursprung der Evangelienüberlieferung* (WUNT II/7) Tübingen ²1984.

Riga, P., "Signs of Glory. The Use of 'sêmeion' in St. John's Gospel," *Interp.* 17 (1963) 402-24.

Rimmon-Kenan, S., *Narrative Fiction: Contemporary Poetics*, London 1983.

Ringwald, A., "γεννάω," *NIDNT*, I, 176-80.

Rinke, J., *Kerygma und Autopsie. Der Christologische Disput als Spiegel johanneischer Gemeindegeschichte* (HBS 12) Freiburg 1996.

Ritt, H., "'So sehr hat Gott die Welt geliebt...' (Joh 3,16). Gotteserfahrung bei Johannes," in: *'Ich will euer Gott werden.' Beispiele biblischen Redens von Gott* (SBS 100) Stuttgart 1981, 207-26.

Robbins, V. K., "From New Criticism to Post-structuralism. Twentieth-Century Hermeneutics," in: Prickett, S. (ed.), *Reading the Text: Biblical Criticism and Literary Theory*, Cambridge 1991, 248-52.

Roberge, M., "Structures littéraires et christologie dans le IVᵉ évangile. Jean 1,29-34," in: Laflamme, R. and Gervais, M. (eds.), *Le Christ hier, aujourd'hui et demain*, Québec 1976, 467-77.

Roberts, J. J. M., "The Old Testament's Contribution to Messianic Expectations," in: Charlesworth, J. H. (ed.), *The Messiah. Developments in Earliest Judaism and Christianity*, Minneapolis 1992, 39-51.

Roberts, R. L., "The Rendering 'Only Begotten' in John 3:16," *RestQ* 16 (1973) 2-22.

Robinson, D. W. B., "Born of Water and Spirit: Does John 3:5 Refer to Baptism?," *RTR* 25 (1966) 15-23.

Robinson, J. A. T., *The Priority of John*, London 1985.

Rodriguez Ruiz, M., *Der Missionsgedanke des Johannesevangeliums. Ein Beitrag zur johanneischen Soteriologie und Ekklesiologie* (FzB 55) Würzburg 1987.

Rogers, J. B. and McKim, D. K., *The Authority and Interpretation of the Bible: An Historical Approach*, Eugene 1999.

Röhser, G., *Prädestination und Verstockung. Untersuchungen zu ihrer Struktur in der biblisch-jüdischen, paulinischen und johanneischen Theologie* (TANZ 14) Basel, Tübingen 1994.

Rolland, P., "Jésus connaissait leurs pensées," *EThL* 62 (1986) 118-21.

Rose, M. (ed.), *Johannesstudien. Interdisziplinäre Zugänge zum Johannesevangelium. Freundesgabe der Theologischen Fakultät der Universität Neuchâtel für Jean Zumstein*, Zürich 1991.

Roustang, F., "L'entretien avec Nicodème," *NRTh* 78 (1956) 337-58.

Rowland, C. C., "John 1.51, Jewish Apocalyptic and Targumic Tradition," *NTS* 30 (1984) 498-507.

——, *The Open Heaven: A Study of Apocalyptic in Judaism and Early Christianity*, London 1982.

Ruckstuhl, E., "Abstieg und Erhöhung des johanneischen Menschensohns," in: Pesch, R. and Schnackenburg, R. (eds.), *Jesus und der Menschensohn. FS Anton Vögtle*, Basel, Freiburg, Wien 1975, 314-41.

——, "Das Johannesevangelium und die Gnosis," in: Ruckstuhl, E., *Jesus im Horizont der Evangelien* (SBAB 3) Stuttgart 1988, 311-26.

—— and Dschulnigg, P., *Stilkritik und Verfasserfrage im Johannesevangelium. Die johanneischen Sprachmerkmale auf dem Hintergrund des Neuen Testaments und des zeitgenössischen hellenistischen Schrifttums* (NTOA 17) Fribourg, Göttingen 1991.

Rudolph, K., *Gnosis*, Edinburgh 1983.

Ruff, P.-Y., "La communauté johannique et son histoire," *RTP* 123 (1991) 79-92.

Saayman, C., "The Textual Strategy in John 3:12-14: Preliminary Observations," *Neotest.* 29 (1995) 27-48.

Safrai, S. and Stern, M. (eds.), *The Jewish People in the First-Century. Historical Geography, Political History, Social, Cultural and Religious Life and Institutions*, 2 Vols., Assen 1974/76.

Sahi, J., "Nicodemus Comes to Christ by Night," in: Duraisingh, C. and Hargreaves, C. (eds.), *India's Search for Reality and the Relevance of the Gospel of John. Papers from a Conference held in Pune in February 1974*, Delhi 1975, 78-79.

Sanders, E. P., *Jesus and Judaism*, Philadelphia 1985.

Sanders, J., *Canon and Community. Guides to Biblical Scholarship*, Philadelphia 1984.

Saxby, H., "The Time-Scheme in the Gospel of John," *ET* 104 (1992) 9-13.

Schenk, W., "Gefangenschaft und Tod des Täufers. Erwägungen zur Chronologie und ihren Konsequenzen," *NTS* 29 (1983) 453-83.

Schenke, L., "Der 'Dialog Jesu mit den Juden' im Johannesevangelium. Ein Rekonstruktionsversuch," *NTS* 34 (1988) 573-603.

——, *Das Johannesevangelium. Einführung – Text – dramatische Gestalt* (UB 446) Stuttgart 1992.

——, "Die literarische Entstehungsgeschichte von Joh 1,19-51," *BN* 46 (1989) 24-57

Schmidl, M., *Jesus und Nikodemus: Gespräch zur johanneischen Christologie* (BU 28) Regensburg 1998.

Schnackenburg, R., "Die Agape Gottes nach Johannes," in: Franke, T. (ed.), *Creatio ex amore: Beiträge zu einer Theologie der Liebe. FS Alexandre Ganoczy zum 60. Geburtstag*, Würzburg 1988, 36-47.

——, *Jesus in the Gospels. A Biblical Christology*, Louisville 1995.

——, "Der Menschensohn im Johannesevangelium," *NTS* 11 (1964/65) 123-37.

——, "Die Messiasfrage im Johannesevangelium," in: *Neutestamentliche Aufsätze. FS J. Schmid*, Regensburg 1963, 240-64.

——, "Die 'situationsgelösten' Redestücke in Joh 3," *ZNW* 49 (1958) 88-99.

——, "Zur Traditionsgeschichte von Joh 4,46-54," *BZ* (1964) 58-88.

——, "Das vierte Evangelium und die Johannesjünger," *HJ* 77 (1958) 21-38.

Schneider, G., "Ἰησοῦς," *EDNT*, II, 180-84.

Schneider, J., "(βαίνω), ἀναβαίνω, καταβαίνω, μεταναβαίνω," *TDNT*, I, 518-23.

Schneiders, S. M., *The Revelatory Text: Interpreting the New Testament as Sacred Scripture*, San Francisco 2000.

Schnelle, U., *Antidoketische Christologie im Johannesevangelium. Eine Untersuchung zur Stellung des vierten Evangeliums in der johanneischen Schule* (FRLANT 144) Göttingen, 1987.

Schoenborn, U., "'Im Wechsel der Worte das Wort'. Oder: Dialog und Offenbarung in Johannes 3," in: Pfürtner, S. M. and Schoenborn, U. (eds.), *Der bezwingende Vorsprung des Guten. Exegetische und theologische Werkstattberichte, FS Wolfgang Harnisch*, Hamburg, Münster 1994, 108-25.

Scholten, C., "Probleme der Gnosisforschung: alte Fragen – neue Zugänge," *IkaZ* 26 (1997) 481-501.

Scholtissek, K., "Antijudaismus im Johannesevangelium? Ein Gesprächsbeitrag," in: Kampling, R. (ed.), *"Nun steht aber diese Sache im Evangelium..." Zur Frage nach den Anfängen des christlichen Antijudaismus*, Paderborn 1999, 151-81.

———, "Ein Vater, der Mit-Liebende sucht. Beobachtungen zum johanneischen Gottesbild," *Beiträge zu Pastoral, Katechese & Theologie* 11 (1999) 25-31.

———, "'Er kam in sein Eigentum – und die Eigenen nahmen ihn nicht auf' (Joh 1,11). Jesus – Mittler und Ort rettender vita communis in Gott nach dem Johannesevangelium," *GuL* 72 (1999) 436-51.

———, *In ihm sein und bleiben. Die Sprache der Immanenz in den johanneischen Schriften* (HBS 21) Freiburg i. Br. 2000.

———, "Ironie und Rollenwechsel im Johannesevangelium," *ZNW* 89 (1998) 235-55.

———, "'Mitten unter euch steht der, den ihr nicht kennt' (Joh 1,26). Die Messias-Regel des Täufers als johanneische Sinnlinie – aufgezeigt am Beispiel der relecture der Jüngerberufungen in der Begegnung zwischen Maria von Magdala und Jesus," *MThZ* 48 (1997) 103-21.

———, "Mystagogische Christologie im Johannesevangelium? Eine Spurensuche," *GuL* 68 (1995) 412-26.

———, "'Rabbi, wo wohnst du?' (Joh 1,38). Die mystagogische Christologie des Johannesevangeliums (am Beispiel der Jüngerberufungen1,35-51). Mit Johannes das Evangelium entdecken (3+4)," *BiLi* 68 (1995) 223-31.

Schonweiss, H. and Hahn, H. C., "Anger, Wrath," *NIDNT*, I, 105-13.

Schottroff, L., *Der Glaubende und die feindliche Welt. Beobachtungen zum gnostischen Dualismus und seiner Bedeutung für Paulus und das Johannesevangelium* (WMANT 37) Neukirchen-Vluyn 1970.

Schreiber, S., "Die Jüngerberufungsszene Joh 1,43-51 als literarische Einheit," *SNTU* 23 (1998) 5-28.

Schulz, S., *Untersuchungen zur Menschensohnchristologie im Johannesevangelium. Zugleich ein Beitrag zur Methodengeschichte der Auslegung des 4. Evangeliums*, Göttingen 1957.

Schwankl, O., *Licht und Finsternis. Ein metaphorisches Paradigma in den johanneischen Schriften* (HBS 5) Barcelona, Basel, Freiburg, New York, Rome, Wien, 1995.

Schwarz, G., "'Der Wind weht, wo er will'?," *BN* 63 (1992) 47-48.

Schweizer, E., *Ego eimi. Die religionsgeschichtliche Herkunft und Bedeutung der johanneischen Bildreden, zugleich ein Beitrag zur Quellenfrage des vierten Evangeliums* (FRLANT 38) Göttingen ²1964.

———, *Erniedrigung und Erhöhung bei Jesus und seinen Nachfolgern* (AThANT 28) Zürich ²1962.

———, "υἱός," *TDNT*, VIII, 363-92.

———, "Zum religionsgeschichtlichen Hintergrund der 'Sendungsformel' Gal 4,4f. Röm 8,3f. Joh 3,16f. I Joh 4,9," *ZNW* 57 (1966) 199-210.

Segal, A. F., "Conversion and Messianism: Outline for a New Approach," in: Charlesworth, J. H. (ed.), *The Messiah. Developments in Earliest Judaism and Christianity*, Minneapolis 1992, 296-340.

Segovia, F. F., "The Journey(s) of the Word of God: A Reading of the Plot of the Fourth Gospel," *Semeia* 53 (1991) 23-54.

———, *Love Relationships in the Johannine Tradition. Agape / Agapan in I John and the Fourth Gospel* (SBL.DS 58) Chico 1982.

——— (ed.), *"What is John?," Vol.1: Readers and Readings of the fourth Gospel* (SBL.SS 3) Chico 1996.

——— (ed.), *"What is John?," Vol.2: Literary and Social Readings of the fourth Gospel* (SBL.SS 7) Chico 1998.

———, "The Significance of Social Location in Reading John's Story," *Interp.* 49 (1995) 370-78.

Seitz, C. R. and K. Greene-McCreight, K. (eds.), *Theological Exegesis: Essays in Honour of Brevard S. Childs*, Grand Rapids 1999.

Sellin, G., "'Die Auferstehung ist schon geschehen'. Zur spiritualisierung apokalyptischer Terminologie im Neuen Testament," *NT* 25 (1983) 220-37.

Selvidge, M. J., "Nicodemus and the Woman with Five Husbands," *Pro* 2 (1982) 63-75.

Shanks, H., *The Mystery and Meaning of the Dead Sea Scrolls*, New York 1999.

Sidebottom, E. M., "The Ascent and Descent of the Son of Man in the Gospel of John," *AThR* 39 (1957) 115-22.

Simon, U. E., "Eternal Life in the Fourth Gospel," in: Cross, F. L. (ed.), *Studies in the Fourth Gospel*, London 1957, 97-109.

Sjöberg, E., "רוּחַ in Palestine Judaism," *TDNT*, VI, 375-89.

———, "Wiedergeburt und Neuschöpfung im palästinischen Judentum," *StTh* 4 (1951) 44-85.

Sloan, R. B. and Parsons, M. C. (eds.), *Perspectives on John. Method and Interpretation in the Fourth Gospel*, Lewiston 1993.

Smalley, S. S., "The Johannine Son of Man Sayings," *NTS* 15 (1968/69) 278-301.

Smith, C. H., "Οὕτως ἐστὶν πᾶς ὁ γεγεννημένος ἐκ τοῦ πνεύματος (Jn 3,8)," *ET* 81 (1969/70) 181.

Smith, D. M., *The Composition and Order of the Fourth Gospel. Bultmann's Literary Theory* (YPR 10) London, New Haven 1965.

———, *Johannine Christianity: Essays on its Setting, Sources and Theology*, Columbia 1984.

———, "Johannine Christianity: Some Reflections on its Character and Delineation," *NTS* 21 (1975) 222-48.

———, "John, the Synoptics, and the Canonical Approach to Exegesis," in: Hawthorne, G. F. (ed.), *Tradition and Interpretation in the New Testament. Essays in Honour of Earl Ellis for his 60th birthday*, Tübingen 1987, 166-80.

———, "Judaism and the Gospel of John," in: Charlesworth J. H. (ed.), *Jews and Christians. Exploring the Past, Present, and Future*, New York 1990, 76-99.

———, "Prolegomena to a Canonical Reading of the Fourth Gospel," in: Segovia, F. F. (ed.), *'What is John?' Readers and Readings of the Fourth Gospel*, Atlanta 1996, 169-82.

———, *The Theology of the Gospel of John*, Cambridge 1995.

Soares-Prabhu, G. M. (ed.), *Wir werden bei ihm wohnen. Das Johannesevangelium in indischer Deutung* (TDW 6) Basel, Freiburg, Wien 1984.

Söding, T., "Wiedergeburt aus Wasser und Geist. Anmerkungen zur Symbolsprache des Johannesevangeliums am Beispiel des Nikodemusgesprächs (Joh 3,1-21)," in:

Kertelge, K. (ed.), *Metaphorik und Mythos im Neuen Testament* (QD 126) Basel, Freiburg, Wien 1990, 168-219.

Spaller, C., "Strukturale Überlegungen zu biblisch-exegetischem Arbeiten," *PzB* 7 (1998) 1-16.

Spriggs, D. G., "Meaning of 'Water' in John 3,5," *ET* 85 (1973/74) 149-50.

Staley, J. L., *The Print's First Kiss. A Rhetorical Investigation of the Implied Reader in the Fourth Gospel* (SBL.DS 82) Atlanta 1988.

——, *Reading with a Passion. Rhetoric, Autobiography, and the American West in the Gospel of John*, New York 1995.

——, "The Structure of John's Prologue: Its Implications for the Gospel's Narrative Structure," *CBQ* 48 (1986) 241-64.

Stamps, D. L., "Rhetorical Criticism and the Rhetoric of New Testament Criticism," *JLT* 6 (1992) 268-79.

Stanley, D. M., "Israel's Wisdom Meets the Wisdom of God," *Worship* 32 (1958) 280-87.

Stasiak, K., "The Man Who Came by Night," *BiTod* 20 (1982) 84-89.

Stemberger, G., *La symbolique du bien et du mal selon saint Jean*, Paris 1970.

Sternberg, M., *The Poetics of Biblical Narrative. Ideological Literature and the Drama of Reading*, Bloomington 1985.

Stibbe, M. W. G., "The Elusive Christ: A New Reading of the Fourth Gospel," *JSNT* 44 (1991) 20-39.

——, *John as Storyteller. Narrative Criticism and the Fourth Gospel* (MSSNTS 73) Cambridge 1992.

——, *John's Gospel* (NTR) London, New York 1994.

——, "'Return to Sender': A Structuralist Approach to John's Gospel," in: Ashton, J. (ed.), *The Interpretation of John*, Edinburgh ²1997, 261-78.

——, "Structuralism," in: Coggins, R. J. and Houlden, J. L. (eds.), *A Dictionary of Biblical Interpretation*, London, Philadelphia 1990, 650-55.

Stimpfle, A., *Blinde sehen. Die Eschatologie im traditionsgeschichtlichen Prozeß des Johannesevangeliums* (BZNW 57) Berlin, New York 1990.

Stowasser, M., *Johannes der Täufer im vierten Evangelium. Eine Untersuchung zu seiner Bedeutung für die johanneische Gemeinde* (ÖBS 12) Klosterneuburg 1992.

Sudbrack, J., "Denn Gott hat die Welt so sehr geliebt, daß er seinen einzigen Sohn dahingab (Joh 3,16)," *GuL* 53 (1980) 382-86.

Suggit, J. N., "John 2,1-11: The Sign of Greater Things to Come," *Neotest.* 21 (1987) 141-58.

——, "Nicodemus – the True Jew," *Neotest.* 14 (1981) 90-110.

Suleiman, S. R. and Crosman, I. (eds.), *The Reader in the Text: Essays on Audience and Interpretation*, Princeton 1980.

Sylva, D. D., "Nicodemus and his Spices (John 19.39)," *NTS* 34 (1988) 148-51.

Talbert, C. H., "Artistry and Theology: An Analysis of the Architecture of John 1,19-5,47," *CBQ* 32 (1970) 341-66.

——, "The Myth of a Descending-Ascending Redeemer in Mediterranean Antiquity," *NTS* 22 (1976) 418-40.

——, *What is a Gospel? The Genre of the Canonical Gospels*, Philadelphia 1977.

Talmon, S., "The Concept of Māšîaḥ and Messianism in Early Judaism," in: Charlesworth, J. H. (ed.), *The Messiah. Developments in Earliest Judaism and Christianity*, Minneapolis 1992, 79-115.

Teeple, H. M., "Qumran and the Origin of the Fourth Gospel," *NT* 4 (1960) 6-25.

Temple, S., "The Two Signs in the Fourth Gospel," *JBL* 81 (1962) 169-74.

Templeton, D. A., *The New Testament as True Fiction: Literature, Literary Criticism, Aes-*

thetics, Sheffield 1999.

Theobald, M., *Die Fleischwerdung des Logos* (NTANF 20) Münster 1988.

Thomas, J. D., "A Translation Problem - John 3:8," *RestQ* 24 (1981) 219-24.

Thompson, J. D., *An Analysis of Present and Future in the Eschatology of the Fourth Gospel, and an Examination of the Theological Relationship between the Two*, Ann Arbor 1967.

Thompson, M. M., *The Humanity of Jesus in the Fourth Gospel*, Philadelphia 1988.

——, "Signs and Faith in the Fourth Gospel," *BBR* 1 (1991) 89-108.

Thüsing, W., *Die Erhöhung und Verherrlichung Jesu im Johannesevangelium* (NTA 21) Münster ³1979.

Tobler, E., *Vom Mißverstehen zum Glauben. Ein theologisch-literarischer Versuch zum vierten Evangelium und zu Zeugnissen seiner Wirkung* (EHS.T 395) Bern, Frankfurt, New York, Paris 1990.

Topel, J. L., "A Note on Methodology of Structural Analysis in Jn 2:23-3:21," *CBQ* 33 (1971) 211-20.

Traets, C., *Voir Jésus et le Père en lui selon l'évangile de saint Jean* (AnGr 159) Rome 1967.

Trilling, W., "Gegner Jesu - Widersacher der Gemeinde - Repräsentanten der 'Welt'. Das Johannesevangelium und die Juden," in: Goldstein, H. (ed.), *Gottesverächter und Menschenfeinde? Juden zwischen Jesus und frühchristlicher Kirche* (ppb) Düsseldorf 1979, 190-210.

Trites, A. A., *The New Testament Concept of Witness* (MSSNTS 31) Cambridge 1977.

Trocmé, E., "Jean 3,29 et le thème de l'époux dans la tradition pré-évangélique," *RevSR* 69 (1995) 13-18.

——, "Jean-Baptiste dans la quatrième évangile," *RHPhR* 60 (1980) 129-51.

Trudinger, P., "The Seven Days of the New Creation in St. John's Gospel: Some Further Reflections," *EvQ* 44 (1972) 154-58.

Trumbover, J. A., *Born from Above. The Anthropology of the Gospel of John* (HUTh 29) Tübingen 1992.

Tsuchido, K., "The Composition of the Nicodemus-Episode John ii 23 - iii 21," *AJBI* 1 (1975) 91-103.

Turner, G. A., "Soteriology in the Gospel of John," *JETS* 14 (1976) 271-77.

Turner, M., "Atonement and the Death of Jesus in John. Some Questions to Bultmann and Forestell," *EvQ* 62 (1990) 99-122.

Ulrich, U., *The Dead Sea Scrolls and the Origins of the Bible*, Winona Lake 1999.

Untergaßmair, F. G., *Im Namen Jesu: Der Namensbegriff im Johannesevangelium. Eine exegetisch-religionsgeschichtliche Studie zu den johanneischen Namensaussagen* (FzB13) Stuttgart 1973.

Uspensky, B., *A Poetics of Composition. The Structure of the Artistic Text and Typology of a Compositional Form*, Berkeley, Los Angeles 1973.

van Belle, G., "Jn 4,48 et la foi du centurion," *EThL* 61 (1985)167-69.

van Bruggen, J., *Jesus and the Son of God: The Gospel Narrative as Message*, Grand Rapids 1999.

VanderKam, J. C., "Righteous One, Messiah, Chosen One, and the Son of Man in 1 Enoch 37-71," in: Charlesworth, J. H. (ed.), *The Messiah. Developments in Earliest Judaism and Christianity*, Minneapolis 1992, 169-91.

van der Watt, J. G., "The Dynamics of Metaphor in the Gospel of John," *SNTU* 23 (1998) 29-78.

——, "The Use of αἰώνιος in the Concept ζωὴ αἰώνιος in John's Gospel," *NT* 31 (1989) 217-28.

van Hartingsveld, L., *Die Eschatologie des Johannesevangeliums. Eine Auseinanderset-*

zung mit Rudolf Bultmann, Assen 1962.

Vanhoye, A., "Les indices de la structure littéraire de l'Épître aux Hébreux," in: *Studia Evangelica II* (TU 87) Berlin 1964.

——, "Interrogation johannique et l'exégèse de Cana," *Bib.* 55 (1974) 157-77.

——, "Notre foi, œuvre divine, d'après le quatrième évangile," *NRT* 86 (1964) 337-54.

van Selms, A., "The Best Man and the Bridegroom from Sumer to St. John," *JNES* 9 (1950) 65-75.

Vellanickal, M., *The Divine Sonship of Christians in the Johannine Writings* (AnBib 72) Rome 1977.

Vermes, G., *An Introduction to the Complete Dead Sea Scrolls*, Philadelphia 2000.

——, *The Dead Sea Scrolls in English*, London 1987.

Via, D., *Kerygma and Comedy in the New Testament. A Structuralist Approach to Hermeneutic*, Philadelphia 1975.

Voelz, J. W., *What Does This mean? Principles of Biblical Interpretation in the Post-Modern World*, Saint Louis ²1997.

Vögtle, A., *Die "Gerechtenfrage" des Menschensohnproblems. Bilanz und Perspektive* (aD 152) Freiburg i. Br. 1994.

von Harnack, A., "Das 'Wir' in den Johanneischen Schriften," in: his *Kleine Schriften zur alten Kirche. Berliner Akademieschriften 1908-1930* (Opuscula IX/2) Leipzig 1980, 626-43.

von Lips, H., "Anthropologie und Wunder im Johannesevangelium. Die Wunder Jesu im Johannesevangelium im Unterschied zu den synoptischen Evangelien auf dem Hintergrund johanneischen Menschenverständnisses," *EvTh* 50 (1990) 296-311.

von Wahlde, U. C., "The Gospel of John and the Presentation of Jews and Judaism," in: Efroymson, D. P., Fisher, E. J. and Klenicki, L. (eds.), *Within Context. Essays on Jews and Judaism in the New Testament*, Collegeville 1993, 67-84.

——, "The Johannine 'Jews': A Critical Survey," *NTS* 28 (1982) 33-60.

——, "Literary Structure and Theological Argument in Three Discourses with the Jews in the Fourth Gospel," *JBL* 103 (1984) 575-84.

——, "The Terms for Religious Authorities in the Fourth Gospel: A Key to Literary Strata?," *JBL* 98 (1979) 231-53.

Vorster, W., "The Reader in the Text: Narrative Material," *Semeia* 48 (1989) 21-39.

Vouga, F., "Antijudaismus und Johannesevangelium?," *ThGl* 83 (1993) 81-89.

——, *Le cadre historique et l'intention théologique de Jean* (BeRe) Paris 1977.

Waldstein, M., "Die Sendung Jesu und der Jünger im Johannesevangelium," *IKaZ* 19 (1990) 203-21.

Walter, L., "Lecture d'Évangile. Jean III,1-21: selon la foi et l'incrédulité," *EeV* 87 (1977) 369-78 and 385-90.

Wanke, J., "Die Zukunft des Glaubenden. Theologische Erwägungen zur johanneischen Eschatologie," *ThGl* 71 (1981) 127-39.

Watson, A., *Jesus and the Jews: The Pharisaic Traditon in John*, Athens, London 1995.

Wead, D. W., "The Johannine Double Meaning," *RestQ* 13 (1970) 106-20.

——, "Johannine Irony as a Key to the Author-Audience Relationship in John's Gospel," in: Francis, F. O. (ed.), *AAR Biblical Literature, 1974*, Missoula 1974, 33-50.

——, *Literary Devices in John's Gospel* (ThDiss 4) Basel 1970.

Webb, R. L., *John the Baptiser and Prophet: A Socio-Historical Study* (JSNT.S 62) Sheffield 1991.

Webster, E. C., "Pattern in the Fourth Gospel," in: Clines, D. J. A., Gunn, D. M. and Hauser, A. J. (eds.), *Art and Meaning: Rhetoric in Biblical Literature* (JSOT.S 19) Sheffield 1982, 230-57.

Weder, H., "L'asymétrie du salut. Réflexions sur Jean 3,14-21 dans le cadre de la théologie johannique," in: Zumstein, J., Kaestli, J.-D. and Poffet, J.-M. (eds.), *La Communauté Johannique et son histoire. La trajectoire de l'évangile de Jean aux deux premiers siècles*, Geneva 1990, 155-84.

——, "Deus Incarnatus: On the Hermeneutics of Christology in the Johannine Writings," in: Culpepper, R. A. and Black, C. C. (eds.), *Exploring the Gospel of John. In Honour of D. Moody Smith*, Westminster, Louisville 1996, 327-45.

Weiss, J., *Jesus' Proclamation of the Kingdom of God*, Ames 1999.

Welch, J. W. (ed.), *Chiasmus in Antiquity. Structures, Analyses, Exegesis*, Hildesheim 1981.

Wellek R. and Warren, A., *Theory of Literature*, London, New York ³1977.

Wengst, K., *Bedrängte Gemeinde und verherrlichter Christus. Der historische Ort des Johannesevangeliums als Schlüssel zu seiner Interpretation* (BThSt 5) Neukirchen-Vluyn ²1983.

——, "Nikodemus. Bemerkungen zu Joh 3,1-5," *NStim* 31 (1978) 38-40.

Weren, W., *Windows on Jesus: Methods in Gospel Exegesis*, Philadelphia 1999.

Wessel, F., "'Der Mensch' in der Verteidigungsrede des Nikodemus Joh 7,51 und das 'Ecce Homo'," *SNTU* 17 (1992) 195-214.

Westermann, C., *The Gospel of John in the Light of the Old Testament*, Peabody 1997.

Wheelwright, P. E., *Metaphor and Reality*, Bloomington, London 1962.

White, H., "The Value of Narrativity in the Representation of Reality," *CI* 7 (1980) 5-27.

White, R. J., *The Kingdom of God in the Fourth Gospel*, Louisville 1982.

Wilckens, U., "Rezension Richter, Georg: Studien zum Johannesevangelium," *ThLZ* 106 (1981) 815-17.

Wilder, A. N., *Early Christian Rhetoric: The Language of the Gospel*, Cambridge 1971.

Willett, M. E., *Wisdom Christology in the Fourth Gospel*, San Francisco 1992.

Williams, C., *He Came Down from Heaven*, Grand Rapids 1984.

Wilson, J., "The Integrity of John 3:22-26," *JSNT* 10 (1981) 34-41.

Wind, A., "Destination and Purpose of the Gospel of John," *NT* 14 (1972) 26-69.

Wink, W., *The Bible in Human Transformation. Toward a New Paradigm for Biblical Study*, Philadelphia 1973.

Witherington, B., III, "Jesus and the Baptist –Two of a Kind?," in: Lull, D. (ed.), *SBL 1988 Seminar Papers*, Atlanta 1988, 225-44.

——, *The Many Faces of the Christ: The Christologies of the New Testament and Beyond*, New York 1997.

——, "The Waters of Birth: John 3.5 and 1 John 5.6-8," *NTS* 35 (1989) 155-60.

Wuellner, W., "Is There an Encoded Reader Fallacy?," *Semeia* 48 (1989) 40-54.

——, "Where is Rhetorical Criticism Taking Us?," *CBQ* 49 (1987) 448-63.

Yamauchi, E., "Gnosticism and Early Christianity," in: Helleman, W. E. (ed.), *Hellenisation Revisited. Shaping a Christian Response within Graeco-Roman World*, London 1994, 29-61.

Zerwick, M., "Veritatem facere. Joh 3,21; 1 Joh 1,6," *VD* 18 (1938) 338-41 and 373-77.

Zimmermann, H., "Die christliche Taufe nach Joh 3. Ein Beitrag zur Logoschristologie des vierten Evangeliums," *Cath(M)* 30 (1976) 81-93.

Zimmermann, M. and R., "Der Freund des Bräutigams (Joh 3,29): Deflorations- oder Christuszeuge?," *ZNW* 90 (1999) 123-30.

Zumstein, J., "Analyse narrative, critique rhétorique et exégèse johannique," in: Bühler, P. and Habermacher, J.-F. (eds.), *La narration. Quand le récit devient communication* (LiTh 12) Geneva 1998, 37-56.

——, "L'Évangile johannique: une stratégie du croire," *RSR* 77 (1989) 217-32.

——, Kaestli, J.-D. and Poffet, J.-M. (eds.), *La Communauté Johannique et son histoire. La trajectoire de l'évangile de Jean aux deux premiers siècles* (MB) Geneva 1990.

Laurent W. Ramambason

Missiology: Its Subject-Matter and Method

A Study of *Mission-Doers* in Madagascar

Frankfurt/M., Berlin, Bern, New York, Paris, Wien, 1999. 208 pp.
Studies in Intercultural History of Christianity. Edited by Richard Friedli,
Jan A. B. Jongeneel, Klaus Koschorke, Theo Sundermeier, Werner Ustorf.
Vol. 116
ISBN 3-631-34602-6 · pb. DM 65.–*
US-ISBN 0-8204-4320-4

Missiology is the study of *mission-doers*, the persons who are active in
Christianisation, with methodological attention to the dialectic of personhood.
Mission, in this approach, is what a mission-doer thinks it is. Mission-doers
are potential facilitators as well as potential hinderers of the cause of Jesus
Christ. They emerge in particular contexts; as the contexts change they
converge and diverge. New contexts for Christianisation may require new
ways of doing it, which in turn may require new people to carry them out.
That is why individual and corporate mission-doers emerge, are renewed
and eventually fade away. The understanding of missiology is illustrated
with reference to the Church of Jesus Christ in Madagascar under the
impact of the Gorbachev transition (1985-93).

Contents: The study of *mission-doers* · Persons who are active in
Christianisation · Methodological attention to the dialectic of personhood ·
Study of '*mission-doers*' in Madagascar under the impact of the Gorbachev
transition (1985-93)

Frankfurt/M · Berlin · Bern · Bruxelles · New York · Oxford · Wien
Distribution: Verlag Peter Lang AG
Jupiterstr. 15, CH-3000 Bern 15
Fax (004131) 9402131
*incl. value added tax
Prices are subject to change without notice.